A HISTORY OF MADNESS IN
SIXTEENTH-CENTURY GERMANY

A History of Madness in Sixteenth-Century Germany

H. C. ERIK MIDELFORT

Stanford University Press
Stanford, California

Stanford University Press
Stanford, California
© 1999 by the Board of Trustees
of the Leland Stanford Junior University

Printed in the United States of America

CIP data appear at the end of the book

For Katarina and Kristian,
  who saw the beginning,
And for Lucy,
  who saw the end.

Acknowledgments

THIS book began twenty-five years ago in the hope of presenting a more circumstantial and credible account of the history of madness in early modern Europe. Fairly early on, I decided to confine my attentions to the German-speaking parts of Europe and to the sixteenth century, but the book continued to expand all the same. Listing all those who have helped me with this project could be almost the same as naming everyone with whom I have discussed it over the years, and yet common decency requires that I thank explicitly those who have made the work possible. Librarians and archivists are often the unsung heroes of academia, so I must recall the remarkable and indispensable contribution made by interlibrary loan services, the Electronic Text Center, and by the reference librarians at the University of Virginia. When abroad, I have found a warm welcome and essential assistance at the Warburg Institute, the Wellcome Institute for the History of Medicine, and the British Library, all in London. In Tübingen, the Institut für Spätmittelalter und Reformation (then under the direction of Heiko Oberman) and the Institut für Geschichte der Medizin (under Gerhard Fichtner) gave me crucial access to their remarkable indexes and collections, as well as a comfortable place to work. While in Marburg, I was cordially assisted by Peter Dilg of the Institute for the History of Pharmacy and by Kurt Goldammer and Hartmut Rudolph of the Paracelsus Edition, and at Haina my project received enthusiastic support from the whole staff of the hospital. In the Bayerische Staatsbibliothek, Munich, Adelheid Oberwegner provided me with a scholarly office that permitted me to get much more accomplished than I otherwise would have. Other chapters or paragraphs rest on help I have received from the Houghton Library at Harvard University, the Beinecke Library at Yale University, the rare book collections of the Bancroft Library at the University of California, Berkeley, the

Library of Congress, the Folger Shakespeare Library, and the National Library of Medicine in Bethesda, Maryland.

Individual scholars and friends have also gently steered me toward treasures they knew about (and away from one or another of my idées fixes). I especially thank Robin Barnes, Phil Benedict, Jürgen Beyer, Peter and Renate Blickle, William Bynum, Stuart Clark, Robert Dawidoff, Peter Dilg, Martin Dinges, Carlos Eire, Gerhard Fichtner, Christopher Friedrichs, Arlene Miller Guinsburg, Chad Gunnoe, Scott Hendrix, John Holloran, Ronnie Po-chia Hsia, Robert Jütte, Joseph Kett, Richard Kieckhefer, Benjamin Kohl, Werner Friedrich Kümmel, Stephan Kuttner, David Lederer, Hartmut Lehmann, Sönke Lorenz, Michael MacDonald, Allen Megill, George Mora, Keith Moxey, Heiko Oberman, Duane Osheim, Steven Ozment, Roy Porter, Roger Reynolds, Tom Robisheaux, Bernd Roeck, Lyndal Roper, Hans-Christoph Rublack, David Sabean, Heinz Schilling, Anne Jacobson Schutte, Gerd Schwerhoff, Winfried Schulze, Bob Scribner, Andrew Scull, Kathy Stuart, David Summers, John Tedeschi, Otto Ulbricht, Merry Wiesner-Hanks, and Gerhild Scholz Williams. Special thanks go to Tom and Kathy Brady for transcribing materials in Strasbourg and for listening to me, to Bill Abbot for perceptively reading through the whole manuscript in a penultimate draft, and to Wolfgang Behringer, who has commented thoughtfully on many pieces of this work.

Portions of this book have appeared as public lectures at the University of Bielefeld, the University of British Columbia, Brown University, the Universities of California at Berkeley, Davis, and Los Angeles, the College of Charleston, Davidson College, Duke University, the University of Giessen, Harvard University, the Folger Institute, the Johns Hopkins University, the University of Minnesota, the National Library of Medicine, the University of Oregon, Pomona College and the Claremont Graduate School, Roanoke College, Simon Fraser University, the University of Tübingen, the University of Washington, Washington University at St. Louis, and at meetings of the American Historical Association, the American Philosophical Society, the Duquesne History Forum, Frühe Neuzeit Interdisziplinär, the German Historical Institute in Washington, D.C., the International Congress of Medieval Studies in Kalamazoo, the Mid-Atlantic Renaissance and Reformation Seminar, the Renaissance Society of America, the Sixteenth Century Studies Conference, and the Society for Reformation Research. I thank all who listened attentively and especially those who through their perceptive questions or comments inspired me to try for greater clarity.

Major funding for my research has come from the John Simon Guggenheim Foundation, the National Endowment for the Humanities, the American Philosophical Society, and from the sesquicentennial fellowship program of the University of Virginia. I am also grateful for University of Virginia summer research fellowships that freed me from teaching and allowed travel abroad.

Before the advent of personal computers, the secretaries of the department of history at the University of Virginia typed and retyped the early chapters. I thank especially Lottie McCauley, Kathleen Miller, Elizabeth Stovall, and Ella Wood. David Seaman and Catherine Tousignant in the Electronic Text Center of the University of Virginia were patient and friendly in helping me create the maps. Danielle Culpepper helped me compile the bibliography. Donald McColl has been skillful and tireless in the task of locating images and securing the necessary permissions. My other graduate students, too, have often alerted me to books, sources, and approaches that have greatly enriched this work.

My family have been consistently supportive over all these years, and I am especially grateful for the encouragement and patience shown by Anne and Lucy. Despite all the help and advice I have received, however, I have perhaps willfully persisted in peculiar attitudes and unwillingly committed particular errors, all of which, I'm afraid, are mine.

HCEM

Contents

Tables and Maps

MAPS

Illustrations

Abbreviations

Carolina, the	Charles V's imperial criminal code of 1532, the *Constitutio criminalis carolina*
HHA	Hospitalsarchiv, Haina
L2 (89)	Paracelsus [Philippus Aureolus Theophrastus Bombast von Hohenheim], *De secretis secretorum theologiae*. MS in the Leiden Rijksuniversiteit Library, Cod. Voss. Chym. 25. Available as a typewritten transcript in the Office of the *Paracelsusedition* at the University of Marburg.
LW	Martin Luther, *Works*. Edited by Helmut T. Lehmann and Jaroslav J. Pelikan. St. Louis, 1955–86. "The American Edition."
Mad Princes	H. C. Erik Midelfort, *Mad Princes of Renaissance Germany* (Charlottesville, Va., 1994)
MP	*Paracelsusedition*, University of Marburg
NLM	The National Library of Medicine, Bethesda, Maryland
OED	*The Oxford English Dictionary*, 2d ed. (1989)
RR	HHA, Receptions-Reskripte
StAM	Hessisches Staatsarchiv, Marburg
StAN	Staatsarchiv Nürnberg, Ratsverlässe
StAW	Stadtarchiv Literalien, Würzburg
SW	Paracelsus, *Sämtliche Werke*. Pt. 1: *Medizinische, naturwissenschaftliche und philosophische Schriften*. Edited by Karl Sudhoff. Munich and Berlin, 1922–33. Pt. 2: *Die theologischen und religionsphilosophischen Schriften*. Edited by

	Wilhelm Matthiessen and Kurt Goldammer. Munich and Stuttgart, 1923–.
WA	*Martin Luthers Werke: Kritische Gesamtausgabe*. Weimar, 1883–.
WABr	WA, *Briefwechsel* (letters)
WATR	WA, *Tischreden* (table talk)

𝓘ntroduction

LATE in the year 1539, a certain Master Peter Mair arrived in the proud and wealthy imperial city of Nuremberg, advertising his ability to cure fools and madmen.[1] Hopeful that this doctor could return madmen "to their senses and reason," the city councilors agreed to let him try. By November 28, this mad-doctor (*Narrenarzt*) had had success with two patients, who were declared healthy enough that "they should return to their women and households." The director of Nuremberg's hospitals was ordered to pay Mair for his treatments.[2] In early December, Mair requested twenty gulden, a considerable sum, in exchange for promised treatment of "awkward people" (*ungeschikte leut*), but the councilors thought it better to pay for results rather than setting him up in a salaried position.[3] Through the first half of 1540, Mair continued to practice as a Narrenarzt, attracting the attention of such noble families as the von Seckendorfs. But this was riskier than trying to heal the poor and unnoticed, and by September 1540, the town councilors had had enough. They charged Mair with malpractice and expelled him: "Send [a messenger] to Peter Mair, the mad-doctor, and tell him that because he has mistreated Maiden von Seckendorf so badly, it no longer pleases our lords [of the council] to tolerate him. He must spend his money elsewhere."[4]

1. This episode may be reconstructed from Staatsarchiv Nürnberg, Ratsverlässe (StAN), nos. 910, 912, and 921. My warm thanks to Dr. Peter Fleischmann for help in locating and reading these materials.

2. StAN, no. 910, fol. 9; see Ernst Mummenhoff, "Die öffentliche Gesundheits- und Krankenpflege im alten Nürnberg," in *Festschrift zur Eröffnung des neuen Krankenhauses der Stadt Nürnberg* (Nuremberg, 1898), pp. 1–122, esp. pp. 59–60.

3. StAN, no. 910, fol. 17v.

4. StAN, no. 921, fol 12v. The episode has been described by Mummenhoff, "Die öffentliche Gesundheits- und Krankenpflege im alten Nürnberg," p. 60, and by George

This episode plunges us into the fascinating history of madness in sixteenth-century Germany. Much that we would like to know is obscure. Who was this Peter Mair, and how did he become known as a Narrenarzt? What were the mental troubles of these "awkward" fools? What sort of treatment, if any, had they received in the hospital? What were Mair's treatments like? What did Nurembergers mean by "fools"? Were they thought to be sick? Or mentally retarded? Or demon-possessed?

In this specific case, the most interesting questions must remain unanswered, because Peter Mair disappears from our sources without a trace. The problems raised in this little story, however, are emblematic of those with which this book is concerned. The history of madness is more than the history of psychiatry, although professional medical views are certainly part of the larger history told here. It is also more than the story of institutional responses to deviance, mental disorder, and weirdness, although institutions, too, figure prominently in some of the chapters of this book. We shall be concerned with the views of healers and town councilors, and with the strategies of hospitals and of healing shrines. Where possible, I have also sought to locate the case histories of individual mad people from various social classes. A basic assumption here is that one cannot understand madness and mental disorder in a society until one understands the social contexts within which madness and mental disorder are diagnosed and treated. And one cannot grasp the ideas about madness held by intellectuals, theologians, physicians, or lawyers until one uncovers the larger context of their thinking, the nodal intellectual points where madness posed deep challenges by calling the very categories of humanity and reason into question.

Before proceeding very far with such topics, the modern reader often expects an author to clarify his or her theoretical presuppositions. Do we have here a study inspired by one of the great founders of modern psychiatry or neurology, or one based perhaps on a skeptical metacritique of all modern theories of mind? Does this study situate itself clearly among the controversial positions in the scholarly minefield of the mind-body problem?

Psychoanalytic and Feminist Approaches:
The Problem of Hysteria

For many scholars the psychoanalytic views of Sigmund Freud, or of the various neo-Freudian or psychodynamic schools, remain the most powerful contribution to twentieth-century ideas about human functioning. For such scholars, it seems literally inconceivable that a Freudian (or Jungian, or Kleinian, or Kohutian) perspective would fail to illuminate the madnesses and the psychiatry of the sixteenth century. Indeed, perhaps they will all turn out to have their uses, even though the dynamic psychologies themselves have seemed lately to be dwindling in scientific and imaginative force with each passing decade. My own position is not one of inveterate or principled hostility to psychoanalytic history, but I do suspect that historians will make the distant past more understandable if they take as a first task the attempt to see a distant world and its problems as people did in that past. I assume that how one sees and interprets the world determines what one expects, and therefore what one experiences, because we often can only experience what we recognize.[5] This makes it important that we try as best we can to grasp the ways in which ordinary people, as well as academics and intellectuals, understood and interpreted their world and the kinds of madness in the world. I emphatically agree with Jean-Pierre Vernant, therefore, when he points out that even Sophocles' Oedipus himself had no "Oedipus complex," because, so far as Oedipus was concerned, such a complex would have involved the only mother and father he knew, namely, Merope and Polybus, his adoptive parents. His later relations and conflicts with Jocasta and Laius (his biological parents) were so unconscious as to be totally beyond his awareness.[6] This simple but profound point should stand as a warning against imposing a false psychodynamic upon the past, and I am frankly more impressed by recent efforts to understand Freud through the literary models (and competitors) that he recognized (and repressed) than by most efforts to "apply" Freudian or neo-Freudian ideas to times and places distant and different from fin de siècle Vienna.[7] Martha Nussbaum has shown that attempts to see the ancient Greeks and Romans through Freudian lenses may diminish what we can actually learn from them. By casting their confident net over all of the past, scholars of psychoanalytic inclination may seriously misinterpret such human experiences as dreams, childhood, conflict, passion, and healing.[8]

5. Roberta Satow, "Where Has All the Hysteria Gone?" *Psychoanalytic Review* 66 (1979): 463–77, at 471.

6. Jean-Pierre Vernant, "Oedipus Without the Complex," in id. and Pierre Vidal-Naquet, *Myth and Tragedy in Ancient Greece*, trans. J. Lloyd (New York, 1988), pp. 85–111.

7. Harold Bloom, *The Western Canon: The Books and School of the Ages* (New York, 1994), pp. 371–94; Mark Edmundson, *Towards Reading Freud: Self-Creation in Milton, Wordsworth, Emerson, and Sigmund Freud* (Princeton, 1990).

8. Martha C. Nussbaum, "The *Oedipus Rex* and the Ancient Unconscious," in *Freud and Forbidden Knowledge*, ed. Peter L. Rudnytsky and Ellen Handler Spitz (New York, 1994), pp. 42–71; and see, more generally, Nussbaum's *The Therapy of Desire: Theory and Practice in Hellenistic Ethics* (Princeton, 1994).

Some of the most flexible psychoanalytic investigators have known this all along. Georges Devereux, for example, was eager to fashion an "ethnopsychiatry" that could take account of the substantial differences among cultures, and to emphasize the existence of culturally specific psychoses, that is, kinds of madness that one finds only in specific societies. As he put it, "the psychologically ill comply rigorously with expectations regarding 'behavior suitable for madmen.'"[9] These considerations suggest that the history of madness must seek to explain how madness was categorized, understood, and experienced in strange societies.[10]

In eschewing the insights of dynamic psychology, however, we do run the risk of making the past seem stranger than necessary. In undertaking this project, we may fall, wittingly or unwittingly, into the program of "defamiliarization" that some modern critics contend is essential to our modern sense of cultural dislocation. To some extent, this step is unavoidable, however, as a corrective to the bland assertions that human "nature" and, with it, human diseases and disorders have been unchanging and universal for millennia. Over the past century, for example, it has been characteristic of the history of hysteria to emphasize its long continuity, reaching back to antiquity. It was, we have been told, an ailment recognized by the ancient Egyptians and Greeks, linked causally to the supposedly wandering womb (*hystera* in Greek) and thus a characteristically female disorder.[11] Recent work has proved, however, that for the ancient Egyptians "the womb lay still."[12] None of the ancient papyri speak at all of a wandering womb, even though scholars of our century have regularly imputed ancient Greek views to the even more ancient Egyptians in a seriously mistaken projection of modern expectations. In a more general assault on received views, Helen King has demonstrated persuasively that hysteria itself was not known to the ancient Greeks.[13] It was at best a "name without a disease," for the Hippocratic physicians did, of course, attribute certain ailments to the curiously

9. Georges Devereux, "Schizophrenia: An Ethnic Psychosis, or Schizophrenia Without Tears," in id., *Basic Problems of Ethnopsychiatry*, trans. Basia Miller Gulati and Georges Devereux (Chicago, 1980), pp. 214–36, at p. 217. On Devereux's problematic project, see *Die wilde Seele: Zur Ethnopsychoanalyse von Georges Devereux*, ed. Hans Peter Duerr (Frankfurt a/M, 1987).

10. Arthur Kleinman, "Anthropology and Psychiatry: The Role of Culture in Cross-Cultural Research on Illness," *British Journal of Psychiatry* 151 (1987): 447–54; id., *Rethinking Psychiatry* (New York, 1988).

11. "L'hystérie a toujours existé, en tous lieux et en tous temps," declared Jean-Martin Charcot (quoted in Étienne Trillat, *Histoire de l'hystérie* [Paris, 1986], p. 272). See also Ilsa Veith, *Hysteria: The History of a Disease* (Chicago, 1965), on roughly the same attitude.

12. Harold Merskey and Paul Potter, "The Womb Lay Still in Ancient Egypt," *British Journal of Psychiatry* 154 (1989): 751–53.

13. Helen King, "Once upon a Text: Hysteria from Hippocrates," in *Hysteria Beyond Freud*, ed. Sander Gilman et al. (Berkeley and Los Angeles, 1993), pp. 3–90. See also Trillat, *Histoire de l'hystérie*, pp. 14–20.

wandering womb, and these disorders were logically called *hysteric* (i.e., characteristic of or caused by the womb). But even the Greeks had no disorder they called *hysteria*, no syndrome or disease with its own identity. Instead, we find a loose grouping of symptoms labeled hysteric: mainly an uncomfortable sensation of suffocation due to pressure from the uterus on the heart, liver, and lungs, a disorder most commonly found among recently widowed women who were suddenly deprived of sexual intercourse. The Hippocratic writings contain no case histories of these uterine disorders, only brief lists of symptoms and remedies.[14] King concludes that the Greek medical tradition did not diagnose any particular disorder as hysteria. Indeed, the term is an amazingly late arrival. The French adjective *hysterique* was first used in print in 1568, and its English equivalent, *hysterical*, dates from 1615.[15] Even the Latin term *hysterica passio* appeared in English texts no earlier than 1603,[16] while the English *hysteria* began its meteoric career in our language no earlier than 1801. Before that, English texts referred to a disorder of "the mother," the rising of the womb and the suffocation, choking, swelling, and fits or seizures generally associated with the supposedly mobile uterus.[17] One need not be an extreme philosophical nominalist to find these late appearances troubling to the conventional notion that hysteria has been recognized for over two millennia. Indeed, the sensational variety of symptoms attached to the "vapors" and to the idea of *hysteria* first expanded rapidly in the eighteenth century.

Scholars have seriously tried to find sixteenth-century hysteria in certain reports of anaesthesia, localized spots of numbness that seem symptomatically akin to certain late-nineteenth-century "hysterical anaesthesias." But upon closer inspection, it turns out that almost all the early reports of numbness came from witchcraft trials in which a person was first accused

14. James Palis, Evangelos Rossopoulos, and Lazaros Triarhou, "The Hippocratic Concept of Hysteria: A Translation of the Original Texts," *Integrative Psychiatry* 3, no. 3 (Sept. 1985): 226–28.

15. The *OED* cites Helkiah Crooke's *Mikrokosmographia: A Description of the Body of Man . . .* (1615) for the earliest use of *hysterical*: "Of, pertaining to, or characteristic of hysteria." See also W. Russell Brain, "The Concept of Hysteria in the Time of William Harvey," *Proceedings of the Royal Society of Medicine* 56, no. 4 (Apr. 1963): 317–24, esp. p. 323, and Mark S. Micale, *Approaching Hysteria: Disease and Its Interpretations* (Princeton, 1995), p. 43.

16. In Samual Harsnet's well-known *A Declaration of Egregious Popish Impostures* (London, 1603). See the excellent introduction by Michael MacDonald to his *Witchcraft and Hysteria in Elizabethan London: Edward Jorden and the Mary Glover Case* (London, 1991), pp. vii–lxiv, esp. pp. xxviii–xxxiv. See also Jeffrey M. N. Boss, "The Seventeenth-Century Transformation of the Hysteric Affection, and Sydenham's Baconian Medicine," *Psychological Medicine* 9 (1979): 221–34.

17. The *OED* cites vague usages from the fifteenth and early sixteenth centuries, but by the early seventeenth century, many authors referred to a disorder called the "mother," meaning the rising or suffocation of (or caused by) the uterus. See, e.g., Edward Jorden, *A Disease Called the Suffocation of the Mother* (1603; repr., Amsterdam, 1971).

of witchcraft and only then found to have one or more areas that were insensitive to a pinprick. Usually, these suspects appear to have been previously unaware of these anaesthetic regions. It would, therefore, be wrong to conclude from such episodes that hysterical women were singled out as witches, because these examples of supposedly hysterical anaesthesia came to light only after a witchcraft trial was well advanced. And no one thought the pricking test was crucial. One might well pass that test and yet be condemned as a witch on other grounds, and one might fail the test and still escape conviction as a witch.[18] But, more important, no one associated such spots of localized lack of sensation with any disorder. There is no indication that such supposed hysterics had ever noticed these numb spots at all. No one thought it a symptom of any disease, let alone a side effect of a "rising mother."[19]

The result for us is that, however much hysteria may trouble the modern history of madness, it plays virtually no role in the history of madness or psychiatry in sixteenth-century Germany.[20] Neither professionals nor the laity, and neither the afflicted nor their comforters, connected mental troubles with uterine troubles, except in cases of deranged feminine sexuality, which was indeed sometimes diagnosed as *furor uterinus*, what later centuries might call nymphomania. This is not to say that German observers were unaware of the many connections between sex, passion, and mental disorder, but I do insist that we must notice exactly which connections they did draw, rather than prematurely congratulating them on almost seeing what we supposedly see so much more clearly.

Renaissance physicians and philosophers often assumed that *melancholia* was more common among men than women, and modern feminist scholarship has begun to pursue this assertion with discrimination.[21] This book does not begin from an explicitly feminist orientation, however, because again I have been concerned to determine first what was construed through the categories of gender and what was not. I have not found, for example, that melancholy as a disease was specifically or even disproportionately

18. Sanford J. Fox, *Science and Justice: The Massachusetts Witch Trials* (Baltimore, 1968).

19. This is my chief objection to the passages dealing with hysteria in the sixteenth century in G. S. Rousseau, "'A Strange Pathology': Hysteria in the Early Modern World, 1500–1800," in *Hysteria Beyond Freud*, ed. Gilman et al., pp. 91–221, esp. pp. 96–101.

20. On the modern history of hysteria, see esp. Roy Porter, "The Body and the Mind, the Doctor and the Patient: Negotiating Hysteria," in *Hysteria Beyond Freud*, ed. Gilman et al., pp. 225–85; Martha Noel Evans, *Fits and Starts: A Genealogy of Hysteria in Modern France* (Ithaca, N.Y., 1991); Mark S. Micale, *Approaching Hysteria*; Janet Beizer, *Ventriloquized Bodies: Narratives of Hysteria in Nineteenth-Century France* (Ithaca, N.Y., 1994); Elaine Showalter, *Hystories: Hysterical Epidemics and Modern Culture* (New York, 1997).

21. Julia Schiesari, *The Gendering of Melancholia: Feminism, Psychoanalysis, and the Symbolics of Loss in Renaissance Literature* (Ithaca, N.Y., 1992).

"gendered" as a female sickness.[22] The medical and hospital records are full of male and female melancholics, and the real story is perhaps more the rise of melancholia as a fashionable diagnosis for both men and women than the invidious labeling of disproportionately more men or more women. One might have thought that at least in the case of demon possession, a feminist analysis would be required, but here, too, my first (and astonished) impression of the German evidence is one of a remarkable degree of "gender equity." At precisely the time when German society was finding and executing thousands of witches, most of them women, demonic possession afflicted males almost as often as females. It is true that the most publicized and most famous episodes involved female demoniacs, but statistically German men were often as likely to suffer possession as women.

The Contribution of Michel Foucault

For the past thirty years, historians of madness have also had to contend with the socio-philosophical criticism of Michel Foucault, whose first famous book was a history of madness in the "classical age."[23] As a mental tone poem, Foucault's work has inspired outpourings from enthusiastic readers and baffled groans from empirically minded skeptics.[24] The most charitable and perhaps most illuminating reading of Foucault's history sees it as a great idealist portrait of the age of reason as an age of confinement, a time when the self-proclaimedly moral and reasonable saw fit to lock up those who seemed less hardworking, less powerful, less moral, and less reasonable.[25] Foucault worked at such a level of symbolist abstraction, however, that empirical criticism never much bothered him or has bothered his disciples. If one finds, for example, that Foucault's image of universal confinement is overdrawn for England, Germany, or even for France,

22. On this question, see Jane E. Kromm, "The Feminization of Madness in Visual Representation," *Feminist Studies* 20 (1994): 507–35. For a sharp rebuke to the thesis that madness was "gendered" in the nineteenth century, see J. Busfield, "The Female Malady: Men, Women and Madness in Nineteenth-Century Britain," *Sociology* 28 (1994): 259–77.

23. Michel Foucault, *L'histoire de la folie à l'âge classique* (Paris, 1961).

24. For those interested in my critique of Foucault's work as a history, subject to the historian's criteria of accuracy, fairness, representativeness, and clarity, see H. C. Erik Midelfort, "Madness and Civilization in Early Modern Europe: A Reappraisal of Michel Foucault," in *After the Reformation. Essays in Honor of J. H. Hexter*, ed. Barbara Malament (Philadelphia, 1980), pp. 247–66. A wide variety of reactions to Foucault's history of madness (and to my reading of Foucault) may be savored in *Rewriting the History of Madness: Studies in Foucault's "Histoire de la folie,"* ed. Arthur Still and Irving Velody (London, 1992).

25. This is the approach of Gary Gutting, "Foucault and the History of Madness," in *The Cambridge Companion to Foucault*, ed. id. (Cambridge, 1994), pp. 47–70.

why then one has misunderstood what Foucault was using the image to accomplish.[26] If one finds that Foucault betrayed Romantic tendencies and a complacent acceptance of conventional periodization, one is told that one has naively bought into the project of Enlightenment, with its belief in progress, or that one has overlooked the radical nihilism of the master. Basic to the Foucaultian perspective is a corrosive suspicion that all historical liberations have actually deployed a subtle exercise of power (often state, economic, or sexual power), and that knowledge itself is a function of power (not that knowledge gives one power, but that power constitutes or constructs "knowledge"). In Foucault's view, power/knowledge itself is subject to unpredictable ruptures, moments of discontinuity in which social practices reorient themselves. While some historians have recommended the bracing tonic offered by these suspicions, Allan Megill describes well the trouble historians have had and will necessarily have in implementing or "applying" Foucault's antidisciplinary perspectives.[27] More important for historians committed to recapturing the texture of the past, the complexity, variety, and competition of various discursive practices in the past, Foucault's work is a radical and dramatic simplification, a reduction of whole generations, countries, and disciplines to symbolic markers in a moral game whose object is the destabilizing of the present. I have not drawn much refreshment from these bitter herbs, but I have occasionally noticed areas in which my laborious conclusions agree with the apparently effortless flashes of Foucault's insight.[28] More often, I have found that the complexity of the sixteenth century defies the idealizing, symbolically reductionist tendencies of the Parisian savant. On topics such as the early modern confinement of the mad, attempts to help or heal the mad, or la-

26. For these criticisms, see Roy Porter, *Mind-Forg'd Manacles: A History of Madness in England from the Restoration to the Regency* (Cambridge, Mass., 1987); Andrew Scull, *The Most Solitary of Afflictions: Madness and Society in Britain, 1700–1900* (New Haven, 1993); E. Köhler, *Arme und Irre: Die liberale Fürsorgepolitik des Bürgertums* (Berlin, 1977); Klaus Dörner, *Madmen and the Bourgeoisie: A Social History of Insanity and Psychiatry* (Cambridge, 1984); Colin Jones, *The Charitable Imperative: Hospitals and Nursing in Ancien Régime and Revolutionary France* (London, 1989); André Cellard, *Histoire de la folie au Québec de 1600 à 1850* (Montreal, 1991); Colin Jones, "Medicine, Madness, and Mayhem from the *Roi Soleil* to the Golden Age of Hysteria (17th–19th Centuries)," *French History* 4 (1990): 378–88; Martin Dinges, "Frühneuzeitliche Armenfürsorge als Sozialdisziplinierung? Probleme mit einem Konzept," *Geschichte und Gesellschaft* 17 (1991): 5–29; Colin Jones and Roy Porter, eds., *Reassessing Foucault: Power, Medicine, and the Body* (London, 1994).

27. Allan Megill, *Prophets of Extremity: Nietzsche, Heidegger, Foucault, Derrida* (Berkeley and Los Angeles, 1985); id., "The Reception of Foucault by Historians," *Journal of the History of Ideas* 48 (1987): 117–41. One of the more successful applications of Foucaultian ideas of discourse, but one that does not fully escape the problems of schematic oversimplification, is Jean-Marie Fritz, *Le discours du fou au Moyen-Âge: Étude comparée des discours littéraire, médical, juridique et théologique de la folie* (Paris, 1992).

28. See, e.g., *Mad Princes*, p. 154.

beling the mad as possessed by demons, I have not found Foucault's obsession with power to be of much assistance. Melancholia as a label and as a diagnosis, as a problem and as a mood, was palpably on the rise during the second half of the sixteenth century. It may be true that the rise of melancholy worked to the advantage of the medical profession, although soon enough physicians of the seventeenth century found that they were having unexpected trouble even in locating black bile (melancholy) in the human body and turned it into the metaphor we still employ today.[29]

Sixteenth-century Germans worried a great deal about sin and the devil, and a wave of scandalous demonic possessions swept over Germany during the latter half of the century.[30] Again, I do not think we can explain the growing currency of demonic explanation as the cunning advance of regulatory power somewhere (or nowhere) in society. I do think we should notice, however, that the theorists of demonic possession were working out the dynamics of a mental disorder that had no organic or physical basis. In that sense, Christian culture, like many other cultures, invented and has preserved the idea and fundamental structures of *mental* illness—that is, of an illness not driven by heredity, hormones, humors, nerves, or cerebral malfunction. The Renaissance physician Paracelsus, too, specifically identified what he called "mental illnesses" (*Geistkrankheiten*), diseases of the soul or spirit that had no organic basis. This book devotes much time and energy to sin and the devil, not only because German people of long ago thought in those terms, but also because modern ideas of the unconscious and of the autonomy of mind from body (and therefore of mental illness from organic disorders) have at least one important root in this line of religious speculation.[31] Rather than "applying" a modern psychological theory, the historian can provide a context for understanding today's competing schools of psychology and psychiatry.[32] I would insist, however,

29. T. H. Jobe, "Medical Theories of Melancholia in the Seventeenth and Early Eighteenth Centuries," *Clio Medica* 19 (1976): 217–31; Stanley W. Jackson, "Melancholia and the Waning of the Humoral Theory," *Journal of the History of Medicine and Allied Sciences* 33 (1978): 367–76; Michael Heyd, "The Reaction to Enthusiasm," *Journal of Modern History* 53 (1981): 258–80; Porter, *Mind-Forg'd Manacles*, pp. 47–52, 176, 281.

30. In "Reforming the Spirit: Society, Madness, and Suicide in Central Europe, 1517–1809" (diss., New York University, 1995), pp. 215–23, 271–98, David L. Lederer shows that the rise in the number of cases of demonic possession continued in Bavaria well on into the seventeenth century.

31. My approach is much indebted to Henri F. Ellenberger, *The Discovery of the Unconscious: The History and Evolution of Dynamic Psychiatry* (New York, 1970).

32. In *From Soul to Mind: The Emergence of Psychology from Erasmus Darwin to William James* (New Haven, 1997), Edward S. Reed provides a philosophically subtle example from the nineteenth century. Certain anthropologists point out that even in modern practice among Third World people, the modern psychiatrist may be therapeutically less effective than exorcists who share the same worldview and language of affliction as their clients.

that a history like this one does not only point toward our age. Through the analysis of madness in a bygone century, we can learn to know another people from a new angle.

Madness as Cerebral Disorder

Of course, it is today again fashionable to declare that the mind is nothing more than the brain, and that "mental disorders," therefore, are only unrecognized somatic disorders.[33] This is partly an empirical problem into which the practicing historian can claim no privileged insight. And yet it remains true on a phenomenological level that all people experience the world and their own minds through the cultural filters and linguistic lenses of their time and place, and of their ethnicity, class, age, and gender. To recapture the experience of people four hundred or five hundred years ago, it will not help us much to apply the constantly evolving diagnostic criteria of the DSM IV (the American Psychiatric Association's *Diagnostic and Statistical Manual of Mental Disorders*, 4th ed., 1994). Arthur Kleinman has noted that some 90 percent of the mental disorders found around the world are not found in the DSM at all. And the modern syndromes and disease categories described there may indeed prompt us to lump together symptoms that Renaissance Germans barely noticed, or whose coherence they did not suspect. Obviously, in a certain sense, we know more about the past than people of the past themselves knew. And so, in this kind of scholarship, as Clifford Geertz has remarked, things may also

---

See, e.g., Leslie A. Sharp, "Exorcists, Psychiatrists, and the Problems of Possession in Northwest Madagascar," *Social Science & Medicine* 38 (1994): 525–42.

33. Books taking this line often ostentatiously reduce the soul to physical categories. See, e.g., Paul Churchland, *The Engine of Reason, the Seat of the Soul: A Philosophical Essay on the Brain* (Cambridge, Mass., 1995); Antonio Damasio, *Descartes' Error: Emotion, Reason, and the Human Brain* (New York, 1994); Francis Crick, *The Astonishing Hypothesis: The Scientific Search for the Soul* (New York, 1994).

34. "The truth of the doctrine of cultural (or historical—it is the same thing) relativism is that we can never apprehend another people's or another period's imagination, as though it were our own. The falsity of it is that we can therefore never genuinely apprehend it at all. We can apprehend it well enough, at least as well as we apprehend anything else not properly ours; but we do so not by looking behind the interfering glosses that cannot connect us to it but through them. Professor [Lionel] Trilling's nervousness about the epistemological complacency of traditional humanism is not misplaced. The exactest reply to it is James Merrill's wrenching observation that life is translation, and we are all lost in it," Clifford Geertz observes in "Found in Translation: On the Social History of the Moral Imagination," in id., *Local Knowledge.: Further Essays in Interpretive Anthropology* (New York, 1983), pp. 36–54, at p. 44. Later in the same essay, Geertz (p. 50) quotes Merrill at greater length:

"Lost, is it, buried? One more missing piece?
But nothing's lost. Or else all is translation

be *found* in translation.[34] The anthropologist or the historian may learn precisely from the process of interpreting another culture, of putting cultural peculiarities into modern Western categories, and of judging them by our own standards (who else's do we have?). And yet the risks of loss and of misunderstanding, of sovereign overconfidence and inattention to detail, are so great that I have generally resisted the temptation to translate late medieval and Renaissance diseases into modern technical terminology or to judge that German society and its ailments with our fraying sense of right and wrong.[35] That is one reason why this book dwells on "madness," for the very word resists specification and defies the subtle professional euphemisms and refinements provided by medicine, law, theology, psychoanalysis, and modern social theory. *Madness* is so general, so vague a term that we find ourselves forced to ask what it meant in any given time or place, and so it well serves the purposes of an empirical historian who aims, as I do, to convey some of the flavor and strangeness of a forgotten culture. If that means that I will not settle such intriguing questions as whether there were any true cases of schizophrenia before 1700,[36] or other equally contentious puzzles, then one can only hope that my concentration on the realities of the sixteenth century will be an adequate compensation. We must also recognize that biological reductionism itself has a long history, and one that does not crucially depend on modern scientific discoveries. It is an attitude with a context and an ancient past.

And every bit of us is lost in it
(Or found—I wander through the ruin of S
Now and then, wondering at the peacefulness)."

citing James Merrill's "Lost in Translation," from his *Divine Comedies* (New York, 1976), p. 10.

35. Another way of dealing with this ambivalence is to tell the story from a variety of points of view, as ethnography, as analysis, and as literary creation. See Margery Wolf, *A Thrice-Told Tale: Feminism, Postmodernism, and Ethnographic Responsibility* (Stanford, 1992).

36. E. Fuller Torrey, *Schizophrenia and Civilization* (New York, 1980); D. V. Jeste, R. del Carmen, J. B. Lohr, and R. J. Wyatt, "Did Schizophrenia Exist Before the Eighteenth Century?" *Comprehensive Psychiatry* 26 (1985): 493–503; N. M. Bark, "Did Shakespeare Know Schizophrenia? The Case of Poor Mad Tom in *King Lear*," *British Journal of Psychiatry* 146 (1985): 436–38; John Ellard, "Did Schizophrenia Exist Before the Eighteenth Century?" *Australian and New Zealand Journal of Psychiatry* 21 (1987): 306–14; Edward H. Hare, "Was Insanity on the Increase?" *British Journal of Psychiatry* 142 (1983): 439–66; id., "Schizophrenia as a Recent Disease," *British Journal of Psychiatry* 153 (1988): 521–31; id., "Schizophrenia Before 1800? The Case of the Revd. George Trosse," *Psychological Medicine* 18 (1988): 279–85; Irving I. Gottesman, *Schizophrenia Genesis: The Origins of Madness* (New York, 1991), esp. pp. 61–81.

Sociological Approaches

Another approach to mental illness is also widely available today. For about a century, sociologists have usually recoiled from psychologically and physically reductive explanations of mental illness, emphasizing not the uniformity but the startling social disparities in rates of suicide, mental disorder, and deviation. Using a careful analysis of statistical data became the hallmark of this new social science, one of whose earliest discoveries was that Protestants everywhere have committed suicide at far higher rates than Roman Catholics. Beginning with his study Le suicide in 1897, Émile Durkheim and his followers were sure that only a sociological explanation could account adequately for these differences, and modern skeptics have humorously referred to this regularity as "sociology's one law."[37] One sort of social history would take this "law" and search for the social conditions that prompted more Protestants than Catholics to take their own lives. But I propose that we not employ modern sociological theory, any more than modern psychological theory, as our guide. Instead, we should recognize that sixteenth-century Lutheran culture positively expected that some anguished souls would fall into despair and perhaps try to commit suicide. From their expectation of religious depression, Lutherans found a place in their mental world for those who could no longer bear to live, and in recognizing suicide, they quickly concluded that German Lutherans were falling into suicide far more often than their Catholic brethren, or at least more often than the Catholics advertised.[38] We cannot assume, therefore, that "social laws" discovered by modern social scientists can reliably guide us through the history of madness. Those laws themselves may be symptoms of their age.

I am suggesting that when the historian looks carefully at his sources, he may find patterns that modify or even challenge the assumptions of modern psychology and sociology. Instead of borrowing ready-made theories and merely applying them to the past, the historian may thus become the conscience of the social sciences,[39] prompting modern theorists and scien-

37. W. Pope and N. Danigelis, "Sociology's 'One Law,'" Social Forces 60 (1981): 495–516; William B. Bankston, H. David Allen, and David S. Cunningham, "Religion and Suicide: A Research Note on Sociology's 'One Law,'" Social Forces 62 (1983): 521–28; Charles E. Faupel, Gregory S. Kowalski, and Paul D. Starr, "Sociology's One Law: Religion and Suicide in the Urban Context," Journal for the Scientific Study of Religion 26 (1987): 523–34.

38. See H. C. Erik Midelfort, "Religious Melancholy and Suicide: On the Reformation Origins of a Sociological Stereotype," in Madness, Melancholy, and the Limits of the Self, ed. Andrew D. Weiner and Leonard V. Kaplan, pp. 41–56 (Madison, Wis., 1996), vol. 3 of Graven Images: Studies in Culture, Law and the Sacred. I am much in sympathy with the work of Barbara T. Gates, Victorian Suicide: Mad Crimes and Sad Histories (Princeton, 1988).

39. I owe the phrase "the conscience of the social sciences" to Joseph F. Kett.

tists to reexamine their own conclusions. But let me emphasize again that this book is first and foremost a history, an account of how people lived and suffered long ago. Even without a specifically modern relevance, such stories are worth preserving.

Madness and Culture

I would not claim, certainly, that this book proceeds boldly where none have gone before. For inspiration, this study looks to models provided by three very different books. The psychologist Louis Sass has pointed to the uncanny similarities between modern schizophrenia and the characteristic postures of "modernism," the aesthetic, moral, and philosophical movement that has had such a far-reaching and destabilizing impact on our world.[40] In Sass's analysis, the typical gestures of modernism involve a flatness of affect, a sense of alienation, and a hyperrationalism that are among the most striking features of schizophrenia too. In the Renaissance, by a parallel process, several characteristic forms of high culture mimicked, mirrored, or helped to "construct" the features of the most common mental disorders, which were generally lumped together as manifestations of melancholia. This is not the place in which to draw out the parallel with Sass's ideas at great length, but one could argue that this book documents an earlier phase of symbiosis between melancholy and "early modernism," with uncanny parallels between the rise of demonic possession, melancholy, and high cultural introspection in the late Renaissance. Along somewhat similar lines, Wolfgang Weber has recently studied the meaning of the rise of "melancholy" and has found that this increasingly popular diagnosis and symbol contributed to newer, more modern concepts of individuality and self-reflection, to the secularization of medicine and of scholarship, and to new concepts of health, work, and leisure.[41] From this perspective, the idea of melancholy was thus linked to deep social, political, and religious processes of modernization and of cultural change, especially in Western European attitudes toward the individual person.

In a very different book, the philosopher Ian Hacking has recently described the modern epidemic of multiple personality disorder (more recently called dissociative identity disorder) as the latest consequence of a movement that began just over one hundred years ago, a movement to re-

40. Louis Sass, *Madness and Modernism: Insanity in the Light of Modern Art, Literature, and Thought* (New York, 1992); see his resumé in id., "Civilized Madness: Schizophrenia, Self-Consciousness and the Modern Mind," *History of the Human Sciences* 7 (1994): 83–120.

41. Wolfgang Weber, "Im Kampf mit Saturn: Zur Bedeutung der Melancholie im anthropologischen Modernisierungsprozess des 16. und 17. Jahrhunderts," *Zeitschrift für historische Forschung* 17 (1990): 155–92.

describe the individual soul as a cluster of memories.[42] As nineteenth-century psychologists secularized and "rewrote" the soul so that they could study it in newly scientific ways, they made it possible for persons to develop more than one identity, to dissociate one set of memories from others, and to make sense of themselves as multiple. In this way, Hacking analyzes the evolution and production of new psychic disorders. In like manner, my book suggests that changes in law, medicine, and theology altered the categories of experience for troubled Germans of the Renaissance. An increased flexibility in the understanding of melancholy, for example, made possible a rise of a whole new series of disorders, nominally linked to the mental diseases described by ancient Greek physicians. These now proliferated at an unheard-of rate in Germany and the rest of Europe because of the theory that any one of the four normal humors might be roasted or burnt and thus transformed into a kind of black bile (*melancholy adust*). Another set of pressures led late Renaissance Germans to detect the presence of the devil far more commonly than people had in the centuries before the Protestant Reformation.

I also hope to document the subtle connections between the study of the soul and the sufferings of those whose "vocabularies of discomfort" developed to take account of a changing world.[43] One point is, however, worth emphasizing: neither Sass nor Hacking has any doubt that however socially or culturally "constructed" a mental disorder might be, the condition is nonetheless "real."[44] Patients are not necessarily "faking it" when they "remember" things that never happened: the suffering is often all too real. This is a point with historical consequences, because it means that we need not adopt a cynical position that might say of demonic possession, for example, that the possessed "learned" to "fake" their demon-obsessed conditions. I think it likely that demonic possession provided troubled persons with the means of expressing their often guilty and morally straining conflicts, a vocabulary of gestures, grimaces, words, voices, and feelings with which to experience and describe their sense that they were not fully in charge of their lives or their own thoughts. One cannot rule out the Protestant or materialist suspicion that demoniacs were being coached by their exorcists and confessors on how best to appear as if possessed, but such charges of fraud and priestcraft only seem compelling if we have prematurely excluded the possibility (or even the probability) that the demon-

42. Ian Hacking, *Rewriting the Soul: Multiple Personality and the Sciences of Memory* (Princeton, 1995).

43. Satow, "Where Has All the Hysteria Gone?" p. 471; Pauline B. Bart, "Social Structure and Vocabularies of Discomfort: What Happened to Female Hysteria?" *Journal of Health and Human Behavior* 9 (1968): 188–93; Showalter, *Hystories*.

44. See in addition Leon Eisenberg, "The Social Construction of Mental Illness" (editorial), *Psychological Medicine* 18 (1988): 1–9.

possessed were actually suffering from a serious disorder of body, mind, and soul.

A third book provided another sort of inspiration. In Nancy Scheper-Hughes's anthropological inquiry into the incidence and shape of mental illness, and especially schizophrenia, in rural western Ireland, I found a model of engaged and empathic ethnography.[45] Her villagers in "Ballybran" are suffering demographic, economic, and cultural assaults that seem to prompt some of them to retreat into anomie or even mental disintegration. Scheper-Hughes movingly describes the way in which severe Irish Catholic attitudes toward the body and sexuality combine with child-rearing practices and farm inheritance customs to place young men under extraordinary strain. She does not argue that the major psychoses found in western Ireland are simply produced "by culture," as if there were no genetic or biological component, but she goes far toward showing that culturally variable factors can play a crucial role in psychiatric epidemiology. One of the great strengths of her study is the wide range of her observations: the Irish sense of sin, religious devotion, and reverence for sainthood, their jokes and habits of ridicule, attitudes toward marriage, work, and education, family relations and sibling rivalry, changes in agriculture and in ways of death, rates of hospitalization and in the willingness to use psychotherapy all shape the incidence of mental trouble and remind us how complicated it is to describe the roles madness can play in any society. In this book, I have no access to the kinds of statistical, epidemiological, and personal information that Scheper-Hughes so ably deploys, but her kind of ethnography can still inspire the attempt to find the hidden links between mental aberrations and the culture in which they appear.

This book sets forth a history of madness that copes with the strangeness and variety of the German past in a way that tries to avoid the trap of translation while still benefiting from the vantage point that four or five hundred years' hindsight has given us. I assume that learning about madness and the limits of reason in a distant century will tell us much about the implicit standards and structures of that society, and also about the lives and troubles of those who were thought to have lost their minds. Becoming sensitive to the language with which madness was once conceived, and to the various approaches and attitudes that the mad once confronted, may serve to make us more aware of how contradictory and conflicted our own modern concepts, attitudes, and approaches are. The chapters that follow outline the dominant metaphors and therapeutic approaches that governed the way sixteenth-century Germans understood, regulated, and treated

45. Nancy Scheper-Hughes, *Saints, Scholars, and Schizophrenics: Mental Illness in Rural Ireland* (Berkeley and Los Angeles, 1979).

those they regarded as mad. Often the root metaphor or basic idea provided a model of etiology, nosology, and therapy all in one parsimonious image, and it was difficult then (as it is difficult today) to escape the persuasive drift of a powerful image. If one held, for example, that madness was essentially a form of humoral disorder, a physical derangement of one's vital juices, it was hard to sympathize with those who held that the most common disorders were actually sinful, ultimately self-destructive, and deliberately self-blinding. And those who worried about epidemics of demonic possession or about the prevalence of "folly" were caught up in equally irreconcilable systems of analysis and understanding. The sixteenth century was rich in the variety of basic metaphors for irrationality, madness, and mental disorder, certainly as rich as our own century. There was no single hegemonic language that channeled all experience into tyrannically narrow categories. The conflicting and competing models of Renaissance madness may be suggestive for students of modern problems, for our age too wrestles with the would-be tyrannies of language and institutions. But I have not written a treatise whose aim is modern enlightenment or moral refinement. Rather, I hope to paint in some of the necessary shadows in our otherwise superficial, flat, and unhistorical ways of understanding where we are today in our experience of madness. There is no evidence that sixteenth-century Germans were mentally better off, or worse off, than we are, but we can profit from learning to see the world and its mental problems from the perspective of a prescientific, preindustrial, premodern people.

The Plan for This Book

Such a history cannot describe Renaissance Germany as a whole or in general. The only way to proceed is through a series of focused investigations of persons or places when abundant source material survives. This has been the strength, for example, of Michael MacDonald's study of the healing practices of a seventeenth-century astrological physician, resulting in a flood of light on religion, magic, mental disorder, and the sociology of troubled Englishmen.[46] The most significant works on demonic possession recently have also been close studies of specific episodes and controversies.[47]

46. Michael MacDonald, *Mystical Bedlam: Madness, Anxiety and Healing in Seventeenth-Century England* (Cambridge, 1981).

47. D. P. Walker, *Unclean Spirits: Possession and Exorcism in England and France in the Late Sixteenth and Early Seventeenth Centuries* (Philadelphia, 1981); Cécile Ernst, *Teufelaustreibungen: Die Praxis der katholischen Kirche im 16. und 17. Jahrhundert* (Bern, 1972); Giovanni Romeo, *Inquisitori, esorcisti e streghe nell'Italia della controriforma* (Florence, 1990); Craig Har-

The dramatic advances in our understanding of witchcraft in the past twenty-five years have come mainly from local studies or careful analyses of specific writers, laws, or outbursts of persecution.[48] On practical grounds, it has seemed wise to limit this study to one national culture and to one (admittedly extended) century: I have endeavored to stay among the German-speaking peoples of the period roughly 1480 to 1620, but I have often availed myself of an American sheriff's right to cross county lines when in hot pursuit of a criminal, and I have, therefore, not always given up the chase when I reached the seventeenth century or when my suspect seemed to retreat into the Middle Ages.

In many of the areas I have examined in this book, the foundation of previous scholarship was almost entirely lacking, and my own investigations have done little more than scratch the surface or dig postholes down into the cluttered archival middens of the past. For this reason, I cannot claim to have treated all of sixteenth-century Germany in anything like the detail required to establish some of my more ambitious claims. Initially, over twenty years ago, I intended to describe the professorial attitudes of academic authors toward madness in all of early modern Europe, in a series of brisk chapters on the scholastic attitudes of theologians, jurists, and physicians. Vestiges of this intention are still visible in this book, but along the way, my crisp little chapters were waylaid by life. I began to wonder just how important, or influential, or widespread were the professorial attitudes I was studying, and I came to think that it would be crucial to establish, if possible, where, when, and how these and other ideas were implemented in social institutions and village practice, in law courts and in hospitals, in churches and in princely courts. In consequence my study has become untidier, but also, I hope, of broader import than a more austere ex-

---

line, *The Burdens of Sister Margaret: Private Lives in a Seventeenth-Century Convent* (Garden City, N.Y., 1994).

48. See, e.g., A. D. J. Macfarlane, *Witchcraft in Tudor and Stuart England* (London, 1970); Christina Larner, *Enemies of God: The Witch-Hunt in Scotland* (Baltimore, 1981); Sylvie Dupont-Bouchat, Willem Frijhoff, and Robert Muchembled, *Prophètes et sorciers dans les Pays-Bas (XVIe–XVIIIe siècle)* (Paris, 1978); Michael Kunze, *Der Prozess Pappenheimer* (Ebelsbach, 1981); E. William Monter, *Witchcraft in France and Switzerland: The Borderlands During the Reformation* (Ithaca, N.Y., 1976); Wolfgang Behringer, *Hexenverfolgung in Bayern: Volksmagie, Glaubenseifer und Staatsräson in der frühen Neuzeit* (Munich, 1987); Rainer Walz, *Hexenglaube und magische Kommunikation im Dorf der frühen Neuzeit: Die Verfolgungen in der Grafschaft Lippe* (Paderborn, 1993); Eva Labouvie, *Zauberei und Hexenwerk: Ländlicher Hexenglaube in der frühen Neuzeit* (Frankfurt a/M, 1991); Walter Rummel, *Bauern, Hexen und Herren: Studien zur Sozialgeschichte sponheimischer und kurtrierischer Hexenprozesse, 1574–1664* (Göttingen, 1991); Gisela Wilbertz, Gerd Schwerhoff, and Jürgen Scheffer, eds., *Hexenverfolgung und Regionalgeschichte: Die Grafschaft Lippe im Vergleich* (Bielefeld, 1994). Wolfgang Behringer provides an exhaustive survey of the historiography of witchcraft in "Zur Geschichte der Hexenforschung," in *Hexen und Hexenverfolgung im deutschen Südwesten*, ed. Sönke Lorenz (Ostfildern, 1994), pp. 93–146.

ercise in intellectual history. I have had to give up any hopes of being complete, since it became clear, for example, that every town in Germany has its own (mostly as yet unwritten) history of hospitals, of deviance, and of demonic possession.[49] By the late sixteenth century, too, each German university produced printed medical disputations on psychiatric topics that would repay closer study than I have had patience for.[50] Much of my task has involved locating original sources that could shed light on topics that had come to seem important. Too many intriguing stories, like that of the Narrenarzt Peter Mair, cannot be pursued, because the sources are too thin. The history of madness has been a favorite topic in the literary histories of early modern Europe, but once the historian moves beyond Burton's *Anatomy of Melancholy* and the literature of folly, beyond Shakespeare's or Cervantes' understanding of madness, once one has considered the iconographic representations of fools in art, it is not immediately obvious where one can find evidence of how madness was ordinarily defined and how the mad were actually treated. So my various postholes, these excursions into legal, medical, religious, and social history, may serve only to suggest the kinds of surviving evidence and the major concepts with which sixteenth-century Germans, at different social levels, responded. I hope that these exploratory digs will be fascinating enough to attract others to the challenge of finding appropriate sources for other aspects of the history of madness. The comparative history of mental hospitals has, for example, only just begun to be written, but abundant sources exist for a better view than that afforded by the most reliable general accounts.[51]

The strangeness of sixteenth-century Germany can be illustrated in the rise and fall of illnesses we no longer experience. Chapter 1 presents three orders of difficulty in approaching the history of madness, three topics that all resist, in one way or another, our anxious efforts to find comfortable parallels in the past, soothing evidence that nothing has really changed. The first example is that of the famous Flemish painter Hugo van der Goes, who suffered a severe mental and moral breakdown. Modern scholars have tried to diagnose his "case," but doing so involves trusting a source that bristles with difficulties. Such interpretive problems are even more troubling in the case of St. Vitus' dance, an acute and sometimes chronic danc-

49. See, e.g., W. Morgenthaler, *Bernisches Irrenwesen: Von den Anfängen bis zur Eröffnung des Tollhauses 1749* (Bern, 1915); Mummenhoff, "Die öffentliche Gesundheits- und Krankenpflege im alten Nürnberg," esp. pp. 73–86.

50. See Oskar Diethelm, *Medical Dissertations of Psychiatric Interest Printed Before 1750* (Basel, 1971), which presents a large but by no means complete bibliography. Further guidance may be found in the still indispensable volumes by Heinrich Laehr, *Die Literatur der Psychiatrie, Neurologie, und Psychologie von 1459–1799* (Berlin, 1900).

51. Dieter Jetter, *Zur Typologie des Irrenhauses in Frankreich und Deutschland, 1780–1840* (Wiesbaden, 1971).

ing mania that rose and fell mainly in the fifteenth and sixteenth centuries. Scholars have never agreed on what this psychosomatic disorder was, but we shall here at least confront a larger share of the evidence than has ever before been presented in English. The third form of strangeness to which I want to attract attention is demonic possession, a culturally sanctioned way of experiencing and understanding acute states of mental alienation. Commonly, of course, modern readers assume that the Middle Ages saw all mental illness as demonic in origin, but this was far from the case. Medieval and early modern thinkers regularly distinguished mental disorders of organic origin from those based on moral, spiritual, or demonic influence. The evidence actually points to an epidemic rise in the second half of the sixteenth century of demonic obsessions, which it is unhelpful to classify as outbursts of hysteria, schizophrenia, dissociative identity disorder, or of other modern mental illnesses. Before we can seek to translate such disorders into our terms, we need to see what they meant in their own historical context.

One of the master categories for experiencing life and its problems in the sixteenth century was sin and alienation from God. Chapter 2 takes up two major thinkers for whom religious notions of madness blended with the more general idea that the world itself was insane. Martin Luther's heightened sense of sin found outlet in a potent image of the world itself as mad, filled with desperate sinners rushing to their own imminent damnation. In the centuries before the scientific revolution made the world seem like an orderly, rational clockwork, a plausible view held that the world and its creatures were actually crazy, self-destructive, and part of the process by which Creation, in its old age, was becoming senile and moribund. Theophrastus Bombastus of Hohenheim, known more simply as Paracelsus, was no Lutheran in theology, but he concurred that the world was mad in a serious sense, and he specifically invoked Luther's example as reformer to present himself as the Luther of medicine. Insanity and mental disorder were one of Paracelsus's prominent concerns throughout his adult life, and his convoluted language merits close analysis. I have undertaken a comparison of the two reformers in chapter 2 not just because of Paracelsus's claim to be a medical Luther, but because he, too, saw sin as the maddening flaw in God's creation. And in his little-known theological writings, he spoke often and movingly of human alienation from God and from the individual's true or spiritual self, an alienation that he called insane. Chapter 2 thus aims to familiarize the reader with the religious notion that madness was woven into the very fabric of a sinful world.

Of course, not all early modern Germans considered life in deeply theological terms. Many a physician simply ignored the religious aspects of mental illness and concentrated on the body. Chapter 3 takes up the theory and practice of Renaissance medicine as we can see it developing in the German lands. Medically speaking, the century of the ostentatiously rebellious anatomist Andreas Vesalius also saw a massive revival of traditional Galenic medicine at the universities, that is, the system of physiology and therapeutics brought together by the famous second-century Greek physician Galen. Sixteenth-century Germany thus provides an excellent opportunity to examine the state of early modern "psychiatry" at a time when ancient medical authority was under attack but experiencing a reflorescence as well. I have called this part of the medical Renaissance the "rise of Galenic observation." Among its practitioners, we find an increased willingness to deploy the technical medical concept of melancholy more widely and effectively than ever before. Medically speaking, the second half of the sixteenth century was increasingly an "age of melancholy." In my book *Mad Princes of Renaissance Germany* (1994), I explore the rise of humoral and specifically Galenic therapies among the one German social group that could always afford the regular attention of university-trained physicians, namely, the princely dynasties of the Holy Roman Empire, ruling families who increasingly took the advice of their learned personal physicians when dealing with their mentally disturbed relatives. I argue there that Renaissance physicians thus helped create the age and the image of the melancholy prince by popularizing the language of melancholy as central to their vocabulary of discomfort.

Turning from medicine to law, chapter 4 deals with the early modern development of the insanity defense, a topic on which the rise of melancholy had a direct and demonstrable impact. For some readers, the surprise will be that there even was an early modern insanity defense, for we moderns have become accustomed to thinking that its development coincided with the intrusion into jurisprudence of sociology or psychology, as we now understand them. But it is evident that the ancient Romans made some accommodation for the insane in their criminal procedures, as indeed have most civilizations. So the problem in chapter 4 was not to discover the origins of legal thinking about the insane but to understand the changes that this well-developed aspect of jurisprudence underwent during the sixteenth century. As it happens, one of the most prominent psychiatric thinkers in early modern Germany was also the most articulate defender of the insanity defense, Johann Weyer, whose defense of witches depended on an adventurous combination of medical, legal, and theological ideas. His arguments triggered a lively discussion, not just among demonologists, but among jurists, too, and left lasting changes in legal practice.

Having considered certain aspects of madness from the points of view of learned theology, medicine, and the law, I turn in chapter 5 to consider a form of mental disorder that was much discussed and even valued in the

Renaissance—namely, folly. The princely courts of Germany and of all Europe maintained troops of retarded and mentally ill persons as court fools, and a well-known literary tradition holds that these fools enjoyed the special privilege of telling the truth to their masters. In trying to uncover what early modern German observers meant by "folly" (*Narrheit, stultitia*), this chapter examines the supposed wisdom of court fools and seeks to discover what the real life of actual court fools may have been like.

Up to this point, my text has considered various sixteenth-century theories, much discussed by Renaissance and Reformation intellectuals, and has sought to trace the connection of these theories to the lives of early modern people. But the last two chapters deal with custodial and therapeutic practices that were not much discussed, at least not by academics at German universities. Throughout the early modern period, simple Catholics sought the supernatural assistance of Christ, Mary, or a patron saint. Often a relative made a vow of pilgrimage on behalf of a deranged or disturbed person, and if relief were forthcoming, a priest at the pilgrimage shrine might record the healing in a register of miracles, a so-called *Mirakelbuch*. Luckily for us, miracles became part of the polemical arsenal of the Catholic Counter-Reformation, and therefore selections from the manuscript miracle registers appeared in print with some regularity throughout early modern times, providing us with an unexpectedly rich source of information about the lives and circumstances of the mad in Catholic parts of Germany.[52] These accounts are also excellent sources for the study of popular attitudes toward the mentally afflicted. Chapter 6 undertakes an account of these pilgrimages by and for the mad.

Another refuge for simple people was the hospital. From their origins in the Middle Ages, hospitals had always provided food and lodging for elderly and helpless urbanites throughout much of the West, but the sixteenth century saw the introduction of new hospitals in Germany that undertook the task of providing care either for new clients or in new ways. Happily, some records survive from Hesse and from Würzburg that allow us to describe both the innovations and some of the constant features in the miserable lives of the mentally afflicted. Chapter 7 tells this part of the story and provides a hitherto unavailable glimpse of some of the actual persons, most of them poor and illiterate, who needed the care of social institutions such as the hospitals. These people are often invisible in printed sources precisely because they were ordinary, illiterate, and politically unimportant. Together with the pilgrims we meet in chapter 6, these hospital residents often came from the lower social orders and had mental troubles that

52. The manuscript registers can sometimes also be found and analyzed, as done in Lederer, "Reforming the Spirit."

reflected their station in life. It is unfortunate that I have not been able to locate dense enough sources for a study of madness among wanderers, beggars, and vagrants in early modern Germany, but at shrines and in hospitals we do at least gain glimpses of how illiterate and powerless peasants and workers experienced and coped with madness and the mad.

Considering the impossibility of reconstructing the epidemiology of early modern madness, it is obvious that one cannot claim that Germany had any more or less mental illness four or five hundred years ago than in our day. And there is no evidence that madness was a greater problem for the Germans than for those in other lands. In order to sustain such comparisons, we would need reliable statistics, but we lack even rudimentary statistical data on the incidence of mental disorder in early modern Germany, even if we could surmount the translation problems to which I earlier alluded. Certainly, if we adopted Luther's standard of madness as blind, resolute, godless sinfulness, his criterion would turn up more madmen than will be found in this book. But as I have explained, there seems little chance of success in trying from this distance to determine whether there were more (or perhaps fewer) schizophrenics, borderlines, or bipolar manic-depressives back then than now.[53]

Madness and Metaphor: Folly, Possession, and Genius

Madness was usually a human catastrophe, but Renaissance culture also gave an exalted interpretation to three specific notions or images of madness: folly, demonic possession, and melancholia. Humanists, theologians, and physicians could interpret these three as if each form of madness incorporated a laudable polar opposite, a form of the irrational that was not harmful but rather offered, so it seemed, access to deeper sources of insight and wisdom than the humdrum workings of consensus, convention, and reason. Placed opposite to selfish folly, for example, was Christian wisdom, which Erasmus and others joined St. Paul in seeing as a form of madness or folly.[54] For these Christians, faith was at its strongest when it took the form of irrational ecstasy. And so folly was not just dangerous or sinful; it could be a source or basis of wisdom. The second image, demonic possession,

53. I have defended this claim at greater length in "Madness and the Problem of Psychological History in the Sixteenth Century," *Sixteenth Century Journal* 12 (1981): 5–12. For a pragmatic argument that reaches the same conclusion, see MacDonald, *Mystical Bedlam*, pp. xii–xiii, 112–13.

54. Michael Screech, "Good Madness in Christendom," in *The Anatomy of Madness: Essays in the History of Psychiatry*, vol. 1: *People and Ideas*, ed. W. F. Bynum, Roy Porter, and Michael Shepherd (London, 1985), pp. 25–39.

with its idea of being taken over by an alien spirit, had its opposite in the workings of "genius," which was still sometimes regarded (as in ancient Rome) as a possessory or tutelary spirit, and in the possibility of angelic vision, which was in the sixteenth century still capable of communicating to rude, humble, and unlettered Christians whatever God asked His people to know. And so spirit possession was not just sickness; it could, too, be the source of the highest wisdom. The third image of madness, melancholy, had its exalted form, as well. Ever since Marsiglio Ficino in fifteenth-century Florence revived Pseudo-Aristotle's Problem 30, no. 1, celebrating melancholy, Renaissance scholars and artists believed that true creativity was necessarily linked to melancholy madness. When we study sixteenth-century madness in its debilitating and crippling forms, therefore, we illuminate some of the most exalted cultural ideals of the Renaissance and Reformation. The high value placed on certain kinds of irrationality also made the definition of madness problematic in the sixteenth century. The discussions engendered by these sorts of problems should sharpen our sense of what early modern Germans were trying to avoid in their lives and enrich our understanding of what they were trying to attain. This is perhaps just another way of saying that madness was a key concept during the Renaissance, emphatically and multiply connected with the best and the worst that men and women could experience.

In succeeding chapters, as I have outlined them, we shall return to these themes, metaphors, and images of madness, but it is also obvious that at least two Renaissance ways of seeing and treating irrationality did not have an exalted form at all. The sinfulness that troubled Luther and Paracelsus (and many other thoughtful Christians) had no brighter side. Luther might humorously counsel his timid colleague Philipp Melanchthon to "sin boldly that grace may abound," but sin itself brought no special access to insight, creativity, or holiness. I have found no apologists for perversity in the sixteenth century, common though they have become in our more enlightened times. And secondly, the commonplace mad, the fools and mentally disordered who were relegated to the care of their families or packed off to pilgrimage shrines or to hospitals, were not credited with a wise folly, or genius, with poetic furor, divine favor, or saintliness. They were simply the helpless, poor, broken down, disabled, confused, simple, villagers or townsmen, sometimes plagued by hallucination or forebodings of their own damnation, occasionally dangerous to themselves or to others, desperately in need of custodial and pastoral care, looking daily for food and shelter. Some of them hoped for a miraculous cure for their affliction. No one thought of them as enjoying an elevated, ecstatic, or sublimely irrational state, and no one consulted them as unwitting oracles. They were a burden assumed by families or by the community, who found themselves required to help their blind neighbors and relatives, along with their crippled, orphans and mentally disabled, until God or His saints sent relief or release from the troubles of this world. It is true that these two ways of seeing the mad, either as essentially sinful or hopelessly helpless, did seem to assimilate them to known categories, so that their contemporaries could deal with their madness. As we shall see, the kinds of image or metaphor through which a disorder was experienced and understood had real consequences for the way one was treated. That much is still true.

CHAPTER ONE

ℋistorical Problems: Sin, St. Vitus, and the Devil

A HISTORY of madness must confront three salient problems in the early modern period. The first is the problem of sources. In our efforts to see how the mad experienced their world and how the world experienced them, we are usually at the mercy of written evidence. In fact, we normally rejoice if we find a long and circumstantial account or a full archival dossier. But historians recognize that their texts can be opaque even when they seem to be unusually full and transparent. This will become clear in the case of the troubled late medieval painter Hugo van der Goes. A second basic problem is the possibility, even the likelihood, that the sixteenth century experienced certain disorders that no longer occur. In cases like the dancing mania, we encounter strange diseases that do not fit into modern diagnostic categories very well. The historian of madness is well advised, especially in such cases, to attend scrupulously to exactly what was said and done with such suffering, rather than leaping to fill the diagnostic vacuum with the confident assurances of the modern psychiatric manual. The third problem is the formidable force of religion in early modern Germany, a force that could encourage certain religious experiences, such as visions, voices, and raptures, that would surely suggest psychosis today. If one's culture encouraged visions and voices, however, it does not make full sense to see these "symptoms" as evidence of illness. Most Christians of the sixteenth century were aware, moreover, that the devil could obsess and possess a person, body and mind, mimicking the worst forms of madness, driving his victims into frenzies and convulsions, and tempting them to suicide. Here was a religious madness that was of purely external and nonphysical origin, but a madness we cannot ignore if we mean to treat the sixteenth century fully and fairly. Physicians were usually content to turn the demon-possessed over to the pastors and exorcists, who were best trained to deal with them, but most physicians left room in their theories for the possible actions of angels and demons. We shall find repeatedly in this book that we cannot make sense of the mental disorders of the sixteenth century without taking such religious conceptions seriously.

Hugo van der Goes

In 1475, or more likely 1477–78, the renowned Flemish painter Hugo van der Goes (1440?–1482) retreated from the world to become a *converso*, or lay brother, in the Red Cloister near Brussels, a move that art historians have almost uniformly interpreted as a sign of his melancholy, depressed temperament.[1] Instead of vanishing into the monastery, however, it is only with his disappearance from the world that much of his internal life comes into view. His monastic life, his achievements and his troubles, were chronicled about thirty years later by his fellow brother Gaspar Ofhuys, in an account that has been subjected over the years to a remarkable variety of interpretations. Van der Goes continued, as a converso, to paint extraordinary pictures and to receive distinguished visitors, including Archduke Maximilian of Habsburg, who became Emperor Maximilian I in 1493. But in 1480 or 1481, while returning from a trip to Cologne, van der Goes suffered a breakdown that merits our closest attention. Writing sometime between 1509 and 1513, Ofhuys reported:

As his brother Nicolaes [a *donatus*, or lay brother in the same monastery] told me at the time, our brother Hugo, during one night on his journey home, was seized by an amazing disease of the phantasy [*mirabilem fantasialem morbum incurrit*], in which he unceasingly said that he was doomed and condemned to eternal damnation. He even wanted to injure himself physically or commit suicide and had to be forcibly restrained by those around him. Because of this strange illness [*infirmitate mirabili*] that trip had a very sad conclusion; then seeking help, they reached Brussels, and the prior, Father Thomas [Vessem or Wyssem, prior of the Roode Clooster] was summoned at once. When he saw and heard all that had happened, he suspected that he [Brother Hugo] was afflicted with the same disease [*morbo*] as had befallen King Saul, and recalling that Saul had been helped by David's playing the harp [1 Sam. 16: 14–23], he ordered lots of music to be made [probably to be sung] and other theatrical performances [*spectacula recreativa*] for Brother Hugo, by which he hoped to drive off his mental phantasies. Despite these efforts, Brother Hugo did not get better; talking madly [*aliena loquens*], he called himself a son of perdition, and thus indisposed he came home [to the Roode Clooster].[2]

1. For the later date of Hugo's entry into the cloister, see Antoine de Schryver, "Hugo van der Goes' laatste jaren te Gent," *Genter Bijdragen tot Kunstgeschiedenis* 16 (1955–56): 193–211.

2. H. J. Sander, "Beiträge zur Biographie Hugos van der Goes und zur Chronologie seiner Werke," *Repertorium für Kunstwissenschaft* 35 (1912): 519–45, at p. 535 ; W. Stechow,

We observe that, in this account, van der Goes's suicidal illness came on suddenly, that Ofhuys described it specifically as an illness, that a musical and theatrical therapy was tried in an effort to lift the painter's spirits, but that at least for some time, he remained sunk in such a religious depression that he was sure that he would be damned. We have no indication in Ofhuys or elsewhere that van der Goes displayed any signs of insanity before the breakdown of 1480 or 1481. Of course, one could say, as many art historians have said, that the painter's turn away from the world and toward the cloister in mid career was itself a symptom of his melancholy. It seems more likely that monastery life merely sharpened the tensions van der Goes felt because he was trying to combine a meteoric career as a famous painter with the self-denying, ascetic life of the cloister.

Ofhuys emphasized that Hugo's fellow monks gave him constant care ("in caritate et compassione noctu dieque"), despite ugly rumors to the contrary, and that after a time, van der Goes recovered completely, returning to the humble life of a converso, leaving the more exalted refectory of the professed monks, and taking his meals with the simple lay brothers. He used his illness as a moral guide, experiencing it as an appropriately humiliating warning not to let his artistic achievements produce a proud heart ("forte cor suum elevatum est, quare deus nolens eum perire, misericorditer ei dimisit hanc humiliativam infirmitatem, qua re vera humiliatus est valde").

Van der Goes may well have been experiencing a much more specific humiliation than what Ofhuys described in general terms. When Nuremberg humanist Hieronymus Münzer visited Ghent in 1495 and there admired the large and famous altarpiece with the Lamb of God by the brothers van Eyck, he remarked that that incredible work had no rivals and went on to describe what he knew of "another great painter" who had tried in his own work to equal the Ghent altarpiece "and was driven mad and melancholy" ("Item quidam alius magnus pictor supervenit volens imitari in suo opere hanc picturam: et factus est melancholicus et insipiens").[3] Münzer did not say who this painter was, but the conclusion seems inescapable that it was Hugo van der Goes, and Münzer's revealing comment that Hugo's illness was grounded in a frustrated rivalry must be fit-

---

Northern Renaissance Art, 1400–1600: Sources and Documents (Englewood Cliffs, N.J., 1966), p. 16, translation somewhat modified in the interest of literal accuracy. See also the translation of William A. McCloy, "The Ofhuys Chronicle and Hugo van der Goes" (diss., State University of Iowa, 1958), pp. 16–26. McCloy presents the best version of Ofhuys's Latin text, pp. 9–15. The best study of the impact of van der Goes's illness upon his art is Bernhard Ridderbos, De melancholie van de kunstenaar: Hugo van der Goes en de Oudnederlandse schilderkunst (The Hague, 1991).

   3. Ridderbos, De melancholie van de kunstenaar, p. 10, citing the text printed in Imaginair Museum Hugo van der Goes (Ghent, 1982).

ted together with Ofhuys's firsthand report on Hugo's fears that he was damned.[4] We may not be far wrong in guessing that for Hugo an initial frustration of artistic pride turned into a morbid obsession with his own sinful pride.

So far we are still in a mental world in which madness had a mainly moral content; we notice that Ofhuys's account first put Hugo's affliction in biblical terms, and the first therapies he described were mainly biblical and spiritual. But Ofhuys also showed a striking interest in physical explanations for Hugo's troubles:

There are many different opinions about the illness of this converso. Some said that it was a kind of *frenesis magna*; others asserted that he was possessed by a demon. Apparently some symptoms of both of these misfortunes were visible, but I have always heard that in all his illness he never wanted to harm anyone except, over and over again, himself. Since this is not the case with phrenetics or with the possessed, I believe that only God knows what it was.[5]

Here we find Ofhuys openly admitting the possibility of either demonic possession or phrenitis as a likely diagnosis, but then showing an apparently striking independence of judgment by rejecting them both. Assuming for the moment that Hugo's illness was natural, Ofhuys went on to display a medical erudition no doubt gained as *infirmarius* of the monastery, saying that there were several natural species of phrenitis, or frenzy:

[S]ometimes it is caused by melancholy foods [i.e., those causing an excess of black bile], sometimes by the drinking of strong wine, which burns the humors and turns them into ashes by the emotions of the soul such as worry, sadness, excessive application to study, or fear. Sometimes such illness stems from the malignity of a corrupt humor that predominates in the body of a man predisposed to such an illness.[6]

Abandoning the model of David and Saul and proceeding now from these physical principles, Ofhuys emphasized that van der Goes was "seriously weighed down by just these passions of the soul, troubled as he was that he could never finish all the paintings he had undertaken," absorbing himself over and over, moreover, "in a Flemish book," and "aggravating his natural inclination by drinking wine—though this was doubtless on ac-

4. The connection between the two descriptions provides the focus for Ridderbos's analysis in *De melancholie van de kunstenaar*.
5. Sander, "Beiträge," p. 536; Stechow, *Northern Renaissance Art*, p. 17; McCloy, *Ofhuys Chronicle*, p. 21.
6. Sander, "Beiträge," p. 536; Stechow, *Northern Renaissance Art*, p. 17; McCloy, *Ofhuys Chronicle*, pp. 12, 22: "Primo dicendo, quod fuerit naturalis et quedam species frenesis. Sunt enim secundum, naturales huius infirmitatis plures speties que generantur aliquando ex cibis melancholicis aliquando ex potatione fortis vini exurentis humores et incinerantis aliquando, ex anime passionibus scilicet sollicitudine, tristicia, nimio studio et timore. Aliquando ex malicia humoris corrupti dominantis in corpore hominis at talem infirmitatem praeparate."

count of his guests."[7] In the course of time, Ofhuys thought, van der Goes may in this way have laid the physical or natural basis for his infirmity.

This detailed description has seemed so clear in its particulars, so clinically detached, so natural, that historians have stumbled over one another to praise Ofhuys's medical and clinical mind. Rudolf and Margot Wittkower call this account "one of the first reliable records of a mentally ill artist."[8] Erwin Panofsky, to take another prominent example, calls the description "a masterpiece of clinical accuracy and sanctimonious malice," sure on the one hand that the medical report was reliable and persuaded on the other that Ofhuys agreed "with those who explained the painter's illness as an act of Providence intended to purify him of the sin of pride."[9] All of these assertions are exaggerations that rest upon misunderstanding. As for clinical accuracy, Ofhuys appears to have been a shrewd and knowledgeable medical observer, but William McCloy has shown conclusively that Ofhuys's description of phrenitis was lifted verbatim from Bartholomaeus Anglicus's thirteenth-century *De proprietatibus rerum*, one of the most popular medico-scientific encyclopedias circulating in late medieval Europe. The crucial passage in Bartholomaeus reads:

[T]hese passions are caused sometimes by melancholy foods, sometimes by the drinking of strong wine, which burns the humors and turns them into ashes by the emotions of the soul such as worry, sadness, excessive application to study, or fear. Sometimes by the bite of a rabid dog or of another poisonous beast. Sometimes [such illness stems] from the corruption of pestiferous and infected air and sometimes from the malignity of a corrupt humor that predominates in the body of a man predisposed to such an illness.[10]

Except for the additional details of venomous animal bites and poisonous airs, Bartholomaeus provided word for word the matrix for Ofhuys's supposedly careful description of van der Goes. If this is true, then it was all too likely as well that Ofhuys would report that Hugo worried excessively about finishing all his artistic projects, studied a book too strenuously, and drank wine to excess. Ofhuys, having become the *infirmarius* of

7. Ibid.
8. Rudolf and Margot Wittkower, *Born Under Saturn: The Character and Conduct of Artists. A Documented History from Antiquity to the French Revolution* (New York, 1963), p. 108.
9. Erwin Panofsky, *Early Netherlandish Painting: Its Origins and Character* (Cambridge, Mass., 1958), 1: 331.
10. McCloy, *Ofhuys Chronicle*, pp. 31–32: " . . . aliquando ex cibis melancholicis aliquando ex potatione fortis vini exurentis et incinerantis humores. aliquando ex anime passionibus. sollicitudine, tristicia, numio [sic] studio. timore. aliquando ex morsu rabidi canis sive alterius canis venenosi. aliquando ex corruptione aeris pestiferi et infecti, aliquando ex malicia humoris corrupti. dominantis in corpore himinis [sic] at talem infirmitatem preparati." McCloy cites Bartholomaeus Anglicus, *De proprietatibus rerum* (Nuremberg, 1483), bk. 7, ch. 6.

the Roode Clooster, probably read up on diseases and madness in the best or only authority available to him and then adapted what he learned to what he knew or suspected of the life of Hugo van der Goes. It is not going too far to say that Hugo had, literally, a "textbook case of insanity," a condition so expected or predescribed by medical authority that we can no longer be sure that the supposedly predisposing conditions of excessive worry, study, and drink existed at all.[11] So much for the masterpiece of clinical description.

The other diagnostic possibility Ofhuys considered was demonic possession, but when he actually got around to a careful consideration of the possible spiritual causes of Hugo's sad condition, he deliberately ignored demons and concentrated instead on the "most benevolent providence of the Lord [ex piissima dei providentia] who tries to call everyone to penance in order that they not perish." From this perspective, Hugo van der Goes needed the humiliation of madness to bring him down from the pride occasioned by his fame as an artist, "for being only human like the rest of us, his heart was elevated by the honors shown to him and by various visits and congratulations."[12] Brought thus sharply to humility, Hugo realized his need for penance, and as soon as he regained his health, he gave up the privilege of dining with the full-fledged monks and was content to take his meals with the lay brothers.[13] Ofhuys regarded this gesture of penitence as truly edifying, but it did not of course suffice to explain the origin of Hugo's mental malady. Therefore just a few lines later he returned to the possibility that brother Hugo had a natural condition, more specifically a "lesion in some blood vessel in the brain, as a result of excessive imaginings, fantasies, and worries." This observation, too, was actually a conjecture based on his medical reading, as Ofhuys admitted:

For it is claimed [aiunt] that there is close to the brain an extremely small and tender vein that is vested with power over imagination and fantasy; therefore whenever imaginations and fantasies overabound in us, this little vein is afflicted; but if it is affected and damaged until it ruptures, the patient falls into phrenitis and madness [frenesim vel amentiam].[14]

11. Lorne Campbell seems to underestimate the importance of McCloy's discovery when he says, "There is no reason, however, to doubt the authority of the information given by Ofhuys on the life of van der Goes" (Colin Thompson and Lorne Campbell, *Hugo van der Goes and the Trinity Panels in Edinburgh* [London, 1974], p. 3, n. 1).

12. "Frater enim iste conversus propter specialem suam artem in nostra religione satis fuit exaltatus famosior effectus quam si in seculo remansisset, et quia homo erat ut ceteri ex honoribus sibi exhibitis visitationibus et salutationibus diversis forte cor suum elevatum est" (McCloy, "Ofhuys Chronicle," p. 13).

13. It is not clear from Ofhuys's account whether Hugo merely returned to the refectory of the *conversi* or whether he now chose to dine with the lowest members of the monastery, the oblates, among whom his half brother Nicholas could be found (ibid., p. 23, n. 31).

14. Ibid., pp. 14, 24.

Clearly Ofhuys regarded Hugo's artistic imagination as dangerous to health, but from his medical report we get a better sense of Ofhuys's reading than we do of van der Goes's ailments.

What was clear to Ofhuys was the sharp antithesis of natural or spiritual causes.[15] It seems odd that Ofhuys did not consider the possibility that God, working providentially to humble the elect, might use natural causes. This would have been a way to join, rather than to split, the two kinds of cause that he discussed. It may be that Ofhuys did not join them because for him the spiritual or providential explanation was actually a substitute for the demonic explanation that he announced but then did not discuss. It was obvious that van der Goes had suffered a morbidly suicidal breakdown, and the devil was, in fact, often invoked as the cause of such assaults, but for reasons we cannot now recapture, Ofhuys preferred the orderly worlds of natural causation and providential planning.

Efforts on the part of art historians to criticize Ofhuys for malice or sanctimony are therefore off the mark, missing as they do the profoundly ascetic, penitential, religious atmosphere of the Red Cloister and of the other monasteries affiliated with the Windesheim Congregation. As Susan Koslow has recently written, "whatever Hugo's psychological dysfunction may have been," its form and expression were "rooted in the social conventions of his time."[16] The religious terrors experienced by van der Goes may well have been the obsessive terrors of the overscrupulous, the awe-filled sense that one can never sufficiently humble oneself before God.[17] Certainly, this was the moral of Ofhuys's tale, and we shall not get the story right if we follow Panofsky in detecting "sanctimonious malice" where we should perhaps rather sense the constant monastic straining, surely shared by van der Goes himself, toward humiliation, penance, fervor, silence, and withdrawal.[18] We should admit that Ofhuys wrote a detailed and circumstantial account of van der Goes's illness, and yet it is remarkable, not because we can reinterpret it now in our modern medical categories, but precisely because the late medieval categories of nature and providence, demons, and the example of Saul, so obviously infused his understanding of what had gone wrong. The passage lifted from Bartholomaeus Anglicus illustrates perfectly the hazards of looking for "objective data" in the medico-moral theorizing of late medieval monasticism. Rather,

15. Ofhuys draws the following distinction: "Esto quod non ex causa naturali hoc infortunium evenit, sed ex dei providentia infallibili, quae procurat electis et praedestinatis (si in errore sunt) materiam penitendi et revertendi" (ibid., p. 14).

16. Susan Koslow, "The Impact of Hugo van der Goes's Mental Illness and Late Medieval Religious Attitudes on the *Death of the Virgin*," in *Healing and History: Essays for George Rosen*, ed. Charles E. Rosenberg (Folkestone, Kent, 1979), pp. 27–50, at p. 30.

17. Wittkower, *Born Under Saturn*, pp. 112–13.

18. Koslow, "Impact of Hugo van der Goes's Mental Illness," p. 42.

we must notice the ways in which culture, here a monastic culture, created and structured the scrupulous madness of men like Hugo van der Goes.

This case of late medieval melancholy highlights one of the major problems we encounter when we try to capture the history of madness. Despite a detailed case description, it seems that we are still far from the "experience" of madness, and equally far from what it may have been like to be Hugo van der Goes, and from what his brethren experienced in their dealings with him. Our primary source, the documentary evidence, is in truth so often dependent upon prior expectations and on other texts that we have trouble penetrating the veil of textuality. Some scholars, for just these reasons, assert that we can never get through to any reality behind the text, but a cautiously optimistic social historian may feel inclined to concede only that historians have always had to cross-examine their sources, and that these documents are neither more nor less reliable than most others. We must not expect our texts to be transparent windows opening up the experience of madness in the past

A Dancing Mania

St. Vitus' dance is usually defined as an epilepsy or a chorea or even more specifically as Sydenham's chorea. In the fourteenth through the sixteenth centuries, however, we find reports of a disease that was not like any epilepsy or chorea treated by doctors today. Wilhelm von Bernkastel, writing in 1491, described a little-known outburst of the malady in 1463. From eyewitnesses, he had heard of an "amazing epidemic" (*plagam*) in which "hopping dancers from many lands came here [to the pilgrimage shrine of Eberhardsklausen], to be healed." Behaving most strangely, "these dancers jumped about in circles, always separately, thinking that they could by exertion and body movement drive out the pains they felt in their heart and viscera. But not getting any better, and thoroughly exhausted, they called upon St. John the Baptist, whose disease [*plagam*] they said this was."[19]

An odd detail is that they could not perceive the color red at all, and yet "as they danced it seemed to them that they saw the head of St. John the Baptist," swimming in blood. Perhaps by reason of its color, pulverized coral, mixed with some liquid, was given to them to drink. Some of the dancers also begged for grains of coral to hang as amulets around their necks. The dance itself was dangerous: "Some of them jumped until their ribs or loins broke, and they died. For some of these persons, the disease

19. This and the following quotations come from Paul Hoffmann and Peter Dohms, *Die Mirakelbücher des Klosters Eberhardsklausen*, Publikationen der Gesellschaft für rheinische Geschichte, vol. 64, no. 179 (Düsseldorf, 1988), pp. 110–11.

lasted half a year, for others less." When the strange hopping and leaping began, it went on day and night until the dancers, totally worn out, fell to the ground. And yet, when wine was poured over their outstretched hands as they lay on their backs, they sprang up with renewed vigor and started hopping and kicking more wildly than before. Wilhelm von Bernkastel and his contemporaries were familiar with epilepsy and called it the "falling sickness," but this was something far stranger. "May God keep this wrath from us!" Folklorists tell us that St. John's disease was the Rhenish version of St. Vitus' dance, but that does not tell us much about what it actually was.[20] From the description as we have it here, the dance was apparently epidemic, but it is worth emphasizing that the dancers were said to have thought that the dance itself, the hopping and leaping, was therapeutic, even though it seems to have become part of the problem.

Frenzied dancing had appeared in epidemic form earlier in the Middle Ages, but in 1373–74, it erupted in Swabia, England, and the Netherlands, spreading then to Hainaut, Flanders, Brabant, the Lower Rhine, Cologne, Utrecht, Tongern, Aachen, and south to Franconia, Metz, and Strasbourg. In 1375, it was found in France and again in Hainaut and Holland. In 1381, it appeared in Augsburg. In 1428, there is a report of dancing women in Zurich and also in the cloister of St. Agnes in Schaffhausen, where a monk danced until he died.[21] Most of these outbursts were very poorly recorded, unfortunately, and so we do not get a clear picture of this odd phenomenon until the major explosion of St. Vitus' dance in Strasbourg in July 1518.

The dancing in Strasbourg apparently began with one woman, about July 14, 1518, but within four days, thirty-four men and women were infected. According to the seventeenth-century chronicle of Oseas Schad, despite efforts to curb the spread of the dancing mania, soon two hundred were afflicted. The Imlin family chronicle claims that within four weeks, more than four hundred were beset with exhausting, uncontrollable dancing; many danced until they fell to the ground unconscious, and some never recovered.[22]

Writing in the early 1520s, the Alsatian humanist Hieronymus Gebwiler described the dance as God's way of forcing modesty and moderation

20. Richard Beitl, *Wörterbuch der deutschen Volkskunde* (Stuttgart, 1955), p. 376.

21. Hellmuth Liebscher, *Ein kartographischer Beitrag zur Geschichte der Tanzwut* (diss., Leipzig, 1931), pp. 7–15. The most extensive discussion is by E. Louis Backman, *Religious Dances in the Christian Church and in Popular Medicine*, trans. E. Classen (London, 1951), pp. 190–234. See also the summary in George Rosen, *Madness in Society: Chapters in the Historical Sociology of Mental Illness* (New York, 1969), pp. 196–204.

22. Alfred Martin, "Geschichte der Tanzkrankheit in Deutschland," *Zeitschrift des Vereins für Volkskunde* 24 (1914): 113–34, 225–39, at pp. 116, 119. Martin mercilessly disposes of ignorant suggestions that this major outburst occurred one hundred years earlier, in 1418. See also the detailed account in Backman, *Religious Dances*, pp. 235–42.

upon the Strasbourgeois, who needed, he said, to crucify their bodies "so that Christ's suffering should not be lost upon us." Gebwiler said that he had seen one woman dance for six days in a row, "and strong men had to replace one another as guards in the job of protecting her from hurting herself." It was a "warning from God that this disease attacked many just from looking on [at her] so much and so often."[23] Aroused by this warning, the Council of Twenty-One ordered two guildhalls to be set aside for the dancers and for them to be provided with guards. Gebwiler remembered that "they danced day and night with those poor people, but toward evening they tied them all onto wagons and took them to St. Vitus of Hohlenstein. And after their pilgrimage there was finished and they were all danced out, they took them home again." The lesson, Gebwiler thought, was obvious. Good citizens needed to "keep some moderation in their dancing, and especially to omit shameful and blasphemous dances; they must never dance in the wrong places or with inappropriate persons, as when they dance in cloisters and nunneries with monks and nuns." If the people of Strasbourg did not improve their conduct, God would surely punish them as he had once punished the Egyptians, "and for our obstinacy He will let us sink in a Red Sea of sins."[24]

By this account, the dancing mania was a moral message straight from God. Gebwiler showed no inclination to interpret the dance as a natural disorder. From other chronicles and from fragments of the city council records, however, it is obvious that there was in fact some dispute about what the disease was and how it should be treated. During the summer of 1518, as the strange dancing continued, physicians testified to the Council of the Twenty-One that the disease was "a natural sickness that came from hot blood." When the afflicted dancers petitioned for a Mass to be said for them, the council consulted with the bishop's vicar, who replied "that this seemed quite unnecessary to him, seeing that the physicians had declared that it was a natural sickness. Accordingly one should try natural means with it." The vicar did concede, however, that if natural remedies failed, "he would order all the preachers [of Strasbourg] to speak out publicly from their pulpits, praying to God and pleading that He send His grace and mercy to us."[25]

23. Karl Stenzel, ed., *Die Straßburger Chronik des elsässischen Humanisten Hieronymus Gebwiler* (Berlin, 1926), p. 74.

24. Ibid., p. 75.

25. *Fragments des anciennes chroniques d'Alsace*, ed. L. Dacheux, vol. 4 (Strasbourg, 1901), p. 252, quoting from the so-called "Annals of Sebastian Brant" compiled by Johann Wencker in 1637; my thanks to Thomas and Kathy Brady for extracting these materials from the "Annals of Sebastian Brant"; they are also printed in Alfred Martin's excellent summary, "Geschichte der Tanzkrankheit in Deutschland," *Zeitschrift des Vereins für Volkskunde* 24 (1914): 113–34, 225–39, at pp. 118–19.

In mid July 1518, it appears, when the dancing mania was still new and relatively unknown in Strasbourg, music and dance were specially ordered as therapy for the dancers. Daniel Specklin recorded in his manuscript chronicle, written in the second half of the sixteenth century:

1518: A dance erupted among the young and the old, so that they danced day and night until they fell down; and more than one hundred danced in Strasbourg at the same time. So they reserved the guildhall of the carpenters and the dyers and set up platforms in the horse market and in the grain market and paid people to stay with them and to dance with them, [accompanied] by fife and drum.[26]

Evidently these measures were a sad failure, for Specklin noted: "All of this helped not at all." Many persons danced themselves to death. Dancing was not a cure; it was the disease itself.

With a change of policy, the Strasbourg council now decided that music was actually making matters worse; music and rhythmic drumming were infecting others to dance uncontrollably. And so the council forbade almost all music until the end of September. In the municipal archive of Strasbourg is preserved an account in Sebastian Brant's own hand:

On the second day after Vincula Petri [i.e., on August 3] anno 18: When sadly at this time a horrible episode arose with the sick, dancing persons, which has not yet stopped, our lord councilors of the XXI turned to the honor of God and forbade, on pain of a fine of 30 shillings, that anyone, no matter who, should hold a dance until St. Michael's Day [September 29] in this city or its suburbs or in its whole jurisdiction. For by so doing they take away the recovery of such persons. The only exception is that if honorable persons wish to dance at weddings or celebrations of first Mass in their houses, they may do so using stringed instruments, but they are on their conscience not to use tambourines and drums.[27]

Stringed instruments may not have seemed so dangerous as percussion instruments because they did not trigger the spasmodic, rhythmic convulsions of this strange dancing. The council had moved as early as July 27 to order several mad dancers to cancel their drumming and to content themselves with the music of stringed instruments.[28] From this point on, it appears that the city councilors were more willing to sanction religious responses to the epidemic. They ordered a Mass in the chapel of Unsere Frau

26. Martin, "Geschichte der Tanzkrankheit," p. 119; L. Dacheux, ed., *Les chroniques strasbourgeoises de Jacques Trausch et de Jean Wencker. Les annales de Sébastien Brant. Fragments recueillis par l'abbé L. Dacheux* (Strasbourg, 1892), p. 148, quoting the "Amazing Cure of St. Vitus' Dance" in Wencker's chronicle.

27. Archive municipale, Strasbourg, R3, fol. 72 recto; my thanks to Thomas and Kathy Brady for transcribing this entry.

28. This is how I interpret the following entry: "5a Mariae Magdalene. Item als etlich frauen und knaben den bössen dantz tantzen, soll die termen [i.e., trommeln?] abstellen und heimlich seitenspiel haben" (Dacheux, *Les chroniques*, p. 240; Martin, "Geschichte," p. 221).

and on August 10 announced that the dancers were to be taken on a pilgrimage to St. Vitus' shrine near Saverne. Each guild was to care for its own frenzied members: "that they be subdued or brought to St. Vitus, and to allow them no sort of stringed music or celebration, no jewelry or beautiful clothes, and also not to let them loose, to run in the streets."[29] Obviously, the Strasbourg councilors had decided that it was time for a general penance. Celebrations with music and holiday clothing were out of place. Loose persons [*leichtfertigen*], meaning probably prostitutes and gamblers, drinkers and ruffians, were "banished from the city for a time."[30] The city also ordered a contribution of a hundred-pound candle and a High Mass, along with three Low Masses, to be sung in the cathedral. Those making the trip to St. Vitus were placed on three large wagons under the care of custodians. When they got near to Saverne, one of the custodians was to ride on ahead and obtain the services of three or four priests, to sing Masses for each group of pilgrims. After each Holy Office, the poor disordered dancers were led around the altar, and each one was to contribute one pfennig. If anyone lacked the requisite pfennig, the city provided money for him or her, and whatever was left over went into the general collection box.[31]

By this point, the city had recognized St. Vitus as the patron of this disease, and reports came back that those who went on the pilgrimage returned fully recovered. According to Specklin's chronicle:

They sent many on wagons to St. Vitus on Hellensteg [i.e., Hohlenstein] beyond Saverne, and others got there on their own. They fell down dancing before his image. So then a priest said Mass over them, and then they were given a little cross and red shoes, on which the sign of the cross had been made in holy oil, on both the tops and the soles. In St. Vitus' name they were sprinkled with holy water. It helped many, and they gave a large contribution. This is why it is called St. Vitus' dance.[32]

If we can trust this part of Specklin's account, it would appear that the pilgrimage to St. Vitus on Hohlenstein involved a successful application of holy water and holy oil to specially prepared red shoes. Again, we notice the color red, which is, with black, perhaps the most powerful color known to folklorists, for whom the bloody tint often connotes health and healing, love, fire, joy, but also the devil, the witch, and the magic by which one might ward off the evil eye.[33]

29. Instructions to the guilds, printed in Martin, "Geschichte," p. 121.

30. Ibid.

31. Ibid., p. 117, and appendices 1 and 2, pp. 122–24.

32. Ibid., p. 121; Dacheux, ed., *Les chroniques*, p. 148.

33. Beitl, *Wörterbuch der deutschen Volkskunde*, p. 647; see *Handwörterbuch des deutschen Aberglaubens* (Berlin and Leipzig, 1927–42, ed. E. Hoffmann-Krayer and Hanns Bächtold-Stäubli, s.v. "rot," vol. 7, cols. 792–834. Backman, *Religious Dances*, pp. 278–81, also speculates on the meaning of red (and especially the hatred of red or the therapeutic use of red) in attacks of St. Vitus' dance.

The shrine of St. Vitus lay in a cave in the Vosges promontory named Vixberg (Veitsberg, Vitus' Mountain), west of Saverne. A narrow path led up to the grotto, which was fitted out as a chapel, to which pilgrims came especially on Easter Monday and on St. Vitus' Day, June 15. Among the most common pilgrims were epileptics, infertile and "hysterical" women, and farmers with sick cattle, as well as those suffering from St. Vitus' dance.[34]

It seems especially noteworthy that even persons living at the time had had so little experience with this dancing mania that they did not know what it was. As we have seen, purely moral explanations collided with the naturalistic explanations of the physicians. At other places, apparently, St. Vitus' dance got its name from its recurrence around mid June, but in Strasbourg, it seems to have obtained its name because it was thought that St. Vitus could help. Daniel Specklin offered a third reason for the name: that someone had cursed the afflicted in St. Vitus' name. "May St. Vitus attack you!" was a frequent anathema among Alsatian authors of the fifteenth and sixteenth centuries.[35] The odd thing here is that St. Vitus could be both the cause and the cure of his disease. Even in this respect, St. Vitus was thought of as behaving much as did other saints, including the Blessed Virgin Mary. Christians have often thought that the saints might punish those who did not adequately venerate them.[36]

The same ambiguity attaches to the use of music. At first it seemed that dancing was what these sick people needed, and the city's Council of Twenty-One ordered fife and drum, guards, and special dance stages. Within two weeks, however, it appeared that music was actually spreading the disorder, and that Strasbourg needed instead to order days of quiet, sober repentance. It was not clear what this sickness was.

One of the most extraordinary features of the dancing mania in Strasbourg was its epidemic progress. It was not always so infectious. We hear of a small group of frantically dancing children in Basel in 1536, and a solitary man caught the dancing mania in Anhalt in 1551.[37] Felix Platter in 1614 described a case of "this disgusting disturbance," as he termed an episode from the Basel of his childhood (during the 1540s): a woman who obsessively and convulsively danced with specially chosen guards ("strong men"), dressed in red, who took turns for almost a full month, dancing and jumping with her day and night until her feet were rubbed raw and she was so exhausted she could no longer stand. At that point she was taken to

34. Martin, "Geschichte," p. 117. On the pilgrimage to the chapel of St. Vitus on Hohlenstein near Saverne, see Backman, *Religious Dances*, pp. 238–42.

35. Martin, "Geschichte," pp. 120–21.

36. Michael Carroll, *Madonnas That Maim: Popular Catholicism in Italy Since the Fifteenth Century* (Baltimore, 1992).

37. Rosen, *Madness in Society*, p. 202.

a local "hospital" (a spital, or nursing home), where she recovered completely. This attack of dancing did not infect others, but again we cannot help noticing the mysterious recurrence of the color red.[38] In his *Praxeos* of 1609, Platter had already described an epidemic version of the disorder, in which not just women but men too were afflicted with dancing that went on for weeks. In that work, Platter noted a possible parallel with a peculiar "jumping condition of the limbs" known to the Arabs, but he opined in conclusion that if this disease was not from the devil, it must come from God Himself as a punishment.[39]

Writing in 1610, the jurist Philipp Camerarius of Tübingen (1537–1624) described a widespread disorder that prompted "a host of dancers not so long ago to take sacrifices to that Saint [Vitus, near Ravensburg in southern Swabia], for they got well with his help and were accustomed to taking refuge here with their dancing."[40] But Camerarius did not give the impression of a real epidemic. So, as it was then understood, this disorder could take an individualized as well as an "infectious" form. Johann Schenck von Grafenberg (1530–1598) described an epidemic form of St. Vitus' dance, but confusingly added details from the southern Italian dance mania called tarantism, which seems to have had a rather different etiology, form, and mythology.[41] Schenck claimed, however, that in the Breisgau in southwestern Germany, the illness came annually in June and that the afflicted gathered

38. Felix Platter, *Observationum, in hominis affectibus plerisque corpori et animo . . . libri tres* (Basel, 1614) , p. 85; *Observationes: Krankheitsbeobachtungen* (Bern, 1963), p. 82; Martin, "Geschichte," p. 122, which cites, in addition to Platter, Johannes Gross, *Kurtze Basler Chronik* (1614).

39. Felix Platter, *Praxeos seu de cognoscendis, praedicandis, praecavendis, curandisque affectibus homini incommodantibus tractatus* (Basel, 1609), pp. 103–4.

40. Martin, "Geschichte," p. 122, citing *Operae horarum subcisivarum, sive meditationes historicae: Centuria altera* (Frankfurt a/M, 1601).

41. One major similarity between St. Vitus' dance and tarantism was the use of music as both the catalyst and the therapy for the dance. In both cases, too, the afflicted danced until they were exhausted. As early as 1611, Sebastian de Covarrubias Horozco commented that the bite of the tarantula "se cura al son de instrumentas, porque el paciente moviéndose al compás del son, dissimula su mal." Quoted in Marius Schneider, "Tarantella," in *Die Musik in Geschichte und Gegenwart*, vol. 13 (Kassel, 1949–86), col. 117. See also Henry Sigerist, "The Story of Tarantism," in *Music and Medicine*, ed. Dorothy M. Schullian and Max Schoen (New York, 1948), pp. 96–116; Jean Fago Russell, "Tarantism," *Medical History* 23 (1974): 404–25. In his *Auszüge aus einem Reise-Journal* (1788–89), Goethe noted that the tarantella was then a dance for girls using castanets and tambourine and employed to cure mental illnesses (*Gemüthskrankheiten*). He observed, however, that the dance itself could turn into a disease and cited the 1771 description by Johann Hermann von Riedesel, who reported a woman of twenty-two who had danced ten hours and another who had danced thirty-six hours without eating or drinking. See Johann Wolfgang Goethe, *Italienische Reise*, pt. 2, ed. Christoph Michel and Hans Georg Dewitz (Frankfurt a/M, 1993), in *Sämtliche Werke*, pt. 1, vol. 15, 2: *Briefe, Tagebücher und Gespräche*, ed. Dieter Borchmeyer (Frankfurt a/M, 1985–), pp. 901–2.

sadly, fearfully, anxiously, and with an oppressed spirit and feel plucking and hopping pain through their whole body as the prelude to and fuel for this malady. They
are convinced that they can never be calmed and relieved if they cannot shake out
this disease by dancing at the shrine of the saint, and their success confirms them in
this. And truly they are as a rule free of this madness for the rest of the year once
they complete this annual dance, which they usually do for the space of three
hours.[42]

Here, obviously, we have a form of chronic and recurrent St. Vitus'
dance that did not drive those whom it afflicted to total exhaustion and
even death, as it had in Strasbourg and Basel. Gregor Horst (1578–1635), a
professor of medicine in Giessen, and at one time the city physician of Ulm,
described a form of St. Vitus' dance that seems to have combined features
of both the chronic (recurrent) and acute forms of the malady:

I recall that I spoke last spring [1624] with several women who annually visit the
chapel of St. Vitus in Drefelhausen, not far from Geislingen [near Weissenstein in
the Ulm territory of Rechberg]. There they dance madly [mit verwirrten Sinnen] all
day and all night until they collapse in ecstasy. In this way they come to themselves
again and feel little or nothing until the next May, when they are again tortured by
a disturbance of their members, according to them, so that they are again forced
around St. Vitus' Day to betake themselves to that place on account of the dance.
One of these women is said to have danced every year for twenty years, another for
a full thirty-two. . . . I got to know an honorable maiden, the daughter of one of our
town's merchants, who has suffered now for some years every spring from a minor
mental disorder and a similar agitation in which she is forced restlessly to move this
or that limb, while her tongue and speech are also often disturbed. She is forced
from place to place, and this lasts for several weeks, in some years [lasting] both day
and night. I'm afraid that much worse may be expected.[43]

Here, Horst described a serious and exhausting malady that nonetheless
seemed to recur every spring. In a learned argument with other commentators, he held that this form of St. Vitus' dance was not a mental or moral
illness (although he seems to have thought that there were such illnesses)
but a basically physical convulsion. Foreshadowing the seventeenth-century turn to neurological explanations, Horst declared:

Some believe that these persons suffer from a mental illness [geistige Erkrankung]
that causes the perverse drive and lust for dancing, but I have concluded that if the
women with whom I spoke last spring are to be believed, these are usually convulsive movements, especially since they maintain that for several weeks before they
came to the chapel of St. Vitus, they suffered from tense pains in all their limbs together with growing fatigue and heavy-headedness, a condition that continued until they came to the customary dancing place and heard the musical instrument that

42. Martin, "Geschichte," pp. 122–23.
43. Ibid., p. 127.

was being struck for them, whereupon they became more and more mentally confused and were forced to dance.[44]

This is a most interesting description, for it rather clearly demarcates an important distinction between mental illness on the one hand and physical disorders of the nervous system or brain on the other. Horst was unwilling to grant that a condition was a *"geistige Erkrankung"* if its origin lay in some physical convulsion or lesion, even though the accompanying symptoms might include serious mental confusion. For the history of the notion of mental illness, and as evidence for the controversial context in which this concept emerged, these remarks are important. But here, too, we are presented with a condition in which frenzied dancing was both a symptom and part of the cure. Music again seemed to be both catalyst and therapy.

Efforts to explain the dancing mania have been as inventive as they have been contradictory. The famous German Renaissance physician Paracelsus exposed his general Christian/medical framework in a subtle and differentiated discussion of the disease. For him there were three sorts of St. Vitus' dance: the first stemmed from imagination (*chorea imaginativa, aestimativa* [dancing arising from the imagination or the judgment]) and was very much the dance as we have found it in other sixteenth-century records; second, there was a *chorea lasciva* (i.e., lustful dancing), involving the senses and the will, but evidently not the imagination or judgment; and, third, Paracelsus recognized a *chorea naturalis* (*coacta*) (forced natural dancing) that had its origin in the body, in certain arteries that could be tickled, prompting involuntary laughter.[45] He emphasized that the disease could be natural or unnatural, bodily or spiritual, coerced or voluntary.[46] The chief advantage of this elaborate diagnostic scheme, as we shall see in the next chapter, was that he could recognize and differentiate moral, religious, emotional, and physical components in St. Vitus' dance. He did not feel the need to reduce everything to any one primordial category. For the explanation of the actual cases of St. Vitus that we have encountered, Paracelsus is actually of some use, because he implied that there was a serious difference between the natural disorder, which modern physicians might categorize as a neurological disorder, and the disorders that arose in one's mind, emotions, and will. He did not, however, pretend to have examined or treated even one case of the disease, and so his categories have a rather flat, schematic, logical flavor.

The farther we get from firsthand experience of the dancing mania, the

44. Ibid.
45. See chapter 2, pp. 116–17, on Paracelsus's treatise *Von den krankheiten die der vernunft berauben* ("Diseases That Rob Men of Reason").
46. Paracelsus, *Von den krankheiten die der vernunft berauben*, in *Sämtliche Werke*, ed. Karl Sudhoff (Munich and Berlin, 1922–33), pt. 1, 2: 392–455, at pp. 408–9, 411.

more adventurous the theorizing becomes. In contrast to medical and moral explanations, the celebrated sixteenth-century French jurist and philosopher Jean Bodin used the condition to illustrate his favorite theory that climate and geography deeply affect human character. On the one hand, he claimed that Mediterranean peoples had a tendency to go mad more often than northerners. This helped explain why Granada in Spain had many hospitals only for the mad.[47] Moreover, madmen in the south had terrible visions; they "preach and speak many languages without learning them, and are sometimes possest with evil spirits, having leane bodies, more like unto ghosts."[48] Northerly climes, on the other hand, engendered a generally sluggish physique and diminished libido. Whereas Africans, Persians, and Peruvians (i.e., in the south) all took many wives, Julius Caesar had reported that in England one might share one woman among ten or twelve men. Northerners were thus naturally conditioned to be chaste. As we can see here, jokes about the sex lives of the English have a long history, but the serious point is that Bodin saw the dancing mania as geographically specific. Northerners tended to be "corpulent and sanguine," and their mental disorders too were different from the furors of the south. Northern European madmen

do nothing but dance, laugh and leape in their fooleries [au leur folie]: and in Germanie it is called the disease of S. Victus [sic], the which is cured by musick: whether that the sweet harmonie thereof doth recall the reason which was distempered, or whether that musick doth cure the infirmities of the bodie by the mind, as the phisick [medicine] doth cure the mind by the bodie, or that evil spirits which do sometimes torment mad men are expelled with this divine harmonie, delighting in nothing but discords.[49]

While Bodin emphasized that St. Vitus' dance was a curiously Germanic ailment, he could not sort out what effect the characteristic music had. Did it work directly on the mind, on the body, or on the demons that might be causing the dancing mania? Bodin did not seem to know that the music could also be an agent in causing the disease itself, but at least he was willing to express a level of uncertainty about this strange disorder. Bodin's observation did advance the discussion of the dancing mania, however, because he focused on the uncanny geographical boundedness of the disorder. Here was a madness that was clearly not universal.

Other scholars have been less well informed but rather more confident

47. Modern historians would be quick to connect Granada's hospitals to the strong medieval Arab-Muslim tradition of caring for the mentally ill in special hospitals.

48. Jean Bodin, The Six Bookes of a Commonwealth, trans. Richard Knolles (1606), ed. Kenneth D. McRae (Cambridge, Mass., 1962), pp. 556–57; cf. Les six livres de la république (Paris, 1583; repr., Aalen, 1977), pp. 681–82.

49. Bodin, Six Bookes of a Commonwealth, p. 556.

in their interpretations. A German tradition of scholarship, for example, interprets St. Vitus' dance as simply a form of epilepsy, ignoring the most prominent forms that the disorder took in the sixteenth century.[50] In the late seventeenth century, Thomas Sydenham (1624–1689) sponsored a neurological interpretation of what had traditionally been thought of as humoral disorders. From this drastically reductive perspective, he declared the dance to be a form of chorea, a twitching and jerking of the limbs.[51] In fact, today St. Vitus' dance is frequently just equated with Sydenham's chorea because St. Vitus' dance "was first well described by the English physician Thomas Sydenham in 1685."[52] Obviously, however, neither of these diagnoses fits the descriptions we have gathered from German sources for the sixteenth and early seventeenth centuries.[53] The frenzied dancers who visited the shrines of St. Vitus, falling under attack every spring, spreading their frenzy occasionally in epidemic fashion, and dancing for days until they dropped, do not conform to any known type of epilepsy. Nor does Sydenham's chorea, an affliction mainly of children between the ages of five and fifteen and of pregnant women, describe the tormented dancers of Renaissance Germany. In the modern chorea, abrupt jerkings and twitches afflict the face, neck, body, and limbs, subsiding completely during sleep. After a few weeks or months, this kind of chorea subsides completely.[54] It is widely held to be a neurological by-product of rheumatic fever. Unless we wish to imagine a quite different epidemiology for rheumatic fever in the sixteenth century, one mainly confined to Germany, and a disease with rather different symptomatology as well, we had best admit that whatever Thomas Sydenham described, it was not the dancing mania as we find it in early modern Germany.

More subtle, or at least more wonderfully vague, is the diagnosis of St. Vitus' dance as a form of hysteria, specifically "chorea hysterica rhythmica."[55] Covering all possible bases, Alfred Martin expands on this notion: "Surely among St. Vitus' dancers were the explicitly mentally ill: some

50. *Handwörterbuch des deutschen Aberglaubens*, ed. Hoffmann-Krayer and Bächtold-Stäubli, vol. 8 (Berlin, 1937), col. 1544, "Veitstanz s. Fallsucht 2, 1168 ff." Richard Beitl, *Wörterbuch der deutschen Volkskunde* (Stuttgart, 1955), p. 781, "Veitstanz s. Veit, Fallsucht."

51. On Sydenham generally, see D. G. Bates, "Thomas Sydenham: The Development of His Thought, 1666–1674" (diss., Johns Hopkins University, 1975); id., "Thomas Sydenham," in *Dictionary of Scientific Biography*, ed. C. C. Gillispie (New York, 1970–80), 13: 213–15. Bates points out that Sydenham devoted hardly any time or space in his writings to the chorea to which modern medicine has attached his name.

52. *Encyclopedia Americana* (Danbury, Conn., 1987), 6: 635.

53. See the similar critique in Liebscher, *Ein kartographischer Beitrag*, pp. 5–6; and Paul Diepgen, *Deutsche Volksmedizin: Wissenschaftliche Heilkunde und Kultur* (Stuttgart, 1935), pp. 88–92.

54. *Encyclopedia Americana* (1987), 6: 636. See also *The Oxford Companion to Medicine*, ed. John Walton, Paul B. Beeson, and Ronald Bodley Scott (Oxford, 1986), 1: 214.

55. Martin, "Geschichte," p. 128.

maniacs (in the modern sense) with a cheerful mood and a great compulsion to move about [*Bewegungsdrang*]; some chronically mad, who danced as a result of delusions; some catatonics, with continuous movements of specific body parts."[56] In Martin's eclectic and comprehensive view, persons with physical ailments "probably started the dancing in Strasbourg," and hysterics then imitated them in large numbers.[57] Such a description at least has the virtue of trying to deal with the evidence as we have it before us. To explain the recurrent epidemic of dancing mania around St. Vitus' Day, Martin goes further in his diagnosis of hysteria:

> The sick who made pilgrimage to chapels of St. Vitus and St. John the Baptist on their days were only the smallest portion of the true St. Vitus' dancers, for they went [to the shrines] if they were sick, not waiting for the saints' days. These were patients with the compulsion of St. Vitus [*Zwangsidee des Veitstanzes*], other kinds of hysterics, especially those with hysterical cramps, those sick with the "small St. Vitus' dance" or Sydenham's chorea (like the girl whom Horst suspected of "much worse"), but then also all kinds of feebleminded, epileptics, and other patients in whom unnatural muscle movements dominated the image of illness.[58]

Without plunging off the cliff of confusion in quite this way, Paul Diepgen and Hellmuth Liebscher contend that St. Vitus' dance was a "psychic epidemic," a "mass psychosis."[59] The dancers were obviously "psychotics in whom a compulsion to imitate lay at the foundation." The dancing mania was for them a "diseased activation of folk belief."[60] Josef Schumacher calls St. Vitus' dance one of the "psychic folk diseases of the German Middle Ages."[61] Criticizing such theories of mass psychosis, George Rosen views the dancing mania as a culturally valid response to stress, similar to religious revivals and primitive revitalization movements.[62] E. Louis Backman, in the most thorough sifting of the evidence, concludes that ergotism, the convulsive cramping disorder caused by rye fungus, *Claviceps purpurea*, was responsible for massive outbursts of St. Anthony's fire and of St. Vitus' dance.[63]

56. Ibid.
57. Hysteria has seemed an attractive diagnosis partly because it was known as the great imitator, a disorder that could look like a multitude of other diseases. See Mark S. Micale, *Approaching Hysteria: Disease and Its Interpretations* (Princeton, 1995).
58. Martin, "Geschichte," p. 129.
59. Diepgen, *Deutsche Volksmedizin*, p. 83; Liebscher, *Ein kartographischer Beitrag*, p. 6.
60. Diepgen, *Deutsche Volksmedizin*, pp. 85–86.
61. Josef Schumacher, *Die seelischen Volkskrankheiten im deutschen Mittelalter und ihre Darstellung in der bildenden Kunst* (Berlin, 1937).
62. Rosen, *Madness in Society*, pp. 195–225. Confusingly, however, Rosen claims that "mental illness as represented by the psychoses is hardly an important element in most of these group occurrences. On the other hand, the singing, drumming, dancing, and other means employed to achieve states of dissociation, trance, or hypnosis do involve psychopathology in a broad sense" (p. 224).
63. Backman, *Religious Dances*, pp. 303–27. The genus Claviceps includes a number of

FIG. 1. Pieter Brueghel the Elder, *The Dancing Pilgrims at Muelebeek*. Courtesy Metropolitan Museum of Art, New York.

Earlier commentators were just as sure that St. Vitus' dance was "a special kind of convulsion that arises from the blood or other humors . . . so that the nerve vessels and the instruments of voluntary motion are excited and stimulated to such amazing and extraordinary movements."[64] Or that in St. John's dance, "secret lusts were excited, and found only too soon an occasion for wild satisfaction. . . . [All sorts] fled their parents and workers their employers in order to revel in the dances of the possessed and to suck in the poison of this psychic infection."[65]

It thus appears that every commentator on this subject has projected a fair share of his own fears, religious and scientific outlook and weltanschauung into the picture. In this confused condition, it is not surprising that the art historians have been at a loss as well. Pieter Brueghel the Elder's famous engraving *Dancing Pilgrims at Muelebeek*, for example, has recently been interpreted as a display, not of ergot poisoning or epilepsy, but of the wild revels of St. John's Day.[66]

Brueghel himself added a note to the drawing explaining: "These are pilgrims who were to dance on St. John's Day at Muelebeek outside Brussels, and when they have danced over a bridge and hopped a great deal they will be cleansed for a whole year of St. John's disease."[67] We notice that the "dancers" are grouped with a woman flanked or controlled by two

---

species. There are three varieties of ergot of rye in Switzerland alone, and other species of *Claviceps* are parasitic on different grasses. They differ in their alkaloidal constituents—and hence, evidently, in their probable effects on someone who ingests them (one outcome being a kind of gangrene, *Ergotismus gangraenosus*, another the *Ergotismus convulsivus* equated with St. Vitus' dance). "In German folklore there was a belief that, when the corn waved in the wind, the corn mother (a demon) was passing through the field; her children were the rye wolves (ergot). . . . [the names] *seigle ivre* ('drunken rye') and *Tollkorn* (mad grain), point to a knowledge of the psychotropic effects of ergot," writes Albert Hofmann (R. Gordon Wasson, Carl A. P. Ruck, and Albert Hofmann, *The Road to Eleusis* [New York, 1978], p. 26). See also A. Hofmann, *Die Mutterkornalkaloide* (Stuttgart, 1964), on research into ergot alkaloids. Hofmann cites G. Barger, *Ergot and Ergotism* (London, 1931), as "the standard monograph on the botany and history of ergot."

64. Johann Heinrich Zedler, *Grosses vollständiges Universal-Lexikon*, vol. 46 (Leipzig and Halle, 1745), col. 1013.

65. J. F. C. Hecker, *Die grossen Volkskrankheiten des Mittelalters: Historisch-pathologische Untersuchungen*, ed. August Hirsch (Berlin, 1865), p. 147.

66. Neil Harding McAlister, "The Dancing Pilgrims at Muelebeek," *Journal of the History of Medicine and Allied Sciences* 32 (1977): 315–19; by the mid seventeenth century, this disorder was now so little understood that when Hendrick Hondius copied Brueghel's drawing as a copperplate engraving, he declared that it "showed how the pilgrims on St. John's Day near Brussels must dance to Meulebeeck; and when they have danced over this bridge . . . they appear to be cured of the falling sickness [epilepsy] for one year" (*Vertooninge Hoe de Pelgerimmen, op S. Ians-dagh, buyten Brussel, tot Meulebeeck danssen moeten; ende als sy over dese Brugh gedanst hebben, ofte gedwungen werden op dese volgende maniere, dan schijnen sy, voor een Iaer, van de vallende Sieckte, genesen te zijn*. Gesneden ende gedruckt van Huyse van Henricus Hondius [The Hague, 1641]).

67. Rosen, *Madness in Society*, p. 202; Backman, *Religious Dances*, pp. 244–47.

men, echoing the folk dance known as the two and one dance. The women in particular seem to be in a kind of trance.

A group of dancing figures under a sculpture of St. Vitus in the great Cologne cathedral is said, by another pair of scholars, to represent "the basic principle of a regulated healing dance in a sanctified place and under the eyes of the patron, St. Vitus."[68] Again we find the curious contradiction that what seems diseased and frenzied to one historian is an example of Apollonian regulation and Christian discipline to another. Was this dancing mania part of the solution or was it a psychic disorder?

This brings us to the crux of the problem, for it seems that even in the sixteenth century, when St. Vitus' dance was still virulent, observers were losing a sense of what it was or how it should be dealt with. Within a generation or two, the dancing mania was almost all gone. Backman argued interestingly that the dancing mania died out once ergotism was recognized as a separate disorder, in the late sixteenth century,[69] but only certain aspects of St. Vitus' dance seem to comport well with the diagnosis of ergotism. Without claiming to have explained this mysterious phenomenon for the first time, I would suggest that it looks surprisingly similar to what Gilbert Rouget in 1980 called a possession cult—that is, a vehement trance induced (in initiates) by music, and sustained and finally terminated by music.[70] In Rouget's terms, such a trance is diametrically opposed to ecstasy in that it is noisy, motoric, social, overstimulated, and lacking in hallucinations. After a possession trance, one does not remember what one has done. Ecstasy, by way of contrast, is generally characterized by immobility, silence, solitude, lack of crisis, loss of sensory perceptions, and by visions or hallucinations. Moreover, ecstatics often, or even usually, remember precisely what has happened to them. No music induces a genuine ecstasy, despite the metaphorical ecstasies of many a music lover. Among the possession states that Rouget describes are the reprobate and the cultivated. Demonic possession is the best example of an uncontrolled, unwanted, frightening possession. Cultivated possession, on the other hand, is closely tied to the cultivated forms of spirit identification possible in many cultures. On this view, tarantism is a possession cult lacking only the name.[71] Initiates in southern Italy or in Spain commonly feel a growing tension and discomfort, which the musician channels, stimulates, and releases through his tarantella. The "tarantella (music and dance) does not have the function of cur-

68. Egon Schmitz-Cliever and Herta Schmitz-Cliever, "Zur Darstellung des Heiltanzes in der Malerei um 1500," *Medizinhistorisches Journal* 10 (1975): 307–16, at p. 313.

69. Backman, *Religious Dances*, pp. 306–7.

70. Gilbert Rouget, *Music and Trance: A Theory of the Relations of Music and Possession* (Paris, 1980), trans. Brunhilde Biebuyck (Chicago, 1985), pp. 8–12. Cf. Rosen, *Madness in Society*, p. 204.

71. Rouget, *Music and Trance*, p. 162.

ing the tarantellee of her hysteria, but on the contrary, provides her with a means of behaving like a hysteric in public," a role that has a cathartic effect.[72] At times it can seem that the music itself has a psycho-physiological effect, and studies have even tried to show that a specific drumbeat can have the effect of trance.[73] Other students have, more plausibly I think, connected the obsessive dancing of the tarantella to rituals of healing in which the sick or neurotic person is "forced" (gezwungen) to dance by a particular kind of music.[74] Students of the tarantella in Italy have discovered that it has a religious form and constitutes a folk exorcism.[75] Fundamentally, however, Rouget's remarkable study points us to the recognition that music is deeply rooted in the essence of trance and "cultivated possession."

> It is due to the music, and because he is supported by the music, that the possessed person publicly lives out, by means of dance, his identification with the divinity he embodies. . . . By playing his "motto," the musicians notify this identity to the entranced dancer, those around him, the priests, and the spectators.[76]

Parts of this theory seem to apply well to the experience of those suffering from St. John's or St. Vitus' dance. Music did seem to induce the weird frenzy of the dancers, a trance that was infectious among at least some observers. In Strasbourg, in 1518, music also seems to have functioned, at first, as part of an intended therapy. But quickly it appeared to the bewildered city fathers that music was making things worse. It was certainly not part of normal late medieval Christian culture to channel "neuroses" into frenzied trancelike dance, and so it is not surprising to find the authorities calling for days of humiliation and penance.

There are certain problems with this interpretation. For one thing, the sources do not present the trance, that painful, exhausting leaping and dancing, as an act of identification with any known divinity or saint. Our St. Vitus' dancers were not identifying with a spider either, as may be said of the dancers of the tarantella. We certainly cannot equate the German dancing mania with Mediterranean tarantism in any simple manner. And yet it may be that what we find in late medieval and early modern Germany is precisely the tail end of a possession cult, a painful, even agonizing, and sometimes fatal, trance that was no longer understood by the educated theologians, physicians, and magistrates as spirit possession or any

72. Ibid., p. 165.

73. Rodney Needham, "Percussion and Transition," Man 2 (1967): 606–14; Andrew Neher, "A Physiological Explanation of Unusual Behavior in Ceremonies Involving Drums," Human Biology 4 (1962): 151–60.

74. Marius Schneider, "Tarantella," in Musik in Geschichte und Gegenwart, vol. 13 (Kassel, 1966), cols. 117–19.

75. Ernesto di Martino, La terra del rimorso (Rome, 1961).

76. Rouget, Music and Trance, p. 323.

known disease, a frustratingly mysterious psychophysical state that also made no sense to "initiates" any more. No wonder Jean Bodin spoke of possible demonic possession. Music and the recurrent color red may have still had the vestigial function of socializing and maintaining or channeling the trance—that seems to be what Johann Schenck von Grafenberg and Gregor Horst were referring to: a cultivated disturbance, an annual dancing disorder, whose function was to calm and relieve the dancers, at least for a year. But for most contemporary observers, the dancing mania appeared both mysterious and insane.[77]

Perhaps St. Vitus' dance was the dying form of a possession cult. Perhaps not. It is important, however, to note that neurotic and psychosomatic complaints continue to rise and decline in history. They do not all fall neatly into permanently valid modern medical categories. In our own century, for example, the classical conversion hysterias have virtually disappeared, even as we now have a novel epidemic of functional eating disorders, idiopathic fatigue syndromes, and multiple personality disorders.[78] Unless we look carefully at the cultures in which a form of madness arises and flourishes, we shall not understand the deviation or even the changing standards of sanity maintained by our ancestors.

The point is a general one. Just as the interpreters of Hugo van der Goes

77. Michael Kleinlawel included the following verse in his 1625 chronicle:

Ein Seltzam sucht ist zu der zeit
Vnder dem Volck umbgangen
Dan viel Leut auß Unsinnigkeit
Zu dantzen angefangen,
Welcher sie allzeit Tag und Nach
Ohn unter laß getrieben
Biß das sie fielen in ohnmacht
Viel sind Todt drüber blieben.

There's been a strange epidemic lately
Going amongst the folk,
So that many in their madness
Began dancing,
Which they kept up day and night,
Without interruption,
Until they fell unconscious.
Many have died of it.

Michael Kleinlawel, *Straßburgische Chronik* (Strasbourg, 1625), pp. 130–31. Again, my thanks to Thomas and Kathy Brady for transcribing these materials more carefully than in the form presented in Martin's *Geschichte*.

78. Mark S. Micale, *Approaching Hysteria: Disease and Its Interpretations* (Princeton, 1995), pp. 169–75; Joan Jacobs Brumberg, *Fasting Girls: The Emergence of Anorexia Nervosa as a Modern Disease* (Cambridge, Mass., 1988); Edward Shorter, *From Paralysis to Fatigue: A History of Psychosomatic Illness in the Modern Era* (New York, 1992); Edward Shorter, *From the Mind into the Body: The Cultural Origins of Psychosomatic Symptoms* (New York, 1994); Ian Hacking, *Rewriting the Soul: Multiple Personality and the Sciences of Memory* (Princeton, 1995); Elaine Showalter, *Hystories: Hysterical Epidemics and Modern Culture* (New York, 1997).

went wrong assuming that they could discover a kind of unmediated medical observational precision in the remarks of Gaspar Ofhuys, and just as the dancing mania has served as a mirror of almost every investigator's favorite diagnosis, so it should be obvious by now that religious assumptions and social conventions are often deeply intertwined in any description from bygone centuries. Madnesses of the past are not petrified entities that can be plucked unchanged from their niches and placed under our modern microscopes. They appear, perhaps, more like jellyfish that collapse and dry up when they are removed from the ambient seawater. To see what madness meant in the sixteenth century, to see how it was experienced and treated, we must learn to swim.

The Madness of Demonic Possession

DEMONOMANIA

If it is difficult to find appropriate medical terminology for understanding the breakdown of Hugo van der Goes, and even harder to interpret the dancing mania of the sixteenth century, there are interpretive problems of yet another order in dealing with the serious loss of integrity and personal control represented by demonic possession. The third problem the history of early modern madness has to deal with is not just the culturally constructed, intertextual dependencies of our sources, and not just the unfamiliarity of baffling disorders, but the overwhelming influence of a religious outlook that assumed that the devil was everywhere, and that madness might have a purely spiritual explanation and a religious solution. The alien voices that spoke forth from the possessed, and the horrible voices and visions heard and seen by the afflicted, make us think at once of schizophrenia or multiple personality disorder, but these Renaissance victims of total breakdown, of suicidal impulses, of seizures and blasphemy, seem too idiosyncratic and culture-bound to fit well into our secular and psychopharmacological notions of neurosis and psychosis.[79] It is not obvious either that, despite their anaesthesias (areas of numbness) and spasmodic, dissociated ragings, they were victims of hysteria or of multiple personality disorder (what is now termed dissociative identity disorder).[80] We shall

79. S. Kemp and K. Williams, "Demonic Possession and Mental Disorder in Medieval and Early Modern Europe," *Psychological Medicine* 17 (1987): 21–29. In his study of "spiritual affliction" in early modern Bavaria, David Lederer emphasizes the often religiously charged language for madness and then examines the vernacular categories then common for mental stress and disorder, finding that even the vague term *Wahnsinn* (madness) was but rarely employed ("Reforming the Spirit," pp. 198–236, 337).

80. For an unconvincing effort to assimilate demoniacs and witches to the history of hysteria, see G. S. Rousseau, "'A Strange Pathology': Hysteria in the Early Modern World,

get further as historians if we confront this form of madness, this demonomania, as it appears in the records of the sixteenth century rather than trying to discover ready-made pigeonholes for disorders that we have not yet
examined closely. Let us begin with a strange case.

On Palm Sunday of 1574, Judith Klatten, a girl from the Neumark (Brandenburg) village of Helpe, took the holy sacrament, in its Lutheran form, as
was her wont, but instead of feeling spiritually nourished that day, she felt
a cold wind rushing around her.[81] Later in the day, she lost consciousness
and was carefully laid in her bed, fully clothed. The comalike trance into
which she fell lasted for weeks, and some sort of diminution of consciousness lasted for months, and, finally, for almost five years. What made her
condition even more remarkable was that to all appearances in all this time
she ate and drank nothing, and consequently excreted nothing. This supernatural fast roused the doubts even of her own father, who reportedly
spied on her to see if she was secretly getting up to take nourishment, but
he saw nothing suspicious. For five years, Judith Klatten hardly spoke, except to respond "ja" or "nein" when she was questioned. And for years apparently she attracted little attention beyond her village. But in the fifth
year of her strange condition, in 1578, the Lutheran pastor Caspar Gloxinus
came out from town to visit her, thinking that she might perhaps be possessed by the devil. But his suspicions too were shattered by the fact that by
now the girl was conscious and prayed properly, confessing her sins. Even
so, she still refused food, and Pastor Gloxinus, now suspecting that she was
a fraud, urged that she be brought into town. And so on August 2, 1578, Judith Klatten was brought the four miles into Arnswalde (now Choszczno in
Poland) and placed in the local "spital," where she was to be observed day
and night.

Under these new and strict conditions, she held out only four days before admitting that she was extremely hungry. After consuming a wine
soup with relish, she told her attendant that over the past five years she

---

1500–1800," in *Hysteria Beyond Freud*, ed. Sander Gilman et al. (Berkeley and Los Angeles,
1993), 91–221, at pp. 96–105, 121–25. The classic attempt along these lines was Jean-Martin
Charcot and Paul Richer, *Les démoniaques dans l'art* (Paris, 1887); I have used the useful edition, *Die Besessenen in der Kunst*, trans. Willi Hendrichs, ed. Manfred Schneider and Wolfgang Tietze (Göttingen, 1988). Ian Stevenson provides a useful overview of some recent
clinical literature in "Possession and Exorcism: An Essay Review," *Journal of Parapsychology*
59 (1995): 69–77. There were, of course, incidents in which contemporary observers tried to
naturalize demonomania by calling it hysteria. See *Witchcraft and Hysteria in Elizabethan
London: Edward Jorden and the Mary Glover Case*, ed. Michael MacDonald (London, 1991).

81. My account depends on Andreas Angelus, *Wider Natur und Wunderbuch: Darin so
wol in gemein von Wunderwercken dess Himmels, Luffts, Wassers und Erden, als insonderheit von
allen widernaturlichen wunderlichen Geschichten grossern theils Europae, fürnemlich der Churfürstlichen Brandenburgischen Marck, vom Jahr 490. biss auff 1597. ablauffendes Jahr beschehen
gehandelt wird* (Frankfurt a/M, 1597), pp. 206–9.

had indeed eaten, but not in any normal fashion: "[L]ittle, tiny men and maids, wearing beautiful ornaments (whom she alone of all the family could see), ran about every day under her bed and brought her food from whatever was being cooked at home or roasted elsewhere."[82]

Judith claimed that she had been sustained over the years by the Little People, but they were not simply her benefactors. "They would gladly have carried her away, except that someone dressed in yellow forbade it. Even so they pressed her hard and hurt her in the side and pushed her eyes shut so that she could not see, as her eyebrows showed."[83]

The pixies or elves helped her maintain the appearance of a miraculous fast by secretly carrying off her excreta in a blue-white basin. But in the end their powers turned out to have limits: "For when they were feeding her for the last time before she was brought into the city, they said amongst themselves that if she stayed on in her village they would gladly [continue to] bring her food, but they couldn't transport food to her over land [i.e., into the city]."[84]

After making these revelations, Judith resumed eating a little, she now spoke a little, and was able to walk, albeit with a limp. Her only fear now was that she might be left at home alone.

The Demonization of the World

There may well be psychohistorians who would undertake to explain what Judith Klatten's visions of the little people may tell us of her mental illness, but what is of more interest to me is what her visions tell us about her culture and about the kinds of delusion and disorder common four hundred years ago. By the 1570s, Germany was experiencing a host of such miraculous or fraudulent fasts,[85] examples either of the way God gave strength to his chosen faithful or of the way the devil, often in league with crafty and malicious priests, deceived the naive and plunged the innocent into superstition. Among Protestants, the latter interpretation had come to

82. Ibid., p. 208: "aber kleine Mänlein und Jungfräwlein, schön Geschmucket, welche keiner im Hause denn sie allein gesehen, weren alle Tage unter dem Bette her auff gangen, und hetten ihr Speise gebracht von allem was sonst im Hause Gekocht oder anderswo gebraten worden."

83. Ibid., p. 208: "Hetten sie auch gerne hinweg getragen, wenns nicht einer im Gelben Kleide widerrahten. Doch hetten sie sie hart gedruckt, unnd an der seiten gelähmt, unnd ihr die Augen zugedruckt, das sie nit hette sehen müssen, wie ihr denn die Augen braun gewesen."

84. Ibid., p. 209: "Item da sie sie auch zuletzt ehe sie in die Stadt gebracht gespeiset, hetten sie untereinander gesaget, Wenn sie im Dorff bliebe, wolten sie ihr wol Speise bringen, aber uber Landt Köndten sie sie nicht Speisen." The substantial town of Arnswalde (now Choszczno in Poland) lay ca. 30 miles north of Landsberg/Warthe (now Gorzów Wielkopolski) and ca. 37 miles east of Stettin (now Szczecin).

85. Johann Weyer, *De lamiis liber: Item de commentitiis jejuniis* (Basel, 1577); on the general phenomenon, see Rudolf M. Bell, *Holy Anorexia* (Chicago, 1985).

prevail, and so it is not surprising that both Judith's father and Pastor Gloxinus suspected fraud, and that the pastor, initially at least, suspected demonic possession. But obviously Judith Klatten's condition was not any normal case of demonic possession. Especially intriguing is her notion that the little people who sustained her over the years could or would not help her if she moved into town. Regardless of how we understand what food she "really" ate between 1574 and 1578, Klatten seems to have been aware that some rural spirits could not survive in the atmosphere of a town, or at the very least that it made for a credible story to assert that her helpers were bound to the world of the village.

In the sixteenth century, many observers agreed that some kinds of spirit were bound to particular waters, others to particular mountains or caves or mines, others still to specific crystals or houses or forests. The writings of Paracelsus, for example, abound with nymphs, sprites, kobolds, elves, dwarves, and fairies.[86] He and his followers held that nature was full of such spirits. Heinrich Kornmann published a Latin treatise in 1611, firmly based on Paracelsan principles, in which he undertook to set forth all the kinds of spirits that inhabit the fires, airs, waters, and earths of our experience, and his example must stand for many.[87] It is equally well known that the miners of Germany had a rich mythology about the Little Men of the Mountain (*Bergmännlein*), who sometimes helped and sometimes exasperated them in their subterranean labors.[88] The world of ordinary experience

---

86. Jodocus Hocker and Hermann Hammelmann, "Der Teuffel selbs," in *Theatrum diabolorum, das ist: Warhafftige eigentliche und kurtze Beschreibunq allerley grewlicher, schrecklicher und abschewlicher Laster, so in diesen letzten, schweren, und bösen Zeiten, an allen Orten und Enden fast bräuchlich*, ed. Sigmund Feyerabend (Frankfurt a/M, 1587), fol. 12ᵛ; Mechtild Josephi Jacob, "Die Hexenlehre des Paracelsus und ihre Bedeutung für die modernen Hexenprozesse: Ein Beitrag zur Geschichte der Entwicklung des Hexenglaubens seit dem Mittelalter unter besonderer Berücksichtigung der Überlieferung aus dem Raum Gifhorn (Braunschweig)" (diss., Göttingen University, 1959); Charles Webster, "Paracelsus and Demons: Science as a Synthesis of Popular Belief," in Istituto nazionale di studi sul Rinascimento, *Scienze, credenze occulte, livelli di cultura: Convegno internazionale di studi, Firenze, 26–30 giugno 1980* (Florence, 1982), pp. 3–20.

87. Henricus Kornmann, *Templum Naturae Historicum, . . . in quo de natura et miraculis quatuor elementorum . . . disseritur* (Darmstadt, 1611); see also Allen G. Debus, *The Chemical Philosophy: Paracelsan Science and Medicine in the Sixteenth and Seventeenth Centuries* (New York, 1977); for a short introduction, see Lynn Thorndike, *A History of Magic and Experimental Science*, vol. 5: *The Sixteenth Century* (New York, 1941), pp. 617–51.

88. Henning Gross, *Magica. Das ist: Wunderbarliche Historien von Gespensten und mancherley Erscheinungen der Geister* (Eisleben, 1600), 1: 35r–36r; Georg Schreiber, *Alpine Bergwerkskultur: Bergleute zwischen Graubünden und Tirol in den letzten vier Jahrhunderten* (Innsbruck, 1956); G. Heilfurth and I. M. Greverus, *Bergbau und Bergmann in der deutschsprachigen Sagenüberlieferung Mitteleuropas*, vol. 1 (Marburg, 1967); P. Wolfersdorf, "Die dämonischen Gestalten der schwäbischen Volksüberlieferung" (diss., Tübingen, 1949). Most of the older literature is cited in the entry "Berggeister," in *Handwörterbuch des deutschen Aberglaubens* (Berlin and Leipzig, 1927–42), ed. E. Hoffmann–Krayer and Hans Bächtold–Stäubli, vol. 1, cols. 1071–83.

in the villages of sixteenth-century Germany was also full of vexatious spirits, who might frighten the cattle, spoil the beer, and keep butter from forming in the churn.

It is hard to find out much in detail about these spirits and goblins and elves, because literate people usually described such ideas as superstition. For orthodox Lutherans and Catholics alike, the world was not full of all sorts of spirits. Rather, there were, fundamentally, only two kinds of spirits in the world: good angels and bad; and of the two, devils were far the more active. Indeed, one of the most pervasive processes across the sixteenth century, and not just in Germany, was the growing demonization of the world.[89] The pious, learned, and literate found that it made better sense of their world to describe the apparent chaos of life and the prevalence of wickedness as a dramatic personal struggle between good and evil, of angels and demons. Because certain kinds of madness came to be experienced and described as demonic possession, we must acquaint ourselves with the rising tide of demons in the world of Reformation Germany.

This process of demonization has been particularly well studied in the area of Lutheran ethics, for here the process resulted in an entirely new genre of literature, the *Teufelbücher*, or devil books, in which all the old vices of vanity, drunkenness, gluttony, lust, gambling, and infidelity were transformed.[90] What Sebastian Brant and his generation around 1500 had attributed to folly, in the *Ship of Fools* and in the *Narrenliteratur* that sprang from Brant's inspired model, was rebaptized and reinterpreted as diabolic, starting in the 1550s, with such demons as Matthäus Friderich's *Sauffteufel* (the devil of drunkenness) and Andreas Musculus's *Hosenteufel*, *Fluchteufel*, and *Eheteufel* (the devils of fancy trousers, cursing, and of marriage).[91] By the 1560s, the genre had become a publishing fad, with as many as twenty-one separate "devils" described (mainly) by hyperorthodox, gnesio-Lutheran moralists.

The odd result of this flurry of Lutheran moralizing was not exactly

89. Wolfgang Behringer provides an excellent example of this point in his *Chonrad Stoeckhlin und die Nachtschar* (Munich, 1994).

90. Max Osborn, *Die Teufelliteratur des XVI. Jahrhunderts*, Acta Germanica, vol. 3, no. 3 (Berlin, 1893); Heinrich Grimm, "Die deutschen 'Teufelbücher' des 16. Jahrhunderts: Ihre Rolle im Buchwesen und ihre Bedeutung," *Archiv für Geschichte des Buchwesens* 16 (1959): 1733–90; Bernhard Ohse, "Die Teufelliteratur zwischen Brant und Luther" (diss., Freie Universität Berlin, 1961); for a meticulously edited selection of devil books, see *Teufelbücher in Auswahl*, ed. Ria Stambaugh (Berlin, 1970–80); for analysis of all the devil tales, see Rainer Alsheimer, "Katalog protestantischer Teufelserzählungen," in *Volkserzählung und Reformation: Ein Handbuch zur Tradierung und Funktion von Erzählstoffen und Erzählliteratur im Protestantismus*, ed. Wolfgang Brückner (Berlin, 1974), pp. 417–519.

91. Barbara Könneker, *Wesen und Wandlung der Narrenidee im Zeitalter des Humanismus: Brant, Murner, Erasmus* (Wiesbaden, 1966); Joel Lefebvre, *Les fols et la folie: Étude sur les genres du comique et la création littéraire en Allemagne pendant la Renaissance* (Paris, 1968).

what the authors earnestly intended. If every vice had not just some foolish blindness at its base, as in the *Ship of Fools*, but a specific devil, then the devil himself could begin to seem foolish, consuming his destructive energies in the effort to tempt mankind to wear large ruffled collars, pointed shoes, pleated shirts, and billowing pantaloons, or coaxing would-be Christians into un-Christian dancing, swearing, disobedience to masters, pensive melancholy, and general laziness.[92] It should be remembered that as the devil became ever more present in the sixteenth century, he assumed an increasingly amazing variety of shapes, ranging from these faintly ridiculous echoes of stock medieval vice and folly figures, on through the threatening sort of devil who seduced wives and widows into witchcraft, and up to figures of fully Satanic, apocalyptic terror. Before drawing too sharp a contrast between the devil of the learned and the demons of the people, therefore, we need to emphasize that even among the learned, and even during the process I have called the demonization of the world, the learned and literate had their own sharp disagreements over just what it meant to say that the devil was active everywhere. Despite divisions among the elite, however, it would be foolish to deny that popular and learned culture diverged even more sharply over just this issue, as the history of witchcraft suggests.

The studies of Norman Cohn, Richard Kieckhefer, and Eva Labouvie suggest that the full European belief in witchcraft (with demonic pact, cannibalism, flight to the Sabbath, the devil's mark, and sexual intercourse with the devil) was a learned fantasy, one that had few if any roots or resonance among "ignorant" villagers, whose witchcraft remained concentrated on the practical advantages to be obtained from cunning men and wise women and on the frightful damage that could be wrought through the *maleficium* of harmful witches.[93] Carlo Ginzburg has objected that ordinary people had their own mythic fantasies of flight and Sabbath and their own mythic terrors, too, but his line of interpretation seems strained.[94]

92. Ohse, "Teufelliteratur," pp. 91–106.

93. Norman Cohn, *Europe's Inner Demons* (London, 1975); Richard Kieckhefer, *European Witch-Trials: Their Foundations in Popular and Learned Culture, 1300–1500* (London, 1976); Eva Labouvie, *Zauberei und Hexenwerk: Ländlicher Hexenglaube in der frühen Neuzeit* (Frankfurt a/M, 1991); and id., *Verbotene Künste: Volksmagie und ländlicher Aberglaube in den Dorfgemeinden des Saarraumes (16.–19. Jahrhundert)* (St. Ingbert, 1992).

94. Carlo Ginzburg, *Ecstasies: Deciphering the Witches' Sabbath* (London, 1990). Anthropologists have argued that cultures where ecstasy is highly valued may have "possession cults" in which men and the elite of society participate; but that cultures where ecstasy is discouraged or devalued often relegate possession to women and the marginal. This distinction seems to work in a rough way for European culture. See David N. Gellner's discussion and application of work of I. M. Lewis in "Priests, Healers, Mediums, and Witches: The Context of Possession in Kathmandu Valley, Nepal," *Man* 29 (1994): 27–48. For criticism of Ginzburg, see Behringer, *Chonrad Stoeckhlin*, pp. 145–50; Klaus Graf, "Carlo Ginzburgs 'Hexensabbat': Herausforderung an die Methodendiskussion der Geschichtswissen-

Pushed to unacceptable extremes in the overly schematic interpretation of Robert Muchembled,[95] this model of competing conceptions of witchcraft (roughly, scholastic vs. popular) has nonetheless prompted a great deal of important work.[96] No one can be content any longer with the bland generalizations of an earlier generation of scholars concerning the common beliefs of an undifferentiated "people." Before we can tell what demonic possession meant in the sixteenth century, we need to clarify whose beliefs we are studying.

And that brings us back to Judith Klatten. What were her own beliefs about the spirits who helped her? Evidently, as a pious girl, she did not share the view that such spirits must be devils, but our source, the *Wider Natur und Wunderbuch* ("Book of Miracles and of Things Contrary to Nature") of Andreas Angelus (Engel), does not permit us to say much more about Klatten's understanding of what had happened to her. If we simply extended the conclusions of some recent witchcraft research, we might emphasize the extent to which Satan was a creature of learned or biblical invention, and minimize the extent to which ordinary, illiterate people feared or even believed in the devil. Such a simple contrast, however, would be unjustified. Just because the commonplace witchcraft beliefs of popular culture did not (or did not until relatively late) stress the devil, it does not follow that popular culture had no devil at all. In fact, the devil was a frequent figure in everyday speech, in slogans, curses, epithets, and aphorisms,[97] and we often find that an ordinary man or woman was regarded as demon-possessed after his or her spouse had invoked the devil by way of a curse.[98]

Reports of Demonic Possession

It is clear that ordinary people experienced and classified some kinds of mental derangement and psychic disintegration as demonic possession. Many of these episodes of demonic possession were so sensational that they could not be concealed, even if anyone had tried to do so. Masses of

---

schaft," *Kea: Zeitschrift für Kulturwissenschaften* 5 (1993): 1–17; Willem de Blécourt, "Spuren einer Volkskultur oder Dämonisierung? Kritische Bemerkungen zu Ginzburgs 'Benandanti,'" *Kea: Zeitschrift für Kulturwissenschaften* 5 (1993): 17–30.

95. Robert Muchembled, *Culture populaire et culture des élites dans la France moderne* (Paris, 1978).

96. See, e.g., the recent work of Eva Labouvie, "Hexenspuk und Hexenabwehr: Volksmagie und volkstümlicher Hexenglaube," in *Hexenwelten, Magie und Imagination*, ed. Richard van Dülmen (Frankfurt a/M, 1987), pp. 49–93; id., *Zauberei und Hexenwerk*; and id., *Verbotene Künste*.

97. See Wolfgang Brückner, "Forschungsprobleme der Satanologie und Teufelserzählungen," in *Volkserzählung und Reformation*, ed. id., pp. 393–416.

98. See Andreas Celichius, *Notwendige Erinnerung Von des Sathans letzten Zornsturm, Und was es auff sich habe und bedeute, das nu zu dieser zeit so viel Menschen an Leib und Seel vom Teuffel besessen werden* (Wittenberg, 1595), fol. G2.

pamphlets, broadsides, *"neue Zeitungen,"* wonder books, and sermons were published before 1600, reporting demonic actions of all sorts.[99] Of course, these sources were first and foremost the creation of their learned, or at least basically literate, authors and reflected the views of an elite culture, but popular views are also evident in these reports and sermons. However tempting the notion, we cannot expect this genre of "popular literature" to provide perfect access to the popular mind.[100] Moreover, such books, sermons, and pamphlets made no claim to list all the cases of possession even for a given town or year. Their pious authors selected examples in order to illustrate a conclusion, and one can search in vain, for example, for Catholic accounts of unsuccessful exorcisms, even though we know that there were many unsuccessful efforts to free victims of demonic obsession.[101] It would be just as foolish to look for Lutheran accounts of successful Catholic exorcisms. It was, moreover, never against the law or even necessarily immoral to be demon-possessed, and so we do not find official registers or jail records of the possessed. No police blotters were filled with these demonic atrocities. Like Judith Klatten, many of the possessed may have lain in obscurity without ever coming to public attention.

Far from aiming at complete or objective reporting, most accounts of demonic possession are zealous polemics.[102] Describing the pitiful case of the

99. While I have examined most of these works, I am aware that important examples may have escaped my attention. Let me here thank Jürgen Beyer for generously sharing his knowledge of sources available in Denmark. He has also shown me his "Wahrhafte Wundergeschicht von neuen Propheten die alle Welt zu rechtschaffener Buße und Besserung aufrufen: Lutherske folkelige profeter i 1500- og 1600-tallet" (thesis, University of Copenhagen, 1990). I would be grateful to extend my acquaintance with relevant works and to adjust my statistics accordingly. I know that manuscript *Mirakelbücher* of various pilgrimage centers often contain otherwise unknown accounts of demonic possession, but I have only dipped into them. David Lederer's recent dissertation,"Reforming the Spirit," provides the first careful analysis of some 1,500 cases of spiritual affliction, including many demonic possessions, in the seventeenth-century records of Benediktbeuern and Pürten. In a sense, most of these miracles were not "public knowledge" (i.e., trumpeted in chronicles, sermons, or pamphlets) as were better-known episodes of demonic possession.

100. See Steven Ozment, "The Social History of the Reformation: What Can We Learn from Pamphlets?" in *Flugschriften als Massenmedium der Reformationszeit*, ed. Hans-Joachim Köhler (Stuttgart, 1981), who seems to ignore some of the chief weaknesses of these sources as windows into the popular mind, while at the same time proving their usefulness for other kinds of social history. On the problems of documentary sources for the study of popular culture, see Peter Burke, *Popular Culture in Early Modern Europe* (New York, 1978).

101. David Lederer ("Reforming the Spirit," pp. 287–327) has studied the manuscript records of cases of demonic possession brought to the attention of the Bavarian shrines of Benediktbeuern and Pürten during the seventeenth century. In these less polemically charged records, one can find numerous examples of unsuccessful exorcism.

102. This is a point made repeatedly by recent scholars. See Cécile Ernst, *Teufelaustreibungen: Die Praxis der katholischen Kirche im 16. und 17. Jahrhundert* (Bern, 1972); D. P. Walker, "Demonic Possession Used as Propaganda in the Later Sixteenth Century," in Istituto nazionale di studi sul Rinascimento, *Scienze, credenze occulte, livelli di cultura: Convegno in-*

ten-year-old daughter of a high-noble family in 1654, the Reverend Johann Conrad Dannhauer of Strasbourg recounts such detailed and theologically correct conversations between the girl and the devil that the modern reader is tempted to conclude that Dannhauer himself composed these dialogues.[103] Similarly, in the Reverend Tobias Seiler's account of the possession and liberation of a twelve-year-old Silesian girl in 1605, the devil enters into such intricate and theologically learned arguments with Seiler and with other observers, over several days, that any modern reader is bound to conclude that Seiler was composing, not only his own lines, but the devil's too.[104] Of course, the devil was expected to be a subtle logician and a keen scholastic controversialist, but few today would believe that the Ancient Enemy was able to show off his theological subtlety through the medium of a child. These can hardly be examples of straight reportage.

Even so, I think that we can catch some glimpses of what these girls actually said and obtain some impression of how they understood and experienced their mental and spiritual troubles, as distinguished from the theological and polemical interpretation imposed upon their words and behavior. For example, Pastor Dannhauer's Strasbourg girl spoke so often and so movingly of death, of wanting to die, of being ready to die, and of seeing God, that we cannot avoid seeing her as a religiously depressed and melancholy child with strongly mystical yearnings. And Pastor Seiler's girl seems to have spoken with the voice of the devil, threatening to leave a terrible stench and warning that he would shit in the pastor's throat to make him hoarse, a threat that prompted the attending cleric to object, "Scheis in die Helle, Gott wird uns dafür behütten" ("Go shit in hell, for God will defend us from that!").[105] Such anecdotes, I think, have the ring of spontaneous reporting. They do not seem to be merely the acidulous products of overheated theological zeal, even if Luther's scatological contempt for the devil persuaded some of his followers to use rough talk with the Enemy. And so I believe that Pastor Seiler provides a roughly accurate account here. It re-

---

ternazionale di studi, Firenze, 26–30 giugno 1980 (Florence, 1982), pp. 237–248, extended in his Unclean Spirits: Possession and Exorcism in France and England in the Late Sixteenth and Early Seventeenth Centuries (Philadelphia, 1981). Anita M. Walker and Edmund H. Dickerman, "'A Woman Under the Influence': A Case of Alleged Possession in Sixteenth-Century France," Sixteenth Century Journal 22 (1991): 534–54. See also Stuart Clark, Thinking with Demons: The Idea of Witchcraft in Early Modern Europe (Oxford, 1997), a pathbreaking synthesis, in which pp. 389–422 develop this theme.

103. Johann Conrad Dannhauer, Scheid- und Absag-Brieff Einem ungenanten Priester auss Cöllen, auff sein Antworts-Schreiben an einen seiner vertrawten guten Freunde, über das zu Strassburg (also titulirte) vom Teuffel besessene Adeliche Jungfräwlin gegeben (Strasbourg, 1654), e.g., fols. A3v, A5r–v, A6v–8v.

104. Tobias Seiler, Daemonomania: Uberaus schreckliche Historia, von einem besessenen zwelffjahrigen Jungfräwlein, zu Lewenberg in Schlesien (Wittenberg, 1605).

105. Ibid., fol. C4v.

mains true, of course, that these literate sources are lenses that distort what they permit us to see, but if we take the shape and color of the lens into account, we may yet be able to say something of what demonic possession was like for the demon-possessed.[106]

One fact on which both the learned and the illiterate would have agreed was the rise in demonic possession in the second half of the sixteenth century. Observers were so impressed with this spread of obsession and possession that they felt compelled to explain why no previous age, with the exception of the age of Christ himself, presented so many frightful examples of the devil's rage.[107] His attacks were a staple feature of the wonder and prodigy literature of the second half of the century. Job Fincel's *Wunderzeichen* (Miraculous Signs), for example, was entirely conceived in the spirit of proving that the rising tide of monstrous births, fiery signs in the heavens, and devilish interventions in the shape of storms, disasters, and demonic possessions gave proof of the imminent end of the world and the urgent need to repent, so long as just a few seconds remained before the end.[108] Johann Weyer's famous attack on witchcraft trials, the *De praestigiis daemonum* (first published in 1563), endorsed this point of view, claiming that in this, the old age of the world, Satan lorded it over the minds of men as never before.[109] Similarly, when a panel of pastors and theologians investigated an epidemic of possessions at Friedeberg and Spandau, near Berlin, in 1593–94, they concluded in their report that such demonic actions were only possible because the second "Advent Christi" was at hand. As in the days of His incarnation, so now too the world swarmed with devils and with possessed persons.[110] After all, it seemed that God had revealed (Rev. 20) that Satan would be turned loose exactly 1,000 years after the reign of

106. I doubt whether the literate and scholarly views and expectations set forth by pastors and other writers so successfully "constructed" the condition of possession that any effort to get at the "facts" would be an illusory "positivist" effort. But the popular view of such matters should have no automatic priority over elite views. In understanding texts, one also needs to read between the lines.

107. For a handy digest of several preachers and theologians who thought so, see Hocker, "Der Teuffel selbs," in *Theatrum diabolorum* (cited in n. 86 above), ch. 14, fols. 22v–26r: "Ursachen warumb der Teuffel jetzund so hefftig tobet und wütet."

108. Job Fincel, *Wunderzeichen: Der dritte Teil, so von der zeit an, da Gottes wort in Deudschland, Rein und lauter geprediget worden, geschehen und ergangen sind* (Jena, 1562); on Fincel generally, see Heinz Schilling, "Job Fincel und die Zeichen der Endzeit," in *Volkserzählung und Reformation*, ed. Brückner, pp. 325–92.

109. Weyer, *De praestigiis daemonum, et incantationibus ac veneficiis Libri sex, postrema editione sexta aucti et recogniti*, 6th ed. (Basel, 1583), col. 43.

110. Andreas Angelus, *Annales Marchiae Brandenburgicae, das ist, Ordentliche Verzeichnus und Beschreibung der fürnemsten ... Jahrgeschichten und Historien, so sich vom 416. Jahr vor Christi geburt, bis auffs 1596. Jahr ... begeben ... haben* (Frankfurt a/O, 1598), pp. 414–26: "Ein kurtz bedencken, was von dem betrübten zustande der bessessenen in Spandow, und von den Englischen Erscheinungen, zu halten, Auch was vor billiche und Christliche Mittel zugebrauchen sein," at p. 417.

Gregory the Great, and 593 + 1,000 = 1593![111] Here we obviously have the clever theological mind at work, but at its base lay the commonplace that there had never before been so many cases of demonic possession. No work set forth this point more successfully than a stout treatise by the ecclesiastical superintendent of Mecklenburg, the well-known Lutheran moralist Andreas Celichius, whose *Notwendige Erinnerung Von des Sathans letzten Zornsturm* ("Necessary Reminder of Satan's Final Raging Storm") (1594; 2d ed., 1595) gathered all of these observations and arguments together.[112] In just the past twelve years, Celichius exclaimed, he had himself witnessed about thirty demoniacs, "some of whom became possessed and convulsive here, but others of whom have come wandering here from Holstein, Saxony, and Pomerania, presenting such horrible spectacles that modest souls have been thoroughly disgusted."[113] To understand such sufferings and to learn how to treat the miserably possessed were, therefore, timely, even urgent, tasks.

With the weight of so much contemporary opinion, it is odd that this phenomenon has never been studied with any care, especially on the basis of the abundant German materials.[114] One reason for this scholarly neglect has been the distinctly provincial view of certain medievalists that demonic possession belongs as a topic to the medievalists. Not so long ago, for example, André Goddu came to the dramatic but silly conclusion that between the years 300 and 1400 A.D., exorcism had been mainly "successful," but that the "failure rate" rose dramatically in the period 1400 to 1700, leading to more stringent tests for true possession and to a much more restricted use of exorcism.[115] The source of such conclusions is Goddu's curiously statistical reading of the *Acta sanctorum*, an inappropriate database for such conclusions. According to Goddu, the *Acta* report only three exorcisms for the sixteenth century, and they were relative failures. But even the vaguest glance at the activities of the Catholic reformers should suffice to persuade a modern observer that the sixteenth century was full of triumphant success stories, trumpeted boldly by proud exorcists and their supporters, who were quick to argue that the repeated Catholic successes in expelling demons pointed to the truth of the Catholic religion and the coming tri-

111. Ibid., p. 417; see Robin B. Barnes, *Prophecy and Gnosis: Apocalypticism in the Wake of the Lutheran Reformation* (Stanford, 1988), for a discussion of this sort of Lutheran numerology.

112. See n. 98 above.

113. Celichius, *Notwendige Erinnerung*, fol. B2r.

114. It was on the minds of nineteenth-century scholars, e.g., Gustav Freytag, "Der deutsche Teufel im 16. Jahrhundert," in his *Bilder aus der deutschen Vergangenheit*, vol. 2 (Berlin, 1927), pp. 114–42; and Johannes Janssen, *Geschichte des deutschen Volkes seit dem Ausgang des Mittelalters*, vol. 6 (Freiburg im Breisgau, 1888), pp. 409–508.

115. André Goddu, "The Failure of Exorcism in the Middle Ages," in *Soziale Ordnungen im Selbstverständnis des Mittelalters*, ed. Albert Zimmermann and Gudrun Vuillemin-Diem, Miscellanea Mediaevalia, vol. 12/2 (Berlin, 1980), pp. 540–57.

umph of the Roman Church.[116] What Goddu's hasty conclusion can teach us, therefore, is the danger of uncritically adopting one kind of source, one genre, and one set of assumptions. This is a real danger for the study of pamphlets and sermons on demonic possession, too, for they present only what was "publicly known" in the sixteenth century. At present, there is no way of proving from archival sources that "public knowledge" corresponded to social reality. It is conceivable that before about 1560, many cases of demonic possession were kept secret or were simply regarded as uninteresting or lacking in value as religious propaganda. Unless the surviving sources distort the picture beyond all recognition, it is clear that demonic possession became epidemic in Germany only after about 1560. Bavaria experienced a wave of demonic possessions that continued well into the seventeenth century, but publicists for pilgrimage shrines did not choose to celebrate their victories in print as Catholic propagandists had done earlier.[117] The publicly known cases of demonic possession in the German-speaking lands from about 1490 to about 1650 are enumerated in table 1.1.

At least thirty-four places were touched by possession between 1490 and 1559, a span of seventy years; but the next twenty years (1560–79) found twenty-five places infected; and the last twenty years of the century (1580–99) added another forty-seven locations (and a generous increase in the size of these demonic outbursts as well). We cannot regard this dramatic increase as simply the illusory artifact of better publicity or the better survival of the appropriate sources, because if such factors were important, we would have a hard time explaining the rapid drop in publicized possession cases in the first half of the seventeenth century, during which I have found only fifteen published examples of demonic possession in the various German territories.[118]

116. See Walker, "Demonic Possession Used as Propaganda"; for Germany, see Martin Eisengrein, *Unser liebe Fraw zu Alten Oetting* (Ingolstadt, 1571). And note the attacks of Johann Marbach, *Von Mirackeln und Wunderzeichen* (Augsburg, 1571), and Martin Chemnitz, *Examination of the Council of Trent*, trans. Fred Kramer (St. Louis, 1971–86), 3: 404; Philip M. Soergel, *Wondrous in His Saints: Counter-Reformation Propaganda in Bavaria* (Berkeley and Los Angeles, 1993). For further examples of this propaganda war, see Petrus Thyraeus, *Daemoniaci, Hoc est: De obsessis a spiritibus daemoniorum hominibus liber unus* (Cologne, 1598); Martin Delrio, *Disquisitionum magicarum libri sex* (Louvain, 1599–1600); Sixtus Agricola and Georg Witmer, *Erschröckliche gantz warhafftige Geschicht welche sich mit Apolonia, Hannsen Geisslbrechts . . . Haussfrawen, so . . . von dem bösen Feind gar hart besessen* (Ingolstadt, 1584); and Georg Scherer, S.J., *Christliche Erinnerung Bey der Historien von jüngst beschehener Erledigung einer Junckfrawen, die mit zwölfftausent sechs hundert zwey und fünfftzig Teufel besessen gewesen* (Ingolstadt, 1583). See also Marc Venard, "Le démon controversiste," in *La controverse religieuse (XVIe–XIXe siècles)* (Montpellier, 1980), 2: 45–60.

117. David Lederer ("Reforming the Spirit," pp. 292–327) has shown that exorcism remained common in Bavaria until official skepticism restricted the use of the ritual in the 1660s.

118. Demonic possessions continued to be publicized well on into the eighteenth century, although historians have not yet studied these controversies carefully. See Beyer,

TABLE 1.1

Published Cases of Demonic Possession in Germany, 1490–1650

	Locations with Individual Possessions			Locations with Mass Possessions			Totals
	Female	Male	Gender Unknown	Female	Male	Mixed Gender	
1490–1559	19	10	0	1	0	4	34
1560–1579	10	4	0	5	1	5	25
1580–1599	17	15	7	1	0	7	47
1600–1650	6	8	1	0	0	0	15
Total	52	37	8	7	1	16	121

When we study the epidemiology of madness, we should look for geographic patterns as well as for evidence of increases. The madness of demonic possession was not rising equally everywhere in the German lands. If we map the extent of obsession and possession, several surprises leap off the page.

The spread and prevalence of demonic possession in Germany from 1490 to 1650, or at least the publicly well known episodes of demonic attack during the period, are charted on maps 1, 2, 3, and 4. It is not a picture that is congruent with the history of witch-hunting, the most severe outbursts of which occurred in the smaller states, and especially in Catholic ecclesiastical territories. With demonic possession, it is especially significant that only thirty-nine towns and villages south of the Main River had any cases at all, and only one of these was a true obsessional epidemic (Eichstätt).[119] In contrast, northern Germany had over eighty-two separate towns with cases of actual or suspected demonic possession, and several of these episodes, especially in the northeast and northwest, were massive outbursts of demonomania. A surprising number of these northern cases came from Lutheran Saxony and Brandenburg, a fact that may be connected to the great gnesio-Lutheran controversy over exorcism at baptism.[120] But only a

---

"Wahre Wundergeschicht von neuen Propheten." Jürgen Beyer was kind enough to photocopy the rich holdings of materials from the late seventeenth century held by the Royal Library in Copenhagen for me. David Lederer found numerous unpublicized cases of demonic possession in seventeenth-century Bavaria, but his dissertation does not present a statistical study of them, and so one cannot be sure of what patterns may have prevailed at shrines such as Benediktbeuern or Pürten (see Lederer, "Reforming the Spirit," pp. 195–96, 271–73).

119. This Eichstätt case from the 1490s was still evoking interest 100 years later: see *Hausbuch des Herrn Joachim von Wedel, Auf Krempzow Schloss und Blumberg Erbgesessen*, ed. Julius Freiherr von Bohlen Bohlendorff (Tübingen, 1882), p. 348.

120. See Bodo Nischan, "The Exorcism Controversy and Baptism in the Late Reformation," *Sixteenth Century Journal* 18 (1987): 31–51; and id., *Prince, People and Confession: The Second Reformation in Brandenburg* (Philadelphia, 1994), pp. 137–44.

tiny number were published concerning outbreaks in the great lands of the Counter-Reformation, Bavaria and Austria.

Proud as he was of the Catholic miracles performed by Our Lady of Altötting, Dr. Martin Eisengrein, writing in 1570, listed only one dispossession of demons in the almost 200 pages of his treatise on that famous pilgrimage shrine.[121] Demonic possession does appear now and then, albeit rarely, in the printed Bavarian and Franconian miracle books, another indication that possession was not a dominant idiom of madness in the south. It may be surprising, but the evidence is clear that famous demonic possessions and controversial exorcisms were largely absent from southern Germany, and especially the Catholic southeast, during the sixteenth century. Can we draw any conclusions about the pressure to be increasingly pious in these regions? Could it be that the Catholic Reformation in those lands did not encourage those pious feelings of doubt, unworthiness, and despair that we sometimes find in monastic culture and in Lutheran Germany alike?[122]

PUBLISHED DEMONIC POSSESSIONS IN GERMANY, 1490–1650

Represented on these four maps are all the "publicly known" cases of demonic possession in the German-speaking lands, 1490–1650. Thus, they include instances recorded in published chronicles, sermons, pamphlets, and news sheets, but they do not portray cases that can be found only in manuscript repositories. It may be that scholars will find other published cases as well, so these maps should be regarded as provisional.

Key to the maps:

→ = movement of a known person from one place to another
♀ = one female thought possessed by the devil
♂ = one male thought possessed by the devil
+ = more than one person thought possessed at one time in the same general place
++ = ten or more persons thought possessed at one time in the same general place
+++ = thirty or more persons thought possessed at one time in the same general place

Note: Cases of demonic possession were reported for Thuringia and Brandenburg, without mention of a specific town or village. Therefore the maps locate those regions without locating these instances exactly.

---

121. Eisengrein, *Unser liebe Fraw zu Alten Oetting*, fol. B3v.

122. By the seventeenth century, to be sure, Bavarians were frequently tempted to commit suicide, and their neighbors often concluded that they had fallen victim to religious doubts and despair (Lederer, "Reforming the Spirit," pp. 360–437).

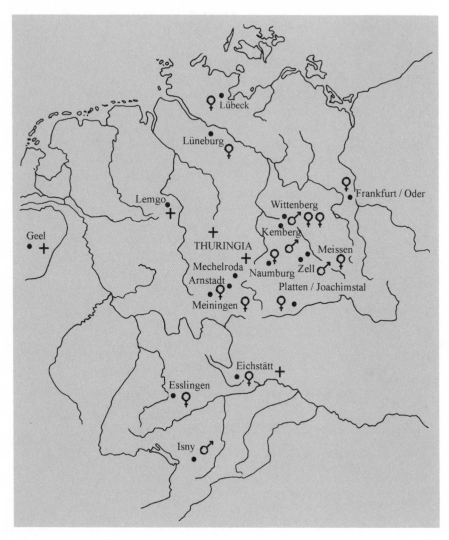

MAP 1. German Cases of Demonic Possession, 1490–1559

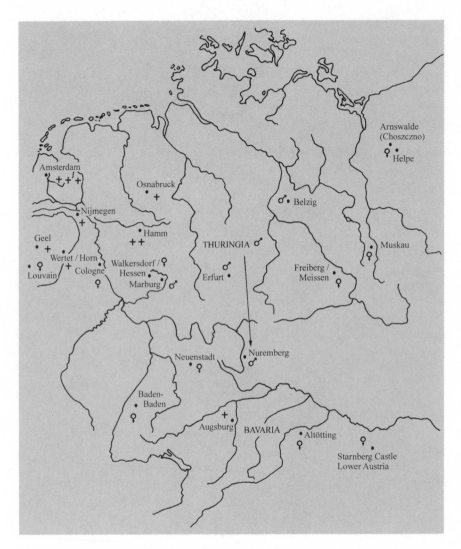

MAP 2. German Cases of Demonic Possession, 1560–1579

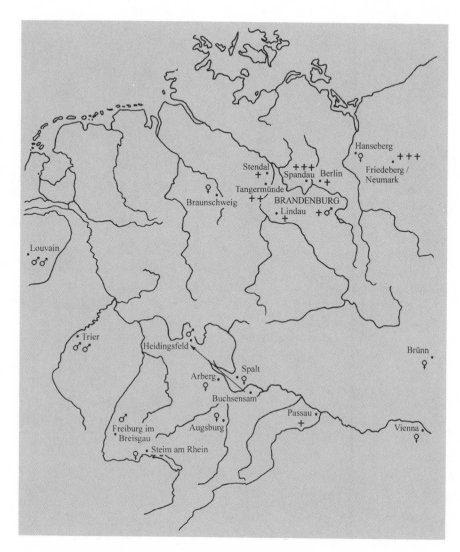

MAP 3. German Cases of Demonic Possession, 1580–1599

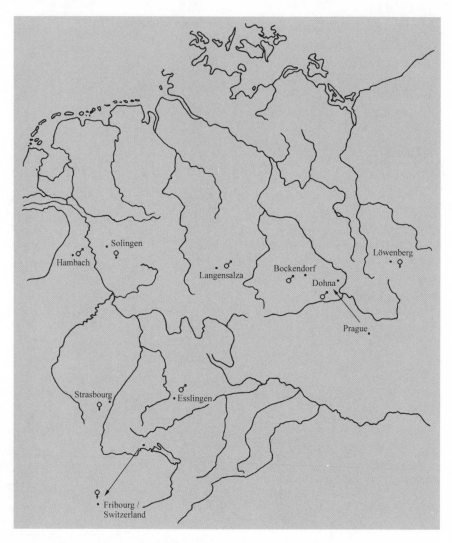

MAP 4. German Cases of Demonic Possession, 1600–1650

Demonic possession occurred most frequently in nunneries and in the most gnesio-Lutheran areas. In both situations, the attempt to live a more God-fearing and perfect life may well have led to stronger temptations, harsher pressures, than those felt in other parts of Germany. This would help to explain the account from Brandenburg in the 1590s in which the devil is said to have strewn coins all over the streets, and whoever picked up a coin became instantly (but not permanently) possessed.[123] Perhaps only a region where the demonic vices of greed, usury, pride, and vanity had been censured for over a generation and with increasingly apocalyptic fervor could have generated such a story. And that in turn suggests that when we speak of "popular" ideas of the devil, we cannot mean *only* those ideas that literate, educated people did not share. By the late sixteenth century, Germans generally, Lutheran and Catholic alike, believed that demonic possession was on the rise, and they may even have taken the rise as a sign of the imminent end of the world. But while accepting this learned interpretation of what they saw around them, ordinary people, and especially Lutherans, also knew how to shape the idiom of possession to some of their own ends.

Time and again, when a rural demoniac could not be helped, he or she would be brought into town, where the spiritual resources of a region were often concentrated, whether in the priests and relics of many a Catholic town or in the large congregations of Lutheran towns, whose Lutheran hymns, and perhaps especially "A Mighty Fortress Is Our God," became the Protestant substitute for exorcism.[124] It appears that the demonomaniac could sometimes be successfully treated this way, combining communal Lutheran prayer, fasting, singing, and large and sensationally orchestrated church services to produce a healing ritual that might be as effective as Catholic exorcisms (which also included communal prayers and the liberal use of holy water, holy relics, the Eucharistic host, waxen images of the Agnus Dei, etc.) in bringing the energumen back to her or his normal mind and normal social relations.

Witchcraft and Demon Possession

Demonic possession became common in Germany just as witchcraft was generally assuming the dimensions of an epidemic as well. It is well known

123. Daniel Cramer, *Das Grosse Pomersche Kirchen Chronicon* (Stettin [Szczecin, Poland], 1628), p. 54.
124. One finds this use of hymn singing, and especially of Luther's famous hymn, in Celichius, *Notwendige Erinnerung* (1595), fol. N4v; Nicolaus Blumius, *Historische erzehlung: Was sich mit einem fürnehmen Studenten, der von dem leidigen Teuffel zwölff Wochen besessen gewesen, verlauffen* (Leipzig, 1605); Angelus, *Annales Marchiae Brandenburgicae* (1598); Hocker and Hammelmann, "Der Teuffel selbs" (1569), in *Theatrum diabolorum*, ed. Feyerabend (1575), fol. 69r; Fincel, *Wunderzeichen*, fol. P3v; and in Seiler, *Daemonomania* (1605).

that Germany experienced relatively few and small witchcraft trials from about 1490 to 1560, but that from then on the panic spread.[125] Were the two sorts of diabolical activity connected? In several well-known cases, the answer is definitely yes. One widespread assumption was that witches could cause another person to become demon-possessed, an assumption so widespread that already in 1563, Johann Weyer devoted book 3 of his *De praestigiis daemonum* (this became book 4 in editions of the work published in 1567 and later) to refuting it as an absurdity.[126] His critique went largely unattended. In the 1583 possession and exorcism of Anna Schlutterbäurin, for example, Anna's grandmother was convicted and executed for causing her granddaughter's possession.[127] Dannhauer's report from 1654 of the miserably possessed girl in Strasbourg rested on the same assumption, and although the girl could not be helped in any decisive way, the witch responsible for her troubles was eliminated, by burning.[128] This was also the most important crime of the witches at Salem, Massachusetts, in 1692, for they, too, were convicted of bewitching (pinching, poking, and "obsessing") the tormented girls of Salem. The problem with proving the guilt of a witch accused of causing the possession of another was that invariably the accusation lay in the mouth of one who was known to be full of the devil, the very father of lies. From the beginning of the great witch-hunts around 1560, therefore, theologians and jurists repeatedly cautioned against taking the accusations of the possessed as serious or credible evidence.[129] And this warning was so widely heeded that we cannot draw any general causal connection between cases of possession and the rising tide of witchcraft prosecutions. In other words, it was not generally *because* of the rising tide of demonic possessions that witch trials became epidemic.

The parallel between demonic possession and witch-hunting is, however, worth exploring in further detail. Even if one did not regularly cause

125. See Gerhard Schormann, *Hexenprozesse in Deutschland* (Göttingen, 1981), and Brian Levack, *The Witch Hunt in Early Modern Europe* (London, 1987), pp. 152–68.

126. Weyer did not add a book to the *De praestigiis* in 1567, as some have assumed; he merely divided book 2 into books 2 and 3. For discussion of the logic of Weyer's argumentation, see chapter 4 in this volume and also my "Johann Weyer in medizinischer, theologischer, und rechtsgeschichtlicher Hinsicht," in *Vom Unfug des Hexen-Prozesses: Gegner der Hexenverfolgung von Johann Weyer bis Friedrich Spee*, ed. Otto Ulbricht and Hartmut Lehmann (Wiesbaden, 1992), pp. 53–64.

127. Scherer, *Christliche Erinnerung*, and Peter Obermayer, "Der Wiener Hexenprozess des Jahres 1583" (diss., University of Vienna, 1963). I am grateful to Heide Dienst for obtaining Obermayer's dissertation for me.

128. Dannhauer, *Scheid- und Absag-Brieff*, fol. A1r–v.

129. E.g., Jodocus Hocker, "Eine Getreuwe, Wolmeynende Christliche warnung, wider die Gottlosen Teuffels beschwerer oder banner, so in diesen ortern herumbschleichen," in *Theatrum diabolorum, das ist: Warhafftige eigentliche und kurtze Beschreibung allerley grewlicher, schrecklicher und abschewlicher Laster*, ed. Sigismund Feyerabend (Frankfurt a/M, 1569), fols. 135r–141v, at fol. 137r. Cf. the attitude of the theologians of Brandenburg in 1594, printed in Angelus, *Annales Marchiae Brandenburgicae* (1598), pp. 414–26, at p. 415.

the other, there are similarities we should not overlook. For example, physicians, jurists, and theologians all agreed that women were more likely to fall into the crime of witchcraft than men, and they cited all the well-known spiritual and physical weaknesses of women, especially post-menopausal women. In their weakness, loneliness, poverty, melancholy, and infidelity, suffering uncontrollable fantasies, and laboring under sexual frustrations, old women made easy victims for the devil, who usually offered them comfort, riches, companionship, dances, feasts, and an active sex life.[130] This much anyone could discover from Renaissance demonological treatises. The match with judicial reality was surprisingly exact. We know that roughly 80 percent of the persons executed as witches in Germany were women, and that older women were more commonly convicted than girls or young married women. What scholars have failed to notice is that the very same medical and theological reasons also existed for expecting demonic possession to predominate among older women.[131] Scholars have been taught, or misled, especially by a few celebrated French episodes, to think that demonic possession was mainly an affair of young women, and especially nuns.[132] Medical theory in the sixteenth century did, of course, regularly note the mental hazards of celibacy for cloistered nuns, but even for physicians, it was old, postmenopausal nuns who were most at risk, owing to their excessive dryness. Young women were regarded as too healthy to be regular victims of the devil, and they constituted therefore a weak link in the chain connecting medico-theological theory and actual cases of demonic possession. If we look carefully, however, we find an even more dramatic breach.

Looking again at table 1.1, we see that in published cases, women did indeed predominate in the relatively quiet period before 1560, although even then I have found four episodes of mass possession (at Geel, Lemgo, Mechelroda, and in Thuringia) in which the sexes were mixed (the pamphlets offer no clue as to the gender ratios).[133] The period 1560–79 matches our common expectations most perfectly, with ten individual female cases and

130. There are examples of such seduction scenes in my *Witch Hunting in Southwestern Germany, 1562–1684: The Social and Intellectual Foundations* (Stanford, 1972).

131. Seiler, *Daemonomania*, fol. F1v; Girolamo Menghi, *Fustis daemonum*; I cite Menghi's edition reprinted in *Thesaurus exorcismorum atque coniurationum terribilium potentissimorum, efficacissimorum cum practica probatissima* (Cologne, 1626), pp. 433–616, at p. 448; see also F. Zacharias, "Complementum artis exorcisticae," in *Thesaurus exorcismorum*, pp. 617–983, at pp. 630–31; Celichius, *Notwendige Erinnerung*, fol. D3r.

132. See Robert Mandrou, *Magistrats et sorciers en France au XVIIᵉ siècle: Une analyse de psychologie historique* (Paris, 1968); Alain Lottin, *Lille, citadelle de la contre-reforme? (1598–1668)* (Dunkirk, 1984), pp. 165–86; Michel de Certeau, *La possession de Loudun* (Paris, 1970).

133. For the pamphlets, sermons, and chronicles on which this table is based, see the works cited in the notes to this chapter and in the bibliography of primary sources at the end of this volume.

five cloisters compared to only four individual cases of men, but even in this period there were one mass possession of boys (thirty boys at Amsterdam in 1566) and five mixed mass possessions (e.g., among the burghers of Hamm). Thereafter, the conventional picture runs into more trouble. For the period 1580–99, male individual possessions ran about equal to the female cases (15 to 17), and we need to add in the extraordinary mass possessions in Brandenburg and, to a lesser extent, Saxony. The reports of eyewitnesses in Brandenburg from the 1590s repeatedly state that the devil seized people and shook them, sending them off into seizures without respect of age or gender.[134] Some 150 persons were afflicted in the Neumark town of Friede-berg, and about 40 fell victim to attacks in Spandau, just west of Berlin. Berlin itself came under siege, as did Stendal, Tangermünde, and the Saxon town of Lindau. Unfortunately, again, we cannot tell the proportions of male and female in these group outbursts, but contemporary pamphlets em-phasize the promiscuous nature of the assaults. Although there were only a few cases after 1600, the new pattern apparently continued, with eight men and six women coming to public attention between 1600 and 1650.

This deviation from learned demonological theory is surprising and in-structive, for it suggests that the theologians, jurists, and physicians of the sixteenth century were in no position hegemonically to evoke or "con-struct" cases of demonic possession in exactly the shapes their reading and traditions led them to expect. Unlike witchcraft, let us recall, it was no crime to be possessed, and perhaps this simple difference left possession more in the hands and minds of ordinary people than the crime of witch-craft, which was, after all, defined, prosecuted, and routinized by the liter-ate magisterial classes of Europe. This means in turn that the actual cases of demonic possession, as we find them in the accounts of publicists of the sixteenth century, were certainly in part, and often in large part, the prod-uct of popular fears, fancies, and images of the devil or of other spirits. Like Judith Klatten's "little people," some of the aspects of real-life demonic possession were thoroughly strange to the biblically, classically, or med-ically trained minds of the literate.

Pursuing this question further, we may look at the preconditions of pos-session, as they were commonly understood. Throughout the sixteenth century, it was widely conceded that the devil might possess both the greatest of sinners and the least sinful of all. In order to display his majesty, God might allow a demonic possession only to show how strong the Chris-

---

134. Cramer, *Grosse Pomersche Kirchen Chronicon*, p. 53; J. C. W. Moehsen, *Geschichte der Wissenschaften in der Mark Brandenburg, besonders der Arzneiwissenschaft*, vol. 1 (Berlin and Leipzig, 1781), pp. 500–502. Jürgen Beyer provides the best account, citing twelve pam-phlets from the year 1594, but emphasizing the elements of prophecy rather than of de-monic possession ("Wahrhafft Wundergeschicht von neuen Propheten," pp. 26–40).

tian sacraments and sacramentals were.[135] Or, of course, God could permit a horrible invasion of demons in order to punish either the sins of the possessed or even of another person. Possession could chasten or test the faithful or simply make a spectacle of the power of the devil, a display often thought necessary in the sixteenth century, when pastors described their congregations as full of godless materialists, Sadducees, swinish Epicureans, and self-satisfied worldlings who refused to recognize the power of God and the reality of the spirit-world.[136] Despite the fact that theoretically almost anyone could be a victim of the devil's assault, it seems that most theologians in the first half of the century were likely to think of possession as a punishment for the sins of the victim. The theological lexicographer Johannes Altenstaig was content to rattle off four routine reasons for demonic possession: for the glory of God, for the punishment of sin, for the correction of the sinner, or for our own erudition.[137] Johann Staupitz simplified this schedule more dramatically in a book on predestination published in 1517: "Obsessio a daemone est poena a deo inflicta horribilis" ("Demonic possession is a horrible punishment inflicted by God").[138] And Martin Luther, too, usually thought of demonic possession as a punishment for, or as an actual instantiation of, sin.[139] (Luther's ideas about madness and the devil are more fully discussed in the next chapter.) Later in the century,

135. Thyraeus, *Daemoniaci*, p. 77.

136. The notion was commonplace; see, e.g., Jacob Heerbrand, *Ein Predig Vom Straal* (Tübingen, 1579), fol. 2 r–v; Angelus, *Wider Natur und Wunderbuch*, pp. 79–80; Jacob Coler, *Eigentlicher Bericht, Von den seltzamen . . . Wunderwercken . . . so sich newlicher Zeit in der Marck Brandenburg zugetragen* (Erfurt, 1595), fols. B3v–D2v.

137. Johannes Altenstaig, *Vocabularius theologiae* (Hagenau, 1517), s.v. *obsessio*: "Permittit autem deus . . . sive ad gloriam suae ostensionem in potestativa eorum eiectione, sive ad peccati correctionem, sive ad nostram eruditionem."

138. Johann von Staupitz, *Libellus de exsecutione aeternae praedestinationis* (1517), ed. Lothar Graf zu Dohna and Richard Wetzel, vol. 14 of *Spätmittelalter und Reformation*, ed. Heiko A. Oberman (Berlin, 1979), ch. 20, para. 183, pp. 244–47.

139. This topic is far too complex to be passed over in a sentence. Chapter 2 deals with Luther's notions of madness in general, but this is the place to note that Luther was perhaps so persuaded that the devil *spiritually* possessed every unregenerate person, inspiring him or her to sinful thoughts and deeds, that he transferred this judgment to those cases of *physical* possession that he dealt with. In practice, with real people, however, Luther could act sympathetically and without this prejudice. The subject is worth more extended consideration, but see, e.g., WABr, no. 3057, Luther to Andreas Ebert (Aug. 5, 1536), vol. 7, pp. 489–90; no. 3398, Luther to Wenzeslaus Link (Oct. 26, 1539), vol. 3, pp. 579–80; no. 3509, Luther to his wife (July 15, 1540), vol. 9, pp. 167–68; and WATR, vol. 3, no. 3739, for Luther's own attempt at exorcism. Recent efforts to deal with this general topic do not concentrate on the question of demonic possession; see Harmannus Obendiek, *Der Teufel bei Martin Luther* (Berlin, 1931); Hans-Martin Barth, *Der Teufel und Jesus Christus in der Theologie Martin Luthers* (Göttingen, 1967); Heiko A. Oberman, *Luther: Man Between God and the Devil* (New Haven, 1989); Jeffrey B. Russell, *Mephistopheles: The Devil in the Modern World* (Ithaca, N.Y., 1986); Jörg Haustein, *Martin Luthers Stellung zum Zauber- und Hexenwesen* (Stuttgart, 1990).

however, the learned personal physician to the Elector Palatine, Johannes Lang, was even willing to opine that true piety actually kept the devil away: "[P]ium enim hominem nec daemon malus, nec fatum tenet."[140] This was a sentiment enthusiastically endorsed by the Freiburg Catholic theologian Jodocus Lorich, who held that the best way to secure one's health and to escape the attacks of the devil was to fear God and lead a pious life, for the devil flees such persons.[141] Would that the world were so simple!

Unfortunately for this comforting theory that the devil worked dutifully as God's jailer and executioner, the published accounts of demonic possession reveal a very different devil, one that positively preferred to attack pious young Christians. A good example is the "gruesome story" from 1559 of a godly girl from Platten, close by Joachimstal in Saxony.[142] She was chaste and modest, went regularly to church, took the sacrament often, and was said to have memorized the gospels. Suddenly, at Shrovetide, she was stricken with seizures so severe that her parents thought she had epilepsy. She lay quietly helpless for four weeks, but after Easter the devil began to erupt, speaking blasphemies from her. Moreover, she began to display such classic signs of possession as eyes that bugged out of her head, a tongue that would stick out the span of a whole hand, and a head that was wrenched around to face backwards. After repeated tortures and extended conversations with the attending pastors, the devil was finally driven out through congregational prayer and hymn-singing by some one thousand common people. Before he left, however, he claimed that God had sent him to plague Anna's body (but not her soul) in order to warn people to give up their godless pride, gluttony, and drunkenness. And as he flew out the window like a swarm of flies he was reported to say: "Alle die nicht gern zu Kirchen gehen, wollen selbst daheimen lesen, zum Sacrament nicht gehen, in Fressen, Sauffen, und Wucher liegen, sind alle mein, mit Leib und Seel" ("All who refuse to go to church, preferring to stay at home to read, rejecting the sacrament, and wallowing in gluttony, drunkenness, and usury— are all mine, body and soul").[143]

So here was another reason for possession, one that the pastors and theologians had not dreamed of: this devil gave a simple smith's daughter the

140. Johann Lang, *Epistolarum medicinalium volumen tripartitum* (Frankfurt a/M, 1589), bk. 3, p. 716.

141. Jodocus Lorich, *Aberglaub: Das ist, kurtzlicher bericht, Von Verbottenen Segen, Artzneyen, Künsten, vermeinten und anderen spöttlichen beredungen . . . von newen ubersehen und gemehrt* (Freiburg im Breisgau, 1593), p. 113.

142. *Eine Grawsame erschreckliche und wunderbarliche Geschicht oder Newe Zeitung, welche warhaftig geschehen ist, in diesem MDLIX. Jar, zur Platten . . . Alda hat ein Schmid eine Tochter die ist vom bösen Feind dem Teufel eingenommen und besessen* (Wittenberg, 1559). This report was also printed at Nuremberg in the same year and was repeated in Fincel's *Wunderzeichen* (Jena, 1562), fols. O7r–P5r.

143. Ibid. as quoted in Fincel, *Wunderzeichen*, fol. P4v.

opportunity to take up the moralizing position of the pious Lutheran *Teufelbücher*, to preach virtue and repentance while at the same time giving vent to her most blasphemous and irreverent ideas.[144] It is possible that her words and indeed the whole account have been corrupted by the pastoral reporter, but it seems more likely that this girl *was* pious and *did* mix blasphemy with pious exhortation.

Hers was not an isolated case. When Veronica Steiner was seized by the devil in 1574, in the castle of Starnberg in Lower Austria, she too possessed two voices, one the deep, coarse, manly voice of the devil, and the other her own tender, reasonable, modest, Christian voice.[145] When using her customary voice, she prayed, praised God, admonished others to pray, sighed over her own sins, and accepted the Catholic faith. But with her devilish voice, she cursed and barked, spat against the Catholic religion and its adherents, and sang unchaste drinking songs or perverted psalms. She too seems to have found in demonic possession a way of expressing the two violently contradictory ways she felt about her religion.

Or take the case of an eighteen-year-old maid from Lutheran Meissen in Saxony, who fell down in fits in 1560, but on recovery would launch into extraordinary prophesies.[146] God had been good to everyone, she reminded her listeners, but no one showed a proper thankfulness, and so God's punishment was surely coming. Girls must give up their vanity, married persons their adultery. Woe to the rich who did not help the poor! Woe to parents who did not discipline their children! And woe to all of Germany for constant drunkenness, gluttony, pride, and the deliberate rejection of godly sermons! This girl fell repeatedly into trances in which she saw God, angels, and hell. Suspicious of this behavior, Hieronymus Weller (a well-known student of Luther's) examined her and had to admit that she uttered "nothing but Scripture and a serious sermon of repentance, which should move us as directly as if it were a good angel's voice."[147] Here was a girl who would certainly have been considered demon-possessed at another time or place, but her piety prevailed in this case. She was allowed, in effect, to preach in this unconventional way.

When the noble Lutheran lady Kunigunde von Pilgram was seized by the devil in 1565, one of the sure signs that this was demonic possession

144. The best work on these visionary and prophetic episodes is Beyer's unfortunately still unpublished "Wahrhafte Wundergeschicht von neuen Propheten" (cited in n. 99 above).

145. Sebastian Khueller, *Kurtze unnd warhafftige Historia, von einer Junckfrawen, wölche mit etlich unnd dreissig bösen Geistern leibhafftig besessen* (Munich, 1574).

146. *Newe Zeytung, Von einem Megdlein das entzuckt ist gewest, und was wunderbarliche Rede es gethan hat* (Nuremberg, 1560).

147. Ibid.: "aber es ist eitel schrifft, als ich vernommen habe, unnd ein ernste Busspredig, welche unns so vil, als eines guten Engels stimb bewegen soll, und ist eigentlich nichts anders, denn ein zeichen von Gott."

was that she wanted to pray but was forcibly restrained by the devil.[148] Both the accounts by Melchior Neukirch of a possession case from Braunschweig in 1595–96 and that by Johann Conrad Dannhauer with respect to the noble girl from Strasbourg (1650–54) allow us to draw the same conclusion, but with even more pathetic detail. In the Braunschweig case, Appolonia, the daughter of Heinrich Stampken, was known to all for her extraordinary Lutheran piety.[149] She loved her catechism, using it in her prayers both morning and night; she attended sermons eagerly, took Holy Communion, received absolution gratefully, and was altogether too good.[150] One day she fell into weakness and depression, a debilitating combination that lasted three-quarters of a year, but then she broke out in fully demonic gestures and speech. With loving pastoral care, she arrived at lucid intervals and admitted that the beginning of her troubles had been when she had heard someone curse her and wish the devil into her. From then on, she had suffered horrible doubts, fearing that perhaps she was not a child of God, perhaps she was not of the elect. These religious doubts had triggered a depression, which in turn opened the door to the devil. Neukirch mobilized the whole congregation of St. Peter's, and others as well, to repeated prayers and hymns, which were printed so that all of Braunschweig could pray at once for her release. Most dramatic and peculiar of all are the prayers composed by Appolonia herself, long stanzas of rhymed verse, of which I shall give only two examples:

> Der Teufel ubt sehr groß Gewalt
> Und plagt mich grewlich mannigfalt
> Nimpt mir all meine Glieder ein
> Reist mich, und macht mir grosse pein
> O Herr hilff mir von dieses quael
> Bewahre meinen Leib und Seel[151]

> The Devil uses great power
> To plague me horribly in many ways
> Seizing all of my limbs,
> Tearing at me and wounding me.

148. Karl von Weber, *Aus vier Jahrhunderten: Mitteilungen aus dem Haupt-Staatsarchiv zu Dresden*, n.s. (Leipzig, 1861), 2: 309–11.

149. Melchior Newkirch, *Andechtige Christliche gebete, wider die Teuffel in dem armen besessenen leuten* (Helmstedt, 1596), fols. A2r–v.

150. I see no reason to doubt that a girl might come to love her catechism, however offensive or peculiar such a devotion might seem to a modern observer. For a skeptical view, see Gerald Strauss, "Comment," in *Religion and Culture in the Renaissance and Reformation*, ed. Steven Ozment (Kirksville, Mo., 1989), pp. 121–30, esp. p. 129. Of course, Pastor Neukirch may have exaggerated Appolonia's piety, but the result only confused the categories more completely: it must have seemed ever less understandable that the devil should attack the innocent vessels of God's grace.

151. Newkirch, *Andechtige Christliche gebete*, fol. D2v.

O Lord relieve me from this torture
And preserve my body and soul.

Gotts Son das Feld behalten muß
Der treib dich Teuffl auß seinem Hauß
Mach wie du kanst, Got ist mit mir
Im gringsten fürcht ich mich nicht für dir.[152]

God's Son will win the field,
And drive you, Devil, from his house
Do your worst, God is with me,
I have no fear of you.

Here was surely a girl who had imbibed rather too freely of the Lutheran teachings that had been offered to her, or perhaps it would be safer to say that she experienced Luther's *Anfechtungen* but had them drawn out over months at a time.

Pastor Dannhauer's noble girl of Strasbourg was just ten when she fell victim to the devil, but the odd thing about her condition was that while her body and her "outer and inner senses" were tortured, she was not fully possessed. Her mind remained clear and Christian, and she remained able, apparently, to curse Satan and order him to leave her. She was persuaded firmly that she was a child of God, having no doubts on that score, but she assured others that it would be better for the godless to experience her pangs in this world. "For they give themselves over to godless gaming, gluttony, and drinking, to whores and lovers, and forget all about God. But how will it turn out for them in the end?"[153] God would punish those who had not borne crosses in this world. She was not content to echo the sermons of the moralizers, however, for this preadolescent also had a strong urge to die. She went on and on, in words that Dannhauer must have put in her mouth, but the basic message may well have been hers: "I'll gladly die if Thou wilt, if it be Thy fatherly will. O dear God I thank you from the bottom of my heart that you are giving me the strength still to escape."[154] In some of her visions, she saw God and his angels.[155]

Here, then, were demonic possessions that produced revival sermons and angelic visions. These afflicted women and girls may have been using the cultural idiom of demonic possession but they were surely extending it

152. Ibid., fol. E7r.
153. Dannhauer, *Scheid- und Absag-Brieff*, fol. A4v: "dann sie ergeben sich dem gottlosen spielen, fressen, und sauffen, dem Huren und Buhlen, und vergessen Gottes. Aber wie wird es ihnen gehen?"
154. Ibid., fol. A7v: "Ich wil gern sterben, wann du wilt, wann es dein Vätterlicher Will ist. Ach lieber Gott ich danke dir von grund meines Hertzens, dass du mir die Krafft giebst, dass ich noch so fortkommen kann."
155. Ibid., fol. B1v.

well beyond what the theological wisdom of the sixteenth century had led anyone to expect. By the 1570s, this was plain to observers such as Georg Walther, pastor of Halle, and even earlier to Veit Dietrich, the short-lived pastor of Nuremberg, both of whom commented on the pious, modest Christianity displayed by many of the possessed when they were given respite from the assaults of the devil.[156]

In these deviations from official expectation, I think we can see what ordinary people experienced using the cultural idiom of demonic possession. They suffered a madness that was a painful liberation from the piety to which they aspired. That is, for many of these victims, diabolic possession gave vent to the agonized religious frustrations, fears, and yearnings of the would-be pious.

In another area, however, a sort of popular confusion arose. In high legal theory, as it developed in the sixteenth century, the difference between the crime of witchcraft and the condition of demonic possession was clear. Witches consciously and voluntarily entered into a pact with the devil, while the possessed passively and involuntarily endured his external and internal assaults. Witches were criminals; the possessed were mad. What could be clearer?

But was it clear what happened to Anna Roschmann in 1563? At the age of twenty, as she lay in her Augsburg bedroom, the evil spirit came to her and asked her to be his, "whereupon she began to act very strangely and as if she had lost her reason."[157] Soon she was showing the symptoms of full, raging possession, but a pamphlet emphasizes that it had begun with an invitation from the devil. Had she entered willingly into a state of demonic obsession? And what shall we think of Anna Barbara of Stein am Rhein, whose own mother had cursed her and caused her to be possessed? Many common folk thought of her as a witch.[158] Truly confusing is the case of Hans Schmidt, a smith's apprentice from Heidingsfeld, near Würzburg. In 1589, at the age of nineteen, Schmidt fell in with bad company and got hold of a book that contained secrets of the magic arts. Realizing its dangers, Schmidt finally burned the book, but he suffered further temptations. Satan offered him money on one occasion and on another tempted him to hang himself, but Schmidt resisted these advances. He tried to live up to his

156. George Walther, *Krancken Büchlein: Woher alle Kranckheiten kommen, Item, warumb uns Gott damit heimsuche: Und wie man sich darinnen Christlich verhalten und in allerley anfechtungen trösten sol* (Wittenberg, 1579), fol. 252r-v.

157. *Eigentliche unnd Warhaffte vertzaichnus, was sich in disem 1563 Jar . . . zu Augspurg, mit eines armen Burgers Tochter daselbst zügetragen, wie sy vomm bösen Geist . . . besessen, und derselbig . . . von Herrn Simon Scheibenhart . . . aussgetriben* (n.p., n.d. [1563]; I have used the copy in the Universitätsbibliothek München).

158. *Neue Zeitung und beschreibung, Was sich mit Anna Barbara, vom Stain geboren, von kuniglichen stamb . . . ist worden . . . wie sie . . . mit 9. Teuflen besessen, auch wider ledig ist worden* (Constance, 1608), fols. A5v–6r.

Christian principles until he was finally possessed by a highly frustrated devil.[159] Here the story began as many a witchcraft seduction tale began, but because of his powers of Christian resistance, the youth was possessed. Indeed, by the late sixteenth century many a suicide attempt was attributed to demonic possession. At times, Martin Luther had explained, suicides did not kill themselves willingly (and did not necessarily go to hell), because they were driven to their deaths by the devil.[160]

To take another example, Appolonia Geisslbrecht was confronted first, in 1583, by a devil who offered her plentiful food, drink, and dance. In this case, she actually accepted the devil's offer, and she was then at once possessed.[161] This looked like a simple case of witchcraft, but the case turned confusingly into obsession, or a form of possession in which she was not fully responsible any more.

Pastor Nicolaus Blum told a similarly confusing story from his parish in Dohna, near Dresden. In 1602, it appeared, God had "permitted" a noble student from Prague to be possessed as punishment for the sin of "Zauberey"—that is, the crime of magic, for which women (and men) were being executed in droves at just that time.[162] Here again it may have been the youth's resistance to Satan that made the difference, but it could also have been his noble and student status.

We know of other adventurous students who signed pacts with the devil, for example, without having to pay the ultimate penalty for their indiscretions. So it was with a desperate twenty-five-year-old whom Pastor Tobias Wagner tried to help in 1643. In a deep depression and eager for money, the young man made a pact with the devil, who then prompted him to attempt suicide. When he was saved from death by his wife, he merely fell into a deeper and more demonic melancholy.[163] Why was this case not treated as witchcraft? Perhaps because of the suicide attempt, perhaps because of the young man's evident depression and desperation. But also perhaps because ordinary people were having trouble keeping the supposedly clear categories of witchcraft and possession clearly separate.

159. Johann Schnabel and Simon Marius, *Warhafftige und erschröckliche Geschicht welche sich newlicher Zeit zugetragen hat, mit einem Jungen Handtwercks und Schmidtsgesellen, Hansen Schmidt genandt* (Würzburg, 1589).
160. H. C. Erik Midelfort, "Religious Melancholy and Suicide: On the Reformation Origins of a Sociological Stereotype," in *Madness, Melancholy, and the Limits of the Self*, ed. Andrew D. Weiner and Leonard V. Kaplan, vol. 3 of *Graven Images* (Madison, Wis., 1996), pp. 41–56.
161. Agricola and Witmer, *Erschröckliche gantz warhafftige Geschicht*, pp. 5–6.
162. Blumius, *Historische erzehlung* (1605), pp. 1–3.
163. Tobias Wagner, *Der Kohlschwartze Teuffel . . . über einem schröcklichen Fall einer Mannsperson die sich in Schwermuth dem Teuffel mit eignem Blut verschrieben* (Ulm, 1643), pp. 73–74. For the demonic temptation to suicide, see esp. Markus Schär, *Seelennöte der Untertanen. Selbstmord, Melancholie und Religion im Alten Zürich, 1500–1800* (Zurich, 1985), and now Lederer, "Reforming the Spirit."

Certainly, that would seem to be the case with the painter Christoph Haiz-mann, whose demonic possession in 1677 was diagnosed by Sigmund Freud as an example of "diabolical neurosis."[164] Haizmann, too, had a pact with the devil, or perhaps two pacts, but he was not treated as a witch; instead, a pilgrimage and repeated exorcisms liberated him from the devil and from his pacts.[165]

So demonic possession came to be experienced as a kind of madness that alienated Christian men and women, and even maids and youths, from the pious thoughts and acts that they had come to think of as their proper characters. Demonic obsession and possession provided a kind of madness in which they could experience the spiritual and mental conflicts within themselves, the contradictory voices and gestures that they could hardly admit existed beneath their Christian appearance. And ordinary people also experienced demonic obsessions when their very piety drove them to desire death or to conclude, despairingly, that they were among the damned. Suicidal demonomania especially afflicted the pious.

In these ways, it appears, German laymen and laywomen constructed an idiom in which to experience and express their religious doubts and their miseries, not an idiom that was purposely taught them by their priests and pastors, but a grammar for their experience of the world, made up of materials partly provided by jurists and theologians. Seen from this perspective, the history of demonomania, of diabolical obsession and possession, is the dark side of the history of piety.

Conclusion

With the melancholy of Hugo van der Goes, we confront a major problem of sources: does a text refer primarily to other texts, or can we winkle out the ways in which it refers to the world as well? With the dancing mania, we have this source problem too, as well as the complex problem of interpretation: just what was St. Vitus' dance?[166] With demonomania, we encounter the spreading madness of demonic possession, in which serious source-related and interpretive problems combine with yet a third sort of

164. Sigmund Freud, "A Seventeenth-Century Demonological Neurosis," in *The Standard Edition of the Complete Psychological Works of Sigmund Freud*, trans. and ed. James Strachey et al., vol. 19 (London, 1961), pp. 67–105; Richard Hunter and Ida Macalpine, *Schizophrenia 1677: A Psychiatric Study of an Illustrated Autobiographical Record of Demoniacal Possession* (London, 1956); Gaston Vandendriessche, *The Parapraxis in the Haizmann Case of Sigmund Freud* (Louvain, 1965); and Lederer, "Reforming the Spirit," pp. 271–2.

165. See my essay on this case, "Catholic and Lutheran Reactions to Demon Possession in the Late Seventeenth Century: Two Case Histories," *Daphnis* 15 (1986): 623–48.

166. Of course, van der Goes also presents serious interpretive problems, but St. Vitus' dance seems to display a different order of difficulty and obscurity.

historical puzzle: the fact that demonic possession was regarded by the clergy as an example of Satan's wrath, but was often experienced by the possessed as suicidal religious doubts, and as frothing, raging seizures of blasphemy and impiety. It was as if the intensely pious culture of Catholic cloisters and of gnesio-Lutheran parishes unintentionally created or cultivated a demonic personality through which the pious could experience and express their temptations, doubts, and repressed attachments to the world.

It is obvious that one of the major ways in which the sixteenth century differed from our own is the deeply felt and broadly all-encompassing religious language of the major thinkers of four or five hundred years ago. The next chapter examines the religious rhetoric of madness as it was developed by two of the most extraordinary thinkers of the entire sixteenth century, Luther and Paracelsus.

$\mathcal{T}$wo Reformers and a World Gone Mad: Luther and Paracelsus

ONE of the reasons the experience of madness in the sixteenth century seems so strange to us is that we have mainly lost the appropriate terms, images, and metaphors with which early modern Europeans looked at and understood the insane. To recover these ideas is the major task of the next few chapters, which deal with religious, medical, and legal attitudes toward mental disorder. The problems highlighted in chapter 1 make it clear that getting at the history of madness requires a detailed knowledge of a spiritual world in which the devil was as much a reality as death.

When we voyage to the sixteenth century without the conceptual comforts of the twentieth, the first differences we are likely to notice are physical. Life was then rougher; hunger, disease and death were closer, transportation more arduous. Because roads were often just rutted paths, even noble ladies rode on horseback rather than in carriages; and ordinary people walked everywhere. The dark of night was not lit up by street lights. The cold of winter was seldom effectively shut out. Smells of rotting manure permeated the bourgeois courtyards of even large towns, while even the finest inns provided only chamber pots for their guests, who slept, often naked, sweaty, and louse-infested, several to a bed.[1]

Spiritually, the age was just as harsh. Traditional and unorthodox thinkers alike agreed that the devil was loose in the world, that Christ's return was, although strictly unpredictable, as imminent as the reign of Antichrist was palpable. In the decrepit waning years of the world, sin was raging as never before. In short, the world was mad. To prove the point, one could pile up anecdotes and quotations from the length and breadth of the sixteenth century, and one could make a huge and various pile.

1. See the brilliant evocation by Lucien Febvre, *Life in Renaissance France* (Cambridge, Mass., 1977).

Instead, I shall pursue another course in this chapter by looking closely at two of the century's most powerful writers and reformers, Martin Luther and Theophrastus of Hohenheim, called Paracelsus, both of whom elaborated a complex rhetoric of madness, a way of talking about all the most serious problems of their age as if they were the product of insanity. The point seems to be worth making in detail, because in our century we have mostly lost a serious moral dimension in our thinking about mental illness. We usually assume that madness confers a medical excuse against accusations of crime and social forgiveness for acts of immorality. Serious moralists today do not discuss sin. When this goes too far, we may sense that something is wrong and overreact, prompting some, recently, to advocate the wholesale abolition of the insanity defense. Secular moralists also assume that if a religious dimension is admitted into the discussion of madness, the ensuing discourse will become mired in the irrational labyrinth of theology. But for Luther and Paracelsus, madness was a vital moral and religious metaphor, capable of extraordinary inflection to cover all sorts of situations. For them, it made sense to say that thought and action could become so evil or degraded or bestial that the sinful person had gone mad. It also made sense to both of them to search the Bible carefully for clues as to the nature of health and reason. If we are to understand this lost world of the sixteenth century, we need to familiarize ourselves with the intense rhetoric of madness generated by two of that century's master moralists.

On the surface, any comparison of Luther and Paracelsus would seem destined to failure; they exhibited such obvious and extreme differences.[2] Luther was a man of institutions, bound to his university and invoking the privileges and obligations imposed upon him by his doctoral degree, even when he no longer felt bound to the Augustinian order of hermits; he was also bound in marriage to a new vision of the dignity of secular life, and dependent on the most ancient sources of the Christian tradition. Even when he felt driven in 1520 to burn the canon law and the papal bull that threatened him with excommunication, Luther was an "obedient rebel."[3]

With Paracelsus one can hardly speak of obedience. He ostentatiously broke with university tradition when he lectured in German at Basel. He prided himself on breaking with the medical tradition of Galen.[4] In theol-

2. Luther and Paracelsus have been compared theologically in Hartmut Rudolph, "Einige Gesichtspunkte zum Thema 'Paracelsus und Luther,'" *Archiv für Reformationsgeschichte* 72 (1981): 34–53, and in Andrew Weeks, *Paracelsus: Speculative Theory and the Crisis of the Early Reformation* (Albany, N.Y., 1997), pp. 1–4, 9–18, 142–44, 161–62.

3. Jaroslav Pelikan, *Obedient Rebels: Catholic Substance and Protestant Principle in Luther's Reformation* (New York, 1964).

4. Paracelsus's contribution and the relation, if any, of magic to the scientific revolution continues to be controversial. See Patrick Curry, "Revisions of Science and Magic," *History of Science* 23 (1985): 299–325.

ogy, he combined belief in the feminine nature of God with mystical and spiritual contentions that rested on a curiously literal and untraditional reading of Scripture.[5] He sided with the German peasants in their attempted revolution of 1525. Recently, it has been plausibly argued that the sources of Paracelsus's demon lore were not so much Neoplatonic and gnostic literature, as eminent scholars had argued, but the oral folk traditions of the peasants among whom he lived.[6] In a certain sense, there were hardly two more dissimilar thinkers in the sixteenth century than Martin Luther and Theophrastus Bombastus.

And yet they drew conclusions with respect to madness that were remarkably similar, using the basic motifs of sin and of demons to explain the hopelessly denatured, alienated, and suicidal character of the world. Both Paracelsus and Luther recognized that the rhetoric of madness, the act of calling another person insane or mad, was essentially connected with deeper questions involving the very definition of what it was to be human. Because the Greeks defined man as the rational animal, the problem of irrationality could take on a new form in the West. The irrational now threatened to be utterly denaturing and dehumanizing. Some of these attitudes remind us of Epicurean, Stoic, and early Christian responses to Aristotelian doctrines, and it will become clear that both Luther and Paracelsus subscribed to certain ancient Greek ideas, but in a radically modified form, holding that the ultimate irrationality was a lack of healthy concern over one's own salvation. From their perspective, resolute, desperate, and deliberate sinfulness was just the sort of madness that made one wonder whether a blind sinner was still fully human.

Although Luther and Paracelsus shared this kind of conclusion, it does not follow that they were close in many other respects. They stand together in this chapter because through them we can get to know their religiously radical approach to the world, and take a step out of the twentieth century back into the sixteenth. For them and for other inhabitants of early modern Germany, the world was not mainly a place of order and reason, of regular and predictable events.

5. Charles Webster, *From Paracelsus to Newton: Magic and the Making of Modern Science* (Cambridge, 1982). Arlene Miller Guinsburg, "The Counterthrust to Sixteenth-Century Misogyny: The Work of Agrippa and Paracelsus," *Historical Reflections* 8 (1981): 3–28.

6. See *Resultate und Desiderate der Paracelsus-Forschung*, ed. Hartmut Rudolph and Peter Dilg (Stuttgart, 1993); Ute Gause, *Paracelsus (1493–1541): Genese und Entfaltung seiner frühen Theologie* (Tübingen, 1993); Hans Jürgen Goertz, *Profiles of Radical Reformers: Biographical Sketches from Thomas Müntzer to Paracelsus*, trans. Walter Klaassen (Scottsdale, Pa., 1982).

Luther and the Rhetoric of Madness

Martin Luther (1483–1546) never wrote a treatise on madness or mental illness, and, as a theologian, he was mainly concerned with religious problems. Still one can say that he was never far from the question of mental
disorder. Scholars have, however, devoted much more attention to Luther's
own supposed mental problems than to Luther's constant concerns about
madness.[7] With the exception of a few old polemical Catholic works that
tried to show that, among other things, St. Thomas Aquinas had a more hu-
mane and balanced approach to the mentally ill than did Luther, there is almost no scholarly literature on this subject.[8]

If we read Luther attentively, however, we cannot fail to be impressed at
how often he commented on mental disorders, his own to be sure, but also
those of his followers and especially those of his opponents, and this is a
clue to the modern scholarly neglect. Luther often blasted his enemies as
fools, madmen, and demoniacs, and their ideas variously as demented,
insane, and rabid; or idiotic, foolish, enraged, phrenetic, maniac, and nonsensical; or crazy, deluded, imbecile, delirious, deranged, furious, demonically inspired, and hopelessly, blindly mad. Scholars have dismissed these
intemperate charges as symptoms of Luther's cultivated gift for invective
and of the violent, even scurrilous, polemics of his day. This scholarly
disregard is unfortunate, because it underestimates Luther's numerous
serious remarks about madness, and also because Luther's invective often
went far beyond the rhetorical norms of his day. His violent language was
not just a crude or superficial symptom of his time, and a closer analysis
reveals that even Luther's loose language, his broadside blasts, make more
sense than scholars have seen.[9] Mark Edwards has shown that when Luther
called some of his enemies "false brethren," he chose words that were
firmly rooted in his own emerging attitude toward the Reformation and
his own place in it.[10] Used just as frequently as the charge of being a false

7. Erik Erikson's *Young Man Luther: A Study in Psychoanalysis and History* (New York,
1958) set the discussion of Luther's neuroses and obsessions on a new level and prompted
a continuing series of studies of Luther's state of mind. See especially Mark U. Edwards,
Luther's Last Battles: Politics and Polemics, 1531–1546 (Ithaca, N.Y., 1983); Harry G. Haile,
Luther: An Experiment in Biography (Garden City, N.Y., 1980).

8. See Julius Bessmer, S.J., "Luthers Anschauungen über die Geisteskrankheiten und
die katholische Lehre," *Stimmen aus Maria-Laach: Katholische Blätter* 84 (1913): 444–45,
474–76.

9. Eric W. Gritsch, *Martin: God's Court Jester* (Philadelphia, 1983); id., "Martin Luther
and Violence: A Reappraisal of a Neuralgic Theme," *Sixteenth Century Journal* 3 (1972):
37–55; M. Brecht, "Der 'Schimpfer' Martin Luther," *Luther* 52 (1981): 97–113; Heiko A.
Oberman, "Teufelsdreck: Eschatology and Scatology in the 'Old' Luther," *Sixteenth Century
Journal* 19 (1988): 435–50.

10. Mark U. Edwards, *Luther and the False Brethren* (Stanford, 1975).

brother, the accusation of madness clearly had other tactical advantages as well. Luther hurled this charge, not just at former disciples (such as the Anabaptists and "Sacramentarians"), but at the Turks, the Jews, Catholics in general and the pope in particular, at monks, scholastics, Arians, Epicureans, atheists, fatalists, Stoics, antinomians, visionary saints, despotic princes, and the many towering examples of unbridled lust and wickedness recorded in the Bible and in secular chronicles.

Luther found such persons mentally ill, not because he thought unreason was humanly normal, but actually because he thought most people were basically reasonable. It is well known that when he first made his evangelical breakthrough and began to publish his revolutionary conclusions, from 1518 to 1523, he expected that the newly recovered light of the gospel would destroy all the shadowy superstitions of popery and confidence in human works righteousness. On the assumption that men were reasonable and that Scripture was clear, Luther at first trusted that the Word would "do it all," and would even persuade ecclesiastical potentates to give up their unrighteous ways. When Luther sadly came to realize that his Reformation would not of itself sweep all errors away, he felt forced to conclude that either Scripture was unclear or unreasoning, obstinate, malicious men were obstructing the obvious dictates of God. Since it seemed blasphemous to think that the Bible was obscure on important points, Luther was understandably attracted to the second conclusion—that his opponents refused to allow Scripture to engage their reason because they were fanatical visionaries and stubborn, sinful, autistic madmen. When the sophists (as he called the scholastics) debated whether God was in this or that category, they were simply "hallucinating."[11] When monks cultivated the contemplative life, they set such unrealistic standards "that no one seemed to be a monk in the true sense of the word unless he had special revelations," visions that were really "satanic illusions pure and simple by which I myself was almost taken in when I was still a monk."[12] Rabbinical interpretations of Scripture were usually false, for the Jews were devilish (following John 8:44), from which "it follows that the Jews are a mad people and given over to a base mind" ("constat esse furiosum populum et traditum in sensum reprobum") (citing Rom. 1:28).[13]

Not all of Luther's opponents had abandoned reason completely, however, for some made the mistake of using (or overusing) reason where it was inappropriate. Reason should not, Luther thought, attempt to dictate

11. Martin Luther, *Lectures on Genesis*: WA, 42: 632; LW, 3: 118; Luther here used the word *delyria*.
12. Ibid.: WA, 43: 667; LW, 5: 346, slightly modified.
13. Ibid.: WA, 44: 218; LW, 6: 293.

to faith. Thus when one of Luther's earliest Catholic enemies, Silvester Prierias, defended the powers of the papacy in 1518, Luther accused him of writing nonsense by being overly logical, "which is nothing other than going mad with reason, as someone [Terence] says."[14] That was also the defect in the sacramentarian position, the claim that Holy Communion could not really or sacramentally offer believers the body and blood of Christ, because it would be too hard to understand. Luther charged that by measuring Christ's words with human understanding, "they have been driven mad by the blind judgment of reason" (*caeco rationis iudicio dementati*).[15]

Although Luther often claimed that his opponents were either mad from lack of reason or from an excess of reason, he did not simply claim that anyone who disagreed with him on any matter was insane. Instead, he meant that he sometimes detected in others a resolute, stubborn, zealous fanaticism that seemed incapable of giving his own arguments serious consideration. In that contentious age, of course, Luther himself seemed to many the very epitome of resolute, stubborn, zealous fanaticism, and Catholic antagonists were not slow to return Luther's charges of demonic possession and mental illness.[16] One man's heroism was another man's madness. I shall not undertake here an exhaustive survey of all of Luther's references to madness. The index to Luther's works compiled at the Institute for Late Medieval and Reformation Studies at the University of Tübingen lists thousands of his references to *furor, insania, mania, dementia, stultitia, Narrheit, Torheit, Unsinn*, and *Wahnsinn*, without even beginning to count the related references to *tristitia, Angst*, and *Anfechtung*. In coming to grips with this unwieldy and hitherto unstudied mass, the best we can hope for is to circumscribe the contours of Luther's thought on madness. Luther's polemical language has already illustrated for us the fact that he did not always choose his words with precision. Even so, one preliminary conclusion is important, that madness could be sinful, and sin could be so unreasonable, so unrestrained, so obsessive, that it was indistinguishable from mental illness. On this point, as it happens, Luther inherited a strong medieval tradition that had interpreted madness as a punishment for sin, and sin itself as a spiritual and mental illness.[17] For biblical theologians

14. *Ad dialogam Silvestri Prieritatis de potestate papae responsio* (1518): WA, 1: 674. For Luther's attitude toward reason in theology, see generally Brian Gerrish, *Grace and Reason: A Study in the Theology of Luther* (Oxford, 1962); and Herbert Olsson, *Schöpfung, Vernunft und Gesetz in Luthers Theologie* (Uppsala, 1971).

15. *Lectures on Genesis*: WA, 44: 377; LW, 7: 105.

16. The psychiatrist on whom Erik Erikson relied heavily for his portrait of the young Luther, Paul J. Reiter, was a Danish Catholic writing in this well-established genre; see Reiter's *Martin Luthers Umwelt und Psychose, sowie die Bedeutung dieser Faktoren für seine Entwicklung und Lehre: Eine historisch-psychiatrische Studie* (Copenhagen, 1937).

17. Penelope B. R. Doob, *Nebuchadnezzar's Children: Conventions of Madness in Middle*

the origins of this equation lay near at hand. The Bible itself is full of references to madness as the divinely inflicted punishment for sin, and to heathen idolatry as madness.[18]

Turning from Luther's general willingness to see sin as madness, we discover that Luther also recognized mental aberrations that later centuries would recatalog as mental illness. Who were these madmen? We may group them into the sick, the demonically possessed, and the outrageous.

THE MELANCHOLY PATRIARCHS

Among those suffering from physical disorders, Luther recognized some as mentally disturbed. One prominent disturbance was melancholy, which was essentially a physical disorder that had serious mental effects. We shall return to the sixteenth-century medical understanding of melancholy in chapter 3, but in this context, it is surprising that Luther often used this medical and completely unbiblical term as a metaphor to excuse the peculiar behavior of some of the saints. In his lengthy lectures on Genesis, delivered in the 1530s, Luther confronted the distasteful story of Lot and his two daughters after the destruction of Sodom and Gomorrah. Thinking that Lot was the last man alive, his daughters decided to replenish the human race by getting him drunk and then having sex with him. The biblical narrator assures us that the saintly Lot remained unaware of what was happening. Rejecting the skeptical rabbinical view that Moses here foolishly demanded that his readers accept what was frankly impossible, Luther insisted that it was indeed possible for holy men like Lot to have intercourse without knowing it.[19]

For it is true that men can become so highly perturbed that they go out of their minds [*fiunt alieno animo*], saying and doing things that they later forget. The mind, as if overwhelmed in great confusion, does not know itself. Thus when Lot had intercourse with his daughters he doubtless felt it, for intercourse is a seizure of the whole body, a purgation of soul and body. But then why does Moses say that he did not feel it? I answer that he was so highly disturbed that he did not remember afterward what he did. We know from experience in lesser matters that melancholics and lovers have such violent emotions that they say and do many things that they no longer remember afterward.

Thus Moses was not describing an impossibility. Lot was a holy man, so wrapped up in vehement thoughts and emotions, and drunk with wine besides, that he was not guilty of incest. "Thus a man can fall into such an af-

English Literature (New Haven, 1974); Judith Neaman, *Suggestion of the Devil: The Origins of Madness* (Garden City, N.Y., 1975).

18. E.g., Wis. 14:23, 28; Isa. 24:6; 1 Kings 20:43; Deut. 28:28; Dan. 4:33.

19. *Lectures on Genesis*: WA, 43: 95–6; LW, 3: 308 (translation modified).

fect of love, hate, sadness, happiness, etc., that he does not know for anger or joy what he says or does."[20]

Luther's view here employed a form of religious or moral insanity defense, one that he applied to the aged Isaac as well. When that patriarch neared the end of his days, he summoned Esau, his elder son, and told him to go hunting to secure the food for the crucial ritual in which he would receive his father's final blessing. While Esau was away, the younger Jacob dressed himself in Esau's clothes, imitated Esau's hairy skin by wearing kidskin on his hands and neck, and came to his father with food. Although Isaac suspected that something was amiss, he was fooled into believing that smooth-spoken Jacob was Esau and thus gave Jacob his irrevocable blessing. The simple explanation for Isaac's mistake is that he was so blind that he had to depend on his senses of smell and touch, but Luther was not satisfied with so simple an answer and postulated instead a mental disturbance. Isaac may have been so intent on holiness that he did not notice other people, "as can be seen in the case of people who have melancholia. While others are talking, drinking, entering or leaving, they neither hear nor see anything; for the thoughts of the heart have been diverted from their senses" (*quia cordis cogitationes sunt abstractae a sensibus*).[21] Melancholics commonly paid no attention to what was presented to their senses, just as St. Bernard had once drunk oil and thought it wine "when he was engaged in earnest meditation." Such distraction was even more severe when a person was spiritually absorbed.

Therefore Isaac is occupied not only with natural thoughts, as lovers and people with melancholia usually are, but also with thoughts that are spiritual. Moreover, even before this Rebecca detected in him melancholia of this kind. It often happened that her husband was unaware of what was going on when she placed food before him.[22]

Never mind that this image of a distracted Isaac does not comport well with the alert Isaac of Gen. 27. It is important to notice the lengths to which Luther was willing to go to defend holy Isaac from the irreverent commentaries of the skeptical rabbis, who imagined, according to Luther, that Isaac had been aware of Jacob's fraud but pretended not to notice. Such worldly readers had "no knowledge of the powers of the Spirit, which are stronger than melancholy thoughts."[23] Luther was using a medical image for his own hermeneutic purposes.

20. Ibid.: WA, 43: 96; cf. LW, 3: 309.
21. Ibid.: WA, 43: 520; LW, 5: 133.
22. Luther added "reddunt eum prorsus stupidum et ekstatikon" (ibid.: WA, 43: 520; LW, 5: 134).
23. Ibid.: WA, 43: 520; LW, 5: 134.

A few days later in his lecture schedule, Luther returned to the theme of the melancholy patriarchs, this time claiming that Jacob, too, was mentally distracted when he mistakenly consummated a marriage to Leah instead of to Rachel, the younger sister whom he thought he was marrying. Such a mistake reminded Luther of Lot and his daughters. "This is strange," he noted. "But it is customary, and in the case of melancholics it is natural when they give serious attention to some endeavor or to thinking about something." Just as melancholics were preoccupied and easily deceived, so Jacob's heart was preoccupied and absorbed in "love and joy."[24] He no longer noticed important details. But how guilty was Jacob? Luther answered that Jacob's ignorance was technically "invincible" and that he was therefore guiltless in any political or legal sense. The medieval schoolmen had regularly argued that invincible ignorance, an ignorance that could not be overcome by prudent attempts to learn the truth, provided a sufficient defense to the charge of sin. Early in his career, however, Luther had confronted this problem of conscience and had concluded that scholastic theology, in its concern with degrees of guilt and with the problem of invincible ignorance, depended on a false notion of conscience. For Luther, any action, even if outwardly good, if performed without faith, was actually wrong, selfish, or sinful, regardless of whether it was outwardly in accord with the law.[25] At first sight, therefore, it appears odd that Luther in his fifties should have reverted to the old scholastic doctrine of invincible ignorance as a means of exculpating the distracted Jacob. Luther appears to have been aware of his problem here, for he went on to note that although invincible ignorance cleared one politically, it was actually of no ultimate concern before God. If this were not so, Luther argued, even the Jews could claim ignorance as an excuse for crucifying Christ. Deftly (and amazingly) sidestepping Jesus' own plea that his Father should forgive his persecutors precisely because they knew not what they did, Luther insisted that the Jews were thoroughly culpable before God. Transferring this argument to the area of mental disturbance, Luther seems to have meant that melancholy obsessions might indeed relieve one of secular, "political" blame, but that the disturbed might still be guilty in some fundamental, theological sense. For these reasons, Luther attacked Catholic casuistry for confusing secular and spiritual guilt.[26] Whenever one was caught in sin, the Christian

---

24. Ibid.: WA, 43: 635–36; LW, 5: 300.

25. Michael Baylor, *Action and Person: Conscience in Late Scholasticism and the Young Luther* (Leiden, 1977), pp. 122, 152–53, 243–45.

26. "In the affairs of government there is room for invincible ignorance, as when someone is at fault because he is encumbered by sickness or is insane. But these ideas should not be carried over into religion and matters of conscience" (*Lectures on Genesis*: WA, 42: 486; LW, 2: 314).

response must be repentance rather than some effort at self-justification. All men, Luther thought, could sympathize with and even pardon a killer:

if he acknowledges it and is troubled about his sin and if he complains that he was deceived and overcome by Satan; but if the deed is excused and defended, as, for example, the Centaurs [i.e., the members of princely courts] and the nobility think that they are permitted to rage against the pitiable throng of peasants with violence and slaughter, both God and man detest that cruelty, and they find no room for forgiveness at all.[27]

Notice that Luther here specifically condemned the terrible rage of the German nobility against the peasants, a rage that Luther had helped to incite during the Peasants' War of 1525. It is also noteworthy that a repentant sinner could claim to have been overcome by Satan but should not make that an excuse for his sinning. Thus the melancholy perturbations of Lot, Isaac, and Jacob might help one to understand their errors without requiring God to forgive them. Luther examined the question of Lot's residual guilt at some length[28] and made the point even clearer with a far-fetched example from the story of Joseph and his brothers. Long after selling Joseph into Egyptian slavery, his brothers came to Egypt seeking grain and failed to recognize their own brother in his role as Pharaoh's governor. Again Luther made difficulties for himself by imagining that Joseph's brothers failed to recognize him, both because Joseph spoke through an interpreter and because "persons subject to melancholy are often absent-minded or, intent as they are on serious thought, neither see nor hear what they have seen and heard."[29] If Luther meant this example seriously, he was implying that Joseph's brothers were all so melancholy or distracted that they could not recognize him. And yet it seemed obvious that Moses regarded them as collectively guilty. Luther regularly invoked the mental disturbance of melancholy to explain and excuse the problematic behavior of the patriarchs.

MADNESS AND ASCETICISM

These examples from Luther's commentary on Genesis suggest just how easily he could pass from regarding melancholy as a physical and emotional state to thinking of delusion as a sinful attitude. Luther did agree with physicians, however, that some mental conditions were simply the result of physical illness. He was quick to note, for example, that the wrong

27. Ibid.: WA, 44: 148–49; LW, 6: 200. Similarly, "drunkenness does not pardon the inebriate, if he sins through his drunkenness" (*Rationis Latomianae . . . confutatio*: WA, 8: 124; LW, 32: 253).

28. *Lectures on Genesis*: WA, 43: 96–99; LW, 3: 309–13.

29. Ibid.: WA, 44: 477; LW, 7: 239.

diet could affect one's mind. If on fast days one found that fish, instead of subduing the flesh as it was supposed to do, actually increased one's wantonness, then one should go back to eating meat and eggs.[30] Severe fasting could have even more dramatic effects:

There are many blind persons, unfortunately, who chastise themselves with fasting, watching and working, all in the opinion that these are good works with which they may earn a great reward. They sometimes do so much that they corrupt their body on that account and make their head crazy.[31]

Citing the moderation of St. Bernard, Luther noted that monks should be aware of the mental dangers of extreme fasts. Although St. Peter urged Christians to set aside drunkenness and carousing, he was not advising that one "fast until crazy."[32] At table, Luther spoke often and naturally of the pleasures of company and of eating. Food and companions could keep one on an even keel. Once he told a story of "a certain bishop, whose sister was so mightily plagued by the spirit of sadness that she could not be consoled. He gave her enough to eat and drink with joy, and presently the whole attack of despair passed."[33] In some cases, it was true, a person actually needed less to eat rather than more. "Thus one should give those who are tempted in the body good things to eat and drink, but the lustful and those troubled by lust should fast."[34] Like all of his contemporaries, Luther recommended these natural remedies for mental affliction as well as exercise, good company, wine, food, and music.[35]

MADNESS: PHYSICAL AND MORAL

Sometimes Luther found it difficult to distinguish true madness from outrageous sin. The question became important with tyrants, because Luther held that Christians must be ready to suffer gross injustice at the hands of evil rulers. But if a prince, king, or lord went mad, "then he should be deposed and confined, for he is no longer to be considered human since he has lost his reason."[36] Here Luther approached a view that we shall find again in Paracelsus, namely, that madness attacked society at its

30. *Von den guten Werken* (1520): WA, 6: 246; LW, 44: 75.
31. Ibid.: WA, 6: 245; LW, 44: 74.
32. *Epistel S. Petri gepredigt und ausegelegt* (1523): WA, 12: 282.
33. WATR, no. 1349. The words Luther used, *Anfechtung* and *tentatio*, are often blandly translated as "temptation," but they carry the forceful idea of an attack, a miserable agony of doubt, verging on despair. See WATR, no. 1347, and Gritsch, *Martin: God's Court Jester*, pp. 11–14, 109–10.
34. WATR, no. 1299.
35. WATR nos. 194, 2545, and 3754; WABr, no. 2113 (May 23, 1534) and no. 2139 (Oct. 7, 1534). See also Carl Schalk, *Luther on Music: Paradigms of Praise* (St. Louis, 1988).
36. Cf. WABr, 8: 367, no. 3297 (Feb. 8, 1539).

root, because it could be literally dehumanizing. If one argued, however, that wicked tyrants were so evil as to be clinically "furious," and that in consequence they, too, should be deposed, Luther disagreed.[37]

> They are not the same. For a madman cannot do or suffer anything reasonable. And there is no hope any more since the light of reason has gone out. But a tyrant still does many things that he knows to be wrong; and he still has conscience and recognition, and there is still hope for him . . . which does not exist with a madman, who is like a block or a stone.

The crucial point here was that true madness was so radically awful that its victims were not just sick. They had lost their status as human beings. We shall see that Luther's views here paralleled those of Paracelsus, and it is not at all difficult to see why he felt that he had to distinguish the physical extinction of reason and conscience (in the mad) from their moral obliteration in sinful men. On another front, Luther was repeatedly concerned to distinguish truly divine visions from mere hallucinations and natural dreams, which, "doctors at times dispute and from which they draw conclusions about the nature of the constitution of the blood or the whole body."[38] True visions were different. "They are not melancholy dreams that have no bearing on reality."[39] Luther obviously did recognize the existence of purely natural hallucinations, but as a theologian he was more concerned to stress the possibility of supernatural mental states like godly visions and satanic delusions. Luther worried in 1522 that men were not paying full attention to the signs God was sending of the last days. Some secular spirits had the audacity to pooh-pooh such signs as purely natural in origin. "Taught by doctors (and believing physicians more than God) they say that one's complexion or melancholy is to blame, or the heavenly planets, or they invent some other natural cause."[40] Physicians, Luther noted, had a disturbing bias toward physical explanations. "Nor do I deny that sometimes such afflictions are helped by the remedies of physicians or even cured. But those who attribute such mental afflictions to natural causes since they are cured by medicine, do not know the power of Satan and that God is more powerful than demons."[41] As a religious thinker, Luther was concerned to protect the autonomy and irreducibility of religious experience.

---

37. *Ob Kriegsleute auch in seligem Stande sein können* (1526): WA, 19: 634.
38. Cf. *Lectures on Genesis*: WA, 44: 389; LW, 7: 122; cf. WA, 44: 248; LW, 6: 332.
39. Ibid.: WA, 43: 592; LW, 5: 237.
40. *Evangelium am 2. Adventsonntag* (1522): WA, 10, I/2: 101.
41. WATR, no. 2267 (2: 385–87).

THE DEVIL

A modern reader will not be surprised to learn that Luther gave the devil a central role in the afflictions of man. Tour guides at the Wartburg Castle in Thuringia have shown the public where Luther threw his inkwell at the Evil One, and traditional Catholic historians used to see Luther as inspired by the devil. Even so, it is striking just how often Luther saw the devil as the prompter of evil, acting not merely as an external tempter, as with Eve, and not simply as a cynical accuser or as a destructive force, as with Job, but also literally as the internal and secret inspiration of evil. The devil thus became an essential part of Luther's rhetoric of madness. The devil possessed evil men, controlling their dispositions, depriving them of freedom to resist, driving them to crimes they had never imagined, and sometimes forcing them into frenzies, convulsions, or suicide. Within such a generous understanding of demonic possession, Luther could describe a madness that subsumed widely different situations and moral problems.

One reason for Luther's emphasis on the devil was his notion that the devil himself was mad—that is, filled with blind rage and unreasoning, uncontrollable fury at the ever-advancing progress of God's plan for His Creation. Ordinary sinful men might have hardships to endure, but they could still hope for eternal life. Satan had no such hope. He felt the constant wrath of God as a present reality and reacted with mad rage.[42] Moreover, this state of constant fury had recently intensified. In his 1535 preface to his commentary on Galatians, Luther noted:

In these most recent and final hours of history he has been provoked into such a rage against the knowledge of Christ in its revived form that men who previously seemed to be possessed by demons and to be insane now seem to have become demons themselves, possessed by even more horrible demons and by an insanity that goes even beyond the demonic.[43]

His own age was uncommonly evil, Luther concluded, because history was in its very last stages. The Church had, of course, always been plagued by devils,[44] and diabolical errors had long been a threat to theological purity.[45] But lately, with history in its last stages and with the Reformation recovery of the gospel, the devil had gone on a rampage, just as he had during the lifetime of Christ: "There are now as many possessed by the devil as in the time of Christ, counting only those as possessed who are physically plagued

42. *Lectures on Genesis*: WA, 42: 145, 146, 149; LW, 1: 195, 200.
43. *Commentary on Galatians*: WA, 40/1: 34–35; LW, 27: 147.
44. *Lectures on Genesis*: WA, 42: 81; LW 1: 213.
45. Ibid.: WA, 42: 101, 178; LW, 1: 134, 135, 240. *Commentary on Galatians*: WA, 40/1: 34–35; LW, 27: 146. *De votis monasticis*: WA, 8: 599–600; LW, 44: 260–61, 285–87.

and tortured by the devil, and not lunatics, fools, or senseless persons."[46] In this passage, Luther distinguished the physically possessed from the mentally ill and the retarded, but more often he spoke of demonic possession as a general condition of willful sin. When Eve was tempted in the garden, for example, she was not rationally persuaded to disobey God; she was deluded: "Because Satan restrains her mind [animum] and eyes, however, she not only does not see death or become aware of it, but gradually she is also more inflamed by her desire for the fruit and delights in this idolatry and sin."[47] Indeed, Adam should have warned his descendants about the consequences of sin, for "when he was deprived of his mind by Satan and believed that he would be like God, he became like Satan himself."[48] The fall into sin had been a fall into unreason. Sin brought fundamental changes in both man and nature. From then on, man's "will is impaired, his intellect depraved, and his reason entirely corrupt and altogether changed."[49] So mankind became sick with a leprosy of the spirit. Human history had thus begun with a lapse into madness.

The next major atrocity in history was the killing of Abel by Cain, a mad murder, which prompted Luther to imagine Cain's furor in some detail. Cain was so incensed at Abel that his mind gave him no rest; he was consumed with a "diabolical madness" (diabolicum furorem) that "distorts the eyes, wrinkles the brow, puffs up the mouth, and supplies the hands with weapons."[50] "Possessed by Satan" (animus a Satana obsessus), Cain craftily lured Abel to his destruction; and we, too, whenever our nature is without the Holy Spirit, are "impelled by the same evil spirit."[51] Amazingly, the modern descendants of Cain, the pope, bishops, and cardinals rage with the same Satanic hatred and murderous intent.[52] Luther repeated the point in countless examples. Satan takes advantage of man in his enfeebled, corrupt, and sinful condition, driving him to further excesses. That explained the wickedness of Sodom, where the men were so mad and frenzied that they spurned women, "as frenzied men are wont to do" (ut furiosi homines solent, sexum contemnunt).[53] It was Satan who produced the madness of Sodom, for when people turn from God, Satan takes over and powerfully suppresses nature, turning men to bestial and unnatural acts. God had to

---

46. "[M]an wolle denn allein fur Besessene rechnen, die leiblich vom Teufel geplaget und gepeiniget werden, nicht die Mondsüchtigen, Narren, Sinnlosen etc." (WATR, no. 830 [1: 403]).

47. Lectures on Genesis: WA, 42: 120; LW, 1: 159.

48. Ibid.: WA, 42: 166; LW, 1: 223.

49. Ibid.: WA, 42: 124–26; LW, 1: 165–66.

50. Ibid.: WA, 42: 193; LW, 1: 261–62.

51. Ibid.: WA, 42: 201–2; LW, 1: 272–73.

52. Ibid.: WA, 42: 192–93; LW, 1: 276, 280.

53. Ibid.: WA, 43: 58; LW, 3: 256–57.

punish the whole town in order "to check the madness that was raging beyond measure."[54]

In a sense, Luther and others who spoke his religiously charged language believed in a moral illness that was so blind and wrongheaded that its victims had no insight into or control over their own evil. While it is true that the modern idea of "mental illness" as a nonphysical, nonorganic disorder, a functional, behavioral, or purely mental disease, has been elaborated only in the past two centuries, yet in Luther's descriptions of sinful perversity one can find several of the elements of what would later be called mental illness. Certainly, there was for Luther's school of interpretation no physiological or psychosomatic explanation for the sin-madness that he found so often among the worst specimens of humanity. A critic might object that Luther and similar moralists did not see such madness as really *sick*, that they were too intent on condemning wickedness to see it as a disease process beyond a person's control. But here we must tread cautiously, because Luther's image of the devil as the inspiration of evil did go some way toward finding the source of wickedness *outside* the person, who was literally beside himself in his sinfulness. We also run the risk of romanticizing the supposedly value-neutral, nonjudgmental modern psychotherapist as the novel formulator of the idea of mental illness as a guilt-free disease of neurosis, obsession, and alienation.

Let us pursue this idea of religious madness more closely. In Luther's view, Laban too was mad and demonically possessed when he pursued Jacob to Gilead. Forgetting that he was the father of Jacob's wives, Laban was not merely "angry or furious in a human way" but "plainly . . . disturbed by a diabolical and infernal madness . . . saturated with the fire of hell."[55] Luther repeatedly attributed thoughts and words to Jacob that had no biblical basis. He was so consumed with the idea that great sins were mad and diabolically inspired that he found examples where the text provided no basis. He regarded Adam, Eve, Cain, Laban, Joseph's brothers, the Sodomites, and a host of other Old Testament sinners as satanically inspired and even possessed.[56] Drawing immediate parallels with his own age, Luther held that God had allowed the Turk and the pope to win "wonderful successes," but then drove them into madness "when they [began to] regard themselves as very wise."[57]

54. Ibid.: WA, 43: 58; LW, 3: 255–56. Nero and Caligula provided further examples of men whose "satanic madness" drove them to effeminacy and uncontrollable desire (*Sathanico furore prorsus effoeminati*) (WA, 44: 443; LW, 7: 195).

55. Ibid.: WA, 44: 26–28, 47; LW, 6: 37–38, 65: "Ideo recte dicit, non humano more irasceris aut saevis: sed plane diabolica et infernali furia percitus es, steckts vol hellisch fewrs."

56. See also ibid.: WA, 44: 274, 279–80; LW, 6: 366, 374.

57. Ibid.: WA, 44: 280; LW, 6: 375.

In addition to this favorite motif of sinful possession, Luther used the idea of demonic possession in other ways. The possessed were sometimes so fearless and unconscious of their condition, for example, that Luther could use them as analogous to Catholic excommunicators, "who puff themselves up and say that their outward ban is to be feared, and with their inner one they damn themselves freely and fearlessly just as with the rejoicing of the possessed, crazy people."[58] Here Luther likened these sinners to men who had lost their autonomy and freedom, their self-consciousness and self-control. In his long 1531 Galatians commentary, Luther took this analogy further. The sinful world, he asserted, was like a man possessed. In both cases society was right in binding them to prevent the spread of wickedness. Indeed, the world itself was mad.

Therefore just as ropes and chains are bound upon men who are possessed and in whom the devil is ruling powerfully to keep them from harming someone, so the whole world, which is possessed by the devil and is being led headlong into every crime, has the magistrate with his ropes and chains, that is, his laws, restraining its hands and feet lest it rush headlong into all sorts of evil.[59]

This image again prompted Luther to consider the guilt of men who had lost their freedom. Could one claim that decent public behavior was a reliable sign of righteousness? Clearly not, "for as a possessed person is not free and mentally balanced just because his hands and feet are bound, so when the world is most restrained by the Law from external acts of disgrace, it is not righteous on that account but remains unrighteous. In fact, this very restraint indicates that the world is wicked and insane."[60] In addition to providing us with a glimpse of how severe cases of demonic possession were controlled, Luther here again blasted his own age as caught in the terrifying grip of satanic possession. That was one reason why he thought human efforts at self-help were bound to fail. Before seeking refuge in Christ's mercy, the human will was so weak, so possessed by the devil, that only the Holy Spirit could effectively intervene. Comparing man's spiritual condition to those "poor people who are physically possessed by the devil," Luther asked, rhetorically, how they could ever hope to free themselves by their own efforts. And if that was obviously hopeless, then how foolish it was for sinful mankind to expect to free itself from spiritual possession.[61] This world was and remained the *Teufels Reich*.

In his reflections on demonic possession, Luther sketched a view of mental disorder that is surprisingly analogous in many of its features to the

58. *Ein Sermon von dem Bann* (1520): WA, 6: 70; LW, 39: 15 (modified).
59. WA, 40/1: 480; LW, 26: 309.
60. Ibid.
61. WATR, no. 6685 (6: 120).

modern idea of a mental illness, which one scholar has recently described as a morbid process characterized by frustration of a person's desire for some symbolized ideal state of affairs, a desire that one has not learned to sublimate or adapt to external reality.[62] Frustration is at the heart of many modern notions of mental illness, but for Luther and his tradition, the notion of frustration of desire was immediately linked with sinful desires and self-assertions. The devil knew how to take advantage of the self-absorbed, possessing them and giving them a horrible vehicle with which to express or even to realize their desires.

The causal connection between frustration and demonic possession, between sin and obsession, and between physical and spiritual possession was not perfect, for Luther held that even relatively innocent persons might be physically possessed by the devil. At table one day, he held forth on the question of whether fools and demonically possessed persons might be saved. Although the devil could indeed "take hold of a body, that does not harm the soul." If a small child who had never sinned were possessed, that was no mark of its damnation but a sign used by God to terrify others. "It is not always true that they sin who are possessed; often the devil possesses pious men, but he does not harm the soul."[63] Elsewhere Luther held that all fools (moriones, Thoren) and those bereft of reason were indeed plagued by the devil, but they were not necessarily damned on that account. The devil tortured their bodies and minds, but only temporally, having no effect on their eternal souls.[64] Sometimes, too, the body was possessed as a punishment for sin. "This is proved by the fact that the devil leaves the possessed body its natural powers and actions, but robs the soul of reason, sense, wit, understanding and all of its powers, as one can easily see in possessed persons."[65] Indeed, if a person claimed to be possessed but still had command of his reason, Luther was skeptical, doubting that it could be a real case of possession. One day a maid from Halle was brought to him, complaining that she was possessed by the devil, but she spoke "sensibly," condemning herself as a "gossip, a contemptuous and abusive blasphemer of the gospel, one whom the executioner should drive out of town." And so she left. We know no more about this apparently overscrupulous and seriously depressed woman, but Luther doubted that she was actually possessed.[66] Early in his career, Luther had expressed a sarcastic contempt for some who frivolously complained of the devil. "For if your wife or servant groans that he or she has been seized by a wandering spirit, hear my advice: you too should seize a wooden cross and sanctify

62. Marshall Edelson, The Idea of a Mental Illness (New Haven, 1971), p. 68.
63. WATR, no. 5731 (5: 333–34).
64. WATR, no. 2267 (2: 387).
65. WATR, no. 6685 (6: 121).
66. WATR, no. 6211 (5: 541–42). See also WATR, no. 5375e (5: 104–5).

his or her backside with strong blows; and you will see that by this finger of God the demon is expelled."[67] Despite his omnipresence, the devil should not be abused as an explanation for every evil.

EXORCISM AND ESCHATOLOGY

Usually, Luther took a more serious approach to the problem of getting rid of the devil. Although Luther conceded that exorcism had been a potent weapon in the days of the apostles, it had been grossly abused by the papacy in an effort to prove the force of priestly ceremony. As a master of deception, the devil had cooperated with the papacy by appearing to be driven out by the mere force of words and ceremony. When a monk at Weimelberg expelled a demon by striking St. Cyriac's bell, for example, the devil was not really *forced* to leave; but he did indeed leave in order that poor superstitious onlookers would be strengthened in their mad belief that the bell itself was holy.[68] In commenting on the Gospel of Matthew, Luther was moved to exclaim:

Who could list all the knavery done in the name of Christ or Mary to drive out devilish spirits! . . . Such spirits arise now and confirm purgatory, Masses for the dead, the service of all the saints, pilgrimage, monasteries, churches and chapels. . . . But all of this comes from the devil in order to maintain his abomination and lies and to hold people charmed and caught in error. . . . It is a small matter for the devil that he allows himself to be expelled, if he wants, by an evil villain; and yet he remains really unexpelled for he thereby possesses people all the more firmly, trapped in his shameful deceit.[69]

Thus it was no wonder that evangelicals could not drive out demons now. The devil could not be expelled by Protestants with their grasp of the true gospel, "for his guile and cunning are known to us and he cannot deceive us."[70] Paracelsus, as we shall see, and later Johann Weyer, were similarly concerned to deny the claims of Catholic exorcists.[71] Despite such arguments, Catholic defenders continued for over one hundred years to score points against Protestants and "atheists" by demonstrating the palpable force of holy water, rosary, and consecrated host against the legions of darkness.[72]

67. *Decem praecepta Wittenbergensi praedicata populo* (1518): WA, 1: 423.

68. WATR, no. 830 (1: 403).

69. *Das fünfte, sechste und siebente Kapitel Matthaei gepredigt und ausgelegt* (1530–32): WA, 32: 525. See also *Von den guten Werken* (1520): WA, 6: 224; LW, 39: 47–48.

70. WATR, no. 830 (1: 403).

71. Annemarie Leibbrand-Wettley, "Zur Psychopathologie und Dämonologie bei Paracelsus und Johannes Weyer," in *Melemata: Festschrift für Werner Leibbrand*, ed. Joseph Schumacher (Mannheim, 1967), pp. 65–73.

72. See D. P. Walker, "The Cessation of Miracles," in *Hermeticism and the Renaissance:*

Luther was not tempted as were some Protestants to deny the reality of demon possession. Instead, as we have seen, he conceded that there were in his day easily as many possessed as in the time of Christ. In reflecting on the reasons for the resurgence of the devil, Luther's thoughts were repeatedly drawn to the Apocalypse. Although the devil was not, strictly speaking, harder to drive out than in earlier days, it was true that men had grown so uncertain and weak in their faith that no one could effectively oppose the devil anymore. Luther held that Christ was allowing evil to multiply in the last days of history. It almost seemed that Christ was no longer guarding his little flock of faithful. The only possible conclusion was obvious to Luther: the Second Coming was at hand.[73] In fact, it appears that Luther's sense of the impending eschaton kept him from skepticism about the awesome power of the devil. He continued to live in a world filled with the demons and apocalyptic expectations of the New Testament. Those Protestants who lost Luther's apocalyptic expectations, however, often found themselves unable to refute Catholic polemicists on their own terms and gave in to the ad hominem suspicion that only human fraud could explain the supposed successes of exorcism.[74] Luther's eschatology thus insulated him in a way from despair when he saw the devil's realm expanding everywhere. Knowing that Christ would soon triumph, Luther could view the rampage of the devil with some equanimity.

A MAD WORLD

As we have seen, the insanity of the world was not merely due to physical illness on the one hand and demonic possession on the other. Rather, men seemed bent on driving their own sinful desires out of control, exaggerating their vices to the point of no return. Pride was a good example. Although all men and women should know that they were children of wrath, of sin, death, and the devil, still they puffed themselves up. It was "impossible not to detest the madness and insanity of the proud. Such people," Luther exclaimed, "rather than those whose mind has been [naturally] disturbed, should be restrained with fetters and chains."[75] Lacking even common sense, the proud did not know themselves, who they were, whence

---

Intellectual History and the Occult in Early Modern Europe, ed. I. Merkel and A. Debus (Washington, D.C., 1988), pp. 111–24.

73. WATR, no. 830.

74. Cécile Ernst, *Teufelaustreibungen: Die Praxis der katholischen Kirche im 16. und 17. Jahrhundert* (Bern, 1972); D. P. Walker, "Demonic Possession Used as Propaganda in the Later Sixteenth Century," in Istituto nazionale di studi sul Rinascimento, *Scienze, credenze occulte, livelli di cultura: Convegno internazionale di studi, Firenze, 26–30 giugno 1980* (Florence, 1982), pp. 237–48, extended in his *Unclean Spirits: Possession and Exorcism in France and England in the Late Sixteenth and Early Seventeenth Centuries* (Philadelphia, 1981).

75. *Lectures on Genesis*: WA, 44: 432; LW, 7: 179.

they came, and what their destined end would be. Poisoned with diabolical pride, their madness "is three or four times greater than that of those
who are not of sound mind, as this affliction is commonly understood."[76]
Men proud of their high office should really bear the title "Three and four
times insane," for they have failed to recognize what all should know.[77]
"Therefore I conclude that this world is nothing else than a prison for mad
and blind men."[78]

It was not only the powerful and worldly who suffered from such insanity. All who built their spiritual houses on their own good works were
trapped in a terrifying "quicksand of their own conceit and dreams." They
could not know the comfort of standing on the rock of Christ. Luther admitted that he had known this madness himself and had seen it "especially
in monasteries," where some poor monks felt such insecurity that "in the
end they go mad with fear and weakness of conscience, and some even fell
into eternal despair."[79] Thus when Luther claimed that his Catholic opponents were mad defenders of a mad doctrine, he did not simply mean that
they were wrong. He meant that the mental and spiritual effects of Catholic
self-reliance were, in his view, spiritually disastrous. One could easily object that Luther's picture was grossly overdrawn, that Catholic doctrine
was not nearly so self-reliant, so dependent on man's efforts to save himself, as Luther claimed, but Luther would then respond, as he often did,
with autobiography. He claimed that for himself, at least, the monastery
had been just such a prison for mad and blind men. He was well equipped
to understand the troubles of Hugo van der Goes. The private visions cultivated by mystics were another form of monastic "madness" he had witnessed while a monk. Theologically, Luther did not rest his doctrine on the
flimsy authority of his own private experience; but much of the force of his
thought and language came from profound reflection on what he had lived
through.

Luther castigated other forms of outrageous madness as well, in the
process expanding what I have called the rhetoric of madness. Even clothing, that shameful mark of Adam and Eve's fall, had become a source of *insane* desires. "People, like donkeys raised for carrying gold, are more intent
on loading themselves down than on adorning themselves."[80] It was no
longer a pleasure, or mere excess, but a "madness among all classes."[81]
Similarly, Adam would be amazed at the "insane gluttony" (*hanc insaniam*

76. Ibid.: WA, 44: 432–33; LW, 7: 179–80.
77. Ibid.: WA, 44: 434; LW, 7: 182.
78. Ibid.: "mundum nihil aliud esse, nisi carcarem furiosorum et caecorum hominum."
79. *Wochenpredigten über Matth.* 5–7 (1530–32): WA, 32: 534.
80. WA, 42: 165–66; LW, 1: 222.
81. Ibid.

gulae) of his descendants.[82] This sin had reached its pinnacle among princes, who "go mad with their gormandizing, prepared as they are to squander and waste without measure and limit."[83] It is clear enough by now that for Luther, such unmeasured and unbridled sin was so alien to all reason that he could easily label it insane. Nor was he hopeful of any improvement. Rather, "this breakdown of morals must be endured in this extreme old age of a mad world" (*in hac extrema delirantio mundi senecta*).[84]

At times Luther tormented himself with senseless fears. Why was it that he still dreaded "the plague, the Turk, danger, or the death of a child? Why am I so insane [*quare sic insanio*] when I have a propitious, protecting, favoring and consoling God?"[85] In addition to documenting clearly the tender feelings he had toward his children, an emotion sometimes associated first with the sentimental burghers of the seventeenth and eighteenth centuries, Luther's concern about his own continuing unreason is of interest. As long as man was in the flesh, he would sin, doubt, and have insane, unreasonable thoughts.

THE USES OF UNREASON

Unreason did have its uses. For one thing, what the world called folly was often the basis of Christian wisdom. Luther was well aware that both John the Baptist and Jesus had been thought possessed by the devil (John 7:20).[86] Indeed, the Jews had often been ready to hurl this charge at those who were immoderate in their attack on the Pharisees.[87] The earliest Christians had seemed drunk and foolish. "Here reason was compelled to conclude that they were completely mad, and the only thing wise men thought was that they were driven along."[88] And yet this was not madness at all, but what Paul had called the "inebriation of faith." Now in the time of the Second Coming, Christians again scoffed at the devil and death: "[T]he world will regard them as insane and out of their senses. . . . But we laugh

82. WA, 42, 157; LW, 1: 210.

83. *Lectures on Genesis*: WA, 44: 560; LW, 7: 351.

84. Ibid.

85. Ibid., WA, 44: 525; LW, 7: 304.

86. *Dictata super Psalterium* (1513–1515): WA, 3: 151, 621; *Rationis Latomianae confutatio* (1521): WA, 8: 46; see Michael Screech, "Good Madness in Christendom," in *The Anatomy of Madness: Essays in the History of Psychiatry*, vol. 1, ed. W. F. Bynum, Roy Porter, and Michael Shepherd (London, 1985), pp. 25–39; id., "The 'Mad' Christ of Erasmus and the Legal Duties of his Brethren," in *Essays on Early French Literature Presented to Barbara M. Craig*, ed. N. J. Lacy and J. C. Nash (York, S.C., 1982), pp. 119–27.

87. *Resolutio Lutheriana super propositione XIII de potestate papae* (1519): WA, 2: 184; *Dominica Judica Sermo* (ca. 1514–20): WA, 4: 614; *Enarrationes epistolarum et evangeliorum quas postillas vocant* (1521): WA, 7: 521, 531.

88. *Lectures on Genesis*: WA, 44: 762; LW, 8: 250.

at the devil and at the pope."[89] The gospel showed that the "wise" were fools and the "fools" were truly wise.[90] The sacraments, which seemed so foolish to reason, were actually instituted to suppress reason: Therefore, for God's sake, the Christian must "be a fool, poor, worthless and despised."[91] Luther was also well aware that he had himself been branded mad and possessed. "What? Do you, reader, think me insane or drunk?" Echoing St. Paul (Acts 26:25), he asserted: "I am not mad, for I speak words of soberness."[92] He admitted that he sometimes acted foolishly, "but it is the wild madness of the papists and the deplorable insanity of the prostitutes, that is the schools of Paris, Louvain, and elsewhere, that extort folly from me."[93] Properly speaking, Christians needed to cultivate a Christian folly, which was at its heart the mystery of Christian faith. This was not really madness. Yet Luther did also concede a genuine role to mental illness and mental disturbance in the religious life.

Far from admiring the insensate or contented tranquillity of a satisfied mind, Luther held that true wisdom was found among "those who are oppressed and in conflict with spiritual trials."[94] Only they could recognize their need for God's consolation. In the Last Days, moreover, not all men would suffer the anxiety and terror of knowing that the end was fast approaching. Most people disregarded the signs from God, "seeing but failing to understand what they see."[95] Only a few would suffer the pangs of true understanding. Indeed, God often chose to strengthen faith by tempting and tormenting believers. Christians should learn to say, "with the father of the possessed boy in the gospel, 'O Lord, Help my unbelief.'"[96] It is widely known that Luther himself suffered attacks of doubt, temptation, sorrow, and depression all his life, but such attacks, he concluded, were not all bad.[97]

In his first lectures on the Psalms, for example, Luther often sympathized with the mental agonies of the psalmist. External troubles were indeed the source of inner peace: "Disturbance according to the flesh is peace of mind. . . . When the flesh is crucified and is not permitted to indulge in its desires but is chastised, then the heart has peace."[98] Still, this was not the

89. Ibid., WA, 44: 763; LW, 8: 252; see also WA, 44: 770; LW, 8: 260–61, and *De abroganda missa privata* (1521): WA, 8: 432.

90. *Kirchenpostille* (1522): WA, 10, pt. 1, sec. 1: 6.

91. WA, 10, pt. 1, sec. 1: 506; see also p. 698.

92. *Acta Augustana* (1518): WA, 2: 18.

93. *De abroganda missa privata*: WA, 8: 432.

94. *Lectures on Genesis*: WA, 43: 542; LW, 5: 165.

95. *Evangelium am 2. Advents sonntag* (1522): WA, 10, pt. 1, sec. 2: 101.

96. *Sermon von dem Sakrament der Busse* (1519): WA, 2: 721.

97. Karl Holl, "Martin Luther on Luther," trans. H. C. Erik Midelfort, in *Interpreters of Luther: Essays in Honor of Wilhelm Pauck*, ed. Jaroslav J. Pelikan (Philadelphia, 1968), pp. 9–34.

98. WA, 3: 525; LW, 11: 7; on Ps. 76:8.

same as actually praising melancholy, as some of the Renaissance humanists did, for Luther held that melancholy persons were not always more
sensitive to religious questions; they could be even less so. In his introduction to Ps. 77, for example, he tried to understand why some people failed
to "grasp the wisdom in which they were created and which shines forth in
them." Irreverent, thoughtless, unreflective souls were "like the horse and
the mule, which have no understanding." They perceived only with their
senses. "Therefore all such souls are melancholic, thick-skinned, of a very
bad constitution, stolid and dull in their feelings."[99] Echoing a theme that
recurs frequently in the history of psychiatry, Luther held that the mad (the
Unsinnigen) were often slower even to feel pain than the average person.[100]
After all, they had lost their senses. The sufferings of Christ were so acute
precisely because he kept his reason "clear, pure, and undefiled" right up
to death, "and the more clearly reason regards death the more horrible it
is. . . . Some men are driven crazy and foolish and don't feel it so
sharply."[101] So some forms of mental agony were good, but a thoughtless
melancholy could be deadening.

MENTAL AND SPIRITUAL DISTURBANCE

In his lectures on Hebrews (1517), Luther was moved to comment on
various sorts of mental and spiritual disturbance. Adopting a tripartite
scheme that we also find in Paracelsus, Luther explained that there were an
inward and an outward rest for the sensual, the rational, and the spiritual
man. The sensual man could be disturbed outwardly by the removal of
sensory objects or inwardly by the addition of confusion to the troubles of
the rational man, "as is clear in the sad and in melancholics."[102] The rational man could be disturbed outwardly if he was sad, but far worse was the
inward disturbance when "alongside the disturbance of the spiritual
man—namely when he is in danger of losing faith and the Word—he himself [i.e., his reason] is also disturbed." This temptation or attack, this *Anfechtung*, was the worst of all (*horribilissima*), since the most profound and
close to hell itself. The spiritual man, finally, could be outwardly disturbed
when his faith was in danger, as when faith, hope, and charity were tested.
This part of man, however, knew no inward disturbance, "for this seventh
day has no evening by which it could pass into another day."[103] Luther here
described various sorts of mental and spiritual suffering, and, as we shall
see, agreed with Paracelsus that the highest and most inward part of man

99. WA, 3: 534; LW, 11: 15.
100. *Wider Hans Worst* (1541): WA, 51: 475; LW, 41: 192.
101. *Predigt am Karfreytag* (Apr. 18, 1522): WA, 10, pt. 3: 73.
102. WA, 57: 3, 159.
103. Ibid.; LW, 29: 162–63.

could not be disturbed or driven insane. If he had conceded that man's essence could be upset, it might have threatened a normal man's humanity, his status as the image of God. While the human mind and body could become bestial and lose their claim to be human, a person's spirit seemed inwardly incorruptible. Melancholy confusion was parallel to but lower than the horrible *Anfechtungen* of reason. Unlike the Renaissance humanists who praised melancholy as the vehicle of genius, Luther saw melancholy as a torment, discovering no virtue in being troubled for its own sake. Mental and spiritual affliction were not for Luther the necessary engines of creativity or the prerequisite for a satisfying intellectual or religious life.[104]

Even so, mental affliction had its uses. Madness could be a sign of sensitivity and openness to God's revelation. In the last days of the world, he thought, the tenderhearted were driven out of their minds by pangs of conscience, "not the coarse large heap of humanity but only the few and usually the most intelligent and sensitive, the good true-hearted people."[105] Never in previous history, he thought, had there been so many madmen. Striking a theme that also haunted social commentators in the nineteenth century, Luther claimed that the growth of madness was itself a sign of how civilization had decayed. Statisticians a century ago often feared conversely that madness was on the rise because of the *advance* of civilization, but the implicit social criticism was similar. In Luther's words: "Although there have always been such persons before, still it was never so widespread and common throughout the world. For from the beginning of the world onwards there has never until now been one-tenth or even one-hundredth of the merely man-made doctrines that rule so widely, so abominably, torturing and killing so many consciences."[106] We can see that although he did not assess madness as a positive good, Luther did link mental suffering to intelligence and sensitivity. As early as 1518, Luther warned especially those of "tender conscience" to beware the doctrine of works righteousness, "for you will go under like someone digging in sand. The more you throw out, the more falls in on you. Therefore many have gone mad, as Jean Gerson says, imagining that they have become a worm or a mouse."[107] If madness was a sign of sensitivity, Luther could be sympathetic. If madness raged without self-doubt, it was an emblem of all that was wrong with the world.

104. It would therefore be a mistake to regard Luther as a forerunner of the Romantics in this regard. For the same point with respect to artists of the sixteenth century, see Rudolf and Margot Wittkower, *Born Under Saturn: The Character and Conduct of Artists. A Documented History from Antiquity to the French Revolution* (New York, 1963).

105. Adventspostille 2, Adventssonntag 1522: WA, 10, pt. 1, 2d half: 102. When Konrad Cordatus suffered severe *Anfechtungen* in 1538, Luther assured him that only the just were so troubled in mind and conscience (WABr, 8, no. 3409: 603–5 [Nov. 22, 1539]).

106. Adventspostille 2, Adventssonntag 1522: WA, 10, pt. 1, 2d half: 103.

107. *Zwei deutsche Fastenpredigten von 1518*: WA, 1: 276.

DESPAIR AND CONSOLATION

Caught in despair, Christians should cry out to God and repent their sins. Perhaps these sensitive souls would respond more readily than the coarse mass. Sadness, grief, depression, these were all marks of being spiritually alive. Although the devil often took advantage of such states, and although sadness drained one's very flesh and bones, "yet a sad spirit is better than being secure in the world."[108] At least the depressed were aware that the human condition was radically wrong. It was true, Luther agreed, that this was slim consolation for anyone caught in deep depression. Referring to his own struggles with depression, Luther once exclaimed at table, "I, Doctor Luther, have been in such high temptations and *Anfechtungen* that they consumed my whole body so that I could hardly breathe, and no one could console me." Worrying that he was alone in his misery, he had wondered, "Am I the only one to suffer this spirit of sadness?" After years of struggle, however, Luther had come to recognize that these bouts of depression served a purpose. "For the spirit of sadness is actually the conscience."[109] Hence Luther did not condemn the depressed, as he often did those whose unreason ran in other directions. Instead, he sought to show them the way out of their misery. Accepting a common monastic proverb, Luther believed that "a melancholy head is the devil's bath," and that "the devil likes melancholy natures and uses them."[110] If left unattended, sadness could produce serious disease. "For if the heart is troubled and sad, physical weakness follows too. . . . Diseases of the soul are real diseases."[111]

The remedies were many. Cheerful company could help disperse the sense of loneliness. Clinging to God's word could allow an escape from morbid introspection. Instead of asking God to spare one from suffering, one should resign oneself to His will. Praising God, especially in song, was a proven method of expelling the devil, "for the evil spirit is a spirit of depression who cannot be driven off with groans and complaints and worrying, but with praising God in which the heart grows cheerful."[112] Later, in a less pious mood, Luther noted that even profane music could drive off gloom and depression.[113] Solitary musings and fasts could only increase the misery,[114] while good food and moderate drink could work wonders. Even humorous preachers were helpful. Christopher von Gross was so funny, for

108. WATR, no. 1347 (2: 61–64).
109. Ibid.
110. WATR, nos. 1349, 2889a and b, 5155.
111. WATR, no. 6024.
112. *Tröstung fur eine Person in hohen Anfechtungen* (1521): WA, 7: 784.
113. WATR, no. 194.
114. WATR, no. 1349.

example, that he could "make all kinds of melancholics happy with his droll wit."[115] Heiko Oberman has recently drawn our attention, too, to the way that Luther used scatological jokes and gestures to embarrass and humiliate the devil. The Enemy of Man was so proud that one could fart in his face to get rid of him, thus showing one's total contempt for him.[116]

In a series of letters to the troubled Prince Joachim of Anhalt in 1534, Luther put this attitude into practical terms, urging the young prince to ride and hunt, to take pleasure in his friends, and not to think that God took pleasure in sad sacrifices.[117] When his depression continued, Luther visited the prince and told him in a letter that he should take comfort in the fact that God was teaching him to endure suffering.[118] In subsequent letters, Luther repeatedly urged a pragmatic combination of religious and physical relief.[119] In the fall of 1534, Luther had a chance to give similar advice to Matthias Weller, who had fallen into a devilish depression. Luther urged him to cheer up. "These are not your thoughts but the suggestions of the miserable devil." He should turn to music, song, and gay company.[120] "If the devil returns and plants worries and sad thoughts in your mind, resist him manfully and say, 'Begone, devil! I must now play and sing unto my Lord Christ.'"[121]

Matthias Weller's brother, Jerome, was also subject to attacks of gloom and depression, especially in 1530, the year he was appointed tutor to Luther's four-year-old son, Johann. Luther wrote him in July of that year urging him to consider his doubts and sadness as the work of the devil. The worst enemies of the gospel, men such as Johann Eck and Huldreich Zwingli, were often left "contented and happy" while true Christians had to suffer. Weller had feared that he would be driven to despair and blasphemy, but Luther urged him to turn his gloom around: "[T]his temptation of the devil . . . is a certain sign that God is propitious and merciful to you."[122] When afflicted by depression, he should scorn the devil, play games, and joke. Recalling his own agony in the monastery and the comforting words of Staupitz, Luther encouraged Weller to see that his mental troubles were actually "more necessary to you than food and drink."[123] One of the devil's favorite tricks was to induce worry about committing sin. So, if the devil said, "Do not drink," Weller should retort, "On this very ac-

115. WATR, nos. 2951, 2965.
116. Oberman, "Teufelsdreck."
117. WABr, no. 2113, May 23, 1534.
118. WABr, no. 2116, June 9, 1534.
119. WABr, no. 2119, June 12, 1534; 2121, June 23, 1534; 2122, June 26, 1534.
120. WABr, no. 2139, Oct. 7, 1534.
121. Ibid.; *Luther: Letters of Spiritual Counsel*, ed. and trans. Theodore G. Tappert (Philadelphia, 1955), p. 97.
122. Ibid., p. 85.
123. Ibid.

count, because you forbid it, I shall drink, and what is more, I shall drink deeply." Luther confided that his own reasons for drinking undiluted wine, talking freely, and eating to excess were to vex the devil, who tried to forbid these things.[124]

What Luther was here prescribing was, in effect, a therapeutic distancing of the depressed person from his own thoughts. By teaching that morbid thoughts of hell and damnation were really from the devil, Luther held out the hope that such worries actually implied that one was bound for heaven. He offered this therapeutic distance, for example, to Elizabeth von Canitz, a former nun whom he was trying to recruit to start a girls' school. "I hear too that the evil one is assailing you with melancholy. O my dear woman, do not let him terrify you, for whoever suffers from the devil here will not suffer from him yonder. It is a good sign."[125]

In our own age, when we are presumed to be the masters and fabricators of our own thoughts, or at least the unconscious producers of our own dreams, temptations, doubts, and unrest, it may be doubted whether Luther's advice could be as effective as it was in his day. But it would be wrongfully present-minded to assume that the critical distance he offered was ineffective then. With the devil a constant reality, the ever-present inspiration of every sin, it may have eased many to learn that depression and doubt, worry and fear, were not grounded in personal failure but in the father of lies.

Aware that his doctrine of the bondage of the human will might cast some Christians into depression concerning their predestination to heaven or hell, Luther often counseled troubled souls to put devilish doubts to one side. It was even a sin to trouble oneself excessively with one's eternal destination. "Nothing but anxiety can be gained from forever tormenting oneself with the question of election. Therefore avoid and flee from such thoughts . . . and direct your attention to Christ."[126] We cannot tell if such advice was helpful in overcoming the depressions often found among Luther's followers. We may suspect, however, that if the troubled in mind or spirit succeeded in gaining some perspective on their own state of mind, they may have experienced some real relief.[127]

To the extent that we can speak of Luther's "psychotherapy," therefore, we might say that he preached a reality that contained balm for the mentally and spiritually troubled. If sinners would only recognize the reality of the God of grace, of the devil, of human weakness, and of the goodness of

124. Ibid., p. 86.
125. Ibid., p. 84.
126. WABr, 11: 165–66; *Luther: Letters of Spiritual Counsel*, ed. Tappert, pp. 137–38.
127. See *Luther: Letters of Spiritual Counsel*, ed. Tappert, pp. 115–24, 130–38, for several excellent examples.

creation, they would not forever drive themselves mad. If the Stoics had only admitted that human passions were real and therefore good (as parts of Creation), they would not have exhausted their minds in folly. When these pagans maintained that courage was an absence of fear and of other passions, "this was insanity and madness and not a virtue."[128] When Thomas Müntzer tried to pretend that he had no natural passions, concealing or suppressing his joy at the birth of a child, for example, and claiming that his old nature had been slain, this was "fanaticism far worse than the delirium of the Stoics."[129] Theological error therefore was not just wrongheaded; it was conducive to real madness. When certain radical reformers began to trust their own visions as if they were divine revelation, Luther claimed that they were more than just wrong: "Some arrived at dementia."[130] Perhaps the most dangerously mad practices were those prompted by self-righteousness. The asceticism of monks led to fasting, physical abuse, and nonsensical arrogance. Here again a wrongheaded theology produced a really wrong head. Similarly, Luther urged marriage as a moderate way of accommodating sexual passion. Speaking of Potiphar's wife, he observed that "when women accomplish nothing with their blandishments and charms, they are driven to madness."[131] By trying to suppress sexual urges, the Catholic religious orders only kindled their own frenzy.[132]

In urging Christians to accept the naturalness of hunger, thirst, affection, and passion, Luther was thus encouraging more than humble submission to the natural limitations of human life; in curbing man's urge to self-glory and self-sufficiency, he also hoped to foster physical and mental health. As we have seen, for Luther, mind and body were so wrapped up in each other, so interdependent, that one could not change one without the other. In ruminating one day on melancholy, he repeated the chestnut that it was the devil's bath, "nor is there any speedier remedy than spiritual joy."[133] True Christian doctrine was a healthful doctrine. Left to their own devices, men would try to work out their own salvation and drive themselves crazy. If they could learn to accept reality and the free grace of Christ, they would be well fortified against the frantic assaults of the devil.

128. *Lectures on Genesis*: WA, 43: 276, cf. 333–34; LW, 4: 195, cf. 276–77.
129. Ibid.: WA, 44: 493; LW, 7: 261.
130. Ibid.: WA, 43: 225; LW, 4: 125.
131. Ibid.: WA, 44: 364; LW, 7: 87.
132. Ibid.: WA, 43: 451–52; LW, 5: 33–37.
133. WATR, no. 5155. The whole reference is of interest: "Melancholia. Est balneum Diaboli, nec est praesentius remedium quam spiritualis laetitia, ut inquit S. Anthonius, contra Diaboli astutias. Tunc quidem dixit: Domine Doctor, credo freneticos non carere Diabolo.—Nihil certius, inquit, nam sic fiunt ferociores, et tamen verum est Diabolum nosse naturas melancholicas; utitur igitur eo instrumento."

Even if his notion of madness in some ways paralleled the modern idea of mental illness, Luther's "therapy" did not depend on an actual change within the suffering person, but rather on a change of attitude between the person and the reality in which he lived. It did not depend on "working through" latent difficulties or in adopting more realistic attitudes toward one's frustrated desires, but instead aimed at diverting attention from desires that were often seen as sinful. It did not always resolve doubts or gloom but rather tried to ignore or transcend them by plunging the sufferer back into a milieu of friends, family, good food and drink, music and games. Above all, it was a spiritual therapy, dependent on God's love and the Christian experiences of repentance, faith, and forgiveness. Paracelsus too spoke this language of spiritual healing.

Paracelsus and Madness in the Microcosm

The man called Paracelsus is perhaps the least known and least accessible major thinker of the sixteenth century. Partly this is because of Paracelsus's own attitude of defiance and deliberate solitude, an attitude that led him to remark, "I do not intend to nourish myself with the caresses of friends."[134] Forced to move from one town to the next, he was not fully understood in his own day. It was only in the generation after his death in 1541 that many of his writings were published, allowing for a better grasp of his ideas, but even then roughly half of his works, those dealing with religious topics, were omitted.[135] Even today, many of these still await their first printing. The confusions about Paracelsus, however, stem also from the ardent scholars who have written about him. Some medical historians have thought they glimpsed the beginnings of modern empirical medicine in Paracelsus's rejection of the ancient Galen and of scholastic medicine. Other medical scholars have reacted angrily to his use of alchemy and astrology and have seen in him only a hodgepodge of nonsense. By emphasizing the chemistry of life, Paracelsus has seemed to some to have founded iatrochemistry and biochemistry, while his herbal formulas, his philosophy of healing, and his psychosomatic principles have inspired modern romantic

---

134. *Sieben Defensiones*, in *SW*, pt. 1, 11: 152.

135. For the spread of Paracelsus's writings and thought, see Allen G. Debus, *The French Paracelsians: The Chemical Challenge to Medical and Scientific Tradition in Early Modern France* (Cambridge, 1991); id., *The Chemical Philosophy: Paracelsan Science and Medicine in the Sixteenth and Seventeenth Centuries* (New York, 1977); Bruce T. Moran, *The Alchemical World of the German Court: Occult Philosophy and Chemical Medicine in the Circle of Moritz of Hessen (1572–1632)* (Stuttgart, 1992); H. R. Trevor-Roper, "The Court Physician and Paracelsianism," in *Medicine at the Courts of Europe, 1500–1837*, ed. Vivian Nutton (London, 1990), pp. 79–94.

and homeopathic physicians, one of whom even undertook a massive three-volume translation of Paracelsus's works into modern German in hopes of making his insights available to modern doctors.[136] Only recently has Paracelsus the alchemist had to make room for the serious philosopher and biblical theologian.[137] Whatever one's general view of the rebel reformer of medicine, no one doubts that the mental illnesses attracted a great deal of his attention. Although Parcelsus was known in his own lifetime for writings on surgery, syphilis, and the plague, his posthumously published treatises reveal a fascination with diseases producing "stones" of various sorts, with women's diseases, miners' diseases, pharmacology, and a host of mental and psychic disorders. Before we turn to the "psychiatric" writings themselves, we must make an effort to grasp Paracelsus's general view of human nature, for he prided himself on grasping things whole, on devising concepts that would relate man the microcosm to the world and universe around him.

136. *Paracelsus: Sämtliche Werke nach der 10-bändigen Huserschen Gesamtausgabe (1589–91), zum erstenmal in neuzeitliches Deutsch übersetzt*, ed. and trans. Bernhard Aschner (Jena, 1926–30). Despite its title, Aschner's edition is far from including the complete works. Instead, Aschner chose those works whose healing philosophy and medical teachings he approved, while rejecting Paracelsus's natural philosophy and theology as being "at most of historical interest," "childish and generally uninteresting"; it would have been "no loss if these works had never reached posterity." Aschner even congratulates himself for having the courage to reject the chaff while keeping the wheat (3: ix). For a critique of Aschner's translation, see *Theophrastus Paracelsus: Werke*, ed. Will-Erich Peuckert (Basel, 1965–68), 1: xii–xvi. For his part, Peuckert emphasized the "pansophic" and magical Paracelsus by including spurious works and by leaving out most of Paracelsus's theology. The best general discussion and critical examination of the authentic and spurious works of Paracelsus remains Karl Sudhoff, *Versuch einer Kritik der Echtheit der Paracelsischen Schriften* (Berlin, 1894–99), partially reprinted as *Bibliographica Paracelsica* (Graz, 1958). Andrew Weeks has argued recently and convincingly, however, for the redating (to a later time) of several of Paracelsus's early medical works (*Paracelsus*, pp. 33–47). For Paracelsus's role as a continuing inspiration for modern philosophy, science, and medicine, see Frank Geerk, *Paracelsus—Arzt unserer Zeit: Leben, Werk und Wirkungsgeschichte des Teophrastus von Hohenheim* (Zurich, 1992).

137. Kurt Goldammer, *Paracelsus: Natur und Offenbarung* (Hannover, 1953); Heinrich Schipperges, *Paracelsus: Der Mensch in der Licht der Natur* (Stuttgart, 1974); Johannes Hemleben, *Paracelsus: Revolutionär, Artzt und Christ* (Stuttgart, 1973); Ernst Wilhelm Kämmerer, *Das Leib-Seele-Geist-Problem bei Paracelsus und einigen Autoren des 17. Jahrhunderts* (Wiesbaden, 1971); *Paracelsus (1493–1541): Keines andern Knecht*, ed. Heinz Dopsch, Kurt Goldammer, and Peter F. Kramml (Salzburg, 1993); *Resultate und Desiderate der Paracelsus-Forschung*, ed. Peter Dilg and Hartmut Rudolph (Stuttgart, 1993). For a bibliography up to 1960, see the careful and extremely helpful work of Karl-Heinz Weimann, *Paracelsus-Bibliographie 1932–1960, mit einem Verzeichnis neu entdeckter Paracelsus-Handschriften (1900–1960)* (Wiesbaden, 1963). The best general introduction to Paracelsus in English is now Weeks, *Paracelsus*, which sets a new standard. The older classic is Walter Pagel, *Paracelsus: An Introduction to Philosophical Medicine in the Era of the Renaissance* (Basel, 1958; 2d ed., Basel, 1982), although Pagel's assumptions regarding Paracelsus's sources are not universally accepted. See Charles Webster, *From Paracelsus to Newton: Magic and the Making of Modern Science* (Cambridge, 1982).

Like many others of his generation, especially outside the walls of the late medieval university, Paracelsus despaired of reason in its scholastic forms and insisted that experience (*erfarenheit*) provided a firmer foundation than speculation (*wenen*).[138] Despite this declared principle, Paracelsus used strong doses of fantasy, intuition, and what he called "theorica" in his own works. We need not join the controversy over whether there are real contradictions in these positions, and it is still less important to claim that Paracelsus thought the way a modern scientist does. It is clear enough that Paracelsus tried to establish the unity of human nature by using medical language to describe ethical and religious matters and by extending moral and biblical language into matters of health. In this respect, he reminds us of Luther and of other sixteenth-century generalists, although these metaphorical flights have caused problems for modern interpreters of Paracelsus. Like Luther, Paracelsus was a gifted writer with a pungent style and a powerful, even uncanny, ability to keep an extended analogy afloat.

PARACELSUS'S VIEW OF HUMAN NATURE

In his repeated efforts to understand the whole of nature and the whole of man, Paracelsus sometimes saw human nature as dual and sometimes as triple. On many occasions, for example, he claimed that man was divided into body and spirit, or into elemental body and sidereal (i.e., astral) body. Apparently realizing that such a dualism might be used to devalue the physical aspects of Creation, however, Paracelsus also elaborated a more complex tripartite view of man, in which body, spirit, and soul were joined.[139] In both systems, Paracelsus taught that man was not to be divided into his functions or labeled by his complexion (whether sanguine, melancholy, etc.). "Man is a world closed in on himself and covered with skin."[140] Or, as he put it elsewhere, "The form of a man is according to his heart, for virtue and mind [*Gemut*] form his body just as the thoughts of the carpenter form a house."[141] Body and soul were inseparable: "What the soul does occurs in the whole body, because body and soul are one thing."[142] This might have implied that individuals were monads cut off from one another,

138. See Charles Nauert, *Agrippa and the Crisis of Renaissance Thought* (Urbana, Ill., 1965); Hiram Hayden, *The Counter Renaissance* (New York, 1950). Weeks, *Paracelsus*, pp. 12–17, 28–32, 88–90, 182–84.

139. See Kämmerer, *Das Leib-Seele-Geist-Problem bei Paracelsus*. It is worth emphasizing that, for Paracelsus, the highest part of man was one's God-given soul and not the spirit-pneuma of the gnostic tradition.

140. *SW*, pt. 1, 11: 178, quoted in Ernst Wilhelm Kämmerer, "Mensch und Krankheit bei Paracelsus," in *Paracelsus: Werke und Wirkung. Festgabe für Kurt Goldammer zum 60. Geburtstag*, ed. Sepp Domandl (Vienna, 1975), pp. 119–24.

141. *Astronomia magna*, in *SW*, pt. 1, 12: 178.

142. *SW*, pt. 2, 4: 139.

and that even at death the soul was inseparable from the body. Paracelsus drew neither conclusion, repeatedly affirming man's social nature, his duty to help his neighbor, the love of Christians for their fellowman, and also the life of the soul after the death of the body. Indeed, he was concerned to value the body and all of physical nature highly.[143] The dichotomy Paracelsus felt most strongly about was ethical, between right and wrong, God and Satan; one should not too quickly assume that his ethical dualism necessarily implied an ontic or substantial dualism. Echoing an orthodox Christian position, he remarked, "Nothing is bad except what we ourselves make bad."[144] Flesh was not less valuable than soul or spirit except when it distracted human beings from their duties. This was why Paracelsus often went far toward spiritualizing matter, on the one hand, and toward materializing the spirit, on the other.[145] Traditional Christianity had often preserved the autonomy and value of nature by insisting on the *ex nihilo* creation of the world, which God had declared to be good. For Paracelsus, the nature of man could not be explained so simply, since the biblical account proved to him that man had not been created *ex nihilo*, but from dust to which had been added the breath of life.[146] Created on the sixth day, man was in fact the only creature to combine the elements and principles of all previous creation. God's word showed man to be a microcosm, a compressed image and occult blend of everything around him, standing between the earth and the stars, between animals and angels. Paracelsus elaborated this theory of the microcosm into a master image that pervades his philosophy.

The macrocosm consisted of three general spheres, the earthly, the heavenly (astral or sidereal), and the divine. Correspondingly, Paracelsus often thought of man as having three natures, a body (or animal), a spirit (or sidereal body), and a divine soul (the image of God). Both the body and spirit were natural, the result of God's miraculous act of creation, binding *limus* (clay) and *astra* (stars) together. These two parts were mortal and corresponded to (1) flesh and blood, and (2) sense and thought.[147] The third part of man was his eternal, immortal, divine soul, the image of God. True wisdom lay in cultivating the divine image, leading a Christian life; yet Paracel-

143. Walter Pagel's magisterial study of Paracelsus seems to exaggerate the gnostic and Neoplatonic desire of Paracelsus to transcend mere flesh (*Paracelsus*, pp. 204–27, 349–50). For an early critique of Pagel that emphasizes Paracelsus's medieval sources, see Gerhard Eis, *Vor und nach Paracelsus: Untersuchungen über Hohenheims Traditionsverbundenheit und Nachrichten über seine Anhänger* (Stuttgart, 1965). Pagel responded in "Paracelsus: Traditionalism and Medieval Sources," in *Medicine, Science and Culture: Historical Essays in Honor of Owsei Temkin*, ed. Lloyd Stevenson and Robert P. Multhauf (Baltimore, 1968), pp. 50–75.

144. *De causis morborum invisibilium*, in *SW*, pt. 1, 12: 275.

145. Pagel, *Paracelsus*, pp. 208, 227.

146. *Astronomia magna*, in *SW*, pt. 1, 12: 36–37, 70.

147. Ibid., pp. 37–38.

sus was far from thinking that a truly wise man could forget or suppress nature and concentrate only on God's scriptural revelations. Instead, man had to use both the Light of Nature and the Divine Light in constructing true wisdom. The Light of Nature was one of Paracelsus's favorite metaphors, and it implied man's ability to see and experience natural truths. The ancients and the heathen had often brought their use of natural reason, the Light of Nature, to high peaks of (mortal) perfection. Paracelsus often used his claim of experience (*Erfarung, Licht der Natur*) to debunk the false teachers of scholastic medicine, who, he thought, depended on logic rather than on observation of the world around them. By denying themselves the advantages of experience and of the Light of Nature, these doctrinaire professorial Pharisees trusted their own fantasies and became fools or even animals, cut off from natural wisdom.[148] Indeed, in his late *Astronomia magna*, Paracelsus claimed that although natural wisdom could exist without divine wisdom (as it had among the ancient heathen), man's possession of divine wisdom was dependent on the natural. For man had to "recognize the eternal from the natural."[149] God, he claimed in another late treatise, took no pleasure in ignorant fools.[150] Every man had a duty to learn, to search, to discover the secrets of nature. God had made man, not for drinking, whoring, and laziness, but for daily exercise and "searching into the secrets of nature in all of the properties that God created in nature."[151]

What arts did the Light of Nature teach? In his scathing *Paragranum* (1530), written in Basel and Nuremberg after sorry experience, Paracelsus claimed that true medicine rested on four columns: natural philosophy, astronomy, alchemy, and virtue.[152] Together these arts were sufficient to destroy the humoral basis of contemporary medicine and to show man the specific causes of specific diseases. In the place of empty speculation, Paracelsus hoped to provide a description of diseases, noting their external origin. Instead of regarding disease as essentially a disturbance of man's inner vapors and fluids, Paracelsus sought an autonomous source of poison, infection, or influence. Armed with the arts provided by the Light of Nature, the physician could understand the diseases of body (*elementischer Leib*) and spirit (*siderischer Leib*). They would not suffice to understand the image of God, man's divine wisdom, for which the Light of the Holy Spirit was necessary; medicine had to remain content within its limits. Accordingly, when Paracelsus dealt with theological themes, he generally took the Bible as his only source and left alchemy and astrology behind.[153]

148. Ibid., pp. 25–28, 58–59.
149. Ibid., p. 29.
150. *Liber de fundamento scientiarum*, in SW, pt. 1, 13: 307–8.
151. *Astronomia magna*, in SW, pt. 1, 12: 59.
152. *Opus paragranum*, in SW, pt. 1, 8: 136–38, 141–42.
153. In fact, late in his short life, he came to question the value of alchemy as a road to

Believing strongly that the stars could reveal the causes of human misfortune and the structure of human life, Paracelsus could easily be accused
of determinism and fatalism. He repeatedly denounced such conclusions
as grossly erroneous, arguing sometimes that the stars neither "inclined"
nor "necessitated" any action. He seems to have meant that the stars corresponded to human actions but had no absolute and direct control over
them, that man and stars were instead bound up in a web of mutual influence. On other occasions, however, he openly urged the power and influence of the stars. After a judicious review of such apparently contradictory
statements, Walter Pagel concluded that there were serious inconsistencies
in Paracelsus's doctrine, and that his attempt to escape from astral determinism was only partly successful.[154] Much of the problem hinged for
Paracelsus on his defense of human freedom. The stars determined no one
absolutely, because the free man could counteract their influence. The wise
man could even "rule the stars."[155] On the other hand, fools and others who
did not sufficiently guard their free will might fall under the attack of a
malevolent star. Even then, the cause was as much in man as in the stars.

Paracelsus was, therefore, not just a medical reformer. His medicine was
so consistently holistic, and his purposes so clearly moral and religious,
that we are confining him in categories that are much too narrow if we see
him merely as a reforming physician. His concerns were overwhelmingly
ethical, and he could easily agree with Luther that sin and sickness were inseparable. The religious writings now finally being published after 450
years of manuscript obscurity make it clear that Paracelsus saw himself
very much as a theologian, even calling himself "Doctor der Theologie und
beider Arzneien."[156] This theological and ethical perspective has often been
neglected in modern attempts to understand Paracelsus's view of disease.
With the mental diseases, the result has been confusion and the unwarranted discovery of contradictions in Paracelsus's thought.

PARACELSUS ON MENTAL ILLNESS

Although the general views of Paracelsus on mental illness can be
quickly summarized, the most careful scholars have felt compelled to concede that their theosophical hero never worked out all of the contradictions
in his teachings on psychiatry. In general, one can say that Paracelsus sponsored a psychosomatic psychiatry that nonetheless gave considerable au-

truth and emphasized the Word of God. See *Liber prologi in vitam beatam*, in *Theophrastus
Paracelsus: Werke*, ed. Peuckert, 4: 141.

154. Pagel, *Paracelsus*, pp. 105, 118.

155. *Astronomia magna*, in *SW*, pt. 1, 12: 41.

156. *Beider Arzneien* referred to a term used at the University of Ferrara, modeled on the
legal degree in canon and civil law, "utriusque juris."

tonomy to both body and spirit.[157] To Paracelsus, it was obvious that the body could affect the mind, and that a diseased mind could harm the body, convictions that have led some scholars to praise him for charting an advance beyond the somaticism or materialism of strict humoral theory. Yet, confusingly, Paracelsus argued in one place that lunacy was a disease to be treated medically but elsewhere that lunatics should be thrust into outer darkness. He seemed to claim that mental illnesses were not caused by evil spirits and that they were, that demon possession was not a disease but also that it was, that human reason was immune to disease but that it could fall into hopeless madness. Walter Pagel repeatedly uses such apparent contradictions to point out weaknesses, confusions, and logical inconsistencies in his hero.[158] E. W. Kämmerer's *Das Leib-Seele-Geist-Problem bei Paracelsus und einigen Autoren des 17. Jahrhunderts* echoes Pagel on this point.[159] And as a general conclusion, it may well be true; there is at any rate no reason why the mass of Paracelsica must be regarded as completely coherent and without inner contradictions. We should not, however, draw that conclusion prematurely with regard to the mental and spiritual illnesses, since Paracelsus commanded an immense gift for metaphor. If one probes behind the image to Paracelsus's intention, one can often detect a surprising coherence in the midst of apparent chaos. Werner Leibbrand and his daughter Annemarie Leibbrand-Wettley glimpse this conclusion when they suggest that some contradictions in Paracelsus's psychiatric doctrines stemmed from his moving from a physical to a Christian framework.[160] Increasingly disillusioned in his mature years with the capacity of human reason to comprehend the world, Paracelsus did shift from an enthusiasm for alchemy, geometry, and natural philosophy to a profoundly Christian, biblical outlook.[161]

Such a shift of attention might help to explain the inconsistency of Paracelsus's various views on madness but does not eliminate it. Careful attention to his ideas on human nature can, however, explain many of the

157. Owsei Temkin, "The Elusiveness of Paracelsus," *Bulletin of the History of Medicine* 26 (1952): 201–17; Iago Galdston, "The Psychiatry of Paracelsus," in id., *Psychiatry and the Human Condition* (New York, 1976), pp. 377–89; Webster, *From Paracelsus to Newton;* Annemarie Leibbrand-Wettley, "Zur Psychopathologie und Dämonologie bei Paracelsus und Johannes Weyer," in *Melemata: Festschrift für Werner Leibbrand,* ed. Joseph Schumacher (Mannheim, 1967), pp. 65–73.

158. Pagel, *Paracelsus,* pp. 150–52; Walter Pagel, *Das medizinische Weltbild des Paracelsus: Seine Zusammenhänge mit Neuplatonismus und Gnosis* (Wiesbaden, 1962), pp. 3–4, 10–11.

159. Kämmerer, *Das Leib-Seele-Geist-Problem,* p. 61; E. Ackerknecht, *Kurze Geschichte der Psychiatrie* (2d ed. Stuttgart, 1967), p. 26.

160. Werner Leibbrand and Annemarie Wettley, *Der Wahnsinn: Geschichte der abendländischen Psycopathologie* (Freiburg im Breisgau, 1961), pp. 201–24, esp. 217–18.

161. See *Liber prologi in vitam beatam,* in *Theophrastus Paracelsus: Werke,* ed. Peuckert, 4: 131–48, esp. pp. 141–44; and (MP) L2 (89), fol. 430a.

TABLE 2.1

Bipartite and Tripartite Divisions of Nature in Paracelsus

I. Bipartite Anthropology

Macrocosm:	Creation (heaven and earth)	God
Microcosm:	Body: *tierisch Vernunft*	Soul: *menschlich Vernunft* (*Bildnus*, Image of God)

II. Tripartite Anthropology

Macrocosm:	Earth	Star	God
Microcosm:	Flesh (Body)	Thought (Spirit)	Soul (*Imago Dei*, Image of God)
	Elemental	Sidereal	Divine
	Mortal	Mortal	Immortal
	Visible	Invisible	Invisible

apparent contradictions in his scattered psychiatric writings. Madness in its many forms fascinated Paracelsus from his earliest writings to his last. Instead of concentrating on just a couple of major treatises on mental aberrations, as scholars have done repeatedly, we need to survey the entire spectrum. When we do so, we shall find that we must recognize both bipartite and tripartite schemes of human nature at work in Paracelsus's thought. At times, it made sense for Paracelsus to emphasize God's transcendence and to see the cosmos in binary terms. At other times, he thought it made better ethical sense to divide the cosmos in three. These two schemes are roughly set out in table 2.1.

The triadic scheme of human nature (body, spirit, soul) gave Paracelsus conceptual room in which to elaborate three forms of mental corruption. It was a flexible system, which allowed him to expound physical (cerebral and physiological) diseases and spiritual (mental) illnesses without threatening the essential humanity (*imago*, *biltnus*) of man. Its hallmark was an emphasis on the *astra* and the sidereal body of man. In classic form, we find it in the great work of Paracelsus's last years, the *Astronomia magna* of 1537 or 1538. Here Paracelsus was mainly interested in the sidereal body of man, his mortal spirit, as it could be understood by the Light of Nature. The basic reason for all mental disease, he argued, was a sinful privileging of the lower parts of human nature. When man ignored or was ignorant of his immortal soul, he was less than perfect, but when he ignored even his sidereal nature, he sank to the level of the beasts, having only a bestial reason. If one acted bestially, it followed that one was indeed "a beast and not a man at all."[162] Those who did not sink so far were sometimes tempted and torn be-

162. *Astronomia magna, SW*, pt 1, 12: 58.

tween their two bodies (body and mortal spirit), becoming so "distracted that they stand on no firm foundation. They produce no well-founded sentence as integrated persons do, for they are mad, beginning many things, but nothing with set purpose; their reason has been corrupted and their elemental body too."[163] Although the focus of this *Great Astronomy* was on the adept, occult wisdom of the stars, at one point Paracelsus made it clear that man really had three wisdoms: bestial, astral, and divine (corresponding to body, mortal spirit, and soul).[164] And each wisdom had its own particular corruption.

What were the diseases of bestial wisdom? Paracelsus had actually described them over a decade earlier in a treatise entitled *On the Diseases that Rob Man of Reason*.[165] With an elaborate but deceptive display of organization, Paracelsus declared that there were five kinds of natural (nondemonic) disease that could destroy reason, and that the fifth was in turn divided into five species.

1. The first type of natural insanity was epilepsy, the falling sickness, which resembled a living earthquake or lightning bolt.[166]

2. The second was mania, a corruption of reason rather than of the senses, occurring either in a healthy body or as the result of some other disease. Worms, for example, might produce mania. But since the cause of mania was physical, Paracelsus here recommended surgical and medicinal cures. The main surgical remedy then in wide use was, of course, bloodletting, and one could release blood from all the extremities if necessary. Such a release of blood "is largely responsible for reducing mania."[167] Draughts of oil of camphor and the quintessences of silver, iron, mercury, and saturn (i.e., lead) could also cool the *"materiam peccantem maniae."*[168]

3. The third was St. Vitus' dance (which Paracelsus also called the lewd dance, *chorea lasciva*), which did not come from saints or God but was the result of cursing, excessive frivolity, or a natural corruption of the imagination. Paracelsus divided St. Vitus' dance into three species. If the dancing mania had been caused by cursing, the remedy was to compose a

---

163. Ibid., p. 65.

164. Ibid., p. 300.

165. *Von den Krankheiten die der Vernunft berauben*, in *SW*, pt. 1, 2: 391–455. The translation by Gregory Zilboorg butchers the treatise; it was published in *Four Treatises of Theophrastus von Hohenheim, called Paracelsus*, ed. Henry Sigerist (Baltimore, 1941), pp. 127–212; Zilboorg made arbitrary and unannounced cuts and added extraneous material, so that one cannot obtain an accurate overview from his translation.

166. See Owsei Temkin, *The Falling Sickness: A History of Epilepsy*, 2d ed. (Baltimore, 1971), pp. 170–77. See also Paracelsus, *De caducis liber I (Von den hinfallenden Siechtagen)*, in *SW* pt. 1, 8: 261–308; id., *Von den Krankheiten die der Vernunft berauben*, in *SW* pt. 1, 2: 393–99.

167. *Von den Krankheiten die der Vernunft berauben*, in *SW* pt. 1, 2: 436.

168. Ibid., p. 438.

waxen image of all of one's curses and evil thoughts and consume them in a fire (anthropologists used to call this sympathetic magic). To counteract frivolity and lascivious thoughts, Paracelsus recommended putting the patient in a dark room and feeding him or her only bread and water, for hunger would create "another frame of mind," driving away unchaste ideas, and the patient would become sober, or even sad.[169] Then a slow relaxation of the prisonlike environment would get rid of the melancholy that had taken the place of frivolity. The third sort of chorea, which Paracelsus called the corruption of imagination, could be treated medicinally with opium, *aurum potabile*, alcohol, quintessence of mandragora, and other material substances.

4. Paracelsus called the fourth disease that deprived one of reason a suffocation of the intellect, a dangerous side effect of other diseases caused, for example, by worms, uterine disorders, and improper food. Its cure was medicinal, using salves and drinks to strengthen the body, because the root of this disease was physical weakness.

5. Finally, the fifth disease complex was *privatio sensuum*, the loss of the senses, and it included five subgroups: lunatics, the congenitally insane, the *vesani* (mad), those afflicted by witchcraft, and the melancholy. Although lumped together because of their defect of sense, the causes of these diseases were different in each case:

(a) Lunatics had fallen (through their own fault) under the influence of the moon; the remedy was to create a chemical-astrological shield to protect the mind, just as a roof can shield our eyes from the sun.

(b) Those insane from birth were the product of careless sexual practice. If parents had intercourse in the midst of passion, their temporary insanity might well be transmitted to the fetus. To avoid this all-too-frequent situation, Paracelsus prescribed cold baths and an artificial coitus "according to nature but not according to the mind or will of insanity."[170] Paracelsus's view of an ideally passionless sexual intercourse may remind us of St. Augustine's contention that Adam, before he fell into sin, could rationally control his sexual organs.[171] While this kind of congenital insanity could have been prevented by a less turbulent sexual encounter between the parents, the remedy for this group of disabled madmen involved strengthening them with quintessences of gold, pearls, silver, coral, antimony, sulfur, mercury, and sapphires.

(c) *Vesani* were often poisoned by food or drink, and Paracelsus recommended trying the same food again. Sedatives might also help.

169. Ibid., p. 441.
170. Ibid., p. 449.
171. St. Augustine, *The City of God*, bk. 14, chs. 16–26.

(d) Those afflicted by witchcraft needed special help described in another treatise on charms.

(e) The melancholy, finally, were those who had gone mad by reason of their own nature or complexion. Although Paracelsus soon came to doubt the very existence of humors like melancholy and the usefulness of ideas like "complexion," he here spelled out cures for excessive sadness (*melancholia, phlegmatica*) and for excessive laughing (*sanguinea, cholerica*).[172] In this treatise the recommended remedy consisted simply of medicines to sober the laughing or to enliven the somber: more opiates, *aurum potabile, manna maris, lolium,* and so on. In a later treatise, Paracelsus also recommended music for these sufferers, because, by encouraging sociability, it counteracts the familiar withdrawal of the melancholy from society.[173] From vastly different points of view, Luther and Paracelsus often drew the same conclusions.

The chief peculiarity of this early psychiatric treatise is its extraordinarily eclectic vision of the causes and cures of mental trouble. Poisons and witchcraft, astral influence, sinful imagination and disordered humors all competed as possible sources of madness. Despite the pretense of elaborate organization, the treatise was hardly one of Paracelsus's stronger attempts at synthesis. Running throughout it was a materialist bias, which emerges, for example, in the lists of chemicals that could be effective remedies. Paracelsus had, in effect, composed a psychosomatic survey of the ailments that could afflict what he would later call the bestial (lower) wisdom; his therapy was emphatically medical, but sharply rejected the Galenic theory of humors and of vague humoral balances, and thus Paracelsus succeeded in conveying the impression that there were many specific mental illnesses with specific remedies available.

These, then, were the mental illnesses, conceived as psychosomatic disturbances of the lower wisdom. Later using implicitly the same triadic scheme, Paracelsus elaborated a further series of middle-level, astral ailments of the middle-level, sidereal wisdom. It is not clear that they should even be called properly *psychic* illnesses at all. In examining the irrational or superrational states (*artes aethereae*) permitting divination and pagan prophecy, the *Great Astronomy* considered an ethereal knowledge called *ebriecatum,* a suggestive term that implied a parallel to ordinary drunkenness (*ebria*). This *ebriecatum* occurred when a person fell into an alien wis-

172. In his *De religione perpetua* (*Theophrastus Paracelsus: Werke,* ed. Peuckert, 4: 157), Paracelsus's major criticism of humoral theory was simply that it was unnecessary. Later in life, he retained melancholy, not as a humor or complexion, but only as a disease: "So doch melancholia nichts ist als eine tolle, unsinnige phantastica krankheit" (*Labyrinthus medicum errantium* [1538], in *SW* pt. 1, 1: 180–81).

173. *De religione perpetua,* in *Theophrastus Paracelsus: Werke,* ed. Peuckert, 4: 165.

dom (*aliena sapientia*) "which makes one confused and mad against all human nature."[174] There were again five species:

1. *ebriecata mania*, exemplified in those who interpreted Scripture in a nonsensical way;

2. *inebriata phrenesis*, as found in those who were always ready to fight and flew easily into rages;

3. *inebriata phantasmata*, as in men who affected strange gestures, behavior, and morals;

4. *imaginatio inebriata*, found among those subject to curious fantasies, such as drunkards who talk to the walls;

5. and, finally, *inebriata immutatio*, the disease of those who were so wrapped up in themselves that they confused friends with enemies. This last sort of astral inebriation produced an autistic and private logic that was unable to reason with anyone else and seems to echo Luther's view of his most determined opponents.[175] Here, Paracelsus conceived of a mental disorder that was a furious inability to see any one else's point of view.

Paracelsus took pains to explain that the drunkenness of which he spoke here was merely an image or metaphor to clarify the disease and had nothing to do with real wine, but like wine the stars could be usefully absorbed and appreciated in moderation.[176] It was up to the individual person to control this astral thirst for *vinum olympi*, however, because too much was dangerous, causing one to stray from both God and the Light of Nature: "[T]hey rave as in a dream, making monkeys of themselves and signifying nothing."[177] Unlike sufferers from ordinary mental diseases, those drunk on a star were often highly regarded as saints or revered as having gifts of prophecy. And yet this was not the divine madness of true prophecy. These astral drunks "leave human nature behind just as does a maniac or phrenetic."[178] Among such intoxicated minds have been celebrated "theologians, preachers, jurists, *Rabulists*, physicians both learned and empiric, soldiers, gamblers etc., and in everything each one has his own peculiar behavior . . . and thus each is [only] self-taught and not instructed by God."[179] This disease of prideful, autistic self-sufficiency was an important category for Paracelsus, since it allowed him to mount a sharper attack than Eras-

---

174. *Astronomia magna,* in *SW,* pt. 1, 12: 107.

175. Ibid., p. 108.

176. Ibid., p. 222.

177. Ibid., p. 213.

178. Ibid., p. 224. Paracelsus repeatedly reminded his readers that this too was a metaphor, and that men afflicted with astral drunkenness still had human understanding and not just a maniacal or phrenetic understanding. The nonsense they spoke was the "firmamental juice" speaking through them.

179. Ibid.

mus could in the *Praise of Folly* by blasting the infatuations of his age, not as mere follies, but as forms of full-fledged madness. Although still human, the sidereally drunk were so far from truth, so persuaded of their own wisdom, and inevitably so popular, that they were dangerous.

The highest wisdom of man in this tripartite scheme resided in his immortal soul, the image of the divine. It was not, strictly speaking, subject to disease or corruption, but sinful men often forgot their highest wisdom and became little better than pigs, unworthy of life.[180] The devil was able to take control of the soul in such cases, producing the madness and states of possession cured by Christ. Like Luther, Paracelsus thought that the devil could take control in two distinct ways, effecting either a total loss of reason and self-control (the classic image of the demoniac foaming at the mouth and thrashing on the ground), or an even more dangerous partial takeover in which the demon-possessed person appeared rational and even saintly but was now full of devilish teachings. Thus the devil controlled greedy merchants, liars, and deceivers more effectively than if he took charge of their bodies and caused them to be thrown into chains. "Only those whom he cannot use at all does he drive on to [full] possession, rage, and madness."[181] Thus at the highest level Paracelsus accorded a dual activity to the devil very like the two kinds of drunkenness (astral or alcoholic), being either moral or physical. Throughout the extended analysis of the *Great Astronomy*, Paracelsus insisted that he was arguing from natural reason and experience, not from revelation. Although the examples of devilish activity might appear to violate this self-imposed limitation, Paracelsus could have reasonably claimed that here he was still only interested in the role of the devil in the corporeal worlds of matter and mortal spirit, and that he had not really examined the world of the soul.

We cannot be sure whether the tripartite anthropology also underlies several treatises that deal mainly with simple corruptions of the body or of the soul. The sidereal body may have been implicit in some of these works without being directly relevant, collapsing the triad into an apparently binary system of the sort that we find explicitly elsewhere. A case in point is the *Opus paramirum* (ca. 1531), in which Paracelsus took careful aim at humoral medicine, arguing that false teachers had invented the four humors from their own fantasy instead of relying on the Light of Nature.[182] Humoral medicine was the product, therefore, of what Paracelsus later called astral drunkenness, that foolish abandonment of sensory knowledge that he blasted in his *Great Astronomy*.[183] Properly understood, mania was indeed a

180. Ibid., p. 306.
181. Ibid., p. 438.
182. *Opus paramirum*, in *SW*, pt. 1, 9: 41.
183. In the *Opus paragranum* of 1530, Paracelsus remarked: "Ist alles nur Wenen bei

hot disease, Paracelsus conceded, but it was not dependent on an imagined choleric complexion. Similarly, Paracelsus agreed with the Galenists that hydrophobia was a moist disease, but he contended it was not particularly hot or cold.[184] Treatment of such physical ailments had to go beyond the Galenic treatment of symptoms. Attacking the cause of the disease by letting blood was far more effective than cooling the maniac with herbs or ice, Paracelsus thought.[185] Although the Galenic idea of a melancholy disposition was gaining in medical popularity as he wrote, he thought it was nonsense, "for the Light of Nature does not even know what melancholy is." Modern scholars have sometimes highlighted such passages as premonitions of a more scientific and empirical medicine, but in the same breath, Paracelsus could turn to the truths of astrology. Thus if one's diagnosis found the patient "saturnine or lunatic in his attitudes, that would be well said," since mores were indeed formed by the Star (*Gestirn*).[186]

Considered in this way, diseases were separate entities with a form and anatomy that could be studied by virtuous physicians ready to trust the Light of Nature.[187] Well beyond the reach of reason and the stars, however, lay the realm of divine diseases, like leprosy, for which God has provided divine remedies (i.e., the apostles). We find in this treatise an anthropology that may have been implicitly triple, but that deals with only two of man's three parts. The stars had their place in it, but they did not here affect a special part of one's mortal substance. Rather, the maniac whose disease could be brought under control by physical means might be under the influence of a star, but that fact did not mean that his sidereal reason was under special attack. Rather than attacking reason, the star-substance Mercury (both in the heavens and in man) might cause (a) sudden death by distillation; (b) by precipitation, the diseases related to podagra (i.e., gout); or (c) by sublimation, the diseases of phrenesis and mania.[188]

We can see that when Paracelsus moved beyond the diseases of the visible body to the mental and spiritual diseases of the *Opus paramirum*, he turned abruptly to the invisible body, whose origin in the breath of life puts it beyond the elements and substances, and clearly beyond the physician. The diseases of the invisible body were logically also invisible; Paracelsus described them in an imperfectly preserved treatise entitled *De causis mor-*

---

euch; dan nur ein Wenen brauchen die cholerischen und phlegmatischen und melancholischen und sanguinischen" (*SW*, pt. 1, 8: 143).

184. *Opus paramirum*, in *SW*, pt. 1, 9: 56–57.

185. Ibid., pp. 59–60. Five years earlier, Paracelsus had recommended herbal remedies himself.

186. Ibid., p. 60.

187. Ibid., p. 64.

188. Ibid., p. 103.

borum invisibilium.[189] Admitting that judging by the *visible* light of nature alone, the idea of a person being possessed by demons was incredible, Paracelsus appealed to what he here called the *invisible* reason (a kind of natural intuition) to grasp a whole series of diseases now labeled *Geist krankheiten* (diseases of the spirit).[190]

As noted, Luther's thinking in places adumbrates modern ideas of mental illness, as opposed to the belief that madness is a somatic disorder. Such foreshadowings are even more evident in Paracelsus's *De causis morborum invisibilium.* As he now imagined matters, this disease complex embraced ailments of spirit (*leibliche Vernunft*) and of the soul, and consequently only nonmaterial remedies came under consideration. To that extent, the treatise is more systematic or coherent, but also more limited, than Paracelsus's earlier treatise *Von den krankheiten die der vernunft berauben* ("Diseases That Rob Men of Reason"). Although he announced a program for dealing in five books with diseases of faith, with impressions of the hidden heaven, with diseases of imagination, with heresy, and with the secret forces that attack corporeal reason, the treatise as we have it has only four books, covering four of these subjects, omitting secret heavenly impressions. Just as *Von den krankheiten die der vernunft berauben* moves easily back and forth across the boundary between body and mortal spirit, so this work on invisible diseases moves effortlessly across the line separating the mortal spirit (*leibliche Vernunft*) from the soul.

Faith, Paracelsus said, is eminently capable of causing disease, because it was so easily abused. Plagues were beyond conventional natural remedies, for example, because they resulted from the abuse of faith.[191] Closer to our topic, Paracelsus urged sharp scrutiny of the cult of saints, because relics were now a source of insane superstition, inasmuch as men bowed

---

189. *De causis morborum invisibilium*, in *SW*, pt. 1, 11: 249–350, esp. pp. 251–58. The programmatic introduction to this treatise (pp. 257–58) is worth quoting in extenso: "[N]och vil mer sollen wir nachforschen, das nicht dem leibe sonder dem ewigen dienstlich ist. dan was dem leibe schadet, das bricht das haus des ewigen; so nun der teufel im selbigen haus wonet so zerrüttet ers. nun ist die ursach billich zu erfaren, warumb er da zu einem werk worden ist. und mags die sichtbarliche vernunft nicht begreifen, so ersuchen wir die unsichtbaren, welche so sie angriffen wird bei seinem liecht, nit minder dan wie die sichtbar ist entgegnet. also dieweil aus den werken ein zal genomen wird, als dan auch bewußt, das ein ietliche practica aus der theorica fliessen sol, so folgen hernach dieselbigen krankheiten in seinen versalen, wie dieselbigen geistkrankheiten mögen bei uns sein, welcher geist doch sichtbar ist bei seinem liecht; dan er ist der halbe mensch. Also wil ich dich leser ermanet haben, das du dich in allen nachfolgenden krankheiten in ein sichtbarn verstant bringest; dan die werk sein alle sichtbar, sichtbar müssen auch ir ursachen sein. Und laß dich das nit betrüben, das die dinge nit alle an der sonne ligen, sonder betrachte wie heimlich got ausserthalb der sonnen ist, und so wir dasselbige sein befunden, das wir hie die unsichtbarn ding unbilich unsichtbar geheißen haben."

190. Ibid., p. 257.

191. Ibid., pp. 265–66.

down to "wooden gods."[192] The devil used such perversions to his own advantage, strengthening belief in the divinity of stars or saints. The chief result of such false beliefs was the spread of sects. Lashing out at the Anabaptists, for example, Paracelsus claimed that they became so attached to particular verses of the Bible that they went mad.[193] "Abusing their mad faith," he asserted, the Anabaptists baptized each other two and three times, saw visions, and eagerly went to their deaths in a way that God had never ordered. "Those who are possessed of the [St. Vitus'] dance have so completely lost their reason that they are reduced to nature, like the Anabaptists, and from their enthusiasm they (both) allow themselves to be burned."[194] In one of his writings on the blessed life, entitled *De religione perpetua*, Paracelsus suggested that music was a potent weapon in the fight against such morbid heresy. Music not only lifted the depressed spirits of melancholy, withdrawn, and despairing persons, as we have already seen; it could also "drive away the spirit 'Afernoch,'" from whom the Anabaptists and similar sects of melancholics arose—those who thought that they had seen heaven and God. For Paracelsus, these were all diseases of the brain and of reason. Just as herbs grew in a garden and could drive out particular diseases, so music was an "herb garden for such fantasies and deranged brain and senses."[195]

Another invisible disease was due to the force of imagination, not on oneself, as in *Von den krankheiten die der vernunft berauben*, but on others, as, for example, the influence of a mother on her developing fetus. Pregnant women should live morally and guard their thoughts, since their imaginations gave shape to their developing children.[196] A lustful imagination produced incubi and succubi, whose unchaste actions remained a sterile matter of spirit only. Yet, here echoing late medieval demonology in this treatise, Paracelsus claimed that nocturnal spirits could carry sperm to produce monsters by having intercourse with witches.[197] Chastity and a pure Christian life were the remedies for this sort of *Geist krankheit*. If one could not control one's lustful thoughts, one should marry, although even that was not an absolutely sure cure.[198] Here again, we can feel the moral

---

192. Ibid., p. 270.

193. Note the parallel here with the astral *inebriata mania* discussed above.

194. Ibid., p. 281.

195. *De religione perpetua* (part of the "vita beata" writings), in *Theophrastus Paracelsus: Werke*, ed. Peuckert, 4: 165. Cf. Kurt Goldammer, "Der cholerische Kriegsmann und der melancholische Ketzer: Psychologie und Pathologie von Krieg, Glaubenskampf und Martyrium in der Sicht des Paracelsus," in *Psychiatrie und Gesellschaft: Ergebnisse und Probleme der Sozialpsychiatrie. Festschrift für Werner Villinger*, ed. H. Erhardt, D. Ploog, and H. Stutte (Bern and Stuttgart, 1958), pp. 90–101.

196. *De causis morborum invisibilium*, in *SW*, pt. 1, 11: 289.

197. Ibid., pp. 299–301.

198. Ibid., pp. 303–304. See also p. 129 below.

and profoundly biblical foundation of much of Paracelsus's thinking on mental illness.

In the last book of this treatise, Paracelsus returned to the subject of heresy, examining those with what he called a morbidly rigid interpretation of Scripture. The devil was always ready to encourage superstition and to foster belief in ceremonies. Although ringing bells, for example, was harmless or even good in itself, and although the pope and his priests enjoyed ceremonies, God wanted the heart. That was why the only effective action against demonic possession was prayer and fasting (Matt. 17:21), a theme to which we shall return.[199]

In this treatise, we observe the metaphor of disease extended to heretical beliefs and sinful desires. In affecting the means of salvation, it appears that Paracelsus was now conceding, the highest realm of the soul could indeed be corrupted, or at least subjected to a dangerous forgetfulness. Yet in general one can say that the implicit tripartite view of man, with its animal, astral, and divine reason or understanding, gave Paracelsus conceptual room in which to describe mental and spiritual illnesses without being constrained by his own framework to regard them all as life-threatening attacks on divine salvation. This extra conceptual space becomes more evident by comparison with a dualist scheme, which did not give Paracelsus the same conceptual parade ground on which to maneuver.

Paracelsus's fullest discussion of madness from a dualist perspective was the *Liber de lunaticis*, to which the great Karl Sudhoff was unable to attach any certain date. It was perhaps a part of the comprehensive *Philosophia magna* that Paracelsus planned but never completed. Will-Erich Peuckert believed that the fragments of this major work should be dated to 1529–32, but their intensely Christian foundation has led others to contend that they must have been written later than that, perhaps at the end of Paracelsus's life. Ute Gause dates the *Liber de lunaticis* to "around 1530."[200] Whatever the date, Paracelsus here asserted that man had two spirits, the spirit of life and the spirit of the *limbus*, or matter into which God had blown the breath of life. "In accord with the spirit of life, man should be a man and not live according to the spirit of limbus, which makes of him an unreasoning creature."[201] With this assertion, Paracelsus wrapped the web of interpretation closely around himself. In these dualist terms, man has to choose whether to be godly or bestial; there is here no middle ground. The *Liber de lunaticis* went over all of the forms of madness (*lunatici, maniaci,*

---

199. Ibid., p. 342.
200. Ute Gause, *Paracelsus (1493–1541): Genese und Entfaltung seiner frühen Theologie* (Tübingen, 1993), p. 109. This work (pp. 109–15) provides the best extended discussion of *De lunaticis*.
201. Paracelsus, *Liber de lunaticis*, in SW, pt. 1, 14: 43.

vesani) again and even touched on cases that Paracelsus did not regard strictly as lunacy (*Narren* and *Tauben*). Repeatedly, this dualist framework imposed a real difference.

Since man's human reason was actually the image of God, it "does not go crazy, and is not subject of disease."[202] Madness was to be found instead among people who either lived according to their natural animal reason or possessed an animal reason that was itself diseased. Paracelsus hastened to point out, for example, that dogs have a reason of their own that leads them naturally to bark and bite when provoked; but when mad, a dog loses even this lower-level "canine reason" and goes about biting indiscriminately. This metaphor clearly isolates what Paracelsus now meant by lunatics: "those who go mad in their bestial reason."[203] Indeed, the difference between folly and madness was that fools (*Narren*, the retarded) were born into an animal spirit and "live like *reasoning* bestial cattle," while the mad "live in a *crazed* bestial spirit; thus fools go mad with reason, what they do is bestial shrewdness. . . . The mad [*Tauben*, from *toben*], however, have that [bestial] reason too, but deranged in its nature."[204]

Although man had two natures, he was responsible for holding his animal nature in check. When successful in setting aside or controlling his bovine, lupine (wolflike), porcine and other bestial tendencies, he was "a pure man who is beyond comparison with any animal."[205] Since even the stars were bestial, man must guard his freedom from them:

For who would admit that Mars belongs to man? No one. Or that Mars is his lord, his incliner, his ascendant? No one. Man is in his essence, free from everything, taking his nature from no one but God, in whose image and spirit [he is formed]. But this is true, that the heavenly stars have a bestial nature.[206]

Only if a man sank to being an animal did he have communion with the stars, and therefore, from this perspective, it was "forbidden to man to use the stars."[207]

Lunacy was now not something that just happened to one; rather it was a self-induced, immoral disease. Just as the sun, moon, and stars shone externally on man, so the

bestial stars look down on the bestial reason of man, penetrate the pores, skin, cells, where the bestial reason is in charge, just as a light can shine into a glass and come out; so the bestial reason, senses, etc., get sick according to whichever bestial star it

202. Ibid., p. 44.
203. Ibid.
204. Ibid.
205. Ibid., p. 46.
206. Ibid.
207. Ibid., p. 47.

is. The *impressiones*, influences, constellations, etc., or whatever they may be called, are all applied to the animal and not to the man. If man lives as befits a man, they are all without effect; if he lives as a beast, however, he is affected like a beast.[208]

Thus fools were led about by a star, and the reasonable or clever (*witzig*) were liable to go mad with their excessive reason, falling into rages like mad dogs during the dog days.[209]

Physicians, therefore, had to be learned in astronomy in order to understand disease; but this was no warrant for dabbling in fortune-telling, augury, and other heathen arts,[210] for these bestial sciences should be deferential and eager to learn from their superior, the image of God.

Every one is taught by God, everyone enlightened who prays and requests in the spirit and not from his animal [nature] from whose spirit one gains nothing. Thus man remains pure and clean, he cannot go mad, cannot go crazy, for he has no cares, no fears, regrets nothing, and is harmed by no one.[211]

With these words Paracelsus here betrayed a basically Stoic view of mental health as a state of ataraxia, the freedom from passion, affection, and disturbance. Unfortunately, in Paracelsus's view, the rebellious animal spirit of man was full of cares, fears, and regrets and if uncontrolled he easily "became mad, silly, senseless, foolish, or doltish."[212] If one followed the higher, properly human reason, one's animal reason would be protected by mental eyelids, but without the supervision or shielding provided by human reason one was mentally blinded by Mars, Jupiter, Saturn or whatever star caught one's fancy, as easily as a fool who goes blind by gazing at the sun.[213]

With this introduction to the origins of lunacy, it should not surprise us to find in the second part of this book a full discussion of the Christian motif of unregenerate man as an animal. In the conceptual framework of this treatise, madness was a state of unregenerate, animal sinfulness. Paracelsus stressed, for example, that John the Baptist had called the Pharisees a brood of vipers (Matt. 3:7) because they had lived as beasts without employing their God-instructed "human spirit." And Jesus, too, had regularly referred to his opponents as dogs, swine, foxes, wolves, and so on, by which he meant that they really were beasts. "Now these are not men as they appear, for if we regard their inner [nature] they cannot disguise what their *limbus* makes them, namely, wolves."[214]

208. Ibid.
209. Ibid.
210. Ibid., p. 48.
211. Ibid., p. 49.
212. Ibid., p. 50.
213. Ibid.
214. Ibid., p. 53.

Pursuing this theme with relentless logic, Paracelsus pointed out that in contrast to Jesus' language regarding unregenerate men, the Lord had used only similes or analogies for his true followers, saying in Matt. 10:16, "I send you forth *like* sheep among wolves" (my emphasis). Christians were truly a new creation, different from (and not just ethically superior to) the blind, sinful, cursed race of reprobates who had not "set aside the bestial," and who therefore drowned in their bestial spirit, becoming "senseless, mad, foolish, deranged." Madness has here become a moral-substantial category to describe the unregenerate.[215] This was a theme to which Paracelsus often returned. In an unpublished work, "On the Secrets of the Secrets of Theology," for example, he glossed Matt. 23:33 by asserting that:

Your names are serpents and vipers, because the new birth of Christians (John 3:3–7) transforms the [true] Christian, who is or will be born of God, like unto the angels. But you are not and will not be of that birth, but of a contrary one. You will become snakes and adders, just as the devil's angels did, and as happened to Leviathan in Paradise.[216]

Addressing the clergy, Paracelsus applied Matt. 3:7 again, saying, "You are an adulterous lot, adders and proud vipers, a race of serpents. Man is not made from animals, but men *become* snakes and basilisks, not sent from God, not men of the new birth, but worms in the pit of hell."[217]

The salvation wrought by God in Christ was for Paracelsus clearly more than a legal declaration of man's forgiveness, more too than merely a new moral capacity, an infusion of the grace necessary to live a God-pleasing life. In systematic terms, as Paracelsus put it in his *Prologue to the Blessed Life*, man of the old creature was literally "bovine, asinine, and bestial," while the true Christian was a new creation; beyond disease and corruption. Like Christ, the Christian was born, not of corruptible flesh, but of the Holy Ghost.[218] So sharp was this distinction that when Christ urged his disciples to preach the gospel to all creatures, he simply meant that they should preach to men who were still dogs, donkeys, and pigs.

Evidently remembering that the madness he was here describing was quite different from the diseases he had earlier discussed in his *Von den krankheiten die der vernunft berauben*, Paracelsus opened the third part of *De lunaticis* with this warning: "There is a big difference between the causes I

215. Ibid., pp. 54–57.
216. (MP) L2 (89), fol. 448b. I am grateful to Dr. Hartmut Rudolph for several discussions on these points. On Paracelsus's theological anthropology, see Gerhild Scholz Williams, "Gelächter vor Gott: Mensch und Kosmos bei Franck und Paracelsus," *Daphnis* 15 (1986): 463–81.
217. (MP) L2 (89), fol. 439b, my emphasis.
218. *Liber prologi in vitam beatam*, in *Theophrastus Paracelsus: Werke*, ed. Peuckert, 4: 137–38; cf. 3: 214.

am here describing and those that also drive people mad, like poisons in the food, etc., which I have attacked in other books. Here my only purpose is to describe those driven mad from heaven, for they are the most common."[219]

On earth there were to be sure many poisons that could produce insanity, such as hemlock, saffron, and "ceredella," but they could also choke and kill, whereas the stars produced only "a chronic mania and not a mortal disease."[220]

Here I speak only of lunatics, since they are very similar to the possessed and are in all things quite close to them. For as causes, the stars, constellations and planets act like spirits, which surpass man so completely that he cannot retain his reason before them, and thus loses it. In this [the stars] are like spirits, which produce a madness similar to that of the possessed, with the only difference being the speed with which spirits act. . . . For one can go blind from looking at a fire, or at the moon, or from the sun; the fire acts most slowly, the moon next, and the sun most rapidly. But in the end the man hurt by fire is as blind as the one hurt by the moon; and those blinded by the moon are as sightless as those destroyed by the sun. . . . And so too with all the mad.[221]

In this passage we may again observe the effect of the dualist framework. Astral influence can now hardly be distinguished from demonic attack, since both were constrained to work in the same general area. Although Paracelsus remembered his triadic scheme in which mental illnesses could spring from bad food or drugs, he now had no time for this confusing or ethically trivial fact. Lunacy was here a moral disease, not one of a group of psychosomatic ailments to be classed as *privationes sensuum*. The cure for lunacy was now Christian faith, not a faith manufactured by human reason, for that too, as an artifact, could "forge the bell of insanity, because it does not come from the divine spirit, and a truly high faith cannot be founded on the beast; and so the star surpasses and destroys it, deranging head and brain."[222] Such pathetic persons had overtaxed their bestial spirits; it was as if one sought to use the sun to help one see, with the result that one went blind instead. Christians needed to take care to keep reason in its place. Luther, as we know, would have applauded sentiments such as these. For Paracelsus, such fanatics ran the risk of driving themselves to suicide.

The astral bestial spirit overcomes man's fleshly bestial spirits, and he goes crazy, mad in himself and as mixed up as a cow that has been hit on the head. Such persons run back and forth, not knowing in their stupidity where they are going, and

219. *Liber de lunaticis*, in *SW*, pt. 1, 14: 57.
220. Ibid., p. 59.
221. Ibid., pp. 59–60.
222. Ibid., pp. 60–61.

flying into rages, some running into fire, others into water. Thus these "believers" have themselves drowned or burned to death because of their deeply bestial understanding.[223]

Instead of seeking martyrdom as heretics, true Christians were to be pure in mind, overcoming even their irrational animal desires for food, drink, and sex. Men who felt lust, even in marriage, were bestial.[224] Here, then, we again find the Stoic ideal of mental health, this time carried to an ascetic extreme.

Unfortunately, it was not always easy to detect these kinds of lunacy. Madmen were generally so trapped in their own nonsense that they thought they were using their reason for high purposes. Like those suffering from astral drunkenness, some even appeared as prophets, who spoke, studied, and fantasied whatever their bestial and corrupted reason presented to them. A physician, for example, often began with the worthy project of understanding disease by understanding the stars. But gaining some fragment of wisdom from astronomy, he came to trust that science for everything, refusing all direction from God and others. "Is he not every bit as mad as those who lie in chains?" There were, Paracelsus asserted, many such mad physicians, alchemists, and artists, who did not need to be chained but who were highly dangerous all the same.[225] "Not every madman aims to kill people or do harm; but even if they do not have such desires, they are not included among the sane or excused from their madness. If anyone is dependent on the stars, he is insane according to what he depends on."[226]

Even husbands who departed from reason and followed the will of their wives were *unsinnig* (insane) since the man was supposed to be master in his house, "and anyone who does not use his own reason is a lunatic and must do what *luna* wants, that is, what his *barbaritz* wants." These ascendants and stars, after all, were not inborn in man: "[W]e take them ourselves according to what we want, and this is the false basis of astronomy and astrology and all of those who cast horoscopes and predict."[227] Merchants, for example, often forgot God's commandments and failed to love their neighbor. Desiring only material things, "he finds an ascendant that shows him the way, for they know it. Is he not mad? Yes, for anyone who abandons his creator must be crazy, mad, possessed . . . and even madder than he who lies in chains who has no reason. Those who have reason . . .

223. Ibid., p. 62.
224. Ibid., p. 63. Marriage was holy and existed only for the production and nurture of children. Paracelsus declared that any other purpose for sex was sodomy and bestiality.
225. Ibid., p. 64.
226. Ibid., p. 65.
227. Ibid.

blind themselves, abandoning God and turning against God, just like the insane whom one fastens in chains."[228]

It is evident that, like Luther, Paracelsus was capable of turning the category of madness into a gigantic moral metaphor. The truly healthy man was the rational Christian whose passions and desires were held in check. From this point of view, sickness was sin.[229] It should not surprise us, therefore, that Paracelsus strictly applied an ecclesiastical model to the cure of such madness (sin). The first step in any healing was to discover the origin of the disease, in other words, to recognize the heavenly sign under which a particular madman had fallen: whether the sun, the moon, Venus, Mars, Jupiter, Mercury, or any of thousands of others.[230] To break a man's mad and bestial understanding one had to explain his situation to him, one had to teach him. If that did not suffice, one was to tell a neighbor and together work with the sick man, hoping for a confession. In the end one should "tell it to the church." If all of these measures were not enough, then "treat him like a heathen [Matt. 18: 17] and throw him into outer darkness, so that he may not with the help of his bestial spirits corrupt the state, the land, and his own house."[231] At this point, modern commentators have shrunk back in dismay at the apparently unenlightened and inconsistent approach Paracelsus seems to have been recommending with regard to the mad. Instead of treating them with love, as he had once recommended, one was now to cast them out![232] What these scholars have missed seeing is the critical change to a more constrictive and dualist framework. In *De lunaticis*, Paracelsus was clearly dealing with madness as a form of resolute sin, not as some physical or psychosomatic ailment. What could be more reasonable in that Bible-trusting age than to treat sin-madness with the remedies of Christ, as proclaimed in Matt. 18? In the end, one had to expel the dangerous sinner from the circle of the faithful. The healthy community was now the church of Christ, from whom the heretic and the disobedient had to be ejected: "For where such bestial prophets rise up there is the devil standing alongside, waiting, driving them on, inflaming the congregation. To save the congregation from corruption they are better among the heathen than in the church."[233]

Examples of such sin-madness include relentless warriors, gamblers, whoremongers, usurers, and magicians.[234] The metaphor of sin as madness

228. Ibid., p. 66.
229. In (MP) L2 (89), fol. 143a, in a thoughtful commentary on Matt. 9:20, Paracelsus admits that sin is not literally equivalent to sickness, although closely parallel.
230. *Liber de lunaticis*, in *SW*, pt. 1, 14: 67.
231. Ibid., p. 68.
232. Pagel, *Paracelsus*, pp. 150–52; Kämmerer, *Das Leib-Seele-Geist-Problem*, p. 61.
233. *Liber de lunaticis*, *SW*, pt. 1, 14: 68.
234. Ibid., pp. 68–69.

suggested that proper treatment of the afflicted involved (1) placing a reasonable man next to the madman as a model for him, since even the mad
sinner had a reasonable side, a conscience, to which one could appeal; or
(2) fasting and praying that God should help directly. A merchant city
councilor who went mad *qua* merchant (i.e., driven by lust for money)
should be approached in his capacity as councilor, for he had a "crack in his
brain"—what we might call a serious moral psychopathology.[235] If talking
did no good, and with rich men it seldom did, one might need to take it to
the church and finally expel him. Where sin had gone so far that reason and
conscience were extinct, one might find a "mad insanity, wild, bestial, constant and beyond relief. Then it is necessary to bind them so that they do
not harm body and soul, themselves and others. We ought to follow our
duty to love our neighbor and guide him in fasting and prayer. . . . Truly,
such people are not far from being possessed," for which the proper Christian response was precisely prayer and fasting.[236] Natural remedies were
fine for merely natural diseases such as mania, but Paracelsus saw this as a
spiritual lunacy for which nature had no remedy. Such astral spirits could
only be combated by God.

And so he concluded his major treatise on the madness of sin. Considered theologically, its chief interest was the basically dualist framework in
which one was either healthy (Christian) or sick (heathen). There was no
room in this scheme for the learned heathen to whom the triadic scheme of
man could accord a special place of earthly honor. No wonder we hear con-
sonances with Luther's melodies throughout.

The same sort of transformation is evident in Paracelsus's dualist treatment of the origins of fools in *De generatione stultorum*, another of the parts
of his projected but never completed *Great Philosophy*. Paracelsus here declared that natural fools (the retarded) existed to teach man humility before
God, who saves people according to his will and not according to our wisdom. Fools were incurable by nature and Paracelsus noted that even Christ
did not heal them. They were, he thought, the result of sin, being among
the misshapen forms that emerged after the fall of Adam and Eve, hominid
forms that included murderers, gamblers, fornicators, monsters, the blind,
and the deaf, as well as fools.[237] Here we are still in the familiar world of *De
lunaticis*. Unlike in his earlier treatise *De morbis amentium*, in which fools
are seen as the curable result of bad eugenic practice, Paracelsus here denied the influence of parents, claiming instead that "Vulcan" and the stars
shaped these fetuses. Fools were those in whom the *vulcani* were still dominant, controlled by the bestial reason and bestial body. A true man used

235. Ibid., p. 70.
236. Ibid., p. 71.
237. *De generatione stultorum liber*, in *SW*, pt. 1, 14: 77.

his bestial body as an instrument, riding it like a horse, thereby breaking the force of the heavens.[238] Vulcan succeeded in making all men drunk in the womb, but fools stayed drunk all their lives, intoxicated with an astral wine that recalls for us the *mania ebriecata* of the *Great Astronomy*. Here, however, Paracelsus urged men to learn from folly. We should not ridicule such persons, but should remember that the prophets, too, were thought to be fools, and that we, who have lost God's image, must learn the folly of Christ.[239]

Repeatedly these treatises seem to contradict the firmly medical advice of *De morbis amentium* and to spurn the products of purely human reason. One reason for this shift may be that Paracelsus became more deeply Christian during the 1530s, as many scholars following Karl Sudhoff have maintained. But Andrew Weeks has argued that the strongly Christian element was present from the beginning of Paracelsus's writing career.[240] Another strong possibility is that the morally attractive dualist framework simply left him no options between sin and health, forcefully suggesting the extended metaphor in which all sickness became a form of sin, and vice versa.

DEMONIC POSSESSION AND EXORCISM

Many of these apparent contradictions are also evident in Paracelsus's copious references to demonic possession. We have already noticed that in Paracelsus's view, the devil took advantage of those who neglected their immortal souls, inspiring some to evil and possessing others physically.[241] Just as disease was metaphorically sinful for Paracelsus, so too diabolic possession might appear as a disease. In the *Opus paramirum*, he had classed it as one of the invisible diseases, and explained that one could actually become possessed by believing oneself possessed.[242] From the intensely Christian position of his later writings, Paracelsus declared that possession was a "great disease" that responded only to the cure of Christ. Christian prayer was a potent remedy.[243] Such references have shocked well-intentioned modern scholars, who had hoped that their "progressive" Paracelsus would hew to the supposedly scientific line he established in his early treatises, when he boldly declared that the diseases that rob men of reason were caused not by demons but by nature.[244] We have already seen,

---

238. Ibid., p. 84.
239. Ibid., pp. 93–94.
240. Weeks, *Paracelsus*, ch. 1 and pp. 71–75.
241. *Astronomia magna*, in *SW*, pt. 1, 12: 432–37.
242. *De causis morborum invisibilium*, in *SW*, pt. 1, 11: 256–57, 279.
243. *Sieben defensiones*, in *SW*, pt. 1, 11: 134.
244. *De morbis amentium*, in *SW*, pt. 1, 2: 393. Weeks, *Paracelsus*, is valuable on this point.

however, that Paracelsus was not actually contradicting himself when he later examined demonic possession. Like other sixteenth-century thinkers, he had little difficulty holding that natural causes could be found for a host of mental aberrations and yet maintaining that the devil also produced frenzy and madness. Paracelsus was not alone on this issue, for most contemporary physicians tried to find a way of dealing with natural causes while leaving room for the devil.

One of the biggest theological problems with regard to demonic possession was that of the freedom of the will. Usually, Paracelsus defended man's freedom against mechanical, astral, and angelic determinism. In an absolute sense, however, only God was free. Before God, man was unfree and had to wait for God, who could also "cripple your grip, cause you to go blind, to go mad, or foolish, to forget where you are, etc."[245] Here would appear to be those divine diseases whose origin was not primarily in human sin but in the inscrutable will of God. Lacking true freedom, human achievements were without true merit. Even if one succeeded in raising the dead, cleansing lepers, or driving out demons, Paracelsus asserted, one could take no credit, for it was God who did it all.[246] Sharpening this point, Paracelsus declared that although the soul had no real freedom, man did have a certain freedom to choose and work at a trade, for example.[247] This distinction may prove that Paracelsus was familiar with some of Luther's or Melanchthon's works, for this was precisely the point they made when arguing that man was not free to choose eternal life but could choose among earthly goods. In any event, it meant that persons physically possessed by demons were examples of God's power and man's weakness. One's Christian duty was to treat them well and not abandon them. "They are miserable people. . . . If God drives the devil out with his power, you will all gain the reward."[248]

In such statements it seems plain that Paracelsus was not concerned with possession as sin or the fruit of sin. Instead, he preached here the love and "happy generosity" that Christ inspired in all his spiritual followers.

How could the devil take over a person? This was one of the main questions treated in the surviving fragment of his book *On Demoniacs and the Possessed*. After Adam fell, he became so similar to Lucifer, the fallen angel, that he was now vulnerable to demonic attack. The spirit of the devil could so overpower man's spirit that he might actually control man's body. Yet possession was not crudely physical: "[H]aving no location, the spirits can-

245. *Liber prologi in vitam beatam*, in *Theophrastus Paracelsus: Werke*, ed. Peuckert, 4: 133.
246. Paracelsus asserted that these three tasks were never given to medicine. See "(Erste) Auslegung über das Evangelikum sanct Mathei" (typescript, MP), L2 (89), fol. 35a.
247. *Liber prologi in vitam beatam*, in *Theophrastus Paracelsus: Werke*, ed. Peuckert, 4: 134.
248. *Liber de felici liberalitate*, in *Theophrastus Paracelsus: Werke*, ed. Peuckert, 4: 201.

not inhabit corporeal things," and so possession was always spiritual.[249] Strictly speaking, therefore, the devil could not cause paroxysms, but he could cause such uncontrolled fear that one might fall down in helpless thrashing.[250] So too when a possessed person foamed at the mouth, Paracelsus argued that this was not the direct action of the devil but a result of fear implanted by the devil.[251] Repeating a theme we have now encountered often, Paracelsus claimed that men were themselves responsible for most cases of demonic possession. As he put it in *De inventione artium*, unregenerate man was essentially a beast, whether dog, wolf, dove, or finch.[252] Only when he was reborn from heaven did his nature leave all bestiality behind: "The devil possesses persons if they are beasts. If they are of heaven then he does not possess them. He seizes only what comes up from below. Look at the possessed persons in the gospel and all the others; they have all been bestial, and using their power the demons have gone into them."

When Jesus cast them out, the Gadarene spirits went over into pigs to show that devils could control only animals. When the devils left, the man was not left in his brutal vulnerable state but was transformed, born again from heaven. Indeed, no man possessed was ever released by the devil without a rebirth in Christ, the new creation of which Paracelsus often spoke.[253]

In this passage, Paracelsus completed an important cycle in his thought. If sickness and especially madness were frequently the result of sin, sin in turn could be the result of diabolic inspiration or possession; the only cure for possession was a rebirth in Christ. From this perspective, we can understand fully why Paracelsus was skeptical of exorcism. He took frequent aim at the false pretensions of exorcists, grouping them with deluded necromancers and conjurers, who ended up actually serving the devil.[254] Exorcisms were useless ceremonies that could in truth constitute a false religion if they went on too long.[255] Although it was true that in biblical times

---

249. *De daemoniacis et obsessis*, in *SW*, pt. 1, 14: 31.

250. Ibid., pp. 36–37. In expressing such ideas, Paracelsus joined a large stream of sixteenth-century thinkers who sought to restrict the physicial effects that one might attribute to the devil. The devil could not even cause the storms that witches attributed to him. See *De sagis*, in *SW*, pt. 1, 14: 11–12. Cf. my *Witch Hunting in Southwestern Germany, 1562–1684: The Social and Intellectual Foundations* (Stanford, 1972), pp. 37–49; Heiko Oberman, *Masters of the Reformation: The Emergence of a New Intellectual Climate in Europe*, trans. Dennis Martin (Cambridge, 1981); Stuart Clark, *Thinking with Demons: The Idea of Witchcraft in Early Modern Europe* (Oxford, 1997), pp. 161–213.

251. *De daemoniacis et obsessis*, in *SW*, pt. 1, 14: 36.

252. *Liber de inventione artium*, in *SW*, pt. 1, 14: 271.

253. Ibid., p. 272. See pp. 120, 126–28 above.

254. *Astronomia magna*, in *SW*, pt. 1, 12: 141–42, 145–46, 148, 270–71.

255. *De religione perpetua*, in *Theophrastus Paracelsus: Werke*, ed. Peuckert, 4: 158–59.

many persons had had the gift of casting out demons, even then it was no proof of godliness. Even Judas Iscariot had had the gift.[256] In the last days, Paracelsus reminded his readers, men would come saying, "Lord, Lord did we not cast out demons in your name?" but Jesus would know them not (Matt. 7:22–23; cf. Mark 16:17). In his own age, Paracelsus contended, by way of contrast, men had grown so faithless that they had lost this power to cast out the devil.[257] What sometimes appeared to be a successful exorcism was simply a trick of the devil, in which he lay still for a time, hoping to strengthen the superstitious belief in exorcisms and other ceremonies.[258] So here, too, Paracelsus echoed the skeptical comments of the Lutheran debunkers of exorcism.

Many of these ideas appear in systematic form in Paracelsus's "Eleven Sermons on the Miracles of Christ with the Possessed," a fascinating series of sermons that is still unpublished. In addition to ridiculing exorcisms, these sermons gave vent to his bitter feelings toward organized Christianity in all of its forms. As an illustration of the wiles of the devil, he pointed to the pharisaical devil's adjutants, "whom we see publicly in the papists and in the Lutherans, Zwinglians, [and] Anabaptists, who allow so many Jewish ordinances to survive."[259] The true, narrow path to God did not need universities, bishops, or pope, whereas the wide path to hell was ornamented with the charms of reason, bells, pictures, officials and a hierarchy, fancy clothing, rents, villages, castles, hounds, falcons, silk, jewels, servants, secular knowledge, and books.[260] The touchstone of one's Christianity was not successful exorcism or any of the distractions of institutional Christianity, but a simple life of good fruits.

As examples of biblical exegesis, these sermons are also of great interest. In a discussion of Mark 9:17–29, Paracelsus held that the dumb spirit who would not leave at the behest of the disciples really represents the "false preachers who withhold the truth," while the boy possessed represented the people who listen to the false preacher and are "possessed" by him. Here and elsewhere, Paracelsus went far toward spiritualizing the personal devil out of existence.[261] At times, too, Paracelsus sought to unite his secular doctrine of dangerous astra with his biblical teachings on demonic possession. Just as the stars could have "complexions" driving a man mercurial, saturnine, martial, venereal, or lunatic,[262] so, too, devils

256. *De daemoniacis et obsessis*, in *SW*, pt. 1, 14: 39–40.
257. Ibid., p. 40; "11 Sermones de miraculis" (MP), L2 (89), fol. 296a.
258. *De daemoniacis et obsessis*, in *SW*, pt. 1, 14: 40.
259. "11 Sermones de miraculis" (MP), L2 (89), fol. 296b.
260. Ibid., fols. 297b–298a.
261. Ibid., fols. 317b–318a.
262. "(Erste) Auslegung über das Evangelium sanct Mathei" (MP), L2 (89), fols. 13b–14a. See pp. 120–21, 125–26 above.

had various personalities or "complexions" (the martial, the lunatic, the saturnine, etc.) and obviously differed in the way in which they possessed a person. In Matt. 8:28, for example, the afflicted men from "the country of the Gergesenes" were possessed by what Paracelsus described as martial devils. Some devils were dumb spirits; others were loquacious *retoricisten teufel*.[263] This variation in demons made a difference in the treatment of the demon-possessed. As Paracelsus noted with respect to Matt. 17:14, devils had a variety of species (*ander und ander geschlecht*), and therefore "the devils cannot all be cast out the same way." Some hung on harder than others, requiring more than purity of faith.

Ultimately, all successful efforts at relief for the demon-possessed included basically only two elements: prayer and fasting, the tools recommended by Christ (Matt. 17:21; Mark 9:29). The potency of prayer was not surprising, since it acknowledged the supremacy of God and implored God for that conversion, or rebirth in Christ, which would free man from his bestial and diabolical servitude.[264] Fasting was harder for Paracelsus to understand, and he tried to see it as a metaphor for the life of repentance; yet Jesus, when he fasted, could not have repented of sin, because he was, of course, without sin.[265] So Paracelsus tried to see fasting as a commitment to higher wisdom, a symbol of sobriety and escape from bestiality.[266] Ultimately, fasting remained an inexplicable but Christ-commanded weapon in the fight against the evil one. Of course, the casting out of devils remained literally a pious hope, since no one living in the sinful declining days of human history could expect to recapture the gift of the apostles.

Conclusion

Paracelsus repeatedly insisted that human beings, as human, were beyond all disease and corruption; the Christian was a new unfallen creation made over in the image of Christ. The corollary of this view was that sickness and demonic possession rendered one distinctly less than human, and Paracelsus could even declare flatly, "Ein krank mensch ist kein mensch" ("A sick man is no man at all").[267] Madness was for him a gigantic symbol for all of

263. "Die andere ausslegung über das Evangelium sanct Mathei" (MP), L2 (89), fols. 142a, 143b.

264. *De daemoniacis et obsessis*, in *SW*, pt. 1, 14: 41; *Liber de inventione artium*, in ibid., p. 272; *Liber de lunaticis*, in ibid., pp. 53–54.

265. *De daemoniacis et obsessis*, in *SW*, pt. 1, 14: 41–42.

266. *Liber de inventione artium*, in *SW*, pt. 1, 14: 272.

267. "Die ander auslegung über den Evangelisten Matthaeus" (MP) L2 (89), fol. 182 b. To get the flavor of Paracelsus's reasoning on this matter, one needs the full context: "der aber krank ist, der ist nit selbst meister, weder zu gutem noch zu bösem . . . der gesund ist

the bestial tendencies that destroyed one's felicity in Christ. This harsh language of rejection did not, however, mean that Paracelsus advocated a program of exile or euthanasia by which his society might rid itself of its subhuman members. For one thing, Paracelsus had no confidence in the spiritual capacities of the state. He thought that Christianity had been in decline ever since the fourth century, when the emperor Constantine had employed Christ as a prop for his state.[268] In addition, true Christians were hard to detect among the mass of hypocrites and anti-Christs who multiplied "in these last days."

Instead of killing or eliminating the subhuman (the mad, the possessed, the sick), one's Christian duty was to love them and to attempt to heal (convert) them to the Way of Life. The physician's calling was a high one precisely because it was so close to that of Christ himself. Referring to the physician's art, Paracelsus declared, "Wo kein lieb ist, do ist keine kunst" ("Where there is no love there is also no art").[269] Even witches, those hateful creatures who were devoted to the devil body and soul, deserved better from Christian society. Instead of burning them to death for their supposed crimes, Paracelsus held, Christians should pray and fast in order to drive out the evil spirit and heal them with Christ.[270]

We are now in a position to see why two figures so widely, even wildly, divergent as Luther and Paracelsus, could agree on certain fundamentals regarding mental, moral, and spiritual health. Both men were rooted in the Western tradition of seeing sin as disease, and disease as often a punishment for or the very embodiment of sin.[271] Luther was surely original in the vehement force with which he attacked the enemies of truth (his truth) as demonic fools, madmen, and self-blinded maniacs. And Paracelsus was surely original in his union of the languages of Scripture, chemistry, and astrology, the symbolic and syncretic net with which he hoped to capture the whole man. His use of both dualist and triadic schemes for understanding the microcosm suited his need to find order in the chaos of life as he found it. But both Luther and Paracelsus, for all their originality, were speaking for sixteenth-century Germans when they assumed that divine salvation

---

im mittel, und hat die urteil frei und verständig. darzue hat er ihm geholfen, daß sie gesund seindt worden, und aber nach der gesundheit volkombnen verstand brauchen, der dann einem gesunden menschen zuhört. ein krank mensch ist kein mensch; ist ein gefangner mensch und soll nichts und ist nichts; und ihm ist nichts zeitlichs nutz . . . Dann wer krank ist, weißt nit. dann wann er gesund wer, er tet ihm anderst. darumb ist er eigentlich seines rechten verstands beraubt, al wol als der besessen."

268. "11 Sermones de miraculis" (MP), L2 (89), fols. 302a–b.

269. *De caducis: Von den hinfallenden siechtagen*, in *SW*, pt. 1, 8: 263.

270. *De sagis et earum operibus*, in *SW*, pt. 1, 14: 13–14.

271. Susan Sontag, *Illness as Metaphor* (New York, 1978); Pedro Lain Entralgo, *Enfermidad y pecado* (Barcelona, 1961).

was an intensely rational, health-giving process, bringing order, restraint, reason, and inner peace to bestial, lunatic, and demonic human beings. At their best, people could understand that they had been created in the image of God and were, therefore, capable of receiving or cultivating a divine rationality. But madness was unfortunately at the very heart of secular reality in the last, declining days of the world, and it should never be forgotten that the ruler of this world was Satan, who went about like a lion, seeking whom he might devour. If one gave in to the world or to a lower nature in one's soul, one was giving in to a frantic and desperate insanity that could destroy and destroy utterly. Sin and demonic possession were not just a matter of disobedient error, thoughtless excess, or foolish pride, but were disfiguring, dehumanizing, utterly alienating conditions. These two German reformers did not agree on much else, but in their moral seriousness, they both saw madness as an ultimate threat to the order and peace to which God called all true believers. In the thoughts of Luther and Paracelsus, we can glimpse some of the deepest assumptions, the often unarticulated or precognitive foundations, on which sixteenth-century Germans (and many other Europeans) tried to construct a Christian understanding of the fallen world and its madness.

Perhaps everyone would agree that Luther used such a highly metaphorical and theologically charged language of madness that there would be little point in trying to find modern psychiatric terminology in which to express his conclusions about the devil, the world, and the enemies of the gospel. Perhaps it will now be clear, too, that Paracelsus had such transparently religious and moral goals that his frequent medical discussions of insanity, stupor, retardation, folly, and suffocation of the mind are best left in their context, lest we blunder into the terrain of theology with the clumsy instruments of modern medicine.[272] Of course, a modern psychiatrist is likely to suffer occasional shocks of recognition in Paracelsus's almost Rabelaisian rambunction of diagnostic categories and therapeutic strategies, but this chapter makes plain how futile it would be to attempt to translate these Paracelsan "lucid intervals," these moments of recognition, into modern medical insights. As Andrew Weeks puts it, Paracelsus "assimilates nature to the mysteries of faith: by carrying over the mysteries of faith into nature."[273]

272. In his own century, opponents of Paracelsus often couched their arguments in religious terms. See Charles D. Gunnoe, Jr., "Thomas Erastus and His Circle of Anti-Paracelsians," in *Analecta Paracelsica: Studien zum Nachleben Theophrast von Hohenheims im deutschen Kulturgebiet der frühen Neuzeit*, ed. Joachim Telle (Stuttgart, 1994), pp. 127–48; Carlos Gilly, "'Theophrastia Sancta': Der Paracelsismus als Religion im Streit mit den offiziellen Kirchen," in *Analecta*, ed. Telle, pp. 425–88.

273. Weeks, *Paracelsus*, p. 162.

It is also obvious that religious language is not the only obstacle we moderns face in trying to understand the ways in which madness was experienced and treated. The professional medical approach can sometimes seem just as strange, and grasping the discourse of sixteenth-century physicians requires a separate chapter.

CHAPTER THREE

Academic "Psychiatry" and the Rise of Galenic Observation

The Early Sixteenth Century

STUDIES of Renaissance psychology, especially when inspired by great Renaissance poets, such as Shakespeare, or painters, such as Albrecht Dürer, have often assumed that starting with Marsiglio Ficino in fifteenth-century Florence, and continuing for almost two hundred years, intellectuals operated unquestioningly with a basic humoral psychology, which they mixed variously with the Platonic writings, Aristotle's *De anima*, and sometimes with Pseudo-Aristotle's *Problems*. Renaissance humanists and academics, we are told, all agreed in finding the roots of madness in an excess of the melancholy humor (black bile). We usually think of this as a crucial "background" for understanding the art and literature of the Renaissance, but as a result, the medical history of the sixteenth century flattens out. Although historians of medicine have celebrated the important innovations in anatomical studies, they have mainly agreed that sixteenth-century medicine and psychology stagnated, trapped in a stultifying humanist scientific tradition and not yet able to muster the imagination required for the medical revolution of the seventeenth century. With no scientific breakthroughs to report, historians of psychology have described the gloomy and virtually static dominance of black bile.[1] Dürer's canonical engraving *Melencolia I*, that brooding portrait of Renaissance genius (Fig. 2), has be-

1. Stanley Jackson's excellent *Melancholia and Depression: From Hippocratic Times to Modern Times* (New Haven, 1986) summarizes much work in this historical tradition. See also Raymond Klibansky, Fritz Saxl, and Erwin Panofsky, *Saturn and Melancholy: Studies in the History of Natural Philosophy, Religion, and Art* (New York, 1964); E. Ruth Harvey, *The Inward Wits: Psychological Theory in the Middle Ages and the Renaissance* (London, 1975); Lawrence Babb, *The Elizabethan Malady: A Study of Melancholia in English Literature from 1580 to 1642* (East Lansing, Mich., 1951); George Sarton, *Six Wings: Men of Science in the Renaissance* (Bloomington, Ind., 1957); Erwin Ackerknecht, *A Short History of Medicine* (Baltimore, 1982);

come for many an emblem for the whole age, reinforcing an uninformed assumption that madness in general and melancholy in particular were prominent as cultural and medical illnesses in early sixteenth-century Germany.

Despite the prominence of folly as a theme in German literature and painting, however, and despite deep artistic and theological ruminations concerning the depressed and melancholy state of the world, German physicians were far from agreed about the origins of mental disorder or the best ways to handle it. The medical treatment of madness—what we might anachronistically call psychiatry—was poorly represented among the medical arts and was not yet part of the rigorous academic tradition in Germany. When German physicians of the early sixteenth century expressed themselves on questions of mental disorder, their writings had a vulgar or popular tone and a naive or simple content that would come to seem distinctly superstitious and incoherent by the professionally esoteric standards of only seventy-five years later. These early Renaissance physicians often ran the risk of drifting away from the medical teachings of the ancients into theology or empirical herbalism. Elsewhere I have argued that in the early sixteenth century, most of the mentally disordered princes of the Holy Roman Empire did not obtain the diagnosis of melancholy or the therapy that such a diagnosis would require, even when they were lucky enough to be attended by a personal physician.[2] So if even the German physicians were little concerned with melancholy, it should not surprise us to find very little melancholy among the German madnesses of the early 1500s. We can confirm this point in almost any of the German medical writings from the early part of the century.[3]

An emblematic example of the early sixteenth century is the controversial Walther Hermann Ryff (d. 1548), a famous medical popularizer, whose numerous works often rashly and radically reduced all illnesses, including madness, to pharmacological problems best treated with fruits, herbs, flowers, wine, and sugar.[4] Although reviled by Conrad Gesner, Leonhart Fuchs,

---

id., *A Short History of Psychiatry*, 2d ed., trans. Sula Wolff, (New York, 1968); "*Komm, heilige Melancholie": Eine Anthologie deutscher Melancholie-Gedichte mit Ausblicken auf die europäische Melancholie-Tradition in Literatur- und Kunstgeschichte*, ed. Ludwig Völker (Stuttgart, 1983); and *The Medical Renaissance of the Sixteenth Century*, ed. R. K. French, I. M. Lonie, and Andrew Wear (Cambridge, 1985).

2. *Mad Princes*, pp. 31–46.

3. Useful bibliographical guides to this large literature include J. B. Friedreich, *Versuch einer Literärgeschichte der Pathologie und Therapie der psychischen Krankheiten von den ältesten Zeiten bis zum 19. Jahrhundert* (Würzburg, 1830); id., *Systematische Literatur der ärztlichen und gerichtlichen Psychologie* (Berlin, 1833); Theodor Kirchhoff, *Grundriß einer Geschichte der deutschen Irrenpflege* (Berlin, 1890); and Heinrich Laehr, *Die Literatur der Psychiatrie, Neurologie, und Psychologie von 1459–1799* (Berlin, 1900).

4. Walther Hermann Ryff, *Warhaffige künstliche und gerechte underweisung und anzeygung,*

and Andreas Vesalius as a vulgarian and plagiarist, Ryff well represented the editorial energies and philosophical naïveté of German medical writers from the early sixteenth century. It is hard to find any order, scheme, or theory behind his references to mental illness, and he seems a perfect illustration of early German Renaissance medicine, so perfect, in fact, that like any extreme example, he seems to stack the deck. Equally telling, however, is the example of Johann Tollat of Vochenberg, who in 1502 published his *Margarita medicine*, in which he laid claim to the help of his adviser, "the most experienced physician, Dr. Schrick," of the "world famous University of Vienna."[5] His short treatise was actually just another list of herbal remedies for a chaotic hodgepodge of human ills and diseases; it lacks even the normal anatomical order that organized medical discussions to range from the ills of the head down to those of the foot. Tollat affirmed that anyone desiring the gift of chastity should inscribe the paternoster on a sheet of paper and carry it with him: "It takes away evil desires and makes one chaste." But if that proved ineffective, "boxwood drives out the devil too, so that he can have no place in the house, and therefore Platearius says one should bless [the house] on Palm Sunday." So useful was boxwood that one could use it for illnesses of the brain as well, if one ground up the leaves and mixed them with lavender water.[6] There were other herbs to use against demons. Carrying *berivica jugrien* (whatever that was) on one's person deprived the devil of all his power; and hanging it over one's door prevented all evil magic. If witches should enter a house so protected, they would complain at once that they had been betrayed and flee. "So with this herb one can gauge which people have the evil spirit in them."[7] Carrying a black agate also rendered the devil powerless, "so that he cannot do what he gladly would . . . And thus Magister Enax says that it is good against diabolical melancholy."[8] We can easily locate other examples of popular

---

Alle Latwegen, Confect, Conserven, eynbeytzungen und einmachungen . . . wie solche in den Apotheken gemacht (Strasbourg, 1540). See the hostile remarks of Lynn Thorndike, *A History of Magic and Experimental Science*, vol. 5: *The Sixteenth Century* (New York, 1941), pp. 442–43. One gains an impression of his output from Richard Durling, *A Catalog of Sixteenth-Century Printed Books in the National Library of Medicine* (Bethesda, Md., 1967), nos. 4014–41.

5. Johann Tollat [von Vochenberg], *Arznei Büchlein der Kreutter, oder Margarita medicine* (Augsburg, 1502); this was a later edition of Tollat's *Ain meisterlichs Büchlin der Artzney für manigerley Kranckheit und Siechtagen der Menschen* ([Memmingen], 1497). I have used the edition entitled *Margarita medicine, ein meisterlichs usserlesens biechlin der artzny für mancherley kranckheit und siechtagen der menschen* (Strasbourg, 1507), citing information from the title page. Tollat's little book was popular for over thirty years. The *Katalog des Bibliotheksverbundes Bayern* lists these additional editions: Erfurt, n.d.; Augsburg, 1507; Strasbourg, 1512; Augsburg, 1514; Nuremberg, 1516; Nuremberg, 1517; Strasbourg, 1518; Augsburg, 1529; Augsburg, 1530; Augsburg, 1532; Leipzig, 1532.

6. Ibid., fol. 10 v.
7. Ibid., fol. 11 v.
8. Ibid., fol. 22 r.

FIG. 2. Albrecht Dürer, *Melencolia I*. Courtesy Metropolitan Museum of Art, New York.

spirit lore in which pharmacy was confused with demonology. It is striking, however, that Tollat appealed to learned authorities in order to construct this oddly eclectic argument. Writings like those of Ryff and Tollat
were more characteristic of German vernacular medicine of the early sixteenth century than medical historians have been comfortable admitting.

In a little book by Johann Schöner of Karlstadt (1477–1547), we again find
brief, vague assertions and a remarkable naïveté with respect to mental disorders. Trained as a theologian, mathematician, and astrologer, Schöner was
eager to publish the diverse recipes and cures he had assembled. From the
outset, he stressed that one had to match any cure to the time of year and to
the twelve signs of the zodiac and the twenty-eight mansions of the moon.
In this respect, he well represents the popularity of astrology in the German
lands of the early sixteenth century. But Schöner proceeded to ignore his
own scholarly precepts and descended to the rank "empiricism" and un-
theoretical, hand-me-down maxims of the common herbalist. "When someone goes mad, he should be often treated with *Meisterwurtz* [*Peucedanum
ostruthium* (L.) Koch] and 'the herb'; soak a cloth in the cooked herb and
bind it to the head, and he will come to his senses. Or give him gentian and
rue seed in vinegar to drink. Or give him swallow's heart in honey to eat."[9]
That was his prescription for all mental disorders, and it is little wonder that
the crudity of vernacular medicine confirmed some academic physicians in
their search for a less popular and more theoretical approach.

We find a more refined and more thoughtful analysis, for example, in
the works of Lorenz Fries (1490?–1531), a physician from Colmar who defended Arab medicine against its contemporary philo-Hellenic humanist
detractors. In Fries we find none of the gross confusion of matter with
spirits that we find in Tollat, none of the desultory herbalism characteristic of Schöner, but instead a systematic effort to interpret all human ills in
physical terms. Even Aristotle had misled many, "not only by slandering
the divine art [of medicine] but also by turning many of his disciples
from the true path."[10] To recover the respect of jurists, philosophers, and
poets for the practice of medicine, Fries insisted that his art was much
more than the often-ridiculed analysis of urine. It was, properly, a holy art
requiring exact knowledge of human nature (e.g., the seven naturals, three
counter-naturals, and six non-naturals). In practice, Fries recommended
a humoral and herbal therapy that counteracted disease by increasing
or decreasing the qualities of hotness, coldness, wetness, and dryness, in
the manner familiar to medical historians from more famous Italian and
French Renaissance medical treatises. As an intellectual construct, this

9. Johann Schöner von Karlstadt, *Ein nutzlichs büchlein viler bewerter Ertzney, lang zeyt
versamlet und züsammen pracht* (Nuremberg: [1528]), fol. E4 r–v.
10. Laurentius Fries, *Spiegel der Artzny* (Strasbourg, 1519), fol. 1 v. I have also used the
expanded edition by Otto Brunfels (Strasbourg, 1532).

sort of medicine marked a real difference from and progress beyond the vernacular chaos of Tollat and the thoughtless empiricism of Schöner. On mental disorder, for example, Fries described the physician's main task as discovering the source of the illness, from which one could deduce a remedy. If a patient suffered headaches from too much black bile, for example, he would very likely be unable to sleep, be full of fears, and show a leaden or pale face, a slow, small pulse, and clear urine. "Treat him by giving him a good routine and see to it that he is not sad." Every morning he was to receive four half-ounces of *oximellis* (a mixture of vinegar and honey) blended with the water of oxtongue (*Picris echioides*).[11] Like others of his generation, Fries also gave melancholy extremely short shrift even though, within a few decades, it became the premier disease of the sixteenth century, encouraging (and responding to) the growth of a dense literature, to which we shall turn in due course.[12]

Fries considered mania a more complex disease. It had a wide variety of causes such as too much wine, the bite of a rabid dog, poisonous air, or even highly seasoned food. Any of the four humors could be corrupted to produce mania as well. If the patient had too much blood, he might "talk constantly, dance, hop about, sing, and be gay, desiring to hear harp music all the time. His pulse is [commonly] fast and hard, his urine red and thick, and his age eighteen to twenty. His complexion is warm and moist, and the season is also warm and moist."[13] On other occasions, it was corrupt choler that caused mania—complaining, screaming, murderous drives. At still other times, phlegm was at fault, producing the delusion that one was surrounded by water or causing a continuous sleep. And finally, of course, black bile or melancholy could induce a mania that was characterized by constant sadness and fearfulness, the sense of being "among dead and monstrous things" and the constant worry "that someone would catch him."[14] With all the confidence of a systematician, Fries provided humoral and herbal prescriptions for all of these serious disorders. Even when dealing with sexual complaints, Fries scrupulously avoided moralizing comment and contented himself with adjusting the patient's bodily fluids.[15] In so doing, he was practicing the physician's reduction, that traditional attitude of somatic interpretation by which medical doctors set themselves off from their philosophical, theological, and juridical colleagues.

When Philipp Melanchthon undertook to describe the soul and its ills,

11. Ibid., fol. 96 r.

12. The only other detailed study of the "rise of melancholy" in the sixteenth century is Noel Brann, "Renaissance Passion of Melancholy: The Paradox of Its Cultivation and Resistance" (diss., Stanford University, 1965).

13. Fries, *Spiegel*, fol. 101v.

14. Ibid., fol. 101v.

15. Ibid., fols. 157v, 160v–162r, 172v.

both physical and spiritual, he seems to have followed Fries's exposition rather closely.[16] Inevitably, this caused Melanchthon some trouble, for a thoroughgoing somatic reductionism could not well be brought to agree with man's nature as a moral or political agent. Sin had to originate in the free will of man and of the devil.[17] Without freedom, man would be no more than a cow, Melanchthon thought, incapable of sin and hence beyond all punishment, even that of God.[18] And so the theologian had at some point to abandon the somatic medical model in order to avoid serious political and theological trouble. For most theologians, as indeed for most persons, man was more than his humors.

But for the medical academic, the charms of somatic reductionism were precisely that it excluded extraneous concerns and allowed a retreat from (or advance beyond) the dolors of common sense. On reflection, it seems that one of the tacitly accepted features of any profession or discipline is a sturdy rejection of what we usually think of as "common sense." As Renaissance German physicians recoiled from the popular culture of vulgar empiricism, they came to appreciate more fully the richness of the ancient Galenic theory. Despite the legendary discoveries of Vesalius and others, academic "psychiatry" in Germany became not less but more Galenist in the second half of the sixteenth century. And one reason for this was that Galen, for some of the same philosophical reasons, had been keen to preserve the realm of human freedom.

The appeal of ancient Galen, however, rested on more than his political correctness. He had a well-deserved reputation for keen observation and systematic rigor, having invented a medicine that attempted to reconcile the even more ancient Plato, Aristotle, and Hippocrates. From Plato, he drew the notion that the body has three chief systems, the heart (or circulatory system), the liver (the alimentary system), and the brain (the nervous system), each of which had connections to mental states. By Aristotle, he was inspired to emphasize hands-on investigation and rigorous logic. From Hippocrates, he derived an effort to find regular patterns in what he observed, the unity, in other words, of reason and experience. The good Galenic doctor was a philosopher.[19] On this basis, Galen could argue, eclectically, that mental disturbances were sometimes due to accidents (such as a blow to the head), sometimes to fevers (producing phrenitis and brain fever), and sometimes to hereditary flaws (which produced retarda-

16. Melanchthon, *Commentarius de Anima* (Wittenberg, 1548), fols. 76r–77r.

17. Ibid., fol. 141v. This is a point developed fully by Sachiko Kusukawa, *The Transformation of Natural Philosophy: The Case of Philip Melanchthon* (Cambridge, 1995).

18. Ibid., fol. 142v. This was a theological commonplace; see Johannes Altenstaig, *Vocabularius Theologiae* (Hagenau, 1517), fol. 184r, s.v. *peccatum*.

19. Vivian Nutton, "The Rise of Medicine," in *The Cambridge Illustrated History of Medicine*, ed. Roy Porter (Cambridge, 1996), pp. 52–81, at p. 62.

tion, for example), but at other times to disturbances of the four bodily juices, or humors. This last point had always been of surpassing theoretical interest to physicians, because it held out the opportunity for theorizing about the connections or correspondences between the four humors (blood, phlegm, yellow bile, and black bile), the four elements (air, water, fire, and earth), the four seasons (spring, winter, summer, and autumn), the four ages of man, and four of the planets: Venus or Jupiter, the moon, Mars, and Saturn.

Keeping these humors in balance was the task of diet and the daily regimen of sleep, play, exercise, human company, sexual activity, and intellection. Too much heat, cold, smoke, moisture, too much study or worry, the wrong foods or beverages, the wrong music, could all affect one's humoral "balance," and thus one's physical complexion or temperament. And when one's bodily humors went out of balance, the result could be mental disturbances such as rage, anxiety, apathy, or deep sadness. If an imbalance lasted too long, or if one lived a life of excess and immoderation, the natural humors could also become overheated or roasted, producing in turn an unnatural, alien humor that Galenic physicians called *melancholia adusta*, or burnt black bile, a dangerous substance that could easily lead to deep depressions, optical and aural hallucinations, sudden outbursts of wrath or weeping, and general madness. The longer these conditions lasted, the harder they were to cure. Revived first by the Arabs, summarized by Avicenna (d. 1037) in his *Canon*, and rejuvenated during the Renaissance, first in Italy, this ancient body of doctrines and methods showed remarkable flexibility and tenacity.[20] It was thus a whole system of inquiry that German physicians revived when they showed a renewed interest in discovering exactly what Galen had meant.

The Rise of Humanist Medicine

This growing German familiarity with Galen, not only among physicians but among classically educated readers generally, is parallel to what we know of medical literature throughout Europe. Although with hindsight we may look back to the sixteenth century searching for signs of experimentation and clinical observation, for rumblings of protomodern discon-

20. The best discussion of the whole Galenic system is perhaps Owsei Temkin, *Galenism: The Rise and Decline of a Medical Philosophy* (Ithaca, N.Y., 1973); see also Per-Gunnar Ottosson, *Scholastic Medicine and Philosophy: A Study of Commentaries on Galen's Tegni, ca. 1300–1450* (Naples, 1984); Nancy Siraisi, *Medieval and Early Renaissance Medicine: An Introduction to Knowledge and Practice* (Chicago, 1990); Harvey, *Inward Wits*; Klibansky, Panofsky, and Saxl, *Saturn and Melancholy*; Werner Leibbrand and Annemarie Wettley, *Der Wahnsinn: Geschichte der abendländischen Psychopathologie* (Freiburg im Breisgau, 1961).

TABLE 3.1
Printed Editions of Avicenna's Canon, 1470–1674

	Latin	Arabic and Hebrew
1470–1500	14	1
1501–1520	15	0
1521–1540	14	0
1541–1560	7	0
1561–1580	5	0
1581–1600	3	1
1601–1620	3	1
1621–1640	1	0
1641–1674	6	2
Total	68	5

SOURCE: Nancy G. Siraisi, *Avicenna in Renaissance Italy: The Canon and Medical Teaching in Italian Universities After 1500* (Princeton, 1987).

TABLE 3.2
Printed Editions of Aristotle, 1466–1600

1466–1480	40
1481–1500	124
1501–1520	211
1521–1540	190
Subtotal	565
1541–1560	576
1561–1580	281
1581–1600	162
Subtotal	1,019

SOURCE: F. Edward Cranz and Charles B. Schmitt, *A Bibliography of Aristotle Editions, 1501–1600*, 2d rev. ed. (Baden-Baden, 1984).

tent with the doctrines of ancient medicine, it can be shown that most medical faculties and most medical writings were as firmly Galenic in 1600 as ever. Nancy Siraisi has even demonstrated the survival of Avicenna's Canon in sixteenth-century Italian medical instruction (table 3.1), while the simplest publication statistics make the same point for Aristotle's corpus (table 3.2).[21]

From tables 3.1 and 3.2, and from the research of Charles B. Schmitt and F. Edward Cranz,[22] it is obvious that there was a surge of humanist editions and translations of Aristotle after about 1535. It is especially noteworthy that there were almost twice as many editions of Aristotle of all sorts from

21. Charles B. Schmitt, *Aristotle and the Renaissance* (Cambridge, Mass., 1983).
22. F. Edward Cranz and Charles B. Schmitt, *A Bibliography of Aristotle Editions, 1501–1600*, 2d rev. ed. (Baden-Baden, 1984).

1541 to 1600 as in the seventy-five year period before 1541. Medical faculties across Europe regarded Aristotle as a fundamental basis for their teaching and research throughout the sixteenth century. Pointing to the great anatomist Fabricius of Aquapendente (1537–1619), Andrew Cunningham has even argued persuasively that an Aristotelian research program was under way in anatomical studies at Padua in the late sixteenth century.[23] Far from being merely an ancient authority, Aristotle was still inspiring novel observations and a research method that aimed at uncovering the "causes of things." I argue in this chapter that many physicians were drawn to a roughly analogous program of "Galenic observation." Such observational research did not directly change the theory or practice of Renaissance "psychiatry," but it prompted physicians in the mid to late seventeenth century to suffer real pangs of anxiety as they came to realize, even without the use of the newly invented microscope, that the melancholy humor could not be identified, isolated, or localized within the human body. Such anxieties lay well off in the future for sixteenth-century physicians, however. For them, Aristotle still provided the crucial definitions and distinctions of causes and categories. *De anima* was one of the most popular Aristotelian texts of all. By 1600, it had been printed in 21 Greek editions, 38 vulgate (medieval) Latin editions, and 99 humanist Latin translations, to say nothing of the two vernacular Italian editions and over fifty scholarly commentaries.[24] There can be little doubt: "everyone" knew Aristotle in 1500; and by 1600, he was even better known. And the revival of Hippocrates and Galen in humanist editions seems to have inspired a late-sixteenth-century surge of what I have called Galenic observation, as we shall see.

Like Avicenna and Aristotle, Galen and Hippocrates also underwent a dramatic Renaissance of new and improved editions. Richard Durling compiled the basic Renaissance Galen bibliography thirty years ago, proving that Galen editions also peaked in the middle of the sixteenth century.

This is also true of Galen's only treatise specifically on melancholy. While not one of Galen's most famous works by any means, *De atra bile* nonetheless enjoyed 22 editions in the Renaissance, and scholars in the late sixteenth century could now more easily than ever before determine just what Galen's views on the sticky black humor were.

From many parts of Galen's *Opera*, one could gather that both yellow bile and black bile (in fact, all four humors) had both natural and corrupt, burnt forms. And one could speak of the normal need for natural black bile

23. Andrew Cunningham, "Fabricius and the 'Aristotle project' in Anatomical Teaching and Research at Padua," in *The Medical Renaissance of the Sixteenth Century*, ed. A. Wear, R. K. French, and I. M. Lonie (Cambridge, 1985), pp. 195–222.

24. Cranz and Schmitt, *Bibliography of Aristotle Editions, 1501–1600*.

as a useful thickener for some of the body's parts.²⁵ From this conclusion, one could extrapolate the further point that a person could suffer from an imbalance or excess of natural melancholy. Black bile, however, could become much more malignant (κακοηθέστερα μὲν πολὺ) when, in a corroded or over-roasted condition, it gained a sharp, vinegary corrosive quality, producing a seething, bubbling fermentation that the overburdened or weakened spleen could no longer cope with.²⁶ So dramatically different was natural black bile from its corrupt and roasted form that Galen even supposed that most of the ancient physicians called the natural form the "black humor" (μέλανα . . . χυμόν) and "not black bile" ('οὐ μέλαιναν χολήν), a name they reserved for the burnt, putrefied, sour form.²⁷ Natural melancholy might have a combined drying and chilling action, as one might guess from the description of the cold, dry humor; but the over-roasted black bile was a "warm substance, able to burn, dissolve, and destroy the flesh."²⁸

By recovering the complexity of Galen's description of melancholy, Renaissance physicians equipped themselves to use the basically simple humoral system to explain (and perhaps, therefore, to notice) a novel variety of symptoms and reactions. Renaissance physicians with their humanist editions of Hippocrates, Galen, and Aristotle, therefore, did more than just guarantee the survival of ancient texts. They created a body of texts far more complex and complete than those the medieval physician had ever had before him. Sixteenth-century academic physicians could now engage in a favorite humanist enterprise, the collation of medical authorities on debated points, and, increasingly, in the disaggregation of one author after another from the mass of hitherto undifferentiated ancient medicine. Unlike medieval scholastics, who often enjoyed finding the harmony of apparently discordant authors (as in the famous project of proving the *concordantia discordantium canonum*), Renaissance academics could revel in the variety of ancient views. Instead of sounding like the naive herbalists of the early sixteenth century, a learned physician could now sound a distinctly humanist note.

When they looked carefully at the ancient physicians, however, humanists could now detect hitherto unsuspected difficulties in the interpretation of key concepts, such as melancholy.²⁹ A comparison of Galen with Hip-

25. Galen *On the Natural Faculties* 2.9.135; trans. Arthur John Brock (London, 1916) (Loeb Classical Library), pp. 209–15.
26. Ibid., 136; Brock trans., Loeb ed., p. 211.
27. Ibid.
28. Ibid., 137; Brock trans., Loeb ed., p. 213.
29. For the following, see R. F. Timken-Zinkann, "Black Bile: A Review of Recent Attempts to Trace the Origin of the Teachings on Melancholia to Medical Observations," *Medical History* 12 (1968): 288–92; and Hellmut Flashar, *Melancholie und Melancholiker* (Berlin,

TABLE 3.3

Printed Editions of Galen, 1473–1600

	De Atra Bile*	Collected Works	Total Galen Editions
1473–1480	0	0	3
1481–1500	1	1	18
1501–1520	1	3	35
1521–1540	5	2	203
1541–1560	9	7	198
1561–1580	4	4	69
1581–1600	2	2	42
Total	22	19	568

SOURCE: Richard Durling, "A Chronological Census of Renaissance Editions and Translations of Galen," *Journal of the Warburg and Courtauld Institutes* 24 (1961): 230–305.
*Includes separate editions and reprints as part of an edition of the collected works.

TABLE 3.4

Printed Editions of Hippocrates, 1473–1650

	Works on or by Hippocrates
1473–1480	6
1481–1500	31
1501–1520	40
1521–1540	109
1541–1560	188
1561–1580	131
1581–1600	119
1601–1620	100
1621–1640	117
1641–1650	61
Total Editions	902

SOURCE: Tabulated from Gilles Maloney and R. Savoie, *Cinq cent ans de bibliographie hippocratique, 1473–1982* (St.-Jean-Chrysostome, Quebec, 1982).

pocrates might show, for example, that while Hippocrates almost always spoke of black bile as a corruption of yellow bile, and therefore as a pathogen, Galen in contrast regularly regarded the black humor as one of the four natural humors. From Galen's point of view, melancholy was a dark, sticky, viscous but normal fluid, whose excess could produce the normal melancholy complexion. The Hippocratic writings surprisingly often assumed the existence of only three humors (blood, phlegm, bile); yet in *De*

1966). The most recent expert review of this problematic substance is in Volker Langholf, *Medical Theories in Hippocrates: Early Texts and the "Epidemics"* (Berlin, 1990), pp. 46–50, 267–69.

natura hominis, the Hippocratic author followed the force of a logical *Systemzwang* and elevated black bile to the status of an independent humor. In the process, he may even have prompted his fellow Greeks to think of autumn (cold and dry, like melancholy) as a separate season for the first time. Careful students of Galen and Hippocrates could not fail to see that black bile was a highly problematic substance, a kind of bile, perhaps, but a separate humor all the same. No wonder so many late Renaissance treatises and disputations were devoted to the bleak humor. Humanist and philological concerns thus encouraged a new attention to melancholy and hence to madness, its forms, and its causes.

German "Psychiatry" at Midcentury: Jason Pratensis

By the mid sixteenth century, this more classical, humanist orientation in Germanic "psychiatry" is amply on display in the work of a Dutchman, Jason Pratensis (1486–1558; originally van de Velde), a physician from Zierikzee, southwest of Rotterdam. Working as the personal physician to Adolf van Bourgondië, margrave of Veere, and serving also as the town physician of Veere, Pratensis not only turned out a series of medical texts dealing with sterility, birth, and the uterus but also found time to publish elegant Latin verses (1530) that earned him a local reputation for refinement.[30] In 1549, he published his last book, *De cerebri morbis*, "On the Diseases of the Brain," a volume of 540 pages divided into 33 chapters and covering every cerebral disorder and disease from headache to dimwittedness, from loss of memory, epilepsy, drunkenness, tremors, and convulsions to frenzy, lethargy, catalepsy, mania, melancholy, and love.[31] A recent author has praised Pratensis for writing "the first neurology book," but the term seems ill considered.[32] Pratensis did not break away from the ancient and medieval humoral tradition to emphasize the nerves in some new way, even though it is true enough that this book was probably the first full-length consideration of all the topics that would later fall within the domain of neurology, as well as much else besides.

Two chapters of *De cerebri morbis* deal directly with madness, mania, and melancholy (i.e., chapters. 17 and 18, pp. 213–94). Pratensis tells us that these two disorders cannot be so easily distinguished as one might suppose, because they proceeded from the same causes. Even so, they differed

---

30. A. J. van der Aa, *Biographisch Woordenboek der Nederlanden* (Haarlem, 1852–78; repr., Amsterdam, 1969), 6, section P: 139–40.

31. Pratensis, *De cerebri morbis* (Basel, 1549).

32. Alan Pestronk, "The First Neurology Book, *De cerebri morbis* . . . (1549) by Jason Pratensis," *Archives of Neurology* 45 (1988): 341–44.

dramatically in their symptoms. Mania was a mental corruption without fever that "carries a man outside his own mind and wretchedly beyond the use of all reason."[33] The afflicted was so out of control that he seemed possessed by demons. In fact, he might well be possessed, for

it happens truly that demons, inasmuch as they are thin and incomprehensible spirits, insinuate themselves into the bodies of men; and thus, hidden in the guts they weaken him secretly, causing diseases. They frighten souls with dreams, and shake minds with furies, so that on the whole it may be wondered whether the madman was attacked by mania or whether he was not rather beaten by the spirit.[34]

Although a demon might in this way play a major role in mania, Pratensis paid no attention to possible religious or spiritual cures for the disorder. He was an academically orthodox humanist physician, after all, and his remedies remained completely physical in the best ancient and medieval tradition. When he analyzed the detailed causes of mania, moreover, demons dropped away. Mania was caused in the main by a corrupt temperament, which in turn was caused by faults in the parental seed, by the ill influence of the stars, and by a noxious environment.[35] Physiologically considered, mania was the product of excessive black bile, an excess that was sometimes temperamental but sometimes resulted when men and women produced and retained too much blood. This condition was more prominent among men than among women, and so men were disproportionately subject to mania. But women, too, could fall into mania if their menses were delayed or stopped.[36] Too much alcohol could prompt mania as well, and so could such aberrant mental states as religious fear, Lutheranism, and the immoderate lust for wealth.[37]

In an effort to preserve intact the whole Western medical tradition, Pratensis defended Avicenna, who with Aristotle had emphasized the psychosomatic significance of the heart, by insisting on the close correspondence of brain and heart.[38] He evidently had little patience with those extreme Hellenists who might wish to jettison all of Arabic medicine in favor of a purified Galenic approach. Pratensis did claim, however, that when surgeons tried to treat fevers, they were all too ready to wield the scalpel (for bloodletting). As ancient Pythagoras had warned: "Fight not fire with a sword." Pratensis, too, was sure that one could usually obtain better effects with diet, herbs, hellebore, cooling herbal baths, and well-regulated exercise and sleep. Wonders could be obtained with dilute white wine; the

33. Pratensis, *De cerebri morbis*, pp. 213–14.
34. Ibid., p. 214.
35. Ibid., pp. 216–21.
36. Ibid., p. 225.
37. Ibid., pp. 228–30.
38. Ibid., pp. 239–40, and see 267, 285–90.

flesh of young (moist) animals, such as veal, lamb, and kid; and the careful administration of concoctions of oxtongue, borage, endive, and chicory. Music could also help: "The elegant joining of sounds restores the soul . . . and calms the tempest of the mind and arrests the hurricanes of its affections."[39] He cited here all the convenient classical and biblical examples.

If these remedies failed, however, Pratensis left no doubt that whips and chains could also be used to control a dangerous maniac. "Unless they are restrained by chains or tamed and controlled by beating with whips, they rise up and attack with blows and battles their own servants, attendants, and anyone they meet."[40] After the best use of baths of flax and mallow and calming milk massages, it sometimes happened that the madman persisted in his "more stubborn vice [*vitium pertinacius*]. . . . They are to be held in chains and forced with whipping (if that seems useful) to pay attention, to learn and to remember, for if no cure has been able to bend them, then a harsher penalty [*poena*] should control them."[41] Here to our surprise we find our author actually using the moral language of vice and punishment (*vitium* and *poena*), although he quickly relented and reminded the physician that he must take care not to fall into an angry frustration that would make him resemble his own frenzied patients.[42]

Melancholy was a disorder stemming from that humor, and so Pratensis devoted several pages to the dark humor before turning to the disease itself. Unlike earlier medical accounts, Pratensis turned immediately to Aristotle's *Problems* and to Marsiglio Ficino's revival of the melancholy paradox, which taught that all men of real distinction suffered from melancholy disorders.[43] Before one concluded too hastily that all men of genius were mad, Pratensis insisted on drawing the crucial distinction between natural melancholy on the one hand and unnatural, corrupt melancholy on the other. The former was a sediment of rightly digested blood, or, to put it more accurately, the denser and drier part of good blood. Such black bile was good for the human body, acting as a glue to hold the other humors together and restraining their labile, flighty tendencies. Those who were melancholy by constitution had an abundance of this natural melancholy and no real deficit of the other humors. Ficino had remarked on the "golden blood verging on purple" of such persons, and Galen, too, had noticed a characteristic sparkle in their blood. Although black bile was naturally cold and dry, it could become warm as it struggled to escape the body (by evaporating?). As it grew warm, it tended to dry off the ashen sadness

39. Ibid., p. 235.
40. Ibid., p. 214.
41. Ibid., p. 256.
42. Ibid.
43. Ibid., pp. 258–60.

of the melancholy and to produce in its stead the clarity, sharpness, and promptness that we associate with great men. The dryness of the humor also kept men healthy and tireless. The melancholy mind (*animus*) with so willing an assistant strives vehemently and with great endurance to find, to comprehend, to see clearly and to judge rightly.[44] No wonder Aristotle had praised the melancholy.

Of course there were dangers, and, as with mania, Pratensis described the dangers in demonic terms: "Thus celestial demons rejoice in this sweet intercourse . . . and desire to dwell in mortals." With immoderate lust they invade and penetrate the inmost parts and settle down and take their delight there, "whirling just as the brightest stars in their region." Inside a person, such celestial demons can drive one mad, as Ovid noted: "O splendid and desirable madness! . . . There's a god in us."[45] In such ecstasies, the demonically melancholy are transported above themselves; they find favor with God, and become inventors of the arts, conservators of the sacred laws, investigators of nature, interpreters of divine mysteries, poets, prophets, and seers. Such men plumb the deepest secrets and grasp the most sublime truths, and afterwards, as Plato said, they are amazed at their own inventions and know not how they did these things.[46]

Having dealt in this way with the Platonic and (pseudo-) Aristotelian paradox of the melancholy genius, a genius that depended as we see, on the condition of natural melancholy and on the influence of celestial demons, Pratensis turned to the disease of melancholy, "an alienation of mind, with fear and sadness but without fever, consisting more in absurd thoughts [*ineptas cogitationes*] than in powerfully contriving disgraceful acts."[47] This disease came from corrupt blood, not from the natural black bile—that is, from a corruption that promoted "torpor, sadness, and desperation."[48] Following the ancient medical tradition, Pratensis described three forms of melancholy disease: (1) the corruption of all the blood; (2) the corruption of only the cerebral blood; and (3) the corruption of the hypochondrion (i.e., the gastric region below the chondrion, or diaphragm). In these diseased forms, the corrupted blood produces dark, swarthy, gloomy thoughts: a flood of terrors, sorrows, and fear of impending death (or even hope for death).[49]

Among the most amazing features of the melancholy mad were their bizarre fantasies. Pratensis assembled a large collection of classical stories

44. Ibid., p. 261.
45. Ibid., p. 262.
46. Ibid., pp. 262–63.
47. Ibid., p. 263.
48. Ibid.
49. Ibid., pp. 264–66.

of this sort, retailing again the accounts of the man who thought himself an earthen vessel and who left the road lest he crash into others; of the man who thought himself a rooster; of the man who thought that he alone, like Atlas, held up the world and feared that he could not sustain it for long; and of the man whose overly scrupulous conscience caused him to seek difficulties when there were none, and who, fearing hell and despairing of heaven, fell into constant weeping.[50] In the classical and medieval medical tradition, such melancholiacs could often be treated through benevolent fraud—that is, by a physician who played along with the patient's fantasy until it could be confronted with its own absurdity or healed by pretense.[51] Sixteenth-century physicians enjoyed displaying both their learning and their medical superiority by telling bizarre tales of therapies, such as pretending to operate on a man who imagined that his nose protruded like an ox foot, or pretending to be dead and allowing oneself to be interred in a sepulchre in order to establish rapport with a man who refused to eat because he thought himself dead. One may doubt that any of these dramatic cures were ever literally implemented in the sixteenth century, but they nicely illustrate a general medical attitude toward the melancholy-mad: that their madness was not without its own internal logic and coherence. Treating them could require the physician to try to discover this logic and to isolate and eliminate the errors on which it rested.

Since melancholy was a physical complaint, it was crucial that the physician determine whether a specific melancholy was of the head, the hypochondrion, or of the whole body, but Pratensis considered this fairly easy to do. Bleedings and changes of regimen could have dramatic results. Many meats, vegetables, and herbs had to be strictly avoided. Cabbage, legumes, and bran bread all fostered too rapid an increase in blood, as did red wine and moist meats. Broths and soups were helpful, however, and so were thin white wine, mild beer, and spices such as cinnamon, anise, and peony seed. Light exercise, bathing in sweet waters, soft, long sleep, and appropriate venereal pleasures were all part of successful therapy. While sexual congress with cold, dry bodies might exacerbate one's melancholy, one might recommend union with warm, moist bodies. This was no panacea, however, "for there are some [men] whom constant sexual intercourse from youth onwards has made more feeble."[52] For those grieving over the loss of a spouse, Pratensis urged physicians to recognize the impact of changes in a patient's erotic life and diet. Simple pleasures, games, and jokes might help someone cope with sadness.

50. Ibid., pp. 270–71.
51. Gill Speak, "An Odd Kind of Melancholy: Reflections on the Glass Delusion in Europe (1440–1680)," *History of Psychiatry* 1 (1990): 191–206.
52. Ibid., p. 276.

Pratensis establishes something like a baseline for us at midcentury. His was a learned "psychiatry" and "neurology" (if one may use anachronistic terms that had not yet been invented). His science tried to reconcile Galen and Avicenna, Aristotle and Hippocrates, but did not rely on clinical observations to any notable degree. Because of his wide reading and broad sympathies, Pratensis was not a doctrinaire fanatic in pursuit of one cure or only one interpretation, and he was evidently not much interested in what his own medical experience might tell him about the nature and cure of madness either. In all of these ways, he represented the best of the early sixteenth-century medical tradition, enlivened by renewed contact with the ancient sources of medicine.

Psychiatric Education at the German University

In its purest forms, humanist medicine continued the classicizing tendencies of Pratensis. We can observe German academic psychiatry at its most theoretical in the new and increasingly popular genre of published medical disputations and inaugural dissertations. These strangely laconic works provide us with a skeleton outline of what was, one may hope, a livelier public occasion. The theses, usually propounded by the presiding professor, are all that remain; we lack any sense of how the student responded to questions and the extent to which he departed, if at all, from his prepared text. These printed disputations began about midcentury but became common after 1570, and they provided neophyte physicians (and their academic sponsors) with a parade ground on which to display their mastery of ancient Greek medical writers, and especially Hippocrates and Galen.[53] Resolving knotty scholastic questions of contradictions among the sources, of obscure terminology, and of problematic interpretation, gave Renaissance German physicians, like their colleagues all over western Europe, an ideal arena in which to discuss and develop a rigorously somatic interpretation of disease, an interpretation that ignored all popular or learned attempts to link disease with sin or immorality, with demons, or with God himself.[54] Their classically natural or physical approach to all human ills may well have constituted a radical foreshortening of the human horizon, but it allowed doctors to create and perpetuate a realm of purely medical learning.

53. See Ewald Horn, *Die Disputationen und Promotionen an den deutschen Universitäten vornehmlich seit dem 16. Jahrhundert* (Leipzig, 1893).

54. For an analysis and classification of 3,553 French psychiatric dissertations, see Arnaud Terrisse, "La psychiatrie en France dans le miroir de la thèse: L'évolution des thèses de médecine psychiatrique françaises du debut du XVIIe siècle à 1934 d'après le fichier des thèses de médecine de la Bibliothèque nationale," *Histoire, Économie et Société* 3 (1984): 247–92.

TABLE 3.5
Medical Dissertations of "Psychiatric Interest," 1550–1650

	Melancholy	Hypochondria	Mania	Phrenesis	Total Dissertations
1550–1580	2	0	0	2	9
1581–1590	3[a]	1	1[a]	6[a]	13
1591–1600	9[b]	1	1[b]	3	33
1601–1610	11	7	1	6	40
1611–1620	12	2	2	8	39
1621–1630	6	8	2	3	40
1631–1640	3[c]	6	2[c]	5	27
1641–1650	6	8	2	6	40
Total	52[a,b,c]	33	11[a,b,c]	39[a]	241

SOURCE: Tabulated from Oskar Diethelm, *Medical Dissertations of Psychiatric Interest Printed Before 1750* (Basel, 1971).
[a] plus one dissertation on melancholy, mania, and phrenesis
[b] plus one dissertation on melancholy and mania
[c] plus one dissertation on melancholy and mania

Nowadays psychiatric topics hardly dominate the general field of medical inquiry, but in the sixteenth and early seventeenth centuries, dissertations on the mental illnesses were surprisingly common, owing no doubt to the fact that these disorders had also figured prominently among the concerns of Galen and Hippocrates.[55] As such psychiatric topics entered the medical mainstream in Germany, the visible influence of Galen actually rose. Of the 241 disputations registered by Oskar Diethelm for the period 1550–1650 (in a list that is far from complete), fully 138 dealt with just four classical disorders: melancholy, hypochondriasis (and hypochondriacal melancholy), mania, and phrenesis (see table 3.5). After 1600, theses on hysteria, another classical topic, became increasingly common as well.[56] It is obvious, however, that the largest fascination was with melancholy. By the last decade of the sixteenth century, of 33 dissertations in Diethelm's list, 10 dealt with disorders of the black bile (as did a further 23 of the 79 dissertations from the period 1601 to 1620). For physicians, this was truly the "age of melancholy," although the theme of melancholy madness remained for a century one of the standard topics for medical humanists and fledgling physicians alike.

What were these dissertations like? Let us examine a few from the Uni-

55. Jackie Pigeaud, *La maladie de l'âme: Étude sur la relation de l'âme et du corps dans la tradition médico-philosophique antique* (Paris, 1981); Giuseppe Roccatagliata, *A History of Ancient Psychiatry* (Westport, Conn., 1986).

56. I have tabulated works listed in Oskar Diethelm, *Medical Dissertations of Psychiatric Interest Printed Before 1750* (Basel, 1971); see also G. S. Rousseau, "'A Strange Pathology': Hysteria in the Early Modern World, 1500–1800," in *Hysteria Beyond Freud*, ed. Sander L. Gilman et al. (Berkeley and Los Angeles, 1993), pp. 91–221.

versity of Tübingen, which were typical of those written and performed at other German universities. The earliest printed Tübingen disputation on madness was the 1580 *Disputatio medica de capite et cerebro hominis* proposed by Andreas Planer, with Helias Waldner of Memmingen as respondent. It was an extraordinary analysis, not so much because of the wide variety of diseases it had to consider (for that was common enough) as because of an obsessive emphasis on the hair. The chief problem in studying the brain, of course, was that physicians of the sixteenth century had no way of observing a living brain directly. They had to infer everything from visible signs, and Galen provided the structure of inference. There were, he had thought, two kinds of sign, the innate and the external, from which one might hope to estimate the condition of the brain. The innate signs consisted of its size and shape (thesis 3), its operations in sensation and sleep (theses 7, 8), the bodily motions prompted by the brain (thesis 9), the mental guides to the brain revealed in the *sensus communis*, fantasy, memory, and thought (theses 11, 12), and finally the process of nourishing the brain, which could be studied indirectly through cerebral excrements of various sorts (theses 14, 15). The external signs were composed of the way in which the brain responded to the six non-naturals: air, sleep, food and drink, rest and exercise, excretion and retention, and the mental affections.

Physicians could also gauge the state of the brain from the heat, toughness, and moisture of the cerebral substance. Too soft, too thick, too hot a brain—all these spelled mental difficulties. How could one judge these qualities? Cerebral excrements in the eyes, ears, nose, and mouth could all be observed, but brain excrement could also flood the lungs, nerves, throat, veins, and stomach, producing an amazing variety of physical ills (theses 32–42). Faced with this bewildering catalog of cerebral symptoms, the physician might turn with some relief to a consideration of the hair, as discussed by the ancients. At first this bizarre suggestion might seem arbitrary, but on reflection the emphasis on hair is a perfect example of what we might describe as a medical retreat from common sense into a system of judgment that could only be based on the secret wisdom of the academy. Since hair sprouted almost from the brain itself, its growth, color, strength, and texture could reveal something crucial about the brain (theses 46–51). A dry brain, for example, produced curly, strong, fast-growing hair, but also baldness. Such persons might be unusually wise. A humid head, on the other hand, resulted in straight hair and no baldness. Such persons were often dull, stupid, and somnolent (theses 68–72). Without the structure of inference provided by Galen, where would this dissertation have been? But without the search for secret coherences, where would any science be?

A very different disputation was that of Daniel Moegling of Tübingen, held at Heidelberg in 1584 with Johann Kuhn (Cuno) as respondent.[57] Beginning with the theological proposition that man was made in God's image, having the use of reason, the formal *quaestio* asked how it was that phrenesis, or brain fever, could push man so far from reason that he became like the wild beasts. Although this opening statement seemed to invite theological commentary on the human nature of the mad, the dissertation quickly entered calmer medical waters by asserting that the cause and cure of such metamorphoses were matters for the physician. Revealing a firm grasp of philosophical complexities, however, Moegling and Kuhn noted that, strictly speaking, the human mind was not liable to death or disease; but so long as it was trapped in this prison of a body (*in hoc ergastulo*), it had to abandon its integrity and attach itself to the inferior faculties of the soul and use the ministry of the interior and exterior senses. Being in this way a composite construction, it became capable of suffering (thesis 1). Here then was a disputation in which major theological and philosophical issues did break the surface, but only in such a way as to justify the medical concern with physical things.

Phrenesis was defined as inflammation of the brain with acute fever and delirium (thesis 4). After distinguishing various sorts of phrenesis, Moegling and Kuhn turned to a detailed consideration of its etiology, symptomatology, and prognosis. Since cure was exceedingly difficult, they noted that the prudent physician would rather avoid the disease altogether (thesis 38). Still, a cure could be effected if the matter of the disease (i.e., the corrupt phlegm) were destroyed or if the source of the corruption itself were corrected. All of these procedures required the use of purges "with a skilled moderation" (*docta moderatione*) (theses 38, 43, 46), or diet, or venesection, or baths (theses 46, 47, 52, 54, 55, 57). Only when the crisis was past and the disease was in retreat did Moegling and Kuhn concede the utility of applying to a feverish head such ancient remedies as split chickens, capons, piglets, and dogs (all alive but with their spines cut), or the fresh lung of a ram, or warm mother's milk (thesis 60). It seems unlikely that Moegling actually held these steps to be effective, and it is noteworthy that he relegated this advice to the stage when the patient was already on the mend.[58] Ultimately, diet and soothing surroundings were of prime importance in helping the patient. Friends, too, could help to calm and flatter him. But if these measures failed to cool the rage, the patient might need chains to confine him. Even so, it was not for the physician to take this last step but for the sick man himself and the attending officials "to make sure that all is done in right order" (thesis 64). This last statement seems to reveal an awareness

57. *Theses de Phrenetide* (Heidelberg, 1584).
58. For a reported use of a split rooster, see the account of Felix Platter, p. 176 below.

of the ethical issues involved in the incarceration or involuntary coercion of the mad. Physicians were to have no part in such decisions, for they were not yet an arm of the state.

In 1588, the Tübingen professor Georg Hamberger presided at another disputation on phrenesis with Balthasar Bruno (Braun) as respondent.[59] Although the dissertation follows the same explanatory scheme as that of Moegling and Kuhn four years earlier, it is striking how much room they found for shifts in emphasis. Hamberger began, for example, by stressing the divergent views of the ancient *prisci medici* (in the *quaestio*). Instead of worrying about corrupt phlegm reaching the head, this disputation concentrated on the dangers of overly thin blood shooting up to the brain and, finding its return blocked, causing inflammation. Brain fever could also be caused by an excess of bright bile (choler), which could turn men into animals, requiring chains. Hamberger was not bothered by the question of who should make such decisions.

In 1602, yet another Tübingen professor, Sebastian Bloss, undertook a discussion of phrenesis with Matthaeus Müller as respondent.[60] Unlike the disputations considered so far, this one cited a fair amount of recent literature instead of commenting exclusively on Galen and Hippocrates. In addition, it showed a lively interest in the effects of brain fever on each of the three internal senses: fantasy, memory, and the common sense (theses 12–20). After agreeing that phrenesis was so dangerous that most patients died, the disputation turned nonetheless to cures; here, amid the common recommendations of bloodletting and purging, was an unusual emphasis on cooling off the patient with special drinks and drugs. Among the prescriptions for oil of roses and violets, lettuce water, and the like, the modern reader may be amused to discover recipes for a medicinal blend of the juice of oranges or lemons and sugar: lemonade? These were truly exotic prescriptions in sixteenth- and early seventeenth-century Germany, for both sugar and citrus fruits were hard to find, except in a well-stocked pharmacy. With this emphasis on drinks and drugs, however, Bloss and Müller were clearly defending an approach to phrenesis that differed from that of their Tübingen predecessors. The Galenic system was a house of many mansions.

Some of the other Tübingen dissertations showed a similarly creative approach to their topics. They did not aim at producing original conclusions; in fact, the basic assumption in most cases was probably that originality was no virtue. And yet the spread of printed disputations understandably encouraged an elite taste for novelty, creativity, or even originality. So long as these occasions were completely oral affairs, a student or his

59. *Disputatio de Phrenetide* (Tübingen, 1588).
60. ΠΕΡΙ ΤΕΣ ΦΡΕΝΙΤΙΔΕ. *De Phrenetide Assertiones Medicae* (Tübingen, 1602).

professor might content himself by answering classical questions with classical answers. But as professors and respondents began to publish these questions and answers, an unspoken urge may have shaped the old materials into new forms, probing and testing the old conclusions. Although this urge did not send physicians rushing to their laboratories for new evidence and controlled experiments, pages as dusty as these medical dissertations evince a fresh effort to arrive at new conclusions or at least to apply the old wisdom to more recent topics.

A good example of this tendency may be found in the 1593 Tübingen disputation of Andreas Planer with Johann Faber (Schmidt) as respondent, *De morbo Saturnino seu melancholia*, which was not content with the ancients but pushed on to consider whether witches were really only melancholy: "The demon can make one melancholic. Melancholy persons possessed by the devil are healed not by use of drugs but by prayers. Not all of the things of hell, but the melancholy themselves are the authors of their own death. Old women with melancholy tend to become witches."

These assertions betray a feeble attempt to keep medicine and theology separate, especially in the claim that the possessed needed prayer rather than medical care. But in the last claim, the authors seem to have agreed with Johann Weyer and his disciples that witches were mainly melancholy, a controversial claim usually taken to imply that their confessions were the worthless products of hallucination. If so, we have here another case of medical reductionism, the invasion of the domains of law and theology by medical thinking. We do not know what was actually said at this point of the disputation; as it stands the utterance is a gnomic reminder of how slender is our knowledge of the past *wie es eigentlich gewesen ist*.

In addition to these unconventional extensions, this disputation also reveals an unusual interest in man as the microcosm, as comprehending, reflecting, and participating in all of the parts and processes of the cosmos. Although the theme was a commonplace among Neoplatonic thinkers, medical writers usually paid it no mind. Here, however, Faber's dedicatory epistle to Duke Ludwig of Württemberg seems to echo Paracelsus in claiming that human diseases were strictly analogous to earthly disturbances. Just as the sun is sometimes eclipsed by the moon, so too the brain is sometimes darkened by phrenesis, delirium, mania, dizziness, suffusions, and cataracts.[61] Melancholy was analogically distinct: it corresponded rather to the windy, cold, dry season of autumn, a time of sad storms. The forging of this Neoplatonic link between melancholy and the cosmos made this disputation unusual, and it is not surprising that it also, like the work of Jason Pratensis in 1549, displayed an interest in the pseudo-Aristotelian claim

61. Andreas Planer with respondent Johann Faber (Schmidt), *De morbo Saturnino seu melancholia* (Tübingen, 1593), fol. A2 v.

that melancholy predisposed one to genius.[62] This medical dissertation approached philosophy and theology so closely that it ran the risk of overstepping the professional boundaries that ensured physicians an autonomous existence as practitioners of a separate discipline.

That danger did not exist for the authors of a 1586 Tübingen dissertation on diseases of the temperament entitled *Disputatio medica de morbis temperamenti*. Andreas Planer presided, with Thomas Schlaier of Tübingen as respondent. Together they analyzed the ways in which heat, cold, moisture, and dryness could become unbalanced and produce a host of psychosomatic disorders. The disputants allowed no moral, ethical, or theological issues to interfere with a strictly medical approach.

It was not only doctors who learned to cite the ancients. One cultural consequence of the rising general popularity of Galen and Hippocrates in the late sixteenth century is that certain medical texts began to reach over from the specialized psychiatric and medical audience to appeal to a much broader audience of cultivated bystanders. On a European scale, we can see this happening with such works as Timothy Bright's *A Treatise of Melancholie* (1586) and André du Laurens's *Discours de la conservation de la veue: des maladies melancholiques: des cartarrhes: et de la vieillesse* (1594; English trans., 1599; Italian trans., 1626). The real high point for such a general Renaissance interest in madness and especially melancholy came about twenty years later and is visible in such amazing repositories of ancient and modern wisdom as Jacques Ferrand's *De la maladie d'amour ou mélancholie érotique* (1610; much expanded in 1623)[63] and Robert Burton's *Anatomy of Melancholy* (first edition, 1621). These works, intended for a general audience, breathe a "modern Galenism" that had not existed a century earlier, an open-minded, erudite, well-informed Galenism that tried to harness, discipline, and integrate divergent strands of myth, allegory, history, philosophy, and medicine.[64] Another result of this "rise of Galenism" in the sixteenth century, therefore, was that melancholy was more widely regarded as a disease, and as a common disease, in 1600 or 1620 than it had been in 1500. The doubt and ferment around the melancholy humor and the melancholy temperament had arisen, not from any new anatomical discoveries or scientific approaches, but from the improved philological abilities and from the improved and much more plentiful texts now available to learned physicians and to the classically educated layman.

It is understandable that the incidence of melancholy madness expanded once educated laymen could read the widely disseminated ancient medical

62. Ibid., fol. C1 v.
63. See now Jacques Ferrand, *A Treatise on Lovesickness*, ed. Donald A. Beecher and Massimo Ciavolella (Syracuse, N.Y., 1990), an exemplary translation and edition.
64. Patricia Vicari, *The View from Minerva's Tower: Learning and Imagination in "The Anatomy of Melancholy"* (Toronto, 1989), pp. 9, 98.

works on melancholy, and once there were enough learned physicians available to deploy this system of diagnosis and treatment. This is nowhere more evident than at the dozens of princely courts of the Holy Roman Empire, where courtiers and anxious family members began increasingly to take the advice of their increasingly influential personal physicians. When Duke Wilhelm II (the Younger) of Braunschweig-Lüneburg (1535–1592) went mad, for example, he was confined to his beautiful new palace at Celle and subjected to an elaborate therapeutic regime that mixed rigorous Galenic remedies for melancholy with daily Lutheran sermons.[65] His court physicians dominated these scenes, but when they failed to obtain results, the pious prince was given adventurous Paracelsan remedies for his sad condition. By the late sixteenth century, every prince who suffered attacks of depression, hallucination, confusion, or insanity was treated in the same way. Duke Albrecht Friedrich of Prussia (1553–1618) and Duke Johann Wilhelm of Jülich-Cleves are only the two best-known examples. But it seemed to some observers a gloomy comment on the state of the declining world that the Holy Roman Emperor himself, the secretive and fearful Rudolf II (1552–1612), was occasionally so afflicted by rage, so frantic with suspicion, so proud in his refusal to marry, that he set his melancholy stamp upon his whole court at Prague. It was indeed the age of the melancholy prince, an age created in large part by the classically trained physicians who diagnosed and treated their mad princes and princesses with the slogans of ancient Greek medicine.

Consultations and the World of Medical Practice

We should not, however, suppose that academic physicians were so hopelessly engaged in philological researches into the works of Galen, Hippocrates, and the other ancient physicians that they spent no time at all in the real world of pain, disease, and death. Indeed, academic physicians were often consulted by town councils, illustrious patients, and other physicians. Their written responses, often published as *Consilia* or *Consultationes medicae*, in fact made up another increasingly common form of medical publication. One simple, although admittedly imperfect, measure of this literature is the massive catalog of the National Library of Medicine in Bethesda, Maryland. Without assuming that the remarkable holdings of this great library are complete or even perfectly representative of all the medical literature published in early modern Europe, one can still learn much about the total output of sixteenth-century medical publications.

---

65. I have treated his case and the others mentioned in this paragraph in *Mad Princes*.

TABLE 3.6

Titles Containing the Words 'Consilia' and 'Consultationes' or Forms Thereof in the National Library of Medicine, 1500–1650

	Germany	Switzerland	Italy	France	Netherlands	Other/ Unknown	Total
1500–1529	1	0	11	2	0	1	15
1530–1559	6	3	14	2	0	0	25
1560–1589	9	15	12	8	0	2	46
1590–1619	48	4	14	6	0	2	74
1620–1650	22	2	20	10	2	3	59
Total	86	24	71	28	2	8	219

Other investigations will have to confirm or disconfirm the impressions I present here based on the book titles dating from 1500 to 1650, as listed in the catalog of the NLM.[66] For this time period, the NLM holds 145 titles containing the word *consilium* or declensions of it and an additional 74 titles containing the word *consultatio* or its declined forms (see table 3.6).

We might imagine that, because of its prominent medical schools, Italy would have led the list as the chief producer of *consilia* and *consultationes*, but, at least in Bethesda, the inescapable impression is that the early modern Germans rose to become the chief publishers of this kind of medical literature. To be sure, Italian publishers held an early dominance of the field down to the 1570s, but then publishers in Frankfurt, Leipzig, Basel, and a few other German publishing centers burst forth with a surprising wave of medical consultations, volumes of detailed advice on specific questions. This increasing attention to the problems of the real world is even more noteworthy when one tabulates the rising frequency of the word *observatio*, or "observation," in the book titles of early modern Europe (looking for both the Latin word and its vernacular equivalents in German, French, and English). Again exploiting the catalog of the National Library of Medicine, one finds fully 254 titles published between 1500 and 1650 in which this key word appears. The rise of empirical observation appears to be nowhere more easily tabulated than in this exercise (table 3.7).

In their rising enthusiasm for "observation," early modern German publishers of medical books led a general European drive for increased attention to empirical detail, to fresh experience with the real problems of this world. Let us take a closer look at this medical literature of consilia and consultations and then at the new genre of "observations."

When physicians got down to cases, they sometimes stopped arguing

66. Here I record my gratitude to James Cassedy and the excellent staff of the NLM for their help.

TABLE 3.7

Titles Containing the Words 'Observation' and 'Observatio' or Forms Thereof
in the National Library of Medicine, 1500–1650

	Germany	Switzerland	Italy	France	Netherlands	England	Unknown	Total
1500–1529	4	0	0	0	1	0	0	5
1530–1559	3	2	0	3	1	0	0	9
1560–1589	11	3	10	9	6	0	1	40
1590–1619	46	3	7	15	21	5	0	97
1620–1650	38	5	6	21	15	17	1	103
Total	102	13	23	48	44	22	2	254

about their ancient texts. A good example is the volume of medical consultations edited in 1598 by Lorenz Scholtz from Rosenau, a physician in Breslau (Wrocław) who lived from 1552 to 1599.[67] This fat folio volume of 1,164
columns contains a sampling of the opinions of forty eminent doctors, including Thomas Erastus, Andreas Vesalius, Jacobus Sylvius, Rembert Dodonaeus, and Theodor Zwinger. In one case, carefully described by Professor Hieronymus Capivacius of Padua, a thirty-six-year-old Styrian woman
had become violently ill and had attacked her own offspring. Of ten children, only two were saved from her murderous assault. Capivacius provided a good, careful, clinical description of this woman's complex symptoms. He noted that she had grown thin after her marriage and had fallen
into epilepsy, melancholy madness, heart tremors, and a variety of further
problems, all of which were exacerbated by the fact that she became too
thin and dry during her paroxysms. A careful regulated regimen of bleedings, purges, pills, syrups, baths, and a controlled diet apparently succeeded in restoring this unhappy woman to health.[68]

Not all consultations were such models of observational medicine, however. A consilium by the famous imperial physician Johann Crato von
Kraftheim (1519–1585) dealt at length with a case of melancholy and covered only theory and therapy without describing the case at all.[69] From the
two following consultations, however, we gather that several physicians,
including Crato, had been sought out with respect to a notable case of
melancholy, and from a couple of the reports, we learn some actual details
of the case. Rembert Dodonaeus, for example, noted that this melancholy
had been acute "ever since 1572." For Julius Alexandrinus, however, the
case presented an opportunity to defend Arab medicine and to point out
that for the learned Arabs, melancholy could originate, not just in the

67. Consiliorum medicinalium, ed. Lorenz Scholtz (Frankfurt a/M, 1598).
68. Ibid., no. 323, cols. 909–15.
69. Ibid., no. 174, cols. 490–97.

spleen, but in the liver or uterus as well.[70] In this case, represented by three complementary opinions, we can sense the range of possibility open to orthodox psychiatric commentary in the late sixteenth century. One might stick to theory, argue about Arabic contributions, or offer careful clinical observations. Therapeutic options, however, remained about what they had been for hundreds of years: a blend of bleeding, purging, baths, herbs, and changes of diet, sleep, air, and so forth. Occasionally, we catch a whiff of the new world of sixteenth-century medicine, though, as in the case of a melancholy nobleman treated by Dr. Matthaeus Stoius, who prescribed the use of Honduran (or Peruvian) sarsaparilla root as a purge. [71] By the late sixteenth century, there was also, as we have seen, a growing concern with hypochondriac melancholy, a flatulent digestive disorder with psychic side effects; numerous consilia described the treatment of this increasingly common kind of melancholy.[72] These were the medical origins of what later centuries would call the neurosis of hypochondria.

In Johann Crato von Kraftheim's own medical consultations, the topic of melancholy often arose. The distinguished imperial physician dealt repeatedly with noblemen who had fallen either into the gastric, hypochondriac version of melancholy or into primary melancholy, which Crato defined as "actio depravata imaginationis, quae laeditur non propter intemperiem, sed ob errorem externum, scilicet ob spiritum animalem tenebricosum" ("a corrupt action of the imagination, which suffers not on account of madness [i.e., rage?] but from an external error, that is, from a dark animal spirit"). Like mania, melancholy was a "delirium without fever" in which "fear and sadness persisted without external causes." The afflicted "seek solitude, enjoy darkness, and have disturbed sleep and sad thoughts."[73] Although Crato did deal with specific cases, he linked them so closely to Galen and Hippocrates, and to the neat and tidy definitions and clinical descriptions he gleaned from his classical sources, that he rarely paused to ask himself whether his experience tallied with what he had read.

Perhaps Crato was modeling his own style of observation and diagnosis on that which he had seen among the Italian physicians. In 1583, shortly before he died, Crato published a large folio edition of the consultations of

70. Ibid., no. 174, cols. 490–97; and no. 175, cols. 498–501.

71. Ibid., no. 177, cols. 504–10.

72. Ibid., nos. 180–92. See also Balthasar Brunner (1533–1604), *Consiliorum medicorum liber unicus ex bibliotheca Jo. Jacobi Strasskirchneri* (Frankfurt a/M, 1727), pp. 33, 34, 71, 336, 395; and *consilia* nos. 5–11. On the interpretation of this kind of melancholy, see Esther Fischer–Homberger, *Hypochondrie: Melancholie bis Neurose: Krankheiten und Zustandsbilder* (Bern, 1970).

73. Johannes Crato von Kraftheim, *Consiliorum et epistolarum medicinalium libri septem*, ed. Lorenz Scholtz (Frankfurt a/M, 1671), bk. 1, no. 104, pp. 483, 499; bk. 2, nos. 16–21, pp. 78–159.

Giovanni Battista Montano of Verona (1498–1551), a volume containing 384 consilia, several of them touching on madness and melancholy. Montano, too, largely contented himself with plugging the observed data into the classical definitions. A disturbed youth, for example, must have been suffering from natural melancholy rather than from melancholy adust, the corrupt burnt or roasted form of black humor, "for where it is adust, maniacs and wild men [*maniaci & furiosi*] are produced." The youth must have been suffering from natural melancholy or some other cold humor, "for, as Avicenna says, melancholy adust makes demoniacs who flee mankind, seeking solitude and inhabiting tombs."[74] While this clarified the differing effects of unnatural and natural melancholy, perhaps, it did not encourage readers or other observers to rethink the categories of their experience or to criticize the traditions within which they had been reared. Montano could disagree with Galen on the cure of melancholy madmen, however, and at one point he emphatically cited his own experience: "I have never seen such ones cured perfectly; partially I concede, but not totally."[75] Doctors were trying to use their consultations to diagnose and to distinguish cases, but we should not think that their contact with the "real world" of disease would necessarily reduce their dependence upon ancient authority. Indeed, it seems appropriate to call their medical research "Galenic observation."

Four Observers: Foreest, Schenck, Weyer, Platter

The literature of "observatio" was different from that of consilia in at least this respect, that it generally admired and relied upon supposedly first-hand experience.[76] The most extraordinary expanding collection of sixteenth-century medical observations was probably that of the "Dutch Hippocrates," Pieter van Foreest (Forestus) (1522–1597), which began as just two books on fevers (1584) but grew to thirty-two books (1606), including treatments of syphilis, a decidedly unclassical subject.[77] Van Foreest noticed the prodromal symptoms of alcoholic insomnia and also recommended lenient treatment of "postpartum frenzy" (*puerpera phrenetica*, something like

74. Ioannis Baptista Montanus (1498–1551), *Consultationes medicae*, ed. Joh. Crato Vratislavensis [Crato von Kraftheim] ([Basel?], 1583), col. 62. The whole consilium (no. 26), cols. 50–74, deals with melancholy disorders.

75. Ibid., col. 65.

76. On the problematic interconnections between medical theory and observation, see Volker Langholf, *Medical Theories in Hippocrates: Early Texts and the "Epidemics"* (Berlin, 1990), pp. 73–76, 179–90, 193–94.

77. *Observationum et curationum medicinalium de febribus ephemeris et continuis libri duo* (Antwerp, 1584); *Observationum et curationum medicinalium liber XXXII, de lue venerea* (Leiden, 1606).

what we call postpartum depression).[78] In book 10 of his *Observations*, he dealt with diseases and disorders of the brain, quoting Jason Pratensis frequently but also offering observations from his own practice in Delft. Cases of melancholy take up seventy pages, and mania thirty-seven more, but he also dealt with isolated cases of lycanthropy, "cynanthropy" (thinking oneself transformed into a dog), love madness, mental retardation, and demonic possession (which he blamed on "a certain thick vapor").[79]

Given the work of Pratensis before van Foreest, and that of his exact contemporary Johann Weyer, we cannot help noticing how active the Low Countries were in cultivating a more exacting interest in mental disturbances. No one has yet offered an explanation for the intense concern with psychiatric topics in a part of the Holy Roman Empire that was just then establishing its claims to independence from the Habsburgs.

Another dramatically successful "observer" was Johann Schenck von Grafenberg (1530–1598), the city physician of Freiburg im Breisgau, whose *Observationum medicarum, rararum, novarum admirabilium et monstrosarum* expanded to seven volumes from 1584 to 1597 and continued to be reprinted down to 1665. Despite its title, Schenck began volume 2 of his work with the customary list of ancient and contemporary sources he had consulted, a long list that included other authors of "observationes" that Schenck excerpted. All the famous physicians of his day were present here, in one way or another, and so the book included much that we modern readers would hardly call "observations." Sometimes the term *observatio* seems to have meant little more than "readings" and Schenck was concerned to impress his reader with his classical erudition. In contrast to scholastic argumentation, however, he claimed that "one should understand how much more experience [*usus*] teaches than reason and authority," as when one actually observes the places in newborn babies that generate stones.[80] Schenck was sometimes proud to claim that he had seen some novelty "with his own eyes" (*vidi ego meis oculis*), apparently appealing to his own experience, but sometimes he was merely quoting someone else's firsthand observations.[81] Observation was all the more necessary, he

78. Maxime Laignel-Lavastine and Jean Vinchon, *Les malades de l'esprit et leurs médecins du XVIᵉ au XIXᵉ siècle: Les étapes des connaissances psychiatriques de la Renaissance à Pinel* (Paris, 1930), p. 38.

79. Petrus Forestus, *Observationum et curationum medicinalium libri tres, Nempe octavus . . . ; Nonus De variis Capitis doloribus; Decimus De universis ac cerebri & meningum eiusdem Symptomatis ac morbis* (Leiden, 1590), nos. 12–19 (melancholy), 20–24 (mania), 25–26 (lycanthropy and cynanthropy), 29–30 (love madness), 31 (stultitia), 50–52 (incubus and demonic possession), p. 375: "vapor quidem crassus."

80. Schenck, *Observationum medicarum, rararum, novarum, admirabilium, et monstrosarum* (7 books in 2 vols.) (Frankfurt a/M, 1600), fol. **6r.

81. Johann Schenck von Grafenberg, *Observationes medicae de capite humano* (1584), p. 292, citing Mathias Cornax. Claiming to have seen what one had only read became a com-

insisted, because his age had seen the birth of entirely new diseases, such as St. Vitus' dance. Schenck described the dancing mania as an "enthusiasm or that amazing kind of madness [*insania*] that has corrupted many of [our] ancestors especially in Germany."[82] Proceeding in the traditional way from head to foot, Schenck dealt with all the diseases of the head in book 1 (*De capite*), a tome of 311 pages and 444 separate *observationes*.[83] He examined cases of spasm, lethargy, epilepsy, apoplexy, stupor, gray hair, bearded women, skull fractures, and a wide variety of mental disorders, including phrenesis, memory loss, lycanthropy, assault by an incubus-demon, melancholia, and mania. While Schenck showed great admiration for Vesalius and the other great anatomists of his day, he displayed no contempt for Galen and the ancients. In fact, he tried hard to fit the most recent discoveries into an essentially Galenic framework. It is not surprising therefore to find Schenck repeating the familiar classical stories of curing melancholy fantasies by establishing rapport with the patient, appearing to accept his or her account of the world, and then, through deception, producing a cure. We learn, for example, of a woman who was sure that she had a snake in her intestines but was cured when her physician produced a serpent that he pretended to have removed from her. A hypochondriac, who thought he was being killed by poisonous toads in his intestines, felt much better after physicians gave him an enema and later showed him the animals in his excrement. Schenck also retailed the well-known story of the man who thought himself dead and refused to eat but was restored to health by actors who pretended to be dead but then offered the suffering melancholic food to eat.[84]

Schenck was much interested in cases in which amatory and sexual disorders led to madness. He told of a mad Italian woman, for example, who was so shameless that she wandered nude and screaming through her city. Spending the night in a workshop, she was raped by fifteen men, with the unexpected result that "her obstructed menses began flowing for the first time in many years, and she went away with her mind restored and feeling great shame."[85] In another case, a middle-aged man married a young wife whose lust for the pleasures of the marital couch was so strong that the poor man dried up and fell into a hot and dry fury. He had to be restrained

---

mon trope. See Frank Lestringant, "L'excursion brésilienne: Note sur les trois premières éditions de l'Histoire d'un voyage de Jean de Lery (1578–1585), in *Mélanges sur la littérature de la Renaissance à la mémoire de V.-L. Saulnier*, ed. Pierre-Georges Castex (Geneva, 1984), 53–72.

82. Ibid., fol. **7v.

83. Schenck first published his *Observationes medicae de capiti* in Basel in 1584. In that first edition, it contained 418 observations.

84. *Observationum medicarum*, observation no. 253, pp. 207–9.

85. Ibid., p. 210.

with chains until he was restored to health by the application of wet poultices and by moist foods.[86]

In addition to his concern with sexual anxieties, Schenck revealed a deep-seated concern with demons. Repeatedly, he told of cases of supposed demonic possession that turned out on medical inspection to be medical problems. Horrible cases of lycanthropy, cribbed from Aetius and Pliny, Jost Fincel and Johann Weyer, all proved to be cases of melancholy, "of which there is little doubt."[87] Stories of nightmare encounters with incubus demons were also susceptible of the same medical account. Borrowing a story from Jason Pratensis, Schenck told of a man who was suffering from a dreadful wasting illness. According to the patient, a woman came to him during the night and pressed his chest so tightly that he could scarcely breathe. Doctors had told him that this was all fantasy, but the man insisted that he was awake during these attacks and in full possession of his faculties. No matter how he struggled, he could not beat off the phantom succubus, and he feared that he was bewitched. To these symptoms were added frightful pains in the bladder and a vile choking sensation. At last his condition improved, not for any medical reason, but because he began to see his situation as funny.[88] Even apparently secure proofs of demonic possession did not persuade Schenck. He related the case of an illiterate woman who spoke fine Latin when she was in the depths of melancholy but who lost this ability when her condition improved.[89]

This last case bears a suspicious resemblance to a remarkable theory pronounced by Levinus Lemnius, a physician from Zirikzee (1505–1568) whose *De miraculis occultis naturae libri iiii* ran through numerous editions. Lemnius made a valiant effort to explain physically and by a Platonic theory of remembrance how it came about that melancholic madmen could sometimes speak foreign languages they had never heard before.[90] We know that Schenck had read Lemnius, for he cited him often, but he claimed to have discovered this case of what we might call "melancholia latinophonia" in Pietro d'Abano's *Commentary* on Aristotle's *Problems*. Wherever he actually found the case, it is a good example of how far a physical reductionist might be willing to go in order to deny the actual influence of demons and demonic possession, even while conceding, if pushed, that demonic possession was possible.

In this connection, Schenck had high praise for Dr. Johann Weyer

86. Schenck, *Observationes medicae de capite humano* (Basel, 1584), observation no. 236, p. 284, citing Giacchino's *Commentary* on Rhazes.

87. *Observationum medicarum . . .* (1600), observation no. 260, p. 212.

88. Ibid., observation no. 252, pp. 205–6, citing Pratensis, *De morbis cerebri*, ch. 26.

89. Ibid., p. 210.

90. Levinus Lemnius, *De miraculis occultis naturae librii iiii* (Antwerp, 1574), bk. 2, ch. 2; id., *The Secret Miracles of Nature in four books* (London, 1658), p. 91.

(1515?–1588), whom he called "the most experienced and most learned physician of our age."[91] There might well have been other contenders for the title of "most learned" in a day when humanist physicians were proud to display their classical learning, but in singling out Weyer's experience, Schenck hit on an essential trait that Weyer shared with the other German physicians we have examined. In the history of Renaissance psychiatry, Weyer has often been given a place of unusual prominence as the heroic founder of clinical or medical psychology, but his psychiatric thinking was mostly conventional. He won fame in his own day and ever since for his energetic attack on witch-hunting and for his tireless debunking of spiritual illusions. But it is quite possible that his impact on legal thought and practice was greater than any influence in medicine, as we shall see in chapter 4.

Weyer did not have a large practice. In fact, as court physician to Duke Wilhelm V of Jülich-Cleves, he may actually have seen fewer patients than doctors with broader responsibilities. But Weyer was unusual in his day because of his passionate appetite for eyewitness observation. He was far from ignoring the works and opinions of the ancients, but like Schenck von Grafenberg, he was convinced that there were diseases and disorders in his time that had been completely unknown to the ancients. In 1567, he published a volume of his "observations" that did rely on his own practice as well as on the opinions of everyone else.[92] And in 1583, he published a German version that described "several hitherto unknown and never described diseases," including the English sweat, syphilis, a kind of "pestilential pleurisy," the "gripes" (Grimmen), St. Anthony's fire (erysipelas, Rotlauff), blackheads, worms, and other disorders that Weyer was sure were symptomatic of the cursed and declining time he lived in, at the very end of human history, weakened by sin and plagued by the God's righteous anger.[93] Of course, it was not literally true that these diseases had never been described before, but the crucial point is that Weyer thought they had all appeared since the days of Galen. Reason enough for going beyond the ancients.

Another reason Weyer believed in using his own eyes was that he had learned to distrust what he read, especially when it came to the supposed wonders and exorcisms of the Catholic clergy. As a vehement Protestant of

91. Schenck, Observationum medicarum (1600), fol. **3v. Weyer also secured a place of honor in the curious volume of celebratory humanist verse by Carolus Utenhovius, Xenia seu: Ad illustrium aliquos Europae hominum nomina, Allusionum (intertextiis alicubi Ioach. Bellaii eiusdem argumenti versibus) Liber primus (n.p. [Basel?], n.d. [1570?]), pp. 104–5, where Weyer is hailed as an anti-Paracelsan.

92. Medicarum observationum rararum liber 1 (Basel, 1567).

93. Johann Weyer, Artzney Buch: Von etlichen bisz anher unbekhandten unnd unbeschriebenen Kranckheiten (Frankfurt a/M, 1583), fols. Aiii r-v, A7 r, B1 v.

Erasmian or perhaps Melanchthonian persuasion, Weyer undertook to debunk the numerous cases of miraculous fasting and of foreign objects supposedly found buried in the bodies of innocent persons. One continues to find scholars who think of Weyer as a Roman Catholic, but the evidence is clear that he sympathized with Protestants and with the Reformation.[94] He gloried in his ability to unmask fraud and expose the cunning of Catholic priests and devils.

It was this zeal for exposing the truth that has made Weyer famous in the history of witchcraft, as we shall see later. In this chapter, it will suffice to examine his medical views of mental disorder. Despite his theological agenda and his legal goal (the suppression of witchcraft trials), his erudition was first and foremost medical. After a youthful apprenticeship with Agrippa of Nettesheim in the 1530s, Weyer studied medicine in Paris and Orleans.[95] At about the age of thirty, he was hired as physician to the city of Arnhem on the Rhine, about twenty miles north of his hometown, Grave. Five years later, around 1550, he took up the office of personal physician to Duke Wilhelm V, a short move up the Rhine to Düsseldorf, and there he lived, except for occasional trips, until his death in 1588. Like most of the other learned physicians of his day, he remained almost completely untouched by the anatomical discoveries of Andreas Vesalius, Michael Servetus, Renato Colombo, and the Paduan school, but he knew enough of Paracelsus to condemn him and his disciples as ignorant empiricists.[96] From Weyer's medical writings, we have already seen, however, that he was open to some kinds of novelty, to new diseases and new remedies. So although he thought that Galen was the "Phoenix of all physicians," and referred to Hippocrates as "peerless," he nowhere felt that they should have the last word on any matter of importance.[97] In his basic medical orientation, Weyer was a perfect specimen of the Renaissance physician, devoted to humoral physiology and firmly convinced that most diseases could be traced back to disorders of the corporal humors and spirits.

Although physicians often tried hard to hew to this classical line, it was

94. See my essay "Johann Weyer in medizinischer, theologischer, und rechtsgeschichtlicher Hinsicht," in Vom Unfug der Hexenprozesse: Gegner der Hexenverfolgung von Johann Weyer bis Friedrich Spee, ed. Hartmut Lehmann and Otto Ulbricht, Wolfenbütteler Forschungen, vol. 55 (Wiesbaden, 1992), pp. 53–64; and also the introduction to Johann Weyer, On Witchcraft, ed. Benjamin G. Kohl and H. C. Erik Midelfort (Asheville, N.C., forthcoming).

95. The best recent account in English of Weyer's life is George Mora's introduction to Witches, Devils, and Doctors in the Renaissance: Johann Weyer, "De praestigiis daemonum," ed. Mora et al. (Binghamton, N.Y., 1991), pp. xxvii–xlv. But still useful is Carl Binz, Doctor Johann Weyer: Ein rheinischer Arzt, der erste Bekämpfer des Hexenwahns (2d ed., Bonn, 1896). See also chapter 4, pp. 198–201, in this volume.

96. Weyer, Witches, Devils and Doctors, pp. 153–54, 319, 407, 423, 475, 557.

97. Ibid., p. 368; Weyer, De lamiis liber (Basel, 1582), ch. 10.

difficult to prove, during the Renaissance, that devils and demons had absolutely no influence on human disease. Like his famous contemporaries
Jean Fernel and Ambroise Paré in France, or Jason Pratensis in the Netherlands, Weyer felt driven to concede that demonic possession did occur and
that diseases could have demonic origins. For believing Christians of his
day, there seemed to be no escaping the biblical stories of unclean spirits,
possessions, and exorcisms, especially those in the New Testament. We
have observed that Johann Schenck von Grafenberg and Levinus Lemnius
went farther in a radically materialist direction, and a bit later so did Reginald Scot of England. But for Weyer and for most Renaissance physicians,
physical action by the devil was always a possibility. Even so, Weyer de-
lighted in showing how rarely one needed to resort to demonic explanations of unusual diseases. Instead, the skeptical doctor had to keep his eyes
open for fraud. Book 4 of Weyer's famous work *De praestigiis daemonum*
starts out with the open declaration that demonic possession often acts like
a melancholy disorder to produce delusions and madness, but through
much of the rest of that book, Weyer took pains to show how unlikely or
even impossible many tales of possession were, and especially to refute the
implication that such unusual conditions, even if caused by the devil, were
actually prompted, initiated, or caused by witches. For Weyer's purposes,
it was not necessary to prove that the devil could not torment men and
drive women mad; it was enough if he could disconnect such actions from
any prior human agency (witchcraft).

Our last example of Renaissance German psychiatry is the famous Basel
physician Felix Platter (1536–1614). After a medical education at Montpellier and Paris, Platter returned to his native Basel in 1557, where he rose
quickly to prominent positions as a professor of medicine, eminent
Vesalian anatomist and theorist of pathology, botanist, city physician, and
pioneer in the field of clinical statistics.[98] Among the subjects to which he
directed his penetrating intellect were mental retardation, melancholy, and
madness. Although he described his medical practice in his theoretically
complex and interesting *Praxeos seu de cognoscendis, praedicendis, praecavendis curandisque affectibus homini* (3 vols., Basel, 1602), a work that was
reprinted over and over well into the eighteenth century, the richest work
for our purposes is his less systematic contribution to observation literature, *Observationum, in hominis affectibus plerisque corpori et animo, func-*

---

98. On his many areas of competence and fame, see *Felix Platter (1536–1614) in seiner
Zeit*, ed. Ulrich Tröhler (Basel, 1991). The best portrait of him remains his own *Tagebuch
(Lebensbeschreibung), 1536–1567*, ed. Valentin Lötscher (Basel, 1976). See now Emmanuel Le
Roy Ladurie, *The Beggar and the Professor: A Sixteenth-Century Family Saga*, trans. Arthur
Goldhammer (Chicago, 1997).

tionum laesione, dolore, aliave molestia et vitio insensis, libri tres (Basel, 1614, 1641, and 1680).[99]

One of Platter's earliest observations, dating from 1560, shortly after his return to Basel, was an investigation of demonic possession. In that year his father, the famous professor Thomas Platter (1499–1582), sent Felix to the house of an exorcist from Lucerne, who made his living by casting out demons, hoping to dissuade him from this "godless" calling.[100] But while he was there a robust demoniac was brought in, stiff as a board, and was dumped on the floor. There he lay, deaf and dumb with twisted legs and hands for several days without eating or drinking and without emitting any bodily substance. Most extraordinary was his head, which was so twisted that it faced exactly backward. Felix Platter was so horrified that he left.[101] The same Catholic exorcist came to Platter that year complaining of such acute hip pains that he could no longer walk. None of Platter's remedies did any good, and finally the priest admitted that his pain had a supernatural cause. Once, when driving forth a demon, the evil spirit had threatened him, as he often did, saying in German: "Priest, I'll pay you back for driving me out." And instantly he was pushed so hard against the stove that his hip was injured.[102]

Certainly nothing in these two accounts justifies P. E. Pilet's modern claim that "Platter refused to consider [mental disturbances] the work of a demon—unlike most of his contemporaries."[103] Historians of medicine must regularly guard against their tendency to see in their heroes the traits they hope and expect to find. While Platter may have shared the common medical assumption that one should first seek physical explanations, he clearly left ample room for demonic influences. In his *Praxis* of 1602, Platter specifically stated that there were two kinds of "mental consternation": natural and supernatural, and under the supernatural he referred to a *sopor sagarum* (bewitched sleep) caused by the devil. Under melancholy, Platter also allowed for *obsessio a daemone*.[104]

99. In addition to the Latin edition, I have used the handy German translation because of its good index: *Observationes: Krankheitsbeobachtungen in drei Büchern. I. Buch: Funktionelle Störungen des Sinnes und der Bewegung*, trans. Günter Goldschmidt, ed. Heinrich Buess (Bern, 1963). For a comparison of the *Praxis* and the *Observationes*, see Oskar Diethelm and Thomas F. Heffernan, "Felix Platter and Psychiatry," *Journal of the History of the Behavioral Sciences* 1 (1965): 10–23.

100. In his diary, Platter also tells this story; there he states that he went to visit the exorcist in Lucerne in order to demand payment of what he owed to Platter's father for his care a year earlier (Platter, *Tagebuch*, ed. Lötscher, pp. 362–63).

101. *Observationes* (1963 ed.), p. 42; 1614 ed., p. 18.

102. Ibid. (1963 ed.), pp. 42–43; 1614 ed., p. 19; *Tagebuch*, p. 362.

103. P. E. Pilet, "Felix Platter," in *Dictionary of Scientific Biography*, ed. Charles C. Gillispie (New York: Scribner's, 1975), 11: 33.

104. H. Christoffel, "Eine systematische Psychiatrie des Barock: Felix Platters 'laesiones

Even if we concentrate on Platter's direct observations, as opposed to his theoretical concessions, there is nothing in his methods to impress modern medical researchers. Read his description of a case of raging frenzy in a very young mother, whose delirium began shortly after giving birth. Her problems began because she was not fully "purified" after her delivery (meaning probably that she retained some or all of the afterbirth). Platter tried bleeding and cupping her, but her violent agitation made these efforts useless; next he turned to syrup of poppy (opium), administered by mouth, and rose oil mixed with vinegar (applied to her forehead), but still she raged.

On January 12 [1593], I had a rooster cut open down the middle and placed still warm and bloody on the top of her head. Shortly thereafter, a clearly visible full, thick steam poured out and upwards from that place. When the rooster was removed, it appeared to have been roasted and to have had an amazingly useful effect. For in the course of January 13, she began to come to herself and to speak quite reasonably and to obey.[105]

Even Platter seems here to have doubted the wonder-working effect of a split-open rooster until, amazingly, it appeared to absorb the burning heat of this suffering woman's phrenitis. Without really knowing what to expect, it seems, Platter knew enough about phrenitis to assume that the chief problem was feverish cranial heat, a heat great enough to cook a chicken and to produce steam. He, too, evidently, saw with his own eyes what his medical training had taught him to look for.[106]

Platter also noticed, however, that medical training and wide reading in Latin sometimes made a specific patient harder to treat. He told the story of a young man who suffered from one of the classic melancholy delusions, that he had a living frog in his innards, a creature that he had swallowed while swimming. For years he lived with this fantasy and no one could talk

---

mentis,' 1602–1736," *Schweizer Archiv für Neurologie und Psychiatrie* 77 (1956): 15–24; id., "Psychiatrie und Psychologie bei Felix Platter (1536–1614)," *Monatsschrift für Psychiatrie und Neurologie* 127 (1954): 213–27; Raymond Battegay, "Felix Platter und die Psychiatrie," in *Felix Platter (1536–1614) in seiner Zeit*, ed. Ulrich Tröhler (Basel, 1991), pp. 35–43, at pp. 39–40. Even the popular J. Karcher, *Felix Platter: Lebensbild des Basler Stadtarztes, 1536–1614* (Basel, 1949), pp. 62–71, got this point essentially right. The best general account of Platter's psychiatry is Diethelm and Heffernan, "Felix Platter and Psychiatry," which includes sections translated from the *Praxis*. Felix Platter, *Praxeos, Seu de cognoscendis praedicendis, praecavendis, curandisque affectibus homini incommodantibus* (Basel, 1609), 1: 32, 67 ("non naturalibus remedii, sed precibus et vitae emendatione curabitur"), 106, 123 ("Nam daemon coactus expellitur theologorum et pioram precibus in nomine JESU").

105. Platter, *Observationes* (1963 ed.), pp. 82–83; 1614 ed., pp. 86–87; for other uses of poultices on the head for madness, see *Mad Princes*, pp. 50, 77, 85, 89.

106. The School of Salerno in the high Middle Ages had frequently recommended such bizarre remedies.

him out of it. He undertook the study of medicine in the hope that he might learn to heal himself, and for seven years he studied in Germany, Italy, and finally in Basel, until he obtained an M.D. cum laude. All of his efforts to kill or to purge the frog came to nothing. In 1609, he came to Platter, who tried to persuade the man rationally that his frog was only a fantasy caused by a belly full of air, and that his belching produced the sounds that he thought were the croaking of a frog. Resisting such explanations, the young doctor tried to prove in writing and then by demonstration that he could feel the movements of his frog, and that when it was hungry he had no peace until he fed it something.

Seizing upon the ancient recommendation of rapport and deception, Platter claims that he tried to give his patient a purgative and then quickly slipped a frog into the chamber pot so as to give the impression that he had freed him of his problem, but "because he was a doctor himself, and knew of all this [deception] very well, he could not be fooled in this way, for he watched everything very carefully."[107] He insisted that Platter use only such strong poisons that really could kill the living frogs, snakes, and worms that could infest a body. And so Platter prescribed absinthe, olive oil, gentian, cumin, oil of peach, and oil of bitter almond—bitter substances that often did kill intestinal worms, Platter remarked. Despite copious emission of mucous and feces, the young doctor insisted on even stronger drugs, culminating in April and May in twenty pea-sized pills of mercury. In this demand for harsh chemicals, he may have switched over to the trendy Paracelsan remedies, which often were tried when milder Galenical herbs had failed.[108] But still the young man insisted that he had a frog inside. Platter lost all patience: "As his complaints of this sort disgusted me, I began to scold him harshly, saying that he was stubborn and that I thought him crazy, inasmuch as he clung to his self-deception and false opinion despite the diagnosis of all his doctors over so many years."[109] Platter also ridiculed his belief by urging that even if he had one or more frogs within him, they would not be able to survive more than an hour, for they would suffocate and be expelled by the intestines. A man who swallowed a live eel had expelled it dead and digested just ten hours later. Herons, too, ate frogs alive, but when they were caught and cut open, the frogs were dead. And finally Platter pointed out that frogs did not live more than two years, whereas his patient claimed to have had the same frog for seven years. This finally turned the trick. Under Platter's barrage of ridicule and criticism, the doctor-patient conceded defeat: "He admitted his folly,

107. *Observationes* (1963 ed.), pp. 57–58; 1614 ed., p. 41.
108. See *Mad Princes*, pp. 66–70, 89–92, 112–17, 146–47.
109. *Observationes* (1963 ed.), pp. 59–60; 1614 ed., p. 43.

thanked me, and was cured of this fantasy."[110] What did the patient say when he got home?

Let us notice in this remarkable case history that Platter first tried to deceive his patient by the recommended methods of rapport and deception, then turned to increasingly harsh and poisonous purgatives, and finally lost all patience and told the young sufferer that he was behaving childishly and foolishly, that if he just thought things through rationally, he would see that he could not have a frog inside himself. If we wanted to discover a theory behind this last kind of therapy, we could compare it to twentieth-century cognitive or rational-emotive therapy, but Platter was not operating from any such theory. As he said, he was tired and disgusted by his learned patient's constant and silly complaining. Sometimes, however, Platter's laughing dismissal of complaints offended those who came to him for help.[111]

Elsewhere in his *Observationes*, Platter turned a sympathetic ear to those plagued by blasphemous thoughts, suicidal temptations, and murderous impulses. Bloodletting and purgatives helped in such cases, he said, even though he frequently described such thoughts as "devilish" and "driven by the demon."[112] Love and intense jealousy also drove Platter's patients so mad that they had to be confined. Fear and frustration, guilt and jealousy, heresy and shocked revulsion at the sight of a man who had hanged himself drove other men and women out of their wits.[113] Impotence and other sexual problems came regularly to his attention, too.[114] Reflecting the sudden popularity of *melancholia hypochondriaca* as a diagnosis, Platter dealt repeatedly with this ailment, noting that such sufferers usually imagined that they were ill in various ways, and "while they do suffer some things that are typical of this kind of melancholy, still most of it is just imagined."[115] They had persuaded themselves that their "stomachs, lungs, livers, kidneys, and, among women, their wombs were weak, corrupt, and full of excrement. In reality, it was nothing of the sort, but a purely melancholy delusion."[116]

Several of Platter's descriptions of mad despair and of deeply melancholy and suicidal observations include stories that live up to our modern expectations of case histories much more perfectly than the other examples we have looked at from the sixteenth century. The reason for this lifelike directness would seem to lie in Platter's certainty that writing a diary was a useful exercise. For in his diary, too, Platter recorded with almost unique

110. Ibid., p. 60; 1614 ed., p. 43.
111. Ibid., pp. 56–57; 1614 ed., p. 39.
112. Ibid., pp. 60–62, 72; 1614 ed., pp. 44–47, 72–73.
113. Ibid., pp. 65, 71, 72, 73, 75, 77–78; 1614 ed., pp. 52–53, 71–80.
114. Ibid., pp. 153–62; 1614 ed., pp. 231–44.
115. Ibid., p. 70; 1614 ed., p. 70.
116. Ibid., p. 71; 1614 ed., p. 70.

confidence the daily events, both ordinary and extraordinary, to which he was exposed. Unlike Weyer, his observations were not aimed at proving or disproving some disputed point of medical or religious doctrine. Instead, they seem to have welled up from Platter's joy in seeing and describing. Often enough, he only saw what he expected to see, of course, and perhaps he was too quick to ascribe psychiatric cures to the herbal and chemical potions he concocted. But I know of no earlier set of "observations" that give us such a lively sense of what it was like in the sixteenth century to be a physician, consulted daily for help in almost any kind of case.[117] They are not so revealing as Montaigne's diary of his trip to Italy, but they do breathe the same air of discovery and of fresh, personal experience.

Conclusion

Observation literature, therefore, began in the sixteenth century to break the bonds of editorial commentary and reproduction apparent in its earlier exemplars. Johann Weyer, Pieter van Foreest, and Felix Platter all came to delight in recording their own firsthand, eyewitness case histories. These Renaissance physicians had not actually hit upon something radically or fundamentally new in the history of medicine, for we know that the praise of firsthand observations goes back at least to Hippocrates and Galen, and had been cultivated by Arab and Western medieval physicians as well. But within the terms of Renaissance German psychiatric writing, there was a dramatic surge of *observationes* and of lengthy case histories between Weyer's *De praestigiis daemonum* of 1563 and Platter's *Observationes* of 1614.[118] None of these works challenged the dominant physiology and psychiatry of Galen; they drew inspiration from ancient medicine rather than seeking to overturn it. Nevertheless, as we have seen, a number of new elements had become prominent in German psychiatry by about 1600.

In addition to the newly detailed descriptions of case histories, perhaps the most notable development toward the end of the century was a rising concern with the devil as a cause of mental disorder, despair, and full-fledged possession. As we have seen, the second half of the sixteenth century saw an epidemic of demonic possessions, and medicine could not re-

117. Ingrid Schiewek, "Zur Autobiographie des Basler Stadtarztes Felix Platter," *Forschungen und Fortschritte* 38, no. 12 (Berlin 1964): 368–72. On the diary as a form, see Peter Boerner, *Tagebuch* (Stuttgart, 1969); Gustav René Hocke, *Das europäische Tagebuch* (Wiesbaden, 1978), esp. pp. 45–69, 560; 563–65, 571–74, 594–96, 601, 606.

118. See, e.g., Chiara Crisciani, "History, Novelty, and Progress in Scholastic Medicine," in *Renaissance Medical Learning: Evolution of a Tradition*, ed. Michael R. McVaugh and Nancy Siraisi, *Osiris*, 2d ser., vol. 6 (1990), pp. 118–39; Danielle Jacquart, "Theory, Everyday Practice, and Three Fifteenth–Century Physicians," in ibid., pp. 140–60.

main immune to this newly potent demonology. German physicians of the early sixteenth century had hardly mentioned the devil, but in Jason Pratensis, the Evil One looms as a possible cause of mania, even though Pratensis ignored this possibility when he dealt with remedies. In Johann Weyer, we find a physician who clearly acknowledged the threat of demonic possession, but who also debunked all the efforts of exorcists to drive out demons. While the devil might be active everywhere, Weyer was also convinced that most supposed cases of possession were cunning frauds, and like other physicians, he sought long and hard for physical explanations before yielding any ground to the theologians. Johann Schenck von Grafenberg was, in truth, so hostile to demonic explanations that he urged the treatment of supposed demoniacs with just the same purges, bleedings, and sweatings regularly reserved for the melancholy. He reasoned that if one could deprive the demon of his favorite bath (black bile), one might accomplish an exorcism by physical means. Theologians understandably reacted in outrage at the temerity and presumption of physicians such as these, but an emerging consensus, even in the Church of Rome, began to hold, by 1600 or thereabouts, that demonic possession had to be rigorously proved by showing in every case at least one supernatural effect, one phenomenon that could have no physical explanation. This conceded most of the practical terrain to physicians, even if the Church insisted on keeping control over the detection of truly demonic possessions.[119] Despite these official fine points, however, ordinary Catholics continued to demand an ever-expanding array of exorcisms.[120]

Among Protestants, too, demonic influence and diabolical possession were by no means gone. This was, after all, the great age of the German witch-hunt, a panic that cost thousands of lives in both Catholic and Protestant territories. Felix Platter testified repeatedly to his experiences with demonic ailments and left room in his "baroque physiology" for direct demonic possession and for the actions of witches. It is noteworthy, however, that in his practice, Platter, like Weyer and Schenck before him, preferred to treat the demonically afflicted with physical and natural remedies. In the end, they were physicians.

119. Jean Céard, *La nature et les prodiges: L'insolite au XVIe siècle, en France* (Geneva, 1977), pp. 354–62; Maxime Laignel-Lavastine and Jean Vinchon, *Les malades de l'esprit et leurs médecins du XVIe au XIXe siècle: Les étapes des connaissances psychiatriques de la Renaissance à Pinel* (Paris, 1930), pp. 43–48. The *Sacerdotale romanum* printed at Venice in 1579 tried to restrict and govern the true signs of possession, but the most restrictive rules were those of 1614 (Adolf Franz, *Die kirchlichen Benediktionen im Mittelalter* [Freiburg im Breisgau, 1909], 2: 561). The basic point could be foolishly exaggerated. Obviously the Church did not withdraw from all areas in which it competed with physicians for influence. See, e.g., Donald A. Beecher, "Erotic Love and the Inquisition: Jacques Ferrand and the Tribunal of Toulouse, 1620," *Sixteenth Century Journal* 20 (1989): 41–53.

120. Franz, *Die kirchlichen Benediktionen*, 2: 585, 648–49.

We can see that with material such as this, Pratensis, Weyer, Schenck, and Platter were moving well beyond their classical and medieval sources. Demonic possession had been banished early on from the medical discourse of classical antiquity, only to return with a new vigor in the sixteenth century. But with the Roman Church's *Rituale romanum* of 1614, the physicians made good their claim to treat most supposedly demonic illnesses. Henceforth demonic possession would be circumscribed in ever-tighter coils of theological definition. Just as theologians came to redefine miracles so that they had to defy all the laws of nature, so, too, in the seventeenth century, high theologians came to credit very few cases of demonic possession. Ordinary Catholic believers (and some Protestants too) were, of course, slow to adopt this newly fastidious approach to the supernatural. Ordinary people might continue to go on pilgrimage or to pray to a saint for wondrous relief from affliction without worrying whether the relief, when it came, was strictly miraculous according to the latest theological definitions. And just so, ordinary Christians, especially in southern Germany and Austria, continued to sense the work of the devil in ailments that the learned had consigned for cure to physicians. These demonic and generally religious explanations, lasting well on into the eighteenth century, help us to understand the survival of miracles and demonic possession long after secular philosophers and rational theologians had cut the theoretical ground out from under belief in the supernatural. This topic will return in chapter 6, which treats the pilgrimages taken by the mad and for the mad.

Having examined the theological and medical languages that dealt with madness in sixteenth-century Germany, we must now take up the procedures and language of the law. In the German insanity defense, we shall find the survival of demons and the rise of melancholy in an exemplary conceptual collision. Perhaps nowhere else can we better scrutinize the religious context that enveloped early modern ideas of madness.

CHAPTER FOUR

𝔚itchcraft and the Melancholy Interpretation of the Insanity Defense

MEDICAL theories of melancholy mental disorder did not only affect medical treatment. By thinking of the mentally disordered as having a *medical* condition, one could also justify the consultation of medical authorities for advice on social policy, as occurs today, or even in legal matters, as began to occur more frequently in the late sixteenth century. To observe this process, one needs to look, not just at what the law said, but also at how it worked in practice. In the waning years of the twentieth century, people sometimes think that the insanity defense is one of the proud achievements of the Enlightenment and of the nineteenth century, or that it must be some sort of modern, "liberal," weak-kneed, tenderhearted, and softheaded approach to crime—as if a tough-minded attitude would ignore a defendant's state of mind either during the commission of a crime or during a trial. It often surprises modern readers to learn that in the West the insanity defense is at least two thousand years old. The ancient Romans, who were not known for their tender hearts or soft heads, had a well-developed set of principles for dealing with insanity, and a careful criminal insanity defense.[1] This jurisprudential tradition was adopted by the Germans, along with most other Western Europeans, in the Middle Ages and applied throughout the early modern period. The largest exception was England, which preserved its common law and had no general "reception" of Roman law. The English therefore had to develop their own insanity defense.[2] This chapter approaches German legal attitudes toward madness by

1. For the basic Roman approach to insanity in matters dealing with contracts, testaments, and witnesses, consult Justinian's *Institutes* 1.10, 1.14.2, 1.23.3, 2.10.6, 2.12.1, and 3.19.8, conveniently translated by Peter Birks and Grant McLeod with the Latin text of Paul Krueger (Ithaca, N.Y., 1987).
2. Nigel Walker, *Crime and Insanity in England*, 1: *The Historical Perspective* (Edinburgh, 1967).

following the twists and turns of the insanity defense in sixteenth- and seventeenth-century Germany.

Insanity and the Law in Germany

We can gain a clear view of how courts and jurists administered the insanity defense before it became thoroughly "medicalized" from the records of a gruesome and notorious murder trial in the duchy of Württemberg. On January 12, 1590, Conrad Herman, a master dyer from Lauffen on the Neckar, in the district of Bietigheim, murdered his wife and attacked his four children in their beds.[3] Neighbors intervened and arrested him, but the question arose at once whether Herman had been so out of his mind that he should perhaps not be punished. Numerous witnesses were interrogated, and the picture that emerged was of a troubled, suspicious, wrathful man, who often talked nonsense and who had accused his wife of being a witch. His wife had feared for her life and tried to take precautions before going to bed on January 12, insisting that the bedroom door be left open and alerting the servant and apprentice, who slept in the kitchen, asking them to come at once to her aid if they should hear any disturbance. She also tried to hide all knives and weapons in the house, all to no avail. Her husband had gone berserk, and now she was dead.

After this basic information was assembled, the learned jurists of the Tübingen legal faculty were consulted for their evaluation, a practice that was becoming routine in early modern Germany in all difficult cases. Citing Justinian's *Digest* 1.18.13–14, the jurists acknowledged that an insanity defense of course existed; but the serious question had to do with Conrad Herman's state of mind at the time of the murder. From the depositions, it seemed clear that he "often displayed melancholy and practiced weird nonsense" ("vilfeltigt erzeigte Melancholii unnd geübte selzame ungerheümbte sachen unnd händel"). And yet the jurists were persuaded that his deadly outburst had occurred during a lucid interval, not because he could justify his horrid deed in any way, but because he knew what he had done. He had tried to hide his murder from the neighbors; he spoke comprehendingly and knowingly of what he had done, and he understood what was said to him ("das er verstending unnd wissendt gewesen, was er

3. For details of the Herman case, I rely on the Württembergisches Hauptstaatsarchiv, A209, Bü. 1425, which contains all the assembled legal documents pertaining to it. I am grateful to Sönke Lorenz for bringing these materials to my attention. I have also drawn on Wendel Rösch's published but unauthorized report, *Warhafftige und Erschröckenliche geschicht, welche sich begeben unnd zugetragen hat* (Tübingen, 1590), a versified account that got the publisher, Alexander Hock, into trouble, because he issued it without Duke Ludwig's permission.

geredt, gethan, unnd warmit er umb gangen, was auch mit im geredt worden"). Over and over, the jurists remarked on the evidence of his "good understanding" both before and after his crime. He had apparently apologized to his wife for his suspicion of her, admitting that he was "not always right in the head" ("das ime ettwan nit recht im Kopf were") and promising to improve himself and to set their household on a new footing. Although his "melancholy disorder" had troubled him a few nights earlier to such an extent that he had not tolerated a single candle, he had seemed better on the twelfth, displaying his "good understanding." The jurists of Tübingen were also troubled by the likelihood (as it seemed to them) that Conrad Herman was only pretending to be mad and had actually given in to the suggestions of the evil spirit: "das er solches vorsäzlich unnd wissentlich, auss angenommener weiss simulatione cuiusdam dementiae gleichwoll uss eingebung dess besen Geists (dem er auss gefastem neidt, unnd zorn, gegen seinem unschuldigen weib zuvil nachgehengt) gethon haben." Herman had killed his wife "fiercely, but, in our opinion, knowingly and intentionally" ("grimmig doch unnsers erachtens wissentlich unnd vorsäzlich").

The key issue for the Tübingen professors was whether Herman had known and intended what he did. No one thought of consulting a physician, because the legal question was framed in such a way that lawyers and laymen themselves could judge the relevant issues. Although the professors spoke of Herman's melancholy and of his "sickness in the head" (*haubtplödigkeit*), he remained, in their view, fully responsible for his actions. And so they recommended on March 28, 1590, that the guilty man be beheaded and his corpse displayed upon the wheel, a sentence that was evidently carried out in early April. Despite the use of a few medical terms, the jurists did not concern themselves with recent disputes about criminal insanity and cited only the ancient texts of Justinian from over one thousand years earlier.

German legal procedures did not remain so purely Roman for long after 1590, because another troubling case seemed to demand a different solution. In April 1596, a desperate Saxon mother took the lives of several of her children. When she came to trial, the local magistrates decided to consult with the legal faculty at the University of Wittenberg. From the report of one of the professors, Peter Heig, we can peer in on the deliberations concerning her case. To the Wittenberg jurists, it was obvious at once that the distracted woman was "not of sound mind but desperate and emotional" ("non integrae mentis, sed desperatae et emotae"). Before committing the crime, she had carried on with absurd and sad words, claiming that her children were about to die of hunger, even though she had "a pot full of meats at home," and her husband agreed that there was enough food for all of them. She had killed her children to spare them an imagined death by starvation. Asked about her apparently "melancholy" state, her husband noted that she had had a slight fever before erupting in "wicked delirium," but this only complicated matters for the Wittenberg jurists, who knew that "physicians assert that melancholy is a disease without fever."[4] On the other hand, the ancient physician Celsus had affirmed that melancholy might begin without fever but then excite a low fever. Still, it was obvious that the poor melancholy woman was not suffering from "manifest insanity such as we usually find in mania and furor. For melancholy, even if present in the highest degree, does not force men into continuous insanity or delirium; rather they act usually more quietly, and in intervals they are less mad, so that sometimes the mind appears not so much disturbed by black bile as defeated."[5]

Professor Heig remarked that in such circumstances, and with such doubts, it was difficult to determine what the proper punishment for so inhuman a deed should be. "It was not clear that the woman committed a crime from some manifest madness [furor], but rather that she was driven to it by excessive sadness and by false imaginings and by despair of life."[6]

Once her deed was done and the neighbors, roused by the shrieks of her other children, had apprehended her, she cooled off a bit "and said that she recognized her crime, alleging all the while that she'd been sleepless and disturbed in the head, which had prevented her from considering the whole matter in her soul." Hence it would have been overly indulgent simply to absolve her of such an inhuman parricide, especially since some jurists held that even raging madness (furor) did not excuse a person fully from the penalties for parricide. Indeed, no one doubted the moral and legal competence of the melancholy:

And as concerns the melancholy, it can be seen that they are not to be classed with the insane at all, nor are they to be excused from punishment; indeed, certain people think that melancholy is the anger of the best geniuses. And the jurisconsults Ulpian and Paul . . . compare the melancholy with those who are immoderately timid, lustful, greedy, and angry; but no one could easily say that they are incapable of making a contract or a will or that they are immune from punishment.[7]

And so it was decided that she should be given an intermediate sentence: she was to be whipped and sent into permanent exile, but not before she had spent some time in jail, so that "ministers of the law and gospel could warn her diligently from the word of GOD concerning her error and bring

---

4. Petrus Heigius, *Quaestiones iuris tam civilis quam Saxonici . . . editae nunc primum cura Ludovici Person,* (Wittenberg, 1601), vol. 2, question 38, p. 332.

5. Ibid., p. 333.

6. Ibid.

7. Ibid., pp. 329–30.

her gradually from despair to faith in divine grace, and so that other things could be added for the care of her body and soul."[8] Thus the public would be avenged and (by her exile) a cause of infamous crime removed. One reason for the mercy shown in this judgment was that "women are by nature in their emotions weaker, and their minds sometimes wander." Heig cited as proof of this point Peter Binsfeld's recent discussion of the confessions of witches. In addition, melancholy affections did allow some mitigation of punishment in criminal cases (Heig here cited the commentary of Claudio Bertazzolio on Bartolus of Saxoferrato). Heig emphasized, however, that more than medical aid was necessary. The gospel brought a spirit of joy that could drive out the sad suggestions of the evil spirit, who sought "first to attack minds and then to trap them in his net." There was no misery, however great, that could tear the faithful from the love of Christ. To this pious conclusion, Heig added an unlawyerly string of Bible verses praising joy in the Lord as a remedy for the griefs of life, supplementing them with a note that Martin Luther, too, had repeatedly praised this kind of joy in his letters.[9] We have seen, indeed, that Luther often recommended religious solutions for mental anguish.

Although Heig analyzed this case in detail in order to show that melancholy persons were not all mad and beyond all punishment, we can observe a number of other important features in this case. First, and most obviously, Heig assumed that if a full *insania* or *furor* could be proved, the suspect should not be punished at all. Like the jurists of Tübingen, he simply assumed the validity of an insanity defense. Secondly, if we inquire into the legal sources of this doctrine, we find Heig citing the ancient Roman law and the Italian commentators on it of the fourteenth, fifteenth, and sixteenth centuries, along with a sprinkling of Spanish, French, and German jurists. His medical understanding came from Galen and from the sixteenth-century physicians Jean Fernel (1497–1558) and Leonhart Fuchs (1501–1566), and his religion, as we have seen, from the Bible and Martin Luther. Repeatedly, however, Heig cited the recently burgeoning literature on witchcraft as generally relevant to the understanding of imagination, intention, and the law, quoting such important contemporary demonologists as Johann Godelmann, Peter Binsfeld, and Jean Bodin. All in all, his understanding of the legal and moral issues was specifically that of the late sixteenth century. His version of the insanity defense could hardly have been composed at any other time.

8. Ibid., pp. 334.
9. Ibid., pp. 334–35.

The Roman and Medieval Insanity Defense

The Württemberg and Saxon jurists did not create the insanity defense ex nihilo. Their citations of ancient Roman law are a fair enough indication that it was traditional. Although it is likely that the ancient Greeks too had some form of insanity defense, the Romans with their flair for legal theory had worked it out in detail. Repeatedly, for example, the Romans assimilated the law dealing with the madman (*furiosus*) to the law regarding infants. The law for one should be the law for the other, because neither had any real understanding of what they did. Already for the Romans, intention was one of the cardinal features of a felony. Without criminal intent, an act might be wrong, but it was not felonious. In one of Justinian's most famous formulations, we read:

If you have clearly ascertained that Aelius Priscus is in such a state of insanity that he lacks all understanding through the continuous alienation of his mental faculties [*in eo furore esse, ut continua mentis alienatione omni intellectu careat*], and if there remains no suspicion that his mother was murdered by him under pretence of madness; then you can abandon consideration of the measure of his punishment, since he is being punished enough by his very madness [*cum satis furore ipso puniatur*].[10]

Careful readers will notice that Justinian here formulated an insanity defense with one peculiarity. After saying that a madman was not to be punished by the law, the *Digest* held that he was still punishable, although not by the state: "furiosus satis ipso furore puniatur." One reason for this peculiarity is perhaps that the ancient Romans did not entirely believe that *furor*, or madness, was merely a state of mental infancy or a purely physical condition.

When Cicero invented the Latin term *furor*, or madness, in the first century B.C., he praised the Romans for making a distinction that the Greeks could not, because the Greeks, in his view, had jumbled dissimilar conditions into the overstressed medico-physical category of *melancholia*.[11] We have seen that Renaissance physicians had their own difficulties with the medical concept of black bile, but the legal problems with the concept were also considerable. *Furor* as a Latin term, on the other hand, had connections to inspiration and to the divine, and Cicero had even noted that "we call it madness [*furor*] when the soul, pulled out of the body by divine impulse,

---

10. *The Digest of Justinian*, 1.18.14, trans. Alan Watson et al. (Philadelphia, 1985), 1: 36. See generally Theodor Mommsen, *Römisches Strafrecht* (Leipzig, 1899), pp. 75–77.

11. *Tusculan disputations* 3.5; I have used the edition and translation by C. D. Yonge, *The Academic Questions, Treatise De Finibus, and Tusculan Disputations of M. T. Cicero* (London, 1880), pp. 367–68.

is excited."[12] *Furor* for Cicero was a raving, prophetic, or poetic frenzy, a "total blindness of mind," that might be greater than madness or other ordinary and culpable perturbations of the mind.[13] The Roman jurists used *furor* to mean insanity, an intellectual and mental alienation, but the religious and Ciceronian origins of Roman thinking on *furor*, and the hint of their survival in the text of the *Digest*, were to leave a lasting impression on the insanity defense as it was deployed in the Middle Ages and in the sixteenth century. As we have seen, German jurists of the 1590s were concerned to discover the exact meaning of *furor* and to discount, as culpable, other disturbed mental states.

To see how and why the early modern German jurists made these distinctions and how they came to change them, we must look briefly at the history of the medieval insanity defense. In the early Middle Ages, we may be fairly sure, even the rudest German barbarians recognized some form of exception or special treatment in cases of insanity. The comfortable notion that Western Civilization has witnessed a steady and wholesome progress (or, for other observers, a namby-pamby liberal decline) in its willingness to consider the legal and moral implications of interior states of human consciousness is a distortion.[14] Certainly, in the history of law, scholars have found no straightforward development from a supposedly primitive concentration on outward acts and results (what the German jurists called *reine Erfolgshaftung*) to a more modern concern with intention.[15] Our twentieth-century view that willful harmdoing is worse than involuntary or accidental harmdoing is, after all, not just a modern example of psychological enlightenment. As Oliver Wendell Holmes remarked, even my dog knows the difference if I intentionally kick him or accidentally stumble over him.[16]

So when we look into the medieval and early modern insanity defense, we should not look for its invention but for its form and its development. How did it work? How often was it invoked? How was it explained? What other concepts did it evoke or depend upon?

When Roman law was revived in the twelfth and thirteenth centuries, the formulation of the criminal insanity defense did not at first command much attention. Even the famous commentator Bartolus of Saxoferrato

---

12. Cic. *De divin.* 1.31.61. Cf. *De divin.* 1.2.4. See also Adrien Audibert, *Études sur l'histoire du droit Romain*, vol. 1: *La folie et la prodigalité* (Paris, 1892), pp. 40–43.

13. Cic. *Tusc. disp.* 3.5.: "mentis ad omnia caecitatem."

14. See the early recognition of this often neglected matter in Wilhelm Eduard Wilda, *Geschichte des deutschen Strafrechts*, vol. 1: *Das Strafrecht der Germanen* (1842; repr., Aalen, 1960), pp. 644–48.

15. David Daube, *Roman Law: Linguistic, Social, and Philosophical Aspects* (Edinburgh, 1969), p. 172.

16. See Karl Binding, *Die Schuld im deutschen Strafrecht: Vorsatz, Irrtum, Fahrlässigkeit. Kurzes Lehrbuch* (Leipzig, 1919), p. 11.

(1314–1357) was content to note, very briefly, that a madman should not be punished, for as Justinian had reasoned, "he is punished enough by his very madness"; but Bartolus added the comment (whose origins lay in canon law) "and thus affliction should not be heaped upon the afflicted."[17] At the same time, it was plain to Bartolus that such persons should not be permitted to roam freely, and, again echoing Justinian, he observed that if family members would not step in to control them, they must be held in jail ("furiosi in carcere detineantur, si alias commode retinere non possunt").[18] His student Petrus Baldus de Ubaldis (1327–1406) was in this matter content to agree with Bartolus, emphasizing that the mad must be put into the custody of responsible men, and that no one should be presumed mad without proof.[19] For the most part, these early commentators were more concerned with property and institutions than with criminal law, and so madness came up mainly in their discussions of contracts and testaments, but in the writings of Albertus Gandinus (born ca. 1245, died after 1310) we find a thoughtful division of crime into three essential components: thinking (intent), acting (attempt), and completing.[20] If this were true, it might easily be argued that a man could kill without intent, and that in such a case, no crime existed in the full sense of the term. Although this line of thought seems to underestimate crimes of neglect and of omission, Gandinus held that it was their lack of intention that excused both children and madmen from punishment. This is a good example of what the assimilation of madness to infancy meant. Gandinus did not repeat the memorable but slightly puzzling Roman phrase that a madman was punished enough by his own madness.[21] Some late medieval canonists went so far as to assert that insanity was a kind of ignorance, which, as Johannes Andreae (1270–1348) remarked, is itself an excuse: "[I]gnorance arising in a defect of mind [*ex defectu scientiae*] is not a sin but a punishment."[22] A statute from Bologna in 1454 echoed this view, asserting that the essence of *furor* was an

---

17. Bartolus de Saxoferrato, *Opera omnia* (Venice, 1570–71), 1: 40.

18. Bartolus de Saxoferrato, *Commentaria in primam digesti veteris partem*, ed. Petrus Paulus Parisii Cardinalis (Lyon, 1550), 1: 46.

19. Baldus de Ubaldis, *Commentaria in digestum vetus* (Lyon, 1562), vol. 1, fol. 63v.

20. This doctrine made its way into German law in the *Klagspiegel* (ca. 1400–1425) and the work of Johann von Schwarzenberg (early sixteenth century), on whom see pp. 193–94. See also Roderich Stintzing, *Geschichte der populären Literatur des römisch-kanonischen Rechts in Deutschland am Ende des fünfzehnten und im Aufang des sechzehnten Jahrhunderts* (Leipzig, 1867) pp. 337–410.

21. Hermann Kantorowicz, *Albertus Gandinus und das Strafrecht der Scholastik* (Berlin, 1907–26), 2: 210–12.

22. Hostiensis (obit 1271) had already said something similar. See the excellent work of Georg Dahm, *Das Strafrecht Italiens im ausgehenden Mittelalter: Untersuchungen über die Beziehungen zwischen Theorie und Praxis im Strafrecht des Spätmittelalters, namentlich im XIV. Jahrhundert* (Berlin, 1931), p. 252.

intellectual defect: "furiosum qui in ea mentis alienatione sit, ut non intelligat vel non intellexerit, quid tunc agat" ("a madman, who is so mentally disturbed that he does not know or understand what he is doing").[23]

Gradually, Italian law and Italian lawyers came to exhibit an exquisite concern for the subtleties of negligence, mistakes, accidental harm, degrees of guilt and mitigating factors in punishment, a concern that was fed by Christianity in general and specifically by canon lawyers, who knew that sin and guilt did not depend on external actions alone, but on the interior condition of the heart.[24] Already by the thirteenth century, canonists had agreed that the deeds of a madman were not to be imputed to him "if the mind is so alienated that the man does not know what he is doing."[25] More broadly, canon lawyers held that a madman could not be held responsible for his deeds because (1) he did not know what he did; (2) he was impelled or forced by some inexplicable necessity; or (3) he was not capable of reason—that is, he was not in charge of himself because he lacked the faculty of deliberation.[26] With such distinctions, the lawyers of the medieval Church went well beyond the ancient Roman jurists in their understanding of the varieties of insanity. Considered abstractly, these three versions of the insanity defense point to three distinct notions of insanity, as (1) a defect of knowledge; (2) an inner compulsion; or (3) a defect of rational capacity. In at least the second and third notions (and possibly implicitly in the first as well), a madman could hardly be said to have free will. He was little more than a beast, which could not sin and could not really deserve punishment.[27] Madness wiped out freedom and thus all imputation of sin. Moreover, the canonists drew an important distinction between the truly insane, who lacked will and could not therefore formulate a criminal intention, and the intellectually impaired, who could not understand the full import of their deeds and therefore, although guilty, could not be so severely pun-

23. Ibid., p. 253.
24. See the excellent works of Woldemar Engelmann: e.g., *Die Schuldlehre der Postglossatoren und ihre Fortentwicklung* (1895; repr., Aalen, 1965), esp. p. 29; *Irrtum und Schuld nach der italienischen Lehre und Praxis des Mittelalters* (Berlin, 1922); and "Der geistige Urheber des Verbrechens nach dem italienischen Recht des Mittelalters," in *Festschrift für Karl Binding* (Leipzig, 1911), 2: 387–610.
25. Gratian and the early glossators of the twelfth century were not entirely clear on this matter, because they admitted that the deeds of a madman could be imputed to him if he had sinfully caused his own madness, here relying on a notion that had originally been used to condemn nocturnal emissions if a man had allowed himself to think lustful thoughts before going to sleep. By far the best discussion of this matter is Stephan Kuttner, *Kanonistische Schuldlehre von Gratian bis auf die Dekretalen Gregors IX.* (Vatican City, 1935), pp. 85–116; the quotation, from Huguccio, is at p. 107, n. 2.
26. Ibid., pp. 96–97.
27. Ibid., pp. 96–97, n. 4. Animals involved in crimes of bestiality were sometimes killed, but canonists were clear that this was not literally a merited punishment.

ished as those of normal understanding.[28] By the end of the fifteenth century, such statements had become commonplaces.[29]

By the mid fifteenth century, criminal jurists had taken over many of the subtle distinctions of the canonists. Perhaps the best example of the increasing skill displayed by legists in dissecting degrees of guilt is the substantial work on crimes, *De maleficiis*, by Angelus Aretinus (1472). In his analysis, we may survey the basic shape of the insanity defense in the late Middle Ages. The essence of a fully criminal act was that one "knowingly and maliciously" intended to harm (*scienter dolose*).[30] But a madman does not fit this criterion, "and he is punished enough by his own madness." What if he does have lucid intervals of sanity? This was a topic that had mainly concerned the ancient Roman jurists when they tried to tell whether a testator's will was legitimate and enforceable, but Aretinus (citing the Accursian Gloss on Justinian's *Digest*) adapted it to criminal concerns: "Even if he does have lucid intervals, if he commits an offense while tormented by his malady, he may not be held responsible" ("[G]lossa dicit quod idem in eo qui habet dilucida intervalla, quia si in illo tempore quo vexatur dolore delinquit, non tenetur").[31] Sympathetically, Aretinus noted that the mad are born for suffering injury ("istae personae sunt aptae natae ad suscipiendum iniuriam") not for causing it in others ("non autem ad inferendum alteri"), and so anyone who injured a mad person should be punished. One of the knottiest problems with the insanity defense, in that age or in ours, was the question of whether an offense was committed during a lucid interval (*scienter dolose*). How could one tell the state of mind of a criminal at the time of his act? Often it was difficult, but Aretinus noted that a previous condition of madness shifted the burden of proof to the accuser, who had to prove that the offense had occurred during a lucid interval ("sic antiquus furor transferat onus probandi in adversarium").[32]

Throughout the sixteenth century, German jurists admired and cited the Italian views we have just outlined, and made little or no effort to construct a peculiarly German law. From their scholarly point of view, such a construction would have been as odd as trying to invent a specifically German medicine. Dealing as the jurists did with Roman law, they held that they

28. Dahm, *Strafrecht Italiens*, pp. 252–53; Kuttner, *Kanonistische Schuldlehre*, p. 165.

29. See their incorporation, e.g., in the most popular confessional manual, the *Summa angelica* by Angelus Carletus de Clavisio (died ca. 1495). I have used the Lyon edition of 1521. The entry s.v. *furiosus* appears on fol. cxxxviii, verso, and cites the most familiar passages from the *Digest* to show that the mad may not be punished, for their madness is punishment enough; that they can suffer injury even though they cannot themselves injure; and that what they do is as if no one did it, since no one was responsible.

30. Aretinus, *De maleficiis, cum additionibus* (Lyon, 1555), p. 315.

31. Ibid., p. 320.

32. Ibid., pp. 320–21.

were treating the very principles of reason itself. And so it should not surprise us to see German jurists regularly citing the opinions of their French and Italian colleagues. Throughout the sixteenth century, the Germans remained mainly faithful to the traditional Italian interpretation of Roman law (the *mos italicus*) rather than to the newer teachings of the *mos gallicus* (the historical school of French Renaissance jurisprudence). One of the founders of the *mos gallicus*, Andrea Alciati, actually thought that efforts to exculpate the mad had gone too far. Alciati agreed with Roman tradition that the madman must not be punished, "for penalties have been set up primarily for the sake of correction, which is meaningless in a madman for he does not understand the matter and must be treated as if he were absent." Claiming that this law applied only to corporal punishment, however, he advanced the novelty that "it is all right that the insane be punished with the penalty of imprisonment (properly speaking) and with the seizure of goods."[33] In so speaking, Alciati flew in the face of late medieval commentary, which he was famous for repudiating on theoretical grounds. Even more seriously, however, Alciati here seemed to reject the words of the *Digest* itself, for that body of ancient legal wisdom had asserted that the criminal lunatic "must be closely confined, and, if you think it advisable, even in chains; this need not be done by way of punishment as much as for his own protection and the security of his neighbors."[34] Alciati's explicit recommendation that a madman could indeed be punished (although not corporally) was not based on any discernible principle of humanist jurisprudence, or on any ancient text of supposedly unpolluted Roman wisdom, but it may have been founded on the modern fear that, left to itself, the insanity defense might get out of hand. Alciati's view also assumed the existence of prisons, essentially a late medieval and modern invention.[35]

I have discovered no German jurists who followed Alciati in his explicit assertion that in some cases the mad could be punished, but if we ask whether these theories were followed in practice, we find that during the fifteenth century, some German jurisdictions proceeded as if they had never heard of Roman law at all, as indeed they may not have. Occasionally, the insane might even be legally executed, as occurred at Breslau (Wrocław) in 1486 and Frauenstädt (Wschowa) in 1490.[36] If any pattern can

33. Andrea Alciati, *Digestorum titulos aliquot, pagina quarta enumeratos Commentaria* (Lyon, 1560), fol. 83r. Cf. Justinian *Digest* 17.124.1.

34. Justinian *Digest* 1.18.14; ed. Watson, 1: 36.

35. For commentators who followed Alciati on these points, see Julius Clarus, *Opera omnia* (Frankfurt a/M, 1576), pp. 294–95; Didacus Covarruvias, *Opera omnia* (Frankfurt a/M, 1583), vol. 1, fols. 63r, 267r–270v; Jacobus Menochius, *De arbitriis iudicum quaestionibus and causis centuriae sex* (Geneva, 1630), "Qua poena furiosus puniatur," p. 605, in which Menochio cites this opinion of Alciati as "verior et receptior opinio."

36. Rudolf His, *Das Strafrecht des deutschen Mittelalters*, pt. 1: *Die Verbrechen und ihre Folgen in allgemeinen* (Leipzig, 1920), pp. 66–67.

be discerned among the actual statutes of late medieval Germany's towns and territories, it is a retreat away from the high medieval notion of holding the custodian responsible for the misdeeds of any madman in his care, a notion we find in such law books as the *Sachsenspiegel* (ca. 1230), the *Blume von Magdeburg* (late fourteenth century) and the *Statutes of Goslar* (mid fourteenth century). In place of such ideas of displaced liability, many fifteenth-century statutes specifically held the unfortunate madman himself responsible for his misdeeds and explicitly sanctioned the punishment of the insane.[37]

The Reception of Roman Law in Germany

What should we conclude? It seems that high legal theory as taught in the Italian schools of the late Middle Ages asserted with uniformity and persuasiveness that the mad should not be punished. It seems just as clear, however, that many German statutes of the later Middle Ages and some actual fifteenth-century trials sanctioned the punishment and even the execution of lunatic criminals. Although the famous sixteenth-century Reception of Roman law in Germany was often only a centralization or clarification of law, on the issue of personal liability and responsibility, it was something more. It marked a decisive turn away from the fifteenth-century practices to which we have just alluded and toward the *mos italicus* of the learned Italian commentators. The Worms legal reform edict of 1498 specifically protected the mad from punishment.[38]

The first major exponent of the new (or newly Roman) view was Johann von Schwarzenberg, the legal scholar who wrote the influential Bamberg criminal code in 1507. With a profoundly religious and ethical concern for the subjective guilt of specific offenders, Schwarzenberg made intention the cornerstone of his jurisprudence. Instead of remaining content with the crude general formulas that had hitherto prevailed, he insisted that individual cases had to be scrutinized carefully to tease out different degrees of legal culpability.[39] Refusing to trust the ignorant interpretations of local judges, Schwarzenberg decreed in the Bamberg code that "if a crime is committed by someone who because of youth or other weakness does not have his wits, the case should in all situations be referred to our council" (Article 205).[40] This explicit comparison of madness to childishness was, of

37. Ibid., pp. 66–68; Eberhard Schmidt, *Einführung in die Geschichte der deutschen Strafrechtspflege*, 2d ed. (Göttingen, 1951), pp. 67–68.

38. Schmidt, *Einführung*, pp. 68, 102–8.

39. Erik Wolf, *Grosse Rechtsdenker der deutschen Geistesgeschichte*, 4th ed. (Tübingen, 1963), pp. 119–20; Schmidt, *Einführung*, pp. 111–13.

40. Wolf, *Grosse Rechtsdenker*, p. 120.

course, traditional in Roman and canon law. Despite its obvious weaknesses as a general analogy, the comparison did make clear a common principle: culpability required that one be *doli capax*—that is, capable of a malicious intention.[41] Because they could not have malice, it made no sense to punish madmen or "infants" below the age of seven. The traditional and complicated history of this rule contained at least one interesting wrinkle. If a child acted with so much cunning and understanding that he did seem to be *doli capax*, then one could claim that his malice filled out his majority, and such a child could be punished as an adolescent or even as an adult.[42] Charles V's imperial criminal code of 1532 (the *Carolina*) picked up this point when it affirmed that malice could "make up for age."[43] Unfortunately for the insanity defense, this scrupulosity with respect to infancy could have caused a great deal of confusion when it came to examining cases of raging or furious madmen. Some of these afflicted souls would surely have showed enough cunning, enough malice, to be treated as legally sane. That is, of course, the great danger with analogies or metaphors: they are often expected to illuminate more than they can.

Over the course of the sixteenth century, therefore, German law came increasingly to include explicit references to Roman law and Roman procedures, and in this process to include large chunks of canon law as well.[44] Nowhere is this more evident than in the history of the crime of witchcraft. As understood by most secular jurisdictions in 1500, witchcraft was the crime of *maleficium*, of harmful magic understood as the production of physical harm through illicit, demonic means. The *Malleus maleficarum* of Heinrich Krämer (Institoris), published in 1487, had, however, tried to shift the focus away from the actual harm done to the spiritual state of infidelity and heresy that made maleficium possible. In the view of the Dominican author, the pact with the devil was the heart of the crime of witchcraft. From a canon-legal point of view, with an emphasis on states of mind and sinful intentions, this shift of understanding was reasonable, but we may well ask why the secular law found it plausible. Some years ago I suggested that the secular courts of Germany came to accommodate the clerical views of Krämer (Institoris) because the secular reasoning of codes such as the *Carolina* was muddled.[45] There was, however, another reason too.

Michael Kunze has recently emphasized that the single most important

---

41. Kuttner, *Kanonistische Schuldlehre*, pp. 124–28.

42. Justinian *Code* 2.42.3 introduced the phrase *malicia supplet aetatem* (Kuttner, *Kanonistische Schuldlehre*, p. 128).

43. "Allso das die Bosheit das allter erfüllet möcht" (*Carolina*, art. 164).

44. See, e.g., Ulrich Zasius's discussion of the three kinds of furiosi, *Opera omnia*, vol. 3, cols. 336–37, paras. 3–5.

45. H. C. Erik Midelfort, *Witch Hunting in Southwestern Germany, 1562–1684: The Social and Intellectual Foundations* (Stanford, 1972), pp. 22–24, 114–17.

German book on law in the sixteenth century, Ulrich Tengler's *Layenspiegel*, was not originally the powerful apology for the *Malleus* that historians have described. When Tengler published his work in 1509, he treated witchcraft only very briefly, as an afterthought to his section on Jewish corruption and usury. In one paragraph, he added that witches and magicians were also heretics who harmed the Christian faith and "especially cooperate with the evil spirit (with God's permission) to cause the elements to clash, making storms and producing many kinds of harm to men and beasts."[46] Tengler concluded that they should "as heretics," be stripped of "all their honors and offices and be excluded from the Christian community," and that "appropriate inquisitions" should determine what punishments or other actions should be added. It is worth pausing to notice that this clause assumed that witches had honors and offices to give up—that they were, in other words, men of wealth and influence, rather than the marginal women who were actually swept up in the great German witch-hunt of the sixteenth and seventeenth centuries. To that extent, Ulrich Tengler's original *Layenspiegel* was useless as a manual for finding women witches, even though he referred learnedly to Roman and canon law and also unspecifically to the *Malleus maleficarum*.[47]

As it happened, this reference to the *Malleus* was far too unspecific for Ulrich's son Christoph, who was a priest and a "doctor of arts and canon law" (*artium et iurispontificii doctori*). When Christoph the theologian undertook to edit a second edition of his lawyer father's work, published in 1512, he made a variety of additions, including the Golden Bull of Charles IV and a large excerpt from the *Malleus maleficarum*.[48] He explained that witchcraft involved such incredible events that some jurists even doubted whether witches existed. As a result, witchcraft was not everywhere prosecuted, and it had lately gotten "completely out of hand" (*merklich überhand*). The *Malleus* had the solution to this overwhelming problem, and Christoph Tengler summarized its provisions in some detail: the use of accusation, inquisition, and torture in ferreting out the evil of witchcraft, a crime now described as mainly committed by women. Instead of one paragraph on witchcraft, the theologically infected *Layenspiegel* of 1512 now had ten pages on the crime, and it was in this form that the *Layenspiegel* was known throughout the first half of the sixteenth century.[49]

46. Ulrich Tengler, *Layen Spiegel: Von rechtmässigen ordnungen in burgerlichen und peinlichen regimenten* (1st ed., Augsburg, 1509); I cite here the revised ed. of Strasbourg, 1582, fols. 125–26; see Michael Kunze, *Der Prozess Pappenheimer* (Ebelsbach, 1981), pp. 175–77.

47. The column note says: "vi mall. male cum ibi no."

48. *Der neu Layenspiegel* (Augsburg, 1512), fols. 159r–163v.

49. The original 1509 edition was reissued in Strasbourg by M. Hupfuff in 1510 and 1511. Christoph Tengler's edition, with his extensive additions, appeared not only in 1512, but also in 1514, 1518, 1527, 1530, 1532, 1538, and 1544.

This infusion of canon law did not, however, immediately affect the insanity defense in the Holy Roman Empire. The renowned Bruges jurist Jost Damhouder declared in 1555, for example, that we excuse the *furiosi et phrenetici* from accusations of murder just as we do children and infants, for they all lack true consent of will and of mind. It was a sign of the sorry times that mere babes of six were now as cunning and malicious as youths of fifteen used to be, but the acts of the mad were nonetheless to be reckoned as if they had been accidental or *sine facto personae*.[50] The only wrinkle Damhouder introduced here was the proviso that "there is no excuse if he commits his crime before falling into furor," just as there were prudent limits to the general rules that sleep and drunkenness excused one from the charge of felony.[51]

Similarly, in 1538, the well-known Frankfurt jurist Johann Fichard claimed that the madman was similar to no one more than to the drunkard, and concluded that in both cases the mind-beclouding condition should mitigate the punishment, if any punishment at all were appropriate.[52] In cases of merely verbal injury such as libel, he said, there could be no crime without the will to injure, and so drunkenness would constitute a full excuse. We can see that Fichard and others were drawing close to an analysis of the actual mental and physiological condition of those accused of crime, but they had not yet turned to medical opinion.

Johann Weyer's Assault

The jurists were not to enjoy their hermetically sealed off isolation from the world of medicine or theology much longer. In 1563, Johann Weyer published the first edition of his extraordinary *De praestigiis daemonum* ("On the Deceits of the Demons") and succeeded in fundamentally altering the terms of legal discourse. This is a large claim and one that runs counter to conventional wisdom on the subject. The profound scholar Friedrich Schaffstein concluded, for example, that between 1550 and 1750 there was no development at all in the area of legal responsibility.[53] Jurists from the end of the period were still repeating the wisdom of 1550, he thought, but as we shall see, the witchcraft controversy had an unexpected impact. Even though medicine did not come up with any decisive or new psychiatric insight in the sixteenth century, the insanity defense was pushed in a new direction by the controversy surrounding Johann Weyer.

50. Jost Damhouder, *Enchiridion rerum criminalium* (Lyon, 1555), fol. 273.
51. Ibid., fols. 274–78.
52. Johann Fichard, *Consiliorum* (Frankfurt a/M, 1590), vol. 1, fol. 130v.
53. Friedrich Schaffstein, *Die allgemeinen Lehren vom Verbrechen in ihrer Entwicklung durch die Wissenschaft des gemeinen Strafrechts* (Berlin, 1930), p. 98.

We have already encountered Weyer's medical views of demonic possession and bewitchment. More important, legally speaking, was Weyer's lengthy and learned argument that the women accused of witchcraft were not guilty of harming anyone, and that they therefore should not be burned to death. Instead, these women (and he thought that witches [*lamiae* or *sagae*] were overwhelmingly women) merely hallucinated or dreamed that they had entered a pact with the devil, that they flew off to the Sabbath with him, that they had sex with him, and so on. Weyer reached this extraordinary conclusion, not by claiming, as a modern skeptic might, that the devil was nonexistent, but paradoxically by affirming that he was far more powerful and deceptive than was usually thought. A host of modern scholars have charged that Weyer was trying to draw a conclusion that his premises unfortunately would not permit. His attack has seemed "logically flimsy."[54] They have held that if the devil was as powerful as Weyer said he was, then witchcraft was not only possible but likely, and Leland Estes has even advanced the remarkable claim that Weyer's approach, by introducing uncertainty, actually fomented witch-hunting rather than dampening it, as he had intended.[55]

To understand Weyer's contribution to the insanity defense, we need to view Weyer's enterprise and argument as a whole, not confining our attention to Weyer's legal views, important though they were. Crucial to the development of Weyer's views was exposure to the best Renaissance thinking on the nature of magic, religion, and heresy.[56] As a trained physician, he could, of course, marshal the opinions of Hippocrates and Galen whenever he wanted to, but it is more striking how willing he was to draw radical religious conclusions from medical evidence. Moreover, Weyer was thoroughly familiar with the Roman tradition of civil and canon law.

54. See H. R. Trevor-Roper, *The European Witch-Craze of the Sixteenth and Seventeenth Centuries and Other Essays* (New York, 1969); E. William Monter, "Inflation and Witchcraft: The Case of Jean Bodin," in *Action and Conviction in Early Modern Europe*, ed. T. K. Rabb (Princeton, 1969), pp. 371–89; Sydney Anglo, "Melancholia and Witchcraft: The Debate Between Wier, Bodin, and Scot," in *Folie et déraison à la Renaissance* (Brussels, 1976), pp. 209–22; Christopher Baxter, "Johann Weyer's 'De praestigiis daemonum': Unsystematic Psychopathology," in *The Damned Art*, ed. Sydney Anglo (London, 1977), pp. 53–75; and id., "Jean Bodin's 'De la démonomanie des sorciers': The Logic of Persecution," in ibid., pp. 76–105, at p. 77.

55. Leland L. Estes, "The Medical Origins of the European Witch Craze: A Hypothesis," *Journal of Social History* 17 (1983): 271–84.

56. On the life of Johann Weyer, one must still consult Carl Binz, *Doctor Johann Weyer: Ein rheinischer Arzt, der erste Bekämpfer des Hexenwahns* (Bonn, 1885; 2d ed., Berlin, 1896). Rudolf van Nahl provides a survey of more recent research in *Zauberglaube und Hexenwahn im Gebiet von Rhein und Maas: Spätmittelalterlicher Volksglaube im Werk Johan Weyers (1515–1588)* (Bonn, 1983), pp. 26–36.

THE SOURCES OF WEYER'S IDEAS

Among Weyer's most important early experiences were the year or two he spent as a servant and assistant to the famous scholar Heinrich Cornelius Agrippa of Nettesheim. As a youth of sixteen or seventeen, Weyer lived with Agrippa in Bonn and came to regard him fondly as "my revered teacher,"[57] using his secretarial position to gain access to occult works that then circulated only in manuscript.[58] From Agrippa, Weyer evidently imbibed a permanent dislike for Aristotle and for the Peripatetic tradition; but he also developed a strong distaste as well for that element in the Platonic tradition that emphasized the power of magical words. In this distaste, Weyer found himself rejecting Agrippa's *De occulta philosophia* and sympathizing rather with Agrippa's later *De vanitate scientiarum*. Late in life, when accused of uncritical dependence on Agrippa, Weyer pointed out that even Agrippa himself had come to reject many of his early occult ideas.[59] Probably more important to Weyer than any specific doctrine of Agrippa's was his mentor's courageous example as a broadly learned, tolerant man with distinct, probably even heretical, religious views. Weyer probably also knew that in 1519, Agrippa had successfully defended a woman accused of witchcraft in Metz; Agrippa had claimed at that time that the woman could not be held for witchcraft solely because her mother had been a witch, for such a conclusion would deny the power of baptism to free Christians from the grip of the devil.[60] Weyer also used this specific argument, but it may be more important that Weyer learned in this way to employ essentially religious arguments in legal cases. As we shall see, much of his later opposition to witchcraft doctrine was religious in nature. From Agrippa, Weyer may have imbibed a broad religious tolerance as well, for Agrippa had been hounded from city to city all his life on account of religious views that were surely unorthodox and may well have been a form of Nicodemite spiritualism.[61] It is of interest that despite the openly magical operations of

57. Weyer, *De praestigiis daemonum* (Basel, 1583), bk. 2, ch. 5, col. 161; id., *Witches, Devils, and Doctors in the Renaissance: Johann Weyer, "De praestigiis daemonum,"* ed. George Mora et al. (Binghamton, N.Y., 1991), p. 111.

58. This was how Weyer came to read Trithemius's *Steganographia*, for example (*De praestigiis daemonum*, bk. 2, ch. 6, col. 168).

59. Johann Weyer, *Liber apologeticus*, in id., *Opera omnia* (Amsterdam, 1660), pp. 625–26, replying to Leo Suavius (Jacques Gohory).

60. Heinrich Cornelius Agrippa, *Opera omnia* (Lyon, 1600?; repr. Hildesheim, 1970), 2: 687–91, at p. 688. On Agrippa's approach to magic, see Paola Zambelli, "Scholastiker und Humanisten: Agrippa und Trithemius zur Hexerei. Die natürliche Magie und die Entstehung kritischen Denkens," *Archiv für Kulturgeschichte* 67 (1985): 41–80.

61. Paola Zambelli, *L'ambigua natura della magica: Filosofi, streghe, riti nel Rinascimento* (Milan, 1991), pp. 121–52; and id., "Magic and Radical Reformation in Agrippa of Nettesheim," *Journal of the Warburg and Courtauld Institute* 39 (1976): 69–103.

De occulta philosophia, Weyer never identified Agrippa as a magician of any sort, preferring to demonstrate (accurately but misleadingly) that Agrippa was not the author of the notorious fourth book of *De occulta philosophia* and insisting that Agrippa had heartily repudiated genuinely dangerous magicians.[62]

Despite his year or two with one of Europe's leading Neoplatonist magicians, therefore, Weyer came away from Agrippa unimpressed by Plato and appalled at learned magic. What he took away from Agrippa was probably a "Nicodemite" ability to keep his religious views to himself, a suspicion that accusations of witchcraft were irreligious, and a tendency to mix religion, medicine, and law into an amalgam that was for his day unusual if not unorthodox.

Second only to the importance of Agrippa for Weyer was his obvious, if always unstated, debt to Martin Luther and the Protestant Reformation. In his published works, Weyer often implied, but only once explicitly admitted, that he was a Protestant, and a hundred years ago Catholic partisans who confined their reading to the *De praestigiis daemonum* were still trying to claim him for the Catholic camp.[63] It is all too evident from his constant attacks on fraudulent priests, false Catholic miracles, possessed convents, superstitious peasants, and phony exorcisms, however, that Weyer could scarcely have been a pious Catholic, not even an "Erasmian" Catholic. Although Erasmus had been able to attack some of these as superstitious in the period 1500–1525, the mood of Catholic Europe hardened against such "liberal" views, especially in the decades after 1560, and Erasmians found it harder and harder to remain faithfully within the Roman fold. So Weyer's scathing and sarcastic attacks on Catholic piety can hardly be construed as vestiges of an Erasmian Catholicism. On the other hand, Weyer's references to Protestants, and especially to Philipp Melanchthon, were warm and admiring, and he dedicated various editions of his works to the Lutheran magistrates of Frankfurt and Bremen. Most telling of all was his open praise for the Countess Anna of Tecklenburg and her whole family for preserving, from the 1520s onward, "the pure teaching of the holy gospel and of true divine service." It was her father, Count Conrad, whom Weyer especially praised for introducing "God's Word and the reformed practice of His holy sacraments" into his territories in 1527.[64] Could there have been a clearer declaration of Weyer's Protestant sympathies?

62. Weyer, *De praestigiis daemonum*, bk. 2, ch. 5, cols. 161–64; id., *Liber apologeticus*, pp. 626–27; cf. Agrippa, *De occulta philosophia*, bk. 1, ch. 39, in *Opera omnia*, 1: 69, where Agrippa sharply condemns the gnostic magi.

63. This effort has not yet ceased. See Rudolf van Nahl, *Zauberglaube und Hexenwahn im Gebiet von Rhein und Maas: Spätmittelalterlicher Volksglaube im Werk Johan Weyers (1515–1588)* (Bonn, 1983).

64. These hitherto unnoticed remarks are to be found in Weyer's *Artzney Buch: Von*

Weyer, in fact, represented at its fullest Lutheran pitch the conclusion that the devil was overwhelmingly powerful and deceptive: for those who thought that they could act with assurance, Weyer pointed out that the devil could exploit and manipulate even sincere actions and intentions. It was not only Lutherans, of course, who held that the devil was the ruler of this world, but Catholics had retained a large measure of confidence in the prescribed rituals of the Church, while Calvinists often argued that the age of miracles was over, and that the devil had a mainly spiritual influence on the world.[65] Lutherans, by way of contrast were often left with the disconcerting view that the devil was loose in the land, that he could indeed work wonders, and that ritual materials and ritual actions such as blessed salt, holy water, and exorcism were powerless. Prayer and fasting were all that could be recommended, and they provided no real assurance or guarantee. For such Lutherans, this world was a dangerous and deceptive place.

The third crucial influence on Weyer's legal views was Erasmus, not the cardboard stereotype of a mild-mannered, liberal, right-thinking man recently ridiculed by Christopher Baxter,[66] but the serious religious thinker for whom the views of the early Church retained an authority undiminished by 1,000 years of Constantinian Caesaro-papism. When Erasmus asked by what right the Church punished heresy with death, he was probing what he saw as the unwarranted merger of ecclesiastical and secular concerns. Jesus' parable of the tares in Matt. 13 made it clear enough, to Erasmus at least, that heretics should not be uprooted from the Christian community for fear of eradicating true Christians as well. This was actually one of the most common arguments for religious toleration in the sixteenth century and one that we should not confuse with modern liberal arguments constructed on relativist or pluralist foundations. The point was that even on profoundly Christian grounds, Erasmus and others like him could not find religious warrant for eliminating those with whom the Church disagreed. Johann Weyer cited Erasmus with some frequency, but nowhere more fervently than on just this point, one that subsumed witchcraft under heresy (just as the late medieval Church had taught) but then asked by what right witch-heretics were to be executed. As we shall see, this Erasmian argument served a crucial function in Weyer's general theory.

The fourth and final area of general influence on Weyer was the Renaissance idea of melancholy, an idea that, as we have seen, was very much on

---

etlichen biß anher unbekandten unnd unbeschriebenen Kranckheyten (Frankfurt a/M, 1583), *Vorrede*, fol. B4v; cf. also fols. 59v–60v, 64r–64v.

65. See D. P. Walker, *Spiritual and Demonic Magic from Ficino to Campanella* (London, 1958); id., *Music, Spirit and Language in the Renaissance* (London, 1985); and H. A. Kelly, *The Devil at Baptism: Ritual, Theology and Drama* (Ithaca, N.Y., 1985).

66. Baxter, "Johann Weyer's 'De praestigiis daemonum,'" pp. 53–75.

the rise among academically orthodox physicians. Already in 1515, the same Andrea Alciati who urged a restriction of the insanity defense had written that many supposed witches had more need of purification by hellebore (the usual purge for excess melancholy) than by fire: "Non paucae helleboro potius quam igne purgandae."[67] At about that time, Agrippa was speculating that the force of the melancholy imagination might be great enough to cause a person to ascend while asleep to places that the waking could hardly attain.[68] By the 1550s, Girolamo Cardano was able to combine these bits and pieces and argue forcefully that witches suffered from melancholy, which drove them to imagine that they did many wondrous and horrible things.[69] When Giambattista della Porta published his famous book on natural magic, *Magiae naturalis*, in 1558, it was becoming widely accepted that various herbs and poisons could cause fearful dreams and hallucinations, and that at least some witches used a special salve that induced a deep trance accompanied by visions of flight to the witches' Sabbath.[70] The theories of melancholy and of hallucinatory drugs, therefore, gave sixteenth-century Europeans a plausible and entirely natural way of explaining away the voluntary confessions made by some of those convicted of witchcraft. They were theories with which Weyer made himself thoroughly familiar, but up until the witchcraft debate unleashed by Weyer in 1563, these ideas had little or no legal impact. What was it that Weyer added to the thought of Agrippa, Luther, Erasmus, Cardano, and Porta?

WEYER'S 'DE PRAESTIGIIS DAEMONUM'

There are many remarkable features of Weyer's book, many respects in which it was a powerful, even if sometimes confused, treatise. For one thing, Weyer recounted his tales and anecdotes with such tongue-in-cheek seriousness that one suspects that he had read Johann Fischart and François Rabelais.[71] Amid a flood of stories concerning gullible peasants, lascivious women, and lusty priests, Weyer retold the stories of Faust and of the Pied Piper of Hamelin, along with tales of monstrous births and mixed fa-

67. Hansen, *Quellen*, pp. 263 f., citing Alciati's *Parergon* of 1515.

68. Agrippa, *De occulta philosophia*, bk. 3, ch. 43, in *Opera omnia*, 1: 440.

69. G. Cardano, *De rerum varietate* (Basel, 1557), ch. 8; cf. Peter Burke, "Witchcraft and Magic in Renaissance Italy: Gianfrancesco Pico and His Strix," in *The Damned Art*, ed. Sydney Anglo (London, 1977), pp. 32–52, at pp. 41, 48.

70. Giambattista della Porta, *Magia naturalis* (1st ed., Naples, 1558); I have used the later edition, *Magiae naturalis libri viginti* (Naples, 1589); cf. Lynn Thorndike, *A History of Magic and Experimental Science* (New York, 1923–58), vol. 6: *The Sixteenth Century*, pp. 418–23; Hans Peter Duerr, *Dreamtime: Concerning the Boundary Between Wilderness and Civilization*, trans. Felicitas Goodman (Oxford, 1985), pp. 1–11.

71. Christopher Baxter calls the flavor "Rabelaisian," a suggestion that would repay closer literary study (Baxter, "Johann Weyer's 'De praestigiis daemonum,'" p. 73, n. 16).

bles from the worlds of Herodotus, Pliny, and Merlin. He called some of his tales true and others fabulous, and occasionally asserted that a story told straight-facedly should be just as firmly believed as a previous story that he had explicitly called fiction.[72] The effect of such legend-mongering word-heaps was to call into question any story for which there was no firsthand evidence. It was an artful literary technique and one that deployed the grotesque as a weapon against the monstrous.

By calling the legends, fables, and traditions of over two thousand years into question, Weyer made it clear that credibility depended on more than just the authority of the storyteller or the plausibility of the story. And he illustrated his skepticism by personally investigating the local scandals and monstrous events of his region, emphasizing throughout his book that his accounts depended upon the testimony of his own eyes or those of other careful observers. In this turn to observational evidence against the dogmatizing of fable and theory, Weyer joined the ranks of the academic physicians who were just then expanding the literature of *observationes*. In his now little-read medical writings, Weyer regularly emphasized the importance of eyewitness observation in detecting new diseases and new syndromes.[73] Experience could trump the whimsical claims of reason.

But Weyer was not content to say that melancholy hallucinations *could* explain the fantastic confessions of witches, or that physical processes *could* explain the odd tumors, lungstones, frosts, and strange mishaps often attributed to the devil, or even that fraud *could* be an explanation for apparently successful exorcisms. Any contemporary controversialist might have coped easily with his arguments if they had rested only on could-have-beens. What made Weyer notably exasperating for his opponents was his claim that he had personally investigated countless weird events and "unnatural" circumstances, and that he had never returned in a state of perplexity. Weyer was one of the early masters of intrepid debunkery. He could say with more than mere plausibility that teenaged girls and young women needed a sex life rather than the austerities of a convent. He could prove that locally celebrated miracles of miraculously extended fasting were fraudulent. His argument seemed incontrovertible when he showed that a case of sexual difficulty rested on natural organic obstacles rather than on *maleficium*. With scathing humor, Weyer reported that he had seen the wax phallus used by Katherine Loe to ward off demonic assaults![74] Readers were invited to laugh at such simplicity. Weyer's empirical arguments could not be refuted with mere reason and clever demonological theory, and his opponents were quick to learn his method of close observa-

72. Weyer, *De praestigiis daemonum*, bk. 1, ch. 16; p. 82.
73. *Medicarum observationum rarum liber I* (Basel, 1567).
74. Weyer, *De praestigiis daemonum*, bk. 5, ch. 36; pp. 635–36.

tion. Jean Bodin, for example, for all his theological, medical, and legal differences with Weyer, also adduced a new body of closely observed material from which to argue for the reality of witchcraft.[75] And that, after all, was the weakness of an argument based on the empirical investigation of wonders and demonic possessions, of monsters and miracles. As often as one showed that a specific case was natural in origin or fraudulent in construction, another observer could reply, truly enough, that that did not make miracles, demonic possession, or witchcraft impossible. It was easy to introduce doubts about witchcraft but hard to prove a case *per impossibile*.

As a result, Weyer could not be secure with a case that rested solely upon the science or medicine of his day. When Reginald Scot, a Kentish gentleman, attempted in 1584 to reformulate Weyer's skeptical assault so that witchcraft became physically impossible, he produced a clearheaded but fanatic Sadducee's account of the world, a world in which witchcraft was impossible because spirits no longer acted physically ("miraculously"). If one had asked how Scot could know that spirits no longer acted and that miracles no longer occurred, his answer came down to bland Calvinist assertion.[76] Johann Weyer was not so brazen. Instead of repudiating the common Bible-based assumptions of his day, he rearranged them into an account of witchcraft in which not spirits but the crime evaporated.

WITCHCRAFT AND HERESY

Instead of claiming, as Scot did, that the Bible no longer provided an accurate picture of the world, Weyer took up the opposite position: that the Bible, properly understood, gave no support to the witch-hunters of the sixteenth century. Employing the tools of humanist philology, Weyer scrutinized the actual words for witchcraft in Hebrew and Greek as used in the Old and New Testaments and concluded, shrewdly, that the Bible knew nothing of pacts with the devil, and that the "witch" of the Old Testament had been essentially a poisoner rather than a heretic. We know that one of the most important transformations in the history of European witchcraft was the late medieval canon legal and theological redefinition of witchcraft as heresy and apostasy, emphasizing the denial of faith rather than harm by hidden, magical means, as earlier laws had understood the crime.

75. Bodin, *De la démonomanie des sorciers* (Paris, 1581).

76. See Leland Estes, "Reginald Scot and His Discoverie of Witchcraft: Religion and Science in the Opposition to the European Witch Craze," *Church History* 52 (1983): 444–56; E. William Monter, "Law, Medicine, and the Acceptance of Witchcraft, 1560–1580," in *European Witchcraft*, ed. id. (New York, 1969), pp. 55–71; Sydney Anglo, "Reginald Scot's Discoverie of Witchcraft: Scepticism and Sadduceeism," in *The Damned Art*, ed. id. (London, 1977), pp. 106–39; Keith Thomas, *Religion and the Decline of Magic* (New York, 1971), pp. 124–25, 570–80.

Weyer was pleased to grasp this transformation with both hands, for it meant that the crime of witchcraft had lost its solid basis in the Word of God. It meant, moreover, that witchcraft should be punished exactly like heresy.

Here, however, Weyer introduced one of his most explosive arguments. Echoing but sharpening Agrippa's argument on behalf of the woman accused of witchcraft in 1519, Weyer exclaimed that if the essence of the crime was the witch's renunciation of her baptism and of Christ, then surely that was a crime that all Christians, including even St. Peter, committed repeatedly throughout their lives.[77] Writing of himself and of all thoughtful believers, Weyer confessed: "We too reject the faith and truly bear witness, and with sound mind, to that which this woman, dulled by age or inconstant by reason of her sex, or unsteady because of her weak-mindedness, or in despair because of a disease of the spirit, is *thought* to have done, either in her imagination or when deluded by the act of the evil one."[78]

Weyer's point, we can see, does not depend here on proving that the witch was insane. Rather, it rested on establishing a bond between every fallible Christian and the suspected apostate. In so doing, he hoped to get the suspected witch off the hook. As a profound Erasmian, Weyer felt the force of Erasmus's plea that Christians should not do all of God's work for Him, that vengeance was after all His, not ours. Heresy, in particular, did not merit the death penalty.

In *De praestigiis daemonum*, book 6, chapter 18, Weyer reprinted in six columns a long section of Erasmus's *Apology* of 1520, in which Erasmus interpreted the parable of the tares to mean that heresy should not be severely punished in this world. Heretics and witches, Weyer argued, needed better religious instruction, to be sure, but their deviations from the Catholic faith should not be capital crimes. In extending Erasmus's argument this way, Weyer brilliantly wielded the double-edged sword of the heresy indictment. Accepting the late medieval reformulation of witchcraft as heresy, Weyer claimed that the only possible crime committed by old women accused of witchcraft was the mental crime of heresy, for which no one should ever be killed. Even the learned magicians of Renaissance Europe (the *magi infames*) were only sinfully, deliberately, and intentionally committing the offense of heresy and blasphemy. From this Erasmian or spiritualizing position, the only criminals worth punishing in this life were the physically dangerous, the *venefici*, the *Giftmischer*, the poisoners.

If this analysis is correct, then recent critics miss the mark when they charge that Weyer merely shifted the capital charge of witchcraft from old

77. Agrippa, *Opera omnia*, vol. 2, pp. 754–57, *Epistolarum ad familiares . . . libri VII*, bk. 2, *ep*. 39–40, on baptism and faith. Cf. *De vanitate scientiarum*, cap. 96.
78. Weyer, *De praestigiis daemonum*, col. 243b.

women to learned (male) magicians.[79] Although outraged by the blasphemies of the magicians, Weyer did not generally urge their execution.[80] Instead, he insisted that if witchcraft were a spiritual crime, like heresy, blasphemy, and apostasy, the proper remedy was spiritual too. Rather than directly showing that witchcraft was impossible, Weyer argued that it was wrong to put witches to death if they were guilty only of religious crimes.

It was an argument of some force in Weyer's day, for the Erasmian tradition in Europe, although in retreat after 1560 or 1570, was never completely routed, especially among Protestants and unorthodox Catholics. Indeed, at just this time (the late 1560s and early 1570s), the Italian reformer Mino Celsi, having fled Italy for the more welcoming atmosphere of Basel, was composing a defense of toleration that exploited Erasmus's, Bernardino Ochino's, and Sebastian Castellio's religious arguments on behalf of heretics but added to them the claim that heretics were as if mad, because they stupidly and dementedly chose error instead of truth. Such heretics should not be punished, Celsi insisted, for their crime stemmed from a depraved intellect rather than from a perverted will, and so they might be restrained if necessary but they were not to be executed, for their madness was punishment enough: "satis enim suo ipsius furore punitur."[81] Here once again we find the claim that heretics, like Weyer's witches, were more deluded and stupid than malicious, and it would be tempting to suggest that Celsi had read Weyer's work, especially considering the fact that Weyer had been published in Basel (by Oporinus) only a few years before Celsi's arrival there. Unfortunately, there is no solid evidence that Celsi had read Weyer. Celsi's language reveals large debts to Erasmus and to Roman law, but he did not pick up a medical vocabulary with which to describe heretics and was content to describe them in the scholastic categories of free will, depraved intellect, and bona fides.[82] Even so, like Weyer's work, Celsi's treatise reveals an openness to the insanity defense as applied to the major cultural issues of his day. On religious grounds, both Celsi and Weyer conceded that the crime of heresy or of witchcraft was conceivable even if it was not recognized in the Bible and even if Christ taught through

79. See, e.g., Anglo, "Melancholia and Witchcraft." Baxter, "Johann Weyer's 'De praestigiis daemonum,'" pp. 57–59, 66–67, 70–71, seems especially confused on this question.
80. Baxter, "Johann Weyer's 'De praestigiis daemonum,'" pp. 59, 70, seems to overemphasize apparent exceptions to this conclusion.
81. Mino Celsi, In haereticis coercendis quatenus progredi liceat: Poems, Correspondence, ed. Peter Bietenholz (Naples, 1982), pp. 45, 345–46. See also Ludwig Fimpel, Mino Celsis Traktat gegen die Ketzertötung: Ein Beitrag zum Toleranzproblem des 16. Jahrhunderts (Basel, 1967).
82. Peter Bietenholz mistakenly denies Fimpel's claim that Celsi based his argument on Roman law and the late medieval commentators: "Mino Celsi and the Toleration Controversy of the Sixteenth Century," Bibliothèque d'Humanisme et Renaissance 34 (1972): 31–47; Celsi, In haereticis, p. 345, n. 7. It is obvious from Celsi's "satis ipsius furore punitur" that he had Roman legal arguments in mind.

his parables of the tares that heresy should not be forcibly uprooted. Compelling as these arguments were in the sixteenth century, Weyer had not yet succeeded in showing that the crime of witchcraft was literally impossible; only when he turned to the argument from law did he find an argument *per impossibile*. And on a legal basis, Weyer went well beyond a reformulation of the insanity defense. He made the amazing claim that witchcraft was an impossible crime.

WITCHCRAFT AND ROMAN LAW

Weyer's references to Roman and canon law are so extensive that one can only admire his legal erudition. In fact, I suspect that he studied law formally at some point in his career, perhaps before he turned to medicine. It is not only that he ranged freely and at will among the massive texts of Justinian, Gratian, and Pope Gregory IX, but more especially that he knew how to seize upon the modern relevance of an ancient ruling, how to apply the principles of the *mos italicus* in order to make the thousand-year-old edicts live again.

In book 6 of *De praestigiis daemonum*, Weyer considered the question of how magicians, witches, and poisoners should be punished. Magicians, he said, were fraudulent, blasphemous, irreligious, and deliberately deceptive. Even so, they did no physical harm with their purely verbal charms and empty rituals. They deserved to be admonished and warned not to disturb the religious peace of their communities. They might be fined and even exiled, but since they did no physical harm, they should not be executed.[83] On the other hand poisoners did real damage and deserved the fullest rigor of the law. Weyer's interesting distinction between *magi infames* and *venefici* has less bearing on the history of madness than his views on witches, the *lamiae*. Witches, he claimed, could not be guilty of the crime of witchcraft for several reasons, some having to do with their mental condition, some with the nature of the alleged acts, and some arising from the law itself. As we have seen, Weyer held that witches were feeble, hallucinating, insane old women, and he cited numerous places in Justinian's *Digest* and in later commentaries where the aged, the feeble, the mentally deranged, and women were shown special leniency.[84]

The cases he cited were well chosen, but the odd thing about this argument is that the most zealous witch-hunters also recognized and even

83. Cols. 655–661.
84. Weyer repeatedly cites the following passages from Justinian on madness: *Digest* 1.18.13–14; 48.9.9; 47.10.3; 9.1.1; 9.2.5; 48.8.12; 26.7.61; 29.7.2.3; 50.17.5; 26.5.12.2; *Code* 4.38.2; on the aged and on women *Digest* 3.2.13; 48.8.4.2; 48.19.16; 29.5.3.7–11; 50.6.5; 48.18.8; 1.5.9; *Code* 5.67; 9.9.29; 1.18.3; 6.9.6; 9.8.5.

stressed the idea that witches were usually aged, feeble, credulous, helpless women. It was precisely their qualities as marginal women that made witchcraft seductively attractive to them. Vigorous men, the witch-hunters often thought, usually had the strength and common sense to resist the temptations of the devil, while old women easily fell prey to demonic entrapment because they had no other social or physical resources. So most of Weyer's legal references to the leniency deserved by old women could cut in the opposite direction as well. This was not true of madness. No witch-hunter, however eager to denigrate women, could afford to concede that witches were out of their minds or driven by forces beyond their control.[85] So bent was Jean Bodin on asserting the sanity of the witches that he constructed a memorably ridiculous argument that women did not usually fall into melancholy disorders, as Weyer had claimed.[86] Although Bodin's position made no medical sense in sixteenth-century terms, it does suggest that Weyer's argument had touched an extremely sensitive nerve in even the best legal minds of Europe.

When Weyer turned to the nature of the alleged acts of the witches, he hit upon an essential element of the crime as most jurists conceived it. The crucial nexus between the terrifying power of the devil and the corrupt will of the witch was the supposed pact with the devil, a notion that scholastic theory had elaborated on the model of the feudal oath of homage. Weyer was on firm biblical ground in pointing out that the Scriptures said nothing of such a contract or pact, but legally speaking he had an even more potent argument in his analysis of the Roman law of contract. If he could show that there was no binding agreement between human and demonic agents, then it would follow that witches could not really order the devil to do anything, nor could the devil require any action of his witches. In essence, their relations would be comparable to those that obtained between the devil and ordinary mortals—that is, the relation of predator and victim. Let us pursue Weyer's legal argument and his legal references more carefully.

It would have been easy, but fairly useless, to argue that Roman law knew nothing of contracts between men and spirits, and so Weyer looked carefully at the nature of contracts of all sorts. He pointed out, for example, that contracts were invalid wherever one party was ignorant of crucial facts

85. See the perceptive remarks of Hans-Peter Duerr, *Dreamtime*, pp. 1–11.
86. Bodin, *De la démonomanie*, fols. 226r–231v; Anglo, "Melancholia and Witchcraft"; Baxter, "Johann Weyer's 'De praestigiis daemonum'"; id., "Jean Bodin's 'De la démonomanie des sorciers,'" Monter, "Inflation and Witchcraft." Noel Brann recognized, as others have more recently, that Bodin's argument was desperate and ill-founded by sixteenth-century standards: see "The Renaissance Passion of Melancholy: The Paradox of Its Cultivation and Resistance" (diss., Stanford University, 1965); see also Jean Céard, "Folie et démonologie au XVIᵉ siècle," in *Folie et déraison à la Renaissance* (Brussels, 1976), pp. 129–47.

because valid contracts depended on *bona fides*.[87] Therefore any contract with the devil was null on grounds that the devil fraudulently withheld information from his intended clients.[88] Moreover, the Roman law of partnership disallowed "leonine" contracts, in which one party could only gain and the other only lose: "Iniquissimum enim genus societatis est ex qua quis damnum, non etiam lucrum spectet."[89] This described exactly the position of witches, who often expected monetary gain or sexual favors, only to be disappointed by the failure of the devil to live up to his promises. Ultimately, the witch stood only to lose and the devil only to gain. Weyer also held that contracts did not bind if they were entered into with *dolus malus* (intentional deceit),[90] which certainly described the action of the devil, who used cunning, tricks, and deception to defraud and seduce the whole world.[91] Had not the ancient Roman jurist Labeo (obit ca. A.D. 10) ruled that contracts were worthless if they sprang from "calliditatem, fallaciam machinationem ad circum veniendum fallendum decipiendum alterum"?[92] In addition, Weyer insisted that pacts with the devil were void since they rested upon force and fear.[93] With a long string of references to Justinian's *Digest*, Weyer made out a case for the sheer *legal* impossibility of witchcraft. Witches could not will what the devil willed; their intentions were necessarily incongruent, resting on the witches' error, ignorance, and lack of a well-formed will (*perfectae voluntati*).[94] From these legal references, it is clear that Weyer's argument was essentially that the devil was so potent, so overwhelming in strength and malice, that any contract with him would have no more force than would a contract between a grown man and an infant. No one would blame a small child for the damage done by an adult, even if the adult claimed that he was merely acting upon the orders of the child. The disparity of wills made the liaison void.[95] This was the relevance of citing the law on contracts made with minors.[96] "Ratione personarum: quia inter quos nulla est communio, inter eos quoque nullum potest esse

---

87. Justinian *Digest* 12.1.41. For a summary of Roman provisions on "pacta" (informal bargains), see W. W. Buckland, *A Text-Book of Roman Law from Augustus to Justinian* (Cambridge, 1921), pp. 524–29.

88. Weyer, *De praestigiis daemonum*, col. 780.

89. Justinian *Digest* 17.2.29.

90. Weyer, *De praestigiis daemonum*, cols. 780–81; Justinian *Digest* 4.3.7.

91. On deceit in Roman contracts, see Buckland, *Text-Book*, pp. 589–90, 714–17.

92. Weyer, *De praestigiis daemonum*, col. 781; Justinian *Digest* 4.2.6.

93. Weyer, *De praaestigiis daemonum*, cols. 782–83; Justinian *Digest* 19.2.15; 19.1.31; 19.2.41; 4.2.1; 4.2.6; *Code* 2.4.13; *Digest* 4.2.9; on fear in Roman contracts, see Buckland, *Text-Book*, pp. 588–89.

94. Weyer, *De praestigiis daemonum*, cols. 780–83; Justinian *Digest* 14.2.8; 2.1.15; 50.17.174; 12.1.12; 39.3.2.6.

95. Weyer, *De praestigiis daemonum*, col. 780.

96. Ibid., cols. 772, 781; Justinian *Digest* 4.4.13; 35.1.5; 50.17.4. On agency in Roman contracts, see Buckland, *Text-Book*, pp. 529–35.

ius. . . . Ratione dissensus, quia semper et de alio et aliter sentit daemon quam homo."[97]

Weyer's assault on the witches' contract was followed up with an assault on the alleged damage willed by the witches. It did not matter that witches might desire to harm their neighbors or even that they might try to incite the devil to harm their communities. The devil really needed no encouragement and could act (with divine permission) without any supposed aid from the witch. Roman law did not punish anyone for merely contemplating a crime, even if the Roman jurists regularly scrutinized intentions to determine the severity of any crime. A naked intention devoid of any action was beyond punishment,[98] for "thoughts are free."[99] One may be surprised to find such a notion in the Roman law, but the ever-practical pagan Romans had no interest in heresy or other crimes of the mind. Moreover, there were certain crimes that simply could not be committed, certain actions that by definition were beyond human ability. One cannot refuse what has not been offered, for example, even if one desires to refuse and goes through the motions of refusing.[100] No one can even seem to will what he actually cannot do.[101] And despite the fact that one could steal houses and crops and even trees, soil, or rocks, Roman law declared that no one could steal real estate: that was an impossible crime although of course one could be defrauded of one's title to a property.[102] So even if one "attempted" to steal landed property, it would be clear at once that this was merely fanciful and absurd.[103] Indeed, anyone who tried to intend or attempt the impossible might be thought mad. "Enimvero huiusmodi cogitationes ac desideria non hominis sani, sed amentia revera sunt."[104] Here we have one of the major reasons why Weyer claimed that witches were mentally disordered. The claim was not merely empirical, as his opponents sometimes thought; it was embedded in Weyer's far more radical claim that witchcraft was an idiotic or lunatic attempt to do the impossible. Weyer was so sure that thinking that one had a pact with the devil (or that one had flown off to the Sabbath and had intercourse with the devil) was evidence of mental illness that he suggested a new way of interpreting malicious thoughts and desires as well. When an accused witch thought of

---

97. Weyer, *De praestigiis daemonum*, col. 780.

98. Justinian *Digest* 26.5.12.2; 33.10.7; *Code* 6.25.5.

99. "Nihil sit liberius," Weyer, *De praestigiis daemonum*, col. 777; Ulpian as quoted at Justinian *Digest* 48.19.18: "cogitationem poenam nemo patitur." Here is an ancient origin for a sentiment often associated with the European Enlightenment: "Die Gedanken sind frei."

100. Justinian *Digest* 50.17.174: "Nolle adire hereditatem non videtur, qui non potest adire"; ibid. 29.2.4.

101. Ibid. 50.1.21.

102. Ibid. 47.2.25.

103. Weyer, *De praestigiis daemonum*, col. 778.

104. Ibid., col. 778.

harming others through witchcraft, Weyer claimed, she was really only harming herself, for the murderous or malicious intent could only rebound upon the subject. With such hurtful intentions, it was as if the mind jammed and the malice exploded internally. Citing the Roman law limiting the praetor's competence to compel himself to do anything, Weyer asserted that such harmful thoughts were harmful only to the one who thought them. Witches actually suffered from their destructive intentions rather than inflicting them.[105] The legal argument is fanciful here, another real stretch beyond what Justinian's jurists had had in mind, but the result for Weyer was a remarkable use of a legal principle to achieve a modern insight into the psychology of hatred.

These audacious claims depended, as we have seen, on an impressive erudition in Roman and canon law. Weyer ingeniously extracted principles of contract law, of agency and voluntary action, and of crimes that cannot exist from the whole range of ancient and ecclesiastical law, often stretching the implications well beyond any ancient intention. His interpretations were occasionally fanciful and often willful, finding current relevance in rulings that had never before been applied to witchcraft or to any crime at all. Anyone who tracks down all of these legal references, however, cannot fail to be impressed at the cogency of the case he built, which did not depend on rationalist skepticism, on an arbitrary disbelief in spirits. Rather, his legal case rested on a profound reverence for the wisdom of the ancient Romans. Indeed, in his zeal to show that witchcraft was an absurdity, Weyer overlooked one major objection that his opponents might have made forcefully. This was that the crucial *pactum cum daemone* was not a contract to be understood in Roman terms at all. In papal formulations of the fourteenth and fifteenth centuries, for example, the witches' pact was often described as an act of "homage" to the devil, a feudal gesture of servitude rather than the compact between well-informed equals that Weyer so impressively debunked.[106] If the pact was an act of homage, perhaps it could only be understood in feudal terms rather than in ancient Roman

---

105. Justinian *Digest* 36.1.13–14; 26.5.4; 46.1.71.

106. Siegfried Leutenbauer, *Hexerei- und Zaubereidelikt in der Literatur von 1450 bis 1530* (Berlin, 1972); Joseph Hansen, *Quellen und Untersuchungen zur Geschichte des Hexenwahns und der Hexenverfolgung im Mittelalter* (Bonn, 1901), pp. 2, 4, 17. For the changes in the Roman law of contract in the feudal period after Justinian, see György Diosdi, *Contract in Roman Law from the Twelve Tables to the Glossators* (Budapest, 1981), pp. 148–228. Richard van Dülmen has pointed out that the witches' pact also had all the characteristics of a marriage vow, and that this analogy would explain perhaps why witches could not revoke their pact, even if they could show that the devil had acted in bad faith and had breached the contract. See "Imaginationen des Teuflischen: Nächtliche Zusammenkünfte, Hexentänze, Teufelsabbate," in Richard van Dülmen, *Hexenwelten: Magie und Imagination vom 16.-20. Jahrhundert* (Frankfurt a/M, 1988), pp. 94–130, esp. pp. 106–8. While this is psychologically illuminating, it was not an explicit issue for most sixteenth-century witchcraft theorists, whether for or against witch trials.

language; Weyer's argument might have had trouble in this context. The way things turned out, however, we need not answer this question, for most jurists between 1550 and 1600 thought about witchcraft in the same Roman terms that Weyer chose. A feudal understanding of the witches' pact is indeed visible in some sixteenth-century drawings of the witches' Sabbath, but lawyers across the Holy Roman Empire had been thoroughly romanized by 1550.

So it seems that Weyer tried to prove on legal grounds that the central crime of witchcraft was impossible, and on religious grounds that the laws governing heresy should ordain only minor disciplinary actions rather than execution. Scholars have doubted whether Weyer's case was as clear as this analysis suggests, partly because they (especially English scholars) have held up Reginald Scot as the model of radical skepticism against which Weyer should be measured. It is plain by now that Weyer's skepticism did not at all rest upon doubting the physical powers of demons, which he did not in principle deny, even if many of the alleged actions of the devils were actually the fraudulent inventions of Catholic priests. But modern readers have not only gone astray in understanding Weyer because they measure him by the standards of Reginald Scot or Jean Bodin. Weyer himself confused his readers in two major ways.

INCONSISTENCIES IN WEYER'S ARGUMENT

Throughout *De praestigiis daemonum,* Weyer took such pains to unmask the fraudulent actions of priests, exorcists, diviners, and magicians that he sometimes seemed to be claiming that the devil could not actually do wondrous acts, that he could not really imitate God's miracles. If readers tentatively draw this conclusion from Weyer's book, they are bound to be appalled and disturbed at the inconsistencies in Weyer's argument when Weyer conceded, as he repeatedly did, that the devil could do much more than merely tempt and delude his human victims.[107] Weyer had probably hoped to prove that the devil was only a deceiver, but countless examples from Holy Scripture constrained him to admit that the devil could physically blind the eyes, scramble the wits, and perturb the humors, ruin crops, predict the future, obsess and possess men and women, afflict them with sores or transport their bodies through the air, stop the milk of cows, prevent butter from forming in churns and wine in vats, and cause painful spasms, wrenching, and seizures that physicians tried in vain to cure.[108] Weyer's attempt to sum up his conclusions regarding the power of demons is thus unintentionally confusing: he declared, on the one hand, that many

107. Weyer, *De praestigiis daemonum,* bk. 1, ch. 10, col. 48; ch. 12, cols. 55–60.
108. Ibid., bk. 1, ch. 12, cols. 58–60.

things were impossible for the devil, whereas, on the other hand, he had already conceded that demonic wonders did occasionally occur.[109] Some of Weyer's objections to the pact with the devil took on just this unsystematic form, as if his claim was that a pact could occur but usually did not. If this were all there was to Weyer's argument, we would have to agree that it was critically flawed.

Weyer also sowed confusion in a second area when he considered the appropriate punishments for witchcraft. Early on in *De praestigiis daemonum* he heaped scorn on the learned magicians (*magi infames*) who befouled Scripture with their claims to know the future, enchant their enemies, raise the dead, summon demons, cast out demons, and generally surpass the powers of nature. Most of what they did was pure illusion and self-delusion, Weyer claimed, and yet his indignation over their blasphemies was so intense that he occasionally implied that the death penalty was appropriate for them. He denounced the *magi* so eagerly that some modern readers have concluded that Weyer merely transferred to them the rage that most of his contemporaries reserved for witches.[110] Certainly Weyer took such pains to distinguish old women accused of witchcraft from the cunning men who practiced various magic arts that one might be forgiven for hastily concluding that he approved of the death penalty for magicians, and that if he did, his argument was hopelessly unsound. Had he not shown that magicians' claims were just as illusory as those of witches?

With a little patience, one can disentangle Weyer's argument from both of these confusions. With respect to the crimes of the *magi*, it is plain that Weyer was indeed appalled at their blasphemies, but he did not argue that magicians should actually be executed. He made it clear enough in book 6 that execution should be reserved for those who physically harmed others with their poisons or in some other way. No one in Weyer's day took seriously the flights of rhetorical excess in which Weyer claimed heatedly that magicians were nefarious criminals, to whom the criminal code should apply in all its rigor. It was only that unlike feeble old women, magicians at least knew what they were doing when they committed heresy and blasphemy. With respect to the powers of the devil, however, Weyer had stum-

---

109. Ibid., bk. 1, ch. 25, cols. 132–35; bk. 3, ch. 3–4, cols. 242–52.

110. Ibid., bk. 6, ch. 1, cols. 653–57; Baxter, "Johann Weyer's 'De praestigiis daemonum,'" pp. 53, 67, 71–72. Citing the Twelve Tables, Weyer claimed that the death penalty was intended for "the magician and poisoner," not the "deluded old woman who is ignorant of all arts; "magus et veneficus hic intelligitur, non: illusa vetula, cunctarum expers artium" (*De praestigiis demonum*, col. 654). Speaking of the local reverence for traveling exorcists, Weyer protested that if anyone tried to prohibit their activities, a cry went up that one was "touching the apple of God's eye." But this is great wickedness deserving of death: "Hoc grande nefas, et morte piandum" (ibid., col. 656).

bled into a more telling confusion. In his own experience, he regularly found natural causes for all of the supposed demonic wonders of his day, but on biblical authority, he dared not conclude that the devil had no physical powers any more. Considering the diabolically infested world of the New Testament, we can see Weyer's problem. It is one that many Christians have had ever since. In one's own experience, one may never meet the devil, and yet the Bible is full of his exploits. Unless one can say on metaphysical or extrascriptural grounds that such devilish actions no longer occur, a literal or fairly straightforward reading of Scripture is bound to prove that the devil has extensive powers.

Weyer never fully resolved this confusion, this conflict between experience and doctrine, but his basic argument did not hinge on it in any event. He could easily concede vast powers to the devil, because the essence of witchcraft was the pact, the agreement between man and devil, and the pact did not depend in any serious way upon the actual physical powers of the devil. The confusion on this score was therefore real but legally inconsequential. On essential points, Weyer's argument was coherent and original.

WEYER'S IMPACT

This is not to say that Weyer won his argument. Instead, many jurists (perhaps most) reacted in shock at the audacity of his claim. Here was a physician who made bold to inform his legal colleagues that a crime they had prosecuted for centuries (in one form or another) was no crime at all, but an impossible absurdity. Physicians today would have similar problems in a modern court of law if as expert witnesses they were to go beyond the assessment of a defendant's state of mind to reflect upon or undermine the actual law under which he is being prosecuted. To borrow the lively analogy of Herbert Fingarette, it is not usually the province of expert cartographers to pontificate on where the borders of any nation ought to be. They are expected rather to draw the borders (to make the distinctions and fine discriminations) that legal and moral authorities decree.[111] So, too, medical experts overstep their authority when they claim that the moral rules and applicable laws of their society are stupid.

Weyer was, therefore, immediately charged with exceeding his competence, with interfering in matters beyond his professional ken, with what some might today call "medical imperialism." And there is indeed some evidence that Weyer did feel strong temptations to reduce legal and theological matters to medical categories, as if the criminal or the sinner merely

111. Herbert Fingarette, *The Meaning of Criminal Insanity* (Berkeley and Los Angeles, 1972), pp. 39–40; see also Herbert Fingarette and Ann Fingarette Hasse, *Mental Disabilities and Criminal Responsibility* (Berkeley and Los Angeles, 1979).

needed medical treatment. In his little treatise on the disease of anger *De ira morbo*, Weyer claimed that the troubles of his day (meaning mainly the brutalities of the Dutch wars with Spain) had produced an "epidemic" of anger. Although conceding that the Stoics were right to counsel men to curb all of their passions, and theologians were surely right to teach humility and forgiveness, Weyer injected a characteristically medical point into this essentially Senecan and Christian tradition. There were, he noted, physical as well as moral causes of anger. First, one could be corrupted in infancy by impersonal or immoral wet nurses, by too much food or luxury, or by wine in one's childhood; or even by too little work and discipline. Second, one might predispose oneself to anger by exercising the wrong humors. Here Weyer praised baths but blasted long vigils and other physical rigors. Sleep was necessary to health; and one should also avoid sweet, sour, or sharp foods, especially sugar, honey, onions, vinegar, pepper, and mustard. Sweet, strong wines were especially productive of anger. Those with bilious livers should purge themselves with rhubarb. Third, sexual intercourse had an important role in calming wrath (among men), for it "empties the over-full body, rendering the body light and virile again, and as far as the spirit is concerned, it dissolves the blocked up force of reason, cuts off the growth of anger, reduces the insane to some degree of modesty and produces hilarity and liveliness."[112] And finally physicians should use music for its medically calmative effect.

Weyer was far from regarding medicine as a replacement for Stoic and Christian counsels, but he did insist that physicians had valuable advice to offer on matters usually left to others. Moderate though he was vis-à-vis anger, his view that modern marvels all had physical explanations and his notion that only the physically dangerous should be punished might be construed as early instances of scientific reductionism. What were jurists to make of Weyer's arguments?

By and large, lawyers ignored or misunderstood Weyer's claim that witchcraft was impossible because the pact with the devil was impossible. This claim depended, as we have seen, on Weyer's extraordinary and unorthodox readings of Roman law. But lawyers could not ignore Weyer's empirical claim that those accused of witchcraft were usually mad. From now on, jurists increasingly felt that they had to take medical testimony seriously. In this sense, Weyer had an amazing impact, even, or perhaps especially, on those who disagreed with him. Moralists and theologians, jurists and political theorists from Jean Bodin to King James VI of Scotland undertook to refute Weyer's offensively reductionist arguments, not by hitting at them directly, but by adding new empirical (often medical) data.

112. *De ira morbo, ejusdem curatione philosophica, medica, et theologica, liber* (Basel, 1577), p. 152.

In the case of Jean Bodin, we have already noticed his peculiar argument that the women accused of witchcraft could not be melancholy because only men were subject to that malady. Although such a claim made philosophical sense if one connected melancholy only with the pseudo-Aristotelian problem topos on human genius, it made no medical sense in Bodin's day, and no one that I know of followed Bodin in this argument. Bodin's sensitivity on this issue does indicate, however, just how crucial the question of melancholy had become.

Another response to Weyer was that of the Swabian jurist (later of Rostock) Johann Georg Godelmann, who published a *Tractatus de magis, venificis et lamiis* in 1591 that adopted Weyer's categories verbatim. Those accused of witchcraft might be *magi* (magicians), *venefici* (poisoners), or *lamiae* (witches), and Godelmann was quick to agree with Weyer that *lamiae* were mainly women who imagined that they had a pact with the devil and that they did all sorts of evil on its basis. The devil attacked women because they were more often "unsteady or flighty, credulous, malicious, ill-humored, melancholy or depressed, but especially old, worn-out women who were foolish and awkward, badly grounded in the Christian faith, and unsound old hags."[113] Their pacts with the devil were only illusory, but necromancers and learned magicians did have a real pact with the devil, which Godelmann believed worthy of severe punishment and even death. While attempting to defend witches from unjust accusations, in other words, Godelmann disagreed with Weyer and left open the argument that at least some persons did have a contract with the devil. Godelmann argued strenuously against abuse of torture and in favor of cautious procedures, but in strictly theoretical terms, he was not the radical opponent of witchcraft trials that Weyer was. Indeed, when modern critics attack Johann Weyer for holding a mixture of confused and inconsistent ideas, they might better aim their indignation at Godelmann. And yet, despite the illogical features of his argument, Godelmann was crucial in the process of restructuring the insanity defense. Precisely because he thought that the witches' pact was a real possibility, Godelmann did not think that one could just assume that supposed witches were mentally ill. This was an empirical question on which medical advice had to be sought.[114]

113. Johann Georg Godelmann, *Von Zäuberern Hexen und Unholden, Warhafftiger und Wolgegründeter Bericht* (Frankfurt a/M, 1592), p. 162. According to Sönke Lorenz, Godelmann anticipated most of this argument in a 1584 Rostock disputation, *Disputatio de magis, veneficis, maleficis et lamiis: Praeside Ioanne Georgio Godelmanno* (Frankfurt a/M, 1584); see his "Johann Georg Godelmann—ein Gegner des Hexenwahns?" in *Beiträge zur Pommerschen und Mecklenburgischen Geschichte*, ed. Roderich Schmidt (Marburg, 1981), pp. 61–105.

114. Godelmann repeatedly raised the question of melancholy, claiming in bk. 2, ch. 2, "Lamiae errant et melancholicis vexantur morbis," and repeating the tag "ubi autem est caput melancholicum, ibi Diabolus habet praeparatum balneum" (*Tractatus de magis, veneficis et lamiis* [Frankfurt a/M, 1591], pp. ii, 10).

Even those who disagreed vehemently had to accept the logic of the analysis here. The vehement witch finder Peter Binsfeld, for example, was openly upset by the number of skeptics at large, men who held that witches should not be punished because their confessions were all fantasy and illusion. He conceded that the devil could pervert the imagination and "make something appear other than it is."[115] And he had to concede that those who dream while asleep or fall into madness are not capable of sin (so long as they are asleep or mad) for sin was "by nature a matter of free will."[116] Even so, he argued strenuously that witches did fly through the air to the Sabbath, and that when the devil deluded their senses and their fantasy, they had already consented to this invasion. Binsfeld recognized that the crux of Weyer's argument was the impossibility of having a pact with the devil. If the pact was impossible, then witchcraft was impossible; consequently, Binsfeld aimed the much longer Latin version of his treatise on witchcraft, *Tractatus de confessionibus maleficorum et sagarum recognitus et auctus*, directly at Weyer.[117] Unlike many modern readers of Weyer, Binsfeld seized perceptively upon the truly novel and dangerous element in Weyer's book: "[H]e refers almost all the evil devices of witches and sorcerers to fantasy, melancholy, and illusion, and judges their league and pact to be imaginary and impossible."[118]

Much of Binsfeld's *Tractatus* is spent in trying to prove on biblical and philological grounds that the demonic pact was possible, and he presented a fully up-to-date legal discussion of witchcraft confessions, accusations, and trial procedure. Repeatedly, he attacked Weyer's understanding of Scripture and of Roman law.[119] Even if Weyer was wrong on these points, however, Binsfeld seems to have felt the force of Weyer's psychiatric claims, for he insisted that despite their possible delusions, witches' confessions were believable. Of course, when a confessed witch accused someone else of witchcraft, the charge was not so credible as it would have been coming from an honorable source, but two or three such accusations would suffice as an *indicium* for torture of the new suspect.[120] Refusing to see things in black and white, Binsfeld elaborated shades of gray.

The key point for the workings of the insanity defense is that Binsfeld

---

115. Peter Binsfeld, *Tractat von Bekanntnuss der Zauberer und Hexen: Ob und wie viel denselben zu glauben* (Munich, 1591) fol. a2v, 25r.

116. Ibid., 31r.

117. Peter Binsfeld, *Tractatus de confessionibus maleficorum et sagarum recognitus et auctus: An et quanta fides iis adhibenda sit* (Trier, 1591). This Latin version bears a title similar to the German treatise cited in n. 115 above, but the Latin *Tractatus* has 633 pages compared with the 75 leaves (and generous font) of the German *Tractat*.

118. Ibid., p. 23.

119. Ibid., pp. 24–27, 395–400, 462, 478, 530–32, 555.

120. Ibid., pp. 248, 260, 280.

exercised exquisite care in judging the extent of guilt in persons suspected of crime. Although he rejected Weyer's claim that witches were necessarily mad, he did not lunge to the opposite extreme like Bodin, who held that witches could hardly be melancholy at all. Binsfeld's repeated arguments with Weyer seem to have jostled him into a more nuanced position on the insanity defense. His flexibility is illustrated by a sympathetic account of a woman who had fallen into desperation, desolation, and weakness of spirit; in this low condition, she had allowed herself to be tempted into witchcraft. Instead of being executed, she was sent into exile, but after a year she came back home, explaining that she had been miserable in exile. Turning herself in to the magistrate voluntarily, she begged to be executed rather than sent away again. Binsfeld took pity on her and insisted that she should not be executed.[121]

Mobilizing Medical Views on the Insanity Defense

This sensitivity to the gray, intermediate areas was what seems to have impressed Peter Heig, who was trying to sort out the degrees of melancholy and madness in the Saxon mother who had killed her children (see pp. 184–88 above). Instead of repeating what had become tired commonplaces about *furor* and *malitia*, Heig seized upon the witchcraft controversy swirling around Johann Weyer and specifically cited the works of Bodin, Godelmann, and Binsfeld to justify punishing the melancholy and seriously deluded woman only mildly and sending her into exile. In modifying the insanity defense to the terms of the witchcraft controversy, Heig made medical testimony or medical thinking a crucial part of the analysis of degrees of guilt. One might be melancholy and desperate and therefore not fully culpable, but also not entirely innocent either.

Heig was not the only one to remake the insanity defense along medical lines. Already in 1594, Dieterich Graminaeus, a well-known scholar and legal counselor to the duchy of Berg, where Weyer had died just six years earlier, wrote to his mad duke, Johann Wilhelm of Jülich-Cleves, that with the world coming to an end, Satan was raging as never before.[122] This made the evaluation of confessions and accusations harder than ever. Graminaeus deplored the recent confusion over witchcraft in the duchy, which had led to the contradictory assertions that witchcraft was all fantasy, on the one hand, and that witches ought all to be executed on account of their horrid offense to God's majesty, on the other. On such questions, Grami-

---

121. Ibid., pp. 568–74.
122. On the madness of Duke Johann Wilhelm, see *Mad Princes*, pp. 98–124.

naeus favored the opinions of Binsfeld and Godelmann, just as Heig had; like Binsfeld, he held that one of the actual causes of witchcraft was "the abandonment of spirit as happens frequently with women, or too much sadness and a contrary timidity."[123] In other words, Graminaeus held that precisely those psychic conditions that Weyer might emphasize in order to get suspected witches off the hook constituted for him the very cause of their crime. Reflecting the changed attitudes in the duchy of Jülich-Cleves, he rejected Weyer's arguments as extreme and even Godelmann's as fatally flawed,[124] but melancholy was for him a plausible defense. Weyer's discourse, if not his conclusions, was beginning to affect legal argument.

Such medico-legal argument is even more evident in the extremely interesting case of Paduan heresy and madness discussed by the renowned jurisconsult Giacopo Menochio (obit 1607) in his collection of legal *consilia*. With an extraordinary display of erudition, Menochio argued that a mad old heretic was not to be punished despite unorthodox opinions that bordered on Protestantism. After a full display of the Roman and canon law on madness and heresy, he switched dramatically to medical opinion, citing Galen, Caelius Aurelianus, Cornelius Celsus, Roderigo Suarez, Cardinal Zabarella, and a variety of modern doctors.[125] It was not enough to speak of *ratio* and *furor*, *ignorantia* and *stultitia*; the question was melancholy, and with a quick gesture, Menochio alluded to medical opinion that held that even the mad might utter sensible things.[126] And so the mere fact that a defendant could speak sensibly did not make him fully responsible for his acts. Once again, medical language was filling in the gray areas. In another opinion regarding the validity of a gift, the question hinged on whether Giovanni Baptista Ricasolo's melancholy was enough to make him mad. Not all melancholiacs were insane, Menochio noted, for (Pseudo-)Aristotle had averred that outstanding men in all fields suffered from black bile without being totally mad. So far as I know, this was the first full discussion of the famous Aristotelian problem in a legal context, and again the medical and physical considerations prompted a more discriminating set of mental gradations than the abstract language of *ratio* and *insania* allowed.[127]

When the Tübingen jurist Christoph Besold (1577–1638) undertook to compile an encyclopedic thesaurus of the legal terms in general use throughout the Holy Roman Empire, his first edition of 1629 did not con-

---

123. Dieterich Graminaeus, *Inductio sive Directorium, Das ist: Anleitung oder underweisung wie ein Richter in Criminal und peinlichen sachen die Zauberer und Hexen belangendt sich zu verhalten* (Cologne, 1594), fol. (i) ii verso and pp. 92–93.

124. Ibid., fol. (i) v verso and pp. 140–57.

125. Jacobus Menochius, *Consiliorum tomi XIII* (Frankfurt a/M, 1676), consilium 81, paras. 218–35, pp. 336–37.

126. Ibid., paras. 232–34.

127. Ibid., consilium 683 (7: 201–5, esp. paras. 13–14, p. 203).

tain any reference to melancholy.[128] As with his earlier works on Roman law, Besold was content to stay within the conceptual framework of Justinian. He dealt with the mad as *furiosi*.[129] But when Besold's *Thesaurus* was reprinted with numerous additions in 1659, it contained a lengthy discussion of melancholy with the familiar medical recommendation that melancholy fantasies could be treated by playing along with them.[130] One reason for the addition was that in 1630 and 1651, the papal physician Paolo Zacchia's writings on forensic psychiatry were published, containing the first full medical discussion of the insanity defense.[131] With a remarkable grasp of the whole legal, theological, and medical literature, Zacchia spoke of melancholy as producing an insanity that was not quite the same as *furor*: "[M]elancholia arises from the natural melancholy humor, *furor* from the unnatural."[132] Certain jurists held that melancholics suffered only in their imaginations, while *furiosi* suffered in their reason, but Zacchia rejected this conclusion, claiming that the melancholy often suffered in their reason as well.[133] Even so, the melancholy were often mad in only one respect or on only one subject, and so they could often testify or be tried for their misdeeds. With explicit mention of Johann Weyer, Zacchia admitted that many supposedly possessed by the devil were actually mad or melancholy: "Among the common people 'demoniac' is the name given to many demented persons."[134] He did not deny that there were true demonic possessions, of course, but claimed: "[T]hose are properly called demoniacs who are driven into insanity from a melancholy weakness, which the demons then use as if it were an instrument to possess them."[135] The most commonly afflicted were "ignorant persons [*idiotas*] and wenches [*mulierculas*], and among the latter especially virgins who are not yet purged by being of mature age and are accounted as demoniacs when they are not."[136] Thus Zacchia doubted most instances of demonic possession and preferred, like

128. *Thesaurus practicus, continens explicationem terminorum atque clausularum, in aulis et dicasteriis Romano-Germanici Imperii usitatarum* (Tübingen, 1629).

129. *Ad tit. I, III, IV, V, et VI lib. I. pandectarum commentarii succincti* (Tübingen, 1616), pp. 55, 176–77.

130. *Thesaurus practicus . . . Additionibus Dn. Joh. Jacobi Speidelii . . . cum novis additionibus . . . Christophori Ludovici Dietherns* (Nuremberg, 1659), no. 40, *melancholi*.

131. Paolo Zacchia's *Quaestiones medico-legales* was first printed in 1621 and expanded in the editions of 1630, 1634, 1651, and 1654. I have used the 1701 Lyon edition. On Zacchia, see Margarete Helms, "Die psychopathologischen Anschauungen bei Paulus Zacchias in Hinsicht auf den Beginn einer forensischen Psychiatrie" (diss., Munich, 1957).

132. Zacchia, *Quaestiones*, vol. 1, bk. 2, title 1, question 9; p. 132.

133. Ibid., p. 132; Helms, "Die psychopathologischen Anschauungen," p. 37; Jean Fernel had also opposed such a distinction. Zacchia cites his *Pathologia*, bk. 5, ch. 6.

134. Zacchia, *Quaestiones*, vol. 1, bk. 2, title 1, question 18, "De daemoniacis, fanaticis, etc.," p. 150.

135. Ibid., p. 151.

136. Ibid.

Weyer, to emphasize humoral imbalances as the root of demonomania. Citing Martin Delrio (who knew the writings of Weyer well), Zacchia pushed his expert discussion in the direction of a cautious forensic medicine, in which the medical condition of witnesses, testators, and suspects was of immediate and obvious importance.

The invasion of the insanity defense by medical thinking was even more evident in the separate question Zacchia devoted to hysteria, the female disorder related to a wandering or "suffocated" uterus. Women were subject not just to female disorders, he said, but to all kinds of insanity; despite the claims of Hippocrates to the contrary, "women rarely avoid melancholy," and it was evident that "for every single demon-possessed man (whom we enumerate in the class of melancholics), six hundred women are possessed by the demon, as [Giovan Battista] Codronchi says (*De morb. venef.* bk. 2, ch. 8). Moreover, this is certain, that when women go mad with melancholy disease, they are far worse off than men: their madness is both more intense and more incurable."[137]

Aside from Codronchi (1547–1628), one cannot tell where Zacchia obtained such an exaggerated view of the numbers of female demoniacs. As we have seen, the German evidence was very different, but a comparison across Europe may yet show that there were dramatic and as yet unexplained regional differences. In any event, it was obvious to Zacchia that medical testimony would often be necessary to clarify the mental state and degree of legal responsibility of melancholy women.

Zacchia's work had a truly European impact, but in Germany the insanity defense had already undergone a kind of medical transformation in the thought of Benedict Carpzov, who was the most important German commentator on criminal law in the seventeenth century. Carpzov (1595–1666) was for forty years a member (and for a time the head) of the famous Leipzig Schöffenstuhl, a panel of judges who heard appeals from all over Germany, but especially from the eastern regions of the Empire, settled in the Middle Ages by Saxons, whose descendants were legally obliged to confer with Saxon judges on countless matters. Carpzov was also a member of various Saxon superior courts, a professor of law in Leipzig, and for eight years a privy councilor at the Dresden court. In 1635, he published the main work on which his fame rested, *Practicae novae imperialis Saxonicae rerum criminalium*.[138] In this book, Carpzov tried to create a German criminal law for the Empire, one that was based more on Charles V's famous criminal code of 1532 (the *Carolina*) than on the Italian commentators. In the process, Carpzov rethought all the basic elements of criminal law, includ-

---

137. Ibid., vol. 1, bk. 2, title 1, question 22, "De suffocatis ex utero," p. 158.
138. Benedict Carpzov, *Practicae novae imperialis Saxonicae rerum criminalium* (1635; 8th ed., Wittenberg, 1684).

ing, of course, the insanity defense. Essentially, Carpzov was still working within the Roman legal tradition, however, and that meant that criminal intent (*dolus*) was still mainly an intellectual affair of knowing what one was doing and what the consequences of one's acts might be. Ignoring the medieval canon lawyers, who, as we have seen, emphasized both the will and the intellect as components of any crime, Carpzov mainly followed the Roman jurists and was relatively unconcerned about the possibility that one's will might be so bound or driven that one could not be deemed responsible for one's acts.[139]

Confronting Johann Weyer's conclusion that all of the old Roman laws concerning *furor* should apply to *melancholia*, Carpzov took refuge in Peter Heig and insisted that melancholy was not the full excuse that raging madness was. One had to make distinctions.[140] There were in his view two sets of rules, one for the *furiosus* and another for the *melancholicus*. Agreeing with the long tradition that I have already outlined, Carpzov held that the *furiosus* should not be punished at all, for his *furor* was punishment enough.[141] Despite his constant emphasis on the intellect, Carpzov said that this made perfect sense, because will was essential to crime, and a *furiosus* acted involuntarily. The Schöffenstuhl in Leipzig also deployed this rule, for example, in March 1623, when it decided that an insane murderer was not to be punished. Following the letter of the Roman law, it decreed further "that he should be taken by his friends and relatives [*von seiner Freundschafft*] to a special place in secure custody, there to be held with chains and bands so that he will not be able further to harm himself or others."[142] This rule was also binding on those who became insane after committing a crime. Punishment of any sort, corporal, capital, or pecuniary, had to wait for the criminal to enjoy a lucid interval.[143] This was true, Carpzov held, not only because madness was "punishment enough," but because the madman had to be treated as if absent or dead, and if the analogy were strict, then one obviously should not punish him so long as he was mad. These rules regarding *furor* had to be applied with great caution, he admitted, for the proof of *furor* was difficult. Carpzov recommended that physicians be consulted to assist in the legal deliberations, but the trouble was, as we can see, that physicians were not trained to recognize *furor*. They could diag-

---

139. For a sharp critique of the shortcomings of Carpzov's understanding of liability and responsibility, see the useful work of Franz Lubbers, *Die Geschichte der Zurechnungsfähigkeit von Carpzow bis zur Gegenwart unter besonderer Berücksichtigung der Doktrin des gemeinen Rechts* (diss., Jena, 1936; published Breslau-Neukirch, 1938), pp. 3–7.

140. For citations of Heig, see Lubbers, *Geschichte der Zurechnungsfähigkeit*, p. 22; Carpzov, *Practicae novae*, 3: 367, 371–72.

141. Carpzov, *Practicae novae*, 3: 368.

142. Ibid.

143. Ibid., p. 369.

nose mania, phrenitis, melancholy, and other diseases, but not the legal category. A similar situation often exists today, of course, when lawyers ask psychiatrists to translate their thinking into the legal categories of responsibility and freedom, and of knowing right from wrong. Citing appropriate references in the familiar Roman texts, Carpzov reminded his readers, however, that even if a madman was declared not guilty because of his *furor*, he was "not to be let go or set free at once, but should be held in custody by his own people and even in chains and shackles if necessary, not as a punishment for any crime but lest he do himself or others some damage."[144] All of this thinking about *furor* was subject to the major limitation that if it could be shown that "the madman was responsible for provoking [*sua culpa*] his own madness," he should be punished, yet not so severely as would be right if he were fully sane and fully guilty.[145] So much for the *furiosi*.

The melancholy were another story. "If a criminal commits a crime on account of melancholy, he should by no means go unpunished, and yet the ordinary penalty should be remitted on that account, and another, milder one can safely be imposed."[146] Such a ruling left the insanity defense in some confusion, but Carpzov maintained that there was an obvious difference between the furious and the melancholy: "The furious are those who lack mind and common sense [*qui mente et sensu communi caret*], while the melancholy are persons of desperate and agitated mind, imagining to themselves and saying absurd and sad things [*homines desparatae et emotae mentis, absurda et tristia sibi fingentes atque dicentes*]."[147]

Carpzov was not speaking of those who were merely melancholy by temperament, those whose humoral temper made them usually fearful, lustful, greedy, or angry. He was speaking of the melancholy-mad, but, picking up the distinction made by Cicero in his *Tusculan Disputations* (see pp. 187–88 above), he insisted that they were not completely insane. Even the melancholy of those suffering strange delusions and tempted to kill themselves had not usually brought them to a "total mental alienation, nor has it flatly deprived them of understanding; and so there is no doubt that they do their misdeed willingly and with malice."[148] Thus a plea of melancholy did not necessarily get one off the hook. As an example, Carpzov recounted the judgment given in 1608 in the case of a woman who confessed that she had murdered her own child. By her account, she had been driven to this deed by a black man who had come to her in a dream; it seemed likely that she had acted out of "sadness, melancholy, and depres-

144. Ibid., p. 370.
145. Ibid., p. 371.
146. Ibid., p. 372.
147. Ibid., p. 371.
148. Ibid., p. 372.

sion" and so the "ordinary" death penalty was remitted. Instead, she was to be tied into a sack with a dog, a rooster, a snake, and a cat and thrown into the water to be drowned. If the place had no suitable water, she was to be executed on the wheel, one of the most gruesome deaths available in an age that specialized in gruesome punishments.[149]

Carpzov clearly felt he had to deal with the subject of melancholy, but he gave melancholics no quarter. Some of his animus against them may have arisen from his sharp and prolonged effort to refute the arguments of Johann Weyer.[150] We can see plainly in Carpzov's case the way in which medical language and medical consultation entered the law of insanity; jurists did not accept the argument as Weyer had posed it, but they did adopt Weyer's terms of discourse, as further interpreted especially by Peter Heig.[151]

Conclusion

With this turn to medical language and medical consultation, the insanity defense entered a strangely modern phase. If lawyers and judges were no longer the best judges of whether a suspect was capable of committing a particular crime or fit to be punished, they began to worry, as they rarely had before, that madness might be feigned. Here, too, of course, there was a Roman legal precedent, as a glance at Justinian's *Digest* 1.18.14 shows.[152] But commentators had largely ignored the possibility of pretense until jurists were compelled by their own language, the language of melancholy, to seek expert medical testimony.

In 1654, for example, Justus Oldecop of Halberstadt wrote a treatise on criminal procedure highly critical of the abuse of torture to extract confessions.[153] One of the major difficulties in current legal practice, he thought, was the ease with which suspects feigned illness in order to avoid jail or torture or punishment. Some simulated demonic possession, while others pretended to be suffering from "enthusiasm" or to be caught up in ec-

149. Ibid.

150. Ibid., 1: 308–16.

151. Lubbers, *Geschichte der Zurechnungsfähigkeit*, p. 22, holds that Heig was the first to see melancholy as a legal problem, but such a view obviously ignores the very sources Heig cites: Binsfeld, Godelmann, and Bodin, all of whom were reacting to Weyer.

152. *Digest of Justinian*, 1.18.14, trans. Watson et al., 1: 36: "if . . . no suspicion is left that he was not simulating insanity when he killed his mother."

153. Justus Oldecop, *Observationes criminales practicae congestae et in quinque titulos . . . tributae*, signed by Oldecop in Halberstadt, January 12, 1654. I have used the 1685 Frankfurt a/O edition published by Jeremiah Schrey and Heinrich Johann Meyer, which contains a remarkable appendix, pp. 349–72, listing 42 cases of innocent persons who were unjustly tortured and condemned.

stasy.[154] Women were especially likely to feign suffocation of the womb or pregnancy. In order to detect and unmask such deceits, one needed expert physicians. Following Paolo Zacchia, Oldecop listed five ways of uncovering fraud, and emphasized especially the role of medical knowledge in distinguishing true from false madness.[155] Gone was Carpzov's tortured Ciceronian distinction between *furor* and mere melancholy madness, a distinction that we can regard as a last desperate effort to retain a legal category separate from the medical. For Oldecop, the real problem was that "there is almost no disease more easily and frequently imitated than insanity."[156] Two kinds of insanity were common, he thought: melancholy plain and simple and melancholy mixed with furor. "There is this certain difference between the two, that the former are quiet, timid, sad, and dejected in spirit, while the later are worked up and in perpetual motion, restless, rash, and wrathful."[157] Both kinds resulted in sleeplessness, and a careful physician would know both well and be able to tell them from the false. Often sleeplessness was a good enough litmus test by itself, "for Celsus rightly says that for the mad sleep is as difficult as it is necessary."[158] Such extreme disorders did not develop overnight but built up with the excess humors over a long period. Without prodromal symptoms, one should remain gravely suspicious of malingering. Moreover, the mad usually exhibited queer opinions, such as thinking oneself dead and therefore avoiding food and drink (taking one of the classic tales of melancholy); deceitful simulators of madness never imitated these opinions, Oldecop thought, but how long would this remain true if Oldecop's descriptions of true madness made their way out of Latin and into the popular imagination?[159] Recognizing this dilemma, he passed on the advice of a "most learned physician" that mad suspects should be whipped, "with this purpose and intention, that if he be truly mad these blows might divert the humors to the beaten parts; but if he really dissimulate, by the strength of those same blows he may recover, even if he doesn't want to."[160] On and on he went with medical tests for true madness. Among his favorite authorities for all of this were Carpzov, Menochio, and Peter Heig, but it should be obvious that Oldecop was coping with a new fear. Now that the insanity defense was medical, how could one be sure that only the mad were protected by it?

He was not the only one to feel this new threat. Just one year later, in 1655, Johann Andreas Frommann published a doctoral disputation on the

154. Ibid., pp. 150–51: "Enthusiasmum pati . . . aut in Ecstasin rapi."
155. Ibid., pp. 153–54.
156. Ibid., p. 158.
157. Ibid., p. 159.
158. Ibid., p. 160.
159. Ibid., pp. 161–62.
160. Ibid., p. 162.

legal treatment of the insane agreeing that melancholy madness was an adequate excuse. Citing a 1623 case out of Carpzov, Frommann analyzed the mental condition of a murderer whom physicians had examined and found to be suffering a "melancholy delirium" so that his head was all "confused and mixed up."[161] Such persons were not to be punished. We observe that while Carpzov raged against the melancholy for not fully qualifying as *furiosi*, Frommann and Oldecop did not share this harsh attitude. But like Oldecop, Frommann was worried about deceit, and he composed a chapter entitled "De ficto et simulato furore."[162] Again, medical opinion was essential in the testing for true madness.

By midcentury these anxieties had become commonplace. In 1672, for example, Samuel Stryk, a professor of law, tried to establish that madness ought actually to be divided, not into species (as Carpzov and Heig had tried to do), but into grades, running from full dementia to melancholy. Medical advice was necessary to distinguish the grades and to weed out the fraudulent, a task made even more complex by the proverb "Sometimes it is wise to simulate madness."[163] Citing Carpzov, Stryk insisted that learned and experienced physicians could make all the difference,[164] and his discussion of melancholy in particular became a treatment of the medical literature.[165] Although he usually accepted the opinions of Zacchia, Heig, and especially Carpzov, Stryk disagreed on the subject of melancholy; in its mildest forms, to be sure, melancholy did not constitute a defense, but in its highest, worst forms (*summa melancholia*) it did obliterate the "rational faculty" and constituted a full insanity defense. Even after their delusions, in quiet moments, these melancholiacs were punished by the awareness that they might go mad at any time: "satis est, ad reliqua quacunque tempore hos insanire paratos esse."[166] This made a neat parallel to the Roman dictum that the *furiosus* was punished enough by his own *furor*, but it made medical judgment absolutely central, since there was no longer a fully autonomous legal judgment of reason, intent, and malice.[167]

Even though the county sheriff's principle of hot pursuit has carried us

161. Johann Andreas Frommann, *Hypotyposis Juris Furiosorum singularis quam deo ter opt. max. miserabilium eiusmodi personarum defensore justissimo dirigente* (Strasbourg, 1655), p. 63.

162. Ibid., pp. 70–83.

163. Samuel Stryk, "Disputatio octava inauguralis de dementia et melancholia (March 8, 1672)," in his *Opera omnia* (Frankfurt a/M and Leipzig, 1743–53), 2: 202–12, at ch. 1, no. 15, p. 204.

164. Ibid., ch. 2, no. 16, p. 206.

165. Ibid., ch. 4, pp. 208–9.

166. Ibid., ch. 5, no. 8, p. 211.

167. For a brief discussion of Stryk, see Lubbers, *Geschichte der Zurechnungsfähigkeit*, pp. 41–44, which criticizes Stryk for failing to follow the pioneering work of Pufendorf on natural law, in which freedom of the will was the central issue. The best recent discussion is Winfried Schleiner, *Medical Ethics in the Renaissance* (Washington, D.C., 1995).

well past the borders of the sixteenth century, this is surely not the place to track the details of the German insanity defense into the eighteenth century. We may, however, at least note that jurists remained anxiously dependent upon a medical understanding of madness. The legal scholar Caspar Heinrich Horn displayed this clearly enough in a consultation given in 1700 on the subject of dementia.[168] Professor Michael Alberti (1682–1757) also tried anxiously to differentiate true melancholy from false by claiming that certain temperaments allowed a lapse into only certain specific madnesses: that only the choleric fell into furor, for example.[169] And by the mid eighteenth century, the insanity defense was subject to widespread abuse, if we may believe the testimony of Jacob Ernest Friedrich Crell, a jurist who charged that many, when accused of a crime, sought out pliant physicians willing to attest to their madness. Injustice and confusion were the result.[170] It was the dawn of the medico-legal world we live in today, but the point of this chapter is that the origin of the medical interpretation of the German insanity defense lies back in the remarkable work of Johann Weyer. In order to defend witches, he had seized upon the exclusively legal language of *furor* and infused it with the medical discourse of melancholy. In the process, jurists gained the ability to see more than the abstract qualities of reason and will. By confronting the medical condition of troubled suspects, legal minds may have been encouraged to cope with an empirical reality that might not fit neatly into scholastic legal categories. It is true, however, that the academic medicine of the sixteenth and seventeenth centuries, just as in our own day, had its own neat scholastic categories. By inviting medically expert testimony, by insisting on medical advice, lawyers and jurists also forfeited some of their independence of judgment. It may have been a good thing, on the whole, but it opened a new loophole for the clever defendant: the pretense of madness. This had always been a possibility, but with the growth of forensic medicine, it appears to have become somewhat easier to employ. In any event, it is a tortuous path from Weyer's witches to Peter Heig's melancholy but culpably murderous mother, and to the fraudulent madmen that worried Carpzov, Oldecop, Frommann, and Stryk. The path traced here suggests a hitherto unsuspected power in the melancholy metaphor, a power that transformed the insanity defense into something closer to what it is today.

168. Caspar Heinrich Horn, *Consultationum responsorum ac sententiarum liber unus in XVI classes distributus* (Dresden and Leipzig, 1711), class VII, no. 24, pp. 393–95. I have not yet located the supposed disputation by Caspar Heinrich Horn (1657–1718) on how the mad should be punished, *Disputatio de poenis furiosorum.*

169. Michael Alberti, *De melancholia vera et simulata* (Halle, 1743).

170. J. E. F. Crell, "Observationes de probatione sanae mentis . . . defend. Iac. Ernest. Frider. Crellius . . . 5 Dec. 1737," in Christoph Ludwig Crell, *Dissertationum atque programmatum Crellianorum fasciculi XII* (Halle, 1775–84), fasc. 5, pp. 731–46, at pp. 732–33.

This legal discourse on madness did not, of course, capture the realities of madness and mental disorder as they were experienced by many early modern Germans, but the effort to decide questions of responsibility was the lawyers' way of asking whether the insane were fully human, a question to which theologians and physicians also devoted their attention. We have seen that in a medical sense, the sixteenth century became the age of melancholy, with its resurgent Galenic theories and numerous melancholy princes. We have also seen that religious writers might understand their world and their age as declining, decrepit, and mad, filled with insane sinners trapped in the jaws of the sin-maddened Serpent. A third way of experiencing madness was that of the jurists, who had thought of madness as akin to childishness, but who, in launching the age of witch-hunting, had embraced both medical and demonological views of madness. One more major conversation or discourse structured the experience of madness. Sixteenth-century Germans tried to understand the fundamental flaw in their lives, the basic sickness of the world, through a fourth master image: the literary and moral category of fools and folly. And like the discourses associated with medicine, theology, and the law, the rhetoric of folly found incarnation in the real world. The sixteenth century saw the institution of the court fool at every minor princeling's court.

CHAPTER FIVE

Court Fools and Their Folly: Image and Social Reality

LONG ago a wise people called the "Lalen" grew so tired of being constantly asked to solve the problems of their princes and neighbors that they decided to dispel their reputation for wisdom and to behave in as foolish a manner as they could. They built a new triangular town hall with no proper doors and no windows; they then tried to bring in sunshine in baskets and buckets, and finally solved the problem of darkness by taking off the roof. When the emperor came to visit, they recognized that he must already have gold and silver aplenty, and so presented him with a common pot of sour mustard. Noticing his unmarried son, they offered the swineherd's daughter to him in marriage. In due course, their cleverly planned foolishness became habitual, and habit became second nature to them: "Consuetudo est altera natura." In the end, they found that they could not be other than the fools they had become. Fear of a cat (a "mousedog") led them finally to burn down their whole town and to scatter to the four corners of the world, spreading their folly to every tribe of the race of man: "And so the name and tribe of Lalen from Laleburg disappeared and was extinguished. And yet their nonsense and folly, which was their best part, survived. Perhaps you and I have even inherited a good portion of it. Who knows if it's not true?"[1]

This story of the Lalen was first published anonymously in Strasbourg in 1597, and immediately in the next year, it appeared with many editorial changes as the story of a people now known as Schildbürger. In one form or the other, in at least twenty-six editions before 1800, the tale was reprinted, retold, refashioned, and even translated into Yiddish, becoming

---

1. *Das Lalebuch: In Abbildung des Drucks von 1597*, ed. Werner Wunderlich (Göppingen, 1982), p. 213. Wunderlich also edited a version in modern German, *Das Lalebuch herausgegeben und in unsere Sprache übertragen* (Stuttgart, 1982).

one of the best-selling "folk-books" of early modern Germany.[2] For some readers, the fun lay in thinking of a place of such resounding stupidity: many cultures tell such stories, after all.[3] For others, the dystopia of the Lalen and Schildbürger allows us to feel the frustration of humanistically educated burghers increasingly exploited by the selfish demands of expanding princely courts.[4] But it is just as true that the *Lalebuch* can be seen as a rewriting of the fall of man, a fall not into sin and perversion but into folly. And in this sense, the fools of Laleburg can stand as emblems of a century that had reveled in folly as the lively image of all that was wrong in life, and sometimes of all that was right.

The Age of Folly

Modern readers will inevitably associate this image of the sixteenth century with the ideas of Michel Foucault, whose dramatic history of madness confronted historians, philosophers, and literary critics with a series of startling and prophetic images in the early 1960s.[5] At the beginning of his history of madness, Foucault painted an unfamiliar picture of late medieval Europe as a time when the fools and the mad were loose in the land. They were not yet excluded from society, marginalized or confined to mental hospitals. Instead, they roamed the roads and went on strange pilgrimages in "ships of fools," bound for distant shrines or simply roving aimlessly. Readers have often assumed that these ships were real, and have found in Foucault's powerful metaphor an apt image of the relaxed relations that then prevailed between reason and unreason. It was the age of the court fool, who

2. *Folk-book* can be a dangerous term if it is taken to mean a book with no author, a book that therefore springs directly from the timeless soul of the people. Hans Joachim Kreutzer has provided a trenchant warning against such romanticizing tendencies in *Der Mythos vom Volksbuch* (Stuttgart, 1977). In recent years, the authorship and even the priority of the *Lalebuch* (the assumption that it came before the *Schildbürgerbuch*) have been questioned, in a dispute that need not detain us. Rupert Kalkofen provides a useful analysis in "*Lalebuch* oder *Schiltbürger*, Anonymus oder Fischart? Die buchgeschichtlichen Untersuchungen von Peter Honegger und Stefan Ertz im Vergleich," *Wirkendes Wort: Deutsche Sprache und Literatur in Forschung und Lehre* 41 (1991): 363–77. The best general discussion of the wide range of research concerning this stream of German literature is Werner Wunderlich, " 'Schildbürgerstreiche': Bericht zur Lalebuch- und Schildbürgerforschung," *Deutsche Vierteljahrsschrift für Literaturwissenschaft und Geistesgeschichte* 56 (1982): 641–85.

3. Hermann Bausinger, "Schildbürgergeschichten: Betrachtungen zum Schwank," in *Wunderseltsame Geschichten: Interpretationen zu Schildbürgern und Lalebuch*, ed. Werner Wunderlich (Göppingen, 1983), pp. 25–58.

4. Stefan Ertz, *Aufbau und Sinn des Lalebuchs* (Cologne, 1965); Heinz-Günter Schmitz, "*Consuetudo* und *simulatio*: Zur Thematik des Lalebuchs," in *Festschrift für Gerhard Cordes zum 65. Geburtstag*, ed. Friedhelm Debus and Joachim Hartig (Neumünster, 1973), 1: 160–76, reprinted in *Wunderseltsame Geschichten*, ed. Wunderlich, pp. 121–41.

5. Michel Foucault, *Histoire de la folie à l'âge classique: Folie et déraison* (Paris, 1961).

also exemplified the rapport between wisdom and folly, while Renaissance poetry and drama confirmed the permeability of the membrane between madness and sanity. No wonder Don Quixote tilted at windmills and King Lear could learn profound lessons from his fool. The Lalen and Schild-bürger had indeed spread throughout the world.

This is not the place for a full discussion of Foucault's *Folie et déraison* or of his lifelong struggle with the oppressive structures of reason.[6] But in our search for the historical languages and social contexts of madness, we must deal with the tangled topic of folly and its crystallization in the office of court fool. We know well enough that literary works and visual images cannot be used as direct representations of reality. And yet their verbal and iconic vocabularies powerfully shape all that we say and see. When we ask, then, what the court fool was "really" like, and how he was seen at court, we have to rely on literary and artistic evidence, at least to some extent, and sometimes we find ourselves in a perfect cabinet of mirrors. We need not give up the quest for referentiality—the historian's search for the social re-ality behind the various images handed down to us—but as we review the surviving evidence, we have to be careful that we are not merely examin-ing the dust on our spectacles.

Renaissance German physicians, as we have seen, diagnosed the trou-bles of their age as an epidemic of melancholy, while religious observers of-ten saw their century as increasingly obsessed with demonic possession. Thoughtful German artists and writers, however, came to believe that mankind was also profoundly threatened by sheer stupidity, or what they called *Narrheit* (folly).[7] When they analyzed the reasons for the deepest troubles and despairs of their age, they were not inclined to blame tyrants and evil magistrates, social conditions, political decisions, or economic and other distant and impersonal forces. Instead, they sought explanations in the "folly" and immorality of their ancestors and contemporaries. In a study of madness, the question arises of whether this sort of folly was an-

6. I attempted such a review in "Madness and Civilization in Early Modern Europe: A Reappraisal of Michel Foucault," in *After the Reformation: Essays in Honor of J. H. Hexter*, ed. Barbara C. Malament (Philadelphia, 1980), pp. 247–66. My views have been criticized by Colin Gordon, "Histoire de la folie: An Unknown Book by Michel Foucault," *History of the Human Sciences* 3 (1990): 3–26; and by Gary Gutting, "Foucault and the History of Mad-ness," in *The Cambridge Companion to Foucault*, ed. id. (Cambridge, 1994), pp. 47–70.

7. The best recent studies of court fools and of early modern folly include Angelika Groß, *"La folie": Wahnsinn und Narrheit im spätmittelalterlichen Text und Bild* (Heidelberg, 1990); Barbara Könneker, *Wesen und Wandlung der Narrenidee im Zeitalter des Humanismus* (Wiesbaden, 1966); and Joel Lefebvre, *Les fols et la folie: Étude sur les genres du comique et la création littéraire en Allemagne pendant la Renaissance* (Paris, 1968). Older but still irreplace-able studies include Karl Friedrich Flögel, *Geschichte der Hofnarren* (Liegnitz and Leipzig, 1789); Barbara Swain, *Fools and Folly During the Middle Ages and the Renaissance* (New York, 1932; repr., Folcroft, Pa., 1976); Enid Welsford, *The Fool: His Social and Literary History* (Lon-don, 1935).

other form of madness. Just as there were those who saw sinful madness as the primeval flaw in God's creation, and just as others might emphasize the devil as the ruler of this world, driving its human denizens to suicide or possessing their bodies in blasphemous frenzies, so there were many, like the authors of the *Lalebuch* and the *Schildbürgerbuch*, who attributed the basic defects of our world to folly (*Narrheit, stultitia*), which they perceived as a mental disorder. Folly was the source of what was wrong.

The fool in the West, however, has never been only a figure of sin, blindness, godlessness, and insane nonsense. In the Christian tradition, the fool is more than the reckless wretch who says in his heart that there is no God, as the Psalmist puts it (Ps. 53). While the Old Testament maintains a relentlessly hostile attitude to folly, the message of the New Testament is ambiguous in its use of the concept. St. Paul taught, for example, that faith required a kind of folly, irrationality, or even madness. And the Russian Orthodox Church has even canonized numerous holy madmen as saints.[8] As a secular figure in the real world, the fool has also represented many things, and not just blindness and limitation. The fools in Rabelais, Cervantes, and Shakespeare are often oracles of insight. Court fools, we are told, were always granted a license to speak the unvarnished truth to those in power, as if they were humble prophets, permitted to say things no courtier would dare to say. The Germans called this license *Narrenfreiheit*, and in English too we speak of the wisdom of fools. Did Renaissance Germans think that madness, for all its misery, also gave access to some otherwise inaccessible wisdom? Were sixteenth-century Germans, especially those at the courts of the emerging early modern states, eager to license and listen to such fools?

The Stereotypes of Folly

To get a grip on the complexity of folly and its connections to the history of madness, we need to examine some of the most popular works of sixteenth-century German literature, for folly literature (*Narrenliteratur*) experienced a boom in Germany that made *Narrheit* perhaps the most fashionable term of the early sixteenth century.[9] The most amazing book in this large genre

8. Michael Screech, *Ecstasy and the Praise of Folly* (London, 1980); id., "Good Madness in Christendom," in *The Anatomy of Madness: Essays in the History of Psychiatry*, ed. W. F. Bynum, Roy Porter, and Michael Shepherd, vol. 1 (London, 1985), pp. 25–39; Ewa M. Thompson, *Understanding Russia: The Holy Fool in Russian Culture* (New York, 1987).

9. Germanists have studied the concept of *Narrenliteratur* for almost two hundred years, going back to the *Narrenbücher* edited by Friedrich Heinrich von der Hagen (Halle, 1811) and Felix Bobertag (Berlin, 1884). The list of the most prominent works in this genre includes late medieval works such as *Salomon und Markolf, Der Pfarrer vom Kalenberg,* and *Peter Leu;* anonymous sixteenth-century works such as *Hans Clawert, Till Eulenspiegel,* the *Lalebuch* of 1597, and the *Schildbürgerbuch* of 1598, as well as the jestbook (*Schwankbuch*) lit-

TABLE 5.1

The Publication History of the 'Narrenschiff,' 1494–1600

	1494–1499	1500–1509	1510–1519	1520–1549	1550–1600	Total
German	13	3	2	4	10	32
Dutch	0	2	0	1	1	4
French	4	3	0	1	1	9
English	0	1	1	0	0	2
Latin/English	0	1	0	0	1	2
Latin	8	6	4	0	2	20
Total	25	16	7	6	15	69

SOURCE: Thomas Wilhelmi, *Sebastian Brant Bibliographie* (Bern, 1990), nos. 171–248.
NOTE: Nine more editions (six in German, two in Dutch, and one in Latin and English) appeared from 1601 to 1787.

was the best-selling *Ship of Fools* (*Narrenschiff*) published in 1494 by Sebastian Brant, a jurist and Strasbourg chancellor. This work obviously gripped the moral imagination of its readers, for it succeeded more extravagantly than any other literary work in Germany until Goethe's *Sorrows of Young Werther*.[10]

For the years between 1494 and 1787, seventy-eight editions of the *Ship of Fools* have been registered, the vast majority before 1510. Brant used the idea of folly or *Narrheit* to cover a host of weaknesses and sins, and this usage became perhaps the dominant moral meaning of the term throughout the sixteenth century.[11] From a Stoic-Christian vantage point, Brant derived all the world's ills from folly—that is, from the human inability to act in one's own best interests and to do what one knows is best. Men and women were not totally helpless, but they regularly succumbed to pleasures and sinful, passionate obsessions, those addictive vices that a fully rational person would avoid. What made Brant's work such a stupendous success was perhaps his relentless application of the word *Narr* to all those

erature generally; and specifically several works by Thomas Murner, Johann Fischart, and Jörg Wickram. In the seventeenth century, one has to include Grimmelshausen's *Simplicius Simplicissimus* and Philipp Cradelius's *Eine Lehr-, Trost-, und Vermahnungs-Predigt bey der Leich- und Begräbniss des weyland albern und unweisen Hans Mieszko* (3d ed., 1692). Such a list only scratches the surface, however, and serious students should consult *Deutsche Schwankliteratur*, ed. Werner Wunderlich (Frankfurt a/M, 1992), and the comprehensive bibliography provided by *Wolfgang Büttners Volksbuch von Claus Narr: Mit einem Beitrag zur Sprache der Eisleber Erstausgabe von 1572*, ed. Heinz-Günter Schmitz (Hildesheim, 1990), esp. pp. 16–19, 355–77.

10. Johann Wolfgang von Goethe, *The Sorrows of Young Werther* (1774; New York, 1989).

11. See a useful exhibition catalog edited by the Universitätsbibliotheken Basel, Freiburg im Breisgau et al., *Sébastien Brant: 500ᵉ anniversaire de 'La Nef des folz,' 1494–1994; 'Das Narren Schyff,' zum 500 jährigen Jubliäum des Buches von Sebastian Brant, 1494–1994* (Basel, 1994).

sinners whose pleasures, vices, and excesses made social and religious life difficult.[12] And no one escaped his critique:

> Dan nyeman ist dem nütz gebrist
> Oder der worlich sprechen tar
> Das er sy wis, und nit ein narr

> Since none who lives from fault is free,
> We see ourselves in every man who'll
> Say he's wise and not a fool.[13]

That is to say, Brant radically simplified the understanding of folly so that it became a shorthand term for his conception of sin, while at the same time linking it to the image of the fool and jester. Immoral fools leaped and pranced as they teetered on the brink of hell.

> Gdenck narr, das es gylt din sel
> Vnd du dyeff fallest jnn die hell
> Wann du mit jr vermeynschaffst dich
> Wer wollust flüht, der würt dort rich

> Remember, fool, your soul's at stake
> And soon in deepest hell you'll bake
> If such lewd women you frequent.
> Shun lust, then blessings will be sent.[14]

With tedious thoroughness, Brant proceeded to pillory all ages and estates, all trades, all immoralities and vices, men, women, and children. All were fools. Brant did not, however, regard folly as an inborn stupidity or natural stolidity, for such an understanding of folly would have blunted the moral critique he leveled at his contemporaries.

In contrast to this single-mindedly rational critique of folly, Erasmus of Rotterdam launched his own more carefully nuanced *Praise of Folly* (*Morias encomion, id est stultitiae laus* [1511]), in which he skewered some of the same targets attacked in Brant's satire; but Erasmus also rehabilitated two forms of folly that Brant had tarred with the broad brush of his general satire.[15] First, as is well known, Erasmus's Dame Folly, Stultitia herself, praises the folly that makes life itself possible: the folly of love, sexual at-

---

12. John Van Cleve provides a useful summary and critique of a large scholarly literature in *Sebastian Brant's "The Ship of Fools" in Critical Perspective, 1800–1991* (Columbia, S.C., 1993).

13. Sebastian Brant, *Das Narrenschiff*, ed. H. A. Junghans and Hans-Joachim Mähl (Stuttgart, 1985), "Ein vorred," lines 38–40; *"The Ship of Fools" by Sebastian Brant*, ed. and trans. Edwin H. Zeydel (New York, 1944), p. 58 (translation modified).

14. *Narrenschiff*, ch. 50, ll. 15–18; *Ship of Fools*, ed. and trans. Zeydel, p. 179.

15. Georg Baschnagel, *"Narrenschiff" und "Lob der Torheit": Zusammenhänge und Beziehungen* (Bern, 1979), pp. 170–79.

traction, affection, family loyalty, and simple bodily pleasures. In this way, Erasmus repudiated the coldly stoic impulses of Brant's poem. For him, folly was human in a positive and not just in a negative sense. Moreover, at the end of his *Praise of Folly*, Erasmus undertook a careful praise of specifically Pauline folly, the irrational, ecstatic madness that carries a Christian beyond his everyday, commonplace rational and empirical bearings and into a mystical relation to Christ that no pagan wise man could have imagined.[16]

Thus Brant saw folly as irrationality, conceived in Christian-Stoic terms as a passionate, selfish, pleasure-seeking, sinful shortsightedness, whereas Erasmus described folly as multivalent irrationality, a lively mindlessness that could be life-giving and even deeply mystical, although in its selfish forms it was as sinful as anything Brant imagined.

Curiously, both Brant and Erasmus ignored or suppressed a common contemporary meaning of folly (*Narrheit, stultitia*), that of natural fools and madmen, the retarded and mentally disordered, who provided everyday examples of folly to poets and theologians. At one point, Erasmus deliberately justified this neglect. Dame Folly explains that there are actually two kinds of *insania*, two sorts of madness or folly:

> One which is sent up from the underworld by the avenging Furies whenever they dart forth their serpents and inspire in the breasts of mortals a burning desire for war, or unquenchable thirst for gold, or disgraceful and wicked lust, or parricide, incest, sacrilege, or some other such plague, or when they afflict the guilty thoughts of some criminal with the maddening firebrands of terror. There is another kind far different from the first, namely the kind that takes its origin from me [Dame Folly] and is most desirable. It occurs whenever a certain pleasant distraction relieves the heart from its anxieties and cares and at the same time soothes it with the balm of manifold pleasures.[17]

But even though Erasmus here acknowledged the moral terrors of mania and furor, he ignored the other kinds of natural mental illness, disorder, mental torpor, and retardation that were to be found all around him in the world. He was so engrossed in the moral task at hand that he had nothing to say about folly as it was commonly perceived in the real world. Another reason for his neglect was that he (and his Dame Folly) wanted to praise the common, daily irrationalities, pleasures, and whims that made life possible, while condemning unusual, antisocial, and terrifying madness. This distinction rested upon the social utility of the mental error in question and

---

16. Screech, *Ecstasy and the Praise of Folly*.

17. Erasmus, *Encomium moriae*, in *Opera omnia*, 4th ser., vol. 3, ed. Clarence Miller (Amsterdam and Oxford, 1979), pp. 116–18, ll. 873–80; id., *The Praise of Folly*, ed. and trans. Clarence Miller (New Haven, 1979), p. 58.

not on some particular condition or failing of the mind itself. And so Erasmus was ill equipped to say much, or anything at all, about natural folly and the nature of fools in the *Praise of Folly*.

For such a description, we can profit from examining the vocabulary of Friar Johannes Pauli, O.F.M., whose *Schimpf und Ernst* (Jests and Lessons [1522]) was one of the early and most popular collections of witty tales and sayings, of jests and stories, that instructed German readers in the art of entertaining narrative. Anecdotes numbers 23 through 54 are about fools (*Von den Narren*) and deal with folly both in the moral senses we have seen in Brant and Erasmus and with the fool as a social type. An example of the latter:

Once upon a time there was a fool whose lord gave him to another [lord]. Two servants were sent to get the fool and bring him home, but as the two servants were walking across a field, they got way ahead for the fool was walking slowly behind. And the two servants repeatedly had to wait for him, and so they scolded him harshly and cursed him. Then up spoke the fool: "A fool does nothing without being beaten." Thereupon the two servants cut a long rod, with which they beat the fool and drove him on ahead. Now the fool had no [long] pants on, and the two servants struck him one time or three on the shins. And when the fool felt the rod, he began to walk so fast, and even to run, so that the two servants could not catch him with their rods.

Many people are just this way. They don't run toward heaven unless they are beaten and driven with sicknesses and pestilence and with other plagues.[18]

Here we see the moralizing Pauli using the now familiar human analogy with fools, to be sure, but in a way that tells us also that such fools "belonged" to one lord or another and might be traded or given as gifts. Pauli also assumed that readers would recognize as foolish the naive but truthful reply of the fool, who invites his own beating. The basic point is that Pauli also portrayed a class of persons whom one could simply call fools. Were they just retarded? Another of his stories helps us with an answer:

Once upon a time a man lost his mind [*von Sinnen kummen*] as a result of sickness and became a fool. Once, as he was walking up and down in the town as he had often done before, young children and youths, large and small, ran after him, leaping and mocking him until he was excited to anger. Then he grabbed one of them by the hair and wrestled with him. Another person was there, who took a stick and struck the fool on the head, opening a wound so that steam and smoke poured forth from his head. And then he [the fool] immediately recovered his senses and wits [*sinnig und witzig worden*], and when he saw himself surrounded by so many youths and children, he was ashamed. And they asked him what it was like when he was out of his mind and saw so many youths around himself. And he answered that he had

18. Johannes Pauli, *Schimpf und Ernst* (1522), ed. Johannes Bolte (Berlin, 1924; repr., Hildesheim, 1972), vol. 1, no. 23, pp. 21–22.

thought that he was the Roman king or emperor and that he had to take part in a great tournament ordered by Alexander the Great, and these [children] were all his servants and retinue, etc.

There is no better medicine for fools or for restoring the senseless to their senses than to open the head and let the steam escape. There is even a little verse to this effect: O medici, mediam capitis pertundite venam! [Doctors, perforate the middle vein of the head!].[19]

Here we can see that Pauli uses the word *Narr* not just for retarded simpletons but for the deranged. We can also see that the simple moral of the tale suggested the advantages of rough treatment, as if sage physicians, too, might give the same advice.

Pauli's fools are not sinful or immoral examples; instead, they are often simpletons who tell the unadorned truth. One dying fool, for example, tells his lord that he does not want to go to heaven because he wants to stay with his lord, which requires him to go where all his subjects agree so evil a lord will go—namely, to hell (no. 46). Another fool solves a thorny problem of precedence between physicians and jurists by noting that when a man is led out to be executed, the executioner always follows him (no. 50). Yet another fool urges that a stingy innkeeper be paid with the mere sound of coins, because he has granted a poor man nothing more than the smell of his roasting meat (no. 48). In examples such as these, we can see the stereotypical contours of the wise fool, but in none of these cases does Pauli speak of fools as jesters—that is, of normal entertainers or witty persons who merely pretended to be simpletons. Pauli's fools are all either retarded, simple, and naive, or else mad, hallucinating, and possessed by the devil. For the purpose of establishing the social context of the fool, it is worth pointing out that here and elsewhere in Pauli's *Schimpf und Ernst*, the fool is not a witty jester but a mentally deficient or disordered man.

Varieties of Fool: Mad, Sinful, Natural, Crippled, and Artificial

We know from other sixteenth-century sources, however, that the social type of the fool included both simpletons and "artificial" jesters who were just pretending to be mad or simple. Perhaps the best-known representation of this sharp distinction is to be found in the elaborate parade of 137 large woodcuts executed between 1512 and 1519 by the Augsburg artist Hans Burgkmair (and others) and known as *The Triumph of Maximilian I*. One woodcut presents spirited horses pulling a car with five jesters (*Schalcks-*

19. Ibid., no. 36, p. 29.

FIG. 3. Hans Burgkmair et al., *Schalksnarren* (Artificial Fools). Woodcut from *The Triumph of Maximilian I*. Vienna, Albertina A.A. K. 10, Mappe 1.

narren) and led by Emperor Maximilian's favorite jester and confidant, Kunz (Conrad) von der Rosen (fig. 3).

In Maximilian's own instructions for the painted version of the *Triumph*, he told his secretary Marx Treitsaurwein that the figure of Kunz von der Rosen was to bear a banner proclaiming his constant efforts to provide the merriest entertainers and jesters for his majesty. Four of the five jester-fools were named by Maximilian: "Lenntz and Caspar, Meterschy and Dyweyndl."[20] From their image in the surviving woodcut, it appears that these were indeed distinct personalities. One of them is shown hitting another, while the last one, seated under the canopy, mimics the roaring, raving demeanor of a maniac. Monkeys, bells, and alcoholic excess enhance the tone of frivolity. About the leader of this wagon, Kunz von der Rosen (born Rößlin in Kaufbeuren), we know much more, and it is plain that he was not a court jester in any conventional sense. Rather, he was the emperor's boon companion, a learned and brave man, who saved Maximilian's life on one occasion. He did not wear fool's clothing and was not a witty

20. Franz Schestag, "Kaiser Maximilian I. Triumph," *Jahrbuch der kunsthistorischen Sammlungen des allerhöchsten Kaiserhauses* 1 (1883): 154–81, at 160. Cf. Hans Burgkmair, *The Triumph of Maximilian I: 137 Woodcuts by Hans Burgkmair and Others* (New York, 1964), the generally reliable translation and edition by Stanley Appelbaum, p. 6, where it appears that Appelbaum has erred in taking *"die paurn"* to be the proper name of a fifth jester.

FIG. 4. Daniel Hopfer, *Kunz von der Rosen*. Kupferstichkabinett. Staatliche Museen zu Berlin–Preußischer Kulturbesitz. Catalog No. B. 87-1. Photo: Jörg P. Anders.

Lustigmacher, although he apparently did enjoy the privilege of telling other courtiers exactly what he thought. His portrait (fig. 4) conveys a sense of his strength and seriousness, and even if one supposes that he actually must have looked different from this idealized image, it is nonetheless good evidence of how he was perceived, and of how he wanted to be perceived.[21]

In contrast to the wagon of professional entertainers depicted in figure 3, the woodcut in figure 5 shows a car containing five natural fools pulled by mules. Maximilian's directions for this image again provide a clue to its interpretation, but we also notice that the woodcut also deviates substantially from what Maximilian prescribed:

Natural Fools: Item, next there should be a small car for these natural fools: Gylyme, Pock, Gülchisch, Caspar, Hanns Wynnter, Guggeryllis. And a mule should pull the car and a small boy shall be driver.

> Another group is drawing near
> Riding, they're the next ones to appear.
> These are the fools of the natural sort,
> Very well known in the Emperor's court.
> They have often seemed so daft
> That at them one just had to laugh.[22]

In Burgkmair's woodcut, there are not the prescribed six but only five natural fools, just as there were five jesters in the previous car, yet it is of greater importance that Emperor Maximilian here too named the specific fools he had in mind for this carriage, surely an indication of the strong personal attachment or perhaps even the affection he felt for them. Pulled by a pair of mules (not one), their cart is a rude, makeshift peasant contraption, and the faces of a couple of these fools betray serious mental deficiency.

Two of these naturals are making music, with a flute and a mouth harp. Most significant for our analysis is the final phrase in the verse quoted above: they were considered so amusing that one just had to laugh *at* them.

---

21. J. Franck, "Kunz von der Rosen," in *Allgemeine deutsche Biographie* (Leipzig, 1875–1912), 29: 195–97; Flögel, *Hofnarren,* pp. 190–203. Charles V favored as "fools" men who were well above average in literacy and achievements: see Gustav Wolf, "Über den Hofnarren Kaiser Karls V., genannt El Conde don Frances de Zuñiga und seine Chronik," *Sitzungsberichte der kaiserlichen Akademie der Wissenschaften. Philosophisch-historische Classe,* vol. 5, sec. 2 (1850), fasc. 6–10, pp. 21–63.

22. Burgkmair, *Triumph of Maximilian I,* ed. and trans. Appelbaum, p. 6. I have modified two lines of Appelbaum's translation, which, for my purposes here, deviate too far from the text. Appelbaum translates: "Their sayings and deeds without reason or rhyme / Have occasioned great laughter many a time." The original verse reads: "Sy haben manche kurtzweil gemacht / so artlich das man Ir hat gelacht" (Schestag, "Kaiser Maximilian I. Triumph," p. 160). Prosaically this could be translated as: "They have often been so entertaining that one laughed at them." In producing a rhyme, however, I too have been unable to avoid deviating from the text.

FIG. 5. Hans Burgkmair et al., *Natürliche Narren* (Natural Fools). Woodcut from *The Triumph of Maximilian I*. Vienna, Albertina A.A. K. 10, Mappe 1.

Unlike the professional jesters, whose jokes and jests were funny, it seems that the natural fools themselves were funny. Even some of their names were ridiculous or even contemptible.[23]

23. It may seem remarkable that the Holy Roman Emperor should have spent time on such minor details, but Maximilian I often saw himself in the symbolic company of fools. In Maximilian's favorite city, Innsbruck, the Goldenes Dachl has a prominent oriel niche sculpture portraying an idealized Maximilian I set between his chancellor and a court fool (fig. 6). See Werner Mezger, *Hofnarren im Mittelalter: Vom tieferen Sinn eines seltsamen Amts* (Constance, 1981), pp. 8–10. See also the well-known copperplate engraving of Maximilian I (1520) by Lucas van Leyden, in which a fool stands above and behind the emperor, holding up a sign with the year and van Leyden's initial, *L* (fig. 7). Here, as elsewhere, the fool points to the folly and vanity of this world: Maximilian had died in 1519 (Mezger, *Hofnarren*, pp. 40–42).

FIG. 6. Niklaus Turing, Maximilian I between a fool and a chancellor. Stone relief. Landesmuseum Ferdinandeum, Innsbruck. Foto Marburg / Art Resource,
New York, Archive no. LA 5658/11.

We can see from these literary and artistic images that Renaissance Germans used the words for fool and folly in a rich and variegated way, which
included the metaphorical and moral sense of folly as a sinful or willfully
stupid, blind, selfish, irrational, impulsive, and passionate demeanor. In
this sense, folly was immoral, and madness thus became one of the basic

FIG. 7. Lucas van Leyden, Emperor Maximilian I with fool. Copperplate engraving. 1520. Vienna, Albertina negative no. 52.043, inv. no. 1926, 2014.

moral categories of the sixteenth century. At the social root of this usage, however, lay perceptions of the fool as a helpless, mentally disordered or retarded person. Since it was common to laugh at the naïveté and difficulties of such persons, the social sense of the fool was extended to include actors, comedians, and jesters, who imitated the ridiculous behavior of the natural fool. We continue to laugh at the type today.

The Social Position of the Fool: Outsiders

Where did these fools fit in the world? Where did thoughtful Germans place them in their social hierarchies? Nowhere do we find a better initial answer than in the *Eygentliche Beschreibung aller Stände auff Erden*, or *Ständebuch*, a collaborative work by the Nuremberg shoemaker-poet Hans Sachs and the Zurich emigrant artist Jost Amman, published by Sigmund Feyerabend in Frankfurt am Main in 1568, which ambitiously claimed to be an *Actual Description of All the Estates on Earth, the High as well as the Low, the Spiritual and the Secular, and of all the Arts, Crafts, and Trades, etc., from the Highest to the Lowest; as well as their Origin, Invention, and Usages*. This *Book of Trades*, as it has become known in English, does not of course live up to its promise to cover all the estates in the whole world,[24] but it is still somewhat puzzling to discover that after a fairly sober (and only occasionally Lutheran) depiction of such estates as pope, king, priest, and nobleman, and after a remarkably detailed presentation of dozens of urban trades such as sieve maker, lockmaker, bookbinder, and hatter, Amman and Sachs turn, at the very end of their book, to four kinds of fool: the *Geltnarr*, the *Fressend Narr*, the *Schalcksnarr*, and the *Stocknarr* (figs. 8, 9, and 10).

The first two of these fools, the *Geltnarr* and the *Fressend Narr*, were drawn from the arsenal of sinful fools that had been popular ever since Brant's *Narrenschiff*. These two images satirize avarice, usury, gluttony, and drunkenness and mark a sharp break from the previous catalog of trades and estates, suggesting that the two authors were also interested in a rank-

24. Jost Amman and Hans Sachs, *Eygentliche Beschreibung Aller Stände auff Erden, Hoher und Nidriger, Geistlicher und Weltlicher, Aller Künsten, Handwercken und Händeln, etc. vom grosten biß zum kleinesten, Auch von irem Ursprung, Erfindung und gebreuchen* (Frankfurt a/M, 1568). Note, however, that when Amman published a book of costumes "from women of high and low estate, and from almost all places . . . such as German, Italian, French, English, Netherlandish, Bohemian, Hungarian," his title corresponded to a genuine interest in the women of the then known world. He drew costumes from Turkey, Moscow, Poland, and even Peru. See the selection printed in *Frauentrachtenbuch von Jost Amman: Mit kolorierten Holzschnitten der Erstausgabe von 1586 und einem Nachwort*, ed. Manfred Lemmer (Frankfurt a/M, 1986). He may have thought, in contrast, that the estates (the *Stände*) of the world were adequately represented by the status hierarchy of western Europe, or, perhaps, that other parts of the world had fundamentally incompatible status hierarchies.

FIG. 8. *Der Fressend Narr* (The Gluttonous Fool). Woodcut from Jost Amman, *Ständebuch* (1568). Vienna, Albertina Cim. V, 15, fol. 111.

ing of moral estates. They here employed the word *Narr* in a severely moral sense and did not actually say anything about the social category of fool in which we are here interested.

With their other two fools, however, the *Schalcksnarr* (literally, a rogue-fool) and the *Stocknarr*, we seem to leave behind the moral connotations of fool to consider two social types, two statuses or trades. Let us look closely at what Amman drew and at what Sachs wrote:

> Der Schalcksnarr
> Ich brauch mancherley Narren weiß
> Darmit ich verdien Tranck und Speiß
> Doch weiß ich durch ein zaun mein Mann
> Mit meim satzwerck zu greiffen an.
> Da ich mit mein närrischen Sachn
> Die Herrschafft kan fein frölich machn
> Mit heuchlerey die Leut ich blendt
> Drumm man mich ein Schalcksnarren nennt

FIG. 9. *Der Schalcksnarr* (The Jester). Amman, *Ständebuch*. A Latin edition of Amman's images, *Panoplia* (Frankfurt: Sigmund Feyerabend, 1568), reverses *Der Schalcksnarr* and *Der Stocknarr*.

> The Jester
> I use the ways of many a fool
> To earn my food and drink
> And yet I can fence in others
> With words that attack them
> So that with my foolery
> I can entertain my lords.
> With hypocrisy I blind them
> That's why I'm called a jester.[25]

Amman chose to present this figure, a man in jester's clothing, with a fool's ass-eared hood, bedecked with bells, a fool's scepter, a (foolish) sawtoothed sword, a club hanging from his belt, a chest bandolier of heraldic (or possibly a pilgrim's) badges, and in his right hand, a mirror. Each of these items

25. Jost Amman and Hans Sachs, *The Book of Trades (Ständebuch)*, ed. Benjamin A. Rifkin (New York, 1973), p. 121.

FIG. 10. *Der Stocknarr* (The Natural Fool). Woodcut from Jost Amman, *Ständebuch* (1568). Vienna, Albertina Cim. V, 15, fol. 113.

had its own iconographic history, and one kind of historical analysis would trace the gradual accretion of these items around the figure of the fool. Instead of following this line, however, I would rather emphasize that the mirror could figure as an image of vanity, of self-knowledge, or even of revelation to others of their own natures. Hans Sachs's verses, however, composed with no apparent connection to Amman's image, give us a self-conscious deceiver, whose hypocrisy and wit were found amusing by the powerful.[26] Neither the picture nor the verses substantiate a claim to any special fool's wisdom nor to any special license to speak the truth.

The very last image in the *Ständebuch* is that of the simpleton:

> Der Stocknarr
> Ein natürlich Stocknarr ich bin

26. The best study of the *Ständebuch* is Rolf Dieter Jessewitsch, *Das "Ständebuch" des Jost Amman (1568)* (Münster, 1987), which considers the problematic relation of text and pictures, pp. 43–49, here esp. p. 49.

Denn ich hab weder Witz noch Sinn
Hab ein groben verstand / der massen
Kan weder hengen noch nachlassen
Ich fahr herauß mit wort und that
Tölpischer weiß / folg keinem raht
Verschon niemand / drumb man mich zelt
Für ein groben Stocknarren helt.

The Natural Fool
I am a natural fool
For I have neither wit nor sense
I have so coarse an understanding
That I can neither stick nor let go.
I journey forth in word and deed,
Foolishly, taking no advice.
I spare no one, and so I'm called
A gross natural fool.[27]

Here, too, Amman's image dramatically interprets what Sachs leaves largely to the imagination. Amman presents a clumsy man in contemporary dress (but with a hat that seems to suggest the court fool's donkey-ears), holding in his left hand a tray of trinkets, including an hourglass, a cup, and a chain of beads, while in his right hand he holds aloft a mirror, in just the same gesture we recognize from the *Schalksnarr*. Is he holding up the mirror of self-knowledge or of vanity? This image of the natural fool is not only similar in certain ways to that of the court fool, however, for Amman's image of the natural fool is also exactly identical to his picture of the peddler, the *Krämer* (from 60 pages earlier).[28] Are we to conclude that the peddler is a fool, or that the simpleton was not different in looks from other honorable estates, or that Amman was simply pressed for time? In one other instance he also employs an image to do double service: to depict the weaver and the tapestry weaver, two trades that, unlike simpletons and peddlers, might indeed have been hard to tell apart at first glance. Hans Sachs's verses do not help us with this puzzle, but it is important that the natural fool claims that he has only a coarse understanding, lacking wit and sense, and that he therefore says whatever comes to mind (*fahr herauß mit wort und that / Tölpischer weiß*) and spares no one. Here then was a characterization of natural folly as a sort of uninhibited crudity, a lack of politesse and finesse.

These two fools establish once again, just as we saw in Burgkmair's *Triumph of Maximilian I*, that in addition to the moral category of sinful fool, sixteenth-century Germans commonly distinguished the professional fool

27. Amman and Sachs, *Book of Trades*, p. 122.
28. Ibid., pp. 122, 41.

FIG. 11. Gerhard Altzenbach, *Ständetreppe* (Ladder of Estates). Early seventeenth century. Germanisches Nationalmuseum, Nuremberg. H.B. 24590.

or jester (sometimes known in English as the artificial fool) from the natural fool, the simpleton, the retarded or mentally disabled. Although Sachs and Amman associated only the *Schalcksnarr* with the courts of ruling lords and princes, the truth is that both kinds of fool were found at court. By the early sixteenth century, in fact, the custom of keeping a natural fool was so widespread that one finds them in the household of almost any rich and powerful family: among bishops and dukes, counts and merchants. Saxon records alone contain the names of over fifty court fools from 1485 through 1679.[29]

What, then, was the social position of the fool? From Amman and Sachs we can see that both the natural fool and the jester stood outside the ordinary ranks of society, and that impression is only strengthened by the dramatic presentation of the hierarchy of this world in a copperplate engraving by Gerhard Altzenbach of Cologne. During the Thirty Years' War, Altzenbach displayed the longing for peace and order of his whole society,

29. Friedrich W. Ebeling, *Friedrich Taubmann: Ein Kulturbild*, 3d ed. (Leipzig, 1884), p. 7.

which he imagined as a series of steps leading up from the lowly estates of peasant and soldier through the more honorable ranks of burgher, nobleman, and bishop, to the most exalted levels of king, emperor, with (again, as in Amman and Sachs) the pope at the very top (fig. 11).

Death stands in the midst of all, didactically aiming his crossbow directly at the viewer and announcing that despite the distinctions of this world, in death all are equal.

> Nun mögt ihr kommen all herbey
> und sehet wer Herr oder knecht sey.
> Bey bettlern undt Bey Obrigkeit
> Mach ich im Lohn kein Unterscheidt.
>
> Let all of you come here to me
> and see who'll lord or servant be.
> 'Tween beggars and the magistrate
> There'll be no difference in their fate.[30]

For the history of madness, it is also noteworthy that at the very bottom of Altzenbach's social pyramid, and not even part of the actual hierarchy, we find the figures of a child and a fool, with the legend beneath the fool: "I am similar only to small children" ("Den Kindern klein gleich ich allein").[31] The notion that the fool was intellectually like a child was, of course, an ancient commonplace, one that lawyers also used, as we saw in chapter 4, but the important point is that both the child and the fool are here recognized as figures essentially without social status, without a rung of their own on the social ladder. In time, children grew into the status of their parents, but fools lived all their lives as social outsiders, as we can gather, too, from the way in which Emperor Maximilian I referred to his jesters and fools specifically by name but, except for Hanns Wynnter, listed them only by their first names or with humorous nicknames. Without a family name or a place of origin, these fools were literally hard to place. They were outsiders.

It appears that cripples, dwarfs, and other misshapen persons were similarly regarded as outside the normal categories of social status, and in fact fools were sometimes portrayed as cripples, perhaps to exemplify their mentally crippled condition. Pieter Brueghel the Elder, for example, painted a group of cripples in 1568, whom he provided with foxtails and leg bells, symbols of folly and of carnival fools (fig. 12).

So close was the identification of cripples with fools that when Peter Wouters described this picture in an inventory completed in 1673, he did not even refer to these figures as cripples. Instead, he saw the painting as

---

30. Werner Mezger, *Hofnarren im Mittelalter: Vom tieferen Sinn eines seltsamen Amts* (Constance, 1981), p. 52.

31. Ibid., pp. 52–54.

FIG. 12. Pieter Brueghel the Elder, *The Crippled*. Oil painting. Louvre, Paris. Foto Marburg / Art Resource, New York.

portraying "Several fools walking on crutches, by the old Brueghel" ("Eenige sottekens op crucken loopende, van den ouden Bruegel").[32] Similarly, when Brueghel himself sketched a series of cripples, he included among them in the top left corner a normal-looking lute-playing man in fool's costume (fig. 13). The fool was a kind of cripple, or the cripple was a fool.

Religious Interpretations of the Fool

One might suppose that, theoretically, a "fool" could also be demon-possessed, too, especially if he or she were suspected of having a familiar spirit, as some people thought was the case with Claus Narr, the court fool of Saxony, to whom we shall turn in a moment. I have not, however, come across any case of demonic possession among the many surviving descriptions of court fools.

32. Ibid., pp. 56–57, citing Gustav Glück, *Bruegels Gemälde* (Vienna, 1932), p. 62.

FIG. 13. Pieter Brueghel the Elder, *Cripples*. Pen and ink. Vienna, Albertina, negative no. 54.268, inv. no. 7798. The attribution of this sketch is uncertain: see Lydia De Pauu-De Veen, "Das Brüsseler Blatt mit Bettlern und Krüppeln: Bosch oder Bruegel?" in *Pieter Bruegel und seine Welt*, ed. Otto von Simson et al. (Berlin, 1979), pp. 149–58.

Paracelsus did give his attention to this question and concluded that the devil might indeed possess fools deprived of reason from birth. In his *Liber de lunaticis*, he held that the difference between folly and madness was that fools were born into an animal spirit and "live like reasoning bestial cattle"—that is, they were not fully human, but they were not necessarily deranged either. The mad, in contrast, "live in a crazy bestial spirit," like mad dogs, and they could be driven in this direction by the devil.[33] As he put it in *De inventione artium*, unregenerate man was essentially a beast (whether a dog, wolf, dove, finch, or serpent, etc.). Only rebirth from heaven could bring a man to leave his natural bestiality behind, a bestiality that the devil could otherwise command, for "the devil possesses persons if they are beasts."[34]

Even if fools were not fully human, however, Paracelsus insisted that they were to be well treated, for they lived to teach man humility before God. In his *De generatione stultorum*, Paracelsus reminded readers that God saves man according to His will and not according to our own wisdom. Fools were incurable by nature, he noted, and even Christ did not heal them. So fools were those in whom the *vulcani* were still dominant, to change the metaphor as Paracelsus often did. A true man learned to use his bestial body as an instrument, riding it like a horse, and thereby breaking the force of Vulcan and the stars. Vulcan did succeed in making all human beings drunk in the womb, and so we are all born fools. But natural fools stayed drunk this way all their lives, intoxicated with astral wine. As such, they were living lessons for men. They did not have a special wisdom, but we should not ridicule them, Paracelsus urged, for even the biblical prophets were thought to be fools, and we who have lost God's image, at least inwardly, must learn the folly of Christ.[35]

Most Germans did not accept or even fully understand the astrological and alchemical religion that Paracelsus developed, but in the lessons to be drawn from folly, he was speaking their language. As we shall see, princes such as the counts of Zimmern regularly took pity on poor witless fools "for the sake of God" and not because they had some secret wisdom. So, too, the category of fool expanded to include cripples, dwarfs, and other misshapen and miserable "mirrors of mankind," whose status as outsiders made them examples to haughty courtiers who stood in danger of forgetting their common humanity. In this way, the natural fool had a religious use even as he took part in the "civilizing process." But what about the

33. Paracelsus, *Liber de lunaticis*, in *SW*, pt. 1, 14: 43–44; cf. *De generatione stultorum*, in ibid., p. 84. And see also pp. 125–32 above.
34. Paracelsus, *De inventione artium*, in *SW*, pt. 1, 14: 271–72.
35. Paracelsus, *De generatione stultorum*, in *SW*, pt. 1, 14: 73–92, esp. pp. 73–74.

artificial fool, the professional jester, who might imitate the pranks of the natural but about whom there was no doubt concerning his wits?

The Courtly Uses of Folly

At court, too, the "fool" might be not just the jester or the mentally retarded. In the broadest sense, the word and the idea included also physically impaired or deformed persons, whose shape was a source of entertainment for the supposedly refined members of the Renaissance court. The court of Duke Wilhelm V of Bavaria at Landshut (before he took over the whole duchy of Bavaria) bought, traded, and collected dwarfs, Turks, and "Moors" (black Africans), as well as simpletons, all evidence of the court's crude delight in the rarities and curiosities of human form and behavior.[36] It was the budding age of the museum-cabinet of natural and artistic curiosities. Fools from the seventeenth and eighteenth centuries included dwarfs and wastrels, such as the dwarf-drunkard Perkeo, court fool at the court of Elector Karl Philipp of the Palatinate (1661–1742), a fool whose great thirst accorded his image a place of humorous honor next to the gigantic wine barrel in the castle at Heidelberg.[37]

What were these court fools used for? Did they indeed enjoy a license to tell the truth? Why should we assume that they even knew "the truth"? Shall we go on to imagine that the rich and powerful of long ago (unlike the rich and powerful of today) had a thirst for truth or wisdom that they could not find among their sycophants, yes-men, and courtiers? Or were such fools really only entertainers and status symbols? To approach these questions, we would normally look for a rich archive or a memoir that might flesh out the stereotypes we have located in literature and art, but I have found no perfect cache of documents from sixteenth-century Germany, and so I turn to several examples of actual court fools of the Renaissance, from southwestern Germany and Saxony, where I shall deal with the most celebrated natural fool (Claus Narr) and then turn to the most extraordinary artificial fool (Friedrich Taubmann).[38]

36. Berndt Ph. Baader, *Der bayerische Renaissancehof Herzog Wilhelms V. (1568–1579): Ein Beitrag zur bayerischen und deutschen Kulturgeschichte des 16. Jahrhunderts* (Leipzig, 1943), pp. 83–87.

37. Wilhelm Muschka, *Opfergang einer Frau: Lebensbild der Herzogin Jakobe von Jülich-Kleve-Berg, geborene Markgräfin von Baden* (Baden-Baden, 1987), p. 211.

38. Unfortunately, one can glean very little reliable information from Ludwig Rosenberger, *Narrenkabinett: Galerie von Hofnarren und lustigen Räten* (St. Michael, Austria, 1978); but see pp. 8–39 for anecdotes about sixteen famous German fools. Not much better is Clemens Amelunxen, *Zur Rechtsgeschichte der Hofnarren*, Schriftenreihe der Juristischen Gesellschaft zu Berlin, no. 124 (Berlin, 1991).

A NATURAL FOOL: CLAUS NARR

Claus Narr is mainly known to us from the remarkable *Volksbuch* of the Saxon pastor Wolfgang Büttner.[39] Although only six copies of the 1572 first edition are known to exist today, the diligent researches of Heinz-Günter Schmitz have recently identified and located copies from twenty-eight further editions down into the mid-eighteenth century, not to mention three more editions that appear bibliographically credible, even though no exemplars have survived.[40] Schmitz also demonstrates that even more editions once existed.

According to Pastor Büttner, Claus Narr came from Rannstädt and served the electors of Saxony, starting with Friedrich the Wise (1463–1525), as well as Bishop Ernst of Magdeburg and Halberstadt. Claus is said to have died during the reign of Elector Johann the Constant (1467–1532), who held the electoral title from 1525 until 1532. Büttner also quoted Claus's occasional remarks about Martin Luther, who became a celebrity only after 1517. The impression that Claus lived on into the 1520s and 1530s was further bolstered by several graphic representations: a pen-and-ink portrait of an old man (fig. 14), often identified as Claus Narr, dated 1521 and controversially attributed to Albrecht Dürer; a life-size stone sculpture of Claus Narr with his dog, completed around 1535 (fig. 15) and brought to the Castle Hartenfels in Torgau, where it served as a cornice support; a stone relief (fig. 16) above one of the first-story windows of the same castle with the inscription KLAVS NAR 1523 or 1533 (one number is worn away); and, finally, a small (169 x 125 mm) oil painting ascribed to Hans Sebald Lautensack, entitled CLAVS NARR VON RANSTEDT and dated 1530 (fig. 17).[41]

These bits of evidence, however, all run counter to the single best account of the life of Claus Narr, a short manuscript biography composed in 1536 by Petrus Ackermann, the deacon and vicar of Weida (Kreis Gera).[42]

39. Wolfgang Büttner, *Sechs hundert / sieben und zwantzig Historien / Von Claus Narrenn. Feine schimpfliche wort und Reden / die Erbare Ehrenleut Clau=sen abgemerckt / und nachgesagt ha=ben / Zur Bürgerlichen und Christ=lichen Lere / wie andere Apo=logen / dienstlich und förder=lich. Mit lustigen Reimen gedeutet und erkleret* (Eisleben, 1572). Americans have difficulties finding this once-famous book because the university libraries at Yale and Berkeley appear to have the only copies in the Western Hemisphere, and it remains amazing that no modern reproduction of the book has yet appeared. Heinz-Günter Schmitz is preparing a facsimile edition.

40. Heinz-Günter Schmitz, *Wolfgang Büttners Volksbuch von Claus Narr: Mit einem Beitrag zur Sprache der Eisleber Erstausgabe von 1572* (Hildesheim, 1990), pp. 309–54. According to this list, at least eighty-six copies of the book survive from all the various editions.

41. For all of these representations, see Schmitz, *Wolfgang Büttners Volksbuch von Claus Narr*, pp. 10–11, 285–301.

42. Franz Schnorr von Carolsfeld, "Ueber Klaus Narr und M. Wolfgang Bütner," *Archiv für Litteratur-Geschichte* 6 (1877): 277–328, at pp. 277–78.

FIG. 14. Albrecht Dürer, bust of an old man wearing a vest (Claus Narr?). 1523.
Pen and ink. Vienna, Albertina negative no. 53.327, inv. no. 3172.

FIG. 15. Claus Narr with dog. Stone sculpture at Castle Hartenfels, Torgau. Manfred Bräunlich, Torgau.

FIG. 16. Claus Narr. Stone relief at Castle Hartenfels, Torgau. 1533? Manfred Bräunlich, Torgau.

Although Franz Schnorr von Carolsfeld published this important account in 1877, very few scholars have taken any notice of it, relying instead (directly or indirectly) on Büttner or on Karl Friedrich Flögel's history of court fools, published in 1789. Ackermann's manuscript biography states emphatically that Claus died in the year 1515 at an age of almost ninety.[43] If he died at so advanced an age, it seems likely, as Ackermann reports, that Claus was originally adopted not by Friedrich the Wise but by Elector Friedrich the Mild of Saxony (1412–1464) in the 1430s or 1440s, especially if there is any truth to Büttner's famous story that the elector adopted (and paid the parents for) Claus, who was then just a youth because the elector was heartily amused by Claus's naively brutal treatment of some geese he was tending.

During his long life, Claus developed quite a reputation for childishly witty sayings, and even for clairvoyance and prophecy. Shortly after

43. This year of death is confirmed by documents in the Weimar Staatsarchiv, detailing the fiscal outlays in 1515 for Claus Narr's funeral, coffin, requiem mass, etc. These documents were discovered by the Church historian Georg Buchwald and published as "Lutherana: Notizen aus Rechnungsbüchern des Thüringischen Staatsarchivs zu Weimar," *Archiv für Reformationsgeschichte* 25 (1928): 1–98, here 93–98. It is a sorry commentary on modern scholarship that, despite Buchwald's decisive evidence, even recent books such as Rosenberger's *Narrenkabinett*, p. 11, continue to repeat the old, disproven notion that Claus lived on into the 1530s.

ANNO D
1530

CLAVS NARR VON RANSTEDT BEII
HERTZOG FRID ZV SAXEN GEW.

FIG. 17. Hans Sebald Lautensack, *Hofnarr Claus von Rannstedt*. Oil painting on wood. 1530. Bayerische Staatsgemäldesammlungen, Munich, inv. no. 5318.

Claus's death, the famous theologian Johann von Staupitz, confessor to Martin Luther, remarked over dinner in Nuremberg that Claus had shown amazing clairvoyant abilities and had probably had a "spiritus" as his helper. Martin Luther, at his dinner table (in his *Tischreden*), spoke often of Claus Narr, mentioning, for example, the same cases of clairvoyance noted by Staupitz and concluding that he "was not just retarded from birth for he also had a little spirit by which he is said to have foretold many things" ("non adeo natura fuit stolidus, sondern hat ein geistlein gehabet, quia multa divinasse dicitur").[44] Johann Agricola also mentioned Claus Narr in his well-known collection of 750 common German aphorisms, and remarkably he too spoke of his supernatural ability: Claus had "predicted many future things, and other things that happened at distant places" ("vil zukunfftiger ding / auch so an andern orten geschehen seind / verkundigt").[45]

This attribute of the fool, the uncanny ability to foresee the future or to know what was going on miles away, was hard to explain, and so it is no wonder that Luther and others suspected the help of spiritual (demonic) forces. In fact, the Roman Catholic *Rituale romanum* of 1614 declared that the ability to know what was happening elsewhere was one of the only truly reliable signs of demonic possession. Nor was Claus Narr unique in this presumed ability. The group with whom Johannes von Staupitz supped in Nuremberg had also heard of a fool of the bishop of Bamberg who "sometimes foretold future events or [knew] things that no one knew" ("bey weilen kunfftig ding oder das nymandt gewist gesagt het").[46] In this sense, then, Claus Narr had a reputation in his own lifetime for being an extraordinary, if not a conventionally wise, fool.

But let us return to the biography of Pastor Ackermann for further clues to the real life of Claus Narr and to the general problem of the wisdom of fools. Ackermann's little work consists of a prologue and several numbered paragraphs, which we can deal with seriatim:

1. The biography places Claus's birth in Roda, near Weickelsdorf (in the modern Kreis Zeitz), and makes him the son of a herdsman. Ackermann claimed that he had been unable to learn anything about the notion that Claus had been born in Ranis (the modern Kreis Pößneck), and a second hand in the manuscript noted: "Others [place his birth] at Rannstedt, but incorrectly" ("Alii zu Ranstad sed falso"). Notice that by setting this tone of disinterested inquiry, Ackermann takes the reader into his confidence and presents himself as a thoroughly objective and factual reporter.

2. Ackermann goes on to tell how Claus punished cattle (*vihe*) and

---

44. Schmitz, *Wolfgang Büttners Volksbuch von Claus Narr*, pp. 13–14, citing Johann von Staupitz, *Sämtliche Werke*, ed. J. K. F. Knaake, *Deutsche Schriften*, vol. 1 (Potsdam, 1867), pp. 42–48; and Martin Luther, WATR, nos. 3018b and 3018a.

45. Schmitz, *Wolfgang Büttners Volksbuch von Claus Narr*, pp. 12–13. Those who added to Pauli's *Schimpf und Ernst* in 1533, in 1546, and in 1555 included anecdotes about Claus Narr but did not mention his prophetic or clairvoyant gifts, perhaps because they were neither immediately amusing nor morally edifying. See Pauli, *Schimpf und Ernst*, ed. Bolte, 2: 3–5, 82–83.

46. Schmitz, *Wolfgang Büttners Volksbuch von Claus Narr*, p. 13.

geese, hanging them as thieves for straying from the common meadow. This showed how infantile Claus was, and the anecdote perhaps survived in transmuted form in Wolfgang Büttner's celebrated story of how Claus had strangled his geese by tucking them all under his belt in an effort to control them.

3. Claus's mother used to tie him to a ring to keep him from getting into trouble, an indication surely that as a child Claus had been difficult to manage.

4. Duke Ernst's father, Friedrich the Mild (d. 1464) adopted Claus after interviewing him. Claus had complained that his mother, whom he called "the old whore" (die alde Hure), had kept him in a sack for nine years.

5. When his brother was arrested for theft, Claus exclaimed: "Off to the gallows with him!" ("Immer an galgen"), but he had wept when he realized at the last moment that his brother was about to be executed, and his brother was only then let go.

6. When they divided Saxony between them in 1485, Elector Ernst and Duke Albrecht had agreed to estimate Claus's value at 3,000 fl. (a very high sum), so that whoever retained him would receive that much less in cash.

7. Claus had reacted to the actual division of Saxony by tearing a satin cape in two, to make the point that dividing their inheritance would ruin Saxony. Here was a striking example of a fool's proverbial "wisdom," to be sure, except that the modern reader may well doubt that it happened.[47] If it was not clear to the dukes in 1485 that dividing Saxony was a bad idea, how should Claus, considering his naïveté and childishness, have had an opinion about such matters of state?

8. Claus interceded with the duke on behalf of his widowed mother, whom he again called an old whore (mein mutter die alt hure), so that she might obtain enough to eat. Here we get a sense of Claus's genuine humanity or childish sympathy.

9. Learning that castles could be starved into submission, Claus began a lengthy fast in an effort to starve everyone out of the castle: evidence of a touching or amusing literalism.[48] And he once sat on some eggs, hissing like a goose; perhaps someone had called him a silly goose?

10. When the court servants placed a foal with his horse, a stallion, and told Claus that his horse had given birth after visiting a whore, Claus beat his horse with a pitchfork but forgave the foal, saying "Oh, you poor little

47. Many of these kinds of foolishness have long been recognized as proverbial bits of folk wisdom. See Stith Thompson, Motif Index of Folk Literature (Bloomington, Ind., 1957), categories J156, J156.4, and J1700–J2749.

48. Pauli's editor of 1545 tells this story about "Bocher," the court fool of the Elector Palatine (Schimpf und Ernst, 2: 49). In his Motif Index, entries J1700–J2749, Stith Thompson refers to this kind of fool as the "literal numskull."

animal, don't be afraid. I won't hurt you. How can you help it that your mother is a whore?" ("Ach du armes tirlein furchte dich nicht ich will dir nichtes thun, was magstu sein, das dein mutter Ein hure ist"). Remembering Claus's words about his own mother, we are struck that Ackermann here represents Claus as showing unusual sympathy for a "bastard" pony. Should we understand that Claus was an outsider without a family name, whose mother was a "whore"? Was he, himself, perhaps of illegitimate birth?

11. Claus once ridiculed the duke's soldiers as cowards and showed them how to reduce to rubble a beautiful oven in the duke's new palace, shouting, "Defend yourselves now, you rascals, defend yourselves! Yes, there you are now! Puff, puff, I got you!" ("Wert euch nun ir boschebichte weret euch ia do liget ir nun, puff puff habe dirs etc"). Claus gave the impression of living at times in a world of quixotic fantasy.

12. Ackermann says that he saw Claus Narr become so annoyed when he got no wine during Shrovetide 1514 at Weida, that he turned to attack his host (exercising what we must suppose to be his *Narrenfreiheit*), saying, "Lord Captain von Hilberg, you have a pious wife, and yet [you have] many whores in the city" ("Her heuptman von hilperg ir habt ein from weib, vnd doch vill huren in der stat"), an outburst that provoked boisterous guffaws.

13. Visiting Bohemia with the court, Claus allegedly found the wine there so good that he would gladly have turned heretic for its sake. This was a good story, but one that Ackermann evidently borrowed from the Bavarian historian Aventinus, who tells it of Duke Ludwig of Bavaria-Landshut's fool. Borrowings like this put us on guard that Ackermann is not actually a straightforward, objective reporter. Like other more formal examples of the *Narrenliteratur*, his history includes extraneous stories that have nothing to do with the "real" Claus Narr.

14. And, in his final anecdote, Ackermann describes his visit to Claus as he lay dying in 1515. According to this account, Claus resisted holy unction and spoke disrespectfully of two friars: "Oh, how mighty are monks in the act of love. . . . The wonder is that the woman survived" ("O quam potentes sunt monachi actu venerio . . . mirum quod super vivebat mulier.") Here is another episode in which Ackermann's invention, and in this case his Lutheran sentiments, apparently colored the scene.[49]

I have given so detailed an accounting because it seems valuable to notice that even in the earliest full account, literary influences, the clairvoyance of hindsight, and Lutheran prejudices of the 1530s dash any hope of finding out how Claus Narr actually lived and behaved. Ackermann pre-

49. Carolsfeld, "Ueber Klaus Narr," pp. 278–83.

sents Claus as farsighted enough to know that the division of Saxony would cause trouble; as bold enough to criticize publicly the infidelity of the captain in charge of a castle where he was staying; and as compassionate enough to pardon a "bastard" pony and to obtain a pension for his widowed mother. In general, however, Ackermann depicts Claus as almost pathetically naive, stupid, and dangerously impulsive. It seems clear enough that the reason the dukes of Saxony valued him so highly was not that he bubbled over with sage advice or with saintly simplicities, but that they were amused by his retarded condition and foolish, childish behavior.

Heinz-Günter Schmitz has also explained why early modern princes were so eager to be entertained. In a common medical theory of the day, the commanding mood of a prince was all too often melancholy: the cares and pressures of office, the sleepless nights, the immoderate diet, and the inflated fantasies of courtiers could all drive a prince to distraction, so disordering his humors that he might fall into that dread combination of fear and sadness (linked with hallucinations and gastric distress) that doctors called melancholy.[50] For example, the Bavarian court preacher and Benedictine monk Wolfgang Seidel (1491–1562) wrote a special warning for princes and lords, pointing out the occupational hazards of their rank: melancholy sadness and "dangerous fantasy."[51] In addition to piety and regular, healthy habits, the prince needed amusement. From this perspective, it was easy to argue that princes and the powerful had more need for jokesters and entertainers, for laughter and comic relief, than any other part of society. One can illustrate this princely desire for the help of fools by looking at Margravine Susanna of Brandenburg-Ansbach (daughter of Duke Albrecht IV of Bavaria and wife of the ruthless Casimir of Brandenburg), who fell into a deep depression over the death of her small son in 1525; to raise her spirits, she asked Sigmund von Schwarzenstein zu Engelburg to lend her his fool, Hänsel, just for three months. Despite the fact that Sigmund, too, was in mourning, having just lost his wife, he lent Hänsel for this limited period. But Hänsel was such a hit at Ansbach that Susanna refused to return him to Sigmund, who a year later was still trying to get his fool back.[52] Susanna asserted for her part that Hänsel liked it better at her court than at Sigmund's, an interesting but unproven claim.[53] The two

50. Heinz-Günter Schmitz, *Physiologie des Scherzes: Bedeutung und Rechtfertigung der Ars Iocandi im 16. Jahrhundert* (Hildesheim, 1972).

51. Wolfgang Sedelius, *Wie sich ain Christenlicher Herr, so Landt unnd Leüt zuo Regieren under im hat, vor schedlicher Phantasey verhueten, unnd in allen noeten troesten soll* (Munich, 1547). See *Mad Princes*, pp. 21–22.

52. Fridolin Solleder, "Markgräfin Susanna und ihr Narr," *Das Bayerland* 47 (1936): 686–89.

53. Margravine Susanna's claim is interesting, in part, because it suggests that the feelings of the fool mattered.

houses almost came to serious difficulties over who had the better claim to Hänsel. When Duke Wilhelm V of Bavaria became depressed in the late 1570s, he frequently borrowed a fool belonging to Hans Fugger of Augsburg.[54] The melancholy of a prince required the nonsense of a fool.

This courtly function of Claus Narr began to be lost, for readers at least, even as early as the first edition of the so-called *Volksbuch* of 1572, for Büttner edited his original model in a variety of ways.[55] As with Ackermann, but now much more vigorously, the biographical aspect began to disappear under the plumped-up contours of a conventional jest book. No longer rooted in the scene at court, Pastor Büttner's Claus moved in the direction of bourgeois or Lutheran fun. Büttner sometimes addresses a bourgeois reader, but he also claims to be telling his funny stories to combat attacks of sadness (*anfechtende Trawrigkeit*) and says that he would have added more but felt constrained to include only virtuous tales that could be repeated in princely chambers and among gracious noble ladies (*Fürstlichen Gemachen und Durchleuchtigen ehren Frawenzimmern*).[56] First, he added a host of stories that had nothing to do with Claus Narr or with the Saxon court at all, with the effect that the book took on the generic character of a normal *Schwankbuch*.[57] He alerts the reader to many of these intrusions and additions, but not to all of them. More important, for our purposes, he attached to each of the 627 stories (actually only 626, and because of a repetition really only 625 stories) about Claus Narr his own simple, moralizing Lutheran verses, *lustige Reime*, as he called them, which would advance the book's general purpose, *Zur Bürgerlichen und Christlichen Lehre*, as he announced on his title page. "Long ago when learned men were supposed to lecture [*Doctorieren*], they wore a black robe with a red trim or border," he notes in a typical example. "Claus recognized this and said, 'See, this one is learned right down to his red border.'"

> Doctrine
> If one is learned because of one's coat
> We'll find a professor in a billy goat
> On whom we hang the proper gown.
> [But] reason is the true scholar's crown.[58]

54. Baader, *Der bayerische Renaissancehof*, pp. 212–13.

55. This whole paragraph is dependent on the scrupulous work of Schmitz, *Wolfgang Büttners Volksbuch von Claus Narr*, esp. pp. 33–79, 305–54.

56. I have used the edition by Nicolaus Bassee's heirs (Frankfurt a/M, 1602), in the library of the University of California at Berkeley. The quotation is from fol. A5v.

57. This generic shift is also apparent on the first page, in which the stories are described this way: "Clauß Narr. Heist kurtzweil, zucht, schimpff und ehr / In rechter maß nach Bürger Lehr" (fol. A1v).

58. Schmitz, *Wolfgang Büttners Volksbuch von Claus Narr*, p. 207: "Lehre. / Wenn manchen macht gelehrt sein Rock / Leicht Doctor würd ein Ziegenbock / Dem man umbhieng ein dapffer Kleid / Vernunfft und Witz gibt glehrte Leut."

The first nine editions of *Claus Narr* continued to print these aesthetically dubious, flat, but supposedly edifying verses. It was only with the cheaper and smaller editions starting in 1645 that these Christianizing moral rhymes were dropped, and only then if at all that *Claus Narr* became a *Volksbuch*. I find Büttner's authorial decisions deeply interesting: Büttner chose to publish anonymously and subverted his text by adding insipid moral rhymes with the intention of castrating the humor or at least diverting attention from the frivolous nature of some of Claus's gestures, stupidities, and pranks. Over and over, Büttner found deep wisdom or simple piety in jokes that surely had a simpler or ruder meaning. When Claus talked to his hat when it fell off and expressed his worry that his head might fall off next, Büttner extracts the moral: "What can't be cured must be endured" ("Laß fahren hin was nicht sein kan").[59] Sometimes, Büttner openly rejects the force of his own story. One one occasion, for example, Claus defended a man who had impregnated a maid, saying that she had previously been only a *Mayd* but was now *Fraw Mutter*. Pastor Büttner, however, drew the opposite conclusion and urged punishment for fornication (*Unzucht*).[60] Such editorializing suggests that Büttner was both fascinated by these stories but apprehensive that they might be turned to secular or even immoral ends. In his foreword, Büttner even explicitly contrasts the moral worth of Claus Narr's words and deeds with the immoral, godless, filthy stories of *Eulenspiegel* and of other "scandalous poems, which are vulgar pulp and books of sin that invoke the devil and prompt one to lust" ("Schandgedichte, das ist schnöde leserey und Sündenbücher, die dem Teufel ruffen und Unzucht suchen").[61] It is true enough that most of the stories of Claus Narr do not reek of the human ordure that we smell in the frequently fecal stories of Till Eulenspiegel,[62] and also that unlike Master Owl Glass, Claus Narr was no amoral merry prankster bent on inflicting his sadistic whims on the conventional and naive. But it is also true that in trying to frame his large collection of stories as if they were mainly useful for Christians and burghers, Büttner ran the risk of losing sight of Claus Narr as embedded in an earthy Saxon courtly culture that was not yet restrainedly Christian or bourgeois.

These considerations prompt me to ask the apparently simple question: What was so funny about the jests of a jester like Claus Narr? His "wisdom" seems to have consisted in (a) occasionally (twice?) foretelling the fu-

---

59. Büttner, *Von Claus Narren* (Frankfurt a/M, 1602), p. 13.
60. Ibid., pp. 73–74, cf. pp. 174–75.
61. Ibid., fol. Aiiiiv.
62. Despite Büttner's disclaimer, however, excrement, farting, and defecation are a major theme of several stories in his collection. See ibid., pp. 56–57, 71, 108–10, 152–55, 185–86, 202, 204, 233, 239, 336, 446, 467–68, 476.

ture or knowing clairvoyantly what was happening elsewhere; and (b) in being an amusing fellow to have around. We need to admit, frankly, that we do not understand the fool's supernatural knowledge, if indeed he ever possessed any gift of clairvoyance. But we may approach the second part of the fool's "wisdom" by asking what was so hilarious. My impression is that Claus Narr and most other court fools seemed funny because they defied the increasingly delicate standards of courtesy, of restrained courtly behavior, of *Höflichkeit*. Claus Narr had a childish ignorance of such adult realities as money, sex, adultery, counting and numbers, metaphoric language, religion, and death. Although Claus possessed a childish modesty, he was a naive and clumsy master of social transgression.

According to the Grimm brothers' famous dictionary, even the German word *unhöflich* (discourteous) dates precisely from Sebastian Brant's *Ship of Fools*. Those new or newly rigorous standards of deportment have been famously studied by the German sociologist Norbert Elias, who found in courtly culture a new set of embarrassments about the body, about cleanliness, excretion, nakedness and sex, about food and drink, about farting and sleeping, invasions of privacy and lapses from elegance, all deviations from smooth gracefulness and from an emerging conformity to aristocratic standards of appearance and deportment. With these newly stringent expectations, we can see why dwarfs, cripples, and hunchbacks could also be counted along with the retarded as fools. Courtly culture was increasingly demanding a smooth behavior and appearance of just the sort that one could not expect of the fool.

FOOLS IN THE CHRONICLE OF THE
COUNTS OF ZIMMERN

Such new norms made the fool seem funny to the court. But that did not mean that one had to let him go his way without punishment. Court fools were often the butt of cruel jokes, the objects of abuse, manipulation, and ridicule. Even the beloved Claus Narr complained of being beaten every Holy Innocents' Day (December 28).[63] As late as 1660, the prince bishop of Bamberg kept a fat, stammering fool at his table, to whom on one occasion he gave hazelnuts and commanded that he crack them by smashing them on the table with his forehead. He let this sadistic joke go on until blood was streaming down the fool's face.[64] From the 1590s comes further evidence that a fool could be ordered into humiliatingly compromising positions. During the madness of Duke Johann Wilhelm, at the court of Jülich-

63. Ibid., p. 41.
64. Adolf Schwammberger, "Von Hofnarren in und aus Franken," *Jahrbuch für fränkische Landesforschung* 34–35 (1974–75): 975–81, at 976.

Cleves, Duchess Jakobe von Baden was accused by the duke's sister Sibylla of committing a variety of crimes and outrages ranging from the casting of magic spells to frequent acts of marital infidelity. But the duchess had, in addition, disgraced herself with the court fool, a man named Martin, whom she "secretly after dinner ordered to her rooms, where, behind closed doors, she tugged at his trousers for two or three hours." Was she playing sexual games with a fool? These were dangerous indiscretions. Witnesses charged that she had "stroked him lovingly, clothed him delicately, painted his face, and given him baths twice a week."[65] The princess had a reputation for frivolity but this was surely too much! The court in Düsseldorf was abuzz with rumors, but for our limited purposes here it is noteworthy that a fool had his part to play in this melodrama, a tragedy that only ended with the bedroom murder of Duchess Jakobe.[66] Here was a fool with whom a lady could play naughty games, but only at the risk of her life.

The historian's task in describing the life of court fools is to find more of this sort of credible evidence of life as it was actually lived, as distinct from the heaps of literary and derivative fantasies that were collected in the jest books of *Narrenliteratur*. We have seen in the case of Claus Narr how quickly the sources fill up with literary stereotypes and pious moralizing. The single best source from which to reconstruct the real lives of German fools may be *Die Chronik der Grafen von Zimmern* ("The Chronicle of the Counts of Zimmern"), which has become famous in the past 150 years because it documents the court life, politics, and daily living conditions in a tiny Renaissance German territory in unparalleled detail. That does not mean, of course, that it offers us a transparent window through which to look at a past social reality. Like any other source, it needs to be interrogated and approached with caution. Obviously, some parts of the *Chronik* fantasized or borrowed anecdotes from elsewhere, just as did the jest books whose literary impulses we confront at every turn.

Fools appear often in the *Zimmerische Chronik*. For example, we are told that Count Johann Wernher von Zimmern, whose residence was at Messkirch among the rolling, half-forested lands between the Upper Danube and the Lake of Constance, had a fool named Wolf Scherer, a man who had been born at Oberndorf on the Neckar. Because of some brain injury, "and because he was foolish [*dorecht*] and such an amazing, perverted person [*ain so wunderbarlicher, verkerter mensch*]," he was generally called Peter Letzkopf (i.e., "Crack-Brain").[67] Even though he owned shoes, he

---

65. Muschka, *Opfergang einer Frau*, p. 332.
66. I sketch the episode in *Mad Princes*, pp. 100–118.
67. Mezger, *Hofnarren im Mittelalter*, p. 66. All of the quotations in this paragraph come from Froben Christof, Graf von Zimmern, and Wilhelm Wernher, Graf von Zimmern, *Die*

went about barefoot summer and winter. Courtiers obviously had a good time abusing this unfortunate man, so much so that on one occasion he fell into a rage and took revenge by stuffing wood shavings into all the palace key holes. But this deed in turn irritated Count Johann so deeply that he banished his fool from Messkirch. According to this decree, Letzkopf was seized and led to the nearby monastery of Wald. To the astonishment of all, later that same day Letzkopf appeared in Messkirch at court again, returning even before the servant who had taken him into exile (the fool had known a shortcut through the woods). When asked to explain himself, Letzkopf set forth a touching confession. Once abandoned at the monastery, the poor man "had sat down on a large stone and had looked around at the wide world in all directions" and concluded that "no place in all the world was so dear to him as Mösskirch." This touching story made Count Johann laugh, and he received Letzkopf back into his good graces again. The life of a natural fool at court was clearly not all beer and skittles, but Peter Letzkopf was evidently something more than a helpless imbecile. It was said that he had been four times to Santiago de Compostela, and that in Rome he had once tricked a blind beggar who had secreted a hoard of forty gold pieces in his cloak into jumping off a bridge into the Tiber (and drowning), while Letzkopf made off with the cloak and the money. Clearly, he was no saint, and "where he was most welcome, there he stayed the least, and if he noticed that he was unwelcome, then no one could get him to leave." He was an amusement and a threat in about equal measure.

The *Chronik* also tells of another fool named Peter, owned and maintained by a Strasbourg prebendary named Schmidtheuser. "Although he was [mentally] no more than a child, he could take care of household tasks," such as buying food at the local market and waiting on table, and was generally regarded as trustworthy, except for his odd delusion that if he put a crab shell or chicken bone on his nose, he would become invisible.[68] Like Letzkopf, he was not just retarded. He suffered not only from mental insufficiency but also from the kind of "melancholy" fantasy that was frequently described in dense anecdotal detail throughout the medical literature of the sixteenth century. In other words, this Peter was probably mentally undeveloped but also disordered (pathologically melancholy). When the prebendary had guests, they sometimes humored foolish Peter's delusion, as doctors frequently recommended throughout the century.

Chronik der Grafen von Zimmern, ed. Hans-Martin Decker-Hauff and Rudolf Seigel (Constance, 1964–), 2: 131–33.

68. This and the other quotations in this paragraph are drawn from *Chronik*, 3: 338–39. On another fool, who was described not as retarded but as *nit recht bei sinnen*, see ibid., p. 310.

Putting on his crab shell, he fancied the guests could not see him. "Where, oh, where, has our Peter gone?" ("Ach, wo ist uns der Petter hinkommen?"), the guests would then exclaim. This pleased Peter enormously, who then betook himself to a corner. One guest lamented, "I fear that our Peter is lost," but another objected, "Hah, that rascal, that thief is probably off stealing another sheep or skinning a cat so that he can sell the pelt to a furrier as if it were a buckskin." Such a charge was too much for the fool, but thinking that he could not be seen, he swallowed his anger. "They kept up this kind of mummery with him a long time. Finally, someone came along and knocked the crab shell off his nose as if by accident and shouted, 'Look, Peter, are you here? We all thought you were away.'" And then Peter laughed and exclaimed, "'Ja, I just came from the fish market where I was doing this or that.'" Our chronicler remarks that Peter had to be teased and enraged periodically, "so that his spirit would get excited, for otherwise he would get sick because of his melancholy, as the proverb says: 'Fools have to be driven and exercised, or else they go rotten and soft from lying around.'" The application of this proverb is of interest here, not only because it reveals that a kind of debased medical thinking had penetrated the nobility even in remote rural corners of Germany, but also because fools were not usually thought to have the humoral disorder of excessive black bile (melancholy). Yet here was a melancholy fool. Generally, sixteenth-century doctors and philosophers agreed that no one was born mad with melancholy, even though many were indeed born "under Saturn," that is, with a tendency toward a melancholy disposition. But in foolish Peter of Strasbourg, folly-as-retardation and the physical category of Hippocratic disease obviously overlapped.

Some of the fools mentioned in the *Zimmerische Chronik* had difficulties in expressing themselves, such as a man named Vischerhanns (Fisher John), who rushed to his master, Count Wilhelm Wernher von Zimmern, in order to be the first to tell him that the count's wife had died. But standing before the count, the poor man was so agitated that he was unable to get out one word, and stammered "Botz, teuz, gnedige hee! sie tommen, sie tommen, gnedige hee, . . . die botten." Realizing that he would get no real news from his fool, the count had to wait an hour for the official messenger's report. Observers found the fool's incapacity as laughable as his apparent expectation that the count would be overjoyed that Vischerhanns had been the first to report the sad news.[69] Like some other anecdotes, this story does not seem to have been borrowed from the *Schwankliteratur*. Does this mean that we can trust the tale?

Some fools were treated as members of the family and must have devel-

69. Ibid., p. 112.

oped a strong sense of family loyalty. Count Johann Wernher took a young, retarded boy named Junghans and raised him, "for the sake of God." It should not surprise us, therefore, that when his widow, Countess Margarethe von Zimmern, was to be displaced from her residence by Count Haug von Werdenberg, Junghans, a "poor, childish, silly person," felt it as an attack on his own mother. In defense of "my dear mother," this "senseless fool" threatened to kill Count Haug with an ax, but he was disarmed by the countess before he could do any harm.[70]

As we can see, the fools mentioned in the *Zimmerische Chronik* were not professional jesters, entertainers, or *Schalksnarren*. They were men with more or less serious mental troubles or deficiencies. Sometimes the idées fixes or "melancholy" delusions of such fools made life hard for everyone. The *Chronik* reports on Count Rudolf von Sulz's fool, who on the face of it seemed normal but had a mania for collecting all sorts of papers. To humor this odd fixation, courtiers used to give him old letters and other irrelevant waste paper. Once, when Count Rudolf was trying to travel incognito, his companion, the fool, seized a package of confidential letters from the count, prompting the count to strike the fool on the finger, sending the poor man off into such a rage that he was uncontrollable for a time. By charging that Count Rudolf had actually stolen the letters from him, that the count was *ein wissentlichen ehrlosen briefdieb*, the fool threatened to blow the count's cover and almost succeeded in having his master thrown in jail.[71]

So it seems that keeping a fool was not just a one-way system of abuse. But it is also clear that princes and courtiers often did tease or irritate their fools, playing on their habits and fixations, sometimes in the announced hope that by going along with the delusions of a man, he might be drawn to see that his ideas were ridiculous. The fool who thought himself invisible found, as we have seen, that courtiers were willing (for a time) to humor this fantasy. The professional medical literature that we examined in chapter 3 is full of classic stories of melancholy men, such as the man who held that he was dead and so refused to eat, but who was cured, we are told, by being placed in a tomb in which another man, wrapped in grave clothes was lying. As soon as they were alone together, the second man asked the melancholy fool, "When do we eat?" and set a good example when food was sent down into the tomb.[72]

70. Ibid., 1: 258–59. On a fool named Michel who regarded Count Johann Wernher as his father, see ibid., 2: 280–81.

71. Ibid., 2: 266.

72. This famous anecdote concerning the melancholic who thought himself dead was attributed also to Claus Narr (Büttner, *Von Claus Narren* [1602], pp. 486–87). Many such stories, originating with the ancient physician Rufus of Ephesus (fl. under Trajan) were collected by Jason Pratensis in *De cerebri morbis* (see pp. 152–56 above) and by Robert Burton in *The Anatomy of Melancholy* (London, 1621). On ancient psychiatry, see J. Pigeaud, *La*

As we have seen, fools were sometimes put to work with simple tasks, but there was always the risk that a fool would not perform as expected. The *Zimmerische Chronik* tells of a swineherd who deliberately led his pigs to feed on poisonous herbs so that he would have fewer pigs to guard.[73] Another fool, admired for his ability to play the bagpipe, fashioned a foxskin blanket for his instrument so that his pipes would not feel cold in the winter.[74] The most common expression used to describe a fool in the *Zimmerische Chronik* is *ain lauters kindt*, "nothing but a child," a phrase that explains perhaps the amusement and the indulgence with which these unfortunates were regarded. The counts of Zimmern did not, however, see their fools as licensed oracles or goofy critics of courtly convention. They were funny specimens of a distorted humanity.

An Artificial Fool: Friedrich Taubmann

One of the more remarkable academic careers in sixteenth-century Germany was that of Friedrich Taubmann (1565–1613), a poet, professor, and "merry counselor" (*lustiger Rat*) to the electors of Saxony (fig. 18).

Over one hundred years ago, Friedrich Ebeling published an excellent study of Taubmann's life and writings, together with a collection of his jests and a bouquet of his Latin poems. It is still today the best work on Taubmann, who was born in 1565 in Wonsees, near Bayreuth in Franconia. The son of a shoemaker, young Friedrich attended a sort of lower *gymnasium* (1578–82) in Kulmbach and then a better school in Heilsbronn (1582–90), before finally obtaining a stipend from the margrave of Ansbach to support university study at Wittenberg, beginning in 1592. Ebeling suspected that Taubmann's poverty and the student-begging that went with poverty taught the boy the habit of ingratiating himself with those in power. Already from his youth, there were stories redolent of the arrogance, effrontery, and brazen discourtesy that came to characterize him in adulthood. I give only one example, drawn from many: When a teacher asked him the elementary grammar question, "Cuius generis est mater?" ("What kind [of word] is *mother*?"), Taubmann shot back: "Mea mater est generis feminini, tua vero erat generis communis" ("My mother is feminine but yours was of the common sort").[75] Remarkably, several of Taubmann's teachers and fel-

---

maladie de l'âme et du corps dans la tradition médicophilosophique antique (Paris, 1981); Helmut Flashar, *Melancholie und Melancholiker in den medizinischen Theorien der Antike* (Berlin, 1966); Stanley W. Jackson, *Melancholia and Depression: From Hippocratic Times to Modern Times* (New Haven, 1986).

73. *Chronik* (cited n. 67 above), 2: 155.
74. Ibid., p. 156.
75. Ebeling, *Friedrich Taubmann*, p. 16.

FIG. 18. Friedrich Taubmann (1565–1613). Frontispiece from Friedrich W. Ebeling, *Friedrich Taubmann: Ein Kulturbild*, 3d ed. (Leipzig, 1884).

low students recognized in him more than just a rebellious and insulting rascal—some thought him brilliant.

At Wittenberg, Taubmann devoted himself to philology, and especially to ancient Latin literature, but he used his time also to read Thomas More's *History of Richard III*, Hector Boethius's *Scotorum historia*, the poetry of Dante, and the stories of Boccaccio. He became an enthusiastic reader of Machiavelli.[76] He also perfected his talents for occasional and spontaneous

76. Ibid., pp. 39–41.

(often humorous) Latin verse. At the same time, he developed an unslakable and stereotypically German thirst and a serious desire to enrich himself. After three semesters, he had earned his baccalaureate, and by 1595, his magister, the highest degree in philology. Although enjoying a generous stipend, Taubmann immediately applied for a full professorship in the faculty that had just promoted him. In fact, he applied for his own teacher's job, noting that Adam Theodor Siber had too much to do to cover poetry, rhetoric, and the Greek language. When the philosophical faculty flatly rejected Taubmann's plea for self-advancement, the twenty-nine-year-old magister showed his true genius. He took his plans to Margrave Georg Friedrich of Ansbach, his old patron, whom he won over, and soon Georg Friedrich was recommending Taubmann to Duke Friedrich Wilhelm of Weimar, administrator of Electoral Saxony from 1591 to 1601. Friedrich Wilhelm in turn ordered the Wittenberg faculty to split Siber's professorship so that Taubmann could obtain the position he wanted. Ducal influence could often solve problems that seemed to have no academic solution.[77]

From then on, Taubmann's career oscillated between the poles of court and university. He enjoyed his fame as a student of Plautus and as a poet, but he realized at once that the court paid better, perhaps four times better, and that the wine was better too.[78] He soon became the *kurzweiliger Rath* (amusing adviser) at the Saxon court of Wittenberg. No one, so far as I know, literally called him a *Hofnarr*, doubtless because, as we have seen, the term implied a series of mental or physical deficiencies. And the term *kurzweiliger Rat* was the same title sometimes used for Kunz von der Rosen, the humorous favorite of Emperor Maximilian I. In effect, Taubmann was the learned jester and amusing confidant of the Saxon prince. He dropped his professorial duties repeatedly in order to travel with the court. He dropped his professorial dignity, too, becoming a wild, scabrous, scandalous, smutty, drunken, nonsensical, but learned buffoon. He never, or perhaps just once, played the moral critic, exercising his *Narrenfreiheit* in order to speak truth to power, and even that one questionable time it was in order to regain the good graces of his lord.[79]

Again, therefore, we are entitled to ask what wisdom he possessed. What sort of fool was he? From his many recorded jests, I shall offer only a few striking examples. At table one day, Taubmann found that he had been given nothing to eat. Although a Latin witticism instantly brought him up to Duke Friedrich Wilhelm's elbow, the court ladies continued to tease him about the incident so mercilessly that Taubmann decided to take revenge. He outfitted the palace ladies' privy with a deep black sack and filled it half-

77. Ibid., pp. 47–49.
78. Ibid., p. 100.
79. Ibid., pp. 84–85, 219–20.

full with pine ashes. The little room was so dark that the fine ladies could not notice that every time they relieved themselves, a cloud of soot besmirched their bottoms. And we must recall that bathing was so infrequent that it was often prescribed as an unusual medical procedure. Remembering this, we can understand Taubmann's certainty that he had trapped the abusive ladies in a deep embarrassment. At table a few days later, when they persisted in their foolishness at Taubmann's expense, he whispered to the duke that he was willing to bet that most if not all of these fine ladies had black bottoms. The duke shook with laughter and told his duchess, who in turn ordered the ladies off to a private room where an inspection could take place. Of course, Taubmann was vindicated and the ladies were humiliated.

Much of his poetry was occasional or festive verse in praise of drink. One went like this:

> Vivendi recte, bibere est et principium et fons
> Hoc tibi teutonici poterunt ostendere mores:
> Poclaque provisum ventrem haut invita sequuntur.

> Drink is the source and beginning of living well
> This the customs of the Germans can show you
> Gladly the glasses follow a well-prepared stomach. [80]

Or these lines:

> Heus-Juvenis: potorum te ipse minorum
> Excerpas numero. Ne, lente invergere poclum,
> Dixere esse satis.

> Hey, son, avoid the company only of lesser drinkers
> Lest you claim it's enough just
> To drain the bowl slowly.[81]

Or these:

> Nec tibi potus erit, qui recto insistere talo
> Audet adhuc, nomenque suum qui novit: et aequo
> Calce pavimentum metatur.

> He is not drunk who can still walk. Nor he who still
> Knows his name, nor he who
> Bestrides the floor with head held high.[82]

Taubmann used his facility with Latin to compose nonsense, too, including verses to a lover, calling her Columba (dove), a play on his name, Taubmann (dove-man),[83] others on the death of a young rabbit, and an-

80. Ibid., p. 328.
81. Ibid., p. 330.
82. Ibid., p. 330–32.
83. Ibid., p. 282.

other for a flea.[84] He seems to have been a master of sprightly Latin verse in honor of the weddings of his friends, and equally ready to blast his enemies with the ferocity of a Juvenal or a Martial.

To the legend of Taubmann were attached a host of jests, witty sayings, and anecdotes, some of which had been told of other fools before him. Once, for example, on a trip through a Catholic territory, Taubmann removed his hat in honor of a crucifix, but later failed to do the same when he passed a gallows. "Why," asked a witty Lutheran courtier, "don't you honor the gallows, too, seeing that it is made of wood as much as was the crucifix?" And Taubmann replied, "Then why do you kiss your wife on her mouth and not on her ass, seeing that they are both of the same flesh?"[85] In fact, generally, Taubmann practiced a kind of impartial rudeness and even-handed discourtesy to all, including his prince.[86] Even sacred things were not safe from his scurrility. It was said that an over-clever nobleman once asked Taubmann what the initials V. D. M. I. Æ. (the Saxon Lutheran motto, *verbum domini manet in æternum*, "The word of the Lord will last forever") meant. Contemptuously, the junker suggested that they should be construed as "Unsern Dreck Müßt Ihr Æssen" ("You will have to eat our shit"). Whereupon Taubmann shot back, "No, no, it has to be turned around: 'Æsst Ihr Meinen Dreck Vorher' " ["First you'll have to eat my shit"]).[87]

Asked once where the greatest fools were to be found, Taubmann replied, "At court, for there each person is the other's fool." Did that include the elector of Saxony, his lord? "Ah," answered Taubmann, "Ille est eximius" ("He is exceptional!").[88]

Such stories go on and on, but let us reflect again on what kind of humor this was. We recall that such transgressions of decorum and propriety seem to have proliferated especially at the court, which pretended to higher standards than the surrounding countryside. Courtiers and princes alike seem to have roared with laughter to see their own standards mocked and flouted. Taubmann was a master of social irreverence, but he was himself almost invulnerable because he did not easily take open offense over attacks on his own supposed honor or dignity. He flourished where quick wits and brazen audacity struck many as refreshing. To a nervous student who intended to praise him but got stuck after the first line:

"Tu Taubmanne vates"

"O Taubmann, you prophet—"

Taubmann responded in rhyming irritation:

84. Ibid., pp. 246, 248.
85. Ibid., p. 190.
86. Ibid., pp. 193–210, for a series of examples.
87. Ibid., p. 207.
88. Ibid., p. 213.

"Tu mihi lambe nates"

"Lick my ass."

In Taubmann's career at the Saxon court, we can perhaps see what the satirical *Lalebuch* of 1597 was talking about. Here was a humanist burgher who found that he was asked for advice by his princely lords, but that the only advice they accepted and understood was scabrous nonsense. In this sense, the court was on its way to becoming the dystopia described by the *Schwankbuch* literature.

Conclusion

Norbert Elias's famous theory of the "civilizing process" includes the notion that modern embarrassments over the body began when courtiers learned to repress or discipline their grosser bodily functions. But so long as the fools found in the *Chronik der Grafen von Zimmern*, so long as Claus Narr or Friedrich Taubmann and their counterparts were at court, this civilizing process had a limit or a counterpoint, a heightening by way of contrast that no one could ignore. Down to the end of the seventeenth century, or even well into the eighteenth century, most German courts kept fools, who were largely retarded naturals but might include increasing numbers of "artificial" fools and even learned jesters as well, along with dwarfs and cripples. Princes and courtiers laughed with them and at them, sadistically abused them, treated them as pets, or regarded them as prized parts of the princely inheritance. Maybe it was just as funny to pervert the humanist wisdom of a professor by rewarding his crudities. But it should be clear by now that the fool did not really enjoy a reputation for wisdom, or even generally for prophetic insight. His discourteous and unintentionally Christian "wisdom," if we can call it that, consisted in reminding all who saw him that he was in his way as human as any courtier.

Observers, of course, remained well aware of the traditional literary and religious connection between folly and wisdom; they continued to look for and expect instances of genuine insight in the fools of their world, but a story out of Pauli's *Schimpf und Ernst* epitomizes the true relations of image and reality. Pauli tells of a Roman fool who was instructed to remain silent when a learned Greek jurist interviewed him:

The Greek from Athens began the disputation by raising one finger, his index finger, as if to say that there was only one God. The fool concluded that he wanted to poke out his eye with his finger, and so the fool raised two fingers, as if to say, "I'll poke out both of your eyes." But it is usual that when one sticks out two fingers one also extends the thumb, and so the Athenian gathered that he wanted to convey the holy trinity in one true God, and that was the reason he held out three fingers. Then the

Athenian lifted up his flat open hand, as if to imply that God the Lord knew and saw all things; but the fool thought that he was about to slap him on the cheek with his open hand, and so in response he made a fist, as if he would hit the Greek on the head. Seeing this the Greek from Athens thought he meant that God had placed all things under his power, and that the judgments of God the Lord were secret and hidden from all the world. . . . And so the Athenian concluded that this was a wise and deeply learned man."[89]

Pauli's delightful little tale surely deflates the traditional notion of the wisdom to be found in fools and suggests that such wisdom was only in the eye of the beholder. The tradition from Erasmus, Rabelais, Cervantes, and Shakespeare, and on through Grimmelshausen and Voltaire's Candide, has ever since continued to work its mischief on our presuppositions. We find it hard to realize that court fools were usually little better than slaves and pets: men (and a few women) who may well have preferred the abuse they received at court to the neglect and abuse they might as easily have received on the road or at home in the village.

When early modern Germans thought of the world as full of madmen and fools, therefore, they were not describing people in a state of mystical ecstasy or possessed of a gentle wisdom. Fools were for them essentially outsiders, to be beaten, manipulated, coddled, and laughed at. Careful observers could mark a difference between the retarded and those who had developed a mental illness, and could certainly tell the difference between the physically deformed, cripples, dwarfs, and the mentally disordered, but the force of their language pushed many early modern Germans to emphasize the alienation, ridicule, and abuse to which fools were all subjected.

One reason folly was so potent an image was that one was born into it and there was little anyone could do about it. It was a natural condition and seemed in its helpless naïveté and blundering to reveal important truths about the human condition. Doctors did not claim to cure retardation; theologians agreed that natural fools remained like children all their lives; lawyers were of one mind in appointing lifelong guardians or custodians to manage their affairs. In contrast, most madnesses were thought to be illnesses or disorders into which one fell, the result of some acute fever, perhaps, or of some gross error in one's diet or love life. If one did not die at once of frenzy or stupor, one might hope for a cure, or at least for some alleviation of one's misery and confusion. And here, too, sixteenth-century Germans often sought and found religious remedies for their mental ills. Chapter 6 looks at prayer, vows, and pilgrimage, whether in gratitude for or hope of a miracle. Christians had long had recourse to these in times of distress, and most Catholic Christians in the sixteenth century continued to do so.

89. Pauli, *Schimpf und Ernst*, no. 32, pp. 26–27.

CHAPTER SIX

*P*ilgrims in Search
of Their Reason

IN THE late Middle Ages, a popular piety flourished so vigorously that some churchmen worried about how to retain control over the sacred.[1] It was the age of the "children's pilgrimage" to Mont St. Michel (1456–59) and of the mass enthusiasm surrounding Drummer of Niklashausen (1476), of bleeding hosts and the cult of Corpus Christi, of the new devotion of the Rosary and an apparently insatiable appetite for preaching.[2] The reader of such accounts could easily come away with the impression that this florid display of religious excess fell victim in the sixteenth century to the combined forces of Protestant and Catholic Reformation, and to what Peter Burke has called the "triumph of Lent."[3] Reading in English, especially, one would conclude that pilgrimage was an essentially medieval form of piety, and that after 1500 the ridicule of Erasmus and Luther's systematic critique undid the venerable practice of pilgrimage.[4] Certainly, this

---

1. Charles Zika, "Hosts, Processions and Pilgrimages: Controlling the Sacred in Fifteenth-Century Germany," *Past & Present*, no. 118 (Feb. 1988): 25–64.

2. Ulrich Gäbler, "Die Kinderwallfahrten aus Deutschland und der Schweiz zum Mont St. Michel, 1456–1459," *Zeitschrift für schweizerische Kirchengeschichte* 63 (1969): 221–331; Klaus Arnold, *Niklashausen, 1476: Quellen und Untersuchungen zur sozialreligiösen Bewegung des Hans Behem und zur Agrarstruktur eines spätmittelalterlichen Dorfes* (Baden-Baden, 1980); Peter Browe, "Die Ausbreitung des Fronleichnamsfestes," *Jahrbuch für Liturgiewissenschaft* 8 (1928): 107–43; Alois Mitterwieser, *Geschichte der Fronleichnamsprozession in Bayern* (Munich, 1930); Miri Rubin, *Corpus Christi: The Eucharist in Late Medieval Culture* (Cambridge, 1991); Heiko Oberman, *The Roots of Antisemitism in the Age of Renaissance and Reformation*, trans. James I. Porter (Philadelphia, 1984); Ronnie Po-chia Hsia, *The Myth of Ritual Murder: Jews and Magic in Reformation Germany* (New Haven, 1988); B. Moeller, "Piety in Germany Around 1500," in *The Reformation in Medieval Perspective*, ed. Steven E. Ozment (Chicago, 1971), pp. 50–75.

3. Zika, "Hosts, Processions and Pilgrimages," pp. 62–63; Peter Burke, *Popular Culture in Early Modern Europe* (New York, 1978).

4. This is the impression given by Jonathan Sumption's otherwise illuminating *Pilgrimage: An Image of Mediaeval Religion* (Totowa, N.J., 1975); and by Benedicta Ward, *Miracles and*

is what Michel Foucault had in mind when he characterized the life of the mad in the late Middle Ages as a wandering quest for reason on the pilgrimage roads and rivers of Europe:

The mad, then had an existence easily wandering [*facilement errante*]. Towns gladly drove them beyond their walls; they were allowed to ramble in the remote countryside or else they were entrusted to a group of merchants and pilgrims. . . . It is possible that those ships of fools that haunted the imagination of the whole early Renaissance were pilgrimage ships, highly symbolic ships of madmen in quest of their reason."[5]

Pilgrimage has seemed so fundamentally medieval that many observers do not notice it in the modern world, even though it remains common.

The Abundance of Miracles

It comes as a salutary shock, therefore, to discover in a recent book on modern pilgrimage that the greatest surge in European shrine formation came in the early seventeenth century.[6] Indeed, pilgrimage continues to be one of the major expressions of Catholic piety today, with certain shrines attracting millions of pious visitors annually.[7] For most Catholic Christians, however, the cultivation of local or regional shrines is more important than the once-in-a-lifetime exertion of a distant pilgrimage to Rome or to Lourdes.[8] William Christian has usefully characterized this piety as "local religion."[9] It was, and indeed is, a religion bound to the locality, to specific places and

the Medieval Mind: Theory, Record, and Event, 1000–1215 (Philadelphia, 1982). So, too, Peter-Michael Spangenberg, Maria ist immer und überall: Die Alltagswelten des spätmittelalterlichen Mirakels (Frankfurt a/M, 1987).

5. Michel Foucault, Histoire de la folie à l'âge classique (Paris, 1972), p. 19; id., Madness and Civilization: A History of Insanity in the Age of Reason (New York, 1965), p. 8. This passage has become controversial, and at Allan Megill's suggestion, I have modified Richard Howard's translation to convey a sense of the ambiguity of Foucault's phrase une existence facilement errante. See also the controversy generated by Colin Gordon, "Histoire de la folie: An Unknown Book by Michel Foucault," History of the Human Sciences 3 (1990): 3–26, and the subsequent discussion in ibid., 27–68 and 327–96, esp. 45.

6. Mary Nolan and Sidney Nolan, Christian Pilgrimage in Modern Western Europe (Chapel Hill, N.C., 1989), pp. 80–114; cf. Ludwig Hüttl, Marianische Wallfahrten im süddeutsch-österreichischen Raum: Analysen von der Reformations- bis zur Aufklärungsepoche (Cologne, 1985).

7. Nolan and Nolan, Christian Pilgrimage, pp. 22–35; Gottfried Korff, Heiligenverehrung in der Gegenwart: Empirische Untersuchungen in der Diözese Rottenburg (Tübingen, 1970).

8. Georg Schreiber, "Strukturwandel der Wallfahrt," in Wallfahrt und Volkstum in Geschichte und Leben, ed. id., Forschungen zur Volkskunde, vols. 16–17 (Düsseldorf, 1934), pp. 1–183.

9. William Christian, Local Religion in Sixteenth-Century Spain (Princeton, 1981); see also David Freedberg, The Power of Images: Studies in the History and Theory of Response (Chicago, 1989), pp. 99–100.

times, rather than floating in the universal, nonlocal, "logocentric" spirituality fostered by Erasmus and much of Protestant Christianity. It is only our modern enlightened ignorance, therefore, that prompts us to assume that pilgrimage ended with the Middle Ages, maintaining an only "fitful existence ever since."[10] But pilgrimage has not simply survived in Catholic Christianity as an eternal constant. Especially in Germany, the Protestant Reformation occasioned a deep crisis in the cult of the saints, stretching from about 1520 to 1570. For fifty years or thereabouts, even in the most devout regions of Catholic Germany, pilgrimage fell on evil days. Beginning with the Catholic Reformation, however, the shrines of Germany and Austria experienced a revival that made the cult of the saints, and especially of the Virgin Mary, more available as a seasonal or occasional option than ever before.[11]

The history of shrines and miracles is of more than just theoretical interest for the history of madness. Foucault was mistaken in his assumption that the roads and rivers of Europe teemed with mad pilgrims mainly in the Middle Ages, but one needs to go beyond the unsatisfying task of arguing with the structure or the details of his idealist history.[12] Luckily for the empirical historian looking for new source material, pilgrimages produced surprising masses of documentation. Most important shrines kept manuscript miracle books that recorded local miracles and other unexpected outpourings of grace. Beginning in the late fifteenth century, the shrines of Bavaria and Austria, and later those of Franconia and the Rhineland, began to publish selections of their recorded miracles in a twofold effort to attract pilgrims to a given shrine (rather than to another) and to prove the efficacy of Catholic doctrine and practice (over against Lutheran and Calvinist unbelievers). Starting generally as little pamphlets with short, four-to-eight line descriptions of wonders and miracles, the genre expanded in the seventeenth century to include hundreds of stories, now told with fully baroque extravagance.[13] The result is a volume of source material that folklorists have been exploiting for over fifty years, but that has remained almost untapped by historians of medicine or by social historians investigating what we used to call "popular religion."[14] Fortunately, this picture is

10. Sumption, *Pilgrimage*, p. 302.

11. Hüttl, *Marianische Wallfahrten*, pp. 37–59; Rudolf Kriss, *Wallfahrtsorte Europas: Unter Mitarbeit von Lenz Rettenbeck* (Munich, 1950). On post-tridentine pilgrimage as part of Bavaria's state-building program, see David Lederer, "Reforming the Spirit: Society, Madness, and Suicide in Central Europe, 1517–1809" (diss., New York University, 1995), pp. 78–123.

12. H. H. Beek offers a corrective to Foucault and outlines the importance of pilgrimage for relief of madness in the Middle Ages and early modern period in *Waanzin in de Middeleeuwen: Beeld van de Gestoorde en Bemoeienis mit de Zieke* (Nijkerk, Neth., 1969).

13. Hermann Bach, "Mirakelbücher bayerischer Wallfahrtsorte: Untersuchung ihrer literarischen Form und ihrer Stellung innerhalb der Literatur der Zeit" (diss., Munich, 1963).

14. The first major recognition of the value of German miracle books for folklore came

now changing as historians begin to realize what remarkable sources these are.[15] Miracle books constitute one of the best early modern records of illness, hardships, and madness among the ordinary, illiterate villagers of Germany.[16]

Compiled by priests, the custodians of local shrines, miracle books naturally embody the prejudices and propaganda of their authors. The published miracle books, set forth as propaganda for specific shrines, do not record the failures of the local shrine, although one frequently finds accounts of pilgrims who had finally come to the right place only after fruitlessly seeking help at other shrines. Most miracle books show only a fleeting interest in who the pilgrim was in ordinary life. How old was he? Was she pious? What sort of family did he come from? How did she hear of the shrine to which she came? And these books almost never follow up a miraculous cure to determine whether a crippling disease returned soon after the pilgrim went home. For early modern pilgrims, it was miraculous enough that even temporary relief could be obtained from Mary and the saints.

The miracle books also show no interest in the vexing question of whether the relief sought was finally and truly miraculous in the high theological sense of defying the laws of nature.[17] Pilgrims recorded their

---

in Georg Schreiber's *Deutsche Mirakelbücher: Zur Quellenkunde und Sinngebung*, Forschungen zur Volkskunde, nos. 31–32 (Düsseldorf, 1938).

15. See, e.g., Steven Sargent, "Religion and Society in Late Medieval Bavaria: The Cult of St. Leonard, 1258–1500" (diss., University of Pennsylvania, 1982); Philip M. Soergel, *Wondrous in His Saints: Counter-Reformation Propaganda in Bavaria* (Berkeley and Los Angeles, 1993); Rebekka Habermas, "Wunder, Wunderliches, Wunderbares: Zur Profanisierung eines Deutungsmusters in der frühen Neuzeit," in *Armut, Liebe, Ehre: Studien zur historischen Kulturforschung*, ed. Richard van Dülmen (Frankfurt a/M, 1988), pp. 38–66, 278–80; Günther Reiter, "Heiligenverehrung und Wallfahrtswesen im Schrifttum von Reformation und katholischer Restauration" (diss., University of Würzburg, 1970); Pierre-André Sigal, *L'homme et le miracle dans la France médiévale: XIe–XIIe siècle* (Paris, 1985); Harry Kühnel, "Integrative Aspekte der Pilgerfahrten," in *Europa 1500: Regionen, Personenverbände, Christenheit*, ed. Ferdinand Seibt and Winfried Eberhard (Stuttgart, 1987), pp. 496–509; Oliva Wiebel-Fanderl, *Die Wallfahrt Altötting: Kultformen und Wallfahrtsleben im 19. Jahrhundert* (Passau, 1982); and Hans Roth, "Die Mirakelüberlieferungen von St. Walburg in Eichstätt aus dem 17. and 18. Jahrhundert," *Sammelblatt des Historischen Vereins Eichstätt* 71–72 (1978–79): 81–110. For a critique of German folklorists' approaches to pilgrimage, see Leopold Schmidt, *Volksglaube und Volksbrauch: Gestalten, Gebilde, Gebärden* (Berlin, 1966), pp. 154–68. The efforts of ethnologists and folklorists to develop an historical perspective are summarized and criticized in Giuseppe Cocchiara, *The History of Folklore in Europe*, trans. John N. McDaniel (Philadelphia, 1981), pp. 467–95, 528–44. See also Gerhard Lutz, "Volkskunde und Geschichte: Zur Frage einer als 'historische Wissenschaft' verstandenen Volkskunde," in *Volkskultur und Geschichte: Festgabe für Josef Dünninger zum 65. Geburtstag*, ed. Dieter Harmening et al. (Berlin, 1970), pp. 14–26.

16. Lederer's "Reforming the Spirit," the first study to concentrate specifically on madness using the manuscript miracle books of Benediktbeuern and Pürten, concludes that these two shrines alone witnessed some 1,500 healing miracles in the seventeenth century.

17. The stress on miracles as defying natural law "was in fact very closely connected

gratitude for "wonders" only if they were unexpected; it was surprise and relief that together constituted the "wondrous," the "miraculous." As the French scholar Pierre Ribon puts it: "People did not despise any method, any technique, any solution. They did not oppose but rather conjoined methods to achieve a better effect. For the sick person the means employed do not matter; only the result counts."[18]

And this points to another unexpected feature of late medieval pilgrimage: to a surprising degree, the pilgrim does not seem to have been religious in any modern spiritual sense. In dozens of late medieval and early modern miracle books, pilgrims from Bavaria, Austria, Franconia, and the Rhineland display no special concern about the state of their souls.[19] They were not usually trying to earn the grace and divine favor necessary for salvation, and they recorded no deep repentance for their sins. For most German pilgrims before 1570, pilgrimage to the shrine of a saint was part of a contractual affair, a vow, that if miraculous aid for some immediate trouble were provided, the grateful recipient of such aid would render homage, honor, and payment in coin or wax to the shrine of the responsible saint. Often miraculous help came as soon as a troubled person vowed a pilgrimage. Prisoners, for example, sometimes found that the Blessed Virgin would release them from jail, freeing them to fulfill their half of the bargain by visiting her shrine. Desperate parents often vowed a pilgrimage if their drowning or mutilated child were restored to life.[20] In such emergencies, the miracle had to come first, but a supplicant might in other cases seek aid for some long-standing difficulty, hoping that a miracle might follow the pilgrimage. Votary pilgrims often felt that they were paying off the

with the movement which had brought about the scientific revolution in England," R. M. Burns points out in *The Great Debate on Miracles: From Joseph Glanvill to David Hume* (Lewisburg, Pa., 1981), p. 13. As such, our miracle books represent a typical prescientific acceptance of "wonders." See also Habermas, "Wunder," and Robert A. H. Larner, *Water into Wine? An Investigation of the Concept of Miracle* (Montreal, 1988), pp. 93–109.

18. Pierre Ribon, *Guérisseurs et remèdes populaires dans la France ancienne: Vivarais Cévennes* (Paris, 1983), p. 166.

19. Their votive gifts suggest, however, that repentance, forgiveness, and reconciliation were prominent features of the pilgrimage. See, e.g., the beautiful book by Lenz Kriss-Rettenbeck, *Ex voto* (Zurich, 1972), pp. 9–16, 274–75.

20. As such sources exist in great abundance, they provide glimpses of the relations between various family members that are often utterly obscure in other sources. It is striking, for example, how often the Bavarian miracle books of the sixteenth century speak of weeping and desperate parents, whose emotional involvement in their children's lives was far from what Lawrence Stone has led us to expect in his *The Family, Sex and Marriage in England, 1500–1800* (London, 1977). Other scholars have also faulted Stone for offering a distorted picture of emotional relations in the sixteenth-century family. See, e.g., Steven Ozment, *When Fathers Ruled: Family Life in Reformation Europe* (Cambridge, Mass., 1983); Michael MacDonald, *Mystical Bedlam: Madness, Anxiety and Healing in Seventeenth-Century England* (Cambridge, 1981); Linda Pollack, *Forgotten Children: Parent-Child Relations from 1500 to 1900* (Cambridge, 1983).

saint or the Virgin for help they had already received, but woe betide those who tried to evade their half of the agreement. Mary was known to have stricken down false bargainers with even worse calamities until a vow was finally satisfied, and this emphasis seems to have become a commonplace in the seventeenth century.[21] In other cases, we find ample evidence of the pilgrimage as petition, an attempt through pious action to obtain relief for intolerable circumstances. And this is the main point here. Pilgrimage was a response to desperate earthly trouble: to apparently incurable disease and frightful, life-threatening accidents, to sickness among one's cattle or to demonic possession. The saints, and especially the Blessed Virgin, could help where doctors and pharmacists had already failed, and the miracle books often took triumphant note of this superiority.[22]

The picture that emerges from this practical Catholicism is of a visceral, this-worldly piety aimed squarely at this-worldly problems. Pious Catholic Christians must have often wondered what Luther and his disciples were talking about with their criticism of works righteousness and of the futility of earning grace. Had not Jesus himself taught his followers to pray for daily bread, an image that might stand for all sorts of requests for earthly advantages and remedies?[23] Did not Christianity offer relief to the sick and poor and troubled of heart?

Protestant criticisms did, however, leave their mark.[24] Beginning with the Counter-Reformation, Catholic defenders of miracle-working shrines insisted that pilgrims should say their confession and attend Mass before they actually visited the shrine itself. Preaching at Altötting in 1571, Peter Canisius, S.J., insisted that a heavenly response to pilgrimage obligated one to a life of piety and repentance.[25] At Flochberg in the county of Oettingen-Wallerstein in the year 1582, the Virgin Mary appeared in visions to a ten-year-old boy afflicted by convulsions. After curing him by means of a strange root, Mary warned the boy to amend his life: "Be pious. Pray. Call upon God. Go diligently to Church. Listen to God's word and complete

21. See, e.g., Paul Hoffmann and Peter Dohms, eds., *Die Mirakelbücher des Klosters Eberhardsklausen*, Publikationen der Gesellschaft für rheinische Geschichte, vol. 64, no. 179 (Düsseldorf, 1988), nos. 754–853. I thank Virginia Mosser for bringing this book to my attention. See also Michael Carroll, *Madonnas That Maim: Popular Catholicism in Italy Since the Fifteenth Century* (Baltimore, 1992).

22. Wilhelm Theobald, *Votiftafeln und Medizin: Kulturgeschichte und Heilkunst im Spiegel der Votifmalerei* (Munich, 1978); id., *Mirakel-Heilung Zwischen Wissenschaft und Glauben* (Munich, 1983).

23. Even the words of the Lord's Prayer could be read in a contractual sense: "Give us this day our daily bread, and forgive us our trespasses as we forgive those who trespass against us."

24. Karl-Sigismund Kramer, "Typologie und Entwicklungsbedingungen nachmittelalterlicher Nahwallfahrten," *Rheinisches Jahrbuch für Volkskunde* 11 (1960): 195–211.

25. Soergel, *Wondrous in His Saints*, p. 261.

your pilgrimage."[26] Increasingly, pilgrimage manuals emphasized the need for true devotion, modesty, and deep spirituality.[27] It was no longer enough simply to turn imploringly to Mary and the saints whenever there was earthly trouble.

As the accounts of each miracle became more and more detailed, as miracle books became a form of pious baroque literature, one also has the impression that they threatened to lose all connection with daily events and real problems as they were experienced by bystanders and participants.

The mad went on pilgrimage throughout the late Middle Ages and early modern period. Indeed, the mad still go on pilgrimage. And the records of their visits to the shrines of their various Catholic regions constitute a fascinating and voluminous body of sources that bring us close to some of the mentally disordered whom we would never meet in other sources.

It is hard to tell from medieval sources just how common it was for the mentally ill to go on pilgrimage. Jonathan Sumption has estimated that "approximately half the miraculous cures recorded by Gregory of Tours [538–594] involved some form of insanity or mental abnormality."[28] Pilgrimage was widely held to be effective against demonic possession, which as we have seen was one of the basic medieval paradigms for delirium.[29] From late medieval sources, nowhere near half of all pilgrims had mental disorders, but the rough figures we can compile are impressive enough. Some shrines actually specialized in curing mental illness. It was common to take the mad to ancient Benediktbeuern, near the Kochelsee in southern Bavaria, for example, where they could place a relic from the head of St. Anastasia upon their own heads.[30] The shrine at the village of Pürten, east of Munich, also specialized in healing mental disorders and spiritual afflictions.[31] Of the one hundred miracles recorded at Aufkirchen am Würmsee (i.e., the Starnberger See) between 1510 and 1637, nine involved the cure of *Unsinnigkeit*, but the numbers were not usually so high. The 1555 miracle book for Andechs, one of the holiest places in Bavaria, lists 142 miracles, of which 7 were miraculous cures of madness, and 4 of the 60 Andechs miracles in 1601 were also of this sort. The three miracle books of Bogenberg, another Bavarian shrine on the Danube near Straubing, record seventeen wondrous cures of the mad.[32]

On first contact with such high numbers, the modern reader may be as-

26. Ibid., p. 353.
27. Ibid., pp. 379–80; Hermann Bach, "Mirakelbücher bayerischer Wallfahrtsorte."
28. Sumption, *Pilgrimage*, p. 85.
29. Ibid., 79–80.
30. Anton Bauer, "Wallfahrten zum Anastasiahaupt in Benediktbeuern," *Heimatbote vom Isarwinkel*, 1936, no. 8.
31. Lederer, "Reforming the Spirit," pp. 195–97.
32. Habermas, "Wunder," pp. 45, 279.

tonished or incredulous in the face of hundreds of supposedly "miraculous" cures, but there were actually many more. The shrine to St. Valentine in Diepoldskirchen (in Lower Bavaria between Passau and Landshut), for example, attracted epileptics in particular because a folk etymology connected the "falling sickness" (*vallendes siechtum*) with Valentine. The miracle book for Diepoldskichen begins in 1420 and lists 2,914 miracles between that date and 1691, 95 percent of them from the period after 1535.[33] The shrine to St. Rasso in Grafrath (Wörth on the Amper, 18 miles west of Munich) recorded 5,173 miracles between 1444 and 1518, and another 7,000 by the end of the eighteenth century, with a characteristic steep decline between 1514 and about 1560.[34] The common claim among Erasmians and Protestant reformers that the age of miracles was over must have struck devout pilgrims from Bavaria and Austria as bizarre and easily disproved. Literally hundreds of shrines sprang up between 1400 and 1700, and each one could demonstrate its power with lists of wondrous cures and "miracles."

LATE MEDIEVAL MIRACLES IN
THE RHINELAND

We can get closer to the mad by looking at several specific miracle books in which we find vivid case histories. One of the most interesting miracle books is that of the monastery of Eberhardsklausen on the Mosel River, downstream from Trier. There Wilhelm of Bernkastel kept a chronicle and register of wonders from 1490 to his death in 1536.[35] He enumerated 765 miracles for the period 1440 to 1536 and celebrated many of them in touching and personal detail.[36] In 1450, for example, a young girl came to the monks' attention who for seven years had had an egg-sized "stone" in her stomach that caused her to be crazy: "[M]ente capta et omni funditus sensu privata est." The relatives who brought her to Klausen, however, regarded her as demon-possessed, asking "whether she was tormented by a demon and perhaps ought to be exorcised." Without answering this question di-

33. Steven D. Sargent, "Miracle Books and Pilgrimage Shrines in Late Medieval Bavaria," *Historical Reflections* 13 (1986): 455–71, at p. 468; B. Spirckner, "Kulturgeschichtliches aus dem Mirakelbuche der Wallfahrt zum hl. Valentin in Diepoldskirchen (1420–1691)," *Verhandlungen des historischen Vereins für Niederbayern* 42 (1906): 173–96.

34. Sargent, "Miracle Books," pp. 458, 464–65; Karl S. Kramer, "Die Mirakelbücher der Wallfahrt Grafrath," *Bayerisches Jahrbuch für Volkskunde*, 1951, pp. 80–102.

35. Matthias Zender, "Mirakelbücher als Quelle für das Volksleben im Rheinland," *Rheinische Vierteljahrsblätter* 41 (1977): 108–23; Hoffmann and Dohms, eds., *Mirakelbücher*, pp. xv–xvii. See also Walter Rummel, "Gutenberg, der Teufel und die Muttergottes von Eberhardsklausen: Erste Hexenverfolgung im Trierer Land," in *Ketzer, Zauberer, Hexen: Die Anfänge der europäischen Hexenverfolgungen*, ed. Andreas Blauert (Frankfurt a/M, 1990), pp. 91–117.

36. The critical edition lists 753 entries, but some of them contain reports of more than one miracle: see Hoffmann and Dohms, eds., *Mirakelbücher*.

rectly, the Blessed Virgin of "Euertzclusen" healed her.[37] In 1455, a woman from Reuland fell into such madness that she gnashed her teeth like a beast at her companions and threatened them with her hands; her terrified friends bound her in chains and put her in jail. "Many of them believed her possessed," wrote Wilhelm of Bernkastel, but he claimed instead that she was "insane," suffering from *mentis defectionem* and a "sick head and a disturbed brain" (*infirmato capite disturbatoque cerebro*). Such persons did not need exorcism, "for if they are brought here and prayers and vows are offered for them, in a short while they get completely well again."[38] Evidently, Wilhelm was concerned about rumors of demonic possession, and indeed, over the years, he noted over twenty other cases in which madness was so furious and bestial that the patient was regarded as possessed. Time and again Wilhelm recorded that "it was believed," "it was feared," "it was thought," or "she seemed" possessed by a demon.[39] In most of these cases, Wilhelm was sure that there was no demon involved, noting, for example, that a mad priest from Xanten acted so strangely that one could easily have believed him possessed, except that "in his insanity he often shrieked, 'Jesus, Jesus,'" which ruled out demonic influence as far as Wilhelm was concerned.[40] Sometimes it was not so easy. A boy was brought to the cloister in 1508 unable to stand up. His father held the view that "he had been badly poisoned by a witch" ("quod per maleficam intoxicatus esset maxime"), but Wilhelm thought it just as likely that he was possessed.[41] Fortunately, the Blessed Virgin of Eberhardsklausen again came to the rescue before this question had to be settled definitively. In the following year, a young man had developed a sudden and vehement hatred of his new wife and came to the shrine at Klausen to be helped. He was exorcised (as if possessed) and cured, and Wilhelm remarked: "I do not know by what work of the devil he was so bewitched," but once the demon was gone, "the young man was very happy, who had seemed insane just before" ("nescio quo opere diaboli sic fuit maleficiatus . . . filius optime contentus erat, qui prius insanire videbatur").[42]

When Wilhelm confessed that he knew not what bewitchment was at hand here, his ignorance was not because of a lack of theory. He cited the recently published *Malleus maleficarum* (1487) often enough to show that he knew its contents well.[43] But the *Malleus* did not really help to settle a 1508

37. Ibid., no. 47.
38. Ibid., no. 51.
39. Ibid., nos. 47, 48, 171, 181, 184, 214, 217, 246, 257, 375, 380, 386, 418, 517, 525, 529, 530, 551, 589, 608, 648, 683.
40. Ibid., no. 175.
41. Ibid., no. 217.
42. Ibid., no. 246.
43. Ibid., nos. 120, 160, and 447; and see the excellent index s.v. *Hexen* and *Teufel*. See, too, Rummel, "Gutenberg, der Teufel, und die Muttergottes."

case in which Wilhelm mulled over the question of whether doctors or churchmen were needed. If the infirmity had a cause (*a casu*), then "the physicians must be consulted," but if it came from witchcraft, then clerics must be called in as the appropriate experts.[44] In 1522, a youth was brought to the shrine who had "fallen into an injury of his fantasy" (*fantasie laesionem*): "[H]e spoke and acted so strangely that he was thought possessed; and it seemed so to me, too, for he was unable to bear the test for the demon-possessed." We do not, unfortunately, learn what these tests consisted of, but Wilhelm conceded that even a pilgrimage to the shrine at Eberhardsklausen brought no immediate relief. When the boy was finally taken home to his father, he got better within two days.[45] Sometimes, however, nothing helped. Wilhelm described the sad case of a nun who:

fell into an amazing melancholy and mad sickness in which she imagined that she had given herself to the devil, had denied God, and needed to kill herself. [At first she seemed to improve somewhat, but then] she fell back into the same melancholy and is today bound in chains as a most wretched person, for she lacks a doctor whom she can trust. Thus just as the disease itself needs an effective doctor, so the suffering person needs a doctor he can trust.[46]

Notice here that Wilhelm of Bernkastel and his contemporaries felt able to distinguish true pacts with the devil from suicidal melancholy, just as on other occasions the question turned on whether a person was bewitched or possessed or sick. We cannot read far in these records without concluding that even late medieval clerics recognized a realm of physical sickness, of medicine and the natural order. Even when they accepted the existence of witches and witchcraft, they did not see the devil everywhere.

Wilhelm's analysis of why the melancholy nun could not benefit from medical treatment is also noteworthy. He was well aware that treating a patient (a *persona paciens*) was more than just treating a disease. If she could not trust any of her physicians, there was no hope for her.

What lingers in the mind from a reading of the miracle book of Eberhardsklausen is the pious matter-of-factness with which the actions of the Blessed Virgin are described. One did not need to know exactly what was wrong before she could be implored to help. In cases of mental disorder, this was a distinctly good thing, because Wilhelm and his fellow monks only rarely had a clear diagnosis of what a desperate or troubled person was really suffering from. The pilgrimage worked by faith and by a show of loyalty, not by knowledge.

Altogether, Wilhelm recorded sixty-seven miraculous cures of mentally

44. Hoffmann and Dohms, eds., *Mirakelbücher*, no. 214.
45. Ibid., no. 648.
46. Ibid., no. 380.

TABLE 6.1

Madness Among the Miracles of Eberhardsklausen, 1440–1536

	(N)	Demon Possession	"As if" Demon Possession	Madness and Schwachsinn	Vomits and Worms	Bewitched	Depression, Melancholy and Suicide	Visions*	Other	Total Mad
1446–1460	(62)	3	0	3	0	0	0	0	1	7
1461–1480	(30)	3	0	0	4	0	0	0	1	8
1481–1500	(70)	1	0	2	2	0	0	3	0	8
n.d., but before 1490	(11)	0	0	0	0	0	0	0	0	0
1501–1520	(472)	2	6	11	3	2	5	7	1	37
1521–1536	(120)	0	2	2	1	0	0	2	0	7
Total	(765)	9	8	18	10	2	5	12	3	67

*Wilhelm of Bernkastel did not regard visions as necessarily mad. In fact, a warning vision of Christ or a consoling vision of Mary was much desired. The table includes visions only because modern psychiatry has often regarded visions, voices, and hallucinations as symptoms of schizophrenia.

disordered persons (table 6.1), representing almost 9 percent of all the miracles he thought worth recording at all. The largest number of mad pilgrims (37) came in the first two decades of the sixteenth century, but those were also the decades when Wilhelm was most diligent in recording miracles of all sorts (472 in all). The highest proportion of mad pilgrims came in the period 1461 to 1480 (8 out of 30 miracles), especially if we may be permitted to include four persons troubled (so they thought) by giant stomach worms, the sort of trouble that a couple of generations later indicated demonic possession, along with a 1463 outburst of "St. John's dance," the Rhenish name for St. Vitus' dance.[47]

MADNESS AND MIRACLES IN FRANCONIA

Turning farther south, we find that Franconia was full of pilgrimage shrines. The folklorist Dieter Harmening has evaluated the cult of thirty-six shrines at which hundreds of miracles were recorded.[48] Along the Main River, much the same pattern emerges as elsewhere, in that an active late medieval piety was disrupted and transformed by the Reformation. From 1531 to 1590 the Franconian miracle books recorded only three miraculous cures, one of them a release from demonic possession. But then, starting in the 1590s the cult of the saints revived, and the miracle books triumphantly advertised hundreds of wondrous divine interventions down to the nine-

47. Ibid., nos. 53, 54, 55, 112, 179; Richard Beitl, ed., *Wörterbuch der deutschen Volkskunde*, 2d ed. (Stuttgart, 1955), pp. 747, 376, 780–81.
48. Dieter Harmening, "Fränkische Mirakelbücher: Quellen und Untersuchungen zur historischen Volkskunde und Geschichte der Volksfrömmigkeit," *Würzburger Diözesangeschichtsblätter* 28 (1966): 25–240.

TABLE 6.2

The Miracles of Franconia, 1450–1650

	(Total Miracles)	Demon Possession	Madness	St. Vitus' Dance
1450–1470	(0)	0	0	0
1471–1490	(39)	0	0	0
1491–1510	(73)	0	1	1
1511–1530	(199)	3	12	0
1531–1550	(1)	0	0	0
1551–1570	(0)	0	0	0
1571–1590	(2)	1	0	0
1591–1610	(26)	0	1	0
1611–1630	(113)	3	10	0
1631–1650	(86)	1	3	0
Total	(539)	8	27	1

teenth century. The contours of Franconian miracle reports appear clearly in table 6.2.

Clearly, miraculous cures were not so widely reported in Franconia as at Eberhardsklausen, which all by itself reached levels that surpass the reports evaluated by Harmening. We cannot tell, however, if this lower level of reporting was owing to a lower level of wondrous cures or to a reduced desire to publicize such divine interventions. It may well be that in religiously divided areas, such as Franconia during the Reformation, Catholic shrines felt some reluctance to publicize their successes for fear of stirring up increased controversy. Or it may be that the Reformation produced so many defections from the ranks of pious Catholics that miracles lost credibility. Whatever the reasons, the Franconian miracle books recorded a total of 539 miracles between 1450 and 1650, in two distinct waves, 1471 to 1530 and 1591 to 1650.

Madness made up almost 7 percent of the cases reported throughout Franconia. As elsewhere, when the person appeared dangerous, he was commonly bound with chains:

[In 1520] the honorable Lorentz Ebernn from Hollerbach in the region of Buchen came here and said, truthfully, that he had suffered from the horrible disease and misery of the plague, and that in this disease he had lost his reason and run out of his house into the street and attacked [*breynt*] people and knocked them down. And so his neighbors came running and caught him and bound him in chains in a "tall" house [*in einen hoge haus*]. There he lay all unreasonable for fourteen days.[49]

In other cases, perhaps fearing such treatment, the mentally troubled took off for the woods:

49. Ibid., p. 73.

In the year [15]22 on the fourth Sunday after Pentecost the honorable Jorg Noezell from Auerswalde near Chemnitz reported that he had been ill for a long time and that during his illness he had lost his mind and reason. Completely naked and without clothes he was so mad that he ran into the forest, where he remained both day and night. In their sorrow his wife and family urged him to visit the church of Mary the Mother of God in Grimmental.[50]

But, more often than not, the truly wild and dangerous found themselves confined, either by their own families or by the authorities. "Seventy years ago there was a son of Schneeberg by the name of Christopher Eib, a vicar in Brussels, who fell into such a delirium that he spent several years locked in iron fetters and chains."[51] Here, too, as in the Rhineland, many were brought on pilgrimage whose madness seemed to be due to demonic possession: "[P]lures putarent, ipsum esse obsessum a daemone."[52] In 1590, the exorcist at Maria im Sand in Dettelbach relieved a woman of a whole host of demons:

[He] began to exorcise the evil enemy and found that there were many more than he had at first assumed: that this possessed woman had more hellish spirits in her than the number of ravens that assemble around a dead animal. When she was asked where she came from and why she was here, they answered that they came from Sicily, "where we persuaded someone to doubt his own salvation, and so he hanged himself." As they were then ordered to leave [the woman], they resisted strongly and behaved contemptuously at being driven so soon from their new resting place. They also spoke foreign languages, and especially Greek. Finally, they realized that they would have to yield to the command of a stronger one, but they asked permission to fly into the ears of some other people. And meanwhile many people had indeed gathered, and regrettably many had come out of idle curiosity; and so the possessed woman was led into the sacristy and exorcised anew. . . . Finally, the Virgin and Mother of God heard their prayer and came close with her help. Thus the enemy was defeated and the whole host of evil spirits was driven out.[53]

Perhaps the strangest case in Franconia was this one, recorded in 1620 but retelling a tale that went back to 1520:

A young journeyman dressed himself in an amazing [multi-]colored fool's costume and went running in the streets, crying out and acting as people do at Shrovetide. But soon God punished him, so that he became a real fool, which he had only pretended to be before. He raged and went crazy, running around and roaring like a lion. No one was safe from him. His madness got more and more out of control, and no one knew what to do. His friends made a vow [to take] him and five virgins to

50. Ibid.
51. Ibid.
52. Ibid.
53. Ibid., p. 74.

Marienweiher, and as soon as he got there, his understanding cleared, he praised God and thanked Him for the grace He had bestowed.[54]

Here we find a real-life example of what was only fantasy in the *Lalebuch* of 1597, in which the pretense of folly became the real thing. "Consuetudo secunda natura," said the moralists of the day, suggesting that immorality or excess could become a permanent mental or moral disorder.

These colorful stories bring us close to the way madness was perceived and understood in the sixteenth century, as mysterious, uncanny, sudden in onset and in remission, possibly of divine or demonic origin, but sometimes "credibly from a drink that he was given,"[55] or from other merely physical causes. In contrast to the learned treatises of physicians and theologians, the simple reports in the early miracle books use a folksy language with which to describe the wonders of a local shrine. They did not aim to impress anyone with their style or expertise but aimed at creating thankful, awestruck devotion to the saint and his or her shrine.

Bavaria: Land of Miracles

Farther to the south, the miracle books are even more numerous, and recorded wonders lie thick on the ground. The 1657 miracle book for the "Holy Mountain of Andechs," southwest of Munich, states that between 1454 and 1657, a remarkable 23,050 miracles were granted to faithful pilgrims who made their way to the "Sacrament of St. Gregory the Great" and, after 1500, to the ever more popular shrine of the Virgin Mary.[56] The actual summary register provided, however, itemized fewer than half that number, 9,049 miracles to be exact. This left a large miscellaneous category, *allerley Widerwärtigkeiten* ("remedies for all kinds of difficulties"), of 14,001 miracles.[57] From the list of specific cases, more than a third (3,403) were miraculous relief from plague and other epidemic diseases; problems with pregnancy and childbirth account for 1,610 more; Andechs also healed the lame (355), the deaf (237), and the blind (868). Naturally, scores of mentally troubled persons also found relief on the Holy Mountain. Fully 221 persons were described as "madmen who have returned to sound reason," and that does not count 175 mute persons (who were often regarded as mentally disturbed or retarded), 188 epileptics, and 23 who suffered from dizziness

54. Ibid., p 69.
55. Ibid., p. 73.
56. Fritz Meingast, *Marienwallfahrten in Bayern und Österreich* (Munich, 1979), p. 56.
57. *Mons Sanctus Andechs, Das ist. Kurtzer Begriff oder Innhalt von den Gnadenreichen H. Berg Andechs* (Munich, 1682).

TABLE 6.3

Pilgrimage Shrines in the Bishopric of Passau

	(N)	To Christ and The Trinity	To Saints	To Mary
		Dedication:		
Founded before the Reformation	(53)	7	29	17
Founded after the Reformation	(127)	13	35	79
Total	(180)	20	64	96

SOURCE: Franz Mader, *Wallfahrten im Bistum Passau* (Munich, 1984), p. 11, and information on the map on the endpaper.

or long-term headaches, all of whom found relief at this most venerable and ancient Bavarian shrine.[58]

When we consider the 5,000 or more miracles from 1444 to 1518 at Grafrath (the shrine to St. Rasso), or the 1,748 miracles reported at St. Leonhard's shrine in Inchenhofen just between 1506 and 1512, or the 2,109 wonders at the hands of St. Richildis at Hohenwart (1486–1520), to say nothing of the hundreds more reported at Aufkirchen on the Würmsee (known today as the Starnberger See) (1510–14), Burgholz (1479–88), or Traunwalchen (near Traunstein, just east of the Chiemsee, 1507–19),[59] there can be little doubt that pre-Reformation Bavaria was in the grip of a major, hitherto unexplained and underexamined popular enthusiasm for the saints and for Mary.[60] In fact, it was mainly the rising cult of Mary that accounted for the startling spread of shrines in late medieval and then especially in seventeenth-century Bavaria and Austria. Unlike other saints, Mary had been assumed bodily into heaven and had thus left very few physical relics behind. Her shrines, therefore, usually concentrated attention on a picture or sculpture of the Virgin, with or without her Son. This rise of Marian piety can easily be illustrated with the summary provided for the bishopric of Passau. Of the 53 shrines founded before the Reforma-

58. Ibid., and Almut Amereller, *Votif-Bilder: Volkskunst als Dokument menschlicher Hilfs-bedürftigkeit, dargestellt am Beispiel der Votif-Bilder des Klosters Andechs* (Munich, 1965): "Summarische Inhalt der Gnaden und Wunderwerken so sich von Anno 1454 bis auff Anno 1657 zu getragen."

59. Sargent, "Miracle Books," pp. 457–58.

60. Scholars have noticed the phenomenon without explaining it: see, e.g., Romuald Bauerreiss, *Pie Jesu* (Munich, 1931); Josef Staber, *Volksfrömmigkeit und Wallfahrtswesen des Spätmittelalters im Bistum Freising* (Munich, 1955); Richard van Dülmen, "Volksfrömmigkeit und konfessionelles Christentum in 16. und 17. Jahrhundert," in *Volksreligiosität in der modernen Sozialgeschichte*, ed. Wolfgang Schieder, *Geschichte und Gesellschaft*, special no., 11 (Göttingen, 1986), pp. 14–30; Ludwig Andreas Veit and Ludwig Lenhart, *Kirche und Volksfrömmigkeit im Zeitalter des Barock* (Freiburg im Breisgau, 1956), pp. 59–63, 178–79.

tion, only 17 were devoted to the Virgin (32%), but among the shrines founded after the Reformation, Mary was the focus of 79 out of 127 (62%).

The rise of Mary was, of course, a pan-European phenomenon.[61] As in many other areas, in German regions, Mary was sought out as a kind of "general practitioner," whom one could invoke in any time of need. In contrast to other saints, who often had specialized areas of responsibility, Mary was available no matter what went wrong. Perhaps it is for this reason that the first printed miracle books were mostly from shrines dedicated to Mary, for these shrines may well have felt that they were in competition with one another.[62] In the southern German and Austrian area, we find advertising campaigns employing printed books, printed pictures, and special pictorial miracle cycles at the major shrines of Mariazell in Styria (the "national shrine of Austria"), Tuntenhausen (southeast of Munich), Altötting (50 miles east of Munich), and Regensburg on the Danube. Between 1490 and 1535, these four Marian centers of devotion developed new means of extending their catchment basins and of attracting pilgrims. Fortunately for the historian, these activities produced a permanent residue of records that we can examine not just for the history of piety but for the history of madness as well.

The first printed miracle book in Bavaria was printed in 1494 or 1495 in Augsburg by Hans Schobser. It describes 25 miracles at the little shrine in Altötting, in the diocese of Passau, where a miracle in 1489 revived a three-year-old boy who had drowned. By taking her little boy at once to the chapel at Altötting, his mother showed such trust in the Virgin that when she laid the corpse on the altar, "The child came to life at once."[63] That same year another child's life was saved after he had fallen from a hay wagon and under its wheels.[64] News of these wonders traveled fast, and by 1503, thousands of pilgrims had begun to seek the aid of the Virgin at Altötting, including the highest nobility of the Holy Roman Empire, and the Emperor Frederick III himself before his death in 1493.[65]

One reason for the wildfire success of this shrine was surely the printed miracle book. Reformation historians have grown used to the fact that Protestant reformers quickly seized upon the newly invented printing press as a medium for their message. Catholic spokesmen were much slower to

---

61. Nolan and Nolan, Christian Pilgrimage, pp. 116–17, 152–56.

62. Franz Falk lists sixteen German shrines that published pamphlets or books to advertise their pilgrimage before the Reformation: "Die Druckkunst im Dienste der Kirche zunächst in Deutschland bis zum Jahre 1520," in Görres Gesellschaft zur Pflege der Wissenschaft im katholischen Deutschland 2 (1879): 58.

63. Robert Bauer, Bayerische Wallfahrt Altötting: Geschichte, Kunst, Volksbrauch, 2d ed. (Munich, 1980), p. 24, quoting the chronicler Johannes Schneitenberger.

64. Ibid., p. 24.

65. Sargent, "Miracle Books," p. 460.

see the advantages of print. We should remember, however, that among the earliest uses of print were the indulgences whose popularity triggered Martin Luther's protest. And in printed miracle books, we have another exceedingly popular Catholic means of cultivating the piety of pilgrimage.

Interestingly, this first Bavarian advertisement featured the cure of madness in three or four of its twenty-five cases. They deserve to be savored here for their folksy idiom.[66] We learn for example that "Hainrich Reicherczsamer, a journeyman weaver from Zlabing [in Lower Austria] fell into a serious disease and lost his reason for three whole days and nights. Vowed [a pilgrimage] here and got well after his oath."[67] Or take Agnes Freybergerin, from the district of Mosburg: "For seven straight years she has been robbed of her reason [*Vernunft*]. So they [her friends and relatives?] invoked Our Lady of Altötting and promised to take her there with a worthy gift. After this vow she got right again [*ist wieder richtig worden*] and told her story. [In the year 14]93."[68] In that same year, "Hanns Jaeger of Würzburg [about 180 miles to the northwest] was robbed of his reason, and for three-quarters of a year, he could not speak. But when Hans Schedelrait from Rattensandtt [Rothensand, south of Bamberg] promised [to bring] the first-named Hanns here, his speech returned and he came here."

Notice that in the last account madness and mutism seem to be equated.[69] This means that we may be justified in adding as a fourth case a certain Mathias from Mutterdorf. He "lay a whole year in mortal illness and there was no hope for him. And for three years he had been robbed of his speech and couldn't talk." His father and mother vowed a pilgrimage and a gift of wax in the shape of a bowl.[70] At once he could speak his native Bohemian tongue, as honorable witnesses testified.[71] In this case, we may notice an early appearance of assurances that the miracle had really occurred, with reference to the testimony of worthy and honorable witnesses, but in general these four cases are perfectly typical of the Bavarian miracle report for the next hundred years or more. Short, truncated sentences or phrases. Formulaic expressions of piety. Just the facts. Madness is represented as a loss of reason, usually with no mention of the devil or of demonic possession. When a cause was suggested, it would seem that madness was often thought of as a concomitant of disease ("fell into a serious disease and lost his reason"). Speechlessness, too, seems to have been

66. Robert Bauer, "Das älteste gedruckte Mirakelbüchlein von Altötting," *Ostbairische Grenzmarken: Passauer Jahrbuch für Geschichte, Kunst und Volkskunde* 5 (1961): 144–51.

67. Ibid., p. 145, no. 5.

68. Ibid., p. 147, no. 15.

69. Ibid., p. 146, no. 10.

70. The bowl shape ("*Gussel*") may have been meant as a symbolic representation of the cranium.

71. Ibid., p. 148, no. 17.

closely associated with madness, and recovery could mean the recovery of speech. In another case, recovery was described as "becoming right again" (*ist wieder richtig worden*). In the early chapters of this book, we have examined the professional idioms of physicians, lawyers, and theologians. We might have expected that because these stories were recorded and published by priests at the shrine, the language of these reports would reflect theological learning or biblical prejudice. But the fifteenth- and sixteenth-century miracle reports are virtually devoid of technical terms and priestly learning. We may surmise that these miracle reports were surprisingly close to the everyday language and thought of weavers and peasants from southern Germany and Upper Austria.[72]

In 1497, the Altötting canon Jacob Issickemer published a much larger account of the miracles of Altötting (54 pages as against only 8). He presents 77 miracles, now organized into edifying chapters on the seven ways in which Mary helps sinful men, women, and children.[73] Aside from the fact that Issickemer's devotional thoughts took up more than one quarter of his book, his text also described the miracles of 1495–97 in much more detail than the telegraphic staccato in the book of 1494–95. Read, for example, the story of "an honorable woman of Nuremberg" who wrote "in her own handwriting" that during one of the nights before St. Michael's Day (September 29), 1496, a strange distress (*Betrübnis*) came over her,

twisting her neck and disturbing and darkening her eyes, as if a skin had grown over them; she growled and gnashed her teeth gruesomely, stamping her feet and clenching her fists and [twisting] all of her limbs; thus she lost her reason [*Vernunft*] and fell into deep unconsciousness. This happened often to her. When she was somewhat more reasonable, she bethought herself to pray and to lift her heart in devotion—but just then something like a mouse ran around before her eyes and robbed her of her reason and gave her the means with which she should kill herself, pushing her constantly into despair. Moreover, she suffered incalculable pains. And yet a grace [came] to her so that she called out to the Mother of God, the Consolation of all the world, and she promised [a pilgrimage] with gifts to Old Öding [Altötting]. And from that moment all her distress left her, and she was fresh and healthy.[74]

Here we have a report of a bestial insanity with hints of demonic subversion in the shape of the mouse that intervened just when this woman thought of praying, a mouse/demon that was directly associated with sui-

72. The ideas of priests and pilgrims, and thus of high and low culture, were strikingly similar in the seventeenth century, argues Gregory Hanlon, "Piété populaire et intervention des moines dans les miracles et les sanctuaires miraculeux en Agenais-Condomois au XVIIᵉ siècle," *Annales du Midi* 97 (1985): 115–27.

73. On Issickemer and his book, see Soergel, *Wondrous in His Saints*, pp. 33–35.

74. Robert Bauer, "Das Büchlein der Zuflucht zu Maria: Altöttinger Mirakelberichte von Jacobus Issickemer," *Ostbairische Grenzmarken* 7 (1964–65): 206–36, at p. 223, no. 61.

cidal despair, which was the worst spiritual condition known to late medieval people. Fortunately, Mary came to the rescue. By 1496, her shrine in Altötting was evidently well known even in Nuremberg, over 100 miles off to the northwest.

Or take the case of Anna Sewsin, the owner of a hammer works in Trausnitz, north of Regensburg:

She was robbed of her senses [ihrer Sinne] for a year and a half, and because of her great fury [grosses Toben], she was put in chains and well secured [to the wall?]. During the first holy days of 1497, her husband called on Mary, etc., promising [to take] her to old Öding with [a votive gift of] a skull made of wax. From that moment on, she began to feel better, so that on the Friday after Pentecost of that year, she came to old Öding with the perfect use of her reason.[75]

Here we notice the now familiar response of chaining and "securing" the mad if they went totally out of control. It is also worth noting that even the ex voto waxen gift symbolized Anna's brain as the source of her madness. At Easter in 1496, Cuntz Schuster of Plauen (180 miles to the north, in Thuringia) and Katharina Hafnerin, from Wertingen (northwest of Augsburg) arrived in Altötting, both with letters officially signed and sealed from their respective cities, documents that praised the Mother of God and explained that each had gone mad, but that through a vow to the Virgin promising a pilgrimage to Altötting, they had "from that moment on retrieved the perfect use of their reason, so that even the huge irons and chains that bound the said Cuntz (because no one trusted that he would stay sane just because he had called out, 'So help me Virgin Mary') had opened immediately as easily as soft cloth is cut by a shears."[76] With pilgrims arriving from distant towns, bearing the official recommendations of their local authorities, Altötting was obviously developing a more than local reputation for helping the mad. It was natural for the Virgin to undo the chains of Cuntz Schuster, since she was well known for releasing convicted criminals from jail, too.

The year 1496 also saw the arrival of Katharina, the daughter of Hans Tremel from Königheim in Franconia.[77] She had been devoted to the Mother of God since childhood, but lately she had been "troubled three times by the evil spirit, who tempted her [once] to hang herself, even placing the rope around her neck; a second time to stab herself, even setting the knife to her throat; and a third time to drown herself, and she even had gone to the water to throw herself in. But always it came into her mind to

75. Ibid., p. 220, no. 44.
76. Ibid., p. 223, no. 60.
77. Bauer suggests that "Kenicken" is Köngen south of Stuttgart, but this is impossible since the text explicitly states that the town is "im Lande zu Francken in Meyntzer Bistum." Königheim, which lies between Wertheim and Mergentheim, seems a likelier location.

pray three Hail Marys, and when she did, she was released." When these attacks did not cease, however, she vowed a pilgrimage of some 180 miles to Altötting, and once there, she felt totally relieved of her suicidal urges.[78]

Hans Hochstetter, a Franconian serving as the city secretary of Pettau (Ptuj) also came to Altötting in 1495 to express his thanks to Mary for relief from the "calamity and distress in which I stood, not knowing then how I should escape," as he wrote in the document that he displayed in the chapel for all to see.[79] Here began the remarkable tradition at Altötting of leaving behind personal descriptions of one's miraculous cures. In this case, then, we are not dependent on the words of some priest, for we have Hochstetter's own description, and it is doubly impressive that he chose words like those we have seen before, "calamity and distress" (*Widerwärtigkeit und Trübsal*), rather than some other more technical vocabulary. We are probably safe in concluding that these early printed miracle books from Altötting preserve the language of the pilgrims themselves, even though the accounts were, of course, abridged to fit the requirements of space on the printed page.

One of the pilgrims to Altötting in 1497 came from distant Kassel in Hesse, where she had borne a defective baby who lacked hands, legs and feet. She was so appalled "that she got the falling sickness, and that, so severely that she fell down [had seizures] up to thirty times night and day," a condition that lasted half a year. While epilepsy, the falling sickness, was not usually thought of strictly as a kind of madness, this case is of interest because the tormenting seizures were thought to have their origin in a monstrous birth. So powerful was the shock of horror.

Although there are other pilgrims of interest in Issickemer's miracle book, the case of Margereth Geschmeydlerin, a citizen of Straubing in Bavaria, is especially instructive. She arrived in Altötting in 1497 bearing a sealed letter from her father confessor affirming that for three years she had had such "disease, distress, physical pain and various temptations [*Anfechtung*] that she often lost control of her effective reason ["ihrer wirklichen Vernunft ungewaltig ist gewesen"] and sometimes was so tempted by the evil spirit (by the decree of God, as should be believed) that she should finally run out and kill herself, by which she would condemn her body and soul to eternal damnation."[80]

In this horrible condition, Geschmeydlerin was urged to pray to Mary in all humility and to undertake the pilgrimage of 50 miles to Altötting. As usual in these accounts, as soon as she made this vow, Mary's intercession was palpable, and "she was released from the abovementioned distress,

78. Ibid., pp. 223–24, no. 62.
79. Ibid., p. 224, no. 63. The oldest surviving votive tablet dates from 1501.
80. Ibid., p. 225, no. 68.

pain, sickness and mortal danger." Georg Brenner, priest of Straubing, went on for twelve more lines describing the humility, piety, and devotion of Margereth, the new turn her life had taken, the love and praise of Mary and her Son, and so on and so forth. Here surely we have an example of a pastoral mind and a professional vocabulary at work, and in consequence we cannot even be sure that Margereth felt tempted by the devil to commit suicide; the priestly filter is here so thick that it obscures our sense of how she herself felt about her troubles. But just this difference from the other reports should strengthen our growing confidence that the "normal" miracle report at Altötting appears in language fairly close to what ordinary persons used.

It is noteworthy that madness figures prominently among the earliest recorded miracles at Altötting. Taking the twenty-five miracles from 1494–95 together with the seventy-seven from 1497, I have found twelve cases of mental disorder. This amounts to almost 12 percent of the reported miracles, a higher proportion than found at Eberhardsklausen, and much higher than was common at the other shrines we have hitherto examined. This emphasis is still visible in the third miracle book from Altötting, an undated booklet of eight pages that would seem to have been published by Andreas Schobser about 1540.[81] Philip Soergel observes that "the largest category of illness in the book is mental illness, which is reported in seven of the 27 miracles."[82] Unfortunately for the history of madness, five of these cases turn out to be persons who were thought dead or unconscious, rather than what we might think of as madness. But one of the reports tells of a distraught mother who attempted suicide after losing both her husband and her eight-year-old son in the space of three weeks. Mary intervened miraculously to deflect the knife and to revive the boy.[83] Another case of madness was Wolfgang Öbinger of Kropfberg, "who lost his reason [Vernunft] and could no longer hear or see." His wife vowed to send him on a naked pilgrimage, "and when he came to the altar of Our Lady's Chapel, he was to take off his clothes and leave the altar completely naked, giving Our Lady his clothes. At once the said Wolfgang became fresh and healthy."[84] Even without the other five cases of unconsciousness, it remains

81. The date is controversial. Maria Angela König, *Weihegaben an U.L. Frau von Altötting* (Munich, 1939), 2: 4, suggests a date of 1520. Robert Bauer, "Das Altöttinger Mirakelbüchlein von 1540," *Ostbairische Grenzmarken* 6 (1962–63): 241–48, argues for 1540, pp. 241 and 246, no. 16; recently Steven Sargent has posited a date of 1512, "Miracle Books and Pilgrimage Shrines," p. 458; but to my mind Bauer's date of 1540 seems more likely.

82. Philip Soergel, "Wondrous in His Saints: Popular Pilgrimage and Catholic Propaganda in Bavaria, 1470–1620" (diss., University of Michigan, 1988), p. 159, n. 84.

83. Bauer, "Das Altöttinger Mirakelbüchlein von 1540," p. 244, no. 17.

84. Ibid., p. 242, no. 4. See Friedrich Zoepfl, "Nacktwallfahrten," in *Wallfahrt und Volkstum*, ed. Schreiber (cited n. 8 above), pp. 266–72; Irmgard Gierl, *Bauernleben und Bauern-*

true that the early Altöttingen miracle reports emphasized madness as one of the conditions for which Our Lady was especially helpful. We cannot be sure that more of the mentally troubled actually went to Altötting than to some other shrines, although this seems to have been the case. It is striking enough that three mad persons were sent by their priest or by their town magistrates with sealed letters of explanation and introduction.[85] But in any event, Altötting did not rival the (later) reputation of Benediktbeuern as the best shrine of all for those with troubled heads.

So far as we know, Altötting published no further miracle books in the sixteenth century,[86] but a large book published in 1644 selected the most dramatic miracles from three manuscript miracle registers then on hand but unfortunately since destroyed. Of the total of 285 miracles reported for the period 1487 to 1643, some 28 reported miraculous relief from madness.[87] A few of these cases help round out our picture of madness as it was represented by pilgrims. One of them from 1527 concerns a certain Leonhard Felbmayr of Degernbach who "lost his mind [Verstand] so completely that he trampled his own child with his feet. But when he came to himself, he was advised to vow [a pilgrimage] to Altötting. And when he did this, he recovered the health of his mind, and his child [the health] of his body."[88] Another miracle, reported from the year 1491, relieved a certain Sigmund Weber of the entire nest of snakes that had so taken over his body that he had lost his understanding (Verstand).[89] Here we find an explicit connection between the disorder of "snakes in one's body" and madness. More often the early miracle reports from 1490 to 1550 simply refer to the coughing or vomiting up of numerous or large snakes or worms without any hint that this may have been a fantasy or a physicalistic explanation for demonic possession.

Canon Issickemer tells the story of one Jacob Punn from Schwäbisch Gmünd, who claimed that he had accidentally drunk water containing snake eggs, and that they had hatched and grown in his stomach and intestines, until he looked like a pregnant woman.[90] Suffering intense pains, he had sought out doctors, who in their helplessness said that he had very little time to live. He vowed a gift of silver and a pilgrimage to Mary of Al-

wallfahrt in Altbayern: Eine kulturkundliche Studie auf Grund der Tuntenhausener Mirakelbücher, Beiträge zur altbayerischen Kirchengeschichte, vol. 21, 2 (Munich, 1960), pp. 113–15.

85. See above in Issickemer's 1497 miracle book, nos. 60 and 68.

86. Robert Bauer (Bayerische Wallfahrt Altötting, p. 62) thinks that Altötting may well have published annual miracle books as Tuntenhausen did, but that they may all be lost. This too is possible.

87. Jacob Irsing, S.J., Historia von der weitberühmbten unser lieben Frawen Capell zu Alten-Oeting in Nidern Bayern, trans. Johann Scheitenberger (Munich, 1644), pp. 100–278.

88. Ibid., pp. 148–49.

89. Ibid., p. 120.

90. Bauer, "Das Büchlein der Zuflucht zu Maria," pp. 226–27, no. 74.

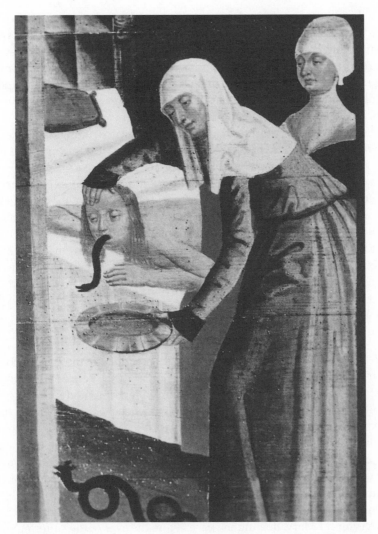

FIG. 19. *Woman vomiting a snake.* Panel painting from the Gnadentafel, Heilige Kapelle, Altötting. 1520. Heilige Kapelle, Altötting.

tötting "and shortly, one after another, some five hundred snakes and adders came forth from him, some of them two to two and a half ells in length [i.e., over a yard]. And thus he became fresh and healthy. . . . So in this way we should learn to flee in strong trust to the Virgin Mary and pray that she save us, and so that we may be relieved from the snakes of hell, from our great heart-gnawing sins, [and] from eternal misery."[91]

91. Ibid., p. 227.

In this description from the 1490s, the metaphorical power of snakes explicitly connects a physical ailment with the mental anguish of demons and "heart-gnawing sins." One of the large panel paintings hung in the chapel's exterior gallery in 1520 depicts another of these wondrous expulsions of huge stomach-serpents, an ailment that seems, for all its apparently explicit detail, to have been a sign of psychosomatic distress, or perhaps a physically articulated form of demonic possession (fig. 19).[92]

In some ways, the most touching of these miracle paintings is the depiction of Margreth, Hanns Eyseleis's daughter from Mündraching. She was said "to have been somewhat unright for about four years" ("ist bey vier jaren etwas unrichtig gewesen"), until her brother vowed to bring her to Altötting and to pay for a sung mass. "And from that hour she came to her reason." The anonymous painter has portrayed a clumsy young woman with wild hair and grotesque fingers, whose foot is chained to the wall. Here we have one of the clearest pictures of what madness meant to ordinary people of the sixteenth century: wild, dangerous, controllable by chains, but curable by divine assistance alone (fig. 20).

THE FORMS OF MADNESS: MIRACLES
AND PROPAGANDA

In trying to characterize the ideas of madness found in the miracle books of early modern Germany, we are also struck by the *lack* of certain forms of mental disorder that have so grown in prominence in modern times that we often assume such persons must be crazy whenever and wherever they are found. The most striking example is visions. No one in these hundreds of miracles was deemed mad because he or she claimed to have seen the Blessed Virgin.[93] Rather, it was thought a special grace to be granted a vision of Christ, Mary, or the saints. Even a vision of the devil could work as a warning and was not prima facie evidence of madness. Six of the fifty-seven large late gothic miracle panel paintings at Altötting (1520) represent holy visions of Mary, floating in space before the eyes of the suffering penitent, apparently invisible to all others.[94] In the 1540 miracle book, Mary appeared in a vision five times in the twenty-seven miracles reported;[95] four

92. Bauer, *Bayerische Wallfahrt Altötting*, p. 64; Philipp Maria Halm, "Die Mirakelbilder zu Altötting," *Bayerischer Heimatschutz* 21 (1925): 1–25. The great miracle altar at Mariazell has a picture of such a snake expulsion, too: see Peter Krenn, "Der große Mariazeller Wunderaltar," *Jahrbuch des kunsthistorischen Instituts der Universität Graz* 2 (1966–67): 31–51.

93. See the remarks of Felicitas D. Goodman on "Visions," in *The Encyclopedia of Religion*, ed. Mircea Eliade (New York, 1987), 15: 282–88; cf. William Christian, *Apparitions in Late Medieval and Renaissance Spain* (Princeton, 1981).

94. Bauer, *Bayerische Wallfahrt Altötting*, p. 64.

95. Bauer, "Das Altöttinger Mirakelbüchlein von 1540," p. 247, and nos. 7, 8, 9, 17, 24.

FIG. 20. *Madwoman: Margreth*, Hanns Eyseleis's daughter. Panel painting from the Gnadentafel, Heilige Kapelle, Altötting. 1520. Hans Strauss, Altötting.

of the twenty-five miracles listed in 1494–95 also reported such a vision;[96] and Issickemer reported blessed visions in fourteen of his seventy-seven miracle cases.[97] Similarly, in the miracle book of Eberhardsklausen, Wil-

96. Bauer, "Das älteste gedruckte Mirakelbüchlein von Altötting," p. 150, nos. 4, 6, 16, 24.

97. Bauer, "Das Büchlein der Zuflucht zu Maria," p. 235, nos. 1, 2, 4b, 5, 6, 11, 24, 40, 43, 48, 64, 65, 66, 75.

helm of Bernkastel reported thirteen visions, but none of them seemed to him to be symptomatic of mental disorder. These were not regarded as hallucinations, and they prompted no investigation.[98]

Another modern image of madness was utterly lacking in these accounts: the megalomaniac who imagined himself to be Alexander the Great, Christ, or some other world-historical figure. In a clever bon mot, Michel Foucault suggests that the madmen of the early modern period, instead of identifying with God, actually denied the existence of God altogether.[99] Unfortunately for this witty idea, not one of the dozens of madmen we meet in these miracle reports was thought mad (or thought himself mad) for failure to believe in God. Indeed, as we have already noticed, religious troubles appear amazingly seldom, and none of these recorded pilgrims seem to have showed much anxiety over doctrinal matters. The one major exception was the religious madness described as demonic despair and the temptation to commit suicide, a desperation that never took the form of denying God but was always an intensely personal feeling of unworthiness, failure, sadness, and what Renaissance doctors quickly diagnosed as melancholy. This was the word used by Wilhelm of Bernkastel in describing the desperate nun who "denied God" (although she did not deny His existence) and felt that she must die.[100] Among the German miracle accounts from the late fifteenth or early sixteenth centuries, not one uses the "educated" term *melancholisch* (melancholy), but by the end of the sixteenth century, the word and the concept were entering the vernacular imagination. As we shall see, these sources, like many others, document what we have called the rise of melancholy.

Altötting advertised its wonders, not only with miracle books and large miracle panel-paintings, but also with lead, silver, and gilded *Pilgerzeichen*, tokens about two inches high depicting the Madonna and Child. Surviving records allow us to estimate that hundreds of thousands of these "pilgrim-badges" were sold as mementos and advertisements of Altötting in the 1490s.[101] Small devotional pictures were perhaps distributed as early as the sixteenth century, too, but apparently the earliest surviving examples date from the seventeenth century. What Altötting lacked in its arsenal of miracle advertisements was any work by a major artist. This was an arena in which other sensationally popular shrines could effectively compete. At Einsiedeln in Switzerland, for example, the Master ES drew exquisite devotional pictures, and at St. Wolfgang am Abersee, one of the leading Ger-

---

98. Hoffmann and Dohms, eds., *Mirakelbücher*, nos. 106, 107, 111, 137, 177, 184, 234, 272, 452, 590, 627, 674, 741.
99. Foucault, *Histoire de la folie*, p. 549; id., *Madness and Civilization*, p. 264.
100. See p. 286 above. Hoffmann and Dohms, eds., *Mirakelbücher*, no. 380.
101. König, *Weihegaben*; Bauer, *Bayerische Wallfahrt Altötting*, pp. 66–67.

man Renaissance artists, Michael Packer, constructed a famous altar. As we shall see in a moment, Regensburg employed the talents of both Albrecht Altdorfer and Michael Ostendorfer, and in 1519 the Alsatian pilgrimage shrine of Marienthal also commissioned a picture cycle of miracles. In Styrian Mariazell, we find a similar array of miracle books, "pilgrim-badges" made of lead and precious metal, devotional pictures, and miracle books going back to the early fifteenth century. But in addition the Benedictine abbot of nearby St. Lambert commissioned a small miracle altar (1512) with six miracle scenes. Scholars surmise that the gallery of large and touching but fairly crude panel paintings at Altötting, dating from 1519 or 1520, was a response to the visual challenge provided by Mariazell. And Mariazell in turn answered the pictures of Altötting and especially of Regensburg with the 1519 construction of a huge "miracle altar" that displayed fifty miracle scenes and celebrated the Styrian shrine's greatest wonders in a more spectacular manner than could be found anywhere else.[102]

Without getting lost in the intricacies of Styrian shrines and miracles, it is worth noting that the expulsion of demons was a well-known specialty at Mariazell. Of the three miracles regularly portrayed there in the fifteenth century, one was an exorcism.[103] The small miracle altar of 1512, with six miracle scenes, also includes an exorcism. The magnificent altar of 1519, commissioned by Abbot Valentin Pierer, likewise depicts an exorcism, that of a "possessed woman [who] killed her own child and her father and mother." This scene of slaughter is at her feet. But "she was brought to [Maria]zell, where a legion of devils [i.e., 6,666 devils] were driven out of her." The painting shows a swarm of winged, scorpionlike demons emerging from the woman's mouth and flying out the window, as a priest, holding a band around her neck, performs the rite by which the demons were banned. An apparition or vision of the Madonna with Child appears in the top right corner. According to Peter Krenn, this miracle dated from 1370.[104] Another picture portrays a wondrous exorcism of a man from Olmütz dating from 1484. In addition, there are pictures of three miraculous cures of the falling sickness (epilepsy) and one of a youth vomiting up an enormous

102. Only forty-seven miracles survive today in the altar as preserved in the Johanneum in Graz. See Peter Krenn, "Der große Mariazeller Wunderaltar von 1519 und sein Meister," *Jahrbuch des Kunsthistorischen Instituts der Universität Graz* 2 (1966–67): 31–51; Leopold Schmidt, "Via sacra: Zur Geschichte der 'Heiligen Straße' zwischen Wien und Mariazell," in *Via sacra: Das Wallfahrtsmuseum in Kleinmariazell*, ed. Helene Grünn, Veröffentlichungen des österreichischen Museums für Volkskunde, vol. 15 (Vienna, 1977), pp. 73–83, at p. 80; Gustav Gugitz, *Österreichs Gnadenstätten in Kult und Brauch* (Vienna, 1955–58), vol. 4: *Kärnten und Steiermark*, pp. 197–201; Peter Krenn, "Die Wunder von Mariazell und Steiermark," in *Die Kunst der Donauschule, 1490–1540: Ausstellung des Landes Oberösterreich*, ed. Otto Wutzel (Linz, 1965), pp. 164–68.

103. Krenn, "Der große Mariazeller Wunderaltar," p. 31.

104. Ibid., illustration 17 and p. 33.

snake.[105] Pictorially, Mariazell was establishing its sovereignty over the whole spectrum of human misfortune, but especially over demons, and over the perhaps related conditions of epilepsy and "serpent possession."

Shortly after completion of the large altar, Abbot Pierer commissioned (ca. 1520) a series of 25 or 26 excellent woodcut miracle pictures, which served to advertise the Styrian shrine's greatest miracles and to counteract the burgeoning fame of Regensburg's "Schöne Maria." These woodcuts, by an unknown master of the Danube School, represent one of the high points of the Austrian Renaissance.[106]

Although they depict the miraculous curing of three cases of epilepsy, these woodcuts do not hint at even one cure of madness.[107] The artistic and popular excitement about miracles and pilgrimage reached such a peak in just these years that if Luther's Reformation had not burst forth upon the German scene at the same time, we would probably remember the years 1510 to 1520 as a time of escalating competition for pious pilgrims.

BEAUTIFUL MARY OF REGENSBURG

In 1519, the already heated competition between Mariazell and Altötting was complicated by a new contender. In Regensburg, in the wake of the cathedral preacher Balthasar Hubmaier's anti-Semitic sermons, the town council seized the political opportunity offered by the death of Emperor Maximilian I to expel the Jewish community in January and February of 1519, and to raze the synagogue and Jewish cemetery. In the midst of this demolition work, a master stonemason, Jacob Kern, fell from a roof and was buried in rubble. Although he appeared dead, the Mother of Grace showed mercy and miraculously restored Kern to health; in gratitude for this sign, the city council decreed that a wooden chapel in the Virgin's honor be erected.[108] At Hubmaier's suggestion, the hastily erected chapel was called the "Beautiful Mary" (schöne Maria), and a wonder-

---

105. Ibid., illustrations 3, 6; p. 33.

106. George Hirth, *Die Wunder von Mariazell: Facsimile-Reproduction der 25 Holzschnitte eines unbekannten deutschen Meisters um 1520* (Munich, 1883); Karl Garzarolli-Thurnlackh, "Die Holzschnitte der Mariazeller Wunder: Ihre Vorläufer und Meister," *Phaidros* 1 (1947): 181–89; Franz Winzinger, *Wolf Huber: Das Gesamtwerk*, vol. 1 (Munich, 1979), p. 170; Charles Talbot and Alan Shestack, eds., *Prints and Drawings of the Danube School* (New Haven, 1969), pp. 67–72; Krenn, "Der große Mariazeller Wunderaltar," pp. 31–51.

107. Hirth, *Die Wunder von Maria Zell*.

108. Carl Theodor Gemeiner, *Regensburgische Chronik: Unveränderter Nachdruck der Originalausgabe. Mit einer Einleitung, einem Quellenverzeichnis und einem Register*, ed. Heinz Angermeier (Munich, 1987), vol. 4, pp. 357–58; note Gemeiner's carefully skeptical remarks on Kern's recovery, p. 358 n. 693. Wilhelm Volkert, "Die Regensburger Juden im Spätmittelalter und das Ende der Judengemeinde," in *Crossroads of Medieval Civilization: The City of Regensburg and Its Intellectual Milieu*, ed. Edelgard E. DuBruck and Karl Heinz Göller, Medieval and Renaissance Monograph Series, vol. 5 (Detroit, 1984), pp. 139–71.

working image of Mary was placed on the altar and a sculpture of her by Erhard Heydenreich outside. Within weeks, rumors of miracles in Regensburg spread like wildfire well beyond the city. Pilgrims began to arrive by the hundreds and then by the thousands. Regensburg's new shrine became the site of the most explosive cult in late medieval Germany.[109] Folksongs told of miracles that opened the eyes of the blind.[110] Hubmaier himself seems to have kept "a kind of diary," in which he recorded and commented on the miracles of 1519.[111] In that year, 10,172 lead images and 2,430 silver pilgrim badges were sold; in 1520, sales of such mementos went up to 109,198 in lead and 9,763 in silver. Leonhard Widman claimed that on St. George's Day alone (April 23, 1520), 50,000 pilgrims arrived and 27,000 of these badges were sold.[112] Albrecht Altdorfer, the renowned artist of the Danube School, made numerous copies of the *Schöne Maria* and illuminated a copy of the papal bull of indulgence (June 1, 1519) on green silk for use in the chapel.[113] During the next year, he painted the large chapel banner that appears, for example, in Michael Ostendorfer's famous woodcut depicting the pilgrimage to the "Beautiful Mary." Altdorfer's workshop also produced miracle woodcuts, probably by the thousands, although only two survive.[114]

With these major talents at work, Regensburg took the lead in attracting pilgrims, especially after it became clear, as it did in Ostendorfer's woodcut, that some pilgrims also experienced dramatic ecstasies. Hubmaier complained that some of the votaries behaved as if mad. He wrote to his friend Wolfgang Rychard, the city physician of Ulm, that he had gone with Regensburg's town councilors to the shrine, where they found an enormous crowd of pilgrims dancing and bellowing like cattle.[115] Ostendorfer's scene of ecstatic frenzy also offended Albrecht Dürer, who wrote on his copy of the print: "This spirit has arisen against Holy Scripture in Regens-

---

109. Torsten Bergsten, *Balthasar Hubmaier, Anabaptist Theologian and Martyr*, trans. W. R. Estep, Jr. (Valley Forge, Pa., 1978), pp. 60–61; Karl Bauer, *Regensburg: Aus Kunst- Kultur- und Sittengeschichte* (Regensburg, 1980), pp. 514–25; Gerlinde Stahl, "Die Wallfahrt zur Schönen Maria in Regensburg," *Beiträge zur Geschichte des Bistums Regensburg* 2 (1968): 35–282; Franz Winzinger, *Albrecht Altdorfer: Graphik. Holzschnitte, Kupferstiche, Radierungen. Gesamtausgabe* (Munich, 1963), pp. 28–32; Soergel, *Wondrous in His Saints*, pp. 56–61.

110. Gemeiner, *Regensburgische Chronik*, 4: 376, n. 727.

111. Ibid., p. 377; this diary seems to have disappeared; see Balthasar Hubmaier, *Schriften*, ed. Gunnar Westin and Torsten Bergsten, Quellen und Forschungen zur Reformationsgeschichte, vol. 29 (Gütersloh, 1962), pp. 12–13; cf. Bergsten, *Balthasar Hubmaier*, pp. 403–4.

112. Winzinger, *Albrecht Altdorfer*, pp. 30–31. Bauer, *Regensburg*, 520–25; Freedberg, *Power of Images*, p. 103.

113. Winzinger, *Altdorfer*, pp. 29–30.

114. Bauer, *Regensburg*, pp. 520–22.

115. Bergsten, *Balthasar Hubmaier*, p. 62; Winzinger, *Altdorfer*, p. 32; Soergel, *Wondrous in His Saints*, pp. 57–58.

TABLE 6.4

Miracles at Regensburg, 1519–1522

Relief from Accidents of all sorts		112 (39 involving children)
Physical assaults, imprisonment		42
Illnesses		562
Eyes	28	
Head	22	
Ruptures	37	
Bladder & Kidney Stones	16	
Crippled limbs	58	
Female disorders	4	
Syphilis	55	
Problems in childbirth	41	
Cramps	23	
"Pest"	20	
Nervous & Mental Illness	19	
Indeterminate	131	
Other		8
Corrections for Repetitions		-3
Total Miracles		721

SOURCE: Gerlinde Stahl, "Die Wallfahrt zur Schönen Maria in Regensburg," *Beiträge zur Geschichte des Bistums Regensburg* 2 (1968): 35–282, appendix.

burg, and has been encouraged by the bishop for the sake of temporal gain rather than stopped. May God help us that we do not dishonor His Mother in this but [honor] Her in Christ, Amen."[116] Sebastian Franck also criticized these falling fits as a crazy fad.[117]

So pictures of miraculous excess could be morally ambiguous, and that was also true of miracle stories. Among the excited pilgrims to Regensburg were some who claimed to have been miraculously cured of ills they had never had. A certain Paul Spitzer of Nuremberg, for example, was thrown in jail when it was learned that though he claimed to have been cured of blindness, he had earlier resided in a hospital that explicitly excluded blind persons.[118] When it was learned, however, that Spitzer had indeed suffered from a discharge that had impaired his vision, the authorities released him.[119] They obviously suspected that not all votaries to their spectacularly popular shrine were sincere. Martin Luther was outspokenly critical of what he saw as "devilish deceit" in the Regensburg excesses,[120] and soon

116. Winzinger, *Altdorfer*, p. 32.
117. Soergel, *Wondrous in His Saints*, p. 58.
118. Gemeiner, *Regensburgische Chronik*, 4: 377.
119. Although in most respects one can use the published version, here again one must consult Philip M. Soergel's earlier and unpublished "Wondrous in His Saints," p. 184.
120. "Address to the Christian Nobility of the German Nation" (1520), WA, 6, 447–48; LW, 44: 185.

Catholic authorities were agreeing with him. By 1522, popular preachers in Dinkelsbühl, Augsburg, and even in Regensburg attacked the validity of the pilgrimage, and beginning in 1524, the Bavarian bishops joined in the effort to close it down.[121] By then, the once popular shrine was attracting only a trickle of pilgrims. After 1522, the pilgrimage withered away.[122]

In its heyday, however, 1519–22, the Beautiful Mary produced hundreds of miracles, recorded in six printed miracle books. Gerlinde Stahl made a careful study of the miracles reported, and what she found is summarized in table 6.4.

The mad did not make up a large portion of those miraculously cured here. Among the nineteen cases of madness, however, we find a now-familiar mix of suicide attempts, demonic visions (as if a person were under assault by the devil), a variety of madmen and women described as "unreasonable" (*unvernünftig*), "senseless" (*unsinnig*), "not right" (*unrichtig*), "crazy in the head" (*doll im haubt*), "bereft of her senses" (*irer sin beraubt*), and mad outbursts labeled "raging" (*toben*) and "fury" (*wüten*). These are the vernacular terms we have found elsewhere in Bavaria and Franconia. There is not a technical or medically specific term among them. Moreover, we find not one case of demonic possession among these 721 tales of miraculous relief. Here, as in the earliest miracle books of Altötting, we hear the most common folk-descriptions of the major ills of the mind, basically uncorrupted by the professional languages of law, medicine, and theology. With sources like these, we get as close to the perceptions of ordinary people as we are ever likely to.

OUR LADY OF TUNTENHAUSEN

Let us look closely at just one more major pilgrimage center, one that was not so internationally renowned as Mariazell or Altötting, and one that did not experience the explosive flash of wild popularity that characterized Regensburg. Perhaps because Tuntenhausen, situated 25 miles southeast of Munich, never achieved the fame of Regensburg or the international drawing power of Mariazell, and perhaps because Tuntenhausen attracted mainly Bavarian and Tyrolean peasants, rather than the nobles and princes who went to Andechs and Altötting, this secluded shrine did not suffer the dramatic decline in intensity of pilgrimage after 1520 or 1530 that we notice at most German shrines before the surge of the Counter-Reformation.[123]

121. Stahl, "Wallfahrt zur Schönen Maria," pp. 77–79.
122. Soergel, *Wondrous in His Saints*, p. 61.
123. Irmgard Gierl, *Bauernleben und Bauernwallfahrt in Altbayern: Eine Kulturkundliche Studie auf Grund der Tuntenhausener Mirakelbücher*, Beiträge zur altbayerischen Kirchengeschichte, vol. 21, 2 (Munich, 1960), p. 140 and appendix 1, a list of the places of origin of pilgrims to Tuntenhausen in the period 1506–1738, pp. 155–60.

Tuntenhausen seems to have been relatively isolated from the major political and religious turmoil of the Reformation. The cult of its church and of
its sculpture of the Virgin with Child began in 1441, but so far as we know,
the Augustinian canons of Beyharting, who had responsibility for the
shrine, only began to publish the greatest wonders of Tuntenhausen in
1506,[124] perhaps inspired by the example of Altötting. Throughout the sixteenth century, however, the miracle books of Tuntenhausen continued to
flow forth. We know of at least thirty different editions before 1600, twenty-
two of them published before 1570.[125] These were almost always short pamphlets of six to eight leaves, containing brief descriptions of forty to fifty
miracles. During the seventeenth century, as was common elsewhere too,
the Tuntenhausen abbots adapted their miracle books to a wealthier read-
ership and produced large, doubtless expensive, volumes with effusive
baroque descriptions.[126] Even with thirty miracle books in the sixteenth
century, the canons of Beyharting often emphasized that they were describing only a small fraction of the miracles that actually occurred. Just between 1530 and 1540, over 6,600 miracles were reported there, although the
books for this decade describe only 527 of them in any detail at all.[127]

As at other shrines, the mad also found their way to Tuntenhausen even
though the usually careful investigation of Irmgard Gierl misleadingly emphasizes the prevalence of demonic possession among the mentally disor-

124. Meingast, *Marienwallfahrten in Bayern und Österreich*, pp. 38–52; Soergel, "Wondrous in His Saints," pp. 32, n. 27; 43; Gierl, *Bauernleben*, pp. 16–19.

125. The years of publication for the surviving Tuntenhausen miracle books are as follows: 1506, 1527, 1530, 1531, 1532, 1533, 1534 (2 different books), 1535, 1536 (2 different
books), 1537, 1538, 1539, 1544, 1547, 1551, 1555, 1561, 1564, 1567, 1569, 1574, 1577, 1579,
1581, 1583, 1584, 1589, and 1597. The editions for 1569 and 1577, listed in Soergel's dissertation, "Wondrous in His Saints," p. 163, n. 92, were unknown to Gierl, *Bauernleben*, p. 11.
Curiously, Soergel does not list the edition of 1577 in his book *Wondrous in His Saints*, p. 32,
n. 27, where he also omits mention of the editions of 1555 and, indeed, all of the editions after 1569, leading to an underestimate of the continuity of pilgrimage to Tuntenhausen
(*Wondrous in His Saints*, p. 72).

126. The edition of 1646, for example, numbered 166 pages and 590 miracles. This was
now a volume that not every peasant pilgrim could afford. Of the 590 miracles there reported, 49 (8.3%) were cases of "despair, temptation [*Angefochtne*], confusion [*Zerritten*], de-
spondency [*Kleinmütigen*], demonic possession, and the Hungarian disease [brain fever
also known as *Soldatenkrankheit*]." The elegant octavo of 1738 describes 150 miracles on 160
pages. Gierl, *Bauernleben*, pp. 33–35.

127. Compare Soergel's dissertation, "Wondrous in His Saints," pp. 166, n. 100, and 170,
n. 106, with his *Wondrous in His Saints*, pp. 72–73. It is not clear why Soergel underestimates
his own findings when he claims that the Tuntenhausen miracle books report about 6,400
miracles for the period 1530–51. By my count, his dissertation provides evidence of over
7,000 miracles for that period. And why are these large figures "not credible" just because
they surpass the hitherto reported record number of miracles at Grafrath (5,173 wonders in
the period 1444 to 1518)? Such large numbers may well have represented the actual instances of "unexpected relief" from misery and disaster that we have seen was the practical meaning of sixteenth-century "wonders."

TABLE 6.5

Madness Among 800 Miracles at Tuntenhausen, 1520–1589

	(N)	Cases of Madness	Devil Involved in Madness
1520s	(58)	1	0
1530s	(388)	26	6
1540s	(36)	3	0
1550s	(33)	1	0
1560s	(43)	2	0
1570s	(91)	6	0
1580s	(151)	9	2
Total	(800)	48 (6.0%)	8 (1.0%)

SOURCE: *Tuntenhausen unser lieben frawen Gotzhaus*, miracle books from the years 1527, 1530, 1532, 1533, 1534, 1535, 1536, 1537, 1538, 1539, 1547, 1551, 1564, 1574, 1579, 1581, 1583, 1584, and 1589.

dered pilgrims to Tuntenhausen. She based her picture too much, perhaps, on the seventeenth-century miracle reports, and as we shall find, there is surprisingly little mention of demons in the records for the sixteenth century.[128] My account does not completely exhaust the Tuntenhausen reports, but here is an evaluation of nineteen miracle books from the sixteenth century.[129] If we break them down by decade (table 6.5), the 1530s stand out as the most active years for miracle reporting there.

Of the 800 published Tuntenhausen miracles that I have studied from the period 1520 to 1589, 48 involved relief from madness. This is 6 percent of all the Tuntenhausen miracles studied for this period, a figure that comports well with the percentages reported at the other shrines we have studied. As we have seen, reports of the cure of madness usually ran between 4 and 8 percent of all the miracles. It is also remarkable that the devil was explicitly involved in only eight of these cases (or 1% of the total). This means, of course, that the vast majority of madnesses reported in the sixteenth century, five-sixths of them, indeed, did not involve any supposed demonic attack. But it is also striking that six cases of demonic affliction were reported during the 1530s. When we look more closely at these six demonic afflictions, we discover that in four of these cases, the devil was playing his familiar role as fomenter of despair and suicide. Rather than a

128. Gierl, *Bauernleben*, p. 98. Lederer also found that seventeenth-century pilgrims in Bavaria were often troubled by problems they characterized as demonic possession ("Reforming the Spirit," pp. 271–327).

129. Each one bears the title *Tuntenhausen unser lieben frawen Gotzhaus* with the year of publication. I present here an analysis of 19 miracle books from the following years: 1527, 1530, 1532, 1533, 1534, 1535, 1536, 1537, 1538, 1539, 1547, 1551, 1564, 1574, 1579, 1581, 1583, 1584, and 1589. To simplify citation, I give only the year.

full-fledged attack of physical possession by the devil, we find a situation like this one in a miracle report from 1530:

A woman from the parish of Neukirchen lay in madness [iren] for six weeks; the evil enemy attacked her (with the thought) [angefochtn] that she should cut herself up and kill herself. She had a knife and an awl secretly with her, and with the knife she gave herself three large wounds on the feet. When her nurse came to her, she hid both the knife and the wounds. So again she took the awl and stabbed herself under the heart; as a result she lay in bed as if dead. Her husband, on the advice of someone else, vowed a wax image, her best dress, and her best veil to Tuntenhausen, together with a Mass; and from that hour onwards, the lady came to herself, and in a short time she was freshly healthy [frisch gesund] through the help and intercession of Mary, the Mother of God.[130]

This story is typical of many from Tuntenhausen. Although the devil played an initial part in the suicidal thoughts of this troubled woman, he soon disappears from the story; this was a demonic temptation but not a full-scale demonic possession. Moreover, help began to arrive from the moment someone else vowed gifts and a pilgrimage to the shrine. The mad were, of course, not generally expected to make their own vows of pilgrimage. Friends and relatives almost always made the vow on behalf of the sufferer.[131]

Although the devil was useful as an explanation of suicidal despair, he played no role in several of the suicide attempts reported among these 800 miracles. Ten of the mental disorders cured by the Virgin of Tuntenhausen involved suicide attempts or suicidal despair, but six of these ten reports make no mention of the devil. Take this remarkable case from 1579:

[A man from Pittenhart (near Traunstein) had a wife who] "lost her senses" [von Sinnen kommen] so that she ran outside under the impression that something was telling her to drown herself ["vermaint, es sprech was zuo ihr, sie soll sich ertrencken"]; her husband vowed [a pilgrimage] with a wax candle-wreath around [her] head ["verlobts ihr Mann mit ainem wäxen liecht umb den Kopff"], but she performed the vow herself with her reason intact.

It is not entirely clear that the husband vowed to make a pilgrimage to Tuntenhausen with a wax candle-wreath on his wife's head, but that seems to be the implication here. I find remarkable the narrative restraint shown by the author, Provost Peter Späditer. We notice that this woman heard the voice of "something," urging her to suicide, and yet Späditer resisted the theologically obvious conclusion that this could only have been the devil.

130. *Tuntenhausen . . . 1530*, fol. A2ʳ. This was a familiar motif elsewhere as well. See, e.g., the case from Neubeuern in 1520 reported by Anton Bauer, "Die ehemalige Marienwallfahrt Neubeuern am Inn," *Das bayerische Inn-Oberland* 33 (1963): 51–94, at 65.
131. *Tuntenhausen . . . 1530*, fol. A2ʳ.

Here again, as elsewhere in these sixteenth-century miracle books, we hear the voices of ordinary people describing their problems in their own uneducated way, with very little priestly suggestion. By now we are becoming accustomed to this vernacular description of madness. Here are some further examples:

A man from the Huoeb in the parish of Aibling was robbed of his senses for ten weeks ["ist seiner synn zehen wochen beraubt gewest"]. [1527]

A maiden from the parish of Ried was not right for three weeks ["ist unrichtig gewest drey wochen"]. [1530]

A woman from Benediktbeuern was robbed of her senses and troubled by the evil enemy, and nothing seemed to help ["ist jrer synn beraubt gewest unnd mit dem pösen veindt behafft, hat nichts wöllen helffen"]. [1530]

The baby of a lady from Munich fell from a bench, and she was so severely shocked that she became "not right," and for eight days ate and drank nothing. ["Ainer frawen von München ist ain kind ab ainer panck gefallen, ist sy so hart erschrocken das sy unrichtig ist worden"]. [1530]

A few of these unfortunates had explicitly religious troubles, such as the mother from Gauting, "who fell into despair because she felt doomed, and denied God and all His salvation, and abused Him as badly as possible, and gave herself to the devil body and soul." Without her extenuating mental condition, she might have been regarded as a witch, but her husband vowed a Mass and a sheep worth eight kreuzer. Thereafter she tried twice to hang herself, but again he rescued her; she tried stabbing herself, and yet he hindered her and laid her in irons. When the pastor recommended a pilgrimage to Tuntenhausen, she suddenly had a vision of a woman with a child, and while on the way to Tuntenhausen, she began to feel better. She returned home "fresh and healthy" (1532, fol. A3). Or consider the religious agony of Anna, "the daughter of Hans Hierschenbeck from Wollenma in the district of Aich [Aichach?], who was in deep agony for six weeks because she could no longer pray, but was crazy [irr] all the time instead." In such misery, they "vowed her with one pound of wax" and instantly she felt better; her attack of "despair [anfechtung] was gone by the help of God and the intercession of Mary" (1583, fol. A3ʳ). This report is evidence of a new terror in Germany. Inability to pray was the frightening negative side of Counter-Reformation piety. It revealed not a suicidal impulse but another deep spiritual problem, and as such it is virtually unique in the miracle literature, although it points in the same direction as the spread of demonic possession among the pious, discussed in chapter 1.

Another woman, a maid from Reichertsheim, fell into heresy. "She was polluted with the unbelief of Anabaptism, and they led her forth with others to be drowned in the Pirg; but she recanted and they let her go. Again she became 'not right' and tried to drown and stab herself; so they locked her up. In jail Mary the Mother of God appeared to her [and urged] her to vow herself to Tuntenhausen . . . and she vowed a Mass and a pilgrimage on her knees with the rope of the martyrs and with a wax wreath." Soon she was healed (1532, fol. A4^v).

Other persons described their suicidal impulses as a *grosse Anfechtung*, a great attack, temptation, and obsession. This was, of course, the very word Luther used to describe his religious agonies, but these Bavarian peasants usually used the word to describe murderous, despairing, or suicidal fantasies (e.g., 1533, fol. A4^r, and 1536, fol. A1^v). Repeatedly, the miracle reports also state that doctors had been visited, all to no avail, an interesting indication that the poor rural population had some access to a local doctor, probably not a university-trained physician, but a professional healer and more than just an amateur herbalist or cunning man. Such sources suggest that doctors with some training were not available only to noblemen and comfortable burghers.[132]

It was not just adults who needed help. "A girl of ten years from Pfländorf was 'not right' from Pentecost through to St. Michael's day [i.e., from roughly May through September], so that they had to put her in chains. She was vowed here [to Tuntenhausen] with two pounds of wax, and afterwards the girl became right again and healthy" (1536, fol. A4^r). At table a father frightened his little boy so horribly that it was feared the child would die. The child turned black. Panic-stricken, the father sought advice from his neighbors and suddenly thought of a pilgrimage to Tuntenhausen. When he got home, the boy was already better (1547, fol. A2^r). A little girl from Prem, four and a half years old, "was not right, but they vowed her with a dress and she got right again" (1547, fol. A5^r).

Madness was often not the only complaint. Reports of persons who went mad in the course of some other disease or as the result of some constant pain were very frequent. A woman from Hohenbrunn, for example,

lay in so severe a sickness that she was robbed of her reason [*vernunfft*] and behaved as if she was possessed. In such a state she was taken to Benediktbeuern [to the relic of St. Anastasia's head] in the hope of obtaining a recovery there, but to no avail. But then she was vowed [by others] to Tuntenhausen with a Holy Mass, a pound of wax, and a pilgrimage, and the above-mentioned woman came again to her reason, was graciously helped, and the vow was carried out to the honor of the Virgin Mary.[133]

132. Gierl, *Bauernleben*, pp. 88–90.
133. 1537, fol. A4^v. For other examples of Tuntenhausen's proud superiority to Benediktbeuern, see *Denkwürdige Miracula unnd Wunderzaichen in Zwölff underschidliche Ordnungen außgethailt . . . zu Tundenhausen* (Munich, 1646), category 2, nos. 24 (1616) and 31 (1643).

In 1564, a woman from the parish of Euernbeck near Pfaffenhofen went mad with the pain from an ulcer, and a boy lost his mind from a constant headache.[134]

Repeatedly, we are reminded that terrors were regarded as extremely dangerous. A maid of sixteen was "very badly frightened on a Saturday night" and went mad for two weeks (1581, fol. B3^r). A maid of fifteen from Inning on the Ammersee became ill after receiving a bad scare while tending cattle (1574, no. 31). In 1546, a ten-year-old girl watched her father's bath-house burn down, "saw the fire and was so terrified that she fell into mortal illness; for eight days she didn't recognize anyone," but a pilgrimage solved this problem as it did with all the other cases reported (1547, fol. A4^r). One striking story concerned a six-year-old child, "who led another child off into the woods and then ran away from him, leaving him alone. And so the child went mad [*von seinen synnen kummen*], and did not know his own mother or others, screaming that a black dog was going to tear him apart" (1532, fol. A4^r).

The Attack on Miracles

Miracle books aimed first and foremost at magnifying the glory of a particular shrine. In the course of the sixteenth century, however, they were also deployed against Protestant religion in all its forms, for the miracles of a saint or of the Virgin seemed to prove the merits of the Catholic persuasion. Just as with exorcisms, so with the miraculous cures associated with vows and pilgrimage, evangelical authors did not simply feel driven to condemn pilgrimage as religiously suspect or as harmful to a deeper piety. Pilgrimages were also blasted from pulpits and in popular pamphlets as devilish priestcraft, as fraudulent, deceitful operations in which simple peasants and crafty clerics conspired to make it seem that God and the saints still responded with miracles if one only performed the requisite works of Catholic piety. Among many evangelical thinkers, there was a growing conviction, even if one that had only the slenderest scriptural basis, that the age of miracles was over. The miracles reported in the Old and New Testaments were usually regarded in the sixteenth century as true miracles. Theologians traditionally argued that they had been necessary for the early Church to make its way among the voices of competing pagan faiths. But Erasmus, most Calvinists, and a growing number of Lutherans held that miracles were no longer necessary, and that God, therefore, no longer dispensed them.[135] To be sure, God continued to answer prayer and to sustain

134. 1564, fols. A2^r and A5^r. See also 1579 fol. B1^r, B1^v, and B2^r.
135. D. P. Walker, "The Cessation of Miracles," in *Hermeticism and the Renaissance: Intel-*

his faithful, but not by contravening His own natural order. This left only a couple of possible explanations for the wondrous cures and interventions reported by gleeful Catholics. For many a Protestant, they were lies, deceptions, or demonic illusions. Human fraud played an important role, it seemed, in all of these Catholic miracles. And so the miracle report found itself on the front lines of the confessional battle.[136] Although this battle really heated up in the second half of the sixteenth century, we catch an early hint of it in the miracle book of 1539 from Tuntenhausen. After reporting a miraculous recovery from a grotesque puncture wound, Abbot Lucas Wagner noted: "Now although the 'new Christians' [i.e., Protestants] with their vile and idle protests deny and despise [our miracles], yet all things are possible for God and for His chosen spirits. For those persons of weak faith, however, the secrets of God are hidden and [the ability] to recognize His works" (1539, fol. A3^r). It remains true even today that miracles occur mainly to and for those who believe in them.

The Protestant assault did make it harder to register as miraculous events that had, or could have, an easy natural explanation. Increasingly in the seventeenth century, the wondrous cure of madness thus came to be ever more bound up with demonic possession and with other signs of supernatural intervention.[137] The miracle books of the seventeenth century also stress the credibility of their reports, emphasizing (and sometimes naming) the worthy, sober, or even noble witnesses who could attest to wondrous events.[138] To illustrate this observation, look at the miracles reported in the Tuntenhausen miracle book for 1646, a volume of 166 pages and 590 miracles, a retrospective look at miracles stretching back to the mid sixteenth century. Of the twelve categories of miracles registered, category

---

lectual History and the Occult in Early Modern Europe, ed. Ingrid Merkel and Allen G. Debus (Washington, D.C., 1988), pp. 111–24. Although pastors might draw these conclusions, it was harder to obtain compliance from Lutheran congregations, who sometimes clung to pilgrimage and procession: see Ernst Walter Zeeden, *Katholische Überlieferungen in den lutherischen Kirchenordnungen des 16. Jahrhunderts* (Münster, 1959), pp. 55–59; Richard Andree, "Katholische Überlebsel beim evangelischen Volke," *Zeitschrift des Vereins für Volkskunde* 21 (1911): 113–25.

136. Soergel, "Wondrous in His Saints," pp. 90–107, 275–334. Cécile Ernst, *Teufelaustreibungen*; D. P. Walker, *Unclean Spirits: Possession and Exorcism in England and France in the Late Sixteenth and Early Seventeenth Centuries* (Philadelphia, 1981); Keith Thomas, *Religion and the Decline of Magic* (New York, 1971).

137. See, e.g., Tiroler Landesausstellung (anon.), *Heiltum und Wallfahrt* (Innsbruck, 1988), pp. 105–12. But this trend is not everywhere visible; cf. Hanns Bachmann, *Das Mirakelbuch der Wallfahrtskirche Mariastein in Tirol als Quelle zur Kulturgeschichte (1678–1742)* (Innsbruck, 1973), pp. 71–75, who lists 28 cases of madness among 945 miraculous cures, and not one demonic possession among them.

138. See, e.g., Fortunat Hueber, *"Zeitiger Granat-apfel." Muenchen 1671: Mirakelbuch des bayrisch-böhmischen Wallfahrtsortes Neukirchen bei Heilig Blut*, ed. Guillaume van Gemert (Amsterdam, 1983), pp. 284–90.

TABLE 6.6

Cures of Madness in the Tuntenhausen Miracle Book of 1646

	Madness as Part of Physical Illness; Brain Fevers	Madness Without Concomitant Physical Illness	Tempted by the Devil (*Angefochten*) Suicidal	Possessed by the Devil
1588–1599	0	5	1	0
1600–1619	3	10	2	1
1620–1639	8	8	1	3
1640–1645	0	4	2	3
Total	11	27	6	7

SOURCE: *Denkwürdige Miracula unnd Wunderzaichen in Zwölff underschidliche Ordnungen außgethailt ... zu Tundenhausen* (Munich, 1646).

two included the mad.[139] Fifty-one persons reported that the Virgin and her shrine at Tuntenhausen had cured their madness. They were distributed as shown in table 6.6.

We notice here what we have seen in other ways as well. The seventeenth century did not see the sudden disappearance of demonic activity. In fact, as with witchcraft trials and as with the celebrated cases of demoniac possession in Lille, Louviers, and Loudun, in some ways the devil seemed even more active in Germany during the seventeenth century, both as the great tempter (to suicide and despair) and as the maddening possessor of body and soul. Notice, too, that the devil was thought to be involved in over half the miraculous cures of madness reported for the six years 1640–45.[140] In Bavaria, as Lederer has shown, a skeptical turn in official policy began to restrict exorcisms only in the 1660s, and exorcism remained prominent until much later at Benedictine shrines.[141]

Those who lived through these years may well have thought that the devil was indeed more active than ever before, but there is also no disputing the important fact that such cases were also rhetorically more effective against Protestants, who generally conceded that the devil was still active in this world even if God had withdrawn and miracles no longer occurred. No wonder Protestant apologists frantically tried to discredit the shrines and miracles of Catholic Europe. And no wonder Catholic apologists and

139. See Gerlinde Stahl, "Die Wallfahrt zur Schönen Maria in Regensburg," *Beiträge zur Geschichte des Bistums Regensburg* 2 (1968): 35–282, appendix.

140. This was true of the twenty-two cases of madness and demonic affliction cured at Inchenhofen from 1560 through 1659 as well, which comprised nine cases of madness, four cases of possession, and nine cases of demonic temptation to suicide (Martin Dallmayer, *Synopsis miraculorum et beneficiorum seu vincula charitatis, Lieb-Bänder und Ketten-Glider, welche berührt ... S. Leonardus ... zu Inchenhofen ... uber dreytausend Wunderzaichen ... geschehen* [Munich, 1659], pts. 5 and 16).

141. Lederer, "Reforming the Spirit," pp. 298–327.

exorcists continued to emphasize that their faith was triumphant against all the ills of this world.

German Catholics, therefore, continued to go on pilgrimage in the seventeenth and eighteenth centuries, very likely in increased numbers.[142] Miracle books became ever more elaborate, developing into an early form of baroque literature.[143] New shrines sprang up, and old ones took a new lease on life. St. Benno of Meissen, for example, was carried from Saxony to Munich in 1576–80 and became a major attraction for Counter-Reformation Bavarians in the seventeenth century.[144] His shrine drew mainly the lame and the blind, but occasionally the mentally disturbed came as well.[145] Some of these reinvigorated pilgrimage centers came to be so specialized that no mad pilgrims were now reported in their miracle books at all. This was the case in many of the shrines around Augsburg,[146] and in the miracle book of Kirchwald, near Nußdorf, for example.[147] Other holy places, such as St. Salvator in Bettbrunn (between Ingolstadt and Regensburg in Lower Bavaria), attracted ever larger numbers of the mad and demon-possessed. About 10 percent of St. Salvator's roughly 2,700 miracles in the years 1584–97 involved relief from demonic *Anfechtung*, diabolic possession, madness, and *Fraiß*, which often meant a frightful choking until the sufferer lost consciousness.[148] Evidently, such choking was related to the other forms of insanity reported in the same chapter. Similarly, the Holy Mountain of Andechs attracted large numbers of deranged pilgrims among the thousands who came seeking relief from all the ills of this world.[149] During

142. Nolan and Nolan, *Christian Pilgrimage*; Günter Bers, *"Das Miraculöß Mariä Bildlein zu Aldenhoven": Geschichte einer rheinischen Wallfahrt, 1685–1985*, Schriften zur rheinischen Geschichte, vol. 6 (Cologne, 1986), Dieter P. J. Wynands, *Geschichte der Wallfahrten im Bistum Aachen* (Aachen, 1986), pp. 13–18; Mader, *Wallfahrten im Bistum Passau*.

143. Hermann Bach, "Mirakelbücher bayerischer Wallfahrtsorte"; Habermas, "Wunder."

144. Soergel, *Wondrous in His Saints*, pp. 181–91; Robert Böck, "Die Verehrung des hl. Benno in München," *Bayerisches Jahrbuch für Volkskunde*, 1958, pp. 53–73.

145. *Gewiß und Approbirte Historia Von S. Bennonis etwo Bischoffen zu Meissen, Leben und Wunderzaichen* (Munich, 1602); *Verzaichnus etlicher furnemmer wunderwerck so sich bey S. Bennonis Heilthumb zu Munchen im Jahr 1601 und 1602 begeben* (Munich, 1604), no. 36, fols. 36^{r-v}; *Umbstendig und warhaffter Bericht was sich zu end deß 1602 und 1603 gantze Jahr bey S. Benno in München für Wunderwerck begeben* (Munich, 1603), no. 23; *Kurtzer Bericht Etlicher Miracul unnd Wunderwercken so . . . 1605 . . . bey S. Bennonis Hailthum in Munchen* (Munich, 1606); *Extract Unnd gründtlicher Bericht, etlichen Gnaden: und Wunderwercken, so . . . Gott, durch das . . . Fürbitt . . . Bennonis . . . gewirckt* (Munich, 1643).

146. Walter Pötzl, *Mirakel-Geschichten aus dem Landkreis Augsburg* (Augsburg, 1979), summarizing 130 miracle stories from the period after 1590.

147. Gerhard Stella, "Das Mirakelbuch von Kirchwald bei Nußdorf. Eine Handschrift in der Bayerischen Staatsbibliothek München (Kloeckeliana 606^b)," *Das Bayerische Inn-Oberland* 42 (1980): 65–111.

148. David Mörlin, *Sanct Salvator Zu Bettbrunn in Bayern: Das ist: Von der alten heiligen Capellen und wirdigem hoch brühmbten Gottshauß . . . S. Salvators zu Bettbrunn* (Ingolstadt, 1597), pp. 154–68.

149. *Etliche WunderZaichen, die Gott der Almächtig auff dem heiligen Berg Andechs . . .*

the Counter-Reformation, many a medieval shrine that had fallen into disuse during the early and mid sixteenth century bounced back with curious specialties. St. Leonard's shrine at Inchenhofen (on the Paar River, fourteen miles northeast of Augsburg), for example, had long been a major medieval pilgrimage center. As the patron of prisoners, St. Leonard had special sympathy for captives and others bound in chains. That probably explains why mad persons in the fourteenth and fifteenth centuries had turned in large numbers to St. Leonard.[150] Of 199 miraculous cures between 1346 and 1447, Steven Sargent reports, seventeen healed the mentally ill and an additional seven relieved the demon-possessed. It is evident, however, that the early years of the Reformation brought the collapse of pilgrimage we have seen so often elsewhere. When the shrine revived in the late sixteenth century, St. Leonard had changed his specialty. He was now the special patron of horses and cattle, a role for which he became famous.[151] According to the amazing *Synopsis miraculorum* of 1659, however, this shift did not spell any real diminution of St. Leonard's sympathy for the mad. Although thousands of miracles were attributed to St. Leonard, this volume describes in some detail 494 miraculous acts of healing, spread out over three centuries. Forty-nine (10%) of these cures involved the mad, the demon-tempted, and the demon-possessed.

In the report of a miracle from 1594, we even hear of "melancholy," a term for mental disorder that rarely appears in our miracle reports. The full entry reads: "A pious and well-respected person, who withheld her name, had fallen into such melancholy and misery that she kept on thinking she had to kill herself."[152] Here it is probably significant that "melancholy" was attributed to a pious woman of the middle classes, not to a peasant. It was a fancy diagnosis, but certainly not one to be proud of, as we may gather from the fact that her name was withheld. We also note in passing that this victim was a woman: melancholy was not a gender-specific ailment. St. Leonard's concern for the mad and the demon-obsessed is also emphasized in the miracle books of the late sixteenth century: 5 of the 39 miracles reported in 1585 (13%) involved madness or near madness, as did 13 of the 118 miracles reported in 1606 (11%).[153] The mad were still pilgrims.

---

gewirckt und erzaigt hat (Munich, 1602); *Mons Sanctus Andechs, Das ist: Kurtzer Begriff oder Innhalt von den Gnadenreichen H. Berg Andechs* (Munich, 1682).

150. Sargent, "Religion and Society," p. 262, table 4; pp. 300–301.

151. Klaus Welker, "Die Inchenhofener Mirakelaufzeichnungen, 1506–1657: Ihr Beitrag zur nachtridentinischen Verehrung des hl. Leonhard als Viehpatron," in *Von Konstanz nach Trient: Beiträge zur Geschichte der Kirche von den Reformkonzilien bis zum Tridentinum. Festgabe für August Franzen*, ed. Remigius Bäumer (Munich, 1972), pp. 635–57.

152. Dallmayer, *Synopsis miraculorum et beneficiorum*, pt. 5 and pt. 16, no. 8.

153. S. *Leonhardus: Etliche gedenckwirdige Miracul und Wunderzeichen* (Munich, 1585); *Vilerley gedenckwürdige Miracula, so sich zugetragen von Anno 99 bis ad Annum sexcentissimum quintum* (Munich, 1606).

Nowhere is this continuation and revival of pilgrimage better known than at Altötting, where St. Peter Canisius (1521–1597), a Jesuit, performed a dramatic exorcism in 1570 upon Anna von Bernhausen, a noble maid-in-waiting to Baroness Sibylla von Fugger of the famous Augsburg family of financiers. Not only was the exorcism carried out with fanfare and in the presence of a noble entourage, it was also memorialized by Martin Eisengrein, a convert from Lutheranism, professor of theology at Ingolstadt, and, since 1567, provost of the collegiate church of Altötting. His book *Unser liebe Fraw zu Alten Oetting* ("Our Lady at Altötting"), which went through at least ten editions between 1571 and 1625,[154] made the remarkable healing powers of the Bavarian shrine known to thousands of readers. Despite official Jesuit efforts to restrict the practice of exorcism and especially to curb the practice of Peter Canisius, the saint found ample evidence of demonic possession in Augsburg. In 1568, when the town fathers forbade any further exorcisms within the confines of the city, his healing practice was moved to Altötting.[155] The elaborate exorcism of 1570 also became the target of a pointed Protestant attack by Johann Marbach of Strasbourg, and a polemical war of tract and countertract broke out.[156] Fervent evangelicals may have been hardened in their contempt for supposedly wonder-working shrines and relics, but the average South German may well have found Altötting all the more attractive because of the controversy.[157]

In any event, the pilgrimage to Altötting revived with a roar. Duke Albrecht of Bavaria undertook his own pilgrimage to Altötting in 1571, one year after Canisius's successful exorcism of Anna von Bernhausen, and the Bavarian dukes soon made it a place of annual pilgrimage. Duke Maximilian I began the tradition of signing a personal pledge in his own blood to the Virgin of Altötting, and the hearts of the Bavarian ducal and royal line have been preserved there ever since 1651.[158] Thus Altötting grew to be the single most important "national" holy place in all Bavaria. Jacob Irsing's miracle book of 1643 (translated into German in 1644) documents the revived importance of Altötting for the pilgrimages of the mad. Like many other mid-seventeenth-century books of wonders, this one is an elegant tome of 278 pages, originally in Latin, containing accounts of miracles from 1487 (*sic*) down to 1643.[159] Table 6.7 summarizes these.

154. Martin Eisengrein, *Unser liebe Fraw zu Alten Oetting* (Ingolstadt, 1571). See Soergel, *Wondrous in His Saints*, pp. 110–42, esp. p. 111.
155. Lederer, "Reforming the Spirit," pp. 272–80.
156. Ibid., pp. 131–42; for more light on Marbach's career and thought, see James Kittelson, "Successes and Failures in the German Reformation: The Report from Strasbourg," *Archiv für Reformationsgeschichte* 73 (1982): 153–75.
157. Veit and Lenhart, *Kirche und Volksfrömmigkeit*, pp. 59–60.
158. Meingast, *Marienwallfahrten*, p. 15; Bauer, *Bayerische Wallfahrt Altötting*, pp. 128–31.
159. Jacob Irsing, S.J., *Historia von der weitberühmbten lieben Frawen Capell zu Alten-Oeting in Nidern Bayern*, trans. Johann Scheitenberger (Munich, 1644).

TABLE 6.7

Madness in the Altötting Miracle Book of 1644

	(N)	Sick with madness	Mad without sickness	Demon-tempted and Suicidal	Demon-possessed
1487–1499	(49)	2	2[c]	1	0
1500–1529	(29)	1[a]	1	0	0
1530–1569	(14)	0	0	0	0
1570–1599	(30)	2	1	0	3
1600–1619	(91)	2	6[b,c]	0	2
1620–1643	(72)	1	3	1	1
Total	(285)	8	13	2	6

SOURCE: Jacob Irsing, S.J., *Historia von der weitberühmbten lieben Frawen Capell zu Alten-Oeting in Nidern Bayern*, trans. Johann Scheitenberger (Munich, 1644).
[a] "Thought" to be possessed
[b] Two regarded as mad *or* possessed
[c] One suicidal, but with no mention of demonic *Anfechtung*

Madness and demon possession make up just over 10 percent of the cases reported in Irsing's *Historia*. As elsewhere, demonic activity was clearly concentrated in the latter part of the period covered, even though it never accounted for the ailments of most of the mad. This miracle book also provides us further evidence of the spread, socially downward, of the language of melancholy. A man tried to drown himself in 1610, but his wife pulled him from the water and persuaded him to go to nearby Altötting. "The husband did this and his melancholy and misery [*Melancholey und Betrübnuß*] left him, and this condition never attacked him again."[160] Similarly, a man from Bolzano in the South Tyrol arrived in 1618, complaining that "he had plunged into such a melancholy and misery that he felt ever since that he must kill himself, for he was beyond salvation."[161] In both of these cases, we find the word *melancholy* used to describe suicidal despair, but there is no hint here of the medical origins of the term, no sense that if one suffered from black bile, one really needed a purge. Instead, it appears that as the concept of melancholy spread downwards socially, it lost its specifically humoral connotations.

Conclusion

In no other sources from sixteenth-century Germany do we confront so many humble stories of madness. The miracle books and shrine chronicles present details from the lives of hundreds of simple men and women, and of some children, who lost their reason, their understanding, or their

160. Ibid., p. 190.
161. Ibid., pp. 220–22.

senses. Rarely was a medical diagnosis used to describe their condition, although these sources frequently emphasized that doctors had been consulted to no avail. At least until the seventeenth century, it was also surprisingly rare that madness was attributed to demonic attack or demonic possession. But as the sixteenth century wore on, suicidal despair was more and more often deemed evidence of a demonic *Anfechtung*, an anguished, despairing temptation to escape this world and to give up. But this usage rarely or never implied that a proper exorcism was in order. That ceremony was used mainly in cases of full-fledged physical possession and occasionally for suspected bewitching.

What may linger in our memories even more than the devil's assaults and suicidal suggestions is the hope held out by the shrines of Catholic Germany, both in the Rhineland and in the southern cultural area of Franconia-Bavaria-Austria, that the troubles of this life were not hopeless.[162] To the permanent scandal of Lutheran and Reformed believers, Catholicism offered tangible relief from pain, disaster, and even madness. These mentally disordered peasants were not simply set adrift on the rivers or roads of Germany, as Foucault famously supposed. Our miracle books record over and over that the mad were confined or restrained until someone, usually a spouse or a relative, but sometimes a neighbor or a group of neighbors, betrothed or dedicated the patient to a saint and vowed a pilgrimage to his or her shrine. Often relief was thought to begin at the moment of the vow, but the pilgrimage, when it finally took place, was a formal affair, often involving a large group of friends and relatives, who joined in thanking the Virgin or another specific saint for whatever help had already arrived.[163] Sometimes a helpless madman was taken from one shrine to the next in search of help. Some pilgrimage centers, such as St. Leonhard am Wald, even had cells with chains especially for madmen and the possessed, so that they could be kept for a time, exposed to the healing powers of the shrine.[164] Other shrines, such as Benediktbeuern in southern Bavaria, developed a reputation as especially effective with the spiritually troubled and mentally disordered. Benediktbeuern's prized relic, a piece of St. Anastasia's skull, may have suggested that her healing force might be concentrated on those with troubled heads. Madmen in need of a shrine did not swarm unhindered and uncontrolled through the countryside, however, but were encouraged or compelled to join the formal ritual of penance and pilgrimage.

162. In the Rhineland, the shrines of Not Gottes bei Rüdesheim and of Bornhofen became almost as important as Altötting or Mariazell in their regions (Veit and Lenhart, *Kirche und Volksfrömmigkeit*, p. 63).

163. Occasionally, the formal procession became a piece of religious theater, with the penitent accompanied by six or more maidens dressed in white (Kriss-Rettenbeck, *Ex voto*, pp. 275 and 394, n. 18).

164. Ibid., p. 29.

It was only in the late seventeenth century, and then decisively in the eighteenth, that the state and the church began to find pilgrimage so disorderly that the practice had to be severely regulated, or even curtailed. Typical of the sixteenth century was the treatment received by a certain Oswald Mayr and his wife from Bavaria, who had the misfortune to lose their minds at the same time in 1584. They were "so far bereft of reason and understanding that they had to be chained like the possessed." For a week they lay bound like wild animals until finally several neighbors took pity on them, vowed a group pilgrimage to Tuntenhausen, and secured relief.[165] Here we have a good example of the way in which madness tested and could strengthen communal bonds. What other hope did such people have in sixteenth-century Germany? As we shall see, occasionally other places of refuge were created for the mad, custodial nursing homes such as the hospitals of many a town and those newly invented in Hesse. Occasionally, too, a medical cure for madness was found. The new hospital in Würzburg pioneered a path in this direction. But usually it was up to family and neighbors to find solutions. Of course, the mad were sometimes bound with chains, not usually as a punishment but in order to restrain them. Of course, the mad sometimes behaved as if possessed—indeed, sometimes they were treated as if possessed, but that did not mean only beatings and the kind of abuse we are usually led to expect. Sixteenth-century Germans were capable of careful distinctions. At no time did demonic possession account for more than a small fraction of the madnesses we find in our records. If we oversimplify the early modern German experience of mental disorder, restricting it to a few categories that serve our political or moral purposes (whatever they may be), we do it an injustice and truncate our own freedom, a freedom that depends in part on knowing our past in all its variety.

165. *Denkwürdige Miracula . . . zu Tundenhausen* (1646), no. 30.

CHAPTER SEVEN

*M*adness as Helplessness: Two Hospitals in the Age of the Reformations

Madness as Helplessness

ONE of the characteristics of the early modern state, observable all over Europe, was an increasing concern about and even care for the troubled, dispossessed, and wretched. Tudor England had its famous Poor Laws, and French, Italian, and German towns reformed their provisions for widows, orphans, and the aged. The German territories were not far behind. A generation ago, there was a lively debate among scholars about whether the Protestants were entitled to take most of the credit for such reforms, a debate that evaporated as it became plain that the changes in question were about as prevalent in Catholic towns as in Protestant ones. Then the controversy shifted to center on the question of whether the new interventions of the state were part of a bourgeois or newly rational attempt to control the poor, and most recently they have been seen as part of the civilizing process or of "confessionalization" and state-building.

In this chapter, we shall examine madness in another of its sixteenth-century costumes. Here we shall look at madness as simple helplessness. Those state and city authorities who began to take an increased interest in the mad poor were not particularly concerned with a specific legal, theological, or medical diagnosis. The key element in their decision to take care of a person was whether the person could work and care for himself or herself, and if not, whether the local family or a network of neighbors could be mobilized to provide the necessary help. This concern for work had little to do with the bourgeois work ethic, however, and a great deal to do with an older European work ethic, which valued those who could sustain themselves.

The madness of the poor was often preconceived by magistrates as simple helplessness, but if no one would support these troubled souls, their plight was hopeless too. Just as at the great pilgrimage shrines, we do not find magistrates idealizing the mad as wise fools or melancholy geniuses. But no pious bureaucrat thought to condemn these sufferers as sinners or suicidal fools, either. No hospital official recorded his perplexity, if he indeed ever was perplexed, about whether a particular applicant was medically ill (according to the many categories described by the medical professors), mentally crippled, or demon-possessed (as described by the theologians). So spacious was the house of helplessness that madness as a social problem usually fitted easily into just one or two of its rooms. And the test of whether a disturbed person could support himself or herself (could "function" or "cope" in the world, as we might say) remains basic to the way social agencies understand the mad today.

The search for the origins of German mental hospitals plunges us into the history of the Protestant Reformation and its Catholic counterpart. Historians a generation ago used to think that the Protestant Reformation transformed Germany all at once, reshaping old attitudes and practices beyond recognition in a matter of months or years. But recently a few scholars have followed the example of Ernst Walter Zeeden in looking for lingering remnants of Catholicism behind a Protestant facade.[1] Until very recently, even in the history of institutions as thoroughly medieval as hospitals, the usual emphasis has been on what was progressive and Protestant about the actions of the newly Lutheran princes of the Holy Roman Empire. This chapter, however, compares the new hospitals of the Protestant landgraviate of Hesse with the new hospital of the bishopric of Würzburg. These two territories became well known for their social welfare systems and especially for their hospitals.[2] While other territories also experimented with new hospitals, in most cases the early documents no

1. E. W. Zeeden, *Katholische Überlieferungen in den lutherischen Kirchenordnungen des 16. Jahrhunderts* (Münster, 1959); Robert Scribner, *Popular Culture and Popular Movements in Reformation Germany* (London, 1987); Ronnie Po-chia Hsia, *Social Discipline in the Reformation: Central Europe, 1500–1750* (London, 1989).

2. On the welfare system in Hesse, see William J. Wright, "Reformation Contributions to the Development of Public Welfare Policy in Hesse," *Journal of Modern History* 49 (1977): D1145 (on demand article); id., *Capitalism, the State, and the Lutheran Reformation: Sixteenth-Century Hesse* (Athens, Ohio, 1988). In general, see David B. Miller, "The Dissolution of the Religious Houses of Hesse During the Reformation" (diss., Yale University, 1971); and John C. Stalnaker, "The Emergence of the Protestant Clergy in Central Germany: The Case of Hesse" (diss., University of California at Berkeley, 1970). Historians of Würzburg have never tried to make out a case for its "modern" social policies, but a case like the one for Hesse could be made and is partly implicit in Alfred Wendehorst, *Das Juliusspital in Würzburg*, vol. 1: *Kulturgeschichte* (Würzburg, 1976). For the evolution of Würzburg's poor laws and ordinances, see Hans-Christoph Rublack, *Gescheiterte Reformation: Frühreformatorische und protestantische Bewegungen in süd- und westdeutschen geistlichen Residenzen*, Spätmittelalter und frühe Neuzeit, vol. 4 (Stuttgart, 1978), pp. 128–43.

longer survive.[3] In other towns, such as Augsburg and Kitzingen, the habit of simply locking up the mad with the inconvenient and the drunk in towers or cells called *Narrenhäuser* ("fools' houses") survived.[4] In Würzburg and in Hesse, however, the archives bulge with records that allow us to see what the hospitals were originally like and how they were slowly transformed into hospitals almost exclusively for the mentally deficient and mentally disturbed.[5] In the Hessian hospital established at Haina, one can examine the process by which a Cistercian monastery was converted into a Protestant hospital. Surviving documents from the Juliusspital in Würzburg also permit a detailed examination of the first several decades of a major Catholic venture in social policy and in therapeutic medicine. This chapter is in this way an exercise in comparative history, a chance to see what Protestants and Catholics did with the same social problem.

The Origins of a Reformation Hospital

To grasp the origins of mental hospitals in Germany, one needs to understand the controversial position of monasteries in the age of the Reformation and the political problems of poor relief. In early modern Germany, that means learning about princes: dukes, counts, margraves, and landgraves. In the landgraviate of Hesse, the hereditary ruler was Philipp, son of Wilhelm II and Anna of Mecklenburg. Born in 1504, he lost his father in 1509 and grew up under the influence of his greedy, ruthless, energetic mother.[6] At the age of fourteen, Philipp was declared old enough to rule

3. This is the case, e.g., in Württemberg, where the documents relating to the notable Stuttgart Hospital, founded in the sixteenth century, were destroyed with most of the city archive during World War II. David Lederer ("Reforming the Spirit: Society, Madness, and Suicide in Central Europe, 1517–1809" [diss., New York University, 1995], pp. 341–59) has pursued the history of the Heilig Geist Spital in Munich, which was specially designated for the spiritually troubled in 1551, but that institution remained inadequate to its assigned tasks until the second half of the seventeenth century.

4. Ann Tlusty, "The Devil's Altar: Drinking and Society in Early Modern Augsburg" (diss., University of Maryland, 1994); Lederer, "Reforming the Spirit," p. 333. The best treatment of poor relief and hospitals in the early modern imperial cities is Robert Jütte, *Obrigkeitliche Armenfürsorge in deutschen Reichsstädten der Frühen Neuzeit: Städtisches Armenwesen in Frankfurt am Main und Köln.* (Cologne, 1984).

5. Paul Holthausen, *Das Landeshospital Haina in Hessen, eine Stiftung Landgraf Philipps des Grossmütigen, von 1527–1907* (Frankenberg i. H., 1907), p. 15. The best summary of the history of the Hessian hospitals from the perspective of the general history of psychiatry is the collection edited by Walter Heinemeyer and Tilman Pünder, *450 Jahre Psychiatrie in Hessen.* (Marburg, 1983).

6. Gustav Freiherr Schenk zu Schweinsberg, "Aus der Jugendzeit Landgraf Philipps des Grossmütigen," in *Philipp der Grossmütige: Beiträge zur Geschichte seines Lebens und seiner Zeit,* ed. Historischer Verein für das Grossherzogtum Hessen (Marburg, 1904), pp. 73–143; H. Stutte, "Landgraf Philipp der Grossmütige von Hessen aus medizinischer Sicht," *Hes-*

Hesse without a regent. No one suspected in 1518 that the young ruler of this centrally placed territory, which stretched from Kassel in the north to Darmstadt, south of Frankfurt, would become the earliest and most zealous secular proponent of the Reformation, indeed, a prince without whom the Lutheran Reformation in Germany is scarcely conceivable.[7] As a youth, his religious concerns, to the slight extent that we can perceive them at all, were thoroughly superficial and conventional. In 1521, he met Luther at the Diet of Worms but failed to take sides on the issue then beginning to divide Germany. In 1522, an observer reported that Philipp "wants to remain in the faith in which he was born and raised until his papal holiness, his Roman imperial majesty, together with the Christian kings, spiritual and secular electors and princes, and the estates of holy Christendom decide on another or a better one."[8] Until 1524, Philipp seemed content to let others decide, but in the summer of that year, a meeting with Melanchthon brought his conversion to the Lutheran cause. In 1523, however, when he attempted to reform the Cistercian monastery at Haina, Philipp was still a conventional Catholic prince, concerned for the welfare of his Catholic territory.

Monks had lived at Haina, about fifteen miles north of Marburg, since the early thirteenth century and had erected one of the most significant early gothic churches in Germany there. A venerable Protestant myth has it that the monasteries, although well run and orderly at first, fell progressively into deeper and deeper corruption, reaching a nadir in the late Middle Ages. This picture is almost always overdrawn, and when one reads in the first Protestant history of Haina that by the beginning of the sixteenth century the monks were godless, lazy, drunken voluptuaries, dedicated to "impietas, luxuria, superbia, discordia," the modern reader can taste an overdose of Protestant bias.[9] With accusations such as these, it is usually difficult to separate fact from bias, but in the case of Haina, we are fortunate in having fairly good records dealing with the monastery before the Reformation. These records enable us to see that even if the Protestant charges of corruption were one-sided and biased, there were also pious Catholics who agreed that Haina fell far short of the Benedictine ideal. In 1508, for example, an ecclesiastical visitation report complained of too much drinking at Haina, too much mixing with the laity, too many violations of the ideal of cloistered isolation, and too relaxed an attitude in gen-

---

sisches Ärzteblatt 30 (1969): 1085–97. I have sketched the political atmosphere in which Philipp grew up in Mad Princes, pp. 41–44.

7. Hans J. Hillerbrand, Landgrave Philipp of Hesse, 1504–1567: Religion and Politics in the Reformation, Reformation Essays and Studies, no. 1 (St. Louis, 1967), p. 37.

8. Cited in ibid., pp. 3–4.

9. Johann Letzener, Historische, kurtze, einfaltige und ordentliche Beschreibung des Closters und Hospitals zu Haina in Hessen gelegen. Auffs newe ubersehen und verbessert (Mühlhausen, 1588), fol. G2r.

eral toward the seriousness of divine services.[10] And on March 22, 1523, Philipp of Hesse reaffirmed his duty to protect the monastery of Haina on condition that it returned to a "spiritual, reformed life."[11] In September of that same year, Philipp complained to the abbot and monks of Haina that he still heard complaints about the many visitors and guests in the monastery, whose meetings disturbed divine services. Giving refuge to a few solitary travelers was appropriate, he concluded, but Haina must stop being a hotel.[12] It turned out that these were problems that did not just go away with the wave of the prince's scepter.

After Philipp was converted to Luther's Reformation, his desires to see the monastery at Haina reformed merged with a more general desire for secular control over morals and church property.[13] In 1524, Philipp promulgated a Hessian *Polizeiordnung* for the control of immorality, and especially drunkenness. In 1526, taking advantage of the decree of the Diet of Speyer that acknowledged that the princes of the empire were responsible for religion in their territories, Philipp held an assembly of secular and ecclesiastical officials at Homberg. This so-called synod recommended sweeping legal changes, including the abolition of monasticism in Hesse, the confiscation of monastic property, and the use of monastic buildings and revenues for public purposes such as schools.[14] Rejected and ridiculed by Luther as just a "pile of laws," the ordinances of the Homberg Synod were never actually put into effect, but they reflected an early Lutheran inclination to put monastic property to common use.[15] In February 1527, Philipp ordered an inventory of all Hessian monasteries (about fifty in all) with a view to sequestering them. By mid December, the inventory and sequestration were formally complete, but some monasteries clung tenaciously to the hope that imperial courts might reverse what seemed to them to be a gross invasion of their rights. Probably the single most dramatic instance of resistance was the long and ultimately futile suit of the abbots of Haina in the Reichskammergericht ("Imperial Chamber Court").[16] As the process of secularization went forward, therefore, Philipp

10. Eckhart G. Franz, ed., *Kloster Haina: Regesten und Urkunden*, vol. 2: (*1300–1560*), *Erste Hälfte: Regesten* (Marburg, 1970), pp. 515–16.

11. Ibid., p. 556.

12. Ibid., p. 557.

13. See Miller, "Dissolution of the Religious Houses of Hess," and Walter Sohm, *Territorium und Reformation in der hessischen Geschichte*, Urkundliche Quellen zur hessischen Reformationsgeschichte, ed. Günther Franz, vol. 1 (Marburg, 1957), pp. 19–20.

14. Karl August Credner, ed., *Philipps des Grossmütigen Hessische Kirchenreformations-Ordnung* (Giessen, 1852), pp. 46–47, 108–10.

15. Sohm, *Territorium und Reformation*, p. 28. Electoral Saxony only began to sequester its monasteries in 1531. On the legal questions, see Hans Lehnert, *Kirchengut und Reformation: Eine Kirchenrechtliche Studie*, Erlanger Abhandlungen zur mittleren und neueren Geschichte, vol. 20 (Erlangen, 1935).

16. For the documents in this long case, see Franz, ed., *Kloster Haina*.

was under steady pressure to find legal and moral grounds to justify his novel measures.

Curiously enough, in order to defeat the monasteries, Philipp and his government found strength in the monastic ethic itself. He accused the monks of selfishness and claimed that his Reformation would return monasteries to a true Christian communalism. As the Hessian territorial estates concluded in October 1527, monastic property "should serve the common weal."[17] The most common immorality was selfishness (*Eigennutz*). Philipp appointed reformers who continued to emphasize the kinds of public tasks to which the selfish monasteries could be dedicated. As a result, most secularized church property was put to charitable or educational purposes, including the founding of Marburg University in 1527. One recent estimate concludes that about 60 percent of secularized monastic revenues in Hesse went for charitable purposes, while the remainder of the money found its way to the court and the central administration.[18] To lend credence to his claim that he was merely restoring a monastic (Christian communal) ethic to the monasteries, Philipp had to be careful to avoid the use of force. Thus, as early as October 1525, Philipp advised the margraves of Brandenburg to allow monks to return to their Franconian monasteries, abandoned during the Peasants' War a few months earlier, and to let them live out their lives there, unless some other, better purpose could be found for the monasteries.[19] In Hesse, Philipp and his agents proceeded as if they were merely reforming the monasteries, returning them to their original purposes.[20] Officials arrived at each monastery or convent and tried to persuade the monks or nuns that Luther's interpretation of the gospel was correct, that the Roman Mass was a form of idolatry, and that monasticism was a selfish form of works-righteous arrogance. Usually, the officials then ordered the abolition of the Mass and offered settlements to those monks or nuns who wished to renounce their vows. Those who wished to live on in the monastery were usually allowed to do so if they willingly conformed to the new dispensation. Abbot Dithmar von Wetter of Haina complained in 1530 that these procedures amounted to force, but Philipp could amiably respond that "on the basis of evangelical preaching the greater part of Haina's monks had asked for settlements," which he could not in good conscience refuse. It was true, he conceded, that the abbot and three or four brothers had absconded without his knowledge, but Philipp insisted that

17. Sohm, *Territorium und Reformation*, p. 40.

18. Carl E. Demandt, *Geschichte des Landes Hessen*, 2d ed. (Kassel, 1972), pp. 226–27.

19. Günther Franz, *Urkundliche Quellen zur hessischen Reformationsgeschichte*, vol. 2: 1525–1547 (Marburg, 1954), p. 12, doc. 11.

20. F. W. Schäfer, "Adam Krafft, der Reformator Hessens," *Archiv für hessische Geschichte und Altertumskunde*, n.s., 8 (1912): 1–46, 67–110, at 85.

he had forced no one.[21] Of the 36 monks and lay brothers at Haina in 1527, 32 accepted settlements.[22]

Four years were to pass before Philipp seized control of the abandoned monastery. During March 1531, Philipp began to outline his plans to convert the monastery at Haina and the Augustinian canonry at Merxhausen into hospitals for the rural poor,[23] and on August 26, 1533, he founded these two hospitals.[24] One cannot tell how long he had harbored such plans, but there were a number of compelling reasons for creating hospitals. First, in emotional terms, was Philipp's proud sense that he stood in a tradition of princes who had always helped the poor, stretching back to his most famous ancestor, St. Elisabeth, who had worn herself out in acts of charity three hundred years earlier, and whose pilgrimage church in Marburg was the first completely gothic church on German soil.[25] Even more compelling may have been his awareness of the needs of the peasants of Hesse. Princes did not then live so far from the smells of the village or the cries of country people that they could remain oblivious to the needs of the elderly poor. The landgrave himself might even have to stop along the road to hear the requests of a poor man. And although most towns had "hospitals" or spitals to serve as nursing homes for their elderly poor, the countryside had none.[26] Finally, Philipp was surely aware that his political claims to Haina and to the other secularized monasteries would be strengthened if he could create from some of them institutions that were so clearly Christian in spirit that monks wishing to recapture them for the Catholic faith would be placed in a morally dubious position.

This last motive informs one of the favorite legends concerning the origins of Haina Hospital. When the evicted abbot of Haina took his case to court, he is said to have received not only the support of the archbishop of Mainz but that of the pope as well. These powerful men secured a hearing before Emperor Charles V, who sent a team of investigators to Haina. The earliest Protestant history of Haina, published in 1588, praised Charles's

21. Franz, ed., *Kloster Haina*, 2: 620.

22. Ibid., pp. 575–78.

23. Ibid., pp. 621–22. There seems to be no basis for Holthausen's claim, in *Landeshospital Haina*, pp. 6–7, that Haina became a hospital in 1527 or 1528.

24. The act of foundation is printed in Franz, *Urkundliche Quellen*, 2: 183.

25. Wilhelm Maurer, "Die heilige Elisabeth und ihr Marburger Hospital," in *Kirche und Geschichte: Gesammelte Aufsätze*, vol. 2: *Beiträge zu Grundsatzfragen und zur Frömmigkeitsgeschichte*, ed. E. W. Kohls and O. Müller (Göttingen, 1970), pp. 284–319; see also "Zum Verständnis der heiligen Elisabeth von Thüringen," in ibid., pp. 231–83.

26. Helmut Siefert, "Kloster und Hospital Haina: Eine medizin-historische Skizze," *Hessisches Ärzteblatt* 32 (1971): 963–83. On hospitals as part of a territorial plan for poor relief, see Dieter Jetter, *Das europäische Hospital, von der Spätantike bis 1800* (Cologne, 1986), and on early madhouses, ibid., pp. 193–98; id., "Zur Entwicklung der Irrenfürsorge im Donauraum," *Medizinhistorisches Journal* 6 (1971): 189–99; id., *Zur Typologie des Irrenhauses in Frankreich und Deutschland (1780–1840)* (Wiesbaden, 1971).

exemplary caution and noted that Landgrave Philipp responded swiftly by converting Haina into a hospital and filling it with "poor people, and the blind, lame, dumb, deaf, foolish, lunatic, mad, possessed, deformed, leprous, and similar sorts of afflicted people."[27] When the investigators arrived in Haina, the superintendent of the hospital, Heinz von Lüder, is said to have lined up all the unfortunate patients of the new hospital and to have asked whether the imperial officials intended to throw them all out and to bring back the proud, gluttonous, useless monks. Our Protestant chronicler tells us that this demonstration had the desired effect.[28] We may note in passing that the mad first appear in his history, along with the blind and the halt, as living symbols of helpless suffering, with undeniable claims on the charity of the commonweal.

Regrettably, I have found no evidence of such an imperial visitation to Haina in the contemporary local records, but this does not mean that the pious story is totally without foundation. During the late 1540s, after Charles V had crushed the Lutheran Schmalkaldic League, fears ran through the Hessian administration that defeat would mean the restoration of the monasteries to Catholic control. On October 7, 1548, for example, the hospital superintendent, Heinz von Lüder, a military captain, wrote to Lieutenant Rudolf Schenck zu Schweinsberg in Kassel, that Haina had 200 "poor propertyless men from Hesse," of whom over 30 were "born fools and blind men," while 10 were "madmen kept under lock and key." It took 50 persons to care for all of these unfortunates.

Now before we bend to the claims of three complaining monks and destroy this Christian work, so useful to our land, we ought to receive those three into the hospital, and up to twenty more, and let them live as monks if they will help with caring for the poor and not themselves insist on governing, especially since about eight former monks are already living there.[29]

In 1548, the threat of a Catholic restoration seemed real enough. Later that month, von Lüder warned repeatedly that if the abbot of Haina were to appear in Haina with an imperial mandate, there would be no way easy to refuse him entry. The professors and rector of the new university were similarly threatened by attempts to restore the abbot. In early 1549, indeed, Charles did go so far as to order the return of Haina to its rightful abbot.[30] But in the long-drawn-out negotiations that followed, Hessian officials insisted that since Haina was not being used for private purposes, Charles should leave the hospital and university alone. Charles remained unper-

27. Letzener, Historische . . . Beschreibung, fol. G3v. Siefert, "Kloster und Hospital Haina," too readily assumes the reliability of this story.
28. Ibid., fols. G4r–H1r.
29. Franz, ed., Kloster Haina, p. 657.
30. Ibid., p. 658.

suaded, but Hesse succeeded in stalling until 1552, when the defeat of Charles turned the tables. Actually, the abbots of Haina pursued their now hopeless case in imperial courts until 1558.[31] In all of these proceedings, there is no evidence of Heinz von Lüder's physically lining up Haina's patients before imperial investigators, but there is no doubt that Hessian officials spent years rhetorically lining them up before Charles. To that extent, the pious legend captures an important fact. One reason the hospital survived is that it could plausibly claim to fulfill certain Christian or even monastic functions more perfectly than the Cistercians who had lived there until 1527. The abbot could only grumble that Philipp's actions were "an open affront to natural, divine, and written law, even if they are 'perfumed with the appearance of God's Word.'"[32]

Legally, therefore, Philipp won the right to establish hospitals in place of monasteries (and using their sources of revenue). Eventually, he created four territorial hospitals for destitute country people, at Haina and Gronau for men and at Merxhausen and Hofheim for women, places well distributed throughout his lands.[33] What sort of place did the mad find there? For a better understanding of these hospitals, one needs to examine the regulations that governed them and to discover, if possible, the actual conditions there. The hospital founded at Haina has remarkable records that permit a careful look at both of these questions.

THE HOSPITAL AS CHRISTIAN COMMUNITY

In the first ordinance for the hospital at Haina, an unknown administrator laid down the basic rules that governed life there for the next two hundred years. The hospital was to take in up to one hundred poor men from the countryside; town dwellers were explicitly excluded, and there was no provision for married couples. Patients were to be admitted solely on grounds of poverty and need, and not in return for money, favors, or friendship. A "brother" was also supposed to be at least sixty years of age, "unless he is so feeble that he is useless and could not otherwise work to earn his bread."[34] These were the admission requirements for a nursing home, rather

31. Ibid., pp. 658–72.
32. Ibid., p. 641.
33. Haina was in Upper Hesse (near Marburg), Merxhausen in Lower Hesse (near Kassel), Hofheim in the Upper County of Katzenelnbogen (near Darmstadt), and Gronau in the Lower County of Katzenelnbogen (near Rheinfels). Scattering them was not done in order to make them more convenient for the inmates, but to support them more easily from local resources.
34. Franz, Urkundliche Quellen, 2: 190. Franz prints most of the ordinance, which he dates after April 29, 1534, on pp. 189–97.

than what we might today expect of a hospital. Moreover, the former monastery was to continue to display a strictly Christian character, accepting only good Christians who maintained a holy way of life worthy of the Christian alms that continued to support the hospital. It is sometimes supposed that the Protestant Reformation broke with the ethic of almsgiving and established community chests instead. However much this may be true elsewhere, the Hessian hospital regulations refer repeatedly to alms as the moral basis of these hospitals, a basis that demanded high moral standards.

The ordinance proceeded to prescribe a semimonastic life of celibacy and regular prayer, work, and lessons for the hospital's inhabitants. Those "brethren" who could still move about were to awaken together at the sound of a bell and spend half an hour washing, combing their hair, and dressing "so that they do not live like pigs in a pen." Nor should they lie in bed once they awakened, "for then the devil is not far, and he tempts the flesh. He scratches and rubs and by much touching of the limbs of the body brings one to luxury and to horrible sins, which occur as Paul says 'in chambering and wantonness'" (Rom. 13:13).[35] The hospital thus took measures to suppress the sexual urges of old men. After half an hour, again at the sound of a bell, the brethren were to gather for prayers in the church, at 5:00 A.M. during the summer, or in the large heated dayrooms at 7:00 A.M. during the winter. There they were to be taught to thank God, who had watched over them during the night. The preacher was to follow with a short lesson from Luther's catechism and with prayers for the peace and welfare of the prince, the governor of the hospital, and for the needs of Christendom. Taking the poor attention span of these old men into account, the pastor was enjoined never to let this divine service exceed half an hour.

Having first sought the Kingdom of God, the hospital's residents were now supposed to busy themselves with light work. The point was not to extract profit from the aged, but "to avoid laziness" by making baskets or brooms, tidying up, working in the garden, splitting wood, watering the meadow, "not for the great usefulness of such work," the ordinance conceded, "but so as not through idleness to give the devil room."[36] Those who were too ill to attend morning prayers could now expect a visit from the pastor, who should repeat his lessons for them, "in order that these people, too, as they leave this world may be prepared and sent to their Father. And it would be good if every day the sick could hear some words of comfort, so long as it is short and full of consolation, so that they might be cheerful and undismayed by death and eager for eternal life."[37]

While the able-bodied were working and the sick were praying, the first

35. Ibid., p. 190.
36. Ibid., p. 191.
37. Ibid.

meal of the day was being prepared, the tables set, and bread and drink put out. "For these two things are almost the most important in the hospital: [1] that one supervise the kitchen to assure that everything is clean, useful, well cooked, and faithfully given to the poor [brethren], and [2] that the poor are visited daily so that they not remain unconsoled."[38] Even a hardened skeptic of the twentieth century may be struck by the quiet humanity of these ideals.

At about 9:00 A.M., when they came together to eat, the brethren were expected to wash, sit down, and pray. During the morning meal, someone was to read parts of the New Testament aloud (but not from the Book of Revelation, which was thought too obscure and upsetting). At the evening meal, the reading was to be from Luther's catechism, all year long, for newcomers had need of this instruction. The ordinance suggested that hospital officials eat at some other time so that they could supervise mealtimes and make sure that everyone was well served. Meat, fish, and cheese were to be served in bowls, from which four men would eat. The cooks were to cut such foods into four pieces per bowl so that the men would "have no cause of discord, since some of them have learned no table manners."[39] After the meal and a prayer of thanks, the men were to have about an hour free for making their beds, tidying up, or resting. Then it was back to work until about 1:00 P.M., when they paused for a lunch of beer and bread with cheese. And then work again, each according to his ability, until the evening meal was served, at about 4:00 or 5:00 P.M.. After supper, the men might relax before going to bed at a set hour.

After prescribing a diet with adequate meat, fish, and vegetables, the ordinances went on to forbid the brethren to go out into the nearby village without good reason, for otherwise trouble and rumors would spread. The fear was that too much worldliness could corrupt such a withdrawn and peaceful community.

The Lord's Supper was to be offered monthly, preferably on one of the holidays of the Church year. Brethren who felt unworthy of the body and blood of Christ were to be excused, and those who felt a special need for more frequent communion should be accommodated. Before anyone was permitted to take the Lord's Supper, however, he had to go before the hospital pastor to give an account of his faith, life, sins, and conscience and to repeat parts of the catechism. The pastor might spend the evenings of an entire pre-communion week examining the spital: "Whoever does not know his Ten Commandments, creed, Lord's Prayer, and so forth, should not be admitted to the sacrament until he learns them, because they are es-

38. Ibid.
39. Ibid., p. 192.

tablished for Christians. And if he does not know about Christ, how can he be called a Christian?"[40]

Those whose consciences were weak should be strengthened with absolution; the hard-hearted should be chastened with God's law and brought to a knowledge of their sins so that they would become capable of receiving the gospel. Brethren who could sing were to be taught psalms and prayers from the Wittenberg Order, which they might sing in church and before the evening meal. "But be sure to take enough time in this task, for old people learn slowly."[41]

To keep this religious community well ordered, the ordinance emphasized the importance of finding an upright, God-fearing man as governor (*Spitalsmeister*). This man, who was regularly described in religious language as *Pater*, could be married or single, but if married, he must have no small children (he would have responsibilities enough). He must agree to spend the rest of his days in the hospital, with the provision that he could count on retiring there. At his death, his estate was to go to the hospital. After describing his daily duties, the ordinance laid stress on maintaining Christian unity and order. Hospital servants, too, were to avoid all argument and discord, for "a kingdom divided against itself cannot stand." And, of course, harmony depended on constant prayer to God, "for where man is, there is the devil also, the enemy of all men."[42]

This hospital made no provisions for medical care, and as we have seen, the founding ordinance assumed that sickness was the last stage before death. The hospital ordinance therefore placed its heaviest stress on religion and on the importance of finding a full-time pastor "who will preach at least one sermon a day, will visit the poor in their sicknesses, comforting them with the Holy Scriptures; at table, if there is no other reader present, he should read to the men something edifying from the Bible and also teach the people Christian behavior and what they need to know as Christians."[43]

The hospital was founded as a kind of Protestant monastery, offering spiritual medicines mixed with appropriate food and work.[44] Superintendent Reinhard Schenck repeated this ideal in his revised ordinance of 1573, when he recommended that "those smitten with illness should not be left alone but should be brought to the common rooms, visited by the pastor,

40. Ibid., p. 193.
41. Ibid., p. 194.
42. Ibid., pp. 194–95.
43. Ibid., p. 142.
44. See the perceptive remarks of Johann Jürgen Rohde, *Soziologie des Krankenhauses: Zur Einführung in die Soziologie der Medizin* (Stuttgart, 1962), pp. 65–69.

comforted with God's Word, and refreshed with special brews and light foods."[45]

A lengthy section of the ordinance regulated the jurisdiction, buildings, forests, agriculture, and financial affairs of the hospital, inasmuch as the revenues to support the new establishments continued to be the seigneurial dues, tithes, and rents collected from the former monastic lands. Just as in the period before 1527, a pious gatekeeper was deemed necessary, a man who would open the hospital to the outside world at 4:00 A.M. in the summer (6:00 A.M. in the winter) and close up at 8:00 P.M. in the summer (7:00 P.M. in winter). It was his duty to control who left and who entered.[46] One of the gatekeeper's jobs again reflects the monastic framework of its origins. A clause near the end of the ordinance considered the problem posed by pilgrims, strangers, and other poor wayfarers and declared that if they asked in the name of God for refuge, they should not be denied food and drink and a room in the guest house by the gate, but, with an eye on monastic abuses, the regulations limited such hospitality to "one night and no longer." If poor servants, widows, and orphans living in the nearby villages came to beg for alms, they too should be given grain or other food, but only after it was clear that they were truly needy and worthy.[47] The monastic ideal of hospitality and almsgiving lived on in the heart of a Protestant institution.

This then was the original ideal outline of life at Haina. The three other territorial hospitals founded by Philipp followed this model, making changes only where necessary. At Merxhausen, for example, because the residents were mostly women, the jobs at which they worked were sewing, knitting, crocheting, and other sorts of "women's work." Interestingly, the Merxhausen regulations omitted all reference to the sexual dangers of luxuriously lingering in bed, but they went on in much more detail about the supposedly female vices of arguing, cursing, envying, grousing, and gossiping. The women at Merxhausen were explicitly told to sit down to table in orderly fashion without clambering over one another. They were strictly warned to remain silent during prayers.[48]

---

45. StAM, 40a XXIV Generalia 2: Reinhard Schenk zu Schweinsberg, "Ordnung wie sich ein jeder Ampts Diener im Hospitall Heina in seinem Ampt verhalten soll (1573)."

46. Since Günther Franz did not reprint this section of the ordinance, one must still consult the manuscript: "Hainaer Hospitals-Ordnung," in StAM, 40a XXIV Generalia 2 (Hess. Kammer), 11 fols., at fol 8r.

47. Franz, *Urkundliche Quellen*, 2: 196.

48. "Hospitals-Fundation," StAM, 40a XXIV Generalia 2, 10 fols., at fols. 2r and 4r.

LIFE IN THE HOSPITAL

The rules for conduct tell us something of the ideals at Haina, but what was life there really like? One source that helps us answer this question is the laudatory Protestant history by Johann Letzener, the Lutheran pastor of Leuthorst, published in 1588, and dedicated to the "Christian Brethren of Poor Lazarus at Haina in Hesse." Letzener takes the reader on a tour of Haina, examining first the buildings that survived from the monastery, including the ambulatory with its many refectory rooms and its chapter house; the dormitory with its easy access to the choir of the church; the infirmary; and the guest house. Other old buildings included the wash house; the kitchen house, with piped-in water; the granary with its mill and bakery, where 32 malters (366 bushels, or 133 hectoliters) of grain were ground and baked weekly; the sawmill; the brewery, with huge stone vats larger than those found in many towns or princely palaces; the dairy, hog shed, sheep barn, and implements barn; the buildings that housed the various craftsmen who had served the monastery earlier and the hospital now (shoemaker, tailor, linen weaver, cloth maker, smith, carpenter, cabinet workers, latheworker, wagoners); and the houses of the various officials of the hospital (pastor, schoolmaster, treasurer, governor, head of the kitchen, and the chief of clothing distribution). There was even a house built by the landgrave for his occasional visits. Of course, the most conspicuous building, visible for miles in the rolling Kellerwald valley of the Wohra, was the early gothic church, built with Cistercian simplicity and lacking even the modest steeple it has today. Letzener praised it as the finest monastic church he had ever seen (fig. 21).[49]

Most of these outbuildings served the hospital as they had the monastery. The largest room (*Brüderstube*) of the old monastery itself was used by brethren who could still walk and do various kinds of work. Another room was reserved for helpless old men and for the blind or epileptic. Unlike the able-bodied, who sat down four men to a bowl, each man in the second room received his own bowl. A third room included the bedridden and diseased and was called the infirmary (*Krankenstube*), where the men were fed by two servants. Some of the mentally ill were also placed in two other rooms. A fourth chamber, known as the vault, housed "several mad and lunatic persons, lying in chains, and also several dumb, deaf, and 'awkward' or retarded (*ungeschickt*) men, for whom special caretakers are appointed."[50] A fifth room contained "eighteen massively strong cells, under which flows a stream, which removes all waste and excrement. And

49. Letzener, *Historische . . . Beschreibung*, chs. 4 and 5.
50. Ibid., fol. J3r.

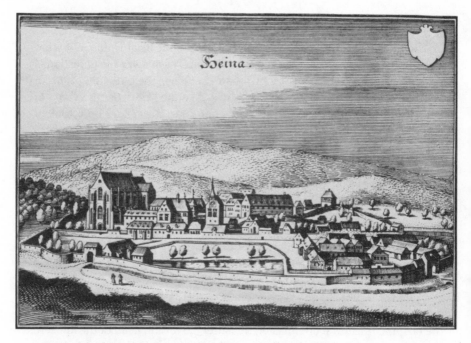

FIG. 21. Matthäus Merian, the hospital at Haina in Hesse. Ca. 1625. Landes-wohlfahrtsverband Hessen, Kassel.

they have three iron ovens placed next to each other so that the poor raving people who lie locked in these boxes may be kept warm."[51]

Special custodians were also appointed for this department. Their job was to care for these dangerously mad people day and night. Situated above these five rooms was a laundry, where eight women washed shirts, linen, and bedding daily for the hospital residents. In addition to the five "wards" here described, Letzener also mentions a sixth, a leprosarium for eighteen men, who lived separately, ate separately, had their own place in church, their own path to church, and their own laundry, with three women assigned to it.

From Letzener's detailed account, it appears that the hospital had found it necessary to add at least a couple of new buildings since 1534.[52] The vault may be the new "block house" mentioned in some of the sixteenth-century records. In Carl Wilhelm Justi's account of 1803, this building had a stone

51. Ibid.
52. Holthausen, *Landeshospital Haina*, pp. 12, 21–32. Carl Wickel, *Gründung und Beschreibung des Zisterzienser-Klosters Haina in Hessen, sowie einiges aus der Geschichte des Klosters und der Anstalt*, 2d ed. (Frankenberg i. H., 1929), has a useful survey of former buildings at Haina.

ground floor with living quarters for the custodian and small rooms only five feet high and eight feet long. In his day, the upper floors were of wood and held "the more reasonable, sometimes only melancholy patients."[53] It is not clear whether the eighteen cells for the mad were in this building, and neither is it known exactly where the leprosarium stood or when it was built. It may have been a medieval monastic structure.[54]

In Letzener's day, Pastor Johannes Pinactus preached twice on Sundays and once on Wednesday and Friday. On the other days of the week, he held only morning and evening prayers. Letzener considered him a worthy servant of the Lord, struggling valiantly against the grossest vices. He employed a sexton to ring the bell, that regular punctuation of the day's routine. As one can see from Letzener's list of chief officers, by the 1580s, a schoolmaster was employed to teach young orphaned boys their catechism and the rudiments of reading, writing, and singing. The ordinance of 1534, of course, had said nothing of orphans or other young boys at Haina; but the new ordinance of 1577, intended for the general superintendent of the four Hessian territorial hospitals, declared that rich persons were not to leave their children at Haina for schooling, "for it ought to be a hospital and not a school, especially since their children always eat the best food, which the poor, needy residents observe and endure with great bitterness."[55] It was a different matter for the foundlings and "similar poor fatherless children who have been transferred here." They should be taught to pray, to read and write, and also to work diligently, so that when they were twelve years old, they could be set out as servants or apprentices and thus not hang around the hospital like "lazy gallows birds."[56]

Letzener's description provides us with a useful vantage point from which to see how the original ordinance of 1534 had been put into practice. Other sources shed indirect light on the same question. From revisions of the hospital ordinances, for example, we can obtain glimpses of real life in contrast to the official ideal. We have already noticed hints in the 1577 ordinance that Haina was so attractive a place that even substantial families were tempted to leave their children there for schooling. Similarly, the ordinances of 1573, 1574, and 1577 all emphasized that the hospital was intended exclusively for rural subjects of Hesse who could not earn a living.[57]

53. Carl Wilhelm Justi, *Das Hospital zu Haina: Versuch einer Darstellung seiner ehemaligen und gegenwärtigen Beschaffenheit* (Marburg, 1803), p. 20.
54. When the monastery was secularized, only one resident was a leper (Franz, *Kloster Haina*, p. 552).
55. StAM, 40a XXIV Generalia 2: "Obervorsteher Ordnung 1577," 6 fols.
56. StAM, 40a XXIV Generalia 2: "Obervorsteher Ordnung 1577"; Reinhard Schenck, "Haina Amts Diener Ordnung 1573"; "Ordnung für Hermann Pauli, 1574."
57. StAM, S60 A: "Salbuch Hessische Hospitäler 1575," instruction by Landgraf Ludwig, July 16, 1575.

These revisions imply that the hospitals were becoming so attractive that persons from Hessian towns or from outside Hesse altogether were attempting to gain admission. As a hospital survey of 1575 noted, officials were to check to see if any unauthorized young, strong, able-bodied persons had been wrongly admitted to the hospitals. The ordinance of 1577 also made the admissions criteria clearer by going beyond the original requirement of disability and poverty to insist that applicants prove that their relatives and friends could not support them. Philipp of Hesse had, after all, intended these hospitals only for poor persons without any means of subsistence whatsoever. This document also discussed the rather unexpected possibility that the sick or disabled might actually improve while in the hospital. If so, they were to leave and find honest work.[58]

Such documents lead one to suspect that regular exceptions were made to the original rules of admission. In addition to the orphaned children already mentioned, the 1575 survey of Haina and Merxhausen reveals, a number of married couples had been granted entry.[59] Indeed, this exception to the original rules became so common that a commission of inquiry in 1627 reported complaints that the married now numbered "40, 50, 100, and even sometimes more than that." To make matters worse, these couples insisted on eating before the poor brethren and on receiving other special privileges. These persons had succeeded in buying places for themselves in the Haina hospital, another practice forbidden by all of the sixteenth-century ordinances and considered harmful to general morale.[60]

Other well-to-do persons found their way into Haina under special circumstances, as in the case of a mentally ill nobleman, Merx von Ramrodt, who was in custody there in 1575, accompanied by two maidservants.[61] Uncontrollable mad persons from towns were often granted admission if it could be shown that there was no other secure place for them. The admission of urban lunatics remained an exceptional practice until 1728, however, when an ordinance allowed for their regular transfer to Haina "if they have a crazed mind and are so wild that they could not be kept in the town hospitals without great danger; and if they have enough wealth not only to pay for their keep but to leave something to the hospitals."[62]

The largest deviation from the original model was the rapid growth of

58. StAM, 40a XXIV Generalia 2: "Obervorsteher Ordnung 1577."

59. StAM, S60 G: "Verzeichnis der personen so zur zeitt im Spittal Heine sint, 16 July 1575."

60. StAM, 40a XXIV Generalia 2: "1627 Bericht der zur Samt-Visitation der Hohen Hospitalien," dated Sept. 26, 1627.

61. StAM, S60 G: "Verzeichnis der personen so zur zeitt im Spittal Heine sint, 16 July 1575."

62. Holthausen, *Landeshospital Haina*, p. 13. Only after 1881 were the mentally ill from Hessian towns sent to Haina as a matter of course.

TABLE 7.1
Hospital Residents in Hesse, 1550–1591
(five-year averages)

	Haina	Merxhausen	Gronau	Hofheim	Men[a]	Women[b]	Total
1550–1555	196	114	66	59	262	173	435
(6 years)	(45%)	(26%)	(15%)	(14%)	(60.2%)	(39.8%)	(100%)
1556–1560	197	157	91	71	288	228	516
	(38%)	(30%)	(18%)	(14%)	(55.8%)	(44.2%)	(100%)
1561–1565	284	213	100	83	384	296	680
	(42%)	(31%)	(15%)	(12%)	(56.5%)	(43.5%)	(100%)
1566–1570	338	273	116	100	454	373	827
	(41%)	(33%)	(14%)	(12%)	(54.9%)	(45.1%)	(100%)
1571–1575	345	313	120	115	465	428	893
	(39%)	(35%)	(13%)	(13%)	(52.1%)	(47.9%)	(100%)
1576–1580	317	354	102	122	419	476	895
	(35%)	(40%)	(11%)	(14%)	(46.8%)	(53.2%)	(100%)
1581–1585	395	396	114	158	509	554	1,063
	(37%)	(37%)	(11%)	(15%)	(47.9%)	(52.1%)	(100%)
1586–1591	391	369	123	173	514	542	1,056
(6 years)	(37%)	(35%)	(12%)	(16%)	(48.7%)	(51.3%)	(100%)

SOURCE: StAM, 40a XXIV Generalia 2: "Summarischer Extract was vom Jhar 50 ahn bis uff das 91sten Jhar in den vier hohen Hospitalien in Hessen . . . underhalten worden." In 1575, the poor at Haina constituted at least 294 of the 346 residents (85.0%); in 1598, they made up 264 of the 323 residents (81.7%); StAM S60 G: "Verzeichnis der Personen so zur zeitt im Spittal Heine sint," July 16, 1575; StAM 40a XXIV Generalia 2: Landgraf Ludwig der Elter to Landgraf Moritz, December 13, 1598. In 1575, the poor at Merxhausen numbered 270 women and 33 men out of 356 (85.1%), not counting the nine persons on leave to visit friends, of whom six were poor. Including them would bring the percentage of poor down to 84.6. StAM S60 H: "Verzeichnus dero personen zu Merxhausen, 15 July 1575."
NOTE: Figures include poor brethren or sisters, officials, and servants.
[a] Haina and Gronau.
[b] Merxhausen and Hofheim.

the hospital, from the 100 originally planned for, to 200 residents and 50 staff in 1548, and to about 312 residents and about 69 staff in 1591.[63] In 1591, the Hessian central administration became concerned at the rising tide of poor and disabled and ordered a survey of the four territorial hospitals. The list they drew up covered the years 1550 to 1591 and revealed that the total hospital population had more than doubled in forty years (see table 7.1). Poor brethren made up about 80 to 85 percent of the figures given here.

It is noteworthy that the numbers of residents increased in all four territorial hospitals, but almost as remarkable was the disproportionate rise of

63. Franz, *Urkundliche Quellen,* 3: 84; Siefert, "Kloster und Hospital Haina"; StAM, 40a XXIV Generalia 2: "Summarischer Extract was vom Jhar 50 ahn bis uff das 91sten Jhar in den vier hohen Hospitalien in Hessen . . . underhalten worden."

Merxhausen and Hofheim, both dedicated to disabled and aged women. In the forty-one years between 1550 and 1591, the hospitals for men almost doubled in size (up 96.2%), while in the same period the women's hospitals more than tripled their size (up 213.3%) and came to have more residents than the men's hospitals. Haina had begun with a clear preponderance, but gradually Merxhausen overtook Haina, until they were roughly equal in size. Nowadays, one might suspect that madness was being "gendered" as female, leading to larger numbers of women inmates, but we must remember that these residents were by no means all mad. The particular reasons for the growing disparities among these hospitals are obscure, but the general reason for this extraordinary growth is not. The landgraves of Hesse repeatedly urged the hospital superintendent and the hospital governors to admit more poor people. As the 1574 ordinance for the new superintendent Hermann Pauli put it, "[A]t all times, but especially in these dizzyingly expensive times, you shall keep as many poor persons as the income of the hospital can possibly support, for the estate of the hospitals ought not to grow by admitting few people; instead, whatever God Almighty grants at any time ought to be shared to the advantage of the poor."[64]

By the 1590s the hospitals at Haina and Merxhausen were jammed full, and yet there were still more poor and disabled who clamored for relief. In 1592, for example, Landgrave Moritz ordered the superintendent, Johann Clauer, to admit to Haina a lame boy who had lost use of his hands and feet, even though "the territorial hospital is already overflowing with disabled persons." In order to find room for the boy, the authorities were to examine all who were there already and expel someone who might be better able to earn a living outside the hospital.[65] In a similar case from 1592, Landgrave Wilhelm told Clauer that he was sure there were some ablebodied men at Haina who could earn their own bread, and that one of them should be expelled to make room for a crippled and truly needy man.[66] There are records of similar orders in 1575, 1592 again, 1598, 1609, and 1616; and they are far from complete.[67] Obviously, the hospitals had admitted too many poor persons and overstrained their resources. On May 31, 1602, Landgrave Ludwig the Elder wrote to his brother Landgrave Moritz that Haina was now losing 2,000 fl. per annum and had to be helped if they hoped to avoid "expelling the wretched and ruthlessly sending even those who qualify for alms (according to the ordinances) out into the coun-

64. StAM, 40a XXIV Generalia 2: "Ordnung für Hermann Pauli, 1574"; repeated verbatim in the 1577 Obervorsteher Ordnung.

65. HHA, "Receptions-Rescripte von den Jahren 1500," Landgraf Moritz to Johann Clauer, n.d. The boy was ordered by Clauer to be admitted on Nov. 2, 1592.

66. HHA, RR, Landgraf Wilhelm to Johann Clauer, June 22, 1592.

67. HHA, "Receptions Rescripte von den Jahren 1500," and also from the cellar room (Klammer), "Ganz alte Receptions Rescripte von den Jahren 1500 u. 1600."

TABLE 7.2
Departures from Haina, 1575

	Brethren (N = 294)	% of Total Brethren	Staff (N = 52)	% of Total Staff
Died	25	8.5	5	9.6
Left Voluntarily	7	2.4	8	15.4
Expelled	9	3.1	0	0.0
Total	41	14	13	25.0

tryside to wander and decay in poverty, hunger, and misery."[68] The hospitals should be pruned back he said, from the current 407 and 380 (Haina and Merxhausen respectively) to 300 and 250, and only the most needy should be admitted.

How long did the average resident remain in the hospital? Some, who arrived as crippled children, might look forward to 40 or 50 years there. Others who arrived after age 60 or 70 probably spent only five or at most ten years there. No records provide a direct answer. In 1575, however, the landgraves conducted a thorough enquiry into the affairs of the hospital and ordered a list of those who died or left the hospital in that year (see table 7.2).

If we assume that 1575 was an average year, we would conclude that about 14 percent of the brethren left each year and 25 percent of the servants or officials. One may perhaps register surprise that only 8.5 percent of the brethren died in 1575, a very low figure considering that they were predominantly aged or disabled. These figures in turn would imply that the average stay was 7.2 years for the average poor brother and 4 years for the average staff member if the hospital had reached a steady state of equal entries and departures.[69]

Records from Merxhausen in 1585 and 1597 indicate departure rates of 24.6 percent for the sisters and 20 percent for the staff, which would indicate shorter average stays in Merxhausen than in Haina (roughly 4 and 5 years respectively). But a note in the same record indicates that 56 of the 67 who died in 1597 had died of plague (*Pestilenz*), which might mean that both 1585 and 1597 were years of extraordinarily high mortality.[70] Of course, these are only averages, which may tell us little about actual condi-

68. StAM, S60 A: "Salbuch Hessische Hospitäler 1575," instruction of July 16, 1575; StAM, 40a XXIV Generalia 2.

69. It can be shown that in a steady state, the average number of years in the hospital for the average person was approximately the inverse of the fraction leaving each year. If an institution were still growing, as the hospital was in 1575, then the average number of years per person would be somewhat less than the inverse of the fraction leaving each year.

70. StAM, 229 HIIIa Landeshospital Merxhausen, Lit. H, no. 2, "Acta generalia die Aufnahme der Hospitalitinnen in das Landeshospital Merxhausen betreffend."

tions. In any event, it is obvious that the country people of Hesse valued the free room and board of the hospitals. Unlike later hospitals elsewhere, which sometimes functioned as workhouses or prisons, the worst punishment for many in Hesse was expulsion from the hospital. And the landgraves were probably correct in thinking that some able-bodied peasants succeeded in slipping away from the harsh world of family and work to the simple comforts of a Christian community.

FOOD CONSUMPTION AND NUTRITION
IN THE HESSIAN HOSPITALS

By the 1570s, the great secular inflation of the sixteenth century had cut severely into the resources of poor people throughout Germany. It is no wonder, then, that many desperate souls sought the security of the semi-monastic hospitals of Hesse. Like the orphanages of early modern Amsterdam, the Hessian hospitals tried to guarantee a diet that was perhaps "monotonous but not meagre."[71] Oddly enough, the food given to residents at Haina can be studied in some detail, enabling us to imagine what an important aspect of life was like both for the mad residents of Hessian hospitals and for the more normal inmates.

We have noted that the hospital ordinances required two main meals a day, with bread and beer for lunch. Ordinarily, there would be no way of knowing whether the hospitals followed these rules, but in 1574, the administration discovered that Haina was consuming much more food per capita than Merxhausen. The landgraves ordered an investigation, which turned up a large mass of information, from which one can draw conclusions about the general state of nutrition in these two hospitals. Similar investigations took place in 1590 and 1621, so that we can give an unusually detailed account of the changing diet at Haina.

The hospitals took special pains to ensure that each resident received an adequate diet of meat, fish, and cheese. The 1534 ordinance specified that on meat days (Sunday, Tuesday, Thursday), two meat courses were to be served in the morning and one in the evening. On fish days (the remaining four days of the week), one course of fish was to be served in the morning and one course of cheese in the evening. Since each meal was to have three courses, vegetable dishes [gemuese] were served to fill out the menu. It is not completely clear what sorts of vegetables were intended, but later records suggest that they were frequently pea soup, barley soup, oatmeal,

71. See Anne McCants, "Monotonous but not Meagre: The Diet of Burgher Orphans in Early Modern Amsterdam," in Research in Economic History 14 (1992), ed. Roger Ransom, 69–116; id., "Consumer Behaviour in an Early Modern Dutch Orphanage: A Wealth of Choice," Journal of European Economic History 22 (1993): 121–42.

TABLE 7.3
*Weekly Diet of Meat, Fish, and Cheese
for Ten Persons in Hessian Hospitals, 1534*

	Courses per Week	Weight per Course	Grams per Person/Day	Calories per Person/Day
Meat	9	3 lb.	186	508
Fish	4	3	83	145
Cheese	4	1	28	119
Total			297	772

NOTE: Here and in other nutritional calculations, no allowance has been made for food wasted and thrown out. The result may be a consistent overestimate of food per person.

or millet. Records from 1574 and 1590 also suggest that the average course of meat was three pounds for a table of ten persons; the course of fish was five herrings per table of ten; and when cheese was served, one pound had to be divided among ten. From these bits of information, one can estimate that hospital inmates' intake of animal proteins and fats took on the profile shown in table 7.3.

We have no information from this early period on how much soup, bread, beer, and other foods the residents were supposed to be given each day, except for a suggestion in the 1534 ordinance that "in addition to meal-times, one should give the hospital people as much bread and drink [beer] as they need."[72] If one guesses that the residents were supposed to be consuming about 2,500 calories per day, then the proportion made up by meat, fish, and cheese was roughly 31 percent.

Using the 1534 ordinance as a gauge, we can see why the investigators of 1574 were alarmed.[73] They found the Haina community of 360 persons consuming 1,580 quarters of rye annually (398,160 lbs; 191,913 kg) or 1.51 kg of bread per person daily (3,620 calories). Other records gave evidence of the same Rabelaisian appetites. The Haina community annually consumed 65 oxen, 22 cows, 94 calves, 441 hogs, and an array of rams, lambs, and goats, to say nothing of the geese, chickens, and eggs, reserved for holidays. Added together, these worked out to an average of about half a pound of meat and sausage per person daily (ca. 712 cal.). Fish added some 54 calories to the average daily diet, and cheese another 276 calories. This diet was supplemented with butter, milk, peas, oatmeal, and small amounts of millet and rice; it was occasionally spiced with poppy seed, cinnamon, ginger, cloves, pepper, saffron, plums, almonds, honey, sugar,

72. Franz, *Urkundliche Quellen*, 2: 192.
73. StAM, 40a XXIV Generalia 2: "Extract zu Heyna und Merxhausen uffgangen . . . 1574."

TABLE 7.4
Diet at Haina and Merxhausen, 1574
(actual consumption)

Food Categories	Haina	Merxhausen
Grains:		
Rye bread[a]	1,318 g.	1,282 g.
@100 g. = 240 cal.	(3,163 cal.)	(3,077 cal.)
Other grains	105 g.	207 g.
@100 g. = 240 cal.	(252 cal.)	(497 cal.)
Wine	30 ml.	15 ml.
@100 ml. = 53 cal.	(16 cal)	(8 cal.)
Beer[b]	1,847 ml.	1,137 ml.
@100 ml. = 20 cal.	(369 cal.)	(227 cal.)
Meat: fresh, pickled, dried	196 g.	124 g.
@100 g. = 273 cal.	(535 cal.)	(339 cal.)
Bacon & sausage	34 g.	14 g.
@100 g. = 520 cal.	(177 cal.)	(73 cal.)
Butter & fats	27 g.	20 g.
@100 g. = 793 cal.	(214 cal.)	(159 cal.)
Innards	56 g.	29 g.
@100 g. = 200 cal.	(112 cal.)	(58 cal.)
Milk	109 ml.	130 ml.
@100 ml. = 66 cal.	(72 cal.)	(86 cal.)
Cheese	65 g.	80 g.
@100 g. = 425 cal.	(276 cal.)	(340 cal.)
Fish	31 g.	29 g.
@100 g. = 175 cal.	(54 cal.)	(51 cal.)
Eggs	.055 egg	.051 egg
@1 egg = 60 cal.	(3 cal.)	(3 cal.)
Sugar & Honey	2 g.	1 g.
@100 g. = 400 cal.	(8 cal.)	(4 cal.)
Average calories per person per day	5,251 cal.	4,922 cal.

[a] Adjusted for payments to day laborers
[b] Diätbier (a light beer, fairly low in alcohol)

raisins, and vinegar. The men of Haina washed all of this down with 1.8 liters of beer daily. The average daily calory allowance in 1574 came to an astounding 5,251 calories a day even after one adjusts for payments to day laborers. Such a lusty diet would be more fit for a winter crew of Minnesota lumberjacks.

Merxhausen's women were only slightly behind Haina, with an average daily calorie consumption of 4,922 (see table 7.4). Merxhausen had noticeably less meat, wine, and other luxury foods, but somewhat more dairy products, and it was understandably more self-sufficient than Haina. In

1574, Haina spent 2,072 fl. 19 alber 3 heller on foods not locally produced, while Merxhausen spent only 858 fl. 15 alber 3 heller on such imported foods.

In an effort to understand the discrepancies between Haina and Merxhausen, the landgrave's officials demanded an explanation from Haina. In their defense, local officials pointed out that Haina had a number of expenses that Merxhausen did not.[74] The Haina ironworks, for example, employed forty men, who came to the hospital for their pay every two weeks and received free food and drink. Similarly, when the local peasants delivered wood to the foundry or to the hospital, they were entitled to half a loaf of bread for each wagon load. Peasants working the hops gardens and hay fields, and those bringing their rents and dues of chickens, geese, grain, or money all got food and drink when they arrived at Haina. Merxhausen apparently employed many fewer of these outside workers and had fewer traditional obligations to its local peasants. In a petulant tone, the Haina defense complained that the hospital was besieged by visitors much more frequently than Merxhausen, and that when nobles and their retinues visited, they usually paid only for their wine. Haina was also a center of administrative personnel (district supervisor, treasurer, kitchen master, grain clerk, clothing clerk, clerks for kitchen and barns) while Merxhausen had only a supervisor and a clerk. The point was that such officials "are fed better than the brothers, who have to content themselves with ordinary fare." In a marginal note, the landgrave added: "Here they really felt the knife!" If these reasons were not sufficient, the Haina officials pointed out that Merxhausen's women ate much less than Haina's men, some of whom truly ate like four persons. In addition, the people locked up at Haina (presumably the mad) "are kept better than the others, and generally the poor are given enough beer and bread. If anyone finishes all of his bread, the waiter sets out more." Strange beggars and the local poor were also a constant drain on Haina's resources. Finally, as if to deal one knockout punch to the suspicion that Haina officials were embezzling food or selling grain on the side, the report claimed that Haina's rye was so inferior that one malter produced only 425 lb. of bread, while one malter of Merxhausen rye produced 617 lb. of bread. Unfortunately, this last argument was too subtle for the landgrave, whose bewildered protest survives in the margin. Apparently no one tested the claim that Haina's rye was inferior, however, until 1621 when a "corn test" was conducted.[75] At that time, officials did indeed discover a difference between the rye at Haina and that at Merxhausen (table 7.5).

74. StAM, 40a XXIV Generalia 2: "Bericht warumb in anno 74 zu Heyna mehr als zu Merxhausen uffgangen."

75. StAM, 40a XXIV Generalia 2: "Heinischen Abschidt und Extract, 1621."

TABLE 7.5
Corn Tests at Haina and Merxhausen, 1621

Grain	Quantity	Yield in Flour	Yield in Bread
Haina rye March 9, 1621	552 lb.	478 lb.	649 lb.
Index	100	86.6	117.6
Haina rye March 15, 1621	288 lb.	252 lb	321 lb.
Index	100	87.5	111.5
Average Haina index	100	87.1	114.3
Merxhausen rye March 5, 1621	509 lb.	435 lb.	635 lb.
Index	100	85.5	124.8

Unfortunately for Haina's argument in 1574, the difference was only on the order of 10 or 12 percent. And it appears that Haina officials were claiming that their rye was so inferior that they actually obtained fewer pounds of bread than the flour with which they began, a claim not worthy of serious scrutiny.[76]

The Haina defense succeeded in persuading the officials of the landgrave that Haina probably used 200 quarters of rye for all of the extraneous purposes mentioned, and that the hospital therefore consumed only 1,380 quarters. This accounts for the significant adjustment of Haina's bread consumption shown in table 7.4.

Apparently in response to the investigation of 1574, officials tried in 1575 to draw up a uniform menu and diet for both hospitals, assuming a combined population of 500 poor persons seated at 50 imaginary tables (table 7.6).[77] This estimate is interesting for a number of reasons. First, it cut the number of meat courses from the nine a week (as recommended in 1534) to six and assumed that each person would eat only two pounds of bread a day, instead of almost three.

The largest and most obvious change was in total calories per person per day, reducing the average daily total from 5,251 to 3,694. The hospitals were hardly being put on short rations, but the recommended reductions reflected the concern of Hessian officials that the hospitals had too much, and that the previous overly generous estimates created opportunities for peculation.

76. One Haina malter of rye grain weighed 552 lb in 1621. It is inconceivable that they should have obtained only 425 lb of bread from so much grain.

77. StAM, 40a XXIV Generalia 2: "Anschlag uff 500 Person zu Heyna undt Merxhausen, Pauperibus" (n.d.); for the date of this estimate, see StAM, S60 F: "Salbuch Hessische Hospitäler 1575: Anschlag uff 500 personen."

TABLE 7.6

Estimates of Food for 500 Poor Persons at Haina and Merxhausen, 1575

Food Categories	grams/person/day		calories/day
Meat (6 courses @ 3 lb. for 10 persons weekly)	124	@ 2.73 cal./g. =	339
Fish (4 courses @ 3 lb. for 10 persons weekly)	83	@ 1.75 cal./g. =	145
Cheese (4 courses @ 3 lb. for 10 persons weekly)	28	@ 4.25 cal./g. =	119
Fats	28	@ 7.93 cal./g. =	222
Bread (4 *Vtl.*/day = 1,000 lb. rye for 500 persons)	964	@ 2.40 cal./g. =	2,314
Other grains and vegetables*	69	@ 3.40 cal./g. =	235
Beer (8 *Maß* for 10 persons)	1.6 l.	@ 2.00 cal./cl. =	320
Average estimated daily calories/person		=	3,694

SOURCE: StAM, 40a XXIV Generalia 2: "Anschlag uff 500 Person zu Heyna undt Merxhausen, Pauperibus" (n.d.).
NOTE: *Vtl.* = *Viertel* (quarter), or 250 lb; *Maß* = measure, about 2 liters.
*peas, oatmeal, barley, millet

It was not easy to regulate the fleshpots of Haina. When a survey of food consumption was again conducted in 1591, examining the year 1590, the average intake was still 5,161 calories a day at Haina and 3,994 at Merxhausen (table 7.7).[78] Eggs, oatmeal, and honey were somewhat more abundant, but meat, cheese, milk, and beer were somewhat less so. The hospitals now diverged even more sharply than they had sixteen years earlier.

We know that the landgraves continued to be concerned about Haina's reputation for gormandizing, especially among the officials and servants of the hospital. When Landgrave Ludwig the Elder wrote to Landgrave Moritz in 1602 about the mounting fiscal problems of the hospitals, he charged that Haina had many unnecessary expenses, including the costs of horses and servants, "to say nothing of the great gluttony of the seventeen persons who work the fields, as well as all sorts of artisans."[79]

What made the good life in the hospital especially embarrassing was the fact that the late sixteenth century was a period of mounting poverty and occasional famine. Starting in the 1570s, "hunger crises" broke out in many parts of the Holy Roman Empire, and they became a periodic feature of the two centuries before the Industrial Revolution.[80] It is no wonder that the Hessian landgraves repeatedly suspected that able-bodied persons were malingering in order to gain access to the fat life at Haina.

78. StAM, 40a XXIV Generalia 2: "Ahnschlag was uff die arme leuth zue Merxhausen in verschienen 90 Jahr, an allerhandt gangen," and "Ahnschlag wass uff die Arme Leuth zu Heyna in verschienen 90 Jahr an allerhandt Victualien gangen." Hospitals elsewhere also served huge amounts of food. See, e.g., Helmut Freiherr Haller von Hallerstein and Ernst Eichhorn, *Das Pilgrimspital zum Heiligen Kreuz vor Nürnberg* (Nuremberg, 1969), pp. 44–50.
79. StAM, 40a XXIV Generalia 2: Landgraf Ludwig der Eltere to Moritz, May 31, 1602.
80. Wilhelm Abel, *Massenarmut und Hungerkrisen im vorindustriellen Deutschland*, 2d ed. (Göttingen, 1977).

TABLE 7.7

Daily Food Consumption at Haina and Merxhausen, 1590

Food Categories	Haina	Merxhausen
Grains		
Rye bread[a]	1,282g.	916 g.
@100 g. = 240 cal.	(3,077 cal.)	(2,198 cal.)
Other grains	257 g.	235 g.
@100 g. = 340 cal.	(874 cal.)	(799 cal.)
Beer[b]	1,600 ml.	1,140 ml.
@100 ml. = 20 cal.	(320 cal.)	(228 cal.)
Meat		
fresh	66 g.	145 g.
@100 g. = 273 cal.	(180 cal.)	(123 cal.)
dry beef	18 g.	24 g.
@100 g. = 400 cal.	(72 cal.)	(96 cal.)
wethers		2 g.
@100 g. = 273 cal.		(5 cal.)
bacon	21 g.	6 g.
@100 g. = 520 cal.	(109 cal.)	(31 cal.)
sausage		
@200 cal./sausage	(2 cal.)	(2 cal.)
Butter & fats	20 g.	18 g.
@100 g. = 793 cal.	(159 cal.)	(143 cal.)
Lard	3 g.	3 g.
@100 g. = 793 cal.	(24 cal.)	(24 cal.)
Milk	139 ml.	103 ml.
@100 ml. = 66 cal.	(92 cal.)	(68 cal.)
Cheese	43 g.	48 g.
@100 g. = 425 cal.	(183 cal.)	(204 cal.)
Fish	24 g.	31 g.
@100 g. = 175 cal.	(42 cal.)	(54 cal.)
Eggs	.123 egg	.124 egg
@1 egg = 60 cal.	(7 cal.)	(7 cal.)
Honey	5 g.	3 g.
@100 g. = 400 cal.	(20 cal.)	(12 cal.)
Average calories per person per day	5,161 cal.	3,994 cal.

SOURCES: StAM, 40a XXIV Generalia 2: "Ahnschlag was uff die arme leuth zue Merxhausen in verschienen 90 Jahr, an allerhandt gangen," and "Ahnschlag wass uff die Arme Leuth zu Heyna in verschienen 90 Jahr an allerhandt Victualien gangen."

[a] Adjusted for payments to day laborers
[b] Diätbier (a light beer, fairly low in alcohol)

TABLE 7.8
Recommended Diet at Haina, 1620–1621

	Hospital Classes				
	I	II	III	IV	V
Meat	463 g.	231 g.	159 g.	72 g.	72 g.
@100 g. = 273 cal.	1,264 cal.	631 cal.	434 cal.	197 cal.	197 cal.
Fish	135 g.	57 g.	0	34 g.	34 g.
@100 g. = 175 cal.	236 cal.	100 cal.	0	60 cal.	60 cal.
Cheese	51 g.	13 g.	19 g.	82 g.	31 g.
@100 g. = 425 cal.	217 cal.	55 cal.	81 cal.	349 cal.	132 cal.
Fats	28.4 g.	28.4 g.	28.4 g.	28.4 g.	28.4 g.
@100 g. = 793 cal	225 cal.	225 cal.	225 cal.	225 cal.	225 cal.
Bread	723 g.	482 g.	˙511 g.	1,393 g.	858 g.
@100 g. = 240 cal.	1,735 cal.	1,157 cal.	1,226 cal.	3,343 cal.	2,059 cal.
Other Grains	93 g.	93 g.	93 g.	93 g.	93 g.
@100 g. = 340 cal.	316 cal.	316 cal.	316 cal.	316 cal.	316 cal.
Beer	2,337 ml.	2,337 ml.	2,337 ml.	2,337 ml.	2,337 ml.
@100 ml. = 31 cal.	724 cal.	724 cal.	724 cal.	724 cal.	724 cal.
Wine	55 ml.	26 ml.	26 ml.	26 ml.	26 ml.
@100 ml. = 53 cal.	29 cal.	14 cal.	14 cal.	14 cal.	14 cal.
Total cal./day	4,746 cal.	3,222 cal.	3,020 cal.	5,228 cal.	3,727 cal.

Key: Class I   Officials
Class II   Officials' Servants
Class III   Prebendaries
Class IV   Hospital Servants
Class V   Poor Brethren and Sisters

A report filed in 1621 fills out our impression of living conditions during the first century of the Hessian hospitals (table 7.8). Examining the consumption of food and drink at Haina in 1620, the report proves that an elaborate five-class system had developed. Taking account of the changed situation, the hospital administration promulgated a "New Dining Ordinance for Haina" on March 16, 1621, a regulation that departed from the original ideal of equality and now declared that the hospital officials should eat at a table where the food was much more luxurious and where wine was regularly served, instead of being reserved just for the six annual church holidays.[81] These men of the elite were granted one pound of meat daily. Their clerks and maids constituted a second class, sitting at a separate table and enjoying a diet much lower in calories, but still very high in meat and fish, with half a pound of meat daily. A third class of *Pröbner* (prebendaries) comprised 24 persons, also known as *Umspeiser* (special diners). They seem to have included 10 special servants and 14 actual

81. The only other persons to receive wine daily were the "sick," who were usually assumed to be at death's door.

"prebendaries," who had been granted entry to the hospital despite their elevated social station, persons for whom the hospitals had never been intended: a schoolmaster, a doctor's widow and child, and educated men with latinate names ("Hartman Scaevola" and "M. Agricola"). They received decidedly more meat than the bottom two classes, averaging one-third of a pound a day. The fourth class comprised 49 hospital servants (including 20 poor brothers and sisters). Their daily work must have been arduous, and in return they received over 5,000 calories daily; but since their social status was poor, they obtained an average of only one pound of meat a week and made up for this meager allotment with cheese and huge amounts of bread.[82] At the bottom of the five classes were 220 poor persons, who ate less than the servants because they were usually elderly and not hired for hard work.

From surviving records, we cannot tell when this classification began, but up to the 1590s, the records do not even hint at a class of *Pröbner*, even though some Hessian officials and pastors had been granted retirement in the hospital as a reward for faithful service.[83] In allowing such a visible and officially sanctioned class system to develop, hospital officials were accommodating social needs never imagined by Philipp of Hesse. Established with a monastic ideal, they fell into a pattern that strangely echoed the abuses of late medieval monasticism. By allowing large numbers of married couples and middle- to upper-class persons to retire to the hospital, they took an important step away from the monastic hospital ideals of poverty, chastity, and equality. As already noted, there had been a complaint in 1627 that large numbers of married residents were claiming privileged places above the poor, unmarried men (p. 338 above). By endorsing this class system in the 1621 Eating Ordinance, officials were admitting that the older ideal of equality was dead. And when the poor were finally restrained from the "gluttony" that characterized the sixteenth century, it was not so much a victory for modesty as a defeat for the ideal of Christian community. This shift also symbolically marks the way in which sixteenth-century humanist goals based on merit often, and not just in German hospitals, gave way to the explicit systems of social privilege of the ancien régime.[84]

82. Recall that all of these figures make no allowance for possible wastage and therefore probably overestimate the amounts of food actually eaten.

83. Franz, *Urkundliche Quellen*, 3: 897.

84. George Huppert, *After the Black Death: A Social History of Early Modern Europe* (Bloomington, Ind., 1986); for this general argument, cf. James V. Skalnik, "Ramus and Reform: The End of the Renaissance and the Origins of the Old Regime in France" (diss., University of Virginia, 1990).

STRAINING FOR A MORAL ORDER

The food consumed at Haina and Merxhausen guaranteed a higher standard of living for these sixteenth-century "welfare recipients" than many working families enjoyed. This fact made hospital officials touchy or even defensive when it came to explaining the existence of the hospital. The obligation to be (and to appear) worthy of charity put residents of the hospitals under a code of behavior much stricter than that imposed on persons living normal lives.

Before one can estimate how hard the hospital tried to meet a higher moral standard than that imposed on the world, one needs to know what standard was imposed upon the world. Fortunately for us, the Haina Hospital Archive has preserved an ordinance issued by Landgrave Philipp for the common inhabitants of Haina and the neighboring lands subject to the jurisdiction of the hospital. The very first clause shows that religious rules played a large role in the outside world as well as in the hospital:

First, God's Word and teaching should be held up before everyone's eyes . . . and all those who are of another faith and doctrine than that taught in the principality of Hesse are not to be tolerated; instead they are to be notorious like those involved in magic, witchcraft, and other works of the devil; and after being publicly rebuked, they may be punished according to the seriousness of their offense.[85]

The people living near Haina were warned that they must not swear by God's wounds, His mother, or His sacraments; the penalties could be severe even for those who tolerated such swearing in others. Those caught working on a Sunday or holiday might have to pay up to two gulden as penalty. During church services, each householder was to see to it that his servants and family attended the service and did not stay at home "practicing knavery and villainy." Infractions were punished at a rate of five shillings for the householder, while servants were to be jailed.

Those notorious for adultery or other immorality were to pay up to ten gulden. Whoring and common fornication were offenses leading to a ten-gulden fine for the householder who tolerated such vices, a two-gulden fine for a male servant, and a one-gulden fine for a maidservant.

Far more serious were fraudulent contracts with the hospital. Anyone cheating the hospital could be fined up to twenty gulden. Abusing the weights and measures could result in a fine of fifty gulden and corporal punishment.

Petty offenses against one's neighbor or against the hospital generally

85. HHA, "Des Hohen Hospitals Policey Ordnung," in a volume of "Hospitals-Ordnungen und Vergleiche," a book of 139 pp. copied in an eighteenth-century hand, pp. 57–93.

cost from six alber (i.e., $1/4$ gulden) to five gulden. No man or woman, for example, could slander another "with immoral, gross words or with any kind of libel or insult" without running the risk of a one-gulden fine.

During a fire, all must help in fighting it or pay a ten-gulden fine. Failure to attend a village court or assembly meeting might trigger a fine of one gulden. Dances of certain sorts were forbidden: "Sunday dancing and other suspect evening dances are herewith completely forbidden; and if this is disobeyed, the men shall pay a fine of one gulden and the woman a fine of thirteen alber."[86]

Such ordinances obviously tried to set a general standard of Christian conduct and communal responsibility, but it is noteworthy that the punishments for false measures, adultery, and fornication were far less severe than those imposed by the imperial criminal code, the *Carolina*.[87]

Although this set of village regulations tried to establish the Christian community as an ideal, there can be little doubt that the hospital, with its regular daily religious observances, strained to maintain a higher moral order. A prayer used at Merxhausen asked God for help in obeying the hospital officials, "and let us not misuse these alms in laziness, lechery, or in other scandalous vices resulting in our eternal damnation."[88] The original ordinance of 1534 read: "And because alms should be given mainly to Christians in need, it is Christian, reasonable, and necessary that the poor who are to be cared for in the hospital shall live in Christian order and maintain a fine and honorable way of life."[89]

Applicants to the hospital emphasized their religious character and their readiness to live "as befits Christian brethren."[90] The preacher at Haina was to urge the poor to hear God's Word not only at the regular services but at special services as well and to inculcate an attitude of constant (*ohn unterlass*) prayer and thankfulness.[91] The hospital seems to have instituted a regular half-hour evening prayer service to balance the one in the morning. The original ordinance of the hospital (1534) required only one sermon a day and stated simply, "after supper and the prayer of thanks, let them rest and have them go to bed at a set time."[92] Already in the undated "Hospitals-Fundation," this thanksgiving was explicitly described as a church ser-

86. Ibid., articles 1, 2, 3, 4, 5, 6, 7, 12, 38, 40, 45, 46.

87. Gustav Radbruch, ed., *Die peinliche Gerichtsordnung Kaiser Karls V. von 1532 (Carolina)* (Stuttgart, 1962), articles 113, 120–23.

88. StAM, 40a XXIV Generalia 2: "Hospitals Fundation" (an undated document of ten fols. intended primarily for Merxhausen), "Ein Gebet," fols. 5v–7r.

89. Franz, *Urkundliche Quellen*, 2: 190.

90. HHA, RR, see, e.g., the cases of Ciriax Fischer (Mar. 19, 1564), Valtin Niphudt (Nov. 8, 1587), Henn Cleinhens (n.d.), Hans Schneider (Wednesday after Invocavit, 1562), Klaus Fischer (Aug. 30, 1581).

91. StAM, 40a XXIV Generalia 2: Schenck, "Haina Amts-Diener Ordnung, 1573."

92. Franz, *Urkundliche Quellen*, 2: 195, 192.

vice set for 6:00 P.M. in the summer, and directly after supper in the large common room during the winter; the prayers were to include special thanks to the territorial prince for his benevolence. And in 1573, Schenck's ordinance described this evening service as a half-hour service with Bible reading and preaching as well as prayers of thanks.[93] Perhaps this was merely a case of ordinary practice becoming more and more explicit in the records, but it seems to indicate an intensified religious life for residents of the hospital, with two services on normal weekdays in addition to special holiday services, the two Sunday sermons, and the extra services on Wednesday and Friday mentioned by Letzener in 1588.

The privileged life of semimonasticism also demanded a higher standard of social behavior. This is why residents of the hospital were not allowed to leave the institution to visit nearby villages. The rule was just as hard to enforce as it had been in the days when Haina was a monastery. In 1573, the superintendent, Reinhard Schenck zu Schweinsberg, observed that some of the brethren at Haina were "involved in all kinds of crafts, commerce, and trading, even on Sundays; and they go out weekly to the villages and attend church fairs and weddings, where they obtain wine and beer and pass the time in drunkenness, immorality [fornication], and wantonness; all of which mightily enrages God at the misuse of alms and gives the fine institution a bad name."[94] To correct this dangerous breach of the rules, the men were threatened with sharp punishments (including jail), and the gatekeeper was not to allow any brother to go out without a special pass, or else he might land in jail as well.

The discrepancy between the good life at Haina and hard times in the countryside, together with the observed failure of hospital residents to live up to the high spiritual standards set for them, may have provoked resentment. This would explain the surprising degree of defensiveness about the value of charity that one observes among pastors and hospital officials in the late sixteenth century. Schenck's 1573 ordinance concluded with the thought that the poor (including the mad) were Christ's representatives on earth. When one neglected them, one neglected one's own salvation. It is surprising that he thought it necessary to say so. Moreover, Johann Letzener devoted the eighteenth chapter of his description of Haina to defending the virtue of charity and attacking those who ridiculed the care of the poor or did not take their responsibilities to the poor seriously. After rehearsing the history of Christian views of charity from biblical writers down to St. Elizabeth of Hungary (and of Hesse), with Socrates thrown in

93. StAM, 40a XXIV Generalia 2: "Hospitals Fundation," and Schenck, "Haina Amts-Diener Ordnung, 1573." Letzener, *Historische . . . Beschreibung*, ch. 16, confirms the existence of a regular evening service in the late sixteenth century.

94. Schenck, "Haina Amts-Diener Ordnung, 1573."

for good measure, Letzener expounded St. Basil's fifth sermon on Ps. 14: "Everything given to the poor is received as an interest-bearing loan by God. And who would not gladly have God as one's debtor?" Taking a cue from St. John Chrysostom's third sermon on Gen. 1, he expanded on this idea: "Whoever receives the poor sets up a loan to God. One party takes the money and uses it. But Another, namely, God, stands as surety and pays a high interest rate, and has moreover promised to repay the principal one hundredfold."[95]

These sentiments represent a venerable Christian tradition of mercy, and doubtless they made an elegant reason for charitable giving, but they sounded very odd in the mouth of a Lutheran clergyman, who in theory rejected works righteousness and ought to have been appalled at the idea that man could have any claim on God. It may be that by preserving the charitable character of Haina and Merxhausen as monastic institutions, these Hessian Lutherans also retained a basically Catholic and monastic attitude toward charity and alms. If so, it was natural that the hospitals also inherited the anticlericalism that had once focused on privileged, leisured monks.[96] This may help explain why hospital administrators and spokesmen constantly defended the communal virtues of caring for the poor and the infirm.

Hospital officials learned to rely on more than the exhortations of the pastor to cope with disorderly residents. In the years after their founding, the Hessian hospitals developed a list of moral regulations with a sliding scale of punishments. The earliest version of such a list of infractions is in the undated, but doubtless early, hospital ordinances for Haina and Merxhausen entitled "Hospitals-Fundation."[97] Here we find frequent mention of punishments for refusal to work; for arguing; for fighting; for carrying bread or beer back to one's room; for cooking one's own food; for making unauthorized things and for selling them; for disobeying an official; for failure to care properly for the sick; for going out walking without permission; for unauthorized loitering or trespassing in the kitchen, cellars, brewery, bakery, laundry, or weaving house; for failure to attend funerals and other special meetings. The women at Merxhausen were especially warned to "maintain modesty and chastity and to avoid all evil society with men both in words and deeds; and anyone discovered in immorality shall be removed from the hospital." As a general rule, the punishments ranged from losing out on a meal to being locked in jail or in the "hole" (*loch*) with only beer and bread to eat. The incorrigible and those who incited others to

95. Letzener, *Historische . . . Beschreibung*, fols. L4v–N1r.
96. See esp. the excellent analysis of Stalnaker, "Emergence of the Protestant Clergy."
97. StAM, 40a XXIV Generalia 2: "Hospitals Fundation" (although undated, the document was clearly composed before 1567).

break the rules were to be dismissed from the hospital.[98] Most of these infractions were construed as breaches of fellowship and community. Failure to accept the religious ground rules of the hospital also led to punishment. If one skipped morning prayers and sermons, for example, one had to miss a meal. If one refused to learn the catechism, one was supposed to be confined in the jail. Stubborn refusal to learn could lead to expulsion, but officials were told to grant newcomers time off from their labors so that they could learn what was expected. Anyone arriving for a meal after prayers had to miss out on the meal unless he had a good excuse. During mealtime, when the Bible or catechism was being read, residents were to be silent. Those who "carried on with their gossip" could be removed from the dining room. Blasphemy was to be punished with whipping for the first offense and expulsion for the second.

Such a list of infractions was not drawn up a priori but was based on close experience with the sometimes unruly old peasants who resided in the hospitals. The rules and regulations underwent little modification during the rest of the sixteenth century. Schenck's 1573 Ordinance made a few additions—for example, urging understanding of the problems that the elderly and feebleminded had in learning their catechisms. The hospital treasurer was told to punish the rebellious and to allow no drunkenness or noisy carousing. The wine steward could help by controlling the wine, thus preventing the men from collecting enough to have drunken parties back in their rooms. It was Schenck who called special attention, we may recall, to the failure of some residents to curb their commercial instincts or their public thirst. From Schenck's Ordinance, one also learns that the hospitals continued to have a problem with guests. In contrast to the earlier ordinances, Schenck declared that these institutions were not hotels but hospitals for the poor. Strangers passing by, therefore, were not to be received by the hospital except on the order of princely councilors or officials, and then only for one meal.[99] By the late sixteenth century, Letzener reports, a sign had been placed at the gate stating that the hospital was no longer a monastery offering lodging.[100] Thus it took over forty years for the monastic ideal of hospitality to disappear as an explicit ideal of the Hessian hospitals. The basic reason for its disappearance, moreover, was that it conflicted with an equally venerable monastic (and hospital) ideal of the Christian community, separated from the world, and using its time for what monks had called *ora et labora*.

The Lutheran Reformation in Hesse did not, therefore, radically or instantly transform all of its monastic institutions and habits of thought.

98. Ibid., fols. 4r–5r, 7v–9r.
99. Schenck, "Haina Amts-Diener Ordnung, 1573."
100. Letzener, *Historische . . . Beschreibung*, ch. 17.

Many Catholic features survived for decades. The Protestant Church recruited most of its early clergy from among the Catholic clergy, and Lutheran reformers continued to hold services in churches that looked Catholic. It took close to a century of propaganda and argument before Protestants and Catholics discovered that they might actually disagree on almost every issue. The Reformation hospitals of Hesse stand as a reminder of this long period of continuity. Although offering no heavenly rewards for entering, they did claim to promote a religious life dependent on the alms of pious Hessians. In a real sense, these "Protestant monasteries" reformulated the Benedictine requirements of poverty, obedience, and chastity, and when, after a century, they fell on evil days, even their corruptions resembled the corruptions of the monasteries from which they had sprung.

MADNESS AND THE RESIDENTS OF HAINA

Although Haina became famous in the nineteenth century as a mental hospital, in its origins it had no such specialization. The hospital received the poor mad as it received the poor blind, the poor crippled, and the poor aged.[101] In fact, on the basis of Letzener's account, scholars have concluded that during the sixteenth century, the mad constituted only a tiny proportion of the residents of Haina. After all, there were only nine mentally ill men chained in the vault and only eighteen cages with fifteen inmates and two custodians in 1575, a year when the total number of brethren was close to three hundred.[102] To assume that as few as 8 percent of the hospital's residents were mentally ill, however, is to forget that the vault and cages were intended only for wild and dangerous persons. Many other mentally disabled persons qualified for admission to the hospital because they were unable to support themselves, without necessarily needing to be bound in chains.

To determine how many mentally ill persons there were at Haina, one would need full descriptions of the various patients, inmates, and residents in the hospital, and generally such sources do not exist for the sixteenth century. As is common with many institutions, we are far better informed about the hospital's finances than about its residents. For Haina and Merxhausen, however, recently discovered bundles of "reception rescripts" enable us to draw a crude profile of the hospital population in the second half of the sixteenth century. These sources become so voluminous for the eighteenth century that they merit separate investigation.[103] Here we shall concentrate on the sixteenth and early seventeenth centuries.

101. This was typical. See Jetter, *Zur Typologie des Irrenhauses.*
102. StAM, S60 G: Salbuch, "Verzeichnis der personen so zur zeitt im Spittal Heine sint, 16 July 1575."
103. I found one package of sixteenth-century reception rescripts in the (uncataloged)

These fading and sometimes crumbling documents reveal more about the concrete human needs served by the Hessian hospitals than any official ordinance or visitor's report can.[104] Here we find the "honest, pious, and Christian" Ciriax Fischer, for example, who petitioned for entry to the hospital at Haina in 1564 because he was eighty years old and physically disabled.[105] And we can read of the three-year-old daughter of Merkell Peters of Lölbach, then deceased, whose widowed mother was too poor to care for her toddler, who was ordered admitted to Merxhausen in 1580, to be raised there until she was old enough to find work.[106] Consider the plight of Hans Orper, a poor old man who fell from his roof while trying to mend it and broke an arm and a leg, so that in 1592, he had to walk with crutches.[107] In a document so torn that the date and addressee are missing, Clauss Spielingk sought help for his two crippled children, whose hands and feet were so disfigured "that they are useless in the world and can do nothing." Their father had remarried in order to give them a mother, but she was now unwilling to care for them, "as any reasonable person will understand, and now their daily presence may cause more misfortune." He offered to pay twenty gulden if the hospital (at Merxhausen, most likely) would receive them.[108] These documents reveal, too, why the original rules were bent or modified. In an undated sixteenth-century appeal, Henn Cleinhens claimed that he had been a resident of Haina for ten years, but

---

Haina Hospitalsarchiv (cited as HHA), and an inquiry led to the discovery of a cellar room ("Klammer") full of such documents. No register of them seems to exist, but they constitute an exceedingly valuable source, especially for the study of eighteenth-century madness.

104. One can legitimately ask how representative this group of 183 cases is. They are not, of course, a sample in the statistical sense at all, but merely the documents that have survived. Still, it may be helpful to compute the percentage they represent of the probable total number of poor in Haina and Merxhausen. Between 1550 and 1591, Haina had an average of 308 residents, and Merxhausen of 274 residents. If one assumes that 80% of these were poor brethren and sisters, we arrive at annual averages of 246 for Haina and 219 for Merxhausen. If one further assumes that these averages held good for the years 1591 to 1622, and an average of ten years in the hospital per person (so that the period 1550–1622 represents 7.2 cohorts of ten years each), then the period 1550 to 1622 saw ca. 7.2 x 246 = 1,771 poor persons in Haina, and 7.2 x 219 = 1,577 poor persons in Merxhausen. This would imply in turn that our documents give us access to information on ca. 8.3% of all the brethren at Haina in 1550–1622 but on only ca. 2.3% of all the sisters at Merxhausen. In the best decades, our probable percentage of retrieval rises to 19.1% for 1561–70 at Haina and 10.5% for 1611–22 at Merxhausen. In other words, even in the best documented decades, probably four-fifths of all cases at Haina and nine-tenths of all cases at Merxhausen have escaped our investigation. As usual, the historian can only carefully study what survives and cultivate the cardinal virtues of faith and hope.

105. HHA, RR, Johann Engelhard and Thomas Moller to Reinhard Schenck, Mar. 19, 1564.

106. HHA, RR, Landgraf Ludwig to Johann Clauer, Sept. 9, 1580.

107. HHA, RR, Landgraf Moritz to Johann Clauer, Dec. 14, 1592.

108. HHA, RR, Clauss Spielingk to unidentifiable landgrave, n.d., witnessed by a pastor and four others.

that he had been expelled after getting dead drunk at Treisa (about twelve miles from Haina). Now he was repentant and vowed to sin no more if only he could be readmitted, for he would surely starve to death outside the hospital.[109] His appeal was accepted. In another exception to the original rules, Anna, the wife of Hans Ammenheusser, asked to join her husband, who was already in Haina, for she was now so old, lame, and poor that she could earn nothing. Instead of remanding her to Merxhausen, Landgrave Ludwig ordered her to join her husband in Haina.[110] Similar appeals describe the desperate circumstances of orphans, epileptics, lepers, the physically deformed, the blind, deaf, and dumb. Several petitioners remarked that recent years had become especially difficult because of the "frightful" rise in prices.[111] Others revealed that the hospital was still regarded as a kind of monastery when they asked to be admitted to the "Gotteshaus" or "Closter" at Haina.[112]

These petitions also form an unparalleled source for the study of mental disorders among the poor, a group who usually escape the view of even the most diligent researcher. Along with the miracle reports that we examined in chapter 6, these petitions put us as close as we are ever likely to get to the sixteenth-century experience of madness. Of the 183 persons for whom a hospital petition survives, 39 were retarded, brain-damaged, or mentally disordered. In some cases, the petition simply remarks, as with Catrin Koch in 1577, that she was now "thoroughly and completely bereft of her senses and reason, and there is no hope of improvement."[113] Another document describes a "crazy and mute" girl admitted to Merxhausen in 1612, but gives us no further details.[114]

If one tries to construct rough categories for these afflicted people, one confronts the often impenetrably vague language of these sixteenth-century documents. We have seen that the academically trained physician of four hundred years ago could regularly distinguish mental retardation, brain damage, senility, and epilepsy from melancholia, mania, and phrenitis. But the authors of these hospital documents had no interest in medical diagnosis; their only intention was to demonstrate that a person needed

109. HHA, RR, Henn Cleinhens to an unidentifiable landgrave, n. d.
110. HHA, RR, Landgraf Ludwig to Johann Clauer, Mar. 6, 1596.
111. HHA, RR, Werner Brosten to Landgraf Philipp, Mar. 6, 1564; Peter Cemmer to an unidentifiable landgrave, n.d.; Anna, Otilia, Barbara, and Elle Mauschnud to Landgraf Philipp, Tuesday after Simon and Jude, 1560.
112. HHA, RR, "Closter zum Haina" in Peter Cemmer to unidentifiable landgrave, n.d.; "Kloster Haina" in Wilhelm von Holtzfeldt to Reinhard Schenck, 1561; "Gotteshauss oder Spittall gehn Heinaw" in Landgraf Ludwig to Johann Clauer, June 4, 1580; "das Gotteshaus zum Heynich" in Adam Bingel to Landgraf Wilhelm, n.d. (1577).
113. HHA, RR, Landgraf Wilhelm to Johann Clauer, Apr. 30, 1577.
114. HHA, RR, Landgraf Moritz to Georg Milchlingen, June 26, 1612.

TABLE 7.9

Frequency of Brain Damage, Retardation, and Mental Illness
Among Applicants to Haina and Merxhausen

Probable Classification	Number of Cases
Retarded or brain damaged at birth	11
Brain damaged in accident	2
Mentally ill, "mad"	16
Senile	1
"Foolishness" produced by epilepsy	1
Indistinct cases	8
Total	39

care, and no professional diagnosis was necessary for that. Unlike jurists, who were increasingly drawn into consulting physicians in order to distinguish melancholia from furor, the Hessian hospitals saw no need for medical language. The bureaucratic language they used was still close to those German vernacular categories regularly used by pilgrims and other ordinary people. Therefore, in several cases, petitioners referred to worthy applicants as "bereft of reason," "senseless," "silly," or "nonsensical." If such a person was a child, we might conclude that he or she was mentally retarded, but we cannot always be sure. When the person was aged, forgetful, and "crazy," we might today think of senile dementia, but this is little better than a guessing game. I have constructed table 7.9 based on such guesswork, however, staying close to the language of these documents.

Although many of these classifications are rough, several of the individual cases cast a bright light into some dark corners of social behavior. Take the case of Steffan Mauschnud, whose four daughters pleaded with Landgrave Philipp late in 1560 to take their father into Haina. He had entered Haina originally as a brother early in 1560, but after fighting there, he had been expelled. His four daughters were trying to care for him, but he fought and argued with them too, demanding food and drink "at all times" and flying into rages, in which he "strikes and tries to strangle us." In this "staggeringly expensive time," the daughters added, they could not afford to keep him. To strengthen their petition they reminded the Landgrave that God would surely reward his charity if he would readmit their father.

Look at another example. On July 18, 1587, a widow asked Landgrave Wilhelm to take pity on her. When her husband died three years earlier, she had been left with six small children, one of whom was "bereft of his senses." He was now fifteen and "so lacking in reason that he is a great domestic affliction and a heavy burden." If pious neighbors had not taken care of him, he would already have drowned or fallen into the fire. And now with prices so high, she could not earn enough to support him. The boy was ordered admitted to Haina on October 10, 1587.

These cases demonstrate that family members and neighbors were expected to care for their own problems and were to seek aid from the territorial prince only when a person became unmanageable. This was clearly the case with Heinrich Senger of Homberg, who fell into a more and more serious madness. The local pastor, Caspar Arcularius, explained that "some years ago Senger had behaved strangely both in words and in deeds, as if he was a madman." The neighbors had tried to practice "Christian love, patience, and sympathy" in tolerating him, but matters had only grown worse. Now in 1593, his reason and human understanding were totally deranged, and he was more than his wife could handle, "who up to now has cared for him not only with great trouble and effort, but also at the risk of life and limb." The neighborhood could "no longer stand to see this miserable specimen, nor could they trust this irrational and senseless person, who might at any hour or moment either kill himself (as he doubtless would have long ago if his wife and neighbors had not kept watch over him) or wound others by hitting, stabbing, burning, etc., and thus produce irreparable damage." Arcularius concluded that Senger must be admitted to Haina, "in order that greater misfortune be avoided and that the poor man be helped." The pastor added, routinely, that God would richly reward such charity "both here on earth and also eternally, in body and soul." Senger was admitted to the stout cells of Haina.

In 1581, a widow burdened with four deformed, retarded, mute children petitioned for relief, saying that their monstrous form and foolish behavior made them useless for work and incapable of learning. Landgrave Wilhelm noted that he had seen these sorry creatures himself and ordered that two of the four should be taken from her and sent to Haina.

Another example of gradually strained neighborhood tolerance was the case of Daniel Hoffmann of Stauffenberg. In his case, the burghermaster and council of Stauffenberg wrote in March 1590 to the captain of Giessen, Rudolf Wilhelm Raw, about six miles away, to inform him that Hoffmann was acting as if possessed. He had been found in his barn with a loaded gun and a handful of flax tow (used for starting fires) under his coat. On other occasions, he had thrown knives and other weapons at his wife and children and had tried to stab them; he had also beaten his wife with his fists and had tried to strangle her. The officials of Stauffenberg commanded him to be restrained in a "blockhouse" or with chains until a more permanent solution could be found. Two weeks later, Hoffmann was confined at Haina, where he would have to stay "until God might send him some improvement."

In 1596, a father in Schmalkalden appealed to Landgrave Moritz on behalf of his son. For three years, the boy had been a singer in church and school, but now he was so "disabled and crazy" that he "cannot well be tolerated here because of the danger." He should be admitted to Haina "until he improves." The superintendent, Johann Clauer, agreed and ordered the boy confined "until Almighty God sends him some improvement."

In mid July 1587, Barba, wife of Jost Bucking from Alsfeld, appealed for the confinement of her husband because he was bereft of his senses. The treasurer of Alsfeld confirmed that Bucking had been mad for four years, when he had begun irritating several citizens with "unnecessary wrangling and hatred, which no one had previously noticed in him since he had been zealous in obeying the church and God's Word' and had always seemed reasonable and beyond reproach." But complaints about him began to pile up:

He began to fantasize, and from day to day got so much worse that at last he went completely out of his mind and in the past had to be kept in chains at great expense and danger. Several times he worked himself free from them, and if dear God had not especially prevented it, he would have done horrible damage with fire or murder.

Bucking had been a wool weaver and had eight children, some of them still small. Although he had been "rather lively" while able to work, ever since he had been chained and bereft of work, he had seemed "all used up." In an earlier letter, Bucking's wife stated that her husband used to beat her whenever he was displeased; and he was wont to go into the barn and stables with fire, clearly endangering not only her but the children and neighbors. Ever since he had been chained, however, they had all been reduced to poverty. He tore all his clothes and any bedding given to him, and there seemed no hope that he would, without God's special mercy, ever recover his reason. On August 29, he was remanded to Haina.

In 1579, the neighbors of Widow Aldehens complained that they were being strained beyond endurance. The widow "had become completely mentally disabled in the past year, and we had to care for her for a time." But then God sent her some improvement, and the local community had hoped that they were free of a great burden. Now she had become much worse again, "and is once again completely disabled and senseless, and she smears herself with excrement so disgustingly and so horribly that no one really wants or dares to stay with her." So the neighbor women made a special chest for her where they kept her day and night. This expedient was expensive, however, and the petitioners claimed that they had neither the incomes nor the husbands to keep up this system much longer. Widow Aldehens was sent to Merxhausen with her children, where she was supposed to stay until God sent some improvement.

A number of things are striking in these cases of madness and mental disorder. First, the petitioners and the Hessian officials often assumed that improvement of mental condition was possible, although in every case the possibility of cure was ascribed to God alone. The hospital did not initiate any special program of therapy. Second, as with the mad pilgrims of the previous chapter, there are surprisingly few instances in which a mad person was thought to be demonically possessed. In these documents, only Daniel Hoffmann came close, and no one seems to have treated him differently just because he acted "as if possessed." It is possible that this almost total lack of concern about demonic possession was a result of Protestant skepticism about possession and exorcism, but as we saw in chapter 1, sixteenth-century Lutherans generally accepted the reality of demonic possession. Perhaps belief in possession had never caught on amongst the Hessians. We do know that in 1575, Landgrave Ludwig advised that a woman considered possessed was "more likely suffering from weakness in her head and silly melancholy thoughts" and urged that she be cared for and comforted with God's Word, "so that she may be discreetly diverted from such heavy thoughts." Here, as elsewhere, demonic possession seems to have functioned as a vivid image to describe depressed thoughts and suicidal temptations. The landgrave had also heard that a certain exorcist named Homberger, from Weidenhausen, had made bold to drive out the evil spirit from her. The landgrave sharply commanded that any such efforts be severely punished; and two Marburg preachers were to talk to Homberger and warn him to give up his own "phantasei."[115]

A third noteworthy fact about all of the 39 cases of mental disability in these Hessian hospital records is that the local community was obviously supposed to exhaust its resources before turning to the territorial administration. Even when spouse and neighbors had been driven to despair with their problem, however, they did not apparently attack, punish, ridicule, or demean the afflicted person, or at least did not openly admit such abuse, if it occurred. They chained or confined the wildly disordered, but only as a last resort and to prevent self-inflicted injury as well as harm to others. There is no evidence that neighbors revered, respected, or were in awe of lunatics and the feebleminded as if they were holy fools or mystical prophets, but the local community was legally required to practice Christian patience and charity.

These case histories are one way of seeing the Haina and Merxhausen hospitals at work. A more general view may be obtained from some elementary statistics, extracted from the surviving reception rescripts. In table

115. The episode is described in Hugo Brunner, "Behandlung einer Geisteskranken im Jahre 1575," *Zeitschrift des Vereins für hessische Geschichte und Landeskunde*, n.s., 24 (1901): 403–4.

TABLE 7.10

Residents Admitted to Haina (H) and Merxhausen (M), ca. 1550–1622

	I		II		III		IV		I & IV		II & IV		I & II		II & III		I & III		Totals	
	H	M	H	M	H	M	H	M	H	M	H	M	H	M	H	M	H	M	H	M
1550–1560	3	0	3	0	1	0	0	0	0	0	0	0	0	0	0	0	1	0	8	0
1561–1570	25	0	2	1	3	0	0	0	1	0	1	0	0	0	0	0	1	0	33	1
1571–1580	12	2	4	2	1	0	1	0	0	0	0	1	0	0	1	1	0	0	19	6
1581–1590	16	1	1	0	8	0	1	0	0	0	1	0	2	0	1	0	0	0	30	1
1591–1600	9	0	7	0	3	0	0	0	1	0	0	0	0	0	2	0	1	0	23	0
1601–1610	5	1	2	2	1	0	1	0	0	0	0	0	0	0	2	0	0	0	11	3
1611–1622	11	11	1	1	4	6	0	2	0	2	1	0	0	0	0	0	0	0	17	22
n.d. (16th c.)	3	0	1	2	1	0	0	0	0	0	0	0	0	1	0	0	0	0	5	3
Total	84	15	21	8	22	6	3	2	2	2	3	1	2	1	6	1	3	0	146	36

Key: I Old, disabled, crippled
II Orphans, deformed children
III[a] Mentally disabled: retarded, mentally ill, brain damaged
IV Blind

Combinations: I & IV = crippled and blind; II & IV = blind orphan, etc.
[a] Haina mentally disabled = 31 (21 %)
Merxhausen mentally disabled = 7 (19%)
Total mentally disabled = 38 (21%)

7.10, I have grouped 182 cases from about 1550 to 1622 into decades and into four broad categories of basic disability (and five categories of combined disabilities):[116]

1. The largest group of residents at Haina and Merxhausen were obviously those men and women often described simply as "old, lame and disabled." This group also includes those suffering from leprosy, physical deformity, deaf-mutism, epilepsy, and desperate poverty.

2. The second broad category includes orphans and disabled, deformed, crippled children.

3. The third category contains cases of mental disability, retardation, madness, and brain damage.

4. And finally, a fourth category singles out the blind, who made up a small but sorry minority in the Hessian hospitals.

The five combinations of these categories have been restricted to simple pairs of equally debilitating afflictions (a sixth possible permutation, combining blindness with mental disability does not occur in these records).

If one examines how the composition of the hospitals changed during the period here under consideration, one can see the contours of the future mental hospital already emerging from the multipurpose original hospi-

116. An additional case, involving a mentally disordered woman who was remanded to Hofheim instead of Merxhausen, has been excluded from these figures.

TABLE 7.11

*The Mentally Disabled as a Proportion of All Hessian Hospital Residents,
in Three Periods, ca. 1550–1622*

	Haina	Merxhausen	Hofheim	Total Patients*	Mental Patients as % of Total
1550–1580	8	1	0	67	13 %
1581–1600	15	0	0	54	28
1601–1622	7	6	1	54	26

SOURCE: Hospitalsarchiv, Haina, Receptions-Reskripte.
NOTE: 8 undated cases from the 16th century have been excluded from consideration in this table.
*N = 175

TABLE 7.12

Male and Female Applicants to Haina and Merxhausen, 1550–1622

		Haina Men	Merxhausen Women
1550–1580	Total Applicants	60	7
	Mentally Disordered	8 (13%)	1 (14%)
1581–1600	Total Applicants	64	4
	Mentally Disordered	18 (28%)	0 (0%)
1601–1622	Total Applicants	17	22
	Mentally Disordered	4 (24%)	6 (27%)
Whole Period	Total Applicants	141	33
	Mentally Disordered	30 (21%)	7 (21%)

tal. By dividing the period ca. 1550–1622 into three roughly equal periods, one observes a marked rise in the proportion of the mentally disabled (table 7.11).

The reasons for this slight but noticeable shift in emphasis at Haina and Merxhausen are far from clear. Perhaps it took forty or fifty years for communities to discover that the hospitals could relieve them of problems that were not strictly speaking poverty and starvation. Perhaps the admissions process was relaxed more frequently for the urban mad as time went by. One cannot at this stage usefully speculate much further until other hospitals have been studied in similar detail.

In modern times, women have generally sought psychiatric care and been sent to mental hospitals at a rate markedly above that for men. If we draw this comparison from these rudimentary data, however, we find that mentally disturbed men and women were admitted to Haina and Merxhausen, respectively, in roughly equal proportions (see table 7.12). No one thought of crippling madness as tied to gender, a conclusion that comports well with the medical theories of the sixteenth century and fairly well, too, with our findings concerning the incidence of demonic possession among men and women in the German lands. Although only women could suffer from *furor uterinus*, and although "hysterical" symptoms were still literally possible only for those with a womb, it also seems that more men than women committed suicide. Madness had not yet been "gendered."

This much is clear. The Hessian hospital system from its very beginnings housed more than a few mentally disabled residents. By 1600, mental patients were common. With the exception of those who were forcibly detained, we can guess that the mad were as relieved as other residents to find a refuge from the world of famine, poverty, and starvation. In contrast to the mental hospitals that functioned as a repressive prison house of reason, whose seventeenth- and eighteenth-century origins Michel Foucault bathed in a garish light, the sixteenth- and seventeenth-century German hospitals that took their cue from Hesse had their origin in monastic institutions whose watchwords were piety and charity. These ideals are obviously not the ideals of modern mental hospitals, but even with all their moralism, they provided comfort for the helpless in ways so attractive that people clamored to be admitted. These people were not part of an experiment in social discipline or victims of a "great confinement."

The Juliusspital

Protestant princes were not the only founders of hospitals in sixteenth-century Germany. Just as Philipp of Hesse hoped to demonstrate a more truly Christian concern for the poor and helpless with his foundations, so too did certain of the Catholic princes during the Counter-Reformation. Perhaps the most famous of these institutions was the hospital established by Julius Echter von Mespelbrunn (1545–1617), prince bishop of Würzburg. Raised to this high dignity in 1573, at the age of only 28, he quickly undertook an energetic program of new foundations, including a university firmly under the control of the Jesuits, and extensive renovations of his princely castle-residence, the Marienberg, buildings that were so full of his architectural spirit that art historians have labeled them "Julius style" and "Echter-gothic." His revolutionary new hospital was only part of an extensive program of Catholic reformation. Long lauded as one of the most forceful counter-reforming bishops of his day, Julius Echter has recently appeared more as an early representative of princely absolutism, whose every move was more clearly prompted by the needs of his state than by the needs of Rome.[117]

---

117. Götz, Frhr. von Pölnitz, *Julius Echter von Mespelbrunn*, Schriftenreihe zur bayerischen Landesgeschichte, no. 17 (Munich, 1934); Ernst Schubert, "Julius Echter von Mespelbrunn (1545–1617)," in *Fränkische Lebensbilder*, ed. Gerhard Pfeiffer, vol. 3 (Würzburg, 1969), pp. 158–93; Gottfried Mälzer, *Julius Echter: Leben und Werk* (Würzburg, 1989).

FIG. 22. Georg Rudolph Hennenberg, the Juliusspital at Würzburg. Oil painting. Courtesy of the Stiftung Juliusspital, Würzburg; photograph by H. Gundermann.

CREATING A COUNTER-REFORMATION
HOSPITAL

Both as Catholic reformer and as secular autocrat, Julius Echter saw an opportunity for grand gestures and much-needed reforms in Würzburg's institutions for social welfare. Although this small town on the Main River already had a long list of tiny spitals in 1570, run by clerical and civic groups, these almshouses were basically old folk's homes rather than what we would call hospitals, and they also served as hospices for pilgrims, as orphanages, and as poorhouses. Like the hospitals of Hesse, their regulations were often those of a cloister, their architecture often specifically monastic.[118] Open to the wealthy as a form of return on investment and to the urban poor as a form of charity, these late medieval hospitals took care of dozens of retired pensioners and a fair number of sick children, orphans, and foundlings. Usually, German towns excluded certain groups from the main spital, providing special houses for the incurable, for the mad, blind, and crippled, and Würzburg was no exception.[119] But in the early 1570s, as we saw in Hesse, the crunch of famine and high prices created new levels of social misery. The tumultuous years of peasant war, dynastic war, and noble rebellion had also done serious damage to the financial resources of Würzburg's hospitals.[120] Immediately after Julius Echter assumed the dignity of bishop, his cathedral canons handed him a plan to respond to these growing social problems by reforming the thirteen hospitals of Würzburg. There would be room enough for the truly needy, the canons thought, if lazy place-holders were eliminated.[121] Julius Echter's ideas were larger and more far-reaching, and he immediately undertook plans for an entirely new hospital.

In early 1574, he turned to the Nuremberg City Council (famous for its Hospital of the Holy Spirit) and asked for an architect to help him with an ambitious scheme. Würzburg's Jewish inhabitants had been expelled in 1560–61, and in 1576, brusquely ignoring the protests of the Jews of Franconia, Julius Echter seized the grounds of the Jewish cemetery, just north of the city walls, and began the construction of his new hospital.[122] By 1579, the

118. Alfred Wendehorst, *Das Juliusspital in Würzburg*, vol. 1: *Kulturgeschichte* (Würzburg, 1976), pp. 17–18.

119. Ibid., p. 18. In Vienna in 1551, for example, the new Hofspital founded by Emperor Ferdinand I explicitly excluded "those who spend their days in gluttony, drunkenness, gaming and such sorts of frivolous, mischievous, annoying activities and thus are the cause of their own poverty and misery; also those persons beset with pestilence, leprosy, syphilis [*Franzosen*], or other diseases called *contagiosos morbos*; and also those who are mad [*unsinnig*]" (Ernst Nowotny, *Geschichte des Wiener Hofspitals* [Vienna, 1978], pp. 23–24).

120. *650 Jahre Bürgerspital zum Heiligen Geist Würzburg* (Würzburg, 1969), pp. 30–31.

121. Pölnitz, *Julius Echter*, p. 278. On the evolution of Würzburg's poor laws and ordinances, see Rublack, *Gescheiterte Reformation*, pp. 128–43.

122. Wendehorst, *Das Juliusspital*, p. 29; Pölnitz, *Julius Echter*, p. 283.

building was far enough along for Echter to be able to issue a charter (March 12, 1579) directing the hospital to care for "all kinds of poor, sick, destitute, and crippled persons in need of surgical or other medical care, as well as abandoned orphans, and then [secondarily?] transient pilgrims and needy persons."[123] We learn that the hospital was to have its own church, mill, bakehouse, kitchen, cellars, granary, stalls, well, gardens, and apartments for various sorts of needy persons, as well as for attendants and the master of the hospital. Only disabled men and women from Würzburg and the prince-bishopric were eligible for entry. Anyone who regained his or her ability to work had to return to the outside world. Orphans were to be cared for until they were old enough to enter school, take up an apprenticeship, or go into service. Pilgrims and other transients were to be allowed only one night before they had to move on. The bishop explicitly forbade the wealthy to buy themselves positions as pensioners, for the hospital was meant for the poor and the sick, not for the leisurely well-to-do.[124] In these respects, the Würzburg solution sounds like the Hessian response of forty years earlier.

From the regulations of 1605–9 (apparently a close copy of the original *Ordnung* of 1579) we learn that Bishop Julius Echter's hospital was to have the character and feel of a monastery, also echoing the four high hospitals of Hesse, and most other German hospitals for that matter. Residents were to undergo a probationary period (like a novitiate), after which they had to purify themselves with a general confession and solemnly swear to attend Catholic services as often as their physical condition allowed. They had to pray three Rosaries daily, to confess and take the Eucharist at the four high holy days of the Church (Maundy Thursday, Pentecost, the Assumption of Mary, and Christmas). Meals were accompanied by prayers, Hail Marys, the Lord's Prayer, and the Creed, as well as readings from Scripture, the *Imitation of Christ*, or the histories of the martyrs. No one was to fall into unnecessary talk.

In addition to regular church services, pensioners were to assemble on Sunday afternoons to rehearse their catechisms and to join a special confraternity of the Rosary for extra devotions.[125] As in Haina, therefore, residents of the Juliusspital were "primarily members of a spiritual community."[126] Healthy pensioners were to take on light jobs in the rooms, gardens, stables, or church of the hospital. Meals were supposed to be generous, even if not adequately varied by modern standards, and the regulations specified that residents were to receive three-quarters of a liter of wine daily. The hospital was to be visited once a month by a barber and his assistants, who bathed and bled everyone.

123. Wendehorst, *Das Juliusspital*, p. 33.
124. Ibid.
125. Ibid., p. 38.
126. Ibid.

THE CARE OF THE MAD

From the outset, again as at Haina and Merxhausen, mentally disordered patients were mixed indiscriminately among the other patients unless they were thought dangerous. The records do not, however, speak of a separation of the sexes, as in the Hessian high hospitals, but also commonplace elsewhere.[127] Violent patients were placed in the "Pilgrims' House" and later in special rooms in the west wing of the spital. Some surviving mid-eighteenth-century records also mention "block houses" for the dangerous.[128] Furious deranged patients were always in the minority among the mentally ill, but Echter instructed that the female inmate in charge of the mad (*Angefochtenen*) should:

[1.] keep the chains and leg-irons, padlocks, and keys to the prison cells in her custody and not allow them to be used or lent or taken elsewhere without her knowledge; and every time they are needed, she is to provide them;

[2.] be responsible for bowls, cups, mugs and similar eating and drinking utensils, and also for the clothing, alms, and whatever else the mad people [*Unbesunnene Leuth*] need; and faithfully care for these things and keep them clean;

[3.] dispense bread, drink, food, and whatever is daily distributed to them, and not seek her own advantage in these matters at all. Whatever they need for their maintenance, [she should] bring to attention without hesitation and in timely manner before they become sick in their prison [*Gefängnuss*];

[4.] adapt herself in every way as much as possible and learn their characteristics so that she may not excite them to more nonsense, rage, frenzy, biting, and fury;

[5.] turn them out from time to time, bathe them and dress them in newly washed clothes, clean out the prison and strew it with fresh straw;

[6.] make a little fire for them in winter, when it is rather cold, and take care that no damage results from the fire and that the crazy people [*Unsinnige*] in the prisons do not hurt themselves on the hot stoves; and therefore visit them often during the day to observe and see to it that there is no straw, clothing, etc., around the stove;

[7.] absolutely not let them have any belt, garter, knife, or any other thing with which they could harm themselves in any way, and, if she notices that someone has any such thing, bring it to attention at once.[129]

From this document we may underline the following points. It is clear that the female pensioner who had the job of looking after the dangerously mad

127. C. Rieger, *Zweiter Bericht (vom Jahre 1905) aus der Psychiatrischen Klinik der Universität Würzburg* (Würzburg, 1905), pp. 9–10, 23.

128. Ibid., p. 155; C. Lutz, "Aufnahme und Verpflegung von Geisteskranken und Epileptikern im Juliushospitale," in *Die Psychiatrie in Würzburg von 1583–1893*, ed. C. Rieger, Verhandlungen der Phys.-med. Gesellschaft, n.s., vol. 27 (1894), pp. 33–37; reprinted in *Erster Bericht vom Jahre 1899 aus der psychiatrischen Klinik* (Würzburg, 1899), pp. 89–93.

129. This document is undated but surely was drafted in the early years of the hospital. C. Lutz, "Aufnahme," p. 9 (65); Wendehorst, *Das Juliusspital*, pp. 155–56. For further discussion of this instruction, see Rieger, *Zweiter Bericht*, pp. 7–11.

might well have had her hands full. She was responsible for the care and safety, the food and cleanliness, the clothing and warmth and comfort of all who were locked up in the hospital's "prison." To be sure, the instruction speaks of chains and leg-irons, but the attendant was also to take the individual characteristics of specific patients into account. While conditions were doubtless harsh, she was expected to be a caregiver as well as custodian, bathing her charges and providing for their clothing, fresh straw, and warm ovens when necessary, all with a view to preventing illness. We surely obtain a glimpse here of the situation into which suicidal and dangerous patients were thrown, but we should not conclude that even these persons had to live in hopeless dungeons. As Conrad Rieger pointed out at the beginning of this century, the Juliusspital could not have been a completely secure place of detention, since 22 of 249 mental patients in this early period (roughly 9 percent) escaped.[130] Only a tiny minority were locked up or put in chains, and even some of these managed to escape. In 1604, we read that a "madman escaped with his chains" (*insanus cum catenis erupit*); in another case, a *mente captus* escaped early on the morning of November 16, 1605, but on December 15, he brought back his chains and was allowed to go home.[131] Despite the evidently lax supervision of the mental patients, only two successful suicides were registered in the first fifty years of the hospital (in 1607 and 1608).[132]

THE HOSPITAL AS A THERAPEUTIC INSTITUTION

Perhaps the most surprising aspect of the Juliusspital is that patients generally stayed only a short time. Most mental patients, like other patients, arrived for stays of a few weeks or a few months. The governors of the hospital displayed a therapeutic optimism that assumed that only the curable would be admitted, that very few would be granted the status of life-pensioner, and that quick results would therefore have to be registered. With amazing frequency, the records speak of "cures." At the remove of four hundred years, it is, of course, impossible for us to tell whether physical or mental improvement was actually visible or whether cures were merely imputed to these troubled persons. Unlike most late medieval German hospitals, however, the Juliusspital was establishing a different ideal of hospital care, one that optimistically intended the treatment and cure of disease and disorder. This ideal is much more visible in the annual records of admissions and dismissals than in documents like the charter of 1579 or the instruction to the woman inmate in charge of the mad.

130. Rieger, *Zweiter Bericht*, p. 14.
131. Ibid., p. 15.
132. Ibid.

Such a therapeutic hospital was not absolutely new in the annals of European medical history. It is well known that early Islamic hospitals had wide-ranging therapeutic goals, and that Byzantine hospitals, too, offered a dramatically medical alternative to the custodial and charitable institutions of the West.[133] Historians have also shown that medically oriented, therapeutic institutions spread during the Renaissance to parts of the Mediterranean world, beginning perhaps with the Ospedale Maggiore in Milan, founded in 1456.[134] At present too little is known of how these hospitals actually functioned, but the sizable medical staff of five doctors, the library, apothecary, and even the plans to compete with the famous medical schools of Pavia, Bologna, Padua, and Salerno, reveal that in Milan, curing the sick was assuming a role at least as important as caring for them.[135] By the late fifteenth and early sixteenth centuries, these ideals were being transplanted to Spain as well as France.[136] The hospital historian Dieter Jetter is doubtless right that the medieval Western ideals of custodial care survived throughout the early modern period and down to 1800; but he has also oversimplified matters with his claim that truly therapeutic hospitals began to replace their custodial ancestors only in the first decades of the nineteenth century.[137] Even though the custodial function grew so dramatically in the Juliusspital that by the eighteenth century, it was mainly a nursing home for the poor and aged, in its origins, as we have seen, it was a *Krankenhaus*, an institution that aimed to cure. It seems likely both from its architecture and from its ordinances that Julius Echter's hospital struck this new theme, not because Islamic or Italian models impressed him, but because of the urgent need to make a dramatic Counter-Reformation statement.

Despite its novel emphasis on treatment and cure of disease, daily life in the Juliusspital was similar in basic form and in development to the Hessian hospitals. As we have seen, life in the Würzburg hospital revolved around moderate work for those who were able, mealtimes filled with pious readings, and the visible effort to glorify God through care for the most

133. Michael W. Dols, "The Origins of the Islamic Hospital: Myth and Reality," *Bulletin of the History of Medicine* 61 (1987): 367–90; Timothy Miller, *The Birth of the Hospital in the Byzantine Empire* (Baltimore, 1985).

134. Ralph Quadflieg, *Filaretes Ospedale Maggiore in Mailand: Zur Rezeption islamischen Hospitalwesens in der italienischen Frührenaissance* (diss., Cologne, 1981). Veröffentlichung der Abteilung Architektur des Kunsthistorischen Instituts der Universität Köln, no. 20.

135. Ibid., p. 44.

136. Catherine Wilkinson, "The Hospital of Cardinal Tavera in Toledo: A Documentary and Stylistic Study of Spanish Architecture in the Mid-Sixteenth Century" (diss., Yale University, 1968), pp. 2–3, 6–9; on the influence of Filarete and the Ospedale Maggiore, see pp. 10–17; Dieter Jetter, *Das europäische Hospital, von der Spätantike bis 1800* (Cologne, 1986), pp. 85–90, 104–8; Katherine Park and J. Henderson, "The First Hospital Among Christians: The Ospedale de Santa Maria Nuova in Early Sixteenth-Century Florence," *Medical History* 35 (1991): 164–88.

137. Jetter, *Das europäische Hospital*, p. 199: "Vom Hospital zum Krankenhaus."

unfortunate. Although residents of the Juliusspital were expected to attend Holy Mass and other Catholic ceremonies, there was no credal or catechetical entrance requirement. One might say that the hospital used a behavioral as opposed to a doctrinal program of Counter-Reformation: patients were expected to thank God, Mary, and all the saints for their care and improvement. It taught Catholicism by practice.

The reason for this sort of "behavioral Catholicism" is surely the fact that in the 1570s, the most prominent citizens of Würzburg were still resolutely Protestant. Decades of halfhearted Catholic measures ordered by Julius Echter's predecessors had had little effect. In contrast, Echter cracked down hard on the city council during the 1580s, and by 1590, his political Counter-Reformation had achieved an unquestioned success. But his iron hand could also wear a velvet glove. In his new hospital from 1580 onwards, the prince bishop was exercising a charitable Catholicism of pious example and orthodox practice.[138]

HOSPITAL PATIENTS

In trying to grasp the conditions of real life for the mad, we can go beyond the general principles on which the hospital was based. Fortunately, the admissions books have largely survived from the earliest years of the Juliusspital. Although missing for some years altogether and mutilated and truncated for other years, these records allow us to describe the hospital population in considerable detail right from the start. The surviving records contain the names and short descriptions of over 4,600 persons admitted in the first fifty years of operation. To get oriented, it is helpful to look at the first ten cases. The register of admissions opens with Margaretha, the daughter of Veit Schneider of Wipfeld, admitted sometime during 1580. She was described as a "forlorn and dejected orphan" (*verlaßene und betrübte Waisen*).[139] After agreeing to be a cheerful and obedient inmate, she was admitted as the first long-term resident of the hospital. About two years later, she was treated by Dr. Wilhelm Upilioni and the two attending barber-surgeons for a crippled arm. We do not know if her arm was already giving her trouble when she entered the hospital, but on March 5, 1582, she was "sent into the wood cure," a treatment from which

138. Rublack, *Gescheiterte Reformation,* pp. 50–75. The hospital also developed into a center for converting the Jews: see Alfred Wendehorst, "Die Juliusspitalpfarrei und ihre Bedeutung für die Gegenreformation," in *Julius Echter und seine Zeit: Gedenkschrift aus Anlass des 400. Jahrestages der Wahl des Stifters der Alma Julia zum Fürstbischof von Würzburg am 1. Dezember 1573,* ed. Friedrich Merzbacher (Würzburg, 1973), pp. 349–74; also Wendehorst, *Das Juliusspital,* pp. 214–21.

139. Stadtarchiv Würzburg, Literalien 2285: Aufnahmebuch Juliusspital 1580–86, 1599–1603, p. 5 (I use the new pagination in blue pencil). I cite this series of sources hereafter as StAW, Lit. 2285.

she emerged on the last day of March. This *Holtz chur*, the *cura ligni*, was extremely popular, at least among those prescribing remedies, during the early years of the Juliusspital, being regularly applied to all manner of patients with crippling ailments, open wounds or sores, and especially the French disease (syphilis). The therapy involved an infusion of guaiacum wood or lignum vitae, which patients drank, and a sweat chamber in which the patient breathed the hot fumes of guaiac resin and suffered his or her body temperature to rise perhaps to as high as 41°C (106°F) or even higher. Although ridiculed by Paracelsus, who favored a mercury cure for syphilis, this guaiac and sweatbath therapy may well have been partially effective against syphilis because the pallid spirochete is even more heat sensitive than the human body.[140] Of the first ten patients whom we can trace in these records, at least six were given the "Holtz chur," often with reports of excellent results. In 1582 alone, at least twenty-six patients, out of the forty-two adults treated that year, were given this "wood cure."

After Margaretha, the records reveal a gap of nine leaves, brutally torn from the bound manuscript, and we pick up the traces of Würzburg admissions with another orphaned girl admitted to the hospital on February 1, 1581. Since each leaf at this time contained the descriptions of four cases, one can estimate that the missing pages probably described thirty-six cases, but of course we cannot say anything about them. Obviously, the hospital was getting off to a cautious or even a slow start, with fewer than forty patients in the first year of operation. In mid March 1581, the records list the arrival of a sick, decrepit old woman, who was given the wood cure five months later but died in January 1582, becoming the first to be buried on the grounds of Julius Echter's new spital.[141]

The fourth patient in the surviving records was a man who came to the spital for his injured hip or thigh. He had better luck with the wood cure and was soon able to return home to his small children. The improvement was only temporary, however, and he later returned for an amputation and was grateful to be accepted once more by the hospital. Next came an unmarried woman, who recovered quickly after the wood cure; and then an unmarried journeyman, who was also soon well enough to go home.

140. Charles C. Dennie, *A History of Syphilis* (Springfield, Ill., 1962), pp. 47–49, 113–18; William J. Brown et al., *Syphilis and Other Venereal Diseases* (Cambridge, Mass., 1970), pp. 11–16. It appears that the attack by Paracelsus was ultimately successful because by 1600 the *cura ligni* was clearly out of favor in Würzburg. By modern standards, Paracelsus was correct in claiming that the guaiac wood itself was no good as a cure for syphilis, but he overlooked the likely beneficial effects of an artificial rise in the patient's temperature, effects that were rediscovered only in the early twentieth century, when Julius Wagner von Jauregg proved that malarial or tertian fevers could dramatically improve the chances of those suffering from syphilitic meningoencephalitis or general paresis. See also Claude Quétel, *History of Syphilis* (Baltimore, 1990).

141. StAW, Lit. 2285, p. 6.

The seventh person listed in the truncated records was "a poor scholar," who was admitted because of his bad knee and other problems. We do not know what happened to him after the almost obligatory wood cure, but he was probably released, because pensioners had to obtain special permission to remain in residence, and there is no surviving record of such a permission. Numbers eight through ten included two men and a woman, who arrived with physical ailments and high hopes of a cure. In at least one of these cases, the wood cure failed outright, and the patient in question was described as still very weak. He had to walk with two canes, and the manuscript mentions that he resolved next to try the healing waters of Wiesbaden.

Such were the first ten cases of whom we have detailed knowledge, five males and five females. By the end of 1581, the Juliusspital had treated them and another thirty-six or so, admitting very few to permanent status as pensioners and sending most of them away after some definite improvement. In its first years, the spital apparently treated no cases of mental disorder, although, as noted, the records are incomplete. In dramatic contrast to the Hessian hospitals, Julius Echter's hospital was looking for curable cases. The permanent barber-surgeons in attendance, the working "wood cure," and, from the 1590s on, the close association with the new university medical faculty make the contrast to the Hessian high hospitals unmistakable. Most of the incurable cases, at least from the towns, were referred to a normal urban or ecclesiastical spital, which usually had medieval roots and served as a nursing home for elderly, often privileged, urbanites.[142] The Hessian hospitals had responded to an obvious need by expanding the idea of the hospital to deal with unfortunate and broken-down peasants and villagers, who were denied access to urban institutions of relief. Bishop Julius Echter von Mespelbrunn was creating a very different institution, however, in which therapy and cure were the main objectives.

In the course of time, however, the custodial functions of the bishop's new hospital rose in importance, so that through much of the seventeenth and eighteenth centuries, pensioners greatly outnumbered the acutely ill.[143] Already in 1621, the spital had 59 male and 76 female pensioners, as well as 21 sick patients, 12 orphans, and 36 servants.[144] But in its origins, the Juliusspital had been dominated by a spirit of what Conrad Rieger called "therapeutic optimism."[145]

142. See, e.g., the referral of a woman, admitted in 1585 but then transferred to the Bürger Spital, ibid., pp. 85–90. For the normal operations of such institutions, see *650 Jahre Bürgerspital* (see n. 120 above).

143. Wendehorst, *Das Juliusspital*, pp. 88–89, 104–5.

144. Ibid., p. 104.

145. Conrad Rieger, "Der therapeutische Optimismus der frühesten Zeiten," in id., *Zweiter Bericht*, pp. 25–67.

In 1582, the new Würzburg hospital stepped up its activity somewhat, admitting 51 patients for longer or shorter periods. Now we begin to find examples of madness. The admissions for 1582 may be broken down into the following categories.[146] Twenty were male and thirty-one female (39 and 61 percent respectively). Just half were crippled, three were blind, nine were orphans, and ten had unspecified disabilities. Three were specifically described as mad or mentally disabled. They included one woman admitted because she was suffering from a "vehement sickness of the head" (*hefftige Hauptkrankheit*); the village mayor of Baltheißheim (in the district of Reigelsberg) who was "healthy in body but crazy from time to time in his head" (*gesundes leibs aber in kopff underweilen Jrrückt*); and a woman of whom it is said (in vague language that recalls the mad of Haina's hospital) that she was admitted "until God should send a remedy," which He evidently did just eleven months later. Of these three, it is true that only the mayor of Baltheißheim was explicitly described as a mental patient, and he was ordered to take instruction from the priest (*dem hern Prediger zu unterweisen bevolen*). But it seems probable that the other two were also mentally disabled. Even so, the mad were not a major element in the first few years of the Juliusspital. A substantial portion of the early admissions presented problems that had no immediate solution, and we find that in 1582, nine children and seven adults were granted the status of pensioner, while ten died in hospital and nineteen were dismissed as cured.[147]

As in the Hessian hospitals, however, the numbers of mad increased in the course of time. We can follow fairly closely the admissions to the Würzburg spital for the first fifty years of its existence, 1580–1629, a period in which the records, despite their current state of mutilation, list close to 5,000 admissions, a large and uniquely interesting mass of patients, from whom one can learn about the stresses of life and the mental troubles of ordinary people in the late sixteenth century (table 7.13).

Looking first at the aggregate picture makes clear that the numbers of mad or mentally disabled rose substantially, both in absolute numbers and as a proportion of the total admissions, from 1580 to 1614, but that this surge leveled off in the last decade and a half under investigation, at just the time when the hospital began to swell far beyond its original limits. It may be that, as in Hesse, the local population of the prince bishop's lands learned in time to refer their mentally disturbed members to the new hospital. At the same time, the hospital may have broadened its sense of therapeutic mission, for we can also notice a dramatic decline in the use of the *Holtz chur* during the 1590s. It went from the status of panacea to a therapy

146. StaW, Lit. 2285.
147. Two of the fifty-one left for no recorded reason, and the fates of four others are unknown. StaW, Lit. 2285.

TABLE 7.13
Admissions to the Juliusspital, 1580–1628

	Total Admitted	Mad Male	Mad Female	Percent Mad
1580–1584[a]	222	6	5	5.0%
1585–1589[c]	218	9	3	5.5
1590–1594	392	16	12	7.1
1595–1599[b]	311	15	14	9.3
1600–1604	495	24	17	8.3
1605–1609	409	16	16	7.8
1610–1614[c]	236	15	2	7.2
1615–1619[a]	697	28	6	4.9
1620–1624[a]	987	27	12	4.0
1625–1628	657	18	21	5.9
Total	4,624	174	108 ·	6.1%

SOURCE: Based on StAW, Lit. 2285 (1580–1586, 1599–1603); Lit. 2286 (1589–1597); Lit. 2287 (1604– 1612); Lit. 2288 (1613–1621); Lit. 2289 (1622–1628); and on C. Lutz, "Aufnahme und Verpflegung von Geisteskranken und Epileptikern im Juliushospitale," in *Die Psychiatrie in Würzburg von 1583–1893*, ed. C. Rieger, Verhandlungen der Phys.-med. Gesellschaft, n.s., 27 (1894), pp. 33–37; reprinted in *Erster Bericht vom Jahre 1899 aus der psychiatrischen Klinik* (Würzburg, 1899), pp. 89–93, which excerpts most of the relevant cases.

[a] 1 year missing
[b] 1 1/2 years missing
[c] 2 years missing

that was only occasionally applied. The heads of the hospital may have learned that some patients responded well to some time away from the daily stresses of life, even if they did not have syphilis or other crippling conditions that seemed to be so well treated with *lignum vitae.*

Table 7.13 also highlights the fact that here men generally outnumbered women among the mental patients by a ratio of about eight to five, but this was a ratio that fluctuated dramatically over the 50-year period we are examining. Whatever our interpretation of these figures, it would be hard to conclude that women were being treated as mad or labeled as sick and incompetent more frequently than men. There was a tendency to grant women the desirable status of pensioner more frequently than men, with the right of unlimited residency, but this fact may be connected to the presumed helplessness of old unmarried women in that day or to the possibility that women were already outliving their spouses in such large numbers that special provisions had to be made for widows.

THE RISE OF MELANCHOLY AND DEMONIC POSSESSION

Even more dramatic than the general rise of the mentally ill among the hospital patients in Würzburg during the first thirty-five years was the

TABLE 7.14
The "Melancholy" as a Proportion of the "Mad," 1580–1628

	Mad		Described as Melancholy		Percent of Mad		
	male	female	male	female	male	female	combined
1580–1584	6	5	0	2	0%	40%	18%
1585–1589	9	3	0	0	0	0	0
1590–1594	16	12	2	0	13	0	7
1595–1599	15	14	3	5	20	36	28
1600–1604	24	17	11	12	46	71	56
1605–1609	16	16	8	9	50	56	53
1610–1614	15	2	10	0	67	0	59
1615–1619	28	6	16	3	57	50	56
1620–1624	27	12	15	5	56	42	51
1625–1628	18	21	13	19	72	91	82
Totals	174	108	78	55	45%	51%	47%

SOURCE: Based on on StAW, Lit. 2285 (1580–1586, 1599–1603); Lit. 2286 (1589–1597); Lit. 2287 (1604–1612); Lit. 2288 (1613–1621); Lit. 2289 (1622–1628); and on C. Lutz, "Aufnahme und Verpflegung von Geisteskranken und Epileptikern im Juliushospitale," in *Die Psychiatrie in Würzburg von 1583–1893*, ed. C. Rieger, Verhandlungen der Phys.-med. Gesellschaft, n.s., 27 (1894), pp. 33–37; reprinted as *Erster Bericht vom Jahre 1899 aus der psychiatrischen Klinik* (Würzburg, 1899), pp. 89–93, which excerpts most of the relevant cases.

general rise of "melancholy" among the mentally ill. Table 7.14 provides the evidence for this conclusion.

We cannot tell from these records if this dramatic rise of melancholy was owing to the possible increase of melancholy as a diagnostic label at the hospital or to an increasing social tendency to see the melancholy as so troublesome, so disordered, that they needed to be sent away to a hospital, or even to the possible growth of a Galenic optimism that led to the increased referral of the so-called melancholy to the Juliusspital. Some combination of these explanations may well have been at work, but they all testify to what we have noticed in other sources and in previous chapters: the distinct rise of melancholy in the waning decades of the sixteenth century. And here there was an increasing level of concern about melancholy, not only among mad princes and other connoisseurs of the latest fashionable medical treatments, and not just among lawyers eager to deploy a new understanding of the insanity defense, but among ordinary people. This rise of melancholy as a label and as an experience was dramatically evident in Würzburg, but nothing comparable is visible in the Hessian hospital records. This discrepancy suggests that the medical resources and close ties to Würzburg's medical faculty contributed to the rising popularity of the melancholy diagnosis there. The Hessian high hospitals, by way of contrast, remained more conservatively committed to a vernacular nosology, to the language and medical understanding of ordinary folk.

If we break these figures down by sex, we find that women were slightly more likely to be described as melancholy than men. "Melancholy" women made up 51 percent of the female patients admitted for madness during the period 1580–1628, while among mad men, 45 percent were described as "melancholy." For both sexes, melancholy became more common as a diagnosis. From 1580 to 1604, only 23 percent of the mentally ill men and 37 percent of the mentally ill women admitted were labeled "melancholy"; but from 1605 to 1628, the melancholy made up 60 percent of the men and 63 percent of the women. In fact, in the mid 1620s (1624–28), fully 72 percent of the male mental cases and 91 percent of the female mental cases are explicitly described as melancholy. A relatively infrequent diagnosis had risen to dominate the experience and perception of mental disorder. On the eve of its collapse as a humoral disorder, melancholy was more popular as a diagnostic category than ever before.[148]

The hospital also had to deal with a wave of demonic possessions among its mentally disturbed patients. In contrast to melancholy, at Würzburg, we are dealing here with a disorder that was clearly gender-specific. Fully 78 percent of the cases that appear in these records (14 of 18) were women (see table 7.15).

Before 1595, the very term *melancholy* appears only three times in the hospital admissions registers. In 1584, for example, Margaretha Wernerin, from a village near Königshofen, was admitted to the hospital with the following description: "[She is] a severe melancholic and behaves strangely in words and actions as if she were possessed."[149] From this language, it is evident that she was not regarded as truly possessed. In the medical language of the time, she might have been suffering from *melancholia daemoniaca*. Veit Müller's wife, Margaretha, "who is crazy or possessed" (*so unbesunnen oder besessen*), was admitted in April 1590, but she was released into the custody of her husband after only ten days, because, it was noted, she had to care for a small child at home.[150] Her case, too, does not look like a real case of possession. Such was also the case with Helena Trotzerin, who arrived at

148. On the general history of melancholia, see Stanley W. Jackson, *Melancholia and Depression from Hippocratic Times to Modern Times* (New Haven, 1986), and chapter 3 above. Michael MacDonald has also noticed the rise of melancholy as a label or diagnosis for the patients of Dr. Richard Napier after the 1621 publication of Robert Burton's remarkable *Anatomy of Melancholy*. See MacDonald's *Mystical Bedlam: Madness, Anxiety and Healing in Seventeenth-Century England* (Cambridge, 1981), pp. 151–60. Such a transformation of vernacular attitudes could not be expected in the Juliusspital during its first decade because the medical faculty were only slowly organized and deployed in Würzburg; medical lectures began in the mid 1590s; Ernst Schubert, *Materielle und organisatorische Grundlagen der Würzburger Universitätsentwicklung 1582–1821*, Quellen und Beiträge zur Geschichte der Universität Würzburg, vol. 4 (Neustadt an der Aisch, 1973), p. 45.
149. StAW, Lit. 2285, Apr. 25, 1584: "so ein grosse Melancholica und wunderbarlich mit wortten und geperden sich ertzaigt gleich ob sy besessen."
150. StAW, Lit. 2286, Apr. 18, 1590.

TABLE 7.15
Demonic Possession in the Juliusspital, 1580–1628

	Male	Female
1580–1589	0	1*
1590–1599	2	8
1600–1609	2	4
1610–1619	0	1
1620–1628	0	0
Total	4	14

SOURCE: Based on StAW, Lit. 2285 (1580–1586, 1599–1603); Lit. 2286 (1589–1597); Lit. 2287 (1604–1612); Lit. 2288 (1613–1621); Lit. 2289 (1622–1628); and on C. Lutz, "Aufnahme und Verpflegung von Geisteskranken und Epileptikern im Juliushospitale," in *Die Psychiatrie in Würzburg von 1583–1893*, ed. C. Rieger, Verhandlungen der Phys.-med. Gesellschaft, n.s., 27 (1894), pp. 33–37; reprinted as *Erster Bericht vom Jahre 1899 aus der psychiatrischen Klinik* (Würzburg, 1899), pp. 89–93, which excerpts most of the relevant cases.
*she was described "as if demon possessed"

the hospital on December 8, 1590, "claiming to be possessed and thinking she could get admitted in that way to the hospital." She was actually exorcised by Father Gerhard, "but nothing was found beyond natural sickness," words implying that exorcism was used here as a diagnostic test, with a negative result. The reverend father ordered her sent away, and on March 4, 1591, she left, thankful for her care and expressing the intention of taking the waters at some mineral spring in the hopes of improving her health.[151]

These cases became more common and more serious in the 1590s. Up to 1604, we find the diagnosis or suggestion of demonic possession in 1591 (twice), 1593, 1595, 1596, 1597, 1599, 1601, 1602, and 1604. In some of these cases, the record simply notes that a maid was *angefochten* (attacked or tempted) (1591), or that a woman was both melancholic and an *energumena ex magia* (demon-possessed as a result of witchcraft) (1601). There may even have been a growing confusion between melancholy and true possession, for we read in the records for 1599 that Appolonia Kreusin was *quasi energumena revera Melancholica* (i.e., "as if demon-possessed with melancholy dreams"), and in those for 1602 of a woman who was *melancholica aut energumena* (melancholic or demon-possessed). Without more detail, we cannot be sure how to interpret such formulas. In other cases, the records are a bit more revealing. In 1593, Caspar Neuber, a barber from Melichstadt, "was admitted to the hospital by our gracious prince. He was possessed by the

151. Ibid., Dec. 8, 1590: "hat furgeben als ob sie besessen sei, vermeinent dadurch in Spittal zu kommen, aber durch Rm Patrem Gerhardum Exorcirt worden aber nichts befunden dan naturlich krankheitten, wirdt von R. G. befholen sie in 2 Tagen abzuschaffen."

evil enemy; he insisted on this for eight days, but nothing was found in him. Instead, it was found that he had imagined it. . . . Modest and sound of mind, he went home." It appears from cases like this that demonic possession had become a popular idiom, and that the authorities, far from imposing their own ideas of the devil and of possession upon an unbelieving populace, were instead skeptical enough that they did not accept popular allegations of demonic possession at face value.

Repeatedly, however, the Juliusspital recorded striking success with the truly demon-possessed. In 1595, for example, Veronica, the wife of Hans Herbst of Hausen, came in, "possessed by many demons. She was freed from them by Father Gerhard through exorcisms and other suitable measures."[152] A similarly mixed therapy helped Kunigundt Schneiderin from Karlburg, "who was very melancholy and behaved strangely as if she were possessed, as she showed in many [ways]. She was restored [to health] by Father Gerhard with medicine, words of consolation and exorcisms, and was sent back grateful to her children."[153] A laconic note records the case of a man who arrived, possessed by a demon, on September 22, 1604. He was exorcised successfully and sent home on October 2. Not all cases were so easy, however, as we learn from the record of Barthel Weigandt, who was from Buthain, near Kitzingen. He arrived at the hospital on September 12, 1596, described as "a strange Stoic and phantast, requesting to be admitted to the hospital and to be freed from the evil enemy (with whom he was not yet possessed). But after he said his confession, he stayed no longer."[154]

The rise of demonic possession in the 1590s corresponds to the beginnings of witch-hunting in southern Germany and especially in the bishopric of Würzburg, where 1596 and 1603 saw the first major waves of prosecution.[155] This correlation is, however, far from exact. The massive witchhunts of 1616–17 and 1626–29 found no parallel among the hospital admissions: between 1609 and 1628, only one of the patients was described as demon-possessed, although an eight-year-old girl, Cordula zu Arnstein, was admitted "because of witchcraft" (*wegen der Hexerei*) for a two-week period in 1617.[156] It is not clear whether Cordula was bewitched or accused of being a witch, but she was evidently not a mentally ill child. The hospi-

152. Ibid., May 28, 1595: "obsessa a multis daemonibus a patre Gerardo ab eisdem liberata per exorcismos aliosque modos convenientes."
153. Ibid., July 5, 1597: "Kunigundt Schneiderin von Carlburg so gar melancholia und seltzam gebern uber sich gehabt und als wer sie besessen, sich in vilen anzaigt hatt, wurde durch artzney verbis consolatoris auch exorcismis per patrem Gerard wider restituirt unnd cum grationibus [*sic*] actione zue ihren kindern verschafft."
154. Ibid., Sept. 12, 1596: "Barthel Weigandt von Buthain bey Kitzingen ein seltzamer Stoicus und phantast bit in spital ihne vom bösen feyndt (damit er noch nit befassen) zue entledigen, do man ihme von der beycht sagte ist seins bleibens nit lenger gewesen."
155. Christel Beyer, *"Hexen-Leut, so zu Würzburg gerichtet": Der Umgang mit Sprache und Wirklichkeit in Inquisitionsprozessen wegen Hexerei* (Frankfurt a/M, 1986).

tal could serve as a safe place for detention. As we have seen, the decline of demonic possession in the hospital did not coincide with a decline of belief in demonic possession, at least not in Bavaria where the pilgrimage shrines at Benediktbeuern and Pürten saw a continuing stream of devil-plagued votants.[157]

THE ATTRACTION OF THE HOSPITAL

The Juliusspital seems quickly to have gained a favorable reputation well beyond Würzburg. The early admissions records show that patients came from as far away as Augsburg (1584), Cologne (1586), Saxony (1586), and Silesia (1584).[158] It is also noteworthy that the hospital did not turn them away as foreigners. A student from Rome was admitted in 1596, and noblemen, too, sought the benefits of the hospital as early as 1589, when Erhard, count of Mellerstaden (Metterstaden?), was admitted, "a poor scholar who because of weakness [had become] rather crazy in the head."[159] Priests and men with learned degrees were also among the hospital's earliest patients (1584, 1585, 1589, 1594, 1597, 1590). So attractive was the Juliusspital that in 1585, we learn, "a crazy mason-journeyman came in over the walls into the hospital and was admitted and restored to health."[160] Needy people were eager to get into such institutions.

The hospital set a firm example of Catholic piety, promptly baptizing any children left at its door (1582), including a boy who had been found in a hedge and maintained by his village for the first nine years of his life.[161] In other cases, the records explicitly state that conversion to Catholicism accompanied the authorized therapy (1584). Not everyone adapted easily to this religious atmosphere. In 1583, a student was treated successfully with the "wood cure," but because of unspecified bad behavior, he was confined for some time on bread and water. Others left or were expelled unthankful for their care (1582, 1583, 1592). Anna, the wife of Veit Müller of Baldersheim, was admitted on April 20, 1590, as "senseless and crazy" (*unbesünnen und im sinn zeruttet*), but she was sent packing eight weeks later "because she refused to confess or take communion." In addition to her men-

156. C. Lutz, "Aufnahme," p. 23.
157. See pp. 60–61 and nn. 117–18 above.
158. StAW, Lit. 2285.
159. StAW, Lit. 2286, Feb. 11, 1589: "Erhard Graf Mellerstaden [Metterstaden?] ain armer schuler wirdt schwachait halber im haupt also etwas verruckt.... Ist mit dankbarkeit, nachdem es besser mit im worden, auß dem Spittal gangen." See also the admission of a noble youth, Tobias ab Hage, July 26, 1590.
160. "Ein wanwitziger Meurers geselle ist uber die mauern inns Spital kommen, wirdt auffgenommen unnd wieder zurecht gebracht" (1585).
161. He gave up his perhaps dishonorable name of Thomas von der Hecken—Hedge Thomas—and took the baptismal name of Nicholas. StAW, Lit. 2285, June 17, 1582.

tal problems, she may have been a Protestant. A certain Bartholomaeus Geeck from Eisleben in Saxony was described as *furiosus* when he was admitted on February 25, 1603. Two weeks later, he had fled (*aufugit 11 Martii*). Still others were evaluated by the spital and referred to other institutions. Not everyone enjoyed the hospital and its uncomfortable wood cure, and one madman protested unhappily in 1594, after he had been assigned a hospital job, that he would rather work for his old master than for the hospital.

Although incurable cases usually went elsewhere, Julius Echter's hospital opened its doors in 1586 to "Laurence N., your Princely Grace's father's former court fool, who died and was buried in the Juliusspital on April 14. He was an old child."[162] Thus we learn that here, as indeed elsewhere, the court fool was regarded as morally and intellectually a child, but one cannot tell from so brief an entry whether this fool was expected to improve in any way from his stay in the Juliusspital. Other natural fools were accommodated in a special *Narrenhaus*, perhaps within the walls of the hospital, as we learn, for example, in the case of Barbara, the daughter of Hans Engler of Essfeld. She was thought to be "out of her senses" and was therefore "in the fools' house" (*nitt bei sinnen . . . ligt im Narrenhaus*) (December 1590). The wife of a co-prefect, also named Barbara, "became completely senseless" and was sent to the *Narrenhaus* in 1589. This building may in fact have been the "prison" for which the "instructions for the care of the mad" (see p. 369 above) were written. From the admissions registers, we can glimpse the selective criteria by which curable patients were accepted into the Juliusspital. What is not clear is how it was decided to admit some orphans and a few elderly women as pensioners, as if to a nursing home; but such persons, classified as *ewige Pfründner* (pensioners for life), were rare in the early years of the hospital, no more numerous than the mad or the orphans, and far less common than the syphilitics and crippled, who were treated with apparent success and in large numbers during the first fifty years of the Juliusspital.[163]

Even so, we must recognize the Juliusspital as a remarkable and novel haven for those mad persons fortunate enough to be regarded as curable. The regime of rest, food, medicine, spiritual consolation and (if indicated) exorcism seems to have done these patients good, responding as they perhaps did to the therapeutic optimism of the Counter-Reformation. Even when they did not recover, the mad may have been glad to end their days there. One such, Balthasar Steichan, was admitted on May 22, 1601; he was

162. StAW, Lit. 2285: "Laurentius N. Ihrer F. G. Vatters seligen Petri Echters gewesener Stultus stirbt und wirdt begraben in Julier Spital für ein altes Kindt den 14 April: 86. anno."
163. The phrases "böse Schäden am Schenkel" or "wegen habende scheden" are by far the most frequent labels attached to the hospital population.

described as a "senseless man," who had "killed his wife with four stab wounds two days ago—she had trusted him too much." He was evidently not punished for his mad deed, but died on September 18, after confessing and taking the sacrament.[164] An autopsy revealed a calcified brain tumor (*tumor stein am kopff*).

Conclusion

Through the exceptional window of these Würzburg *Aufnahmebücher*, we have been able to glimpse the varieties of madness as they presented themselves to a newly founded hospital. Only rarely was it necessary to bind or chain these persons; in the first fifty years, there was only one madman (*furiosus*) of whom it is explicitly remarked that chains were necessary to restrain him (*insanus cum catenis*). Much more typical were the "melancholy and *verrückt*" who were treated usually for a few weeks or months and released "mit zimlicher vernunft," "nach zimlicher gesundheitt," "mit gutter Vernunfft gesundheitt und dancksagung," "wider bey guttem verstandt"; "ut cunque compos mentis," "bene curatus et integer," or "curatus gratusque." Perhaps the most truthful verdict on these surprisingly frequent cures came to the surface in the 1601 case of the melancholy possessed woman (*energumena ex magia*) who arrived in the Juliusspital on July 8 and left, "grateful and *we hope* [emphasis added] restored to health" ("abiit grata et quod speramus curata"), on November 9. Certainly, some patients found the hospital a welcome source of care and understanding. One is startled to read that, in 1597, Elizabeth Kauffmennin from Hackenhausen in the diocese of Mainz was admitted "melancholy because her parents forbade her to marry." She was given medicines and other (unspecified) help, but the best therapy for her may simply have been the frank recognition of what the problem was.[165]

As in Hesse, Würzburg presented a hospital that was clearly a welcome relief from the hard times of the last decades of the sixteenth century. Here the mad were not beaten or abused; they were not forced to work for their suppers, although moderate jobs were found for those who could manage them. They were certainly not part of any "great confinement," but were rather given whatever medication or therapy seemed professionally indicated. Perhaps because the hospital explicitly sought only curable cases, the rate of cure was extremely high. This is not the place to pursue the later history of the Juliusspital, but it is worth mentioning that when modern teach-

164. StAW, Lit. 2285, May 22, 1601.
165. StAW, Lit. 2286, April 28, 1597: "so melancholica propter impeditum a parentibus matrimonium worden."

ing clinics were first established in Germany in the 1790s, the Bamberg model that became famous rested in part on the earlier successes of Würzburg's Counter-Reformation sanatorium. There is an irony in the fact that Philipp of Hesse, while moving his territory into the new world of evangelical social institutions, managed to create a hospital system that was medieval in inspiration, whereas Julius Echter von Mespelbrunn, in trying to stem the tide of Protestantism, created a hospital that, at least in its origins and ideals, looked forward with religious and therapeutic optimism.

$\mathcal{E}$pilogue

WHEN Germans of the sixteenth century encountered thoughts and behavior that made no sense, they were quick to conclude that the problem was madness, but they disagreed sharply over the causes. Basic to everyone's understanding of insanity was the assumption that it might well have physical origins in congenital retardation, brain disease, cerebral injury or tumors, or in more general disorders of the temperament or of the whole body. Physicians made this set of assumptions more specific and more classical by claiming to locate and to give Greek names to the specific bodily juices or humors whose excess or deficit might be at the root of mania, phrenitis, melancholia, or the other less common, but no less well recognized, mental disorders. Even when they did not find a physical cause for madness, early modern Germans knew of other natural processes by which one might be driven crazy. The chapters of this book have illustrated, for example, the widespread notion that a sudden terror might produce so great a shock that one might be driven mad. A bad marriage was another noted source of insanity.

In addition to these naturalistic assumptions, however, sixteenth-century Germans also shared a belief that willfully disobeying the laws of God or flagrantly devoting oneself to a life of sin could be mentally destabilizing. Theologians crystallized these views by speaking of sin as a disease that might, if unchecked, reduce a person to the status of a beast, hardly human any longer except in outward form. Another way of talking about nonphysical and unnatural causes of madness was to speak of the devil, the archenemy of God and humankind, who was always eager to recruit souls for hell and to obsess the minds of the pious, especially with thoughts of suicide. At his most fearsome, the devil might totally possess the body and mind of his victims, producing a demonomania that was beyond human help, but that Catholic priests might exorcise and Lutherans might combat with prayers, fasting, and congregational singing. In this emphasis on sin and the devil, pious Germans recognized that their mental troubles were not all reducible to physical ailments.

The chapters of this book have also shown that both the diagnosis of melancholy and the recognition of demonic possession became dramatically more common in the late sixteenth and in early seventeenth centuries. The scientific and medical language of melancholy did not displace the language of sin and the devil, in part because theologians were quick to say that the devil actually preferred to attack the melancholy (*melancholia balneum diaboli*). Lawyers and jurists, it is true, increasingly had to consult physicians in order to clarify their understanding of the minds of mad defendants, but in an age of rapidly rising witchcraft trials, this turn to a medical understanding of the insanity defense certainly did not point to a declining belief in the devil among the members of the bar. The rise of melancholy among university-trained physicians did not lead most of them to discard the nonphysical analysis of demonic obsession and possession. Sometimes, indeed, they found it convenient to have a plausible excuse for the failure of natural remedies,[1] and physicians might easily grant that the devil could mimic the worst sorts of madness. The diagnosis of melancholy rose in part because academic physicians were better trained to recognize it in all its variety. The same explanation may help account for the rise of demonic possession in the late sixteenth century. As pastors bemoaned the swinish worldliness of their congregations and the massive corruption of a mad world perched on the brink of the apocalypse, and as both Catholic and Lutheran communities strove to enforce higher standards of belief and behavior, some parishioners snapped under the moral strain and became possessed by the devil. This state of siege and of mental oppression, occasionally even prompting thoughts of suicide, made more cultural sense in 1600 than it had a century earlier.

Folly continued to be a separate condition, not adequately reducible to humoral disorders, sinful choices, or the actions of the devil. There are times when folly (*Narrheit, stultitia*) appears to have been nothing more than the sixteenth-century term for congenital mental retardation, but this is only true of the folly of those described as "natural" or "born" fools. In essence, the fool was a dwarf, cripple, or an eternal child, naive and silly, ignorant and amusing, easily abused and suffering from a condition that was just as easily imitated, as clowns and comedians have always known. Hundreds of princely and episcopal courts retained one or more fools for entertainment and for the edification that may be derived from seeing hu-

1. I have treated a good example of this sort of professional buck-passing in *Mad Princes*, pp. 118–22.

manity stripped of its pretensions to reason and civilization. Indeed, as the civilizing process advanced at court, forcing courtiers and aristocrats to keep secret their grosser bodily functions and to cultivate novel sorts of shame and embarrassment over breaches of an ever-stricter code of decorum, the court fool represented a welcome relief from the constant need to be proper. Like pilgrims to a healing shrine and like residents of the newly founded Hessian hospitals, these court fools were not given the benefit of a medical diagnosis. Indeed, they were not treated medically or even pastorally. Nor were they generally looked to as sources of wisdom, even though, like children, they might occasionally naively state an obvious fact that was in danger of vanishing under layers of polite denial and courtly protocol.

Madness was, therefore, a diverse experience in sixteenth-century Germany, one that ill comports with schemes that simplify and try to characterize the age with just a few bold strokes of the pen. The mad were usually recognized as suffering from a desperate and dangerous affliction, and in need of food and shelter, support and protection, and sometimes strict confinement. Families and neighbors were regularly called on to take care of their local mad. Relatives relied on jails and hospitals only if they could prove that they were unable to manage on their own. Sometimes they might vow a pilgrimage in exchange for miraculous healing, and on other occasions they may have been able to send a miserable, helpless person to a therapeutically optimistic hospital, hoping for healing. Prayers, hymns, and exorcisms were apparently helpful in some instances, while changes of diet, air, sleep patterns, music, and sexual relations, or a regimen of drugs (herbal or chemical), must occasionally have been effective, too. But usually madness remained an irremediable condition, and most hospitals continued to recognize that sad fact by organizing custodial care and pastoral comfort without much hope of psychic healing unless God should choose to intervene directly.

Without pushing the comparison too strenuously, one can see that in their way, sixteenth-century Germans were as ambivalent and confused about madness as most of us are four hundred years later. Bookstores today display scores of books that offer to resolve the problems of mind and body, defend the nonorganic autonomy of the mind and of human freedom (and, by extension, the existence of mental diseases), or explain the mind as nothing more than how the brain works. The brain either is or is not a computer. The soul is either a vestige of superstitious religious language or a symbol of the way that we, as conscious and ethical beings, transcend some of the constraints of nature. Like Renaissance Germans, we too have our simplifiers, eager to prove that the mental illnesses are all hereditary, or all organic, or all socially and culturally constructed. Our modern culture, too, provides a great variety of therapies, often depending as much on the details of one's insurance plan as on one's priest, psychotherapist, or social worker. Our age is, of course, different from the past in many ways, but we should resist the powerful temptation to oversimplify the past with the same zeal that we resist those who oversimplify the complexities and confusions of our world. This book has documented a century in which attitudes toward madness changed, and the changes certainly had direction. Medical theories became more systematic and more influential even as demonic possession became more common and demonological theories became more devoted to the collection of empirical evidence and trustworthy, eyewitness accounts. The experience of madness, both among the mad and among those who observed the mad, thus shifted slowly toward categories more like those with which we live today. Should we call these changes progress? As a moral discipline, history should perhaps rather contribute to a healthy cultural humility. Overcoming our sense that we know better what is human and rational, or bestial and mad, may be one of the melancholy satisfactions conveyed by a history of madness drawn from so long ago.

REFERENCE MATERIAL

Bibliography

PRIMARY SOURCES

Archives and Manuscript Collections (with Abbreviations)

Haina Hospitalsarchiv (HHA), Receptions-Reskripte (RR)
Leiden: Rijksuniversiteit Library, Cod. Voss. Chym. 25: Paracelsus, *De secretis secretorum theologiae*
Marburg: Hessisches Staatsarchiv Marburg (StAM)
Marburg: University of Marburg, *Paracelsusedition* (MP) typescript of Leiden Cod. Voss. Chym. 25: De secretis secretorum theologiae; typescript of Paracelsus's unpublished religious writings
Nuremberg: Staatsarchiv Nürnberg, Ratsverlässe (StAN)
Stuttgart: Württembergishes Hauptstaatsarchiv
Tübingen: Institut für Spätmittelalter und Reformation, Lutherindex
Würzburg: Stadtarchiv Literalien (StAW)

Printed Sources

Agricola, Sixtus, and Georg Witmer. *Erschröckliche gantz warhafftige Geschicht welche sich mit Apolonia, Hannsen Geisslbrechts . . . Haussfrawen, so . . . von dem bösen Feind gar hart besessen.* Ingolstadt, 1584.
Agrippa, Heinrich Cornelius, von Nettesheim. *Opera omnia.* "Lyon" [probably Germany, 1600?]; repr. Hildesheim, 1970.
Alberti, Michael. *De melancholia vera et simulata.* Halle, 1743.
Alciati, Andrea. *Digestorum titulos aliquot, pagina quarta enumeratos Commentaria.* Lyon, 1560.
Altenstaig, Johannes. *Vocabularius Theologiae.* Hagenau, 1517.
Amman, Jost. *Frauentrachtenbuch von Jost Amman. Mit kolorierten Holzschnitten der Erstausgabe von 1586 und einem Nachwort.* Edited by Manfred Lemmer. Frankfurt a/M, 1986.
Amman, Jost, and Hans Sachs. *Eygentliche Beschreibung Aller Stände auff Erden, Hoher*

und Nidriger, Geistlicher und Weltlicher, Aller Künsten, Handwercken und Händeln, etc. vom grosten biß zum kleinesten, Auch von irem Ursprung, Erfindung und gebreuchen. Frankfurt a/M, 1568.

———. *The Book of Trades (Ständebuch).* Edited and with an introduction by Benjamin A. Rifkin. New York, 1973.

Angelus, Andreas. *Wider Natur und Wunderbuch. Darin so wol in gemein von Wunderwercken dess Himmels, Luffts, Wassers und Erden, als insonderheit von allen widernaturlichen wunderlichen Geschichten grossern theils Europae, fürnemlich der Churfürstlichen Brandenburgischen Marck, vom Jahr 490. biss auff 1597. ablauffendes Jahr beschehen gehandelt wird.* Frankfurt a/M, 1597.

———. *Annales Marchiae Brandenburgicae, das ist, Ordentliche Verzeichnus und Beschreibung der fürnemsten . . . Jahrgeschichten und Historien, so sich vom 416. Jahr vor Christi geburt, bis auffs 1596. Jahr . . . begeben . . . haben.* Frankfurt a/O, 1598.

Anglicus, Bartholomaeus. *De proprietatibus rerum.* Nuremberg: Anton Koberger, 1483.

Aretinus, Angelus. *De maleficiis, cum additionibus.* Lyon, 1555.

Aschner, Bernhard, ed. and tr. *Paracelsus: Sämtliche Werke nach der 10-bändigen Huserschen Gesamtausgabe (1589–91), zum erstenmal in neuzeitliches Deutsch übersetzt.* 3 vols. Jena, 1926–1930.

Baldus, Petrus. *Commentaria in digestum vetus.* Lyon, 1562.

Bartolus de Saxoferrato. *Commentaria in primam digesti veteris partem.* Edited by Petrus Paulus Parisii Cardinalis. Lyon, 1550.

———. *Opera omnia.* 11 vols. Venice, 1570–71.

Bericht eines Edelmannes in einem Stetlein Beltzig genant mit Namen Anthonius Seele, welcher gar schwere und erschreckliche Anfechtungen hat. N.p., 1562.

Besold, Christoph. *Ad tit. I, III, IV, V, et VI lib. I. pandectarum commentarii succincti.* Tübingen, 1616.

———. *Thesaurus practicus, continens explicationem terminorum atque clausularum, in aulis et dicasteriis Romano-Germanici Imperii usitatarum.* Tübingen, 1629.

———. *Thesaurus practicus . . . Additionibus Dn. Joh. Jacobi Speidelii . . . cum novis additionibus . . . Christophori Ludovici Dietherns.* Nuremberg, 1659.

Binsfeld, Peter. *Tractatus de confessionibus maleficorum et sagarum recognitus et auctus: An et quanta fides iis adhibenda sit.* Trier, 1591.

———. *Tractat von Bekanntnuss der Zauberer und Hexen: Ob und wie viel denselben zu glauben.* Munich, 1591.

Bloss, Sebastian (*praeside*), and Matthaeus Müller (respondent). *ΠΕΡΙ ΤΕΣ ΦΡΕΝΙΤΙΔΕ: De Phrenetide Assertiones Medicae.* Tübingen, 1602.

Blumius, Nicolaus. *Historische erzehlung: Was sich mit einem fürnehmen Studenten, der von dem leidigen Teuffel zwölff Wochen besessen gewesen, verlauffen.* Leipzig, 1605.

Boaistuau, P. *Le theatre du monde ou il est faict ung ample discours des miseres humaines . . . Weltlicher Schawplatz darinn Menschliche jammer, kummer und Ellend außgefürt.* Würzburg, 1587.

———. *Histoires prodigieuses, extraicts de plusieurs fameux autheurs . . . nouvellement augmentées de plusieurs histoires.* Antwerp, 1594.

Bobertag, Felix, ed. *Narrenbuch.* Berlin, 1884.

Bodin, Jean. *De la démonomanie des sorciers.* Paris, 1581.

———. *Les six livres de la république.* Paris, 1583. Reprint, Aalen, Ger., 1977.

————. *The Six Bookes of a Commonwealth.* Translation by Richard Knolles of *Les six livres,* 1606. Edited by Kenneth D. McRae. Cambridge, Mass., 1962.

Bohlen von Bohlendorff, Freiherr Julius, ed. *Hausbuch des Herrn Joachim von Wedel, Auf Krempzow Schloss und Blumberg Erbgesessen.* Tübingen, 1882.

Brant, Sebastian. *"The Ship of Fools" by Sebastian Brant.* 1494. Translated by Edwin H. Zeydel. New York, 1944.

————. *Das Narrenschiff.* 1494. Edited by H. A. Junghans and Hans-Joachim Mähl. Stuttgart, 1985.

Brunfels, Otto. *Spiegel der Artzny.* Strasbourg, 1532.

Brunner, Balthasar (1533–1604). *Consiliorum Medicorum liber unicus ex bibliotheca Jo. Jacobi Strasskirchneri.* Frankfurt a/M, 1727.

Burgkmair, Hans. *The Triumph of Maximilian I: 137 Woodcuts by Hans Burgkmair and Others.* With a translation of descriptive text, introd., and notes by Stanley Appelbaum. New York, 1964.

Burton, Robert. *The Anatomy of Melancholy.* London, 1621.

Büttner, Wolfgang. *Sechs hundert / sieben und zwantzig Historien / Von Claus Narrenn. Feine schimpfliche wort und Reden / die Erbare Ehrenleut Clausen abgemerckt / und nachgesagt haben / Zur Bürgerlichen und Christ-lichen Lere / wie andere Apologen / dienstlich und förderlich. Mit lustigen Reimen gedeutet und erkleret.* Eisleben, 1572. Frankfurt a/M, 1602.

Cardano, Girolamo. *De rerum varietate.* Basel, 1557.

Carpzov, Benedict. *Practicae novae imperialis Saxonicae rerum criminalium.* 1635. 8th ed. 3 vols. Wittenberg, 1684.

Celichius, Andreas. *Notwendige Erinnerung Von des Sathans letzten Zornsturm, Und was es auff sich habe und bedeute, das nu zu dieser zeit so viel Menschen an Leib und Seel vom Teuffel besessen werden.* Wittenberg, 1594, 1595.

Celsi, Mino. *In haereticis coercendis quatenus progredi liceat: Poems, Correspondence.* Edited by Peter Bietenholz. Naples, 1982.

Chemnitz, Martin. *Examination of the Council of Trent.* Translated by Fred Kramer. 4 vols. St. Louis, 1971–86.

Cicero, Marcus Tullius. *The Academic Questions, Treatise De Finibus, and Tusculan Disputations.* Edited by C. D. Yonge. London, 1880.

Clarus, Julius. *Opera omnia.* Frankfurt a/M, 1576.

Clavisio, Angelus Carletus de. *Summa angelica.* Lyon, 1521.

Coler, Jacob. *Eigentlicher Bericht, Von den seltzamen . . . Wunderwercken . . . so sich newlicher Zeit in der Marck Brandenburg zugetragen.* Erfurt, 1595.

Covarruvias, Didacus. *Opera omnia.* Frankfurt a/M, 1583.

Cradelius, Philipp. *Eine Lehr-, Trost-, und Vermahnungs-Predigt bey der Leich- und Begräbniss des weyland albern und unweisen Hans Mieszko.* 3d ed. N.p., 1692.

Cramer, Daniel. *Das Grosse Pomersche Kirchen Chronicon.* Stettin [Szczecin, Poland], 1628.

Crell, Jacob Ernest Friedrich. "Observationes de probatione sanae mentis . . . defend. Iac. Ernest. Frider. Crellius . . . 5 Dec. 1737." In Christoph Ludwig Crell, *Dissertationum atque programmatum Crellianorum fasciculi XII.* Halle, 1775–84.

Crooke, Helkiah, *Microcosmographia: a description of the body of man: together with the controversies thereto belonging.* London, 1615.

Dacheux, L., ed. *Les chroniques strasbourgeoises de Jacques Trausch et de Jean Wencker.*

Les annales de Sébastien Brant. Fragments recueillis par l'abbé L. Dacheux. Strasbourg, 1892.

——. *Fragments des anciennes chroniques d'Alsace.* Vol. 4. Strasbourg, 1901.

[Dallmayer,] Martin [abbot of Inchenhofen]. *Synopsis miraculorum et beneficiorum seu vincula charitatis, Lieb-Bänder und Ketten-Glider, welche berührt . . . S. Leonardus . . . zu Inchenhofen . . . uber dreytausend Wunderzaichen . . . geschehen.* Munich, 1659.

Damhouder, Jost. *Enchiridion rerum criminalium.* Lyon, 1555.

Dannhauer, Johann Conrad. *Scheid- und Absag-Brieff Einem ungenanten Priester auss Cöllen, auff sein AntwortsSchreiben an einen seiner vertrawten guten Freunde, über das zu Strassburg (also titulirte) vom Teuffel besessene Adeliche Jungfräwlin gegeben.* Strasbourg, 1654.

Delrio, Martin. *Disquisitionum magicarum libri sex.* Louvain, 1599–1600.

Denkwürdige Miracula unnd Wunderzaichen in Zwölff underschidliche Ordnungen außgethailt . . . zu Tundenhausen. Munich, 1646.

Du Laurens, André. *Discours de la conservation de la veue: Des maladies melancholiques: des cartarrhes: et de la vieillesse.* Tours, 1594. English trans., London, 1599. Italian trans., Naples, 1626.

Eigentliche unnd Warhaffte vertzaichnus, was sich in disem 1563 Jar . . . zu Augspurg, mit eines armen Burgers Tochter daselbst zügetragen, wie sy vomm bösen Geist . . . besessen, und derselbig . . . von Herrn Simon Scheibenhart . . . aussgetriben. N.p., n.d. [1563].

Eine Grawsame erschreckliche und wunderbarliche Geschicht oder Newe Zeitung, welche warhaftig geschehen ist, in diesem MDLIX. Jar, zur Platten . . . Alda hat ein Schmid eine Tochter die ist vom bösen Feind dem Teufel eingenommen und besessen. Wittenberg, 1559.

Eisengrein, Martin. *Unser liebe Fraw zu Alten Oetting.* Ingolstadt, 1571.

Erasmus, Desiderius. *Encomium moriae.* 1509. In *Opera omnia,* 4th ser., vol. 3. Edited by Clarence Miller. Amsterdam and Oxford, 1979.

——. *The Praise of Folly.* 1509. Translated by Clarence Miller. New Haven, 1979.

Etliche Wunderzaichen, die Gott der Almächtig auff dem heiligen Berg Andechs . . . gewirckt und erzaigt hat. Munich, 1602.

Extract Unnd gründtlicher Bericht, etlichen Gnaden: und Wunderwercken, so . . . Gott, durch das . . . Fürbitt . . . Bennonis . . . gewirckt. Munich, 1643.

Ferrand, Jacques. *De la maladie d'amour ou melancholie erotique.* Paris, 1610. Expanded ed., Paris, 1623.

——. *A Treatise on Lovesickness.* Edited by Donald A. Beecher and Massimo Ciavolella. Syracuse, N.Y., 1990.

Fichard, Johann. *Consiliorum.* 2 vols. Frankfurt a/M, 1590.

Fincel, Job. *Wunderzeichen: Der dritte Teil, so von der zeit an, da Gottes wort in Deudschland, Rein und lauter geprediget worden, geschehen und ergangen sind.* Jena, 1562.

Forestus, Petrus. *Observationum et curationum medicinalium de febribus ephemeris et continuis libri duo.* Antwerp, 1584.

——. *Observationum et curationum medicinalium libri tres, . . . nonus de variis capitis doloribus; decimus de universis ac cerebri & meningum eiusdem symptomatis ac morbis.* Leiden, 1590.

——. *Observationum et curationum medicinalium liber XXXII, de lue venerea.* Leiden, 1606.

Franz, Eckhart G., ed. *Kloster Haina: Regesten und Urkunden*. Vol. 2: *(1300–1560), Erste Hälfte: Regensten*. Veröffentlichungen der Historischen Kommission für Hessen und Waldeck, 9, Klosterarchive, vol. 6. Marburg, 1970.

Franz, Günther. *Urkundliche Quellen zur hessischen Reformationsgeschichte*. Vol. 2: *1525–1547*. Marburg, 1954.

Fries, Laurentius. *Spiegel der Artzny*. Strasbourg,1519.

Frommann, Johann Andreas. *Hypotyposis Juris Furiosorum singularis quam deo ter opt. max. miserabilium eiusmodi personarum defensore justissimo dirigente*. Strasbourg, 1655.

Galen. *On the Natural Faculties*. Translated by Arthur John Brock. London, 1916.

Gemeiner, Carl Theodor. *Regensburgische Chronik: Unveränderter Nachdruck der Originalausgabe. Mit einer Einleitung, einem Quellenverzeichnis und einem Register*. Edited by Heinz Angermeier. 4 vols. Munich, 1987.

Gewiß und Approbirte Historia Von S. Bennonis etwo Bischoffen zu Meissen, Leben und Wunderzaichen. Munich, 1602.

Godelmann, Johann Georg. *Disputatio de magis, veneficis, maleficis et lamiis. Praeside Ioanne Georgio Godelmanno*. Frankfurt a/M, 1584.

———. *Tractatus de magis, veneficis et lamiis*. Frankfurt a/M, 1591.

———. *Von Zäuberern Hexen und Unholden, Warhafftiger und Wolgegründeter Bericht*. Frankfurt a/M, 1592.

Goethe, Johann Wolfgang. *Italienische Reise*. Part 2. Edited by Christoph Michel and Hans Georg Dewitz. Frankfurt a/M, 1993. In *Sämtliche Werke*, pt. 1, vol. 15, 2: *Briefe, Tagebücher und Gespräche*, ed. Dieter Borchmeyer. Frankfurt a/M, 1985–.

Graminaeus, Dieterich. *Inductio sive Directorium, Das ist: Anleitung oder underweisung wie ein Richter in Criminal und peinlichen sachen die Zauberer und Hexen belangendt sich zu verhalten*. Cologne, 1594.

Gretser, Jacob. *Heylsamer Oelbrunn der Hl. Junckfrawen S. Walburgen*. Ingolstadt, 1621.

Gross, Henning. *Magica. Das ist: Wunderbarliche Historien von Gespensten und mancherley Erscheinungen der Geister*. 2 vols. Eisleben, Ger., 1600.

Gross, Johannes. *Kurtze Basler Chronik*. Basel, 1614.

Grosscurdt, Justus. *Warhaffter Bericht von einer Frawen aus Solingen welche vorm Jahr leider vom bösen Geist besessen*. Statthagen, 1618.

Hagen, Friedrich Heinrich von der, ed. *Narrenbuch*. Halle, 1811.

Hamberger, Georg *(praeside)*, and Balthasar Bruno (Braun) (respondent). *Disputatio de Phrenetide*. Tübingen, 1588.

Harsnet, Samuel. *A Declaration of Egregious Popish Impostures*. London, 1603.

Heerbrand, Jacob. *Ein Predig Vom Straal*. Tübingen, 1579.

Heigius, Petrus. *Quaestiones iuris tam civilis quam Saxonici . . . ditae nunc primum cura Ludovici Person*. 2 vols. Wittenberg, 1601.

Hirth, George. *Die Wunder von Mariazell: Facsimile-Reproduction der 25 Holzschnitte eines unbekannten deutschen Meisters um 1520*. Munich, 1883.

Hocker, Jodocus, with additions by Hermann Hammelmann. "Der Teuffel selbs." In *Theatrum diabolorum, das ist: Warhafftige eigentliche und kurtze Beschreibung allerley grewlicher, schrecklicher und abschewlicher Laster*, ed. Sigismund Feyerabend. Frankfurt a/M, 1569 (repr. 1575, 1587), fols. 1–146.

Hoffmann, Paul, and Peter Dohms. *Die Mirakelbücher des Klosters Eberhardsklausen*.

Publikationen der Gesellschaft für rheinische Geschichte, vol. 64, no. 179. Düsseldorf, 1988.

Horn, Caspar Heinrich. *Consultationum responsorum ac sententiarum liber unus in XVI classes distributus.* Dresden and Leipzig, 1711.

Hubmaier, Balthasar. *Schriften.* Edited by Gunnar Westin and Torsten Bergsten. Quellen und Forschungen zur Reformationsgeschichte, vol. 29. Gütersloh, Ger., 1962.

Hueber, Fortunat. *"Zeitiger Granatapfel."* Muenchen 1671: Mirakelbuch des bayrischböhmischen Wallfahrtsortes Neukirchen bei Heilig Blut. Edited by Guillaume van Gemert. Amsterdam, 1983.

Irsing, Jacob, S.J. *Historia von der weitberühmbten unser lieben Frawen Capell zu Alten-Oeting in Nidern Bayern.* Translated by Johann Scheitenberger. Munich, 1644.

Justinian. *The Digest of Justinian.* Edited and translated by Alan Watson et al. Philadelphia, 1985.

————. *Justinian's Institutes.* Translated by Peter Birks and Grant McLeod, with the Latin text of Paul Krueger. Ithaca, N.Y., 1987.

Karlstadt, Johann Schöner von. *Ein nutzlichs büchlein viler bewerter Ertzney, lang zeyt versamlet und züsammen pracht.* Nuremberg, 1528.

Khueller, Sebastian. *Kurtze unnd warhafftige Historia, von einer Junckfrawen, wölche mit etlich unnd dreissig bösen Geistern leibhafftig besessen.* Munich, 1574.

Kleinlawel, Michael. *Straßburgische Chronik.* Strasbourg, 1625.

Kornmann, Henricus. *Templum naturae historicum, . . . in quo de natura et miraculis quatuor elementorum . . . disseritur.* Darmstadt, 1611.

Kraftheim, Johannes Crato von. *Consiliorum et epistolarum medicinalium libri septem.* Edited by Lorenz Scholtz. Frankfurt a/M, 1671.

Krämer, Heinrich (Institoris). *Malleus maleficarum.* 1487. Edited by André Schnyder. Göppingen, 1991.

Kurtzer Bericht Etlicher Miracul unnd Wunderwercken so . . . 1605 . . . bey S. Bennonis Hailthum in München. Munich, 1606.

Lang, Johann. *Epistolarum medicinalium volumen tripartitum.* Frankfurt a/M, 1589.

Lemnius, Levinus. *De miraculis occultis naturae librii iiii.* Antwerp, 1574.

————. *The Secret Miracles of Nature in four books.* London, 1658.

Letzener, Johann. *Historische, kurtze, einfaltige und ordentliche Beschreibung des Closters und Hospitals zu Haina in Hessen gelegen. Auffs newe ubersehen und verbessert.* Mühlhausen, Ger., 1588.

Lorich, Jodocus. *Aberglaub: Das ist, kurtzlicher bericht, Von Verbottenen Segen, Artzneyen, Künsten, vermeinten und anderen spöttlichen beredungen . . . von newen ubersehen und gemehrt.* Freiburg im Breisgau, 1593.

Luther, Martin. *D. Martin Luthers Werke: Kritische Gesamtausgabe.* 101 vols. to date. Weimar, 1883–. Cited as WA.

————. *Briefwechsel.* Cited as WABr.

————. *Tischreden.* Cited as WATR.

————. *Works* ("The American Edition"). Edited by Helmut T. Lehmann and Jaroslav J. Pelikan. 55 vols. St. Louis, 1955–86. Cited as LW.

————. *Letters of Spiritual Counsel.* Edited by Theodore G. Tappert. Philadelphia, 1955.

Marbach, Johann. *Von Mirackeln und Wunderzeichen.* Augsburg, 1571.

Melanchthon, Philipp. *Commentarius de Anima.* Wittenberg, 1548.

Menghi, Girolamo. *Fustis daemonum.* In *Thesaurus exorcismorum atque coniurationum terribilium potentissimorum, efficacissimorum cum practica probatissima,* pp. 433–616. Cologne, 1626.

Menochius, Jacobus. *Consiliorum tomi XIII.* Frankfurt a/M, 1676.

———. *De arbitriis iudicum quaestionibus et causis centuriae sex.* Geneva, 1630.

Moegling, Daniel (*praeside*), and Johann Kuhn (Cuno) (respondent). *Theses de Phrenetide.* Heidelberg, 1584.

Mörlin, David. *Sanct Salvator Zu Bettbrunn in Bayern: Das ist: Von der alten heiligen Capellen und wirdigem hoch brühmbten Gottshauß . . . S. Salvators zu Bettbrunn.* Ingolstadt, 1597.

Mons Sanctus Andechs, Das ist: Kurtzer Begriff oder Innhalt von den Gnadenreichen H. Berg Andechs. Munich, 1682.

Montanus, Ioannis Baptista. *Consultationes medicae.* Edited by Johann Crato Vratislavensis [Crato von Kraftheim]. [Basel?] 1583.

Neue Zeitung und beschreibung, Was sich mit Anna Barbara, vom Stain geboren, von kuniglichen stamb . . . ist worden . . . wie sie . . . mit 9. Teuflen besessen, auch wider ledig ist worden. Constance, 1608.

Newe Zeytung, Von einem Megdlein das entzuckt ist gewest, und was wunderbarliche Rede es gethan hat. Nuremberg, 1560.

Newkirch, Melchior. *Andechtige Christliche gebete, wider die Teuffel in dem armen besessenen leuten.* Helmstedt, Ger., 1596.

Nutton, Vivian. "The Rise of Medicine." In *The Cambridge Illustrated History of Medicine,* ed. Roy Porter, pp. 52–81. Cambridge, 1996.

Oldecop, Justus. *Observationes criminales practicae congestae et in quinque titulos . . . tributae.* 1654. Frankfurt a/O, 1685.

Operae horarum subcisivarum, sive meditationes historicae: Centuria altera. Frankfurt a/M, 1601.

Paracelsus [Philippus Aureolus Theophrastus Bombast von Hohenheim]. *Sämtliche Werke.* Pt. 1: *Medizinische, naturwissenschaftliche und philosophische Schriften.* Edited by Karl Sudhoff. Munich and Berlin, 1922–33. Pt. 2: *Die theologischen und religionsphilosophischen Schriften.* Edited by Wilhelm Matthiessen and Kurt Goldammer. Munich and Stuttgart, 1923–. Cited as SW.

———. *Four Treatises of Theophrastus von Hohenheim, called Paracelsus.* Edited by Henry Sigerist. Baltimore, 1941.

———. *Theophrastus Paracelsus: Werke.* Edited by Will-Erich Peuckert. 5 vols. Basel, 1965–68.

———. *Register (Indices) der Wörter, Begriffe, Namen und Bibelstellen zu den Bänden IV bis VII (Auslegungen zum Alten Testament).* Edited by Kurt Goldammer et al. Stuttgart, 1995.

Pauli, Johannes, O.F.M. *Schimpf und Ernst.* 1522. Edited by Johannes Bolte. 2 vols. Berlin, 1924. Reprint, Hildesheim, 1972.

Planer, Andreas (*praeside*), and Johann Feber (Schmidt) (respondent). *De morbo Saturnino seu melancholia.* Tübingen, 1593.

Planer, Andreas (*praeside*), and Helias Waldner (respondent). *Disputatio medica de capite et cerebro hominis.* Tübingen, 1580.

Planer, Andreas (*praeside*), and Thomas Schlaier (respondent). *Disputatio medica de morbis temperamenti.* Tübingen: 1586.

Platter, Felix. *Praxeos seu de cognoscendis, praedicandis, praecavendis, curandisque affectibus homini incommodantibus tractatus.* Basel, 1609.

————. *Observationum, in hominis affectibus plerisque corpori et animo libri tres.* Basel, 1614.

————. *Observationes: Krankheitsbeobachtangen in drei Büchern.* Translated by Günter Goldschmidt. Edited by Heinrich Buess. Bern, 1963.

————. *Tagebuch (Lebensbeschreibung), 1536–1567.* Edited by Valentin Lötscher. Basel, 1976.

Porta, Giambattista della. *Magia naturalis.* Naples, 1558.

————. *Magiae naturalis libri viginti.* Naples, 1589.

Pratensis, Jason. *De cerebri morbis.* Basel, 1549.

Radbruch, Gustav, ed. *Die peinliche Gerichtsordnung Kaiser Karls V. von 1532 (Carolina).* Stuttgart, 1962.

Rösch, Wendel. *Warhafftige und Erschröckenliche geschicht, welche sich begeben unnd zugetragen hat.* Tübingen, 1590.

Ryff, Walther Hermann. *Warhaffige künstliche und gerechte underweisung und anzeygung, Alle Latwegen, Confect, Conserven, eynbeytzungen und einmachungen . . . wie solche in den Apotheken gemacht.* Strasbourg, 1540.

S. Leonhardus: Etliche gedenckwirdige Miracul und Wunderzeichen. Munich, 1585.

Schenck, Johann. *Observationes medicae de capite humano.* Basel, 1584.

————. *Observationum medicarum, rararum, novarum, admirabilium, et monstrosarum.* 7 books in 2 vols. Frankfurt a/M, 1600.

Scherer, Georg, S.J. *Christliche Erinnerung Bey der Historien von jüngst beschehener Erledigung einer Junckfrawen, die mit zwölfftausent sechs hundert zwey und fünfftzig Teufel besessen gewesen.* Ingolstadt, 1583.

Schickhard, Philipp. *Zwo christliche Predigten uber Buß unnd Belehrung eines Jünglings, welcher sich . . . dem bösen Geist auff siben Jahr lang, mit Leib und Seel ergeben gehabt.* Stuttgart, 1615.

Schnabel, Johann, and Simon Marius. *Warhafftige und erschröckliche Geschicht welche sich newlicher Zeit zugetragen hat, mit einem Jungen Handtwercks und Schmidtsgesellen, Hansen Schmidt genandt.* Würzburg, 1589.

Scholtz, Lorenz. *Consiliorum medicinalium.* Frankfurt a/M, 1598.

Schreckliche Zeitung, warhafftiger und gründtlicher Bericht was sich zugetragen hat mit einem Wirten im Düringerlandt. Erfurt, 1560.

Sedelius [Seidel], Wolfgang. *Wie sich ain Christenlicher Herr, so Landt unnd Leüt zuo Regieren under im hat, vor schedlicher Phantasey verhueten, unnd in allen noeten troesten soll.* Munich, 1547.

Seiler, Tobias. *Daemonomania: Uberaus schreckliche Historia, von einem bessessenen zwelfjährigen Jungfräwlein, zu Lewenberg in Schlesien.* Wittenberg, 1605.

Sohm, Walter. *Territorium und Reformation in der hessischen Geschichte.* Urkundliche Quellen zur hessischen Reformationsgeschichte, ed. Günther Franz, vol. 1. Marburg, 1957.

Staupitz, Johann von. *Sämtliche Werke.* In *Deutsche Schriften,* vol. 1. Edited by J. K. F. Knaake. Potsdam, 1867.

————. *Libellus de exsecutione aeternae praedestinationis (1517).* Edited by Lothar Graf zu Dohna and Richard Wetzel. Vol. 14 of *Spätmittelalter und Reformation,* ed. Heiko A. Oberman. Berlin, 1979.

Stenzel, Karl, ed. *Die Straßburger Chronik des elsässischen Humanisten Hieronymus Gebwiler*. Berlin, 1926.

Stryk, Samuel. "Disputatio octava inauguralis de dementia et melancholia (March 8, 1672)." In *Opera omnia*. 14 vols. Frankfurt a/M and Leipzig, 1743–53.

Tengler, Ulrich. *Layen Spiegel: Von rechtmässigen ordnungen in burgerlichen und peinlichen regimenten*. Augsburg, 1509. Rev. ed., Strasbourg, 1582.

———. *Der neu Layenspiegel*. Augsburg, 1512.

Thyraeus, Petrus. *Daemoniaci, Hoc est: de obsessis a spiritibus daemoniorum hominibus liber unus*. Cologne, 1598.

Tollat von Vochenberg, Johann. *Margarita medicine, ein meisterlichs usserlesens biechlin der artzny für mancherley kranckheit und siechtagen der menschen*. 1497. Strasbourg, 1507.

Tuntenhausen unser lieben frawen Gotzhaus. N.p. Editions consulted: 1506, 1527, 1530, 1532, 1533, 1534 (two eds.), 1535, 1536 (two eds.), 1537, 1538, 1539, 1544, 1547, 1551, 1555, 1561, 1564, 1567, 1569, 1574, 1577, 1579, 1581, 1583, 1584, 1589, 1597.

Umbstendig und warhaffter Bericht was sich zu end deß 1602 und 1603 gantze Jahr bey S. Benno in München für Wunderwerck begeben. Munich, 1603.

Utenhovius, Carolus. *Xenia seu. Ad illustrium aliquos Europae hominum nomina, Allusionum (intertextiis alicubi Ioach. Bellaii eiusdem argumenti versibus) Liber primus*. N.p. [Basel?], n.d. [1570?].

Verzaichnus etlicher furnemmer wunderwerck so sich bey S. Bennonis Heilthumb zu Munchen im Jahr 1601 und 1602 begeben. Munich, 1604.

Vilerley gedenckwürdige Miracula, so sich zugetragen von Anno 99 bis ad Annum sexcentissimum quintum. Munich, 1606.

Wagner, Tobias. *Der Kohlschwartze Teuffel . . . über einem schröcklichen Fall einer Mannsperson die sich in Schwermuth dem Teuffel mit eignem Blut verschrieben*. Ulm, 1643.

Walther, George. *Krancken Büchlein: Woher alle Kranckheiten kommen, Item, warumb uns Gott damit heimsuche: Und wie man sich darinnen Christlich verhalten und in allerley anfechtungen trösten sol*. Wittenberg, 1579.

Weyer, Johann. *Medicarum observationum rararum liber 1*. Basel, 1567.

———. *De ira morbo, ejusdem curatione philosophica, medica, et theologica, liber*. Basel 1577.

———. *De lamiis liber: Item de commentitiis jejuniis*. Basel, 1577.

———. *Artzney Buch: Von etlichen biß anher unbekandten unnd unbeschriebenen Kranckheiten*. Frankfurt a/M, 1583.

———. *De praestigiis daemonum, et incantationibus ac veneficiis Libri sex, postrema editione sexta aucti et recogniti*. 6th ed. Basel, 1583.

———. *Opera omnia*. Amsterdam, 1660.

———. *Witches, Devils, and Doctors in the Renaissance: Johann Weyer, "De praestigiis daemonum."* Edited by George Mora et al. Binghamton, N.Y., 1991.

———. *On Witchcraft*. Edited by Benjamin G. Kohl and H. C. Erik Midelfort. Asheville, N.C. In press.

Widl, Adam. *Divus Sebastianus Eberspergae Boiorum propitius*. Munich, 1688.

Wundergeschicht, Offenbarung und Geschichte einer entzuckten Kindbetterin welche zwelff stunden ist Todt geligen unnd vom Geist umbher gefüret, darnach wider lebendig worden. Augsburg, [1569].

Wunderlich, Werner, ed. *Das Lalebuch: In Abbildung des Drucks von 1597*. Göppingen, Ger., 1982.

———, ed. *Das Lalebuch herausgegeben und in unsere Sprache übertragen*. Stuttgart, 1982.

———, ed. *Deutsche Schwankliteratur*. 2 vols. Frankfurt a/M, 1992.

Zacchia, Paolo. *Quaestiones medico-legales*. 1621, 1630, 1634, 1651, 1654. 3 vols. in 1. Lyon, 1701.

Zacharias, F. "Complementum artis exorcisticae." In *Thesaurus exorcismorum atque coniurationum terribilium potentissimorum, efficacissimorum cum practica probatissima*, pp. 617–983. Cologne, 1626.

Zimmern, Froben Christof, Graf von, and Wilhelm Wernher, Graf von. *Die Chronik der Grafen von Zimmern*. Edited by Hans-Martin Decker-Hauff and Rudolf Seigel. 3 vols. Constance, 1964–.

SECONDARY SOURCES

Aa, A. J. van der. *Biographisch Woordenboek der Nederlanden*. Haarlem, 1852–78. Reprint, Amsterdam, 1969.

Abel, Wilhelm. *Massenarmut und Hungerkrisen im vorindustriellen Deutschland*. 2d ed. Göttingen, 1977.

Ackerknecht, Erwin. *Kurze Geschichte der Psychiatrie*. 2d ed. Stuttgart, 1967.

———. *A Short History of Psychiatry*. Translated by Sula Wolff. 2d ed. New York, 1968.

———. *A Short History of Medicine*. Baltimore, 1982.

Alsheimer, Rainer. "Katalog protestantischer Teufelserzählungen." In *Volkserzählung und Reformation: Ein Handbuch zur Tradierung und Funktion von Erzählstoffen und Erzählliteratur im Protestantismus*, ed. Wolfgang Brückner, pp. 417–519. Berlin, 1974.

Amelunxen, Clemens. *Zur Rechtsgeschichte der Hofnarren*. Schriftenreihe der Juristischen Gesellschaft zu Berlin, no. 124. Berlin, 1991.

Amereller, Almut. *Votif-Bilder: Volkskunst als Dokument menschlicher Hilfsbedürftigkeit, dargestellt am Beispiel der Votif-Bilder des Klosters Andechs*. Munich, 1965.

Andree, Richard. "Katholische Überlebsel beim evangelischen Volke." *Zeitschrift des Vereins für Volkskunde* 21 (1911): 113–25.

Anglo, Sydney. "Melancholia and Witchcraft: The Debate Between Wier, Bodin, and Scot." In *Folie et déraison à la Renaissance*, pp. 209–22. Brussels, 1976.

———, ed. *The Damned Art*. London, 1977.

———. "Reginald Scot's Discoverie of Witchcraft: Scepticism and Sadduceeism." In *Damned Art*, ed. id., pp. 106–39.

Arnold, Klaus. *Niklashausen, 1476: Quellen und Untersuchungen zur sozialreligiösen Bewegung des Hans Behem und zur Agrarstruktur eines spätmittelalterlichen Dorfes*. Baden-Baden, 1980.

Audibert, Adrien. *Études sur l'histoire du droit Romain*, vol. 1: *La folie et la prodigalité*. Paris, 1892.

Baader, Berndt Ph. *Der bayerische Renaissancehof Herzog Wilhelms V. (1568–1579): Ein Beitrag zur bayerischen und deutschen Kulturgeschichte des 16. Jahrhunderts*. Leipzig, 1943.

Babb, Lawrence. *The Elizabethan Malady: A Study of Melancholia in English Literature from 1580 to 1642*. East Lansing, Mich., 1951.

Bach, Hermann. "Mirakelbücher bayerischer Wallfahrtsorte. Untersuchung ihrer literarischen Form und ihrer Stellung innerhalb der Literatur der Zeit." Ph.D. diss., Munich, 1963.

Bachmann, Hanns. *Das Mirakelbuch der Wallfahrtskirche Mariastein in Tirol als Quelle zur Kulturgeschichte (1678–1742)*. Innsbruck, 1973.

Bächtold-Stäubli, Hanns, and E. Hoffmann-Krayer, eds. *Handwörterbuch des deutschen Aberglaubens*. 10 vols. Berlin and Leipzig, 1929–42.

Backman, E. Louis. *Religious Dances in the Christian Church and in Popular Medicine*. Translated by E. Classen. London, 1951.

Bankston, William, B. H. David Allen, and David S. Cunningham. "Religion and Suicide: A Research Note on Sociology's 'One Law,'" *Social Forces* 62 (1983): 521–28.

Bark, N. M. "Did Shakespeare Know Schizophrenia? The Case of Poor Mad Tom in King Lear." *British Journal of Psychiatry* 146 (1985): 436–38.

Barnes, Robin B. *Prophecy and Gnosis: Apocalypticism in the Wake of the Lutheran Reformation*. Stanford, 1988.

Bart, Pauline B. "Social Structure and Vocabularies of Discomfort: What Happened to Female Hysteria?" *Journal of Health and Human Behavior* 9 (1968): 188–93.

Barth, Hans-Martin. *Der Teufel und Jesus Christus in der Theologie Martin Luthers*. Göttingen, 1967.

Baschnagel, Georg. *"Narrenschiff" und "Lob der Torheit": Zusammenhänge und Beziehungen*. Bern, 1979.

Bates, D. G. "Thomas Sydenham." In *Dictionary of Scientific Biography*, ed. C. C. Gillispie, 13: 213–15. 16 vols. New York, 1970–80.

———. "Thomas Sydenham: The Development of His Thought, 1666–1674." Ph.D. diss., Johns Hopkins University, 1975.

Battegay, Raymond. "Felix Platter und die Psychiatrie." In *Felix Platter (1536–1614) in seiner Zeit*, ed. Ulrich Tröhler, pp. 35–43. Basel, 1991.

Bauer, Anton. "Wallfahrten zum Anastasiahaupt in Benediktbeuern." *Heimatbote vom Isarwinkel*, 1936, no. 8.

———. "Die ehemalige Marienwallfahrt Neubeuern am Inn." *Das bayerische Inn-Oberland* 33 (1963): 51–94.

Bauer, Karl. *Regensburg: Aus Kunst- Kultur- und Sittengeschichte*. Regensburg, 1980.

Bauer, Robert. "Das älteste gedruckte Mirakelbüchlein von Altötting." *Ostbairische Grenzmarken: Passauer Jahrbuch für Geschichte, Kunst und Volkskunde* 5 (1961): 144–51.

———. "Das Altöttinger Mirakelbüchlein von 1540." *Ostbairische Grenzmarken* 6 (1962–63): 241–48.

———. "Das Büchlein der Zuflucht zu Maria: Altöttinger Mirakelberichte von Jacobus Issickemer." *Ostbairische Grenzmarken* 7 (1964–65): 206–36.

———. *Bayerische Wallfahrt Altötting: Geschichte, Kunst, Volksbrauch*. 2d ed. Munich, 1980.

Bauerreiss, Romuald. *Pie Jesu*. Munich, 1931.

Bäumer, Remigius, ed. *Von Konstanz nach Trient: Beiträge zur Geschichte der Kirche von den Reformkonzilien bis zum Tridentinum. Festgabe für August Franzen*. Munich, 1972.

Bausinger, Hermann. "Schildbürgergeschichten: Betrachtungen zum Schwank." In *Wunderseltsame Geschichten: Interpretationen zu Schildbürgern und Lalebuch*, ed. Werner Wunderlich, pp. 25–58. Göppingen, 1983.

Baxter, Christopher. "Jean Bodin's 'De la démonomanie des sorciers': The Logic of Persecution." In *Damned Art*, ed. Anglo, pp. 76–105. London, 1977.

———. "Johann Weyer's 'De praestigiis daemonum': Unsystematic Psychopathology." In *Damned Art*, ed. Anglo, pp. 53–75. London, 1977.

Baylor, Michael. *Action and Person: Conscience in Late Scholasticism and the Young Luther.* Leiden, 1977.

Beecher, Donald A. "Erotic Love and the Inquisition: Jacques Ferrand and the Tribunal of Toulouse, 1620." *Sixteenth Century Journal* 20 (1989): 41–53.

Beek, H. H. *Waanzin in de Middeleeuwen: Beeld van de Gestoorde en Bemoeienis mit de Zieke.* Nijkerk, Neth., 1969.

Behringer, Wolfgang. *Hexenverfolgung in Bayern: Volksmagie, Glaubenseifer und Staatsräson in der Frühen Neuzeit.* Munich, 1987.

———. *Chonrad Stoeckhlin und die Nachtschar. Eine Geschichte aus der frühen Neuzeit.* Munich, 1994.

———. "Zur Geschichte der Hexenforschung." In *Hexen und Hexenverfolgung im deutschen Südwesten,* ed. Sönke Lorenz, pp. 93–146. Ostfildern, Ger., 1994.

Beitl, Richard, ed. *Wörterbuch der deutschen Volkskunde.* 2d ed. Stuttgart, 1955.

Beizer, Janet. *Ventriloquized Bodies: Narratives of Hysteria in Nineteenth-Century France.* Ithaca, N.Y., 1994.

Bell, Rudolf M. *Holy Anorexia.* Chicago, 1985.

Bergsten, Torsten. *Balthasar Hubmaier, Anabaptist Theologian and Martyr.* Translated by W. R. Estep, Jr. Valley Forge, Pa., 1978.

Bers, Günter. "Das Miraculöß Mariä Bildlein zu Aldenhoven": Geschichte einer rheinischen Wallfahrt, 1655–1985. Cologne, 1986.

Bessmer, Julius, S.J. "Luthers Anschauungen über die Geisteskrankheiten und die katholische Lehre." *Stimmen aus Maria-Laach: Katholische Blätter* 84 (1913): 444–45, 474–76.

Beyer, Christel. "Hexen-Leut, so zu Würzburg gerichtet": Der Umgang mit Sprache und Wirklichkeit in Inquisitionsprozessen wegen Hexerei. Frankfurt a/M, 1986.

Beyer, Jürgen. "Wahrhafte Wundergeschicht von neuen Propheten die alle Welt zu rechtschaffener Buße und Besserung aufrufen: Lutherske folkelige profeter i 1500- og 1600-tallet." M.A. thesis, University of Copenhagen, 1990.

Bietenholz, Peter. "Mino Celsi and the Toleration Controversy of the Sixteenth Century." *Bibliothèque d'Humanisme et Renaissance* 34 (1972): 31–47.

Binding, Karl. *Die Schuld im deutschen Strafrecht: Vorsatz, Irrtum, Fahrlässigkeit. Kurzes Lehrbuch.* Leipzig, 1919.

Binz, Carl. *Doctor Johann Weyer: Ein rheinischer Arzt, der erste Bekämpfer des Hexenwahns.* Bonn, 1885. 2d ed., Berlin, 1896.

Blasius, Dirk. *Der verwaltete Wahnsinn: Eine Sozialgeschichte des Irrenhauses.* Frankfurt a/M, 1980.

Blécourt, Willem de. "Spuren einer Volkskultur oder Dämonisierung? Kritische Bemerkungen zu Ginzburgs 'Benandanti,'" *Kea: Zeitschrift für Kulturwissenschaften* 5 (1993): 17–30.

Bloom, Harold. *The Western Canon: The Books and School of the Ages.* New York, 1994.

Böck, Robert. "Die Verehrung des hl. Benno in München." *Bayerisches Jahrbuch für Volkskunde,* 1958: 53–73.

Boerner, Peter. *Tagebuch.* Stuttgart, 1969.

Boss, Jeffrey M. N. "The Seventeenth-Century Transformation of the Hysteric Affection and Sydenham's Baconian Medicine." *Psychological Medicine* 9 (1979): 221–34.

Brain, W. Russell. "The Concept of Hysteria in the Time of William Harvey." *Proceedings of the Royal Society of Medicine* 56, no. 4 (April 1963): 317–24.

Brann, Noel. "The Renaissance Passion of Melancholy: The Paradox of Its Cultivation and Resistance." Ph.D. diss., Stanford University, 1965.

Brecht, M. "Der 'Schimpfer' Martin Luther." *Luther* 52 (1981): 97–113.

Browe, Peter. "Die Ausbreitung des Fronleichnamsfestes." *Jahrbuch für Liturgiewissenschaft* 8 (1928): 107–43.

Brown, William J., et al. *Syphilis and Other Venereal Diseases*. Cambridge, Mass., 1970.

Brückner, Wolfgang. "Forschungsprobleme der Satanologie und Teufelserzählungen." In *Volkserzählung und Reformation: Ein Handbuch zur Tradierung und Funktion von Erzahlstoffen und Erzahlliteratur im Protestantismus*, ed. id., pp. 393–416. Berlin, 1974.

Brumberg, Joan Jacobs. *Fasting Girls: The Emergence of Anorexia Nervosa as a Modern Disease*. Cambridge, Mass., 1988.

Brunner, Hugo. "Behandlung einer Geisteskranken im Jahre 1575." *Zeitschrift des Vereins für hessische Geschichte und Landeskunde*, n.s., 24 (1901): 403–4.

Buchwald, Georg. "Lutherana: Notizen aus Rechnungsbüchern des Thüringischen Staatsarchivs zu Weimar." *Archiv für Reformationsgeschichte* 25 (1928): 1–98.

Buckland, W. W. *A Text-Book of Roman Law from Augustus to Justinian*. Cambridge, 1921.

Burke, Peter. "Witchcraft and Magic in Renaissance Italy: Gianfrancesco Pico and His Strix." In *Damned Art*, ed. Anglo, pp. 32–52. London, 1977.

———. *Popular Culture in Early Modern Europe*. New York, 1978.

Burns, R. M. *The Great Debate on Miracles: From Joseph Glanvill to David Hume*. Lewisburg, Pa., 1981.

Busfield, Joan. "The Female Malady: Men, Women and Madness in Nineteenth-Century Britain." *Sociology* 28 (1994): 259–77.

Carolsfeld, Franz Schnorr von. "Ueber Klaus Narr und M. Wolfgang Bütner." *Archiv für Litteratur-Geschichte* 6 (1877): 277–328.

Carroll, Michael. *Madonnas That Maim: Popular Catholicism in Italy Since the Fifteenth Century*. Baltimore, 1992.

Céard, Jean. "Folie et démonologie au XVIᵉ siècle." In *Folie et déraison à la Renaissance*, pp. 129–47. Brussels, 1976.

———. *La nature et les prodiges: L'insolite au XVIᵉ siècle, en France*. Geneva, 1977.

Cellard, André. *Histoire de la folie au Québec de 1600 à 1850*. Montréal, 1991.

Certeau, Michel de. *La possession de Loudun*. Paris, 1970.

Charcot, Jean-Martin, and Paul Richer. *Die Besessenen in der Kunst*. Translated by Willi Hendrichs. Edited by Manfred Schneider and Wolfgang Tietze. Göttingen, 1988.

Christian, William. *Apparitions in Late Medieval and Renaissance Spain*. Princeton, 1981.

———. *Local Religion in Sixteenth-Century Spain*. Princeton, 1981.

Christoffel, H. "Psychiatrie und Psychologie bei Felix Platter (1536–1614)." *Monatsschrift für Psychiatrie und Neurologie* 127 (1954): 213–27.

———. "Eine systematische Psychiatrie des Barock: Felix Platters 'laesiones mentis,' 1602–1736." *Schweizer Archiv für Neurologie und Psychiatrie* 77 (1956): 15–24.

Churchland, Paul. *The Engine of Reason, the Seat of the Soul: A Philosophical Essay on the Brain*. Cambridge, Mass., 1995.

Clark, Stuart. *Thinking with Demons: The Idea of Witchcraft in Early Modern Europe*. Oxford, 1997.

Clarke, Basil. *Mental Disorder in Earlier Britain: Exploratory Studies*. Cardiff, 1975.

Cocchiara, Giuseppe. *The History of Folklore in Europe*. Translated by John N. McDaniel. Philadelphia, 1981.

Cohn, Norman. *Europe's Inner Demons: An Enquiry Inspired by the Great Witch-Hunt*. London, 1975.

Cranefield, Paul. "Psychology as an English Word." *American Notes and Queries* 4 (1966): 116–17.

Cranz, F. Edward, and Charles B. Schmitt. *A Bibliography of Aristotle Editions, 1501–1600*. 2d rev. ed. Baden-Baden, 1984.

Credner, Karl August, ed. *Philipps des Grossmütigen Hessische Kirchenreformations-Ordnung*. Giessen, Ger., 1852.

Crick, Francis. *The Astonishing Hypothesis: The Scientific Search for the Soul*. New York, 1994.

Crisciani, Chiara. "History, Novelty, and Progress in Scholastic Medicine." In *Renaissance Medical Learning: Evolution of a Tradition*, ed. Michael R. McVaugh and Nancy Siraisi, pp. 118–39. *Osiris*, 2d ser., vol. 6 (1990).

Cunningham, Andrew. "Fabricius and the 'Aristotle project' in Anatomical Teaching and Research at Padua." In *The Medical Renaissance of the Sixteenth Century*, ed. A. Wear, R. K. French, and I. M. Lonie, pp. 195–222. Cambridge, 1985.

Curry, Patrick. "Revisions of Science and Magic." *History of Science* 23 (1985): 299–325.

Dahm, Georg. *Das Strafrecht Italiens im ausgehenden Mittelalter: Untersuchungen über die Beziehungen zwischen Theorie und Praxis im Strafrecht des Spätmittelalters, namentlich im XIV. Jahrhundert*. Berlin, 1931.

Damasio, Antonio. *Descartes' Error: Emotion, Reason, and the Human Brain*. New York, 1994.

Daube, David. *Roman Law: Linguistic, Social, and Philosophical Aspects*. Edinburgh, 1969.

Debus, Allen G. *The Chemical Philosophy: Paracelsan Science and Medicine in the Sixteenth and Seventeenth Centuries*. 2 vols. New York, 1977.

————. *The French Paracelsians: The Chemical Challenge to Medical and Scientific Tradition in Early Modern France*. Cambridge, 1991.

Demandt, Carl E. *Geschichte des Landes Hessen*. 2d ed. Kassel, 1972.

Dennie, Charles C. *A History of Syphilis*. Springfield, Ill., 1962.

Deufert, Wilfried. *Narr, Moral und Gesellschaft: Grundtendenzen im Prosaschwank des 16. Jahrhunderts*. Bern, 1975.

Devereux, Georges. "Schizophrenia: An Ethnic Psychosis, or, Schizophrenia Without Tears." In id., *Basic Problems of Ethnopsychiatry*. Translated by Basia Miller Gulati and Georges Devereux, pp. 214–36. Chicago, 1980.

Diepgen, Paul. *Deutsche Volksmedizin: Wissenschaftliche Heilkunde und Kultur*. Stuttgart, 1935.

Diethelm, Oskar, and Thomas F. Hefferman. "Felix Platter and Psychiatry." *Journal of the History of the Behavioral Sciences* 1 (1965): 10–23.

Diethelm, Oskar. *Medical Dissertations of Psychiatric Interest Printed Before 1750*. Basel, 1971.

Dilg, Peter, and Hartmut Rudolph, eds. *Resultate und Desiderate der Paracelsus-Forschung*. Stuttgart, 1993.

Dinges, Martin. "Frühneuzeitliche Armenfürsorge als Sozialdisziplinierung? Probleme mit einem Konzept." *Geschichte und Gesellschaft* 17 (1991): 5–29.

Diosdi, György. *Contract in Roman Law from the Twelve Tables to the Glossators*. Budapest, 1981.

Dols, Michael W. "The Origins of the Islamic Hospital: Myth and Reality." *Bulletin of the History of Medicine* 61 (1987): 367–90.

Doob, Penelope B. R. *Nebuchadnezzar's Children: Conventions of Madness in Middle English Literature*. New Haven, 1974.

Dopsch, Heinz, Kurt Goldammer, and Peter F. Kramml, eds. *Paracelsus (1493–1541): Keines andern Knecht*. Salzburg, 1993.

Dörner, Klaus. *Madmen and the Bourgeoisie: A Social History of Insanity and Psychiatry*. Cambridge, 1984.

Duerr, Hans-Peter. *Dreamtime: Concerning the Boundary Between Wilderness and Civilization*. Translated by Felicitas Goodman. Oxford, 1985.

———, ed. *Die Wilde Seele: Zur Ethnopsychoanalyse von Georges Devereux*. Frankfurt a/M, 1987.

Dülmen, Richard van. "Volksfrömmigkeit und konfessionelles Christentum in 16. und 17. Jahrhundert." In *Volksreligiosität in der modernen Sozialgeschichte*, ed. Wolfgang Schieder, pp. 14–30. *Geschichte und Gesellschaft*, special no., 11. Göttingen, 1986.

———. "Imaginationen des Teuflischen: Nächtliche Zusammenkünfte, Hexentänze, Teufelsabbate." In id., *Hexenwelten: Magie und Imagination vom 16–20. Jahrhundert*, pp. 94–130. Frankfurt a/M, 1988.

Dupont-Bouchat, Sylvie, Willem Frijhoff, and Robert Muchembled. *Prophètes et sorciers dans les Pays-Bas (XVIᵉ–XVIIIᵉ siècle)*. Paris, 1978.

Durling, Richard. "A Chronological Census of Renaissance Editions and Translations of Galen." *Journal of the Warburg and Courtauld Institutes* 24 (1961): 230–305.

———. *A Catalog of Sixteenth-Century Printed Books in the National Library of Medicine*. Bethesda, Md., 1967.

Ebeling, Friedrich W. *Friedrich Taubmann: Ein Kulturbild*. 3d ed. Leipzig, 1884.

Edelson, Marshall. *The Idea of a Mental Illness*. New Haven, 1971.

Edmundson, Mark. *Towards Reading Freud: Self-Creation in Milton, Wordsworth, Emerson, and Sigmund Freud*. Princeton, 1990.

Edwards, Mark U. *Luther and the False Brethren*. Stanford, 1975.

———. *Luther's Last Battles: Politics and Polemics, 1531–1546*. Ithaca, N.Y., 1983.

Eis, Gerhard. *Vor und nach Paracelsus: Untersuchungen über Hohenheims Traditionsverbundenheit und Nachrichten über seine Anhänger*. Stuttgart, 1965.

Eisenberg, Leon. "The Social Construction of Mental Illness" (editorial). *Psychological Medicine* 18 (1988): 1–9.

Ellard, John. "Did Schizophrenia Exist Before the Eighteenth Century?" *Australian and New Zealand Journal of Psychiatry* 21 (1987): 306–14.

Ellenberger, Henri F. *The Discovery of the Unconscious: The History and Evolution of Dynamic Psychiatry*. New York, 1970.

Engelmann, Woldemar. *Die Schuldlehre der Postglossatoren und ihre Fortentwicklung*. 1895. Reprint, Aalen, Ger., 1965.

———. "Der geistige Urheber des Verbrechens nach dem italienischen Recht des Mittelalters." In *Festschrift für Karl Binding*, 2: 387–610. Leipzig, 1911.

———. *Irrtum und Schuld nach der italienischen Lehre und Praxis des Mittelalters.* Berlin, 1922.

Erikson, Erik. *Young Man Luther: A Study in Psychoanalysis and History.* New York, 1958.

Ernst, Cécile. *Teufelaustreibungen: Die Praxis der katholischen Kirche im 16. und 17. Jahrhundert.* Bern, 1972.

Ertz, Stefan. *Aufbau und Sinn des Lalebuchs.* Cologne, 1965.

Estes, Leland L. "The Medical Origins of the European Witch Craze: A Hypothesis." *Journal of Social History* 17 (1983): 271–84.

———. "Reginald Scot and His Discoverie of Witchcraft: Religion and Science in the Opposition to the European Witch Craze." *Church History* 52 (1983): 444–56.

Evans, Martha Noel. *Fits and Starts: A Genealogy of Hysteria in Modern France.* Ithaca, N.Y., 1991.

Falk, Franz. "Die Druckkunst im Dienste der Kirche zunächst in Deutschland bis zum Jahre 1520." *Görres Gesellschaft zur Pflege der Wissenschaft im katholischen Deutschland*, no. 2. Cologne, 1879.

Faupel, Charles E., Gregory S. Kowalski, and Paul D. Starr. "Sociology's One Law: Religion and Suicide in the Urban Context." *Journal for the Scientific Study of Religion* 26 (1987): 523–34.

Febvre, Lucien. *Life in Renaissance France.* Cambridge, Mass., 1977.

Fimpel, Ludwig. *Mino Celsis Traktat gegen die Ketzertötung: Ein Beitrag zum Toleranzproblem des 16. Jahrhunderts.* Basel, 1967.

Fingarette, Herbert. *The Meaning of Criminal Insanity.* Berkeley and Los Angeles, 1972.

Fingarette, Herbert, and Ann Fingarette Hasse. *Mental Disabilities and Criminal Responsibility.* Berkeley and Los Angeles, 1979.

Fischer-Homberger, Esther. *Hypochondrie: Melancholie bis Neurose: Krankheiten und Zustandsbilder.* Bern, 1970.

Flashar, Helmut. *Melancholie und Melancholiker in den medizinischen Theorien der Antike.* Berlin, 1966.

Flögel, Karl Friedrich. *Geschichte der Hofnarren.* Liegnitz and Leipzig, 1789.

Foucault, Michel. *Histoire de la folie à l'âge classique: Folie et déraison.* Paris, 1961. 2d ed., 1972.

———. *Madness and Civilization: A History of Insanity in the Age of Reason.* New York, 1965.

Fox, Sanford J. *Science and Justice: The Massachusetts Witch Trials.* Baltimore, 1968.

Franck, J. "Kunz von der Rosen." In *Allgemeine deutsche Biographie*, 29 (1889): 195–97. 56 vols. Leipzig, 1875–1912.

Franz, Adolf. *Die kirchlichen Benediktionen im Mittelalter.* 2 vols. Freiburg im Breisgau, 1909.

Freedberg, David. *The Power of Images: Studies in the History and Theory of Response.* Chicago, 1989.

French, R. K., I. M. Lonie, and Andrew Wear, eds. *The Medical Renaissance of the Sixteenth Century.* Cambridge, 1985.

Freud, Sigmund. "A Seventeenth-Century Demonological Neurosis." In *The Stan-*

dard Edition of the Complete Psychological Works of Sigmund Freud, trans. and ed. James Strachey et al., 19: 67–105. London, 1961.

Freytag, Gustav. "Der deutsche Teufel im 16. Jahrhundert." In *Bilder aus der deutschen Vergangenheit*, 2: 114–42. Berlin, 1927.

Friedrich, J. B. *Versuch einer Literärgeschichte der Pathologie und Therapie der psychischen Krankheiten von den ältesten Zeiten bis zum 19. Jahrhundert*. Würzburg, 1830.

———. *Systematische Literatur der ärztlichen und gerichtlichen Psychologie*. Berlin, 1833.

Fritz, Jean-Marie. *Le discours du fou au Moyen-Âge: Étude comparée des discours littéraire, médical, juridique et théologique de la folie*. Paris, 1992.

Gäbler, Ulrich. "Die Kinderwallfahrten aus Deutschland und der Schweiz zum Mont St. Michel, 1456–1459." *Zeitschrift für schweizerische Kirchengeschichte* 63 (1969): 221–331.

Galdston, Iago. "The Psychiatry of Paracelsus." In *Psychiatry and the Human Condition*, pp. 377–89. New York, 1976.

Garzarolli-Thurnlackh, Karl. "Die Holzschnitte der Mariazeller Wunder: Ihre Vorläufer und Meister." *Phaidros* 1 (1947): 181–89.

Gates, Barbara T. *Victorian Suicide: Mad Crimes and Sad Histories*. Princeton, 1988.

Gause, Ute. *Paracelsus (1493–1541): Genese und Entfaltung seiner frühen Theologie*. Tübingen, 1993.

Geerk, Frank. *Paracelsus—Arzt unserer Zeit: Leben, Werk und Wirkungsgeschichte des Teophrastus von Hohenheim*. Zurich, 1992.

Geertz, Clifford. "Found in Translation: On the Social History of the Moral Imagination." In id., *Local Knowledge: Further Essays in Interpretive Anthropology*, pp. 36–54. New York, 1983.

Gellner, David N. "Priests, Healers, Mediums, and Witches: The Context of Possession in Kathmandu Valley, Nepal." *Man* 29 (1994): 27–48.

Gerrish, Brian. *Grace and Reason: A Study in the Theology of Luther*. Oxford, 1962.

Gierl, Irmgard. *Bauernleben und Bauernwallfahrt in Altbayern: Eine kulturkundliche Studie auf Grund der Tuntenhausener Mirakelbücher*. Beiträge zur altbayerischen Kirchengeschichte, vol. 21, 2. Munich, 1960.

Gilly, Carlos. "'Theophrastia Sancta': Der Paracelsismus als Religion im Streit mit den offiziellen Kirchen." In *Analecta Paracelsica: Studien zum Nachleben Theophrast von Hohenheims im deutschen Kulturgebiet der frühen Neuzeit*, ed. Joachim Telle, pp. 425–88. Stuttgart, 1994.

Gilman, Sander L., Helen King, Roy Porter, G. S. Rousseau, and Elaine Showalter, eds. *Hysteria Beyond Freud*. Berkeley and Los Angeles, 1993.

Ginzburg, Carlo. *Ecstasies: Deciphering the Witches' Sabbath*. London, 1990.

Glück, Gustav. *Bruegels Gemälde*. Vienna, 1932.

Goddu, André. "The Failure of Exorcism in the Middle Ages." In *Soziale Ordnungen im Selbstverständnis des Mittelalters*, ed. Albert Zimmermann and Gudrun Vuillemin-Diem, pp. 540–57. Miscellanea Mediaevalia, vol. 12/2. Berlin, 1980.

Goertz, Hans Jürgen. *Profiles of Radical Reformers: Biographical Sketches from Thomas Müntzer to Paracelsus*. Translated by Walter Klaassen. Scottsdale, Pa., 1982.

Goethe, Johann Wolfgang von. *The Sorrows of Young Werther*. New York, 1774. Reprint, 1989.

Goldammer, Kurt. *Paracelsus: Natur und Offenbarung*. Hannover, 1953.

———. "Der cholerische Kriegsmann und der melancholische Ketzer: Psychologie und Pathologie von Krieg, Glaubenskampf und Martyrium in der Sicht des

Paracelsus." In *Psychiatrie und Gesellschaft: Ergebnisse und Probleme der Sozialpsychiatrie. Festschrift für Werner Villinger*, ed. H. Erhardt, D. Ploog, and H. Stutte, pp. 90–101. Bern and Stuttgart, 1958.

Goodman, Felicitas D. "Visions." In *The Encyclopedia of Religion*, ed. Mircea Eliade, 15: 282–88. New York, 1987.

———. *How About Demons? Possession and Exorcism in the Modern World*. Bloomington, Ill., 1988.

Gordon, Colin. "Histoire de la folie: An Unknown Book by Michel Foucault." *History of the Human Sciences* 3 (1990): 3–26.

Gottesman, Irving I. *Schizophrenia Genesis: The Origins of Madness*. New York, 1991.

Graf, Klaus. "Carlo Ginzburgs 'Hexensabbat': Herausforderung an die Methodendiskussion der Geschichtswissenschaft." *Kea: Zeitschrift fur Kulturwissenschaften* 5 (1993): 1–17.

Grimm, Heinrich. "Die deutschen 'Teufelbücher' des 16. Jahrhunderts: Ihre Rolle im Buchwesen und ihre Bedeutung." *Archiv für Geschichte des Buchwesens* 16 (1959): 1733–90.

Gritsch, Eric W. "Martin Luther and Violence: A Reappraisal of a Neuralgic Theme." *Sixteenth Century Journal* 3 (1972): 37–55.

———. *Martin: God's Court Jester*. Philadelphia, 1983.

Groß, Angelika. *"La folie": Wahnsinn und Narrheit im spätmittelalterlichen Text und Bild*. Heidelberg, 1990.

Gugitz, Gustav. *Österreichs Gnadenstätten in Kult und Brauch*. 5 vols. Vienna, 1955–58.

Guinsburg, Arlene Miller. "The Counterthrust to Sixteenth-Century Misogyny: The Work of Agrippa and Paracelsus." *Historical Reflections* 8 (1981): 3–28.

Gunnoe, Charles D., Jr. "Thomas Erastus and His Circle of Anti-Paracelsians." In *Analecta Paracelsica: Studien zum Nachleben Theophrast von Hohenheims im deutschen Kulturgebiet der frühen Neuzeit*, ed. Joachim Telle, pp. 127–48. Stuttgart, 1994.

Gutting, Gary. "Foucault and the History of Madness." In *The Cambridge Companion to Foucault*, ed. id., pp. 47–70. Cambridge, 1994.

Habermas, Rebekka. "Wunder, Wunderliches, Wunderbares: Zur Profanisierung eines Deutungsmusters in der frühen Neuzeit." In *Armut, Liebe, Ehre: Studien zur historischen Kulturforschung*, ed. Richard van Dülmen, pp. 38–66, 278–80. Frankfurt a/M, 1988.

Hacking, Ian. *Rewriting the Soul: Multiple Personality and the Sciences of Memory*. Princeton, 1995.

Haile, Harry G. *Luther: An Experiment in Biography*. Garden City, N.Y., 1980.

Hallerstein, Helmut, Freiherr Haller von, and Ernst Eichhorn. *Das Pilgrimspital zum Heiligen Kreuz vor Nürnberg*. Nuremberg, 1969.

Halm, Philipp Maria. "Die Mirakelbilder zu Altötting." *Bayerischer Heimatschutz* 21 (1925): 1–25.

Hanlon, Gregory. "Piété populaire et intervention des moines dans les miracles et les sanctuaires miraculeux en Agenais-Condomois au XVIIᵉ siècle." *Annales du Midi* 97 (1985): 115–27.

Hansen, Joseph. *Quellen und Untersuchungen zur Geschichte des Hexenwahns und der Hexenverfolgung im Mittelalter*. Bonn, 1901.

Hare, Edward H. "Was Insanity on the Increase?" *British Journal of Psychiatry* 142 (1983): 439–66.

———. "Schizophrenia as a Recent Disease." *British Journal of Psychiatry* 153 (1988): 521–31.

———. "Schizophrenia Before 1800? The Case of the Revd. George Trosse." *Psychological Medicine* 18 (1988): 279–85.

Harley, David. "Explaining Salem: Calvinist Psychology and the Diagnosis of Possession." *American Historical Review* 101 (1996): 306–30.

Harline, Craig. *The Burdens of Sister Margaret: Private Lives in a Seventeenth-Century Convent.* Garden City, N.Y., 1994.

Harmening, Dieter. "Fränkische Mirakelbücher: Quellen und Untersuchungen zur historischen Volkskunde und Geschichte der Volksfrömmigkeit." *Würzbürger Diözesangeschichtsblätter* 28 (1966): 25–240.

Hartig, Michael. *Inchenhofen.* 2d ed., Munich, 1955.

Harvey, E. Ruth. *The Inward Wits: Psychological Theory in the Middle Ages and the Renaissance.* London, 1975.

Haustein, Jörg. *Martin Luthers Stellung zum Zauber- und Hexenwesen.* Stuttgart, 1990.

Hayden, Hiram. *The Counter Renaissance.* New York, 1950.

Hecker, J. F. C. *Die grossen Volkskrankheiten des Mittelalters. Historisch-pathologische Untersuchungen,* ed. August Hirsch. Berlin, 1865.

Heilfurth, G., and I. M. Greverus. *Bergbau und Bergmann in der deutschsprachigen Sagenüberlieferung Mitteleuropas.* Vol. 1. Marburg, 1967.

Heiltum und Wallfahrt. Innsbruck, 1988.

Heinemeyer, Walter, and Tilman Pünder, eds. *450 Jahre Psychiatrie in Hessen.* Marburg, 1983.

Helms, Margarete. "Die psychopathologischen Anschauungen bei Paulus Zacchias in Hinsicht auf den Beginn einer forensischen Psychiatrie." M.D. diss., Munich, 1957.

Hemleben, Johannes. *Paracelsus: Revolutionär, Artzt und Christ.* Stuttgart, 1973.

Heyd, Michael. "The Reaction to Enthusiasm." *Journal of Modern History* 53 (1981): 258–80.

Hillerbrand, Hans J. *Landgrave Philipp of Hesse, 1504–1567: Religion and Politics in the Reformation.* Reformation Essays and Studies, no. 1. St. Louis, 1967.

His, Rudolf. *Das Strafrecht des deutschen Mittelalters, erster Teil: Die Verbrechen und ihre Folgen in allgemeinen.* Leipzig, 1920.

Hocke, Gustav René. *Das europäische Tagebuch.* Wiesbaden, 1978.

Holl, Karl. "Martin Luther on Luther." Translated by H. C. Erik Midelfort. In *Interpreters of Luther: Essays in Honor of Wilhelm Pauck,* ed. Jaroslav J. Pelikan, pp. 9–34. Philadelphia, 1968.

Holthausen, Paul. *Das Landeshospital Haina in Hessen, eine Stiftung Landgraf Philipps des Grossmütigen, von 1527–1907.* Frankenberg i. H., 1907.

Horn, Ewald. *Die Disputationen und Promotionen an den deutschen Universitäten vornehmlich seit dem 16. Jahrhundert.* Leipzig, 1893.

Hsia, Ronnie Po-chia. *Society and Religion in Münster, 1535–1618.* New Haven, 1984.

———. *The Myth of Ritual Murder: Jews and Magic in Reformation Germany.* New Haven, 1988.

———. *Social Discipline in the Reformation: Central Europe, 1500–1750.* London, 1989.

Hunter, Richard, and Ida Macalpine. *Schizophrenia 1677: A Psychiatric Study of an Illustrated Autobiographical Record of Demoniacal Possession.* London, 1956.

Huppert, George. *After the Black Death. A Social History of Early Modern Europe.* Bloomington, Ind., 1986.

Hüttl, Ludwig. *Marianische Wallfahrten im süddeutsch-österreichischen Raum. Analysen von der Reformations- bis zur Aufklärungsepoche.* Cologne, 1985.

Imaginair Museum Hugo van der Goes. Ghent, 1982.

Jackson, Stanley W. "Melancholia and the Waning of the Humoral Theory." *Journal of the History of Medicine and Allied Sciences* 33 (1978): 367–76.

———. *Melancholia and Depression: From Hippocratic Times to Modern Times.* New Haven, 1986.

Jacob, Mechtild Josephi. "Die Hexenlehre des Paracelsus und ihre Bedeutung für die modernen Hexenprozesse: Ein Beitrag zur Geschichte der Entwicklung des Hexenglaubens seit dem Mittelalter unter besonderer Berücksichtigung der Überlieferung aus dem Raum Gifhorn (Braunschweig)." Ph.D. diss., Göttingen University, 1959.

Jacquart, Danielle. "Theory, Everyday Practice, and Three Fifteenth-Century Physicians." In *Renaissance Medical Learning: Evolution of a Tradition*, ed. Michael R. McVaugh and Nancy Siraisi, pp. 140–160. Osiris, 2d. ser., vol. 6 (1990).

Jaeger, C. Stephen. "Melancholie und Studium: Zum Begriff 'Arbeitsethik,' seinen Vorläufern und seinem Weiterleben in Medizin und Literatur." In *Literatur, Artes und Philosophie*, ed. Walter Haug and Burghart Wachinger, pp. 117–40. Tübingen, 1992.

Janssen, Johannes. *Geschichte des deutschen Volkes seit dem Ausgang des Mittelalters.* 8 vols. Freiburg im Breisgau, 1883–94.

Jessewitsch, Rolf Dieter. *Das "Ständebuch" des Jost Amman (1568).* Münster, 1987.

Jeste, D. V., R. del Carmen, J. B. Lohr, and R. J. Wyatt. "Did Schizophrenia Exist Before the Eighteenth Century?" *Comprehensive Psychiatry* 26 (1985): 493–503.

Jetter, Dieter. "Zur Entwicklung der Irrenfürsorge im Donauraum." *Medizinhistorisches Journal* 6 (1971): 189–99.

———. *Zur Typologie des Irrenhauses in Frankreich und Deutschland (1780–1840).* Wiesbaden, 1971.

———. *Das europäische Hospital, von der Spätantike bis 1800.* Cologne, 1986.

Jobe, T. H. "Medical Theories of Melancholia in the Seventeenth and Early Eighteenth Centuries." *Clio Medica* 19 (1976): 217–31.

Jones, Colin. *The Charitable Imperative: Hospitals and Nursing in Ancien Régime and Revolutionary France.* London, 1989.

———. "Medicine, Madness, and Mayhem from the Roi Soleil to the Golden Age of Hysteria (17th–19th Centuries)," *French History* 4 (1990): 378–88.

Jones, Colin, and Roy Porter, eds. *Reassessing Foucault: Power, Medicine, and the Body.* London, 1994.

Justi, Carl Wilhelm. *Das Hospital zu Haina: Versuch einer Darstellung seiner ehemaligen und gegenwärtigen Beschaffenheit.* Marburg, 1803.

Jütte, Robert. *Obrigkeitliche Armenfürsorge in deutschen Reichsstädten der Frühen Neuzeit: Städtisches Armenwesen in Frankfurt am Main und Köln.* Cologne, 1984.

Kalkofen, Rupert. "*Lalebuch* oder *Schiltbürger*, Anonymus oder Fischart? Die buchgeschichtlichen Untersuchungen von Peter Honegger und Stefan Ertz im Vergleich." *Wirkendes Wort: Deutsche Sprache und Literatur in Forschung und Lehre* 41 (1991): 363–77.

Kämmerer, Ernst Wilhelm. *Das Leib-Seele-Geist-Problem bei Paracelsus und einigen Autoren des 17. Jahrhunderts.* Wiesbaden, 1971.

———. "Mensch und Krankheit bei Paracelsus." In *Paracelsus: Werke und Wirkung. Festgabe für Kurt Goldammer zum 60. Geburtstag,* ed. Sepp Domandl, pp. 119–124. Vienna, 1975.

Kantorowicz, Hermann. *Albertus Gandinus und das Strafrecht der Scholastik.* 2 vols. Berlin, 1907–26.

Kaplan, Benjamin. "Possessed by the Devil? A Very Public Dispute in Utrecht." *Renaissance Quarterly* 49 (1996): 738–59.

Karcher, J. *Felix Platter: Lebensbild des Basler Stadtarztes, 1536–1614.* Basel, 1949.

Kelly, H. A. *The Devil at Baptism: Ritual, Theology and Drama.* Ithaca, N.Y., 1985.

Kemp, S., and K. Williams. "Demonic Possession and Mental Disorder in Medieval and Early Modern Europe." *Psychological Medicine* 17 (1987): 21–29.

Kieckhefer, Richard. *European Witch-Trials: Their Foundations in Popular and Learned Culture, 1300–1500.* London, 1976.

King, Helen. "Once upon a Text: Hysteria from Hippocrates." In *Hysteria Beyond Freud,* ed. Gilman et al., pp. 3–90. Berkeley and Los Angeles, 1993.

Kirchhoff, Theodor. *Grundriß einer Geschichte der deutschen Irrenpflege.* Berlin, 1890.

Kittelson, James. "Successes and Failures in the German Reformation: The Report from Strasbourg." *Archiv für Reformationsgeschichte* 73 (1982): 153–75.

Kleinman, Arthur. "Anthropology and Psychiatry: The Role of Culture in Cross-Cultural Research on Illness." *British Journal of Psychiatry* 151 (1987): 447–54.

———. *Rethinking Psychiatry.* New York, 1988.

Klibansky, Raymond, Fritz Saxl, and Erwin Panofsky. *Saturn and Melancholy: Studies in the History of Natural Philosophy, Religion, and Art.* New York, 1964.

Köhler, E. *Arme und Irre: Die liberale Fürsorgepolitik des Bürgertums.* Berlin, 1977.

Koldewey, Friedrich. *Der Exorzismus im Herzogtum Braunschweig seit den Tagen der Reformation.* Ph.D. diss., Jena, 1893.

König, Maria Angela. *Weihegaben an U.L. Frau von Altötting.* 2 vols. Munich, 1939.

Könneker, Barbara. *Wesen und Wandlung der Narrenidee im Zeitalter des Humanismus: Brant, Murner, Erasmus.* Wiesbaden, 1966.

Korff, Gottfried. *Heiligenverehrung in der Gegenwart: Empirische Untersuchungen in der Diözese Rottenburg.* Tübingen, 1970.

Koslow, Susan. "The Impact of Hugo van der Goes's Mental Illness and Late Medieval Religious Attitudes on the Death of the Virgin." In *Healing and History: Essays for George Rosen,* ed. Charles E. Rosenberg, pp. 27–50. Folkestone, Kent, 1979.

Kramer, Karl-Sigismund. "Die Mirakelbücher der Wallfahrt Grafrath." *Bayerisches Jahrbuch für Volkskunde,* 1951, pp. 80–102.

———. "Typologie und Entwicklungsbedingungen nachmittelalterlicher Nahwallfahrten." *Rheinisches Jahrbuch für Volkskunde* 11 (1960): 195–211.

Krenn, Peter. "Der große Mariazeller Wunderaltar von 1519 und sein Meister." *Jahrbuch des Kunsthistorischen Instituts der Universität Graz* 2 (1966–67): 31–51.

———. "Die Wunder von Mariazell und Steiermark." In *Die Kunst der Donauschule, 1490–1540: Ausstellung des Landes Oberösterreich,* ed. Otto Wutzel, pp. 164–68. Linz, 1965.

Kreutzer, Hans Joachim. *Der Mythos vom Volksbuch.* Stuttgart, 1977.

Kriss, Rudolf, and Lenz Rettenbeck. *Wallfahrtsorte Europas.* Munich, 1950.

Kriss-Rettenbeck, Lenz. *Ex voto.* Zurich, 1972.

Kromm, Jane E. 'The Feminization of Madness in Visual Representation." *Feminist Studies* 20 (1994): 507–35.

Kühnel, Harry. "Integrative Aspekte der Pilgerfahrten." In *Europa 1500: Regionen, Personenverbände, Christenheit*, ed. Ferdinand Seibt and Winfried Eberhard, pp. 496–509. Stuttgart, 1987.

Kunze, Michael. *Der Prozess Pappenheimer*. Ebelsbach, 1981.

Kusukawa, Sachiko. *The Transformation of Natural Philosophy: The Case of Philip Melanchthon*. Cambridge, 1995.

Kuttner, Stephan. *Kanonistische Schuldlehre von Gratian bis auf die Dekretalen Gregors IX*. Vatican City, 1935.

Labouvie, Eva. "Hexenspuk und Hexenabwehr. Volksmagie und volkstümlicher Hexenglaube." In *Hexenwelten, Magie und Imagination*, ed. Richard van Dülmen, pp. 49–93. Frankfurt a/M, 1987.

———. *Zauberei und Hexenwerk: Ländlicher Hexenglaube in der frühen Neuzeit*. Frankfurt a/M, 1991.

———. *Verbotene Künste: Volksmagie und ländlicher Aberglaube in den Dorfgemeinden des Saarraumes (16.–19. Jahrhundert)*. St. Ingbert, Ger., 1992.

Laehr, Heinrich. *Die Literatur der Psychiatrie, Neurologie, und Psychologie von 1459–1799*. 4 vols. Berlin, 1900.

Laignel-Lavastine, Maxime, and Jean Vinchon. *Les malades de l'esprit et leurs médecins du XVIe au XIXe siècle: Les étapes des connaissances psychiatriques de la Renaissance à Pinel*. Paris, 1930.

Lain Entralgo, Pedro. *Enfermidad y pecado*. Barcelona, 1961.

Langholf, Volker. *Medical Theories in Hippocrates: Early Texts and the "Epidemics."* Berlin, 1990.

Larner, Christina. *Enemies of God: The Witch-Hunt in Scotland*. Baltimore, 1981.

Larner, Robert A. H. *Water into Wine? An Investigation of the Concept of Miracle*. Montreal, 1988.

Lederer, David L. "Reforming the Spirit: Society, Madness, and Suicide in Central Europe, 1517–1809." Ph.D. diss., New York University, 1995.

Lefebvre, Joel. *Les fols et la folie: Étude sur les genres du comique et la création littéraire en Allemagne pendant la Renaissance*. Paris, 1968.

Lehmann, Hartmut. "Frömmigkeitsgeschichtliche Auswirkungen der 'kleinen Eiszeit.'" In *Volksreligiosität in der modernen Sozialgeschichte*, ed. Wolfgang Schieder, pp. 31–50. *Geschichte und Gesellschaft*, special no., 11. Göttingen, 1986.

Lehnert, Hans. *Kirchengut und Reformation: Eine Kirchenrechtliche Studie*. Erlanger Abhandlungen zur mittleren und neueren Geschichte, vol. 20. Erlangen, 1935.

Leibbrand, Werner, and Annemarie Wettley. *Der Wahnsinn: Geschichte der abendländischen Psychopathologie*. Freiburg im Breisgau, 1961.

Leibbrand-Wettley, Annemarie. "Zur Psychopathologie und Dämonologie bei Paracelsus und Johannes Weyer." In *Melemata: Festschrift für Werner Leibbrand zum siebzigsten Geburtstag*, ed. Joseph Schumacher, pp. 65–73. Mannheim, 1967.

Lepenies, Wolf. *Melancholy and Society*. Translated by Jeremy Gaines and Doris Jones. Cambridge, Mass., 1992.

Le Roy Ladurie, Emmanuel. *The Beggar and the Professor: A Sixteenth-Century Family Saga*. Translated by Arthur Goldhammer. Chicago, 1997.

Leutenbauer, Siegfried. *Hexerei- und Zaubereidelikt in der Literatur von 1450 bis 1530*. Berlin, 1972.

Levack, Brian. *The Witch Hunt in Early Modern Europe*. London, 1987.

Lewinstein, S. R. "The Historical Development of Insanity as a Defense in Criminal Actions." *Journal of Forensic Science* 14 (1969): 275–93.

Lewis, I. M. *Ecstatic Religion: A Study of Shamanism and Spirit Possession*. 2d ed. London, 1989.

Liebscher, Hellmuth. "Ein kartographischer Beitrag zur Geschichte der Tanzwut." M.D. diss., Leipzig, 1931.

Lloyd, Daniel Edward. " 'Natura,' 'Ratio,' and 'Usus': The Thematic Unity of the *Lalebuch*." Ph.D. diss., University of Wisconsin, 1991.

Lorenz, Sönke. "Johann Georg Godelmann—ein Gegner des Hexenwahns?" In *Beiträge zur Pommerschen und Mecklenburgischen Geschichte*, ed. Roderich Schmidt, pp. 61–105. Marburg, 1981.

———. *Aktenversendung und Hexenprozeß: Dargestellt am Beispiel der Juristenfakultäten Rostock und Greifswald (1570/82–1630)*. 2 vols. Frankfurt a/M, 1982–83.

———, ed. *Hexen und Hexenverfolgungen im deutschen Südwesten: Aufsatzband*. Karlsruhe and Ostfildern, Ger., 1994.

Lottin, Alain. *Lille, citadelle de la contre-reforme? (1598–1668)*. Dunkirk, 1984.

Lubbers, Franz. *Die Geschichte der Zurechnungsfähigkeit von Carpzow bis zur Gegenwart unter besonderer Berücksichtigung der Doktrin des gemeinen Rechts*. Diss., Jena, 1936. Breslau-Neukirch, 1938.

Lutz, C. "Aufnahme und Verpflegung von Geisteskranken und Epileptikern im Juliushospitale." In *Die Psychiatrie in Würzburg von 1583–1893*, ed. C. Rieger. Verhandlungen der Phys.- med. Gesellschaft, n.s., 27 (1894): 33–37. Reprinted in *Erster Bericht vom Jahre 1899 aus der psychiatrischen Klinik* (Würzburg, 1899), pp. 89–93.

Lutz, Gerhard. "Volkskunde und Geschichte: Zur Frage einer als 'historische Wissenschaft' verstandene Volkskunde." In *Volkskultur und Geschichte: Festgabe für Josef Dünninger zum 65. Geburtstag*, ed. Dieter Harmening et al., pp. 14–26. Berlin, 1970.

MacDonald, Michael. *Mystical Bedlam: Madness, Anxiety and Healing in Seventeenth-Century England*. Cambridge, 1981.

———, ed. *Witchcraft and Hysteria in Elizabethan London: Edward Jorden and the Mary Glover Case*. London, 1991.

Macfarlane, A. D. J. *Witchcraft in Tudor and Stuart England*. London, 1970.

Mader, Franz. *Wallfahrten im Bistum Passau*. Munich, 1984.

Maloney, Gilles, and R. Savoie. *Cinq cent ans de bibliographie hippocratique, 1473–1982*. St.-Jean-Chrysostome, Quebec, 1982.

Mälzer, Gottfried. *Julius Echter: Leben und Werk*. Würzburg, 1989.

Mandrou, Robert. *Magistrats et sorciers en France au XVIIᵉ siècle: Une analyse de psychologie historique*. Paris, 1968.

Martin, Alfred. "Geschichte der Tanzkrankheit in Deutschland." *Zeitschrift des Vereins für Volkskunde* 24 (1914): 113–34, 225–39.

Martino, Ernesto di. *La terra del rimorso*. Rome, 1961.

Maurer, Wilhelm. "Die heilige Elisabeth und ihr Marburger Hospital." In *Kirche und Geschichte: Gesammelte Aufsätze*, vol. 2: *Beiträge zu Grundsatzfragen und zur Frömmigkeitsgeschichte*, ed. E. W. Kohls and O. Müller, pp. 284–319. Göttingen, 1970.

———. "Zum Verständnis der heiligen Elisabeth von Thüringen." In *Kirche und*

Geschichte: Gesammelte Aufsätze, vol. 2: *Beiträge zu Grundsatzfragen und zur Frömmigkeitsgeschichte*, ed. E. W. Kohls and O. Müller, pp. 231–83. Göttingen, 1970.

McAlister, Neil Harding. "The Dancing Pilgrims at Muelebeek." *Journal of the History of Medicine and Allied Sciences* 32 (1977): 315–19.

McCants, Anne. "Monotonous but not Meagre: The Diet of Burgher Orphans in Early Modern Amsterdam." *Research in Economic History* 14 (1992), ed. Roger Ransom, 69–116.

——. "Consumer Behaviour in an Early Modern Dutch Orphanage: A Wealth of Choice." *Journal of European Economic History* 22 (1993): 121–42.

McCloy, William A. "The Ofhuys Chronicle and Hugo van der Goes." Ph.D. diss., State University of Iowa, 1958.

Megill, Allan. *Prophets of Extremity: Nietzsche, Heidegger, Foucault, Derrida*. Berkeley and Los Angeles, 1985.

——. "The Reception of Foucault by Historians." *Journal of the History of Ideas* 48 (1987): 117–41.

Meingast, Fritz. *Marienwallfahrten in Bayern und Österreich*. Munich, 1979.

Merkel, Friedemann. *Geschichte des evangelischen Bekentnisses in Baden von der Reformation bis zur Union*. Karlsruhe, 1960.

Merrill, James. *Divine Comedies*. New York, 1976.

Merskey, Harold, and Paul Potter. "The Womb Lay Still in Ancient Egypt." *British Journal of Psychiatry* 154 (1989): 751–53.

Mezger, Werner. *Hofnarren im Mittelalter: Vom tieferen Sinn eines seltsamen Amts*. Constance, 1981.

Micale, Mark S. *Approaching Hysteria: Disease and Its Interpretations*. Princeton, 1995.

Midelfort, H. C. Erik. *Witch Hunting in Southwestern Germany, 1562–1684: The Social and Intellectual Foundations*. Stanford, 1972.

——. "Madness and Civilization in Early Modern Europe: A Reappraisal of Michel Foucault." In *After the Reformation. Essays in Honor of J. H. Hexter*, ed. Barbara Malament, pp. 247–66. Philadelphia, 1980.

——. "Madness and the Problem of Psychological History in the Sixteenth Century." *Sixteenth Century Journal* 12 (1981): 5–12.

——. "Catholic and Lutheran Reactions to Demon Possession in the Late Seventeenth Century: Two Case Histories." *Daphnis* 15 (1986): 623–48.

——. "Johann Weyer in medizinischer, theologischer, und rechtsgeschichtlicher Hinsicht." In *Vom Unfug der Hexenprozesse: Gegner der Hexenverfolgung von Johann Weyer bis Friedrich Spee*, ed. Hartmut Lehmann and Otto Ulbricht, pp. 53–64. Wolfenbütteler Forschungen, vol. 55. Wiesbaden, 1992.

——. *Mad Princes of Renaissance Germany*. Charlottesville, Va., 1994.

——. "Religious Melancholy and Suicide: On the Reformation Origins of a Sociological Stereotype." In *Madness, Melancholy, and the Limits of the Self*, ed. Andrew D. Weiner and Leonard V. Kaplan, pp. 41–56. Vol. 3 of *Graven Images*. Madison, Wis., 1996.

Miller, David B. "The Dissolution of the Religious Houses of Hesse During the Reformation." Ph.D. diss., Yale University, 1971.

Miller, Timothy. *The Birth of the Hospital in the Byzantine Empire*. Baltimore, 1985.

Mitterwieser, Alois. *Geschichte der Fronleichnamsprozession in Bayern*. Munich, 1930.

Moehsen, J. C. W. *Geschichte der Wissenschaften in der Mark Brandenburg, besonders der Arzneiwissenschaft*. Vol. 1. Berlin and Leipzig, 1781.

Moeller, B. "Piety in Germany Around 1500." In *The Reformation in Medieval Perspective*, ed. Steven E. Ozment, pp. 50–75. Chicago, 1971.

Mommsen, Theodor. *Römisches Strafrecht*. Leipzig, 1899.

Monter, E. William. "Inflation and Witchcraft: The Case of Jean Bodin." In *Action and Conviction in Early Modern Europe*, ed. T. K. Rabb, pp. 371–89. Princeton, 1969.

———. "Law, Medicine, and the Acceptance of Witchcraft, 1560–1580." In id., *European Witchcraft*, pp. 55–71. New York, 1969.

———.*Witchcraft in France and Switzerland: The Borderlands During the Reformation*. Ithaca, N.Y., 1976.

Moran, Bruce T. *The Alchemical World of the German Court: Occult Philosophy and Chemical Medicine in the Circle of Moritz of Hessen (1572–1632)*. Stuttgart, 1992.

Morgenthaler, W. *Bernisches Irrenwesen: Von den Anfängen bis zur Eröffnung des Tollhauses 1749*. Bern, 1915.

Möseneder, Karl. *Feste in Regensburg: Von der Reformation bis in die Gegenwart*. Regensburg, 1986.

Muchembled, Robert. *Culture populaire et culture des élites dans la France moderne*. Paris, 1978.

———. *Sorcières: Justice et société aux 16ᵉ et 17ᵉ siècles*. Paris, 1987.

Mummenhoff, Ernst. "Die öffentliche Gesundheits- und Krankenpflege im alten Nürnberg." In *Festschrift zur Eröffnung des neuen Krankenhauses der Stadt Nürnberg*. Nuremberg, 1898.

Muschka, Wilhelm. *Opfergang einer Frau: Lebensbild der Herzogin Jakobe von Jülich-Kleve-Berg, geborene Markgräfin von Baden*. Baden-Baden, 1987.

Nahl, Rudolf van. *Zauberglaube und Hexenwahn im Gebiet von Rhein und Maas: Spätmittelalterlicher Volksglaube im Werk Johan Weyers (1515–1588)*. Bonn, 1983.

Nauert, Charles. *Agrippa and the Crisis of Renaissance Thought*. Urbana, Ill., 1965.

Neaman, Judith. *Suggestion of the Devil: The Origins of Madness*. Garden City, N.Y., 1975.

Needham, Rodney. "Percussion and Transition." *Man* 2 (1967): 606–14.

Neely, Carol T. "Recent Work in Renaissance Studies. Psychology: Did Madness Have a Renaissance?" *Renaissance Quarterly* 44 (1991): 776–90.

Neher, Andrew. "A Physiological Explanation of Unusual Behavior in Ceremonies Involving Drums." *Human Biology* 4 (1962): 151–60.

Nischan, Bodo. "The Exorcism Controversy and Baptism in the Late Reformation." *Sixteenth Century Journal* 18 (1987): 31–51.

———. *Prince, People and Confession: The Second Reformation in Brandenburg*. Philadelphia, 1994.

Nolan, Mary, and Sidney Nolan. *Christian Pilgrimage in Modern Western Europe*. Chapel Hill, N.C., 1989.

Nowotny, Ernst. *Geschichte des Wiener Hofspitals*. Vienna, 1978.

Nussbaum, Martha C. "The Oedipus Rex and the Ancient Unconscious." In *Freud and Forbidden Knowledge*, ed. Peter L. Rudnytsky and Ellen Handler Spitz, pp. 42–71. New York, 1994.

———. *The Therapy of Desire: Theory and Practice in Hellenistic Ethics*. Princeton, 1994.

Obendiek, Harmannus. *Der Teufel bei Martin Luther*. Berlin, 1931.

Oberman, Heiko A. *Masters of the Reformation: The Emergence of a New Intellectual Climate in Europe*. Translated by Dennis Martin. Cambridge, 1981.

——. *The Roots of Antisemitism in the Age of Renaissance and Reformation.* Translated by James I. Porter. Philadelphia, 1984.

——. "Teufelsdreck: Eschatology and Scatology in the 'Old' Luther." *Sixteenth Century Journal* 19 (1988): 435–50.

——. *Luther: Man Between God and the Devil.* Translated by Eileen Walliser-Schwarzbart. New Haven, 1989.

Obermayer, Peter. "Der Wiener Hexenprozess des Jahres 1583." Ph.D. diss., University of Vienna, 1963.

Ohse, Bernhard. "Die Teufelliteratur zwischen Brant und Luther." Ph.D. diss., Freie Universität Berlin, 1961.

Olsson, Herbert. *Schöpfung, Vernunft und Gesetz in Luthers Theologie.* Uppsala, 1971.

Osborn, Max. *Die Teufelliteratur des XVI. Jahrhunderts.* Acta Germanica, vol. 3, no. 3. Berlin, 1893.

Ottosson, Per-Gunnar. *Scholastic Medicine and Philosophy: A Study of Commentaries on Galen's Tegni, ca. 1300–1450.* Naples, 1984.

Ozment, Steven. "The Social History of the Reformation: What Can We Learn from Pamphlets?" In *Flugschriften als Massenmedium der Reformationszeit,* ed. Hans-Joachim Köhler. Stuttgart, 1981.

——. *When Fathers Ruled: Family Life in Reformation Europe.* Cambridge, Mass., 1983.

Pagel, Walter. *Das medizinische Weltbild des Paracelsus: Seine Zusammenhänge mit Neuplatonismus und Gnosis.* Wiesbaden, 1962.

——. "Paracelsus: Traditionalism and Medieval Sources." In *Medicine, Science and Culture: Historical Essays in Honor of Owsei Temkin,* ed. Lloyd Stevenson and Robert P. Multhauf, pp. 50–75. Baltimore, 1968.

——. *Paracelsus: An Introduction to Philosophical Medicine in the Era of the Renaissance.* Basel, 1958. 2d. ed., Basel, 1982.

Palis, James, Evangelos Rossopoulos, and Lazaros Triarhou. "The Hippocratic Concept of Hysteria: A Translation of the Original Texts." *Integrative Psychiatry* 3, no. 3 (September 1985): 226–28.

Panofsky, Erwin. *Early Netherlandish Painting: Its Origins and Character.* Cambridge, Mass., 1958.

Park, Katherine, and J. Henderson. "The First Hospital Among Christians: The Ospedale de Santa Maria Nuova in Early Sixteenth-Century Florence." *Medical History* 35 (1991): 164–88.

Pelikan, Jaroslav. *Obedient Rebels: Catholic Substance and Protestant Principle in Luther's Reformation.* New York, 1964.

Pestronk, Alan. "The First Neurology Book, *De cerebri morbis* (1549) by Jason Pratensis." *Archives of Neurology* 45 (1988): 341–44.

Pigeaud, Jackie. *La maladie de l'âme: Étude sur la relation de l'âme et du corps dans la tradition médico-philosophique antique.* Paris, 1981.

Pilet, P. E. "Felix Platter." In *Dictionary of Scientific Biography,* ed. Charles C. Gillispie, 11 (1975): 33. 18 vols. New York, 1970–90.

Pollack, Linda. *Forgotten Children: Parent-Child Relations from 1500 to 1900.* Cambridge, 1983.

Pölnitz, Götz, Freiherr von. *Julius Echter von Mespelbrunn.* Schriftenreihe zur bayerischen Landesgeschichte, no. 17. Munich, 1934.

Pompey, H. *Die Bedeutung der Medizin für die kirchliche Seelsorge im Selbstverständnis der sogenannten Pastoralmedizin: Eine bibliographische-historische Untersuchung bis Mitte des 19. Jahrhunderts*. Freiburg im Breisgau, 1968.

Pope, W., and N. Danigelis. "Sociology's 'One Law.'" *Social Forces* 60 (1981): 495–516.

Porter, Roy. *Mind-Forg'd Manacles: A History of Madness in England from the Restoration to the Regency*. Cambridge, Mass., 1987.

———. "The Body and the Mind, the Doctor and the Patient: Negotiating Hysteria." In Gilman et al., *Hysteria Beyond Freud*, pp. 225–85. Berkeley and Los Angeles, 1993.

Pötzl, Walter. *Mirakel-Geschichten aus dem Landkreis Augsburg*. Augsburg, 1979.

Quétel, Claude. *History of Syphilis*. Translated by Judith Braddock and Brian Pike. Originally titled *Le mal de Naples*. Baltimore, 1990.

Quadflieg, Ralph. *Filaretes Ospedale Maggiore in Mailand: Zur Rezeption islamischen Hospitalwesens in der italienischen Frührenaissance*. Veröffentlichung der Abteilung Architektur des Kunsthistorischen Instituts der Universität Köln, no. 20. Ph.D. diss., Cologne, 1981.

Reed, Edward S. *From Soul to Mind: The Emergence of Psychology from Erasmus Darwin to William James*. New Haven, 1997.

Reiter, Günther. "Heiligenverehrung und Wallfahrtswesen im Schrifttum von Reformation und katholischer Restauration." Ph.D. diss., University of Würzburg, 1970.

Reiter, Paul J. *Martin Luthers Umwelt und Psychose, sowie die Bedeutung dieser Faktoren für seine Entwicklung und Lehre: Eine historisch-psychiatrische Studie*. Copenhagen, 1937.

Ribon, Pierre. *Guérisseurs et remèdes populaires dans la France ancienne: Vivarais Cévennes*. Paris, 1983.

Ridderbos, Bernhard. *De melancholie van de kunstenaar: Hugo van der Goes en de Oudnederlandse schilderkunst*. The Hague, 1991.

Rieger, C., ed. *Die Psychiatrie in Würzburg von 1583–1893*. Verhandlungen der Phys.-med. Gesellschaft, n.s., 27 (1894). Reprinted in *Erster Bericht vom Jahre 1899 aus der psychiatrischen Klinik* (Würzburg, 1899).

———. *Zweiter Bericht (vom Jahre 1905) aus der Psychiatrischen Klinik der Universität Würzburg*. Würzburg, 1905.

Roccatagliata, Giuseppe. *A History of Ancient Psychiatry*. Westport, Conn., 1986.

Rohde, Johann Jürgen. *Soziologie des Krankenhauses: Zur Einführung in die Soziologie der Medizin*. Stuttgart, 1962.

Romeo, Giovanni. *Inquisitori, esorcisti e streghe nell'Italia della controriforma*. Florence, 1990.

Rosen, George. *Madness in Society: Chapters in the Historical Sociology of Mental Illness*. New York, 1969.

Rosenberger, Ludwig. *Narrenkabinett: Galerie von Hofnarren und lustigen Räten*. St. Michael, Austria, 1978.

Roth, Hans. "Die Mirakelüberlieferungen von St. Walburg in Eichstätt aus dem 17. and 18. Jahrhundert." *Sammelblatt des Historischen Vereins Eichstätt* 71–72 (1978–79): 81–110.

Rouget, Gilbert. *Music and Trance: A Theory of the Relations of Music and Possession*. Paris, 1980. Translated by Brunhilde Biebuyck. Chicago, 1985.

Rousseau, G. S. "'A Strange Pathology': Hysteria in the Early Modern World, 1500–1800." In Gilman et al., *Hysteria Beyond Freud*, pp. 91–221. Berkeley and Los Angeles, 1993.

Rubin, Julius H. *Religious Melancholy and Protestant Experience in America*. New York, 1994.

Rubin, Miri. *Corpus Christi: The Eucharist in Late Medieval Culture*. Cambridge, 1991.

Rublack, Hans-Christoph. *Gescheiterte Reformation: Frühreformatorische und protestantische Bewegungen in süd- und westdeutschen geistlichen Residenzen*. Spätmittelalter und frühe Neuzeit, vol. 4. Stuttgart, 1978.

Rudolph, Hartmut. "Einige Gesichtspunkte zum Thema 'Paracelsus und Luther.'" *Archiv für Reformationsgeschichte* 72 (1981): 34–53.

Rudolph, Hartmut, and Peter Dilg, eds. *Resultate und Desiderate der Paracelsus-Forschung*. Stuttgart, 1993.

Rummel, Walter. "Gutenberg, der Teufel und die Muttergottes von Eberhardsklausen: Erste Hexenverfolgung im Trierer Land." In *Ketzer, Zauberer, Hexen: Die Anfänge der europäischen Hexenverfolgungen*, ed. Andreas Blauert, pp. 91–117. Frankfurt a/M, 1990.

———. *Bauern, Hexen und Herren: Studien zur Sozialgeschichte sponheimischer und kurtrierischer Hexenprozesse, 1574–1664*. Göttingen, 1991.

Russell, Jean Fago. "Tarantism." *Medical History* 23 (1974): 404–25.

Russell, Jeffrey B. *Mephistopheles: The Devil in the Modern World*. Ithaca, N.Y., 1986.

Safley, Thomas Max. *Charity and Economy in the Orphanages of Early Modern Augsburg*. Atlantic Highlands, N.J., 1997.

Sander, H. J. "Beiträge zur Biographie Hugos van der Goes und zur Chronologie seiner Werke." *Repertorium für Kunstwissenschaft* 35 (1912): 519–45.

Sargent, Steven D. "Religion and Society in Late Medieval Bavaria: The Cult of St. Leonard, 1258–1500." Ph.D. diss., University of Pennsylvania, 1982.

———. "Miracle Books and Pilgrimage Shrines in Late Medieval Bavaria." *Historical Reflections* 13 (1986): 455–71.

Sarton, George. *Six Wings: Men of Science in the Renaissance*. Bloomington, Ind., 1957.

Sass, Louis. *Madness and Modernism: Insanity in the Light of Modern Art, Literature, and Thought*. New York, 1992.

———. "Civilized Madness: Schizophrenia, Self-Consciousness and the Modern Mind." *History of the Human Sciences* 7 (1994): 83–120.

Satow, Roberta. "Where Has All the Hysteria Gone?" *Psychoanalytic Review* 66 (1979): 463–77.

Saunders, A. C. de C. M. "The Life and Humour of Joao de Sá Panasco, o Negro, Former Slave, Court Jester and Gentleman of the Portuguese Royal Household (fl. 1524–1567)." In *Medieval and Renaissance Studies on Spain and Portugal in Honour of P. E. Russell*, ed. F. W. Hodcroft et al., pp. 180–91. Oxford, 1981.

Schäfer, F. W. "Adam Krafft, der Reformator Hessens." *Archiv für hessische Geschichte und Altertumskunde*, n.s., 8 (1912): 1–46, 67–110.

Schaffstein, Friedrich. *Die allgemeinen Lehren vom Verbrechen in ihrer Entwicklung durch die Wissenschaft des gemeinen Strafrechts. Beiträge zur Strafrechtsentwicklung von der Carolina bis Carpzov*. Berlin, 1930.

Schalk, Carl. *Luther on Music: Paradigms of Praise*. St. Louis, 1988.

Schär, Markus. *Seelennöte der Untertanen: Selbstmord, Melancholie und Religion im Alten Zürich, 1500–1800*. Zurich, 1985.

Scheper-Hughes, Nancy. *Saints, Scholars, and Schizophrenics: Mental Illness in Rural Ireland*. Berkeley and Los Angeles, 1979.

Schestag, Franz. "Kaiser Maximilian I. Triumph." *Jahrbuch der kunsthistorischen Sammlungen des allerhöchsten Kaiserhauses* 1 (1883): 154–81.

Schiesari, Julia. *The Gendering of Melancholia: Feminism, Psychoanalysis, and the Symbolics of Loss in Renaissance Literature*. Ithaca, N.Y., 1992.

Schiewek, Ingrid. "Zur Autobiographie des Basler Stadtarztes Felix Platter." *Forschungen und Fortschritte* 38, no. 12 (Berlin 1964): 368–72.

Schilling, Heinz. "Job Fincel und die Zeichen der Endzeit." In *Volkserzählung und Reformation*, ed. Brückner, pp. 325–92. Berlin, 1974.

Schings, Hans-Jürgen. *Melancholie und Aufklärung: Melancholiker und ihre Kritiker in Erfahrungsseelenkunde und Literatur des 18. Jahrhunderts*. Stuttgart, 1977.

Schipperges, Heinrich. *Paracelsus: Der Mensch in der Licht der Natur*. Stuttgart, 1974.

Schleiner, Winfried. *Melancholy, Genius, and Utopia in the Renaissance*. Wiesbaden, 1991.

———. *Medical Ethics in the Renaissance*. Washington, D.C. , 1995.

Schmidt, Eberhard. *Einführung in die Geschichte der deutschen Strafrechtspflege*. 2d ed. Göttingen, 1951.

Schmidt, Gustav Lebrecht. *Justus Menius, der Reformator Thüringens*. 2 vols., Gotha, 1867.

Schmidt, Leopold. *Volksglaube und Volksbrauch: Gestalten, Gebilde, Gebärden*. Berlin, 1966.

———. "Via sacra: Zur Geschichte der 'Heiligen Straße' zwischen Wien und Mariazell." In *Via sacra: Das Wallfahrtsmuseum in Kleinmariazell*, ed. Helene Grünn, pp. 73–83. Veröffentlichungen des österreichischen Museums für Volkskunde, vol. 15. Vienna, 1977.

Schmitt, Charles B. *Aristotle and the Renaissance*. Cambridge, Mass., 1983.

Schmitz, Heinz-Günter. *Physiologie des Scherzes: Bedeutung und Rechtfertigung der Ars Iocandi im 16. Jahrhundert*. Hildesheim, 1972.

———. "*Consuetudo* und *simulatio*: Zur Thematik des Lalebuchs." In *Festschrift für Gerhard Cordes zum 65. Geburtstag*, ed. Friedhelm Debus and Joachim Hartig, 1: 160–76. Neumünster, 1973. Reprinted in Wunderlich, ed., *Wunderseltsame Geschichten*, pp. 121–41. Göppingen, 1983.

———. "Das Melancholieproblem in Wissenschaft und Kunst der frühen Neuzeit." *Sudhoffs Archiv* 60 (1976): 135–62.

———, ed. *Wolfgang Büttners Volksbuch von Claus Narr: Mit einem Beitrag zur Sprache der Eisleber Erstausgabe von 1572*. Hildesheim, 1990.

Schmitz-Cliever, Egonand Herta. "Zur Darstellung des Heiltanzes in der Malerei um 1500." *Medizinhistorisches Journal* 10 (1975): 307–16.

Schneider, Marius. "Tarantella." In *Die Musik in Geschichte und Gegenwart*. Kassel, 1949–86.

Schoeneman, Thomas J., Suzanne Segerstrom, Paul Griffin, and David Gresham. "The Psychiatric Nosology of Everyday Life: Categories in Implicit Abnormal Psychology." *Journal of Social and Clinical Psychology* 12 (1993): 429–53.

Schormann, Gerhard. *Hexenprozesse in Deutschland*. Göttingen, 1981.

Schreiber, Georg. "Strukturwandel der Wallfahrt." In *Wallfahrt und Volkstum in Geschichte und Leben*, ed. id., pp. 1–183. Forschungen zur Volkskunde, vols. 16–17. Düsseldorf, 1934.

———. *Deutsche Mirakelbücher: Zur Quellenkunde und Sinngebung*. Forschungen zur Volkskunde, vols. 31–32. Düsseldorf, 1938.

———. *Alpine Bergwerkskultur: Bergleute zwischen Graubünden und Tirol in den letzten vier Jahrhunderten*. Innsbruck, 1956.

Schryver, Antoine de. "Hugo van der Goes' laatste jaren te Gent." *Genter Bijdragen tot Kunstgeschiedenis* 16 (1955–56): 193–211.

Schubert, Ernst. "Julius Echter von Mespelbrunn (1545–1617)." In *Fränkische Lebensbilder*, ed. Gerhard Pfeiffer, 3: 158–93. Würzburg, 1969.

———. *Materielle und organisatorische Grundlagen der Würzburger Universitätsentwicklung, 1582–1821*. Quellen und Beiträge zur Geschichte der Universität Würzburg, vol. 4. Neustadt an der Aisch, Ger., 1973.

Schuh, Barbara. *"Von vilen und mancherlay seltzamen Wunderzaichen": Die Analyse von Mirakelbüchern und Wallfahrtsquellen*. St. Katharinen, Ger., 1989.

Schumacher, Josef. *Die seelischen Volkskrankheiten im deutschen Mittelalter und ihre Darstellung in der bildenden Kunst*. Berlin, 1937.

Schwammberger, Adolf. "Von Hofnarren in und aus Franken." *Jahrbuch für fränkische Landesforschung* 34–35 (1974–75): 975–81.

Schweinsberg, Gustav, Freiherr Schenk zu. "Aus der Jugendzeit Landgraf Philipps des Grossmütigen." In *Philipp der Grossmütige: Beiträge zur Geschichte seines Lebens und seiner Zeit*, ed. Historischer Verein für das Grossherzogtum Hessen, pp. 73–143. Marburg, 1904.

Schwerdfeger, Gerhard O. "Die Erbanlagen bei Ludwig II. und Otto von Bayern aus genealogischer Sicht: Eine kritische Bestandsaufnahme und neue Forschungsergebnisse." *Genealogisches Jahrbuch* 35 (1995): 11–42.

Screech, Michael. *Ecstasy and the Praise of Folly*. London, 1980.

———. "The 'Mad' Christ of Erasmus and the Legal Duties of his Brethren." In *Essays on Early French Literature Presented to Barbara M. Craig*, ed. N. J. Lacy and J. C. Nash, pp. 119–27. York, S.C., 1982.

———. "Good Madness in Christendom." In *The Anatomy of Madness: Essays in the History of Psychiatry*, vol. 1: *People and Ideas*, ed. W. F. Bynum, Roy Porter, and Michael Shepherd, pp. 25–39. London, 1985.

Scribner, Robert. *Popular Culture and Popular Movements in Reformation Germany*. London, 1987.

Scull, Andrew. *The Most Solitary of Afflictions: Madness and Society in Britain, 1700–1900*. New Haven, 1993.

650 Jahre Bürgerspital zum Heiligen Geist Würzburg. Würzburg, 1969.

Sharp, Leslie A. "Exorcists, Psychiatrists, and the Problems of Possession in Northwest Madagascar." *Social Science & Medicine* 38 (1994): 525–42.

Shorter, Edward. *From Paralysis to Fatigue: A History of Psychosomatic Illness in the Modern Era*. New York, 1992.

———. *From the Mind into the Body: The Cultural Origins of Psychosomatic Symptoms*. New York, 1994.

Showalter, Elaine. *Hystories: Hysterical Epidemics and Modern Culture*. New York, 1997.

Siefert, Helmut. "Kloster und Hospital Haina: Eine medizin-historische Skizze." *Hessisches Ärzteblatt* 32 (1971): 963–83.

Sigal, Pierre-André. *L'homme et le miracle dans la France médiévale: XIᵉ–XIIᵉ siècle*. Paris, 1985.

Sigerist, Henry. "The Story of Tarantism." In *Music and Medicine*, ed. Dorothy M. Schullian and Max Schoen, pp. 96–116. New York, 1948.

Siraisi, Nancy G. *Avicenna in Renaissance Italy: The Canon and Medical Teaching in Italian Universities After 1500.* Princeton, 1987.

———. *Medieval and Early Renaissance Medicine: An Introduction to Knowledge and Practice.* Chicago, 1990.

Skalnik, James V. "Ramus and Reform: The End of the Renaissance and the Origins of the Old Regime in France." Ph.D. diss., University of Virginia, 1990.

Sluhovsky, Moshe. "A Divine Apparition or Demonic Possession? Female Agency and Church Authority on Demonic Possession in Sixteenth-Century France." *Sixteenth Century Journal* 27 (1996): 1039–55.

Smith, Pamela H. *The Business of Alchemy: Science and Culture in the Holy Roman Empire.* Princeton, 1994.

Soergel, Philip. "Wondrous in His Saints: Popular Pilgrimage and Catholic Propaganda in Bavaria, 1470–1620." Ph.D. diss., University of Michigan, 1988.

———. *Wondrous in His Saints: Counter-Reformation Propaganda in Bavaria.* Berkeley and Los Angeles, 1993.

Solleder, Fridolin. "Markgräfin Susanna und ihr Narr." *Das Bayerland* 47 (1936): 686–89.

Sontag, Susan. *Illness as Metaphor.* New York, 1978.

Spangenberg, Peter-Michael. *Maria ist immer und überall: Die Alltagswelten des spätmittelalterlichen Mirakels.* Frankfurt a/M, 1987.

Speak, Gill. "An Odd Kind of Melancholy: Reflections on the Glass Delusion in Europe (1440–1680)." *History of Psychiatry* 1 (1990): 191–206.

Spirkner, B. "Kulturgeschichtliches aus dem Mirakelbuche der Wallfahrt zum hl. Valentin in Diepoldskirchen (1420–1691)." *Verhandlungen des historischen Vereins für Niederbayern* 42 (1906): 173–96.

Staber, Josef. *Volksfrömmigkeit und Wallfahrtswesen des Spätmittelalters im Bistum Freising.* Munich, 1955.

Stahl, Gerlinde. "Die Wallfahrt zur Schönen Maria in Regensburg." *Beiträge zur Geschichte des Bistums Regensburg* 2 (1968): 35–282.

Stalnaker, John C. "The Emergence of the Protestant Clergy in Central Germany: The Case of Hesse." Ph.D. diss., University of California at Berkeley, 1970.

Stambaugh, Ria, ed. *Teufelbücher in Auswahl.* 5 vols. Berlin, 1970–80.

Stechow, W. *Northern Renaissance Art, 1400–1600: Sources and Documents.* Englewood Cliffs, N.J., 1966.

Stella, Gerhard. "Das Mirakelbuch von Kirchwald bei Nußdorf: Eine Handschrift in der Bayerischen Staatsbibliothek München (Kloeckeliana 606b)." *Das Bayerische Inn-Oberland* 42 (1980): 65–111.

Stevenson, Ian. "Possession and Exorcism: An Essay Review." *Journal of Parapsychology* 59 (1995): 69–77.

Still, Arthur and Irving Velody, eds. *Rewriting the History of Madness: Studies in Foucault's "Histoire de la folie."* London, 1992.

Stintzing, Roderich. *Geschichte der populären Literatur des römisch-kanonischen Rechts in Deutschland am Ende des fünfzehnten und im Anfang des sechzehnten Jahrhunderts.* Leipzig, 1867.

Stone, Lawrence. *The Family, Sex and Marriage in England, 1500–1800.* London, 1977.

Strauss, Gerald. "Comment." In *Religion and Culture in the Renaissance and Reformation*, ed. Steven Ozment, pp. 121–30. Kirksville, Mo., 1989.

Stutte, H. "Landgraf Philipp der Grossmütige von Hessen aus medizinischer Sicht." *Hessisches Ärzteblatt* 30 (1969): 1085–97.

Sudhoff, Karl. *Versuch einer Kritik der Echtheit der Paracelsischen Schriften*. Berlin, 1894–99.

———. *Bibliographica Paracelsica*. Graz, 1958.

Sumption, Jonathan. *Pilgrimage: An Image of Mediaeval Religion*. Totowa, N.J., 1975.

Sushrut, Jadhav. "The Cultural Origins of Western Depression." *International Journal of Social Psychiatry* 42 (1996): 269–86.

Swain, Barbara. *Fools and Folly During the Middle Ages and the Renaissance*. New York, 1932. Reprint, Folcroft, Pa., 1976.

Talbot, Charles and Alan Shestack, eds. *Prints and Drawings of the Danube School*. New Haven, 1969.

Temkin, Owsei. "The Elusiveness of Paracelsus." *Bulletin of the History of Medicine* 26 (1952): 201–17.

———. *The Falling Sickness: A History of Epilepsy*. 2d ed., Baltimore, 1971.

———. *Galenism: The Rise and Decline of a Medical Philosophy*. Ithaca, N.Y., 1973.

Terrisse, Arnaud. "La psychiatrie en France dans le miroir de la thèse: L'évolution des thèses de médecine psychiatrique françaises du début du XVIIᵉ siècle à 1934 d'après le fichier des thèses de médecine de la Bibliothèque nationale." *Histoire, Économie et Société* 3 (1984): 247–92.

Theobald, Wilhelm. *Votiftafeln und Medizin: Kulturgeschichte und Heilkunst im Spiegel der Votifmalerei*. Munich, 1978.

———. *Mirakel-Heilung Zwischen Wissenschaft und Glauben*. Munich, 1983.

Thomas, Keith. *Religion and the Decline of Magic*. New York, 1971.

Thompson, Colin, and Lorne Campbell. *Hugo van der Goes and the Trinity Panels in Edinburgh*. London, 1974.

Thompson, Ewa M. *Understanding Russia: The Holy Fool in Russian Culture*. New York, 1987.

Thompson, Stith. *Motif Index of Folk Literature*. Bloomington, Ind., 1957.

Thorndike, Lynn. *A History of Magic and Experimental Science*. 8 vols. New York, 1923–58.

Timken-Zinkann, R. F. "Black Bile. A Review of Recent Attempts to Trace the Origin of the Teachings on Melancholia to Medical Observations." *Medical History* 12 (1968): 288–92.

Tiroler Landesausstellung. *Heiltum und Wallfahrt*. Innsbruck, 1988.

Tlusty, Ann. "The Devil's Altar: Drinking and Society in Early Modern Augsburg." Ph. D. diss., University of Maryland, 1994.

Torrey, E. Fuller. *Schizophrenia and Civilization*. New York, 1980.

Trevor-Roper, H. R. *The European Witch-Craze of the Sixteenth and Seventeenth Centuries and Other Essays*. New York, 1969.

———. "The Court Physician and Paracelsianism." In *Medicine at the Courts of Europe, 1500–1837*, ed. Vivian Nutton, pp. 79–94. London, 1990.

Trillat, Étienne. *Histoire de l'hystérie*. Paris, 1986.

Tröhler, Ulrich, ed. *Felix Platter (1536–1614) in seiner Zeit*. Basel, 1991.

Trossbach, Werner. "'Klee-Skrupel': Melancholie und Ökonomie in der deutschen

Spätaufklärung." In *Die Kehrseite des Schönen*, ed. Karl Eibl (*Aufklärung* 8, no. 1): 91–120.

Ulbricht, Otto, and Hartmut Lehmann, eds. *Vom Unfug des Hexen-Processes: Gegner der Hexenverfolgung von Johann Weyer bis Friedrich Spee*. Wiesbaden, 1992.

Universitätsbibliotheken Basel und Freiburg im Breisgau et al., eds. *Sébastien Brant: 500ᵉ anniversaire de 'La Nef des folz,' 1494–1994; 'Das Narren Schyff,' zum 500jährigen Jubiläum des Buches von Sebastian Brant, 1494–1994*. Exhibition catalogue. Cover title: *La Nef des folz = Das Narren Schiff*. Basel, 1994.

Van Cleve, John. *Brant's "The Ship of Fools" in Critical Perspective, 1800–1991*. Columbia, S.C., 1993.

Vandendriessche, Gaston. *The Parapraxis in the Haizmann Case of Sigmund Freud*. Louvain, 1965.

Veit, Ludwig Andreas, and Ludwig Lenhart. *Kirche und Volksfrömmigkeit im Zeitalter des Barock*. Freiburg im Breisgau, 1956.

Veith, Ilsa. *Hysteria: The History of a Disease*. Chicago, 1965.

Venard, Marc. "Le démon controversiste." In *La controverse religieuse (XVIᵉ–XIXᵉ siècles)*, 2: 45–60. Montpelier, 1980.

Vernant, Jean-Pierre. "Oedipus Without the Complex." In id. and Pierre Vidal-Naquet, *Myth and Tragedy in Ancient Greece*, pp. 85–111. Translated by J. Lloyd. New York, 1988.

Vicari, Patricia. *The View from Minerva's Tower: Learning and Imagination in "The Anatomy of Melancholy."* Toronto, 1989.

Völker, Ludwig, ed. *"Komm, heilige Melancholie": Eine Anthologie deutscher Melancholie-Gedichte mit Ausblicken auf die europäische Melancholie-Tradition in Literatur- und Kunstgeschichte*. Stuttgart, 1983.

Volkert, Wilhelm. "Die Regensburger Juden im Spätmittelalter und das Ende der Judengemeinde." In *Crossroads of Medieval Civilization: The City of Regensburg and Its Intellectual Milieu: A Collection of Essays*, ed. Edelgard E. DuBruck and Karl Heinz Göller, pp. 139–71. Medieval and Renaissance Monograph Series, vol. 5. Detroit, 1984.

Walker, Anita M., and Edmund H. Dickerman. "'A Woman Under the Influence': A Case of Alleged Possession in Sixteenth-Century France." *Sixteenth Century Journal* 22 (1991): 534–54.

Walker, D. P. *Spiritual and Demonic Magic from Ficino to Campanella*. London, 1958.

——. *Unclean Spirits: Possession and Exorcism in England and France in the Late Sixteenth and Early Seventeenth Centuries*. Philadelphia, 1981.

——. "Demonic Possession Used as Propaganda in the Later Sixteenth Century." In Istituto nazionale di studi sul Rinascimento, *Scienze, credenze occulte, livelli di cultura: Convegno internazionale di studi, Firenze, 26–30 giugno 1980*, pp. 237–48. Florence, 1982.

——. *Music, Spirit and Language in the Renaissance*. London, 1985.

——. "The Cessation of Miracles." In *Hermeticism and the Renaissance: Intellectual History and the Occult in Early Modern Europe*, ed. Ingrid Merkel and Allen G. Debus, pp. 111–24. Washington, D.C., 1988.

Walker, Nigel. *Crime and Insanity in England*. Vol. 1: *The Historical Perspective*. Edinburgh, 1967.

Walton, John, Paul B. Beeson, and Ronald Bodley Scott, eds. *The Oxford Companion to Medicine*. 2 vols. Oxford, 1986.

Walz, Rainer. *Hexenglaube und magische Kommunikation im Dorf der frühen Neuzeit: Die Verfolgungen in der Grafschaft Lippe.* Paderborn, Ger., 1993.

Ward, Benedicta. *Miracles and the Medieval Mind: Theory, Record, and Event, 1000–1215.* Philadelphia, 1982.

Weber, Karl von. *Aus vier Jahrhunderten: Mitteilungen aus dem Haupt-Staatsarchiv zu Dresden.* N.S. Leipzig, 1861.

Weber, Wolfgang. "Im Kampf mit Saturn: Zur Bedeutung der Melancholie im anthropologischen Modernisierungsprozess des 16. und 17. Jahrhunderts." *Zeitschrift für historische Forschung* 17 (1990): 155–92.

Webster, Charles. *From Paracelsus to Newton: Magic and the Making of Modern Science.* Cambridge, 1982.

———. "Paracelsus and Demons: Science as a Synthesis of Popular Belief." In Istituto nazionale di studi sul Rinascimento, *Scienze, credenze occulte, livelli di cultura: Convegno internazionale di studi, Firenze, 26–30 giugno 1980,* pp. 3–20. Florence, 1982.

Weeks, Andrew, *Paracelsus: Speculative Theory and the Crisis of the Early Reformation.* Albany, N.Y., 1997.

Weimann, Karl-Heinz. *Paracelsus-Bibliographie 1932–1960, mit einem Verzeichnis neu entdeckter Paracelsus-Handschriften (1900–1960).* Wiesbaden, 1963.

Welker, Klaus. "Die Inchenhofener Mirakelaufzeichnungen, 1506–1657: Ihr Beitrag zur nachtridentinischen Verehrung des hl. Leonhard als Viehpatron." In *Von Konstanz nach Trient,* ed. Bäumer, pp. 635–57. Munich, 1972.

Welsford, Enid. *The Fool: His Social and Literary History.* London, 1935.

Wendehorst, Alfred. "Die Juliusspitalpfarrei und ihre Bedeutung für die Gegenreformation." In *Julius Echter und seine Zeit: Gedenkschrift aus Anlass des 400. Jahrestages der Wahl des Stifters der Alma Julia zum Fürstbischof von Würzburg am 1. Dezember 1573,* ed. Friedrich Merzbacher, pp. 349–74. Würzburg, 1973.

———. *Das Juliusspital in Würzburg.* Vol. 1: *Kulturgeschichte.* Würzburg, 1976.

Wickel, Carl. *Gründung und Beschreibung des Zisterzienser-Klosters Haina in Hessen, sowie einiges aus der Geschichte des Klosters und der Anstalt.* 2d ed. Frankenberg i. H., 1929.

Wiebel-Fanderl, Oliva. *Die Wallfahrt Altötting: Kultformen und Wallfahrtsleben im 19. Jahrhundert.* Passau, Ger., 1982.

Wilbertz, Gisela, Gerd Schwerhoff, and Jürgen Scheffer, eds. *Hexenverfolgung und Regionalgeschichte: Die Grafschaft Lippe im Vergleich.* Bielefeld, Ger., 1994.

Wilda, Wilhelm Eduard. *Geschichte des deutschen Strafrechts,* vol. 1: *Das Strafrecht der Germanen.* 1842. Reprint, Aalen, Ger., 1960.

Wilhelmi, Thomas. *Sebastian Brant Bibliographie.* Bern, 1990.

Wilkinson, Catherine. "The Hospital of Cardinal Tavera in Toledo: A Documentary and Stylistic Study of Spanish Architecture in the Mid-Sixteenth Century." Ph.D. diss., Yale University, 1968.

Williams, Gerhild Scholz. "Gelächter vor Gott: Mensch und Kosmos bei Franck und Paracelsus." *Daphnis* 15 (1986): 463–81.

Windholz, George. "The Case of the Renaissance Psychiatrist Peter Mair." *Sixteenth Century Journal* 22 (1991): 163–72.

Winzinger, Franz. "Zum Werk Wolf Hubers, Georg Lembergers und des Meisters der Wunder von Maria Zell." *Zeitschrift für Kunstwissenschaft* 12 (1958): 71–73.

———. *Albrecht Altdorfer: Graphik. Holzschnitte, Kupferstiche, Radierungen. Gesamtausgabe.* Munich, 1963.

———. *Wolf Huber: Das Gesamtwerk.* 2 vols. Munich, 1979.

Wittkower, Rudolf, and Margot Wittkower. *Born Under Saturn: The Character and Conduct of Artists. A Documented History from Antiquity to the French Revolution.* New York, 1963.

Wolf, Erik. *Grosse Rechtsdenker der deutschen Geistesgeschichte.* 4th ed. Tübingen, 1963.

Wolf, Gustav. "Über den Hofnarren Kaiser Karls V., genannt El Conde don Frances de Zuñiga und seine Chronik." *Sitzungsberichte der kaiserlichen Akademie der Wissenschaften. Philosophisch-historische Classe,* vol. 5, sec. 2 (1850), Heft 6–10, pp. 21–63.

Wolf, Margery. *A Thrice-Told Tale: Feminism, Postmodernism, and Ethnographic Responsibility.* Stanford, 1992.

Wolfersdorf, P. "Die dämonischen Gestalten der schwäbischen Volksüberlieferung." Ph.D. diss., Tübingen, 1949.

Wright, William J. "Reformation Contributions to the Development of Public Welfare Policy in Hesse." *Journal of Modern History* 49 (1977), D1145 (on demand article).

———. *Capitalism, the State, and the Lutheran Reformation: Sixteenth-Century Hesse.* Athens, Ohio, 1988.

Wunderlich, Werner. "'Schildbürgerstreiche': Bericht zur Lalebuch- und Schildbürgerforschung." *Deutsche Vierteljahrsschrift für Literaturwissenschaft und Geistesgeschichte* 56 (1982): 641–85.

———. *Wunderseltsame Geschichten: Interpretationen zu Schildbürgern und Lalebuch.* Göppingen, 1983.

Wynands, Dieter P. J. *Geschichte der Wallfahrten im Bistum Aachen.* Aachen, 1986.

Zambelli, Paola. "Magic and Radical Reformation in Agrippa of Nettesheim." *Journal of the Warburg and Courtauld Institute* 39 (1976): 69–103.

———. "Scholastiker und Humanisten: Agrippa und Trithemius zur Hexerei. Die natürliche Magie und die Entstehung kritischen Denkens." *Archiv für Kulturgeschichte* 67 (1985): 41–80.

———. *L'ambigua natura della magica: Filosofi, streghe, riti nel Rinascimento.* Milan, 1991.

Zedler, Johann Heinrich. *Grosses vollständiges Universal-Lexikon.* 64 vols. Leipzig and Halle, 1732–50.

Zeeden, Ernst Walter. *Katholische Überlieferungen in den lutherischen Kirchenordnungen des 16. Jahrhunderts.* Münster, 1959.

Zender, Matthias. "Mirakelbücher als Quelle für das Volksleben im Rheinland." *Rheinische Vierteljahrsblätter* 41 (1977): 108–23.

Zika, Charles. "Hosts, Processions and Pilgrimages: Controlling the Sacred in Fifteenth-Century Germany." *Past & Present,* no. 118 (Feb. 1988): 25–64.

Zoepfl, Friedrich. "Nacktwallfahrten." In *Wallfahrt und Volkstum in Geschichte,* pp. 266–72. Forschungen zur Volkskunde, 16–17. Düsseldorf, 1934.

Index

In this index an "f" after a number indicates a separate reference on the next page, and an "ff" indicates separate references on the next two pages. A continuous discussion over two or more pages is indicated by a span of page numbers, e.g., "57–59." *Passim* is used for a cluster of references in close but not consecutive sequence.

Library of Congress Cataloging-in-Publication Data

Midelfort, H. C. Erik
    A history of madness in sixteenth-century
  Germany / H.C. Erik Midelfort.
        p.   cm.
    Includes bibliographical references and index.
    ISBN 0-8047-3334-1 (cloth : alk. paper)
    ISBN 0-8047-4169-7 (paperback : alk. paper)
    1. Mental illness—Germany—History—16th
century.   2. Social psychiatry—Germany—History—
16th century.   I. Title.
    RC450.G3M528   1999
    618.89′00943′09031—dc21   98-16558

Original printing 1999
Last figure below indicates year of this printing:
09 08 07 06 05 04 03 02 01 00